KARL POLANYI
IN
VIENNA

KARL POLANYI IN VIENNA

The Contemporary Significance of
The Great Transformation

Kenneth McRobbie, Kari Polanyi Levitt
Editors

Montreal/New York/London

Copyright © 2006 BLACK ROSE BOOKS

No part of this book may be reproduced or transmitted in any form, by any means electronic or mechanical including photocopying and recording, or by any information storage or retrieval system—without written permission from the publisher, or, in the case of photocopying or other reprographic copying, a license from the Canadian Reprography Collective, with the exception of brief passages quoted by a reviewer in a newspaper or magazine.

Black Rose Books No. II341

National Library of Canada Cataloguing in Publication Data

Karl Polanyi in Vienna : the contemporary significance of The great transformation / Kenneth McRobbie, Kari Polanyi Levitt, editors. -- 2nd ed.

(Critical perspectives on historic issues ; v. 8 ISSN: 1195-1869)

Part 1 includes papers originally presented at the Fifth Karl Polanyi International Conference held in Vienna, May 1999.

ISBN: 1-55164-259-X (bound)   ISBN: 1-55164-258-1 (pbk.)
(alternative ISBNs 9781551642598 [bound]   9781551642581 [pbk.])

1. Economic history. 2. Polanyi, Karl, 1886-1964 Great transformation. 3. Polanyi, Karl, 1886-1964. 4. Europe, Eastern--Economic conditions. 5. Duczynska, Ilona. I. McRobbie, Kenneth, 1929- II. Levitt, Kari III. International Karl Polanyi Conference (5th : 1999 : Vienna, Austria) IV. Series.

HB102.P64K37 2005   330.9   C2004-905036-2

Cover design: Associés libres

Cover photograph, by Kenneth McRobbie, shows a group of participants from the 5th Polanyi Conference in a courtyard of the Karl Marx Hof (designed by architect Karl Ehn and constructed in the mid 1920s).

	BLACK ROSE BOOKS	
C.P. 1258	2250 Military Road	99 Wallis Road
Succ. Place du Parc	Tonawanda, NY	London, E9 5LN
Montréal, H2X 4A7	14150	England
Canada	USA	UK

To order books:
In Canada: (phone) 1-800-565-9523 (fax) 1-800-221-9985
email: utpbooks@utpress.utoronto.ca
In United States: (phone) 1-800-283-3572 (fax) 1-651-917-6406
In the UK & Europe: (phone) 44 (0)20 8986-4854 (fax) 44 (0)20 8533-5821
email: order@centralbooks.com
Our Web Site address: http://www.web.net/blackrosebooks

Printed in Canada

TABLE OF CONTENTS

Introduction
    Kenneth McRobbie, Kari Polanyi Levitt xvii

PART ONE: THEMES FROM THE WORK OF KARL POLANYI
FIFTH INTERNATIONAL KARL POLANYI CONFERENCE, VIENNA, 1994

THE CONTEMPORARY SIGNIFICANCE OF THE GREAT TRANSFORMATION

Chapter One: *The Great Transformation* from 1920 to 1990
    Kari Polanyi Levitt 3

Chapter Two: Globalization and *Haute Finance—Déja Vu?*
    Eric Helleiner 12

Chapter Three: The Continuing Crisis of Democracy
    Michele Cangiani 32

Chapter Four: The Case for Control Over Cross-Border Capital Flows
    Fred Block 47

Chapter Five: Re-reading Polanyi: Towards a Second Great
Transformation?
    Björn Hettne 60

Chapter Six: Conditions for Re-launching Development
    Samir Amin 73

Chapter Seven: Vision and Expression: Literature and *The Great
Transformation*
    Kenneth McRobbie 85

TRANSITIONS FROM PLANNED TO MARKET ECONOMIES

Chapter Eight: On the Economic Implications of (Mis)understanding
Markets in Transition Countries
    J.A. Kregel 108

Chapter Nine: From Planned Economy to Market Economy in the Former East Berlin
    Birgit Müller 116

Chapter Ten: Survival Strategies in Post-1989 Bulgaria
    Yulian Konstantinov 132

Chapter Eleven: Changing Modes of Economic Integration in Bulgarian History
    Tanya Chavdarova 146

Chapter Twelve: Financial Stabilization and Social Destabilization in Hungary
    László Andor 160

Chapter Thirteen: The Privatization of the State: The British Experience
    Alan Scott 135

IDENTITIES, CULTURE, CITIZENSHIP, AND DEMOCRACY

Chapter Fourteen: Of Social Spaces, Citizenship, and the Nature of Power in the World Economy
    André C. Drainville 192

Chapter Fifteen: Individualism, Identities and Inclusionary Citizenship in Western Political Culture
    Gregor Matjan 213

Chapter Sixteen: The Constitution of Work Time
    Reinhard Pirker 224

Chapter Seventen: Democratizing Capital: Alternatives to Market-led Transition
    Marguerite Mendell 234

Chapter Eighteen: Reciprocity and the Informal Economy in Latin America
    Larissa Adler Lomnitz 246

PART TWO: KARL POLANYI AND ILONA DUCZYNSKA
ILONA DUCZYNSKA POLANYI

Chapter Nineteen: Ilona Duczynska: Sovereign Revolutionary
    Kenneth McRobbie 255

Chapter Twenty: Ilona Duczynska and Austro-Marxism
    Alfred Pfabigan 265

Chapter Twenty-One: This is the Voice of Radio Schutzbund!
  Barbara Striker..272

Chapter Twenty-Two: From Girl Revolutionary to Old Dissident
  György Konrád...275

Chapter Twenty-Three: From Central Europe, Three Friends Remember
  Eva Cjzjk, Erzsébét Vezér, György Litván....................281

Chapter Four: The Polanyis Discover a Poet
  György Bodnár, Ferenc Juhász..............................288

MEMORIES OF KARL POLANYI IN VIENNA (1920–1936)

Chapter Twenty-Five: The Early Formation of Karl Polanyi's Ideas
  Eva Gábor...295

Chapter Twenty-Six: "I First Met Karl Polanyi in 1920..."
  Ilona Duczynska Polanyi...................................302

Chapter Twenty-Seven: Letter to a Friend, 1925
  Karl Polanyi..316

Chapter Twenty-Eight: Karl Polanyi, Ozkár Jászi, at the *Bécsi Magyar Újság*
  János Gyurgyák..319

Chapter Twenty-Nine: Editorial Meetings of the *Oesterreichischer Volkswirt* (1928)
  Richard A. Bermann..325

Chapter Thirty: Vorgartenstrasse 203: Extracts from a Memoir
  Felix Schaffer...328

Chapter Thirty-One: Mechanisms of the World Economic Crisis 1931–1933
  Karl Polanyi..347

Chapter Thirty-Two: "Old, Badly Peeled, Half-Raw Potatoes" and Peter F. Drucker's Other Myths About Karl Polanyi
  Kenneth McRobbie..359

Chapter Thirty-Three: Tracing Polanyi's Institutional Political Economy to its Central European Source
  Kari Polanyi Levitt.......................................378

List of Contributors..392

To the Memory of
Karl Polanyi
and Ilona Duczynska

Karl Polanyi and Ilona Duczynska Polanyi, in Vienna, in the 1920s.

Karl's father, Mihaly Pollacek with daughter Laura, mother of Michael, Eva (Zeisel) and George Striker.

Cecilia Wohl Polanyi, mother of Laura, Adolf, Karl, Michael and Sophie Polanyi, a familiar figure in Budapest intellectual and cultural circles, where she was affectionately known as 'Cecil Mama.'

A forradalom történetéhez.

Ilona Duczynska and (first husband) Tivadar Sugár who sparked the revolution in Budapest by writing and distributing anti-war literature in munitions factories and army barracks. They were tried, imprisoned, and freed by the victorious revolution in October 1918.

Karl Polanyi with daughter Kari, Vienna, 1925.

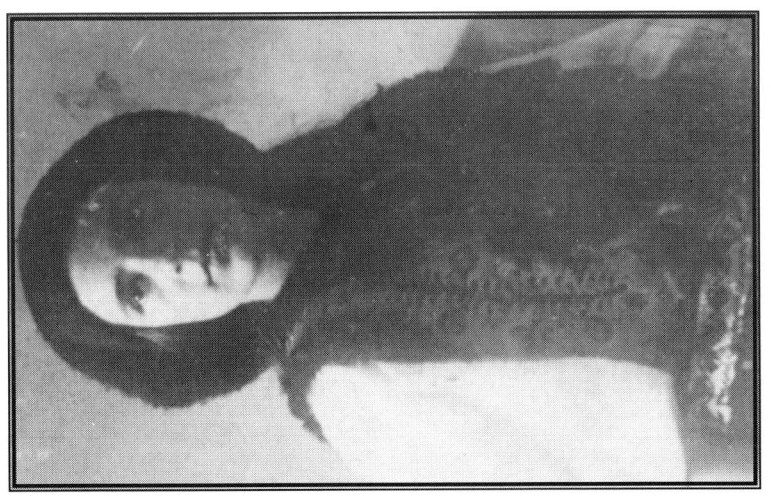

Ilona Duczynska as a young woman.

University students in the Vienna Woods, February 11, 1934, the day before the outbreak of a week of intense fighting between the workers' defense militia (Schutzbund) and the army. On the extreme left, George Striker, in front Barbara Striker, with Kari Polanyi, who was sent to England two weeks after this photo was taken.

Underground publications of the Schutsbund, outlawed by the clerico-fascist regime after February 1934. Ilona Duczynska participated in their production and distribution and criticized the social democratic leadership for their rejection of the advice of General Koerner on tactics. (See her Workers in Arms, *Monthly Review Press, 1978.)*

Left to right: Michael and Karl Polanyi with Karl's close friend Leo Popper, in Budapest, before World War I.

The Protestant Dorotheer Kirche, Vienna, where Karl and Ilona married, in February 1923.

Advertisement for the Oesterreichische Volkswirt, *in* The Economist, *May 26, 1934.*

The Polanyi brothers (left to right) Karl, Adolf, and Michael, with sisiter Laura Striker, in a family re-union in London.

INTRODUCTION
Kenneth McRobbie, Kari Polanyi Levitt

The first and larger part of this volume contains a selection of papers presented at the Fifth International Karl Polanyi Conference held in Vienna from November 10 to 13, 1994. The Conference was jointly organized by the Polanyi Institute of Political Economy of Concordia University, Montreal, and the Socioeconomic Research Unit of the Austrian Academy of Sciences, and was hosted by the Dr Karl Renner Institute. The second part of this volume consists of unpublished documentary material consisting principally of personal recollections of the life and work of Karl Polanyi and his wife Ilona Duczynska in Vienna from 1919 to 1933.

It was our hope that this Conference would light a spark, however small, to restore the memory of Karl Polanyi in intellectual circles of post-war Vienna. Though his work is now cited internationally with increasing frequency, the significance of the social embeddedness of markets has not apparently penetrated the intellectual defences of economic orthodoxy at the Austrian Academy of Sciences. We regret that the name of the socio-economic research unit which co-sponsored our Conference has been changed to eliminate its former designation as "socio-economic," at a time when investigations into the social institutions which sustain markets are moving to the frontiers of social science research.

The Conference marked the 50th anniversary of the publication of *The Great Transformation* (1944), a work recently rated as one of the hundred most important books of the 20th century. The resurgence of radical neoliberalism has given new relevance—and urgency—to Polanyi's critique of "market society." The other theme of the Conference was "Freedom in a Complex Society," the subject of the last chapter of *The Great Transformation*, and a life-long preoccupation, dating back to Polanyi's early formative years in Hungary. Some one hundred and fifty scholars from Europe, North America and the developing world were in attendance, together with family members, friends and former students of Karl Polanyi, and some eighty papers were presented.

THE CONTEMPORARY SIGNIFICANCE OF THE GREAT TRANSFORMATION

We have grouped the material in the first part of the book according to theme, commencing with that which was the principal concern of the Conference. Kari Polanyi-Levitt's welcoming address has been expanded to draw comparisons between the world economic crisis of the 1930s and the currently unfolding financial and economic crisis of the 1990s. She suggests that two books published in 1945 in England—Polanyi's The Great Transformation and Hayek's The Road To Serfdom—were conceived in socialist Vienna of the 1920s. They represent opposing views on the central problematic of our day—the freedom of capital and the freedom of citizens to exercise political democracy.

With reference to Polanyi's The Great Transformation Eric Helleiner challenges the widely held view that financial globalization is technologically driven, irreversible, and beneficial. Drawing on previous work, he argues that the liberalization of cross-border capital flows was encouraged and facilitated by Anglo-American policy. He suggests that countervailing defensive measures to restore a degree of social control over capital are gathering support at the international, national, regional and local levels. In this connection the paper engages in a comprehensive discussion of the feasibility of the Tobin Tax. In conclusion Helleiner identifies the target of Polanyi's critique as the "Austrian school" of neoliberalism led by Hayek and Von Mises. Polanyi, he wrote, encountered this school during his intellectually formative years in Vienna after World War One, and his 1944 book stands as one of the first sustained critiques of this school whose influence is increasingly substantial and global in scope.

In a paper on a similar theme, Fred Block argues that the slowing down of growth and the rise in unemployment in the major industrial countries are due to the high cost of borrowed funds and reductions in state expenditure driven by the fiscal burden of debt servicing. The liberalization of global finance and the development of new financial instruments have enabled investors to obtain high rates of return on financial investments without incurring risks associated with the long term commitment of funds to the real economy. He concludes that three types of reform of the international financial system are required: a return to more stable exchange rates, measures to increase the transaction costs of foreign exchange markets (such as the Tobin Tax), and international agreement on the re-imposition of national capital controls.

Björn Hettne recalls Polanyi's warnings against what he called the "hazards of planetary interdependence" associated with global market expansion. He develops the case for a regionalized world system of relatively closed rather than aggressively competing regions, which may serve as a protective shield against an enforced global culture of middle-class consumerism and mass poverty. Large enough to have a degree of economic efficiency, the New Regionalism may prove more stable and peaceful than a liberal world order which historically has revealed a tendency to collapse.

Hettne details five respects in which the New Regionalism differs from the old, and suggests that a "developmental regionalism" may provide solutions for development problems of the South.

The New Regionalism finds favour with Samir Amin who repeats his previously stated support for the "construction of a polycentric world" as a framework within which negotiated interdependence can be organized in a way which offers dominated peoples and classes improved conditions of participation in production, and access to better conditions of life. For small and medium states this implies action at the regional level, and collective negotiation between regions. Like Hettne, he points the reader to Polanyi, who understood that history is not shaped by infallible laws of economics, but is the product of social reactions to the effects of these laws.

Michele Cangiani reviews Polanyi's writings of the 1920s and 1930s and finds support for the belief that the social organization of the economy should be rescued from market rationality, and be determined by free individuals in the context of democratic institutions. Polanyi maintained that the "self regulating market" was a utopia, which was in any event rendered obsolete by 20th century capitalism that generated new demands for conscious democratic control over the economy. The primacy of economic democracy and cultural and political control over narrowly economic functions is no less relevant at the end of the 20th century than it was when Polanyi made this analysis.

The continuing appeal of *The Great Transformation* may partly be explained, Kenneth McRobbie suggests, by its visionary character deriving from Polanyi's passionate conviction as to humanity's social and cultural needs. That he was able to articulate the vision so effectively was due to his profoundly "humanistic," particularly literary background which enabled him to deploy stylistic techniques and verbal resources in order to render comprehensible changes of almost inconceivable magnitude.

TRANSITIONS FROM PLANNED TO MARKET ECONOMIES

Jan Kregel observed that western advisors to former state socialist regimes seem to be unaware of the distinction between substantive and formal definitions of the market; they assume that effectively functioning economic institutions will emerge spontaneously by privatization. Similarly they appear to believe that democratic political institutions will likewise develop autonomously. Not only have these not emerged in the constituent republics of the former Soviet Union, but the economic "reforms" which separate the economic from the social, political and military spheres, as László Andor shows, have created new potential and actual conflicts in East Euope. They have resulted in increasing political, social and financial insta - bility, and a significant rise in the exposure of individuals to criminal activity.

The unreality of policies based on the market principle alone is illustrated by the experience of Bulgaria. There the collapse of state economic structures has revealed economic sub-structures of "embeddedness." Yulian Konstantinov presents evidence that economic activity continues to be embedded in traditional aspects of cultural and ethnic life of majority and minority communities. In a companion paper which ranges across various periods of history, Tanya Chavdorova demonstrates the continuation of historic patterns of reciprocity and re-distribution in the emerging market economy of Bulgaria.

Birgit Müller shows how the "freedom of the market" introduced existential insecurity to workers in former East Berlin enterprises. They discovered that the market created a discipline which destroyed their former state of what Polanyi called "leisure in security." In a complementary piece on the "freedom of capital" from state intervention, Alan Scott argues that the British experience of privatization actually increased the power of the state *vis à vis* the population. New regimes of regulation and direction have enabled the state to dispense "largesse" to favoured enterprises, while also acquiring new powers of regulation, controlling "the parameters within which actors act autonomously."

IDENTITIES, CULTURE, CITIZENSHIP AND DEMOCRACY

In accordance with increasing interest in the role of "civil society" and the devaluation of the state in the management of economies, a number of papers addressed topics of "Identities, Culture, Citizenship and Democracy." Reinhard Pirker argues that the individual cannot be considered an autonomous irreducible unit of analysis, because institutions influence the formation of goals and interpretations of the world. Individuals are constrained to actively pursue their interests within the limitations created by such conditioning. Pirker elaborates the argument with respect to the concept of "working time"—an instituted creation of modern industrial society, unknown to mankind during millennia of agricultural societies which preceded modernization.

The locus of human existence is increasingly the space of the world economy, within which, as André Drainville shows, the individual is pressing for extended political rights rather than yielding to the hegemony of social formations representing "the new world order." The paper explores the capacities of what Robert Cox has called the *nébuleuse* of international organizations to resolve three problems: the transition of East Europe to "market democracy," the management of international migration, and the third phase of the debt crisis. The ultimate objective is the political invention of a *cité*—and thus a *droit de cité*—in the world economy.

Gregor Matjan addresses similar issues. He argues that it is the the right of individuals to defend their way of life against the systemic powers of both state and market. To utilitarian individualism, Polanyi posits expressive individualism which could lead to greater openness of society and to cultural pluralism. The more freedom there is in the globalized economy and private (life style) relationships, the more governments react with in stitutional closure, immigration laws, and restriction on access to social welfare. In this context, "radical egalitarianism" may have potential for controlling globalized capitalism and national bureaucracies. When confronted by inadequate performance of dominant economic and social institutions, the individual retreats into forms of associative endeavour. The downsizing of the welfare state has given rise to a variety of counter movements which Marguerite Mendell terms "the third sector." To provide for their needs, people are building alternative institutions, recognizing that these must be embedded to form a "social economy," to challenge the prevailing economic agenda. Indeed, such a "third sector" may embrace also the middle class. Larissa Lomnitz describes how in Latin America, not only the poor but also the middle classes complement the formal economy with informal exchanges; above all, reciprocity has emerged parallel with the formal market economy.

ILONA DUCZYNSKA POLANYI

On the closing day of the conference, a session was devoted to Ilona Duczynska Polanyi whose role was acknowledged in Polanyi's *The Great Transformation*: "To my beloved wife Ilona Duczynska I dedicate this book which owes all to her help and criticism." Following his death in 1964, she was actively engaged in encouraging and negotiating the translation of Polanyi's books into several languages. Although Polanyi never returned to Vienna, Duczynska later resided there for part of each year in connection with her research and with her activities in Hungary.

All those who spoke about Duczynska in the panel "Ilona Duczynska: Sovereign Revolutionary" knew her personally. Barbara Striker, a relative, recalled her own role in moving "Radio Schutzbund" (an illegal mobile radio transmitter) from apartment to apartment to avoid detection, to broadcast messages written by Duczynska to sustain the Vienna workers following the defeat of February 1934. Alfred Pfabigan reviewed Duczynska's controversial portrait of General Körner as the "democratic bolshevik," which became a cult book of the "new left" in the 1970s, whose central thesis concerned the feasibility of alternative tactics of armed struggle based on small autonomous units.

Duczynska's life as exemplar to a younger generation of Hungarians is well expressed by the historian György Litván. He recounts how, in the 1970s, she would alight in Budapest from her battered Volkswagen as if stepping out of a "time machine" that transported her from the past to a present of expectant youth: new friends, students and intellectuals. Erzsébet Vezér's recollections of Duczynska convey her exceptional modesty of manner, her tolerance, and her sureness of literary judgment coupled with shrewdness in assessing persons, as in the case of her instantaneous attraction to the eminent Catholic existentialist poet, János Pilinszky. Finally from Vienna, Eva Czjzek, translator of the Hungarian novelist László Németh, recalls Duczynska's simple warmth as a companion, and her formidable capacity for work under all conditions; she recalls visiting her during one of her numerous bouts of illness in the *Wiener Allgemeiner Krankenhaus*, where she found her propped up on pillows, at work on a stack of manuscripts which she was translating.

A second panel on "The Polanyi's choice of Poets" revealed how Duczynska the scientist and political activist, like Polanyi the (reluctant) lawyer turned economic historian, were of a generation for whom the classics of world literature, beginning in her case with the Russian novel, were the natural reading matter of their adolescence, both of them early falling under the spell of the revolutionary avant garde lyric poet Endre Ady. The conference heard contributions from two of Hungary's leading writers. The novelist György Konrád evoked aspects of Duczynska's early life: a childhood spent between two cultures (impoverished Austrian and landed Hungarian gentry), and her plan in 1917 to assassinate the Prime Minister (thwarted only by his resignation)—and meditates on great lives that time turns to ashes, yet which memory can blow into a flame. The other literary figure in attendance was Ferenc Juhász, the poet whose work has been praised by W.H. Auden and George Steiner. Juhász was "discovered" by the Polanyis and introduced to the English-speaking literary world in the anthology *The Plough and the Pen* (1963) which they edited, Duczynska later collaborating on a volume of translations of his selected poems. For the occasion of the conference, Juhász composed a prose poem which he dedicated to the Polanyis, a work representative of his unique surrealist blend of folklore and science. The literary critic György Bodnar then described the nature of the poetic achievement of Ferenc Juhász in accounting for the profound effects his poetry had on the Polanyis.

The introduction to the section on Duczynska provides an outline of her remarkable life of action: her organizational role in the anti-war movement in Budapest in 1917-18; her participation in the second Comintern Congress in 1920 and later in Vienna in the illegal Schutzbund, the para-military arm of the Austrian Social Democratic Party, about which she wrote a monograph; her aeronautical research in Britain during the war; her interest in land reform and peasant conditions world wide (including field work in villages in Hungary and Mexico); her growing involvement with Hungarian affairs which led her in 1956 to begin compiling, together with her husband, a literary anthology; and finally support, both moral and practical, for young dissidents who she believed desired a socialism with a human face—convinced, it has to be said, that only a truly socialist society could have the lineaments of humanity. Throughout she was sustained by an iron will, one that also helped sustain others, and a resolve after the death of her husband to see that his manuscripts found editors and publishers and that his work should appear in translation.

A BUS TOUR OF "RED VIENNA"

Following the Conference, on a cloudy Sunday afternoon, a tour bus set out from the Dr Karl Renner Institute toward the city centre. For a few hours, conference participants were transported back in time to "Red Vienna" of the 1920s. There was a commentary by a specially commissioned—and very well informed—Austrian tour guide, with simultaneous translation by Kari Polanyi-Levitt, who added personal reminiscences as the bus wound its way through the streets of Vienna. The city's older architectural splendors co-exist with a large number of newer well-designed public housing projects—large and small—constructed by the socialist city administration in the 1920s, now renovated and considered among the more desirable dwelling units. These *Gemeindehauser*, as they are called, were financed and subsidized by heavy property taxes imposed on private residences. In pre-1914 Austria, living conditions of the working class had been appalling; tuberculosis, the disease of poverty, was epidemic.

The bus stopped and people got out to admire the most famous of these complexes—the Karl Marx Hof—whose imposing semi-circular arches in mellowed red and blue stucco enclose spacious inner landscaped gardens, in one of which the statue of "The Sower" stands on a tall pedestal. The building takes up a large city block, but each section is designed on a human scale. It was, and remains, a model of public housing. For a week, starting on Monday February 12, 1934, the workers of Vienna heroically defended these buildings. Days and nights of heavy shelling left pockmarks on walls, visible for decades. By the end of the week, socialist Vienna was history; the leaders of the Social Democratic Party were in exile in Prague. The only organized force which could have resisted Hitler when he marched into Austria in 1938, was destroyed by native conservative forces.

Polanyi took with him undying memories of what a socialist administration could do for the quality of life of an urban population. He was convinced that Red Vienna's civic administration had provided the best and most modern urban environment of any working class, together with remarkable social, cultural and recreational services. And this in a small, defeated country with a high rate of unemployment. Tribute is paid in an endnote to *The Great Transformation* where Polanyi wrote that "the great experiment" of Vienna's attempt to transcend the market economy "remains one of the most spectacular cultural triumphs of western history." (pp. 287-288)

Thereafter the bus passed landmarks linked with the Polanyi family. There came into view the turn-of-the-century building which had housed the offices of the *Oesterreichische Volkswirt*, the scene of weekly editorial meetings. It passed by the Café Bauernfeld, later utilized for a dramatic rendezvous in the film version of Graham Greene's "The Third Man." The bus took a sharp right turn at the Belvederegasse where the young Polanyi and his cousin Ervin Szabó had often stayed in the Klatchko family apartment, a stop-over for rest and recuperation for Russian revolutionaries of all parties and tendencies. Close by was another apartment house with a plaque of the former occupant that showed Josef Stalin in profile, possibly the only such memento in all of Europe. In response to Krushchov's request that it be removed, the Austrians, sticklers for legality, pointed out that on the insistence of the Soviet (then occupying) authorities, a guarantee of the plaque's perpetual existence had been written into the constitution.

In the deepening shadows of the late afternoon faces were pressed to the bus window as it passed the apartment house at Vorgartenstrasse 203, set back behind a small garden. This is where the Polanyi family had lived. Kari Polanyi-Levitt pointed out her elementary school, which had not changed in appearance in 60 years; when she mentioned the secondary school she had attended, the tour guide informed us that this was the school also attended by former Chancellor Bruno Kreisky.

KARL AND ILONA POLANYI IN VIENNA 1920-1936

"Karl Polanyi in Vienna" represents a sort of "repatriation" of Karl Polanyi to the city in which he lived and worked in the 1920s until the accession of Hitler to power in Germany in 1933 cast the shadow of impending fascism over Austria. As the "Red" (socialist) member of the editorial team of the *Volkswirt*, the changing political landscape could no longer accommodate his views. His employment was terminated and he left for London in November 1933. His daughter was sent to join him in March 1934, following the events of the previous month. His wife stayed to participate in the illegal work of the Schutzbund, until ill health caused her to leave for England in 1936.

The move from Vienna to England was Polanyi's second political emigration. The first was in 1919 when he arrived in Vienna from Budapest as one of several thousand refugees from the counter-revolutionary White Terror of Horthy's Hungary. He was then 33 years old and suffered from a serious illness contracted during the Great War in which he served as a cavalry officer on the Eastern (Russian) front. Before the war, Polanyi was a well-known figure in Budapest intellectual circles, founding president of the Hungarian student movement known as the Galilei Circle, and editor of the free thinking journal *Századok*. He first met Ilona Duczynska in 1920 in a *pension* which accommodated refugees from the Hungarian counter-revolution.

Karl and Ilona were married in 1923 and soon after set up house in the Vorgartenstrasse, where they lived until their emigration to England. Although both were born in or near Vienna—the old cosmopolitan Vienna of the Austro-Hungarian empire—their critical formative life experiences were Hungarian, rather than Austrian. In Vienna Ilona studied engineering at the Technical University. Both Polanyis were nominal members of the Austrian Social Democratic Party, but neither played an active role in Austrian politics, until February 1934 which Ilona, as already mentioned worked with the (then illegal) Schutzbund. They were however enthusiastic supporters of the socialist municipal administration of Vienna whose pioneering housing, cultural and community developments attracted international attention in the 1920s.

In Vienna Polanyi earned his living by journalism, initially with the Hungarian emigré paper *Bésci Magyar Ujság* edited by his friend Oscar Jászi who later emigrated to the United States. In 1924, Polanyi was invited to join the staff of the leading Austrian economic weekly *Der Oesterreichische Volkswirt*, as senior editor with special brief for international economic and political affairs. His weekly columns documented the unfolding world economic crisis, whose origins he ascribed to efforts by the victorious powers to re-instate the pre-1914 liberal economic order. In Vienna Polanyi first encountered (Austrian) economics, and engaged in debates on the feasibility of socialism with its formidable academic exponents in the leading academic journal of the day. He gave public lectures on guild socialism and participated in adult educational activities. For many years he conducted a "private seminar" on the economics of socialism which met in the family apartment. Felix Schaffer, whose memoirs we reproduce was a regular and faithful participant. But economics was not the only, or even the principal subject of discussion in this "salon" where Zeisel, Lazarsfeld, Popper, Kolnai and many others gathered to discuss philosophy, literature, and politics. It was in Vienna that Polanyi began to formulate ideas which influenced his later teaching and research in England and the United States.

The documentation which constitutes the second part of this volume is rich in insights into Polanyi's life and intellectual concerns in the Vienna of the 1920s. The first item is an extended version of a paper by Éva Gábor of the Michael Polanyi Philosophical Association, which recounts Karl Polanyi's stature as a leading intellectual in pre-1914 Budapest. Next is a lengthy manuscript of unpublished biographical material by Duczynska in which she recounts Karl Polanyi's memories of his childhood and youth and the circumstances of their first meeting. The "Letter to a Friend" that follows was written by Karl Polanyi to Richard Wanke in 1925. Preserved by his widow for five decades, it was anonymously returned to Duczynska in a Budapest hospital in the mid-1970s. Then comes an account of editorial meetings of the *Oesterreichische Volkswirt* by Richard Bermann which provides a unique insight into the journal's personalities and practices by a member of the editorial team.

Last but not least, we reproduce extracts from Felix Schaffer's memoirs, a detailed and reliable account of the intellectual and personal lives of the Polanyis, their family and friends, from 1924 when Schaffer first encountered Polanyi to their last brief meeting in London in 1939. Days later, the Schaffer family sailed to New Zealand where a new life took shape. With a doctorate in economics from the University of Vienna, Schaffer became Professor of Economics at the University of Wellington. Kari Polanyi-Levitt can attest to the accuracy of every detail of Schaffer's description of the Polanyi household: his vignettes of family members and digressions on people and places are equally remarkable. His extensive account of conversations with Polanyi—from which only small extracts are included here—is an invaluable source of research material on Polanyi's (ultimately unsuccessful) attempts to construct a model of a democratic associational socialist economy using the tools of Austrian neoclassical economics.

In England, Polanyi found his *métier* as educator. From 1934 until his departure for Bennington College in the United States in 1940, he worked as tutor for the Workers Educational Association, the adult education outreach programmes of the Universities of Oxford and London. This opened up new vistas, both academic and personal. The assigned courses plunged him into intensive study of English economic and social history. Direct contact with English working-class life dispelled long held illusions of the Anglophilia typical of his generation of continental intellectuals. In England he encountered the "dark satanic mills" of the industrial revolution, which scarred the landscape with coal pits and slums, and stripped the working classes of their heritage of pre-industrial traditional culture. His lecture notes, carefully preserved by his wife, are rough early drafts of *The Great Transformation*. The insights gained in Vienna now found expression in a historical interpretation of the origins and consequences of the "utopian" project of the organization of economic life by self-regulating markets. But that is another story, for another day, for others who might some day organize a Karl Polanyi conference in Britain, and produce a volume on "Karl Polanyi in England."

As to the division of labour of the editors, both collaborated in the design of the book, and the selection of conference papers. Kenneth McRobbie undertook responsibility for correspondence with contributors and related editorial duties. Additionally, he has enriched this volume by sharing material he has collected in preparation for a book-length biography of Ilona Duczynska Polanyi. Kari Polanyi-Levitt who initially proposed that the Fifth Polanyi Conference be held in the city of her birth and that of her parents, provided selected extracts from a 100-page manuscript by Felix Schaffer, and translated this and other material from the German. We extend our thanks to Black Rose Books, for encouraging us to depart from convention by attaching memoirs to a collection of conference proceedings.

Kenneth McRobbie and Kari Polanyi-Levitt
Vancouver and Montreal, July 1999

PART ONE

THEMES FROM THE WORK OF KARL POLANYI

FIFTH INTERNATIONAL
KARL POLANYI CONFERENCE

Vienna, 1994

THE CONTEMPORARY SIGNIFICANCE
OF
THE GREAT TRANSFORMATION

Chapter One

THE GREAT TRANSFORMATION FROM 1920 TO 1990
Kari Polanyi Levitt

The International Karl Polanyi Conference held in Vienna in 1994 coincided with the 50th anniversary of the publication of *The Great Transformation* (1944) and the 30th anniversary of the death of my father. Friedrich Hayek's *The Road To Serfdom* was published in the same year. *The Great Transformation* was well received in the United States but attracted no interest in England where it was published in 1945 as *The Origins of Our Times*. Hayek's polemic against socialism of any variety suggested that the election of the Labour Party could set Britain on the road to totalitarianism. It attracted mixed reviews in England, but met with disbelief and ridicule in the United States where "New Deal" Keynesians were firmly established in the economics profession. Prior to the ideological shift associated with the Cold War and the McCarthy witch hunts of the early 1950s, there was more tolerance for Hayek's views in Britain than in the United States.

For the next twenty five years the Keynesian consensus of "embedded" liberalism achieved an unprecedented increase in the material standard of living under state-managed welfare capitalism, within the political framework of the Cold War, and the capacity of the United States to adhere to the Bretton Woods order and finance general economic expansion. The third quarter of the 20th century has been described as the Age of Keynes. Hayek had to wait 50 years to claim ideological patrimony over the last quarter.

The neo-liberal counter-revolution following economic and political turmoil in the 1970s is too well known to require elaboration. Suffice it to say that in the Age of Hayek the 19th century liberal economic order was refurbished and presented as an inevitable trend toward a globalized world of winners and losers, requiring the subordination of all aspects of social and cultural life to intensified economic competition. Hayek's libertarianism furnished the "globalization" agenda with an ideology dressed in the language of economics. Yet Polanyi's prophetic warning of the perils of the "utopia" of a generalized "self-regulating" market cast a lengthening shadow over the neo-liberal vision of universal capitalism.

Hayek was hostile to market intervention of any form, including Keynesian policies of macro-economic management and deficit financing. His radical neo-liberalism was grounded in the belief that economic planning was incompatible with individual liberty. For Polanyi the freedom of the individual required the subordination of capital to social control. He believed that the measures taken by the western powers to re-construct the 19th century economic order in the years following the First World War, were directly responsible for the political, social and financial turmoil which projected the capitalist world into economic breakdown in the 1930s. Fascism, Stalinist communism and the New Deal were protective national reactions to save societies from economic and social disintegration. He thought (hoped?) that the lessons of the interwar period would result in the transformation of the 19th century liberal economy into some form of planned and regulated economic order, under the guidance of the nation state.

The opposing views of Hayek and Polanyi on the place of the economy in society were debated in Vienna in the 1920s in an exchange between Hayek's mentor and patron Ludwig von Mises and socialist economists, including Karl Polanyi. The debate on "socialist accountancy" in the pages of the principal academic German-language journal of the day, turned on the feasibility of constructing a socialist economy without market-determined prices.[1] It played against the background of mass unemployment and fiscal austerity, as stabilization and adjustment policies to protect the gold denominated value of currencies depressed living standards of the populations of small and weak countries in Central and East Europe. Polanyi was an enthusiastic admirer of the socialist municipal administration of "Red Vienna" which provided state-of-the-art public housing for the working classes, while Hayek championed the interests of Vienna's bourgeoisie whose property taxes financed these programmes.[2] It was a classic contest between "social" and "economic" priorities.

In the 1920s, the Austrian or Vienna school of economics attracted the attention of English and American conservative economists. Hayek, then a promising younger disciple of that school, was brought to the London School of Economics by Lionel Robbins to counter the economic doctrines of Keynes and his associates in Cambridge. A reading of Hayek's mature work reveals a radical liberal vision of the economy as a structure "arising without design from human interaction." The "macroeconomics of the last fifty years" is demonized as a "delusion...the nearest thing to the practice of magic...by professional economists whose extensive use of mathematics has unduly impressed politicians lacking in mathematical education." But the 19th century liberal El Dorado, once described by Eric Hobsbawn as "the anarchism of the bourgeoisie...which had no place for the state," did not arise "without design from human action."

According to Polanyi, nothing could be further from the truth. In *The Great Transformation* he showed that the "laissez faire" liberal economic order was designed by the early English political economists and instituted by the power of the state. "Free" labour markets to force workers to accept employment on conditions offered by the capitalists, were legislated and enforced, on penalty of starvation or the poor house—a fate worse than prison. Workers attempting to defend themselves by combining in trade unions were deported to penal colonies. In a frequently quoted passage Polanyi explained that "laissez faire was planned"—while the protective reaction of society against the discipline of the market was "spontaneous." We note similarities with "free trade" imposed on developing countries by powerful international institutions, on penalty of denial of access to markets and finance. Nor did England acquire the largest empire in all human history in a proverbial "fit of absent mindedness." Prior to 1914, Britain's formal and informal colonies of conquest and settlement yielded backflows of rentier incomes of 8 to 9 per cent of GNP which fed the life style of the English upper classes, and the wealth of the City of London as premier financial center of the world and anchor of the international gold standard.

In describing the role of international finance in restoring rightist regimes in Central and Eastern Europe, Polanyi noted that:

> Vienna became the Mecca of liberal economists on account of the brilliantly successful operation on Austria's *krone* which the patient unfortunately did not survive. In Bulgaria, Greece, Finland, Lithuania, Estonia, Poland and Rumania the restoration of the currency provided counter revolution with a claim to power. In Belgium, France and England the left was thrown out of office in the name of sound monetary standards. An almost unbroken sequence of currency crises linked the indigent Balkans with the affluent United States through the elastic band of the international credit system which transmitted the strains of the imperfectly restored currencies first from Eastern to Western Europe, and then from Western Europe to the United States until the United States itself was engulfed in the premature stabilization of European currencies. (pp.23-24)

Like Kindleberger's classic interpretation of the origins of the Great Depression, Polanyi's account turned on the dynamics of unsustainable structures of external indebtedness.

The international gold standard was a mechanism which imposed deflationary measures on debtor countries to protect the value of financial assets of creditors and the interests of the City of London and Wall Street. Keynes understood better than any other economist that the inter-war gold standard favoured the propertied classes at the expense of the labouring classes: "The gold standard, with its general regardlessness of social detail, is an essential emblem of those who sit in the top tier of the machine." His scathing indictment of "The Economic Consequences of Mr Churchill" and the Bank of England which subjected British miners to the "economic juggernaut" of deflationary policies to defend the overvalued pound in the 1920s is a classic of economic literature. Polanyi's account of the vulnerability of the small and weak peripheral states of Central and East Europe to a pull on the "golden thread" reads like a pre-view of the IMF stabilization and adjustment programmes of the 1980s and 1990s. There was hardly an internal crisis in Europe that did not reach its climax on an issue of the external value of the currency. By means of deflation, mass dismissal of public servants, wage repression and persistent unemployment, currencies were stabilized and fixed in terms of gold, to guarantee debt service to foreign bond holders. In the succession states of Central Europe international creditors instituted regimes of external supervision under the auspices of the League of Nations operating from Geneva.

Polanyi came to England to seek work after he had to resign from the editorial team of Austria's leading economic and financial weekly. Following the accession of Hitler to power in Germany in 1933, the journal could no longer keep an outspoken socialist on staff. It is our contention that Polanyi's Vienna years played a significant role in the formulation of the principal argument of *The*

Great Transformation. His position as senior editor of the *Osterreichische Volkwirt* from 1924 to 1933 with responsibility for international affairs, placed him in the eye of the storm of the political and economic upheavals of continental Europe. From this observation post he followed the unravelling of attempts by the western powers to restore the pre-1914 economic order and its eventual break-down in 1931, when a financial crisis which started with the collapse of a major bank in Vienna spread westward to England and the United States. His articles, now available in Italian translation by Michele Cangiani,[3] constitute a detailed account and analysis of political and financial events of the inter-war period—summarized in Part One of *The Great Transformation* as "Conservative Twenties; Revolutionary Thirties." The closing paragraph of this chapter links Polanyi's earlier journalistic observations of the world economic crisis with his subsequent encounter with English social and economic history. Like Marx, who came to England a century before him, Polanyi found the "origins of our times" in the birthplace of industrial capitalism, in 19th century England:

> Market society was born in England—yet it was on the Continent that its weakness engendered the most tragic complications. In order to comprehend German fascism, we must revert to Ricardian England. The Industrial Revolution was an English event. Market economy, free trade, and the gold standard were English inventions. These institutions broke down in the Twenties everywhere—in Germany, Italy or Austria the event was merely more political and more dramatic. But whatever the scenery and the temperature of the final episodes, the long run factors which wrecked that civilization should be studied in the birth-place of the Industrial Revolution, England. (p. 30)

Emigration to England and the shock of the discovery of the de-culturalization and immiseration of the working classes in the homeland of industrial capitalism constituted a critical experiential input to the central chapters of the book. The legacy of Blake's "dark Satanic mills"—the slums of London, Birmingham and Manchester, the coal valleys of Wales, the hopelessness in the faces of England's two and a half million unemployed, and the crass class structure of Britain—stood in contrast to the higher quality of life of the working class in (economically much poorer) socialist Vienna. England, it should be remembered, was at that time richer than any other European country, whereas post-war Austria suffered persistent high unemployment. In Polanyi's formative years, England was the Mecca of the intelligentsia of Central Europe—a role played on a world scale by the United States after the Second World War.

In England, my father earned his living as extramural tutor for the Workers Education Association from 1934 until 1940, when he was invited to spend three years in the United States where the book was written. His lecture notes, on loan to the Karl Polanyi Institute at Concordia University in Montreal, constitute a preliminary outline of *The Great Transformation*. Part One of the book draws on Polanyi's Vienna observations on the 19th international economic order which, in his view, terminated in 1931-33. Much of the material in Part Two which constitutes the main body of the book, derives from his interpretation of English social and economic history, a subject he regularly taught in WEA evening course classes.

The central thesis of *The Great Transformation* was that the civilization which collapsed in the 1920s was "economic" in a different sense from that in which all societies have been limited by the material conditions of existence. It was "economic" in the distinctive sense that it chose to base itself on a motive never before raised to the level of justification of action and behaviour in everyday life, namely individual gain. Market economy grew to maturity in England, spread to Europe and to America and eventually, Polanyi wrote, "it shaped daily issues into a pattern the main traits of which were identical in all countries of western civilization." (p.30) "Identical" is perhaps an overstatement. The differences in the way capitalism has impacted on different societies are not unimportant. On re-reading the cited passage about the English origins of the key institutions of liberal capitalism, one is struck by the continuity of an Anglo-Saxon political culture which has elevated the institutions of private property, private enterprise, and private profit to normative ends in and of themselves, and the fiction of "economic man" to a pseudo-scientific shibboleth. In the Anglo-American political culture, the worth, value and social status of an individual is judged by the market price he or she is able to command. In contrast, the difference in remuneration between top management and shop floor labour is very much less in Japan or Europe than it is in the United States.

In Britain, barely one third of workers now have full-time tenured jobs. The rest, according to a *Guardian* report in the mid 1990s, "have been plunged into uncertainty and conditions that 19th century factory workers would have recognized." Britain ranks bottom of the league of OECD countries in terms of the protection of labour. British employers "can treat labour more as a disposable commodity and displace the risk of fluctuating demand onto their workers. They meet the very high financial returns demanded by the City of London by pushing labour into abysmal insecurity and increasing poverty." The Anglo-American variety of capitalism is individualistic as no other national capitalism is. Time-horizons are shorter, time preference stronger, expected rates of return higher, and rates of saving lower than is the case in continental Europe or in Japan. It is this Anglo-American version of shareholder capitalism which is being forced on developing countries by the concerted pressure of capital markets sustained by the International Monetary Fund and the combined power of the major OECD countries.

In this model, holders of financial assets are favoured over debtors and borrowers by restrictive monetary policies and high interest rates. Policy makers with an eye on bond market ratings and speculative attack on currencies, have a reflexive bias toward deflation. Years of restrictive monetary policies in the major OECD countries have put thousands of productive enterprises into bankruptcy, enabling gigantic corporations to merge, consolidate and grow ever more powerful. Growth in the real economy has been sluggish over the past 15 years, unemployment rising, non-financial corporate profits declining, commodity prices weakening, and the purchasing power of low-income consumers falling.

In developing countries, restrictive monetary regimes, fiscal austerity, deficit reduction, dismantling of subsidies, and erosion of social infrastructure were accompanied by large devaluations, on the theory that a change in the external value of the currency could "switch" production from domestic to export markets as simply as the flow of traffic can be diverted by a road sign. Throughout the 1980s, countries were pressured to open their markets to imports, and divert resources from domestic to export markets to finance imports and service external debt. The privatization of public capital, initiated by Thatcher in Britain, was added to the arsenal of IMF/World Bank adjustment measures in the later 1980s. Countries were judged by their success in implementing structural reforms, with little regard for the consequences. The patient was considered to be improving so long as the medication was administered as prescribed. The means became ends. Economics became ideology. Accelerated liberalization of cross border flows was urged on developing countries as a way to attract capital and sustain economic growth. In the mid-1990s Mexico and South Korea were rewarded for financial liberalisation by acceptance into the OECD, the club of the rich and powerful. The admission price proved to be very costly to both these countries. It is now acknowledged that financial opening to vast and unregulated flows of short-term capital was a major cause of the "Asian crisis."

Global finance seemed to have acquired a life of its own, as a mass of disembodied money swirling around the globe, descending from the skies to mount attacks on currencies, gave political leaders and their public servants sleepless nights waiting for the reaction of the markets. In developing countries, billions in reserves have been bled out of central banks, billions in asset values have been destroyed, and millions of workers have fallen into poverty and chronic insecurity. Global capital markets have acted as gigantic engines of inequality transferring wealth from the weak to the strong, from debtors to creditors, wage earners and tax payers to the holders of paper claims, from productive to financial activity. The "market-friendly" model of winners and losers is not only inequitable in the distribution of the gains from growth. It is economically, politically, socially and ecologically unstable, and ultimately unsustainable.

The power of the media has created the impression that this is a technologically driven trend beyond the control of national or international policy intervention. To survive in this globalized world, we are told, countries must subordinate domestic concerns to competition in external markets. But "global markets" are not the autonomous creation of a technological revolution in communication, but were instituted by deliberate policy action in the (creditor) interests of the owners of financial claims to income and capital gains. The move to financial liberalization which destroyed the Bretton Woods order, was led by the City of London and subsequently received the support of the United States which has benefited from the position of the dollar as the major reserve currency of the world economy. The role of British and American policy in freeing financial markets from national control is documented in an excellent study by the Canadian political economist, Eric Helleiner.[4] The United States has been able to postpone adjustment to the loss of competitiveness by attracting large net capital inflows, reminiscent of Britain's ability to finance an import surplus by the backflow of overseas interest and profits in the late 19th and early 20th century.

Unrestricted international capital movements are eroding the fiscal base of the welfare state and the capacity of countries to sustain full employment policies, as Keynes knew it would. This is why he advocated permanent capital controls as an essential feature of the Bretton Woods system. For Keynes "the great problem of the age was to free modern industrialization from the fetters of financial capitalism."[5]

The Bretton Woods institutions have long ceased to play the roles originally assigned to them. They have been subverted to bulldoze economic and social protective structures of weak indebted countries. Countries have been forced to dollarize internal prices so that food and other basic necessities of life cost the same in Jamaica as they cost in New York or Toronto, where average incomes are ten to twenty times higher. Debt servicing has priority over developmental expenditures, and real resource transfers from debtor to creditor countries in the form of export surpluses are reminiscent of the economics of colonialism.

Since the demise of the Bretton Woods system in the early 1970s, the international economy has become less stable, growth momentum weaker, real interest rates higher, unemployment chronic, competition fiercer, and income inequalities within and between states very much greater. Exchange rates are no longer governed by trade flows, but by capital movements, including speculative attacks on currencies and destabilizing capital flight which drain the exchange reserves of central banks of countries attempting to stave off impoverishing devaluations. In the 1980s, countries with balance of payment problems were urged to restrict money supply, devalue the currency and increase exports. The case for devaluation was made with regard to the trade account: for exporters, a devaluation lowers costs and increases revenues in local currency. In the 1990s, exchange rates are increasingly volatile, driven by surges of large short-term cross border capital flows.

Interestingly, the IMF has lost its earlier enthusiasm for devaluations. The guardians of the international capitalist order are desperately trying to protect the asset value of foreign placements from melt down by the devaluation of currencies. They intervene in the market to defend the interests of international creditors and lenders. Not trade, but the stability of the international financial order is now the priority. We note the trend toward "independent" central banks and currency board linkages of domestic money to the dollar. Central banks, which used to be instruments of Keynesian anti-cyclical policies of full employment, have reverted to their original vocation of "price stability" at any cost. These institutional devices are attempts to re-create the "automaticity" of the old gold standard. However, conditions today resemble the 1930s, when the tensions between the "social" and the "economic" blew the gold standard out of the water. *The Great Transformation* is an eloquent warning of the consequences of subordinating societies and cultures to finance. It points to the urgent need to impose limitations on the market and to defend, protect and restore the capacity of societies to shape economic institutions in accordance with the diversity of social and cultural priorities of peoples.

By the time *The Great Transformation* was re-issued in 1957, Polanyi had retired from Columbia University where he taught a course in general economic history from 1947 to 1953, and engaged in research on economic life in primitive and archaic societies. He challenged prevailing "formalist" orthodoxies which applied the methodology of neo-classical economics to the study of pre-capitalist societies. The "formalist-substantivist" debate initiated by Polanyi and his associates established his scholarly reputation in the area of economic anthropology, and secured him an academic foothold in the institutionalist camp of American social sciences.[6] He was at that time in the seventh decade of his life. He entered academic life too late to found a school. In so far as there were followers, they were a small number of former Columbia graduate students in anthropology and sociology.[7]

The long detour into economic anthropology was a test of the principal thesis of *The Great Transformation*. Polanyi's "substantivist" argument maintained that in all previous human societies, the economy was submerged (embedded) in social relationships. Prior to the rise of industrial capitalism, markets were never more than accessories of economic life. In that regard, the generalized market economy of modern industrial capitalism stands revealed as an exception. In the course of the past 200 years, economic life has been progressively disembedded from the societal and cultural matrix. As "improvement" (read "efficiency") conquered "habitat" (read "security"), as labour, land and money became commodified, the economy acquired an existence of its own, driven by (economic) "laws" of its own, whether conceived in neo-classical or Marxist terms. "Such an institution," Polanyi wrote, "could not exist for any length of time without annihilating the human and natural substance of society. It would have physically destroyed man and transformed his surroundings into a wilderness." (p.2) Stripped of social, cultural and ecological support systems, he wrote, people will perish from hunger, pestilence, violence and neglect. Fifty years ago the language might have seemed excessive. Today, as man-made disasters of famines, wars, new diseases and environmental degradation threaten the destruction of the social, cultural and ecological fabric which sustains life on earth, the words are prophetic.

Polanyi was certainly premature in dismissing "market economy" and "market society" from the stage of history. But was he wrong in his analysis of the dangers inherent in the elevation of "the economic instance" over all other aspects of human endeavour and human existence? Is there really no alternative to global neo-liberalization? Have nation states—even large ones—been fiscally emasculated into helplessness and passivity by the dictates of global money markets? These questions are crucial, and they are the reason why *The Great Transformation* has surfaced from relative obscurity and why Polanyi's critique of market economy has attracted the attention of an increasing number of scholars and social activists. A remarkable number of people have reported the excitement with which they read *The Great Transformation* and the influence it had on their thinking. The book became a minor classic, rated one of the greatest works of the twentieth century. Translations began to be made. The first was a Spanish pirate edition (Buenos Aires, 1947) followed by Japanese (1956), Italian (Einaudi, 1974), German (1977), Portugese (Rio de Janerio 1980), Turkish (1986), Swedish (1989) and most recently Hungarian (1997) translations. Interest was minimal in Western Europe. The French translation (Gallimard) did not appear until 1983. Recently, however, European scholars have manifested renewed interest in Polanyi. In the 1990s, Karl Polanyi was cited with increasing frequency in the literature of international political economy, economic sociology, development studies, ecology, and even by the occasional mainstream economist.

The transformations we are witnessing today are playing out on a global scale. They are complex, dangerous and indeterminate. The challenge now is to reclaim the state for society as an instrument to contain and discipline creditors, investors and transnational corporations, to redistribute the gains from growth, to assure basic needs including the need for economic security, to re-launch development by debt cancellation, to assert the primacy of inclusion and social justice over exclusion and inequality, and to elevate "social" and "cultural" over exclusively "financial" and "economic" priorities. In the process of the mobilization of popular movements, a variety of alternative political, social and economic institutions will emerge. Hayek was right in insisting on the role of price-making markets as an essential mechanism in complex modern economies. But he was wrong in universalizing the market principle. Polanyi's insistence on reciprocity and redistribution as mechanisms of economic integration which both sustain and contain the play of market forces is a brilliant insight confirmed by his research on the organization of economic life in diverse societies and civilizations, including modern industrial capitalism. For social scientists, he opened a research agenda for investigation of the place of the economy in society. For social and political activists, he pointed to social justice and solidarity as the fundamental principles of equitable and sustainable economic systems, embedded in the cultural diversities of the planet.

NOTES

1. P. Rosner, "Karl Polanyi on Socialist Accounting," in Kari Polanyi Levitt (ed.), *The Life and Work of Karl Polanyi*. Montreal: Black Rose Books, 1990, pp. 55-65; M. Mendell, "Karl Polanyi and Feasible Socialism," in *The Life and Work of Karl Polanyi*, pp. 66-77.
2. K. Polanyi Levitt and M. Mendell, "Hayek à Vienne," in Diane Ethier and Gilles Dostaller (eds.), *Friedrich Hayek. Philosophie, Economie et Politique*. Quebec: ACFAS, 1989.
3. Michele Cangiani, *Chronache della grande trasformazione*. Turin: Einaudi, 1993. Also see Michele Cangiani, *Polanyi : EUROPA 1937, Guerre esterna e guerre civili*. Rome: Donzelli Editore, 1995.
4. Eric Helleiner, *States and the Reemergence of Global Finance: From Bretton Woods To the 1990s*. Ithaca and London: Cornell University Press, 1994.
5. Dudley Dillard, "The Keynsian Revolution and Economic Development," *Journal of Economic History*, Vol. VIII. No.2, November 1948.
6. Karl Polanyi, Conrad Arensberg and Harry Pearson (eds.), *Trade and Market in the Early Empires*. New York: Free Press, 1957.
7. Two books by Polanyi's former students were significant in disseminating his ideas. George Dalton edited a well known selection of Polanyi's writings under the title *Primitive, Archaic and Modern Economies: Essays of Karl Polanyi*. Boston: Beacon Press, 1968. Harry Pearson edited unpublished Polanyi texts, including some of his Columbia lectures on "General Economic History," as *The Livelihood of Man*. New York: Academic Press, 1977.

Chapter Two

GLOBALIZATION AND *HAUTE FINANCE—DÉJÀ VU?*
Eric Helleiner

Karl Polanyi's 1944 book *The Great Transformation* has long been considered a classic within the field of international political economy. Interest in his work, however, has undergone a considerable revival in recent years among IPE scholars studying economic globalization. While the conventional wisdom holds that the current globalization of market forces is something fundamentally new, Polanyi's book is seen to be useful in reminding us of an important historical precedent: the spread of the "self-regulating" market on an increasingly global basis in the nineteenth century.

It is hardly surprising that *The Great Transformation* has received particular attention from those studying the financial dimensions of globalization in the current age.[1] One of the more interesting aspects of Polanyi's book is his analysis of the central position of a globally-integrated financial system in the nineteenth-century world economy. Many scholars today see important parallels between this analysis and their own efforts to study global financial markets today. The world of "haute finance" that Polanyi described is seen to have emerged once again to play a key role in the global political economy.

As financial specialists return to Polanyi's work for insights, it is important to recall his central objective in the work. As he emphasizes at the outset, the book is not intended as a detailed historical study.[2] Rather, Polanyi saw it as an interpretative work whose principal objective was to call into question liberal accounts of the rise and fall of the liberal international economic order of the nineteenth century. Two such arguments were his target. First, he sought to challenge their thesis that the nineteenth-century market economy emerged as a result of inevitable or "natural" economic forces. He argued an opposite case: "There was nothing natural about *laissez-faire*; free markets could never have come into being merely by allowing things to take their course...*laissez-faire* itself was enforced by the state."[3] Second, he questioned the liberal assumption that the nineteenth-century market-based economic order was socially sustainable. Whereas liberals blamed the decline of that order on short-sighted special interests, Polanyi argued that it had been destined to fail because society could not tolerate the instabilities and upheavals that accompanied an economic order organized around the "self-regulating market." From his perspective, the liberal project had been a "utopian" one that had inevitably provoked spontaneous social "countermovements" that pushed successfully for the reassertion of social control over markets, beginning in the late nineteenth century and culminating in the 1930s.

If Polanyi's work is to be useful to scholars studying financial globalization today, it is not likely to be so at the level of historical description.[4] Indeed, many more detailed and superior studies of "haute finance" in the pre-1930s world exist for them to turn to. Rather, his work is useful in prompting us to question two prominent liberal arguments about the contemporary financial globalization trend: 1) that the trend is a natural product of technological and market developments, and 2) that it is sustainable. Indeed, it is perhaps a sign of the hegemony of economic liberalism in the current age that these arguments are increasingly accepted outside of liberal circles as well. A modern-day Polanyian analysis would be expected to challenge each of these arguments. Financial globalization would not be seen as an inevitable and "natural" economic trend, but rather one that had been cultivated by state decisions and political choices. The trend would also not be seen as sustainable. Instead, it would be expected to induce various social countermovements that begin to bring financial markets back under a degree of social control. Can these two Polanyian arguments be made convincingly in the contemporary context?

In this paper, I suggest that they can. Of the two arguments, the first has so far attracted much more attention among scholars who have discussed the potential relevance of Polanyi's thought to studies of financial globalization. In the first section of the paper, I summarize very briefly the arguments that I and others have made about the central role that states played in constructing the current global financial order. In Polanyian fashion, these arguments suggest that today's globalized financial order is best seen as having been actively "made" by state decisions rather than having been the inevitable product of technological and market developments.[5] In fact, I suggest that states can even be seen to have been driven by certain political pressures similar to those which Polanyi suggested were significant in creating the nineteenth-century world market order.

In the second section of the paper, I explore the relevance of Polanyi's second argument to the study of financial globalization. This requires a more extended discussion since it has been less explored within existing scholarship to date, and because it is a more difficult and controversial argument to make. The view that the new liberal global financial order is here to stay is a widely accepted one. Indeed, even many of those quite sympathetic to Polanyi's general argument have questioned whether the financial globalization trend could be successfully challenged by Polanyian-style social countermovements. As I will endeavour to point out, however, there are some important ways in which Polanyi's argument can be seen to be quite relevant in the contemporary context. I suggest that the financial globalization trend has in fact already begun to induce various "counter-movements," although their strategies for reining finance in under a form of social control differ somewhat from those in the pre-1939 period.

Having demonstrated how Polanyi's thought might be applied in analysing the contemporary financial globalization trend, I conclude the paper by highlighting its broader importance for scholars of international political economy (IPE) at the moment. In an era when economic liberalism is in the ascendent, Polanyi is seen to offer an alternative way of thinking about the global political economy which has appeal beyond the narrow confines of one or other of the usual critics of economic liberalism. I suggest that the particular attraction of his argument today may reflect the fact that, while living in Vienna, he was one of the first thinkers to take seriously enough, to devise a critique of, the neoliberal "Austrian" school, one which provided intellectual backing for the current revival of economic liberalism. In addition to challenging liberal arguments, the kind of Polanyian argument presented in the paper is also seen to be useful in suggesting a resolution to the theoretical debate between Ethan Kapstein and John Ruggie concerning the role of the state in this age of financial globalization.[6]

"*LAISSEZ-FAIRE* WAS PLANNED": RECONSTRUCTING GLOBAL FINANCIAL MARKETS
Any Polanyian interpretation of the postwar globalization of finance must begin where Polanyi's book left off: in the year 1944 when the Bretton Woods conference was held. On the occasion of the fiftieth anniversary of Bretton Woods last year, the suggestion was sometimes made that the contemporary global financial order was a product of the visions and plans of the conference participants. But a closer look at the Bretton Woods discussions reveals this argument to be misleading. The kind of neo-liberal thinking and policies which have emerged as dominant in financial circles today had little standing at the Bretton Woods conference. Instead, as John Ruggie has pointed out, the Bretton Woods negotiators drew many of the same lessons from the prewar experience as did Polanyi concerning the social unsustainability of a liberal international financial order.[7] The arguments of *The Great Transformation* were in this sense much more in keeping with the spirit of the conference than that other 1944 book that has become so influential today, Friedrich Hayek's *The Road to Serfdom*.

Ruggie describes the Bretton Woods negotiators as guided by an "embedded liberal" ideology; that is, they were committed to building a modified liberal order that was more compatible with social stability, one in which the economy was less "disembedded" from society than the nineteenth-century liberal order that Polanyi described. A key mechanism by which economic relations were to be "embedded" in society within the Bretton Woods framework was through the use of capital controls. As I have emphasized elsewhere, these controls were not only explicitly permitted but even encouraged under the IMF's Articles of Agreement.[8] The radical nature of the Bretton Woods endorsement of capital controls at the time needs to be recognized. Few states had employed capital controls in the pre-1914 liberal era, and it had not been until the 1930s that extensive capital control regimes had begun to be constructed across the industrial world. Far from turning their backs on these interventionist experiments of the 1930s, the Bretton Woods architects sought to construct an international economic order that legitimized them and incorporated them within an international framework of rules. In this sense, this aspect of the Bretton Woods agreement can be seen as a culmination of Polanyi's long "countermovement" against the liberal financial practices of the nineteenth century. As John Maynard Keynes put it: "What used to be a heresy is now endorsed as orthodox."[9]

In so doing, the negotiators sought to build an international economic order in which finance was the "servant"—not the "master"—of society. In Polanyian terms, this was to be a more socially "embedded" international financial order, an order that was more compatible with social stability than its nineteenth-century counterpart. Capital controls would help to minimize the socially disruptive influence of speculative and "disequilibrating" capital movements on exchange rates and trading patterns. Equally important, capital controls would help to protect the policy autonomy of the institution which was seen as central in promoting social stability in the postwar world: the new Keynesian welfare state. Without capital controls, independent macroeconomic planning could be disrupted by speculative and disequilibrating cross-border financial movements. Similarly, the domestic financial regulatory structures put in place in many countries during the 1930s and 1940s in order to facilitate industrial and microeconomic planning would be undermined if domestic savers and borrowers had access to foreign financial markets. As welfare expenditures expanded, governments could also no longer permit the practice of corporations and wealthy citizens moving their earnings to countries with lower tax burdens in order to evade domestic taxation. More broadly, the Bretton Woods architects also sought to prevent the policy agenda of democratic governments from being thwarted by capital flight motivated by "political reasons" or a desire to evade "the burdens of social legislation."[10]

This is not to say that the Bretton Woods negotiators opposed all private financial movements. The activities of the IMF and World Bank were in fact explicitly designed to help promote movement of "productive" capital and equilibrating financial flows. But because of the fear of disequilibrating and speculative flows, states were granted the right to control *all* financial movements. Each state would be allowed to decide which financial movements were desirable and which were not. "Embedded liberalism" was thus tilted heavily in the "embedded" direction in this sector.

The globalization of financial markets in recent years has brought into being a very different kind of financial world from that planned for at Bretton Woods. Prominent in neo-liberal circles is the view that financial globalization has been an inevitable product of technological and market developments. But a growing body of scholarship in the field of IPE has begun to develop an alternative explanation. While acknowledging that technological and market developments have encouraged the globalization process, this scholarship emphasizes that today's integrated global financial order should be seen to have been more actively "made" by states. Louis Pauly, for example, argues: "A global village does not just spring up: it must be created. Politics within distinct state structures remains the axis around which international finance revolves."[11] Similarly, Geoffrey Underhill notes: "the emergence of apparently unregulated international capital markets was intimately related to political decision—(or non-decision-) making."[12]

Prominent in this IPE literature have been references to Polanyi's work. Both Pauly and Underhill, for example, begin their studies with the quotation from *The Great Transformation* cited at the start of this paper: "There was nothing natural about *laissez-faire*; free markets could never have come into being merely by allowing things to take their course...*Laissez-faire* itself was enforced by the state." To present a convincing alternative explanation of financial globalization, this kind of Polanyian approach must identify both how states actively created the contemporary global financial order and why they did so. Since these issues have already been addressed in detail within the growing body of IPE scholarship, there is no need to present a discussion of them in this paper. Rather, in what follows, I seek to highlight how some of the key themes that emerge in this literature parallel Polanyi's analysis of the politics that underlay the creation of the liberal international economic order in the nineteenth century.

Central to the way in which states actively created the current globalized financial order was their decision to dismantle the capital controls established under the Bretton Woods order. As I have explained elsewhere, the process of liberalizing controls on international financial transactions began with the regulatory support provided by the U.S. and Britain in the 1960s for the early growth of the eurodollar market in London. It then accelerated after the mid-1970s when states across the OECD region began to abolish completely their postwar systems of capital controls, again led by the U.S. and Britain. By the 1990s, an almost fully liberal financial regime had emerged among OECD countries and many Southern countries had also followed their lead, providing regulatory support for "offshore" euromarket operations and liberalizing their own capital controls.[13]

Why have states actively reconstructed a globally-integrated liberal financial system? One explanation for the financial liberalization trend has been the growing prominence in financial policymaking circles of neo-liberal ideas. Although some analysts are inclined in downplay the role of ideas in the making of history, Polanyi's work assigns a central role to the growing power of economic liberalism in his explanation of the rise of the nineteenth-century liberal international economic order. In the contemporary period, the influence of the ideas of the "Austrian" school of neo-liberals—the modern-day successors to Adam Smith and David Ricardo—also is hard to deny across a wide spectrum of economic policy issues. Interestingly, these neo-liberals have focused more attention than their nineteenth-century counterparts on the need to convince policy makers of the case for "free finance." No doubt this has reflected their response to the use by states in the post-war period of much more extensive capital control regimes than were ever witnessed by nineteenth-century liberals. From a neo-liberal perspective, these capital controls inhibited the efficient global allocation of capital and undermined the freedom of individuals to diversify their assets across borders. They also permitted governments to pursue "unsound" inflationary and high tax policies without being properly disciplined by international financial markets. In the Hayekian words of one set of authors, the abolition of capital controls thus came to be seen as a key part of the broader neoliberal project, to produce a "U-Turn on the Road to Serfdom."[14]

The neo-liberal movement found its earliest and strongest support in the U.S. and Britain, as is evident from the leading role these two countries played in the liberalization process. These two countries also supported financial liberalization because each would derive special benefits from financial globalization. Once again, there is a parallel to the history analyzed by Polanyi. Like British promotion of free trade in the nineteenth-century, the enthusiasm of the U.S. for financial liberalization from the 1960s onwards stemmed in part from recognition that it held a "hegemonic" position in a globally integrated financial order that could be used to its advantage. In particular, U.S. officials recognized that mobile capital could be attracted to help finance U.S. budget and current account deficits because of America's unique position as a safe haven for global investors, the international prominence of the dollar, and the depth and liquidity of U.S. financial markets. British financial officials also recognized that a more globalized financial order would bring extensive international financial business to London's financial markets given the City's long history and expertise as an international financial centre.

In Britain and the U.S. as well as elsewhere, a further factor that encouraged financial liberalization was the growing transnationalization of business. Just as the nineteenth-century liberal movement derived strength from an emerging bourgeois class across Europe, corporations with increasingly transnational interests played a leading role in supporting neo-liberal initiatives to dismantle post-war capital controls in the 1970s and 1980s. As their cross-border activities grew, these transnational firms became increasingly frustrated with the way such controls restricted their freedom of action at the global level. The transnationalization of business was particularly important in eroding the support of industrial interests for capital controls. In many countries during the early post-war years, industrial firms had often supported national capital controls strongly when they were opposed by the financial community. But as their interests become more transnational, these industrial interests increasingly came to endorse financial liberalism.

One further development that IPE scholars have cited in explaining financial liberalization was a competitive deregulation dynamic. Once the U.S. and Britain had taken the initial decision to liberalize and deregulate their financial markets, other countries were prompted to follow their lead to prevent footloose financial business and capital from being lured away to the more attractive British and U.S. markets. Without a competitive response, their financial systems risked being rendered minor backwaters in the emerging global financial order, a development that would result in lost jobs and tax revenue as well as a weakening of the competitiveness of nationally-based industrial firms.

The point of this very brief overview is to emphasize that Polanyi's ideas can be seen as useful not just in the way they have been employed so far by IPE scholars: that is, as a reminder that the contemporary financial globalization trend has been a product of active state decisions to liberalize capital controls. His analysis is also useful in pointing to these state decisions as having been prompted by some similar political developments as the ones that encouraged the construction of the nineteenth-century liberal international economic order. In part, financial liberalization reflected the political project of the inheritors of nineteenth-century liberal economic ideas. As in the nineteenth century, liberal advocates also derived considerable support from the "hegemonic" goals of dominant economic powers as well as from social forces seeking freedom to operate in a global market economy. Only the competitive deregulation dynamic—a phenomenon encouraged by the heightened mobility of money in a world of global telecommunications—appears to have had little parallel in the nineteenth-century experience.

A SOCIAL RESPONSE—EMERGING COUNTERMOVEMENTS?
If the first of Polanyi's arguments appears relevant to the contemporary context, what about the second? A Polanyian analysis would suggest that the new liberal global financial order has ushered in a world of social instability and upheaval which, in turn, will begin to induce social "countermovements" that will

successfully place global financial markets under a degree of social control. Interestingly, this argument has attracted much less attention than the first. Many have highlighted the social upheavals caused by the contemporary global financial order, both in terms of exchange rate and trade instability, and in terms of the lost policy autonomy of the Keynesian welfare state. But Polanyi's argument that this situation will initiate social responses that lead to a kind of re-regulation process has had few supporters. The new liberal global financial order, it is said, is here to stay, especially given the difficulties involved in regulating the new global markets. Indeed, even many of those very sympathetic to Polanyi's analysis seem inclined to accept this latter view. As Phil Cerny puts it, "Polanyi's 'Great Transformation' is over."[15] In this section, I argue that Polanyi's second thesis deserves a closer look. Indeed, I suggest that there is already considerable evidence to support it.

GLOBAL RESPONSES: THE BIS REGIME AND THE TOBIN TAX
The first piece of evidence is the fact that a re-regulatory movement has already been underway since the mid-1970s. This movement has been led not by populist social forces, but rather by the G-10 central banks working within the Bank for International Settlements (BIS). Their goal has been a simple one: to minimize the risk of financial crises in the new globalized financial context. They have succeeded in recent years in constructing an increasingly elaborate supervisory and regulatory regime over international financial markets, including most recently the 1988 uniform capital adequacy regulations on international banks. In addition to its growing sophistication, this regime has also extended its geographical reach well beyond the G-10 countries to include the various "offshore" financial centers which are often said to be impossible to regulate.[16]

Although central bankers may seem unlikely leaders of a Polanyian style countermovement, it is important to recall that Polanyi's analysis gave them a central role in the late nineteenth century. He noted that the first form of countermovement in the monetary sphere in that era was led by elite groups who demanded that central banks actively intervene in the unregulated financial order to protect firms from unstable, fluctuating business conditions and financial crises. In Polanyi's words, the emergence of active central banking marked the first form of "monetary protectionism" from the liberal financial order.[17]

Polanyi argued that this development was important not just in and of itself in reducing socially disruptive financial instability, it was also significant in setting the scene for a second, more interventionist form of countermovement in the financial sphere. By highlighting the fact that financial issues were issues of public policy, the rise of central banking opened a political space for other more populist social groups to demand that money and finance be regulated in a more serious way to serve broader social goals. The new central banking mechanisms not only showed that such regulation was possible but also provided institutional frameworks which could be used to pursue such regulation.

One can see certain parallels in the current era. The BIS regulatory and supervisory regime can be seen to have acted already as a kind of limited form of countermovement that aims to lessen instability and reduce the risk of socially disruptive financial crises.[18] At the same time, the regime may also be creating a political and institutional space for more extensive forms of intervention in the global financial order. This is most apparent if one looks at the debates surrounding the "Tobin tax" proposal.

This proposal represents the most prominent initiative today to restore the kind of Polanyian financial vision that had been present at Bretton Woods. First put forward in the 1970s by the economist James Tobin, the initiative would introduce a very small tax (perhaps 0.25%) on all foreign exchange transactions. In quite Polanyian terms, Tobin has argued that the tax would discourage short-term, speculative cross-border financial movements that are causing socially-disruptive adjustments to trade patterns and exchange rates as well as a reduction in the policy autonomy of governments. At the same time, the tax would not prevent more desirable long-term, more productive financial movements since its level would be quite insignificant as a cost item. Tobin's ideas are thus very much in keeping with the kind of "embedded liberal" framework of thought that was dominant at Bretton Woods. International financial markets are not to be discouraged entirely. Rather, they are simply to be regulated in ways that are more compatible with social stability than the fully liberal order that has emerged today. In Tobin's famous phrase, the objective is simply to "throw some sand in the well-greased wheels" of international financial markets.[19]

What many find attractive about Tobin's proposal is that it provides a more effective mechanism for realizing these embedded liberal goals than the mechanism put forward at Bretton Woods. The Bretton Woods negotiators endorsed the use of comprehensive capital controls, suggesting that individual governments should decide which financial movements should be allowed to take place and which should not. Tobin's proposal substitutes a minor tax for such cumbersome capital controls, and leaves it to market actors to decide which financial movements are worth pursuing in this context. Moreover, multinational businesses outside of the financial sector are much less likely to be opposed to the tax than to Bretton Woods-style capital controls since the level of the tax would be almost insignificant to them. A further key benefit of the tax, according to its proponents, is that it would provide considerable revenue which might be used domestically to fund social programs or internationally to address global inequities or common global problems.

Opponents of the Tobin tax have been quick to dismiss it on the pragmatic grounds that it could never be implemented in an effective fashion.[20] Unless the tax is introduced in all the financial centres at once, they point out that market actors will simply move their footloose financial activities to centres where it is not applied. The prospects of the tax ever being implemented are thus said by opponents of the tax to be next to zero given the difficulties of getting all states to implement it. In particular, they anticipate that collective problems would plague cooperative initiatives in this area since individual states—particularly the small offshore centers—would find it tempting to keep their markets free of the tax while others implemented it.[21]

But these critics have overstated the potential political difficulties involved in the implementation of the Tobin tax. To begin with, as advocates of the tax have pointed out, the existence of the BIS regulatory and supervisory regime demonstrates the possibility of achieving the level of cooperation necessary to impose a standard form of regulatory practices on financial actors around the world.[22] As noted above, this regime covers not just the leading financial centers but also the various offshore financial centers that critics argue would be unlikely to go along with a global re-regulatory initiative. The BIS regime has thus been helpful to Tobin tax advocates in exactly the way that Polanyi predicted: it has demonstrated that international financial regulation is politically possible, and that it is thus a legitimate subject of public policy debate. Also in keeping with Polanyi's predictions, some Tobin tax advocates have suggested that the specific institutional frameworks that have been constructed through the BIS regime could even be directly useful in implementing the tax.[23]

The number of countries that would need to be involved in implementing the Tobin tax is also less than sometimes suggested by critics. Foreign exchange trading is, after all, highly concentrated in a few financial centers of the world at the moment: seven financial center countries account for eighty per cent of the trading.[24] Foreign exchange trading is concentrated in this way for good reason. It relies on dense networks of informational, accountancy, and legal services that only such centers can provide in a concentrated and reliable form.[25] The likelihood of foreign exchange trading business fleeing in massive quantities to lightly regulated offshore financial centers is thus exaggerated.[26] Moreover, as Richard Cooper points out, even if this threat were to arise, the leading financial centers could threaten to withdraw key services from jurisdictions that did not abide by the tax. He concludes: "it would not be necessary to get universal agreement on the tax. It would suffice to stipulate that disputes arising over foreign exchange transactions could not be adjudicated in countries of the leading financial centers unless the tax had been paid. Since it takes years to establish a reputation for fair and impartial dispute settlement, a small tax would be unlikely to drive transactions to tax-free countries without such reputations."[27]

If cooperation in implementing the tax is required between only the leading financial centers, collective action problems would seem to be no worse than those associated with macroeconomic coordination. Indeed, they may even be easier to resolve because of the potential leadership role of the U.S. and Britain in the Tobin tax's implementation. If the tax is to be successfully introduced, it is particularly important that it be supported by Britain and the United States because they house the most important foreign exchange markets in the world. This position not only ensures that their cooperation is essential for the tax to be effective, it also gives them a form of "structural power" that could be used to encourage all foreign governments to introduce the tax.[28] The potential effectiveness of this structural power was demonstrated in the negotiations leading up to the 1988 capital adequacy agreement, when Britain and the U.S. threatened to block access to their financial markets to any banks whose governments had not agreed to the new regulations. Given the centrality of these markets to any major bank in the world, the threat was enormously effective in encouraging foreign governments to agree to the British and American proposal.[29] The U.S. government used the same weapon to encourage foreign governments to agree to its new reporting requirements relating to drug money in the late 1980s and early 1990s.[30] In these episodes, the U.S. and Britain have thus shown that leadership can play a key role in overcoming the collective action problems which exist in initiatives to regulate international financial markets.

The likelihood that these two countries might use their power to support the Tobin tax is, of course, difficult to predict. Such a move would represent a reversal of their leadership role in supporting financial liberalization over the last two decades. Still, the possibility should not be ruled out, especially as the structural position of these countries changes in the global political economy. In the US, support for the proposal already exists[31] and one can imagine it growing if there were a crisis of confidence in the dollar (a crisis that could be provoked in the coming years by developments such as the creation of a European common currency).[32] The dollar crisis in 1978-79, for example, led to considerable discussion in the U.S. government about the need to reduce the country's vulnerability to speculative international financial movements.[33] A similar crisis today might lead to a stronger regulatory response from the U.S. government given the new political prominence of isolationist sentiments and attacks on the liberal world economy in U.S. political circles in the post-Cold War era.

The British government might also be more inclined to accept regulation of London's financial markets as London's financial status shifts from bring primarily an offshore eurodollar market centre to more of a regional financial centre within Europe. As European cooperation accelerates, Britain may also find itself increasingly on the receiving end of unwelcome Europe-wide regulatory proposals on finance. Indeed, this possibility has already been raised by the Brussels proposals in 1989 for a Europe-wide withholding tax, the reciprocity provision in the second banking directive, and German speculation about the need for the future European central bank to impose Europe-wide reserve requirements.[34]

A Polanyian analysis might predict, however, that the most important development to generate support for the Tobin tax in the US, Britain and elsewhere would be the social instability and upheavals that Tobin and others argue are produced by the new global financial order itself. Certainly, social responses to the declining policy autonomy of governments in the face of global financial markets seem visible, most recently and perhaps most dramatically in the nation-wide strikes in France in late 1995. Journalist Erik Izraelewicz summed up a common interpretation of the strikes at the time: "For the first time in a rich country, we are having a strike against globalization, a massive and collective reaction against financial globalization and its consequences."[35] At the 1996 Davos Forum, the world's elite also were treated to a lecture from the Forum's founders who insisted that they "start taking the backlash against globalization seriously." As they noted (perhaps too melodramatically), "[t]he mood in these [industrial] democracies is one of hopelessness and anxiety. This can easily turn into revolt, as December's unrest in France showed."[36]

Analyses such as these should obviously be viewed somewhat cautiously. Often the social protests described are reactions to developments that are unrelated to financial globalization. As neoliberals are increasingly keen to point out, the negative consequences of financial globalization are frequently exaggerated, especially the consequences in terms of the lost policy autonomy of governments.[37] But even if recent social movements have sometimes misdirected their protests, the increased focus on "financial globalization" as a target against which to protest is worthy of note at a political level. Indeed, it is this very development that presumably has encouraged neoliberals to begin to emphasize that the declining power of the state in a globalized financial world has been overstated.[38]

Although "financial globalization" has increasingly become a target of criticism in political circles, this development has not as yet translated into large-scale public campaigns for the implementation of the Tobin tax. Indeed, the distribution of the costs and benefits of financial liberalism would seem to work against such a development.[39] The costs associated with international financial liberalism—the loss of policy autonomy, exchange rate instability—are, after all, quite dispersed in their impact and relatively abstract from the standpoint of domestic social groups. By contrast, some of the benefits are highly visible and concentrated in their impact, such as the freedom provided to businesses to operate at the international level without cumbersome capital controls or the attraction of financial capital to domestic markets. The consequence is that initiatives to promote the Tobin tax to date have tended to encounter enormous opposition from the financial community, without at the same time generating considerable countervailing interest and enthusiasm from the general public.

There is, however, one circumstance in which these political dynamics associated with international financial regulation seem to be altered: during and in the wake of foreign exchange crises. Such crises have the effect of raising the political profile of international financial issues and, more specifically, highlighting the costs associated with financial liberalism. The 1931 international financial crisis demonstrated this in a particularly dramatic way. More recently, the European exchange rate crisis of 1992-93 and the Mexican financial crisis of late 1994 generated widespread public debate on the drawbacks of financial liberalism. The Tobin tax proposal attracted considerable attention and a growing number of prominent supporters in the wake of these recent crises. Tobin's ideas began to be actively discussed in leading media outlets as well as in multilateral forums such as the UNDP, UNCTAD, the ILO and the UN Social Summit, and the preparatory discussions for the 1995 G-7 summit. Interest in the proposal also began to be expressed by a number of governments, such as those of Canada, France, and Australia.[40] Undoubtedly, the revenue benefits of the tax only increased the attractiveness of the proposal from the standpoint of these governments, since all are grappling with substantial fiscal deficits.[41]

If foreign exchange crises generate Polanyian-style countermovements against unfettered financial liberalism, one can anticipate that re-regulatory initiatives such as the Tobin tax are likely to attract growing support in the coming years. For as the volume of foreign exchange trading expands, states are finding it more and more difficult to contain such crises. As the IMF reported in the wake of the European exchange rate crisis, the volume of foreign exchange trading now dwarfs the intervention capacities of the world's leading central banks. The trend towards increased cross-border investing by pension funds and other institutional investors also appears likely to accelerate the volume of trading.[42] This provides a further reason to view sceptically the argument that the Tobin tax initiative has no chance of ever being implemented.

REGIONAL, NATIONAL, AND LOCAL RESPONSES

If the BIS regime and the Tobin tax initiative represent two examples of nascent countermovements at the global level, other developments below that level would also seem to accord with Polanyi's predictions. One of these is the formation of regional financial zones, of which the European Monetary System is the most well developed. A central rationale for the formation of the EMS in 1979 was a kind of Polanyian one: that of establishing a regional "zone of monetary stability" in the increasingly volatile global financial environment. Like the BIS regime, this initiative represents only a relatively limited form of countermovement in that it has not sought to inhibit capital mobility. Indeed, European financial politics have moved in a decidedly neo-liberal direction since the formation of the EMS. Not only have EC countries fully liberalized capital movements under the Single European Act, the Economic and Monetary Union initiative also embodies a very neo-liberal conception of the position of money in society. But once again, following Polanyi's analysis, European monetary and financial cooperation can be seen to be creating regional financial structures that might be used for a more interventionist purpose over the longer term. In particular, the prospect has been raised—most recently by Jacques Delors at the end of the 1992-93 exchange rate crisis—of the introduction of region-wide exchange controls vis-à-vis the rest of the world, an initiative that would have been difficult to take seriously not so very long ago.[43]

In addition to global and regional developments, there are also forms of a Polanyian countermovement against financial globalization that are increasingly evident at the local level. Perhaps the most prominent involves the growing popularity of "local currency" experiments. Since the early 1980s, hundreds of these local currencies have been created across the world in countries ranging from Australia to Sweden. These local monetary experiments have involved the creation of currencies which are usually denominated in the national currency but are not convertible into it. They serve simply as a means of exchange within a clearly defined local community network. According to their proponents, these forms of money not only help reduce the vulnerability of local communities to the global financial "casino" but also act as a kind of local form of "capital control" since money is encouraged to remain within the local community. By facilitating economic transactions in poor communities that are starved of cash, local currencies are also seen to provide a primitive "stimulus" to such communities.

Interestingly, many local currency advocates draw directly on Polanyi's thought to support their monetary initiatives. They argue that these forms of money are restoring a sense of social "embeddedness" to the functioning of money, a characteristic that national currencies appear to have increasingly lost in the contemporary global financial environment.[44] Instead of "embedding" money in society through the mechanism of the state's regulation of money, however, they prefer to pursue this goal through voluntarist community initiatives. Here again Polanyi's work is cited, particularly his strong endorsement of Robert Owen's community-oriented "labour notes" in the early nineteenth century.[45] The preference for voluntarist non-state initiatives among local currency advocates is no longer motivated by quite the same "utopian socialist" goals as Owen, however. Instead, it often reflects a "green" critique of the nation state, a critique which suggests that the nation-state has never been terribly responsive to the democratic aspirations and true needs of local communities.[46] It can also simply reflect a defeatist view that the state no longer has the power to regulate money effectively in this age of globalization.[47]

A final type of countermovement within the contemporary global financial order is represented by the growth of nationalist groups which attack the new globalized financial markets for undermining national autonomy and sovereignty.[48] These groups appear to want to reimpose capital controls at the national level in order to restore the kind of world that existed in the middle decades of this century. In some instances, the politics of these groups are quite right of centre (e.g., Jean Marie Le Pen in France or Pat Buchanan in the US) and their rhetoric can be reminiscent of critiques of the power of "haute finance" from the interwar period. Indeed, the broader political messages of nationalist groups on the right often bear a considerable resemblance to the right-wing forms of countermovement that Polanyi analyzed in that earlier era.

Their emergence appears to provide some evidence to confirm Susan Strange's prediction that political movements arousing "strong and violent nationalist emotions" similar to those in the 1930s are likely to result from the "casino-like" atmosphere of risk and uncertainty that she argues exists in this age of global finance.[49] Indeed, the parallels between Strange's analysis and Polanyi's in this respect are worth noting. A central objective of Polanyi's book was to explain the rise of fascism in Central Europe during the interwar period. In particular, he sought to formulate a critique of the liberal argument (well outlined in Hayek's *The Road to Serfdom*) that the rise of fascism had been a product of collectivist thinking and the decline of liberal values. According to Polanyi, it was in fact liberals themselves who were partly to blame for the rise of fascism since their "utopian" project of disembedding the economy from society had induced an inevitable social response of which the fascist movement was one strand. As Polanyi put it: "In order to understand German fascism, we must revert to Ricardian England."[50]

It is interesting to note that nationalist movements calling for capital controls—whether of a left-[51] or right-wing variety—are the only type of "countermovement" today that appears to be pursuing a form of politics that is focused on unilateral behaviour by a single nation-state. The building of the BIS regime, for example, has involved complex forms of international cooperation. Advocates of the Tobin tax are also involved in transnational forms of political activism because of their recognition that all states must be encouraged to introduce the tax at the same time. The initiatives in the European Community have also involved innovative forms of supranational political cooperation at the regional level. Similarly, the local currency movement is reasserting the importance of sub-national political and economic spaces in a context where the nation-state appears less capable of preserving social stability.

This multi-levelled feature of contemporary countermovements contrasts with the period analyzed by Polanyi when countermovements focused most of their energies on a national form of politics. For the left and right alike, in that earlier era, social control over money and finance was to be achieved primarily through the unilateral activities of each individual nation-state. Not until the Bretton Woods meeting was there a serious initiative to move these activities to a different level. And even then, the Bretton Woods proposals on capital controls simply sought international legitimation and support for inward-looking national regulatory initiatives of individual states. Indeed, this was exactly the kind of international activity that Polanyi himself advocated at the end of *The Great Transformation*.[52]

The difference between the two periods appears to reflect recognition of the large hurdles to be overcome in building political support for unilateral nationally-based responses to financial globalization. The high degree of economic interdependence ensures that the costs associated with the implementation of tight effective national capital controls would be considerable. Given the transnationalization of business over the past two decades, unilateral national capital controls will be opposed strongly by large and powerful segments of the business community, and such controls will also be more easily evaded by firms operating transnationally.[53] Technological change has also made unilateral nationally-based re-regulatory strategies more difficult. This is not because the technical capacity of states to monitor financial cross-border financial transactions has necessarily decreased in an age of information technology. Indeed, electronic money transfers leave traces that make them potentially easier to track by state authorities than traditional money flows.[54] Rather, the importance of technological change is that the new mobility of financial capital in a world of global telecommunications has ensured that unilateral regulatory initiatives will be strongly opposed on the grounds that they will place domestic financial markets at a competitive disadvantage vis-à-vis foreign financial markets.

More broadly, many of those involved in countermovements have recognized that the nation state as a political-economic entity has been challenged in a more serious way by those constructing the contemporary world market economy than was the case in the nineteenth century. The liberal international economic order of the previous century was in fact constructed at the same time that economic liberals were *strengthening* the nation-state by building nationally-consolidated markets and national legal-bureaucratic institutions to support these markets. In the monetary and financial sphere, for example, the international gold standard was a monetary order built solidly on the foundation of new national currency structures and national central banks that liberals constructed during the nineteenth century.[55] During that era, the world market economy was an "inter-national" economic order created clearly on the foundation of strong territorially-bound nation states.

By contrast, neo-liberals in the last third of the twentieth century have shown less commitment to the nation state as a political-economic institution in their drive to build a global market order. They have, for example, embraced political-economic innovations such as the "offshore" eurocurrency markets and regional integration initiatives which have undermined the power and economic territoriality of the nation state. They have also often sought to weaken national institutions that served to "embed" markets and bind the state and the national citizen to an ideology of "welfare-nationalism" from the late nineteenth century onwards.[56] The result, as John Ruggie, Eric Hobsbawm and others have noted, has been the emergence of a global economy with a different, more deterritorialized structure than its nineteenth-century counterpart.[57]

In this context, a countermovement that seeks to reestablish social controls over the market with a unilateral nationalist project encounters additional barriers to the ones already mentioned. In the financial realm, unilateral national capital controls will not easily prevent speculation against the national currency in offshore eurocurrency markets. In contexts such as Western Europe or North America, such controls will also likely challenge commitments associated with regional integration initiatives. A countermovement relying on political appeals to concepts such as sovereignty and nationalism may also generate less enthusiasm and resonate less effectively than in the era Polanyi studied because these concepts are being challenged in broader ways.

To summarize, then, Polanyi's prediction that countermovements will emerge in an effort to protect society from the instability of the "self-regulating market" appears to be beginning to be borne out in the contemporary global financial realm. The countermovements are also as varied in their social base as they were in the period analyzed by Polanyi. In addition to these similarities between the two eras, however, there is also an important difference: many of the contemporary movements are less attracted to unilateral nationalist strategies for pursuing "monetary protectionism." They seek to re-embed the market via activities at the local, regional and global levels as well.

The obvious difficulty facing many of these contemporary countermovements is that, in seeking alternative levels at which to pursue their Polanyian goals, they also are counting on alternative senses of "society" emerging in response to the challenges of the self-regulating market. Instead of the "nation" as the agent of the Polanyian countermovement in the pre-1945 period, many contemporary countermovements are suggesting that "societies" also exist at a global, regional, and local level that can and will respond in the ways they hope. Indeed, much of their activity seems devoted to efforts to cultivate these alternative senses of society. How successful this kind of political project can be remains an open question.[58]

One final point must be made about the prospects for the contemporary liberal global financial order. As Polanyi points out, the immediate cause of the collapse of the international gold standard in the pre-1939 era was not the activity of the countermovements he analyzed. Rather, it was the international financial market crisis of 1931. Any analysis of the future of the contemporary global financial order must thus also acknowledge the possibility of this kind of market crisis happening today. In Kindleberger's words, financial markets are, after all, particularly prone to "panics, manias, and crashes."[59] Although the BIS regime has reduced the likelihood of major crises, it has not altogether eliminated the possibility of their occurring. Indeed, Polanyi's analysis of the pre-1939 period suggests that the probability of such a calamitous crisis may increase the more critics of economic liberalism attempt to subject money and finance to forms of social control. According to his account, the emergence of countermovements from the late nineteenth century on increasingly impaired the self-regulating character of global markets in ways that encouraged greater and greater market instability. In the financial sector, it is certainly true that the collapse of the international gold standard in the interwar period was accelerated by the growing demands of right- and left-wing critics of liberalism for more active political control over monetary and financial policy. As Barry Eichengreen has recently shown, these demands encouraged increasingly disruptive speculative financial movements, as the "credibility" and predictability of government financial policy came into question.

Equally important, they also rendered more difficult the efforts of central banks to cooperate autonomously in containing international financial crises.[60]

A similar set of developments might be provoked if some contemporary countermovements—especially the nationalist variants and those seeking regional closure in Europe—were to gain considerably in political strength.

CONCLUSION

A Polanyian analysis presents an important alternative perspective on the historical origins and future prospects of the contemporary global financial order to that offered by neo-liberals. From this vantage point, the contemporary global financial order did not emerge only as a product of market and technological developments. It was also consciously "made" by the decisions of states to dismantle capital controls that had been in place during the mid-decades of this century. A Polanyian interpretation also calls into question the durability of the new liberal global financial order by drawing attention to the emergence of various countermovements that are seeking—some with more success than others—to restore a degree of social control over the global financial realm.

To apply Polanyi's ideas to the contemporary context is not to suggest that history is simply repeating itself. As I have argued, a crucial difference between the pre-1939 period and the contemporary era is the role of the nation state in both the creation of a global market order and the reaction to it. In the period described by Polanyi, the liberal project and the rise of the countermovements it induced were intricately connected with the growth and consolidation of the nation state. In the contemporary period, the globalization trend as well as the reactions to it appear to be playing a role in undermining the nation-state's strength and legitimacy as a political-economic unit.

This is not to suggest that states are vanishing as powerful actors in the current era. As I argued in the first section of this paper, financial globalization in recent years should not be seen as a process somehow beyond their control. Rather, states have authored the globalization trend. Indeed, as Stephen Krasner and Janice Thomson suggest, states have often acquired greater powers in the process of constructing and enforcing the rules on which the new global economy operates.[61] What *is* being challenged, however, is a specific historical form of state—the nation state—which was organized around a particular notion of economic territoriality, state-citizen relations, and political identity.[62]

In drawing this distinction, I find a way to agree with the arguments put forward by both John Ruggie and Ethan Kapstein in their debate about the implications of financial globalization for the nature of the world order.[63] Ruggie's argument that the trend is encouraging radically new forms of economic space and territoriality is certainly borne out by developments such as the emergence of the euromarket. At the same time, Kapstein is also correct to point out that states retain a position of primacy in global financial markets including the "offshore" euromarkets. To my mind, their debate is less a debate than a discussion in which they are talking at cross-purposes. As I have suggested, their two positions can be reconciled by simply acknowledging that it is only a certain historical form of the state—rather than the state itself—that is being eroded by financial globalization.[64]

If the Polanyian interpretation of financial globalization presented in this paper may help in resolving this theoretical conundrum, it is also useful in the more straightforward way noted at the outset: namely, that it offers a somewhat different view of the financial globalization trend to that presented by many neo-liberals. What label best describes the perspective from which Polanyi's position is derived? This is a difficult question to answer, since his work seems to appeal equally to a number of different "schools" within the field of IPE. Realists have been attracted to his emphasis on the centrality of the state in creating and sustaining markets.[65] Those on the traditional left cite his work to back their argument that a society built on market principles is not socially sustainable.[66] As I have noted elsewhere, many contemporary greens are also attracted to his critique of the large-scale nature of political and economic life in the industrial age.[67] And liberals from a more "embedded liberal" tradition have found his critique of unfettered markets useful.[68]

The current resurgence of interest in Polanyi's work is presumably linked to this very fact. In an age when economic liberalism is dominant, Polanyi offers a critique of its ideas that appeals equally to various schools of thought that feel uneasy about this turn of events. If his perspective is hard to pin down, the target of his criticism is certainly very clear from the footnotes in the text of *The Great Transformation*: namely, the "Austrian school" of neo-liberals led by Hayek and von Mises. Polanyi encountered this school during his intellectually formative years in Vienna after World War One, and his 1944 book stands as one of the first sustained critiques of the school. It is perhaps for this reason above all that his perspective is attracting renewed interest in an era when the influence of the Vienna school has become increasingly substantial and global in scope.

NOTES

Portions of this paper appeared as part of a discussion forum in *Studies in Political Economy* 49 (Autumn 1995). I am grateful for comments on earlier drafts to: Greg Albo, David Andrews, Barry Buzam, Helge Hveem, Kate McNamara, Kenneth McRobbie, Leo Panitch, Tony Porter, Bent Sofus-Tranoy, Michael Webb, and Robert Wolfe.

1. His work is cited prominently in many recent works on international finance. See for example various articles in Phil Cerny, (ed.), *Finance and World Politics*. Aldershot: Elgar, 1993; James Hawley, "Protecting Capital From Itself: U.S. Attempts to Regulate the Eurocurrency System," *International Organization* 38, 1984, pp. 131-65; Lou Pauly, *Opening Financial Markets*. Ithaca: Cornell University Press, 1988; Geoffrey Underhill, "Markets Beyond Politics? The State and the Internationalization of Financial Markets," *European Journal of Political Research* 19, 1991, pp. 197-225; Tom Notermans, "The Abdication from National Policy Autonomy," *Politics and Society* 21, 1993, pp. 133-67; Barr Eichengreen, *Globalizing Capital*. Princeton: Princeton University Press, 1996.
2. Karl Polanyi, *The Great Transformation*. New York: Rinehart, 1944, p.2, "Ours is not a historical work."
3. Polanyi, *The Great Transformation*, p.139.
4. As I have noted elsewhere, however, some of his historical arguments about the significance of national currencies for the consolidation of the nation state are in fact unique and worthy of attention today. See Eric Helleiner, "Historicizing Territorial Currencies: Monetary Structures, Sovereignty and the Nation-State," Mimeo, 1996.
5. A "Polanyian" perspective should not neglect the role of technological change. In *The Great Transformation*, Polanyi assigns the Industrial Revolution a central role in his analysis.
6. See John Ruggie, "Territoriality and Beyond," *International Organization* 47, 1993, pp. 139-74; Ethan Kapstein, "Territoriality and Who is 'US'," *International Organization* 47, 1993, pp. 501-3, and Ruggie's reply in the same issue, pp. 503-5.

7. John Ruggie, "International Regimes, Transactions and Change: Embedded Liberalism in the Postwar Economic Order," *International Organization* 36, 1982, pp. 379-415.
8. Eric Helleiner, *States and the Reemergence of Global Finance*. Ithaca: Cornell University Press, 1994, Ch.2.
9. Quoted in Helleiner, *States and the Reemergence*, p.25.
10. Quoted in Helleiner, *States and the Reemergence*, p.34.
11. Pauly, *Opening Financial Markets*, p.2.
12. Underhill, "Markets Beyond Politics?," p.203.
13. Helleiner, *States and the Reemergence*. The following discussion draws heavily on the analysis I present here. For citations to the relevant IPE literature, see the references in this book.
14. Richard McKenzie and Dwight Lee, *Quicksilver Capital*. New York: The Free Press, 1991, Ch.10.
15. Phil Cerny, "The Dynamics of Financial Globalization," *Policy Sciences* 27, 1994, p. 339. Cerny does seem to leave open the option of future change, adding that "a new Great Transformation will be required at a global, supranational level if values other than the establishment of a global self-regulating market are to be realized." But his analysis suggests that he is very sceptical about the prospects for such a development.
16. See for example Ethan Kapstein, *Governing the Global Economy*. Cambridge: Harvard University Press, 1994; Tony Porter, *States, Markets and Regimes in Global Finance*. Basingstoke: Macmillan, 1993.
17. Polanyi, *The Great Transformation*, p. 202. See Ch.16 for his discussion of the ideas I summarize in this paragraph and the next.
18. Some analysts, however, question the extent to which it is in fact successfully achieving this goal. See for example Soichi Enkyo, "Authorities and the Market: The Case of the BIS Standards" in Roger Morgan *et al.*, *New Diplomacy in the Post-Cold War World*. London: Macmillan, 1993.
19. James Tobin, "A Proposal for International Monetary Reform," *Eastern Economic Journal* 4, 1978, p. 158.
20. In this way critics have employed what Albert Hirschman calls the "futility thesis" in opposing the Tobin tax; that is, reform is rejected on the basis that it could never be implemented effectively. To a lesser extent, critics of the Tobin tax have also drawn on the "perversity thesis," a second traditional line of argument against reform initiatives that Hirschman identifies (in *The Rhetoric of Reaction*. Cambridge: Harvard University Press, 1991). According to this second traditional line of argument, reform initiatives are rejected because they are predicted to produce the exact opposite of the results intended. In this instance, some critics of the Tobin tax have suggested that it may lead to an increase in exchange rate volatility—rather than a decrease—because of reduced liquidity in foreign exchange markets (see for example P. Shome and J. Stotsky, *Financial Transactions Taxes*, IMF Working Paper no.77, 1995). This second argument, which assumes that the tax is too effective, is not compatible with the first which assumes that the tax will be futile, and it has been used less frequently by critics.
21. Some critics also predict large-scale evasion via the use or creation of financial instruments that are not covered by the tax but which could serve a similar function as spot foreign exchange transactions. For a critique of this view, see the comments of James Tobin, Barry Eichengreen and Charles Wyplosz in their respective contributions to M. Ul Haq, I. Kaul, I. Grunberg, (eds.), *The Tobin Tax*. Oxford: Oxford University Press, 1996, pp. xv, 31, 278.
22. For examples of Tobin tax advocates citing the precedent of the BIS regime, see John Langmore, "Restructuring Economic and Financial Power," *Futures* 27, 1995, p.192; William Grieder, "The Money Question," *World Policy Journal* 5, 1988, pp. 609-611.
23. See for example Grieder, "The Money Question," pp. 609-611; David Felix, "The Tobin Tax Proposal," *Futures* 27, 1995, p.207. In a similar vein, a recent UNCTAD paper by Yilmaz Akyuz and Andrew Cornford ("Regimes for International Capital Movements and Some Proposals for Reform," May 1994) discusses the potential usefulness of the BIS regime for an initiative that would apply capital charges to banks' open positions in foreign exchange as a possible alternative to Tobin's specific tax proposal. They note (pp. 22-3): "This approach has the advantage of relying on regulations analogous to those already proposed as part of the current initiative of the Basle Committee on Banking Supervision concerning standards for the supervision of banks' market risks including those due to their positions in foreign exchange. Although this initiative is more narrowly directed at objectives regarding the prudential supervision of banks, it would none the less cover the very transactions through which banks can engage in currency speculation."
24. David Felix, "Financial Globalization versus Free Trade: The Case for the Tobin Tax," mimeo, November 1995, p. 43. These countries are: the UK, the US, Japan, Singapore, Switzerland, Hong Kong, and Germany.

25. See for example Nigel Thrift, "On the Social and Cultural Determinants of International Financial Centres" in S. Corbridge, N. Thrift and R. Martin, (eds.), *Money, Power and Space*. Oxford: Blackwell, 1994.
26. For a more detailed discussion, see Felix, "Financial Globalization," pp.43-44.
27. Richard Cooper, "What Future for the International Monetary System?" in Pierre Siklos, (ed.), *Varieties of Monetary Reforms*. London: Kluwer Academic Publishers, 1994, p. 141. Peter Kenen also suggests that authorities could tax foreign exchange transactions with financial centers that were not implementing the tax at a very high rate (Peter Kenen, "The Feasibility of Taxing Foreign Exchange Transactions" in M. Ul Haq et al, *The Tobin Tax*).
28. See Susan Strange, *Casino Capitalism*. Oxford: Blackwell, 1986.
29. Kapstein, *Governing the Global Economy*, Ch.5.
30. Eric Helleiner, "Handling 'Hot Money': U.S. Policy Towards Latin American Capital Flight in Historical Perspective," *Alternatives* 20, 1995; Eric Helleiner, "Liberalism, State Power and the Regulation of Illicit Activity in Global Finance" in R. Friman and P. Andreas, (eds.), *The State and the Illicit Global Economy* (forthcoming).
31. Langmore ("Restructuring," p.192) cites a U.S. opinion survey showing that roughly two-thirds of respondents supported the introduction of the tax. He also notes interest in the proposals among such prominent White House officials as Larry Summers (the U.S. Undersecretary of the Treasury for International Affairs) and Joseph Stiglitz (a member of the President's Council of Economic Advisors).
32. See for example Lou Pauly, "The Politics of European Monetary Union: National Strategies, International Implications," *International Journal* 47, 1992.
33. Helleiner, *States and the Reemergence*, pp. 131-9.
34. Eric Helleiner, "Post-Globalization: Is the Financial Liberalization Trend Likely to Be Reversed?" in R.Boyer and D.Drache, (eds)., *Global Markets: Do Nation-States Have a Future?* New York: Routledge, 1996.
35. Quoted in *The Globe and Mail*, Dec. 7, 1995, p.A18.
36. Klaus Schwab and Claude Smadja, quoted in Thomas Friedman, "Beware Traders, We All Have Our Zyuganovs," *International Herald Tribune*, February 8, 1996.
37. See for example "The Myth of the Powerless State," *The Economist*, October 7, 1995, pp.15-16.
38. Ironically, key sources of these overstatements in the past were neoliberals themselves keen to invoke the "myth of the powerless state" to justify their preference for a limited state role in the economy.
39. Helleiner, *States and the Reemergence*, pp. 203-5.
40. See Langmore ("Restructuring," pp.192-3); Helleiner, "Post-Globalization."
41. As David Felix ("The Tobin Tax," p. 205) notes, in this age of anti-tax populism, governments such as these are searching for sources of tax revenue that are not "politically suicidal." In his words, "[a] tax on foreign exchange speculation may meet this specification, since in U.S. political jargon, it's a tax on 'Wall Street' not 'Main Street'."
42. Helleiner, "Post-Globalization."
43. Lionel Barber, "Delors pushes for monetary 'fortress Europe'," *Financial Times*, September 18, 1993.
44. Abraham Rotstein and Colin Duncan, "For a Second Economy" in Daniel Drache and Meric Gertler (eds.), *The New Era of Global Competition*. Kingston: McGill-Queen's University Press, 1991; Ross Dobson, *Bringing the Economy Home from the Market*. Montreal: Black Rose, 1993.
45. See for example Paul Ekins, "Local Currency," in P. Ekins (ed.), *The Living Economy*. London: Routledge and Kegan Paul, 1986.
46. See for example Eric Helleiner, "International Political Economy and the Greens," *New Political Economy* 1, 1996.
47. It is worth noting that local currencies have proliferated at various moments in history when the state's capacity to manage money effectively was eroded. During the early 1930s, for example, local currencies were used extensively in the U.S. and in countries across Europe. See for example Wayne Weishaar and Wayne Parrish, *Men Without Money*. New York: Putnam's, 1933.
48. This phenomenon is noted, for example, by Louis Pauly, "Capital Mobility, State Autonomy and Political Legitimacy," *Journal of International Affairs* 48, 1995, p. 384; Michael Loriaux, *France After Hegemony*. Ithaca: Cornell University Press, 1991, p.307.
49. Strange, *Casino Capitalism*, p. 192.

50. Polanyi, *The Great Transformation*, p.30. Indeed, Strange's entire book has interesting parallels with Polanyi's work. Her critique of the existing financial order is that it encourages a degree of social upheaval and instability that is unsustainable and also "politically unacceptable to a free society." (p.191) This was also the key concern for Polanyi.
51. See for example Andrew Glyn, "Capital Flight and Exchange Controls," *New Left Review* 155, 1986; Leo Panitch, "Globalisation and the State," in R.Miliband and L.Panitch (eds.), *Socialist Register*. London: Merlin Press, 1994.
52. Polanyi, *The Great Transformation*, pp.253-4.
53. See for example John Goodman and Lou Pauly, "The Obsolescence of Capital Controls," *World Politics* 46, 1993; Strange, *Casino Capitalism*, p. 190. Even supporters of such proposals have been forced to acknowledge these difficulties. See for example Glyn "Capital Flight."
54. Notermans, "The Abdication," p. 151; Helleiner, "Liberalism, State Power."
55. Helleiner, "Historicizing Territorial Currencies."
56. For the historical roots of "welfare-nationalism," see Robert Cox, *Production, Power and World Order*. New York: Columbia University Press, 1987. Indeed, in the monetary and financial sector, neo-liberals such as Hayek have increasingly called into question the need for the very national currencies and national central banks that their liberal counterparts in the nineteenth century built. See for example F. Hayek, *The Denationalization of Money*. London: Institute for Economic Affairs, 1976.
57. John Ruggie, "Territoriality and Beyond"; Eric Hobsbawn, *Nations and Nationalism Since 1780*. Cambridge: Cambridge University Press, 1990, pp. 25, 182. See also Benjamin Cohen, "Phoenix Arisen," *World Politics* 48, 1996, pp. 295-6.
58. For a sceptical view see L. Panitch, "Globalisation and the State." For a more optimistic view see David Held (ed.), *Cosmopolitan Democracy*. Cambridge: Polity Press, 1995. For a discussion of how Held's ideas might apply to the financial sector see Eric Helleiner, "Democratic Governance in an Era of Global Finance" in M. Cameron and M. Molot (eds.), *Canada Among Nations, 1994-95: Democracy and Foreign Policy*. pp. 279-98, Ottawa: Carleton University Press, 1995.
59. Charles Kindleberger, *Manias, Panics and Crashes*. New York: Basic Books, 1978.
60. Barry Eichengreen, *Golden Fetters*. Oxford: Oxford University Press, 1992.
61. Janice Thomson and Stephen Krasner, "Global Transactions and the Consolidation of Sovereignty" in J. Rosenau and E.O. Czempiel (eds.), *Global Changes and Theoretical Challenges*. Lexington: Lexington Books, 1989. See also Panitch, "Globalisation and the State."
62. For a broader discussion of this argument, see Helleiner, "Historicizing Territorial Currencies."
63. Ruggie, "Territoriality and Beyond"; Kapstein, "Territoriality and Who is 'US'."
64. Ruggie chooses to associate the practice of "territoriality" with the seventeenth-century Westphalian state, whereas I am more inclined to agree with Anthony Giddens that it was linked to the nineteenth-century nation state. For a more extended discussion, see Helleiner, "Historicizing Territorial Currencies."
65. See for example Robert Gilpin, *The Political Economy of International Relations*. Princeton: Princeton University Press, 1987.
66. See for example Stephen Gill, "Theorizing the Interregnum," in B. Hettne (ed.), *International Political Economy*. London: Zed Books, 1995.
67. Helleiner, "IPE and the Greens."
68. See especially Ruggie "International Regimes." Similarly, Charles Kindleberger cites *The Great Transformation* as one of the key works of the twentieth century ("The Great Transformation," *Daedalus* 103, 1973, pp. 45-52). Although he criticizes Polanyi for ignoring the extent to which societies *must* adjust to market changes, Kindleberger is appreciative of Polanyi's concern at the costs of this adjustment process when it is too rapid or far-reaching. This view is similar to that of Tobin who justifies the need for a foreign exchange tax on the following grounds: "National economies and national governments are not capable of adjusting to massive movements of funds across the foreign exchanges, without real hardship and without significant sacrifice of the objectives of national economic policy with respect to employment, output, and inflation." (Tobin, "A Proposal," p. 154).

Chapter Three

THE CONTINUING CRISIS OF DEMOCRACY
Michele Cangiani

Karl Polanyi shared with the political culture of "Red Vienna" the notion that the overcoming of the crisis of liberal capitalism would lead to real, not illusory, freedom. The problem of the social organization of the economy would be raised in its political aspect; rescued from market rationality, it would be worked out by free individuals in the context of democratic institutions.

A DEMOCRATIC UTOPIA

Already in 1922, in the essay in which he maintains the possibility and efficacy of "social accounting"—i. e., of an economy democratically addressed and ordered in an uncentralized socialist system—Polanyi says that the capitalistic economy cannot "by its very nature" be oriented "in the direction of social utility," cannot, except by chance, achieve "social productivity." The capitalistic organization of production, having profit as its aim, lacks the necessary "sense organ" (*Sinnesorgan*) which can perceive and understand individual needs and social evaluations. Moreover, the process of production has a "retroactive effect on society's life" and on individual needs, the latter becoming altered and even corrupted, or created on an illusionary basis.[1] Neither society nor the individual is able to control the goals and the means of the production process; on the contrary, the economic system is *autonomous* and constitutes a permanent and severe constraint upon social institutions and individual existence.

It had become obvious to Polanyi that the "self-regulating market" existed no longer and perhaps had never fully existed. Later, in *The Great Transformation*, he would write that it was a "utopia." The concept of a "self-regulating market" has anyway in Polanyi's theory a very different meaning from the model of perfect competition of economic theory in which individual producers are free and consumers are sovereign. In Polanyi's "self-regulating market" the freedom of individuals is illusory, since they are deprived of control over the conditions of their own existence. What Polanyi has in mind is not an abstract economic model, but a historical form of social organization, i. e., capitalism. The "liberal utopia" and, in particular, the theory of free competition and price equilibrium are for him ideological constructs; they reflect the conditions and problems of the initial phase of capitalism, and found only partial contrasting institutionalization in the 19th century.

A fundamental thesis of *The Great Transformation* is that such a utopia had been rendered obsolete by the very development of capitalist society. Conscious and democratic control of the economy could then stand out as a topical need. This need had been the object of Polanyi's analyses in the early 1920s, when he made explicit reference to Otto Bauer's "functional" socialism and to Guild Socialism. This is the background to his observation on "freedom in a complex society," and on "power and economic value" as "a paradigm of social reality" in the last chapter of *The Great Transformation* and later, on the need for a conscious and responsible "planned intervention of producers and consumers themselves."[2]

Let us call this Polanyi's own democratic utopia. We must be mindful of the wide appeal of this utopia in the first half of our century which Polanyi shared with G. D. H. Cole, Harold Laski, R.H. Tawney and others. By 1934, in England where democracy had not been completely abolished as in other European countries, Polanyi continued to wonder how it would be possible "to lead democracy toward its maturity." He not only observed but also collaborated in initiatives devoted to the enlargement of public reflection on social problems, with the purpose of providing the individual with the instruments of knowledge and self-goverment. In an article of that year Polanyi reminds us that an autonomous and informed public opinion is the foundation of democracy, and that the issues at stake are nothing less than the "mutual relation between the political and the economic spheres": the possibility of matching political democracy with a corporative industrial organization.[3] A year and a half later, he greeted the "experiment" of the Tennessee Valley Authority as an example of how society might control the economy rationally and democratically; in no other way can the employment of natural resources attain an optimum from the point of view of social welfare and ecological equilibrium. He considered the free-market rhetoric of the opposition to the T.V.A. as representing the interests of great corporations whose power and political influence had nothing to do with free competition.[4]

The currents of democratic thought to which Polanyi's conception was tied were characterized by two combined requirements: economic democracy based on industrial democracy, and the restoration of the primacy of the cultural and political over the economic function. The case for such a restoration was made by R.H. Tawney[5] by whom Polanyi was influenced. Later, in 1933, Josef Fischer—a Czech sociologist and philosopher, member of the Prague Circle, and close to Austro-Marxism—saw the principal cause of "the crisis of democracy" in the inversion process by which the capitalistic economic system became autonomous and thus was able to dominate the higher social functions of culture and politics. According to Fischer, individuals should regain control of the means and modes of life, starting with their own work. On these foundations society could construct the means of self-government, which consists, first of all, in the capacity to define the goals and methods of production. In short, the development of democracy implies the overcoming of the autonomy of the economy. Democracy would otherwise be limited, at most, to the formal right to vote and to the conflict of group interests, whereas the issue of the economic system as such would not be raised.[6]

After World War I, in Red Vienna and elsewhere, the debate on democracy, its preconditions, and procedures became intense. In Austria universal suffrage and the success of the Socialists gave the impression that the problem of democracy could be solved. If democracy could acquire control over the political sphere, it could be extended to the economy. Otto Bauer later wrote, after reactionary and fascist forces had come to power, that the defeat of such a democratic strategy confirmed the analysis on which it was grounded: a fundamental factor in the "crisis of democracy" was the contradiction between political constitution and social organization, between political equality of civil rights and economic command by capitalists.[7]

In England, where political democracy seemed capable of resistance, Laski's ideas were very similar: economic and social institutions, which are controlled by "aristocratic and plutocratic power," have to be rendered consistent with political democracy. But Conservatives attempted, on the contrary, to make a socialist government *constitutionally* impossible.[8] A statement of Polanyi's expresses precisely the ideas he shared with Bauer and Laski: "democracy cannot be maintained under the conditions of present-day life, unless the principles of democracy are extended to the whole of society, including the economic system itself. This is commonly called Socialism."[9] As both were writing in exile, Bauer in 1936 and Polanyi in 1937, both were painfully conscious that in most European countries the crisis of democracy ended with the abolition of political democratic institutions.

THE "MARKET SYSTEM" AND CAPITALISM

It is clear from his later works that for Polanyi the transition towards a "mature," effective, accomplished democracy depends on the overcoming of two basic features of capitalistic society: capitalist organization of production which cannot but reproduce class division, and the autonomy of the economy. It is interesting that he seems to point to the bond between the two. He writes, for example, that only when "the use of labour power could be universally bought and sold" did it become evident that "the broader range of vital social interests" was deeply affected and restricted by the market mechanism and the profit motive.[10] And again, he points out that the market-society, where "the motive of economic gain" has been "absolutized," "becomes an organism that is, in all essential regards, subservient to gainful purposes."[11]

As these two features of capitalist society are linked, so their consequences are convergent: they lead to the incapacity of the social system to face and even to perceive the problems it produces by its own development. The motive of profit, class exploitation, and lack of democracy bring about tendencies toward disorganization, social entropy. "The ruling classes had committed the error of extending the principle of uncompromising class rule to a type of civilization which demanded the cultural and educational unity of the commonwealth if it should be safe from degenerative influences."[12] This statement is concerned specifically with the defeat of the Chartist Movement. But it belongs to a more general argument developed by Polanyi in the early 1920s, which anticipates systems theory: the capacity of the social-economic system to perceive modifications in the internal and external environment, and to respond adequately to them, depends on the nature of the organization of the system itself. The more democratic the organization, the more information will be available. Therefore, "the capacity organizations have to perform their function depends on the quantity of active democracy present in daily life." This applies to any organization, to a factory as well as to a political party and the state. The latter should be the complex "functional" organization of multiple others, corresponding to various functions or "ambits of life."[13] In short, the pursuit of optimization by an economic system depends on the definition of social ends.

This definition depends on social organization; the more democratic the organization, the more (socially) profitable the definition. Of course, the development of democracy at any level of social life would not necessarily mean the disappearance of all conflicts in the production process, between producers and consumers, and in regards to defining social aims. Nevertheless, what is essential is that their resolution should not be constrained by either economic "automatisms" or the reproduction of a given power structure (as was the case also in "administrative" socialist systems).[14]

One could say that this is Polanyi's solution of the issue—left open by Max Weber—of the criterion for evaluating "substantive economic rationality" (i. e., that which, in opposition to "formal" economic rationality, concerns economic ends to the extent that the motives, by which they are determined, are different from mere formal, market-economic rationality).[15] It is worthy of note that it is a criterion which does not presuppose any given value. But a general principle—opposed to the pessimistic current of modern political philosophy—must be presupposed: the more individuals are free, the more they are able *socially* to seek their own welfare. The more democratic the organization of society, the more it is open to rational choices made by freely associating individuals. Some years later, Karl Mannheim would reformulate the problem of the shrinkage of "substantive rationality"—defined as "the capacity of acting intelligently in a given situation"—because industrial society presupposes the concentration in a few hands of the means of production and knowledge, and therefore of the power of making choices on behalf of the whole of society.[16]

The above considerations show that Polanyi's view is deeply influenced by the socialist and democratic way of conceiving the overcoming, but also the fulfilment, of liberalism, typical of a particular historical conjuncture in the years around World War I. Yet the problems posed by Polanyi encompass modern capitalist society in its entirety; they affect the very condition of modern man.

There is in *The Great Transformation* a typical interplay between more general and less general concepts. For instance, "the smashing up of social structures in order to extract the element of labor from them,"[17] which began in the 16th century and is not yet over, pertains to the whole historical development of capitalism. At a less general level, Polanyi analyzes the instituting of the labour market—fully accomplished in England by the 1830s—as a fundamental element of the *"laissez-faire* policy" of the liberal "market system." This system, then, has to be understood as one of the forms of the capitalistic organization of society. In fact, Polanyi calls it sometimes "the 19th century society" or "the Victorian system" (considered as the expression of British supremacy). The institutional framework of the liberal "market system" would be finally and *irreversibly* transformed after 1929. With regard to the labour market, the diffusion of collective bargaining or the National Labor Relations Act signed by Roosevelt in 1935 may be mentioned as examples of new institutions; so too may the authoritarian legislation of fascist regimes. No one could say, however, that the market system in its broadest meaning, corresponding to the *general* definition of capitalism as a market-centered society, had been supplanted either in the 1930s or today.[18]

Distinguishing between different levels of conceptualization allows for a better understanding of the object of the theory of "transformation": the move from one stage of capitalism to another. From the liberal market system, where there was a *separation* between economic and political institutions, to the corporative system, where this separation comes to an end, while the capitalistic *autonomy* of the economy persists and even has opportunities for becoming more deeply rooted. After 1945 Polanyi continued to maintain that there were *still two tendencies*: towards democratic "planned intervention" as mentioned above, or towards a society "more intimately adjusted to the economic system," dominated by big business, and by privileged and managerial elites.[19] The general and deeply felt need for democracy is not presented as finding expression in any kind of "countermovement" against market self-regulation or intervention in the economic system. If we re-read *The Great Transformation*, bearing in mind the two levels of conceptualization and the object of Polanyi's theory mentioned above, we must conclude that we are being warned that after the end of the market system *stricto sensu* the road to democracy is still long, perhaps even longer and more difficult.

THE CORPORATIVE TRANSFORMATION

Polanyi's articles of the interwar period—about which it is not possible here to go into any great detail—provide evidence of the persistence of his utopian democratic conception: it urges recognition of any social or political attitude which could be interpreted as evidence of its historical plausibility, and it serves as a yardstick to measure how much, and why, the opposite tendency is in fact prevailing. Fascism can then be interpreted as abolition of "the political state" and even of the modern concept of society—a society made up of free and responsible individuals now "considered as producers, and as producers alone."[20] Hitler's slogan of the "primacy of politics over economy" thus stands for its opposite: the capitalist economy is to be maintained and re-structured, even if this demands the abolition of political democracy. The economic and political institutions, which characterize the liberal form of capitalism, are overcome, but capitalism is not. This was Polanyi's conclusion in 1933, when he considered the possible consequences of Hitler's taking of power, his programme for "corporative construction" of the economic system, and the irony that the labour market was displaced by authoritarian discipline and state-controlled allocation of workers.[21] Moreover, as Polanyi specifies, chiefly in articles published in 1934 in the periodical *New Britain*, the abolition of democratic representative institutions gives to capitalistic economic power the possibility of more immediate and effective control over political decisions.

The transformation presupposes a stable hegemony of the ruling class also in the countries where democratic institutions had not been abolished. This is made clear by Polanyi in his articles on Great Britain. In 1926, for instance, he regarded the failure of the General Strike as the ruling class's opportunity to end a long period of social struggle to its own advantage.[22] Even a measure of "socialization" of the economy became feasible—on the initiative and under the control of the ruling class and, in particular, the existing economic power. Political democratic institutions underwent a corresponding transformation. In 1931 Polanyi emphasized that, in forming the so-called National Government, the Labour leader Macdonald "broke with the tradition of democracy—to the disadvantage of the working classes."[23] Then, when the fear of a "popular government" had past, such important institutions of the market system as the gold standard and free trade could be abandoned, and disturbing political "interferences" in the economy could be suitably transformed. Polanyi refers, for instance, to the proposals of the Conservative Harold Macmillan, which, if implemented, could have led to a sort of *"bourgeois* planned economy" through "voluntary self-administration and self-defense of industry."[24] The Trade Unions and the Labour Party, in their turn, discussed a plan which was criticized by the Labour left and described as "democratic-corporatist" by Polanyi, since it replaced the strategy of socialist socialization and political control of the economic system by assigning to trade unions the task of arbitrating conflicts and representing group interests of different categories of workers within the limits of corporate ends decided elsewhere.[25]

Industrial rationalization was to go hand-in-hand with social peace. In 1928 Polanyi discussed the reforms proposed in *Britain's Industrial Future*, the report published by the Liberal Industrial Enquiry. Besides ways to achieve industrial restructuring and more direct involvement of the state, the report recommended recognition of trade unions as representatives of workers' interests. Moreover, it suggested that constant attention be paid to the moods of the workers and to actively diffusing belief in *community* rather than in *conflict* of interest between labour and capital. Polanyi draws attention to the idea of "industrial co-operation" as a sort of "psychologistic pragmatism": the workers' opinions about their condition, and their attitudes toward the power structure, seemed to be more important than the reality.[26]

This was in accord with Josef Schumpeter's 1929 lecture at a meeting of German industrialists where he argued that those belonging to "the leading stratum of economic life" should undertake *social* as well as economic leadership, committed to diffusing the *"belief"* (Schumpeter's stress) that the common good is the purpose and the result of their entrepreneurial activity.[27]

The problem still was how to endow the workers with that "co-operative spirit" which, according to G. D. H. Cole, would have characterized work under a guild-socialist system[28]—but without socialism, without "industrial democracy." In 1934, when hopes for the development of democracy had given way to disillusion, Polanyi wrote that the interplay between democratic political institutions and capitalist command of the economy, which existed in the first stage of the development of capitalist society, had now been converted into reciprocal incompatibility.[29] One year later Schumpeter, moving from different if not opposite political views, expressed himself similarly: "The ideas of political democracy which [the *bourgeois*] made his own in the time of his servitude proved incompatible with the essentially monarchical ideas underlying the organization of business."[30] In his last article, Schumpeter regrets that the rational *forma mentis*, diffused by capitalism itself, tends "to destroy those loyalties and those habits of super- and subordination that are nevertheless essential for the efficient working of the institutionalized leadership of the producing plant."[31]

ANOTHER THEORY OF DEMOCRACY
These samples or symptoms of Schumpeter's point of view are worthy of consideration when we interpret the refutation of the "classical" modern theory of democracy which he expounded in *Capitalism, Socialism, and Democracy* (1942). Neither the common good, he declared, nor the way to achieve it can be "uniquely determined," for the concept of "the will of the people or the *volonté générale* that the utilitarians made their own vanishes into thin air."[32] Political decisions cannot be traced back to the will of independent and rational

individuals; as problems become more general and remote, intelligence and moral standards diminish.

On the basis of this criticism, Schumpeter suggests "another theory of democracy." The identifying mark of democracy is its *modus procedendi*: the struggle for the people's vote has to be competitive. The voters behave like consumers, and the party managers behave like entrepreneurs, offering political goods. Normally competition is oligopolistic and suppliers create the demand. The electorate's choice cannot but be shaped, "and the shaping of it is an essential part of the democratic process."[33] In the long run "no amount of retrospective common sense will alter the fact that in reality [the people] neither raise nor decide issues but that the issues that shape their fate are normally raised and decided for them."[34]

Schumpeter's theory was representative of liberal thinking around the time of World War II. Another famous example of this tendency is *The Road to Serfdom*, published by F.A. Hayek in the same year as *The Great Transformation*. Polanyi's thesis is that the former connection between capitalistic development and the development of freedom and democracy no longer applies. Hayek's thesis is the opposite: market (capitalistic) freedom constitutes the true ground and only guarantee of liberty and democracy. This thesis was the better qualified to prevail, since it better accorded with the "universal capitalism"[35] supported by the U.S.A., despite the fact that the hypothesis of perfect competition was unrealistic.

The new liberalism took advantage of the defeat of socialist movements, of the victory over fascism, and of the global confrontation with communism. During the War discussion was still of the crisis of classical liberalism. The Polanyi Hayek-Schumpeter debates were continued in England and the U.S.A. whither they had emigrated, in terms of the dispute that had begun in "Red Vienna" that was heir to great achievements in all fields of cultural life[36] from the late 19th century until the forced exodus of the 1930s. Other scholars were involved in this dispute, including Otto Neurath who elaborated theories and projects relating to the functioning of a socialist society before the Great War, and who in 1945, at the end of his life, criticised Hayek's book from a point of view close to Polanyi's.[37]

Hayek's ideas would have direct political influence in the 1970s,[38] when neo-liberal policies appeared as a solution to the crisis of post-war development. Schumpeter's theory of democracy is, in its turn, still considered a turning-point in the history of political thought. However, the success of both Hayek's and Schumpeter's theories may be because they reflect in a simplified way actual tendencies in contemporary economic and political life, rather than having consistency and a capacity for explanation. Schumpeter's refutation of the "classical" theory is no more than a substituting of one general concept of man and society for another. But the refutation and the new theory proposed thus remain too abstract. Not only does Schumpeter not take into account the general features of modern capitalistic society and the different historical stages of its development, in both his criticism of "classical" theory and his "other" theory politics seems to be separated from the economy, and political power from economic power. Capitalistic autonomy of the economy is not defined as such in historically concrete terms, but is mirrored in a general, abstract and individualistic concept of the economy, as well as of politics. It thus neglects the changing historical relations between capitalistic economy and capitalistic democracy.

Schumpeter traces the classical concept of democracy back to Utilitarianism, since the latter presupposes, according to him, the existence of individuals naturally capable of acting in accordance with their perfectly rational wills and with each other. Such a simplified view, of course, disregards two centuries of political and theoretical struggles. His theory is basically utilitarian because of the explicit transposition operative in his model of the competitive market applied to politics, and because of his "methodological individualism." If the economy is not conceived as a social and historical form of organization, the consequence is the *natural* separation between politics and the economy. There is a link between Schumpeter's political theory and the way he conceives the economy. His individualistic method implies the premise that economic behaviour can be analyzed in general and in itself. This connected with the belief that economic development, together with the profit motive which animates it, is *per se* in the common good and is the common end of society as a whole. On the one hand, power relations within productive organizations are but a hierarchy of technically established functions requiring the unconditional "loyalty" of the staff. On the other, a democratic political process is incapable of mapping out the goals of the economic system and controlling its working.

LIBERALISM AFTER LIBERALISM

The great crisis of liberal capitalism culminated in the 1929 crash, and the unavoidable transformations it led to emphasized the impossibility of the separation between economic and political institutions. But Schumpeter and other political thinkers probably kept to such separation because it seemed the only escape from the radical alternative as expressed by Polanyi in 1935: "Basically there are two solutions: the extension of the democratic principle from politics to economics, or the abolition of the democratic 'political sphere' altogether."[39]

The conviction that democracy leads to socialism was shared in those years by socialist thinkers, and by conservatives and fascists: by Othmar Spann, "the Liberals of the Mises school" (who, according to Polanyi, are inclined to condone fascism "as the safeguard of Liberal economics,")[40] and Carl Schmitt who asked in 1932 for "a stronger state and a sound economy."[41] Schumpeter, however, perpetuates the liberal paradox, wanting to protect the autonomy of the economy from political intervention, and to restrict democracy to a formally free electoral competition, while also acknowledging the obsolescence of the liberal utopia: "No social system can work which is based exclusively upon a network of free contracts between (legally) equal contracting parties and in which everyone is supposed to be guided by nothing except his own (short-run) utilitarian ends."[42] Thus, he seems to regret the loss of an earlier pre-modern hierarchical organicism which has nothing to do with separation of the economic and political spheres. He regrets the weakening of the good old pre-modern hierarchical mind, and of such "protective social strata" as the aristocracy and the traditional peasantry on which the bourgeoisie used to rely for social order. Some aspects of his political theory are representative of the dark, but well known, side of liberalism. He imagines a sort of post-modern "moral economy," where the workers feel deeply involved in their productive function, have confidence in the managerial leadership, and are persuaded that production is by its very nature directed toward the common good. He presupposes a bounded and "formal" concept of the "common good": namely, economic development to which "the motive of economic gain" gives life. Weber's problem of "substantive" economic rationality is thus not solved, but by-passed. Democracy, deprived of the means of devising cultural and political purposes for economic activities by autonomous and conscious individuals, formally amounts to nothing more than electoral competition.

Recent history has shown that electoral competition and political life in general become filled with all sort of illusions and rituals, if they do not concern themselves with the actual conditions of social life, particularly economic activity. The concentration of power inherent in the capitalistic mode of production remains obscured by rhetoric about the national interest. The autonomy of the (capitalistic) economy imposes itself as a technical requirement of production. That emotionalism and plebiscitarianism take the place of rational judgment in political processes Schumpeter partially aknowledges. Significantly, he ascribes them to human nature, without raising the question of their connection with a given historical form of social organization.

It is worth remembering that fascism, according to Polanyi, is both a conjunctural way out—when an economic and political crisis leads to incompatibility between capitalism and "the form of democracy"—and a *general tendency* toward the destruction of the very "substance of democracy": toward "a structural order of society which rules out the dependence of the whole on the conscious will and purpose of the individuals constituting it." In the view of this order, the autonomous organization of "public opinion based on democracy in small groups" is to be undermined or prevented.[43] The anti-democratic tendency does not disappear with the defeat of fascist regimes. Society continues to be faced with the two alternative "solutions" mentioned by Polanyi: if democracy is not extended to the organization of economic life, it cannot but be reduced, even though not abolished as in fascist regimes. In post-liberal market societies the democratic ideals of the first stage of capitalism—emancipation of individual economic behaviour, and exercise of political rights by the individual within political institutions formally separated from the economic sphere—are inadequate. The problem of the economy is by now its overall organization, in which political institutions are inevitably involved. If the purpose and outcome of this involvement are not the expansion of democracy, then they are the opposite: the concentration of economic power tends to dominate the whole of society, and in particular to have a direct and growing influence on politics. Individuals are thus deprived of political competence in respect of the conditions of their existence—a competence which is the basic requisite of *substantive* democracy. From the point of view of the formal conception, which relegates democracy to the sphere of electoral competition for political power, these tendencies of post-liberal society do not constitute a problem; they are not even perceived.

Schumpeter's democratic procedure on the one hand maintains and deepens the gap between political elites and the masses, and on the other denies society the capacity to solve the problems it is faced with. In addition to being within the exclusive competence of a political elite, political decisions are also instrumental to success in the political market; they are *not* taken because they are considered the best solution to a given problem.

Schumpeter's theory undoubtedly fits in with the prevailing tendency of contemporary politics. The investment of political power in marketable commodities—generally forms of economic advantages to be sold to interest groups in exchange for votes—yields a power surplus. Reform becomes more and more difficult, expecially if such "commodities" as social and moral welfare or environmental equilibrium, and not economic profitability and corporate interests, are the aim. This tendency is reinforced by the increasing capacity of interest groups to have direct entry to different levels of state administration: the more political parties must compete on this ground, the less convenient does it become for them to propose general programs.

The situation created by this tendency seems to be the main reason for the emptying of the political sphere and for the increasing disaffection towards politics. On the occasion of the mid-term elections in the U.S.A. in November 1994 some commentators spoke of a "political jam" or of a "lock effect," of political paralysis due chiefly to the power which organized interests have over government through the Congress and the parties. In the election campaign of November 1996 there was an astonishing absence of debate on governmental projects of restructuring public assistence and reducing welfare expenditure. The absence of democratic and effective debate about actual problems deflects discussion, exaggerates the importance of communication techniques, and makes convenient appeals to emotional rather than rational choice. Appeal to voters' most regressive ideological attitudes—for instance, concerning immigration and crime—moves public opinion toward conservative or "new" (i.e., coming from outside the existing parties) candidates.

In the Italian elections of spring 1994 a new party presented itself to the voters for the first time and received more votes than any other. In reality, it is not a party, but rather a label; the word "party" does not even appear in its name "Forza Italia." Under this label, a notorious finance tycoon organized a successful campaign with the aid of managers and consultants from his own corporations, plus various show business personalities and others attracted by hopes of a lasting job. The very structure of traditional parties was missing. Inside this political business organization, roles and positions were not even formally elective, and cannot therefore have anything to do with any sort of debate about different analyses and strategies. Outside it, the relationship established with the voters, or rather "consumers," is confined to advertising, mostly through television networks, some directly owned by the "chief," who enjoys in Italy monopolistic power also in the field of advertising. It is not the firm that bestows certain of its characteristics upon a party; rather, such a party had from its inception been a firm. Besides, it is sometimes difficult to distinguish the party's political activity from the economic interests and activities of the trust. This political phenomenon is perhaps only an Italian exaggeration. Yet Fascism seemed at the beginning to be no more than that in the epoch of counterrevolution after World War I.

The very development of capitalistic modern society created several obstacles to democratic political life. The loss of autonomy of individuals in mass society has been stressed by sociologists, from C. Wright Mills and Riesman to more recent studies on the risks inherent in the increasing importance of the mass media, and on the "de-structuring" of the "public sphere." Economists like Berle and Galbraith have called attention to the problem of *political* power which business corporations acquire through the mere fact of their size. Daniel Bell has expressed concern about the difficulty political theory and practice have in confronting the increasing extent and complexity of problems in "post-industrial society."

A further problem has become very apparent recently: the decay of the state as the primary subject and sphere of politics. The realm of a more or less democratic political life still remains that of the national state, while the entire globe is the realm of autonomous market forces, financial capital, and big corporations. A thousand billion dollars move around the world every day, while the monetary reserves of even countries of the G-7 group represent only a third of that figure. A truly shocking article by Kristin Dawkins explains how international organizations, such as the International Monetary Fund and the WTO (World Trade Organization), are in fact serving the freedom of big corporations to seek profit everywhere, without state-set limits concerning social and ecological safeguards. Chiapas peasants see NAFTA as a menace to the possibility of agrarian reform, to democracy, and even to their livelihood, while the President of the USA manages to get that agreement approved by promising contracts and economic advantages to two dozen congressmen in exchange for their vote.[44]

In conclusion, it seems difficult, to say the least, to maintain as Schumpeter does that the exigence of democracy—understood as a constant endeavour to enhance the individual's capacity to determine social choices of importance to his own life—is unrealistic simply because it presupposes an unrealistic concept of man, of society, and of politics, and not because it is at odds with a historically given form of social organization. Besides, it is worth noting that this exigence of democracy was by no means alien to classical liberalism, whereas it is denied by liberal thinkers like Schumpeter of the post-liberal epoch. Post-liberal liberalism keeps to formally democratic procedures and rituals, but never seeks the development of liberty as the *positive* liberty of the individual, as the ability and responsibility of all to control the natural and social conditions of their own existence.

POST-LIBERAL DEMOCRACY

Leaving aside general tendencies and the struggle concerning democracy which characterize our century, Schumpeter's viewpoint makes it difficult to understand the transformation that capitalistic society has undergone since the 1930s. His fear is that "the private-enterprise system" will not be able to endure, owing to such political interventions as stabilization policies, income redistribution, price regulation and anti-trust measures, public control over labour and money markets, and the creation of public enterprises for the satisfaction of social needs, together with security legislation.[45] We know that, in reality, the "private-enterprise system" did not come to an end together with the market system in the strict sense of liberal-competitive capitalism; it was not destroyed by the diffusion of organized and managerial capitalism, and the forms of political intervention in the economy adopted for instance by the New Deal—which Schumpeter condemns. Polanyi's view is completely different: he fully endorsed, for example, the opinion of the Secretary of Agriculture, Henry Wallace, that Roosevelt's policy, and even the principle that "industry is a public matter," allowed capitalism to persist, reinforce itself, and develop.[46]

Schumpeter grounds his political theory on the presupposition of the general validity and applicability of the concept of the separation of political institutions from economic ones. But this separation was specific to the character of liberal capitalism; it has been undermined by the political power acquired by the working class through the democratic franchise, by political "interference" in the economy, and by the growth of big corporations and trade unions. In post-liberal capitalism, in fact, not only do the economic corporate power blocs, together with state intervention, condition the market: they also have a growing and more direct influence on political decisions. The latter, in turn, concern more directly and massively the economic sphere, especially since the transformation of the 1930s swept away liberal institutions and prejudices. As a result, political representative institutions tend to be by-passed; these institutions, and therefore the voters as such, lose control over the most important political choices.

Schumpeter's comparison of a political party with a business organization implicitly proposes a further problem, one already raised by Fischer, and recently dealt with by Niklas Luhmann: to what extent do political organizations, and the political system as a whole, pursue their own corporate interest, and correspondingly select the input from and the output to their environment? According to Luhmann, the political system becomes more "self-reflexive," i.e., more concerned with its own preservation and less sensitive to the problems of its social environment. This tendency of the political system is only apparently a paradox; actually, it is consistent with the overlapping of the economic and political spheres. As the main or exclusive purpose of political organizations tends to become their own subsistence, and not the detection and solution of social problems, they cannot but consider the *existing* power structure, which in our society is essentially economic, as a vital support, an unavoidable premise. And vice versa: the autonomy of the economy and its sway over the whole of society tend to restrict the democratic political process, as Schumpeter realized, to a market-like operation, in which the supply of political goods takes place with general indifference shown to their quality, and, above all, with the understanding that the capitalist market system can never be questioned as such.

In the 1970s and 1980s several scholars tried to define democratic corporatism and to analyse comparatively its working in Western industrialized countries. The traits of the new, post-liberal phase of capitalist society have been differently pinpointed and interpreted. Sometimes the organization of conflicting functional interests is stressed, sometimes the representation of organized interests at the state level, sometimes the decision and implementation of state policies. Corporatism is interpreted either as a way of making democracy work and of securing pluralistic representation and concertation, or as a way of bureaucratizing the organization of interest groups and by-passing parliamentary representation. It is seen either as the best solution for reducing distributive conflicts and matching the market system with the self-protection of society, or as the suppression of the political effectiveness of class struggle and the circumventing of the need for bringing the economic system under the control of political democratic procedures.

The working classes acquired, to a limited extent and often at the expense of peripheral and marginal workers, political weight and material rights. As they obtained the democratic franchise in the epoch of liberal capitalism, so they supported democratic pluralism in the epoch of corporate representation. But, as is stressed by C. B. Macpherson, democratic-corporative society cannot but ask us "to forgo any fuller measure...of democratic control." Organized group interests are allowed to seek "to maintain their slice of the pie," but not to "question the methods of the bakery."[47]

As we have seen, Polanyi views democratic corporatism as a kind of capitalistic transformation, in which some features of fascist corporatism are present without a total overthrow of political democracy. With reference to the above-mentioned two levels of concepts in his theory, we may say that the overcoming of the 19th century market system and liberal democracy by no means implies fulfillment of the tendency toward democracy and the abolition of the autonomy of the economy. Even if we consider the most notable achievements of post-liberal capitalism—such as the maintaining of pluralistic interest representation, and the welfare state—these do not open, in general and by themselves, the road toward democratic control of the economic system. Moreover, these achievements were dependent on economic growth which had been created by World War II. But by now even the Swedish budget has severely cut expenditures on social services, education, health and agriculture. In fact, operation of the neocorporative system became more difficult from the early 1970s on when the world economic crisis started, the end of which we are still unable to see. As after 1929, the economic crisis jeopardizes the remains of democracy.

FROM ONE CRISIS OF DEMOCRACY TO ANOTHER

It seems then advisable to raise the question of a new transformation, as a result of the crisis of post-war development and of conflict between two opposing tendencies. As we have seen, these are not new and have been stressed in particular by Polanyi with reference to the crisis of liberal capitalism. However, they acquire new meaning and new potentiality on account of the irreversible results of historical processes. The first tendency, according to Macpherson, leads towards "a genuinely democratic participatory system"; the second towards "some kind of corporative plebiscitarian state."[48]

The first tendency rests on acknowledgment of the structural inability of the capitalist market system to solve the problems of human life in an industrialized world. Both the crisis of post-war development and the potentialities of the new industrial revolution based on informatics point to the need to go beyond the market mechanism and offer genuine economic choices in the democratic political sphere. Not only the question of the quality of economic development and distributive justice should be raised, but all aspects of social life should be discussed. Macpherson calls to mind, on that subject, all the institutions that determine "the chances of the full use and development of human capacities."[49] These chances are at present blocked by the consecration of all social forces to the vain attempt to resolve economic crisis, by the collapse of politics, and by the degradation of culture. In the contemporary world there is, in fact, a growing interdependence between the development of democracy, the diffusion of knowledge and responsibility about social choices, and the possibility of containing entropy, of stopping the increase of disorder, in the first place economic.[50] We have seen that this interdependence is typical of the political philosophy shared by Polanyi. We must acknowledge, however, that Schumpeter's theory, mirroring certain actual features and achievements of contemporary capitalist society, reminds us that it is necessary to confront "democratic utopia" with reality.

The second tendency seems, in fact, the most likely. Post-liberal corporative democracy has failed, both from an economic and from a political viewpoint. Increasing economic demands of the people, which have been fostered by

Keynesian policies and served as a means for securing social peace, can no longer be satisfied. Yet democratic attitudes and institutions, to the limited extent that they were promoted, have been hindered. Moreover, political organizations have become more and more involved in exclusively economic competition between interest groups over the size of their slice of the pie, and in the endeavour to maximize not only their own political power, but also, and not always legally, their own economic assets. As a result, democracy and even political life itself have become discredited. Reactionary forces are ready to avail themselves of this situation. The managerial, elitist, hierarchical, authoritarian aspects of post-war corporatism seem increasingly to be replacing the pluralist, cooperative welfare aspects. Class compromise seems economically untenable, and the system of democratic equilibrium between different social forces, needs and institutions—which characterizes for instance the 1948 Italian Constitution—seems politically out of fashion. Even the memory of industrial democracy is becoming lost, while industrial organization theorists tend to ignore the existence of power conflicts in favour of a pre-modern interiorization of the hierarchical principle and of an organic identification of workers with the organization and with goals fixed by management. Industrial and financial corporations acquire increasing independence from state and political control, while political institutions are more directly influenced and even invaded by corporate capital.

This tendency undermines, simultaneously and correlatively, both democracy and the very ability of the social system to work out and even to recognize its problems. We cannot exclude, anyway, the possibility of a reaction, which would be set in motion by the need to recover this ability, which would recognize the autonomy of the economic system as a fundamental problem, and which would seek new forms of social life and democratic political processes.

NOTES

1. K. Polanyi, "Sozialistische Rechnungslegung," *Archiv für Sozialwissenschaft und Sozialpolitik*, IL, 1922, pp. 387-92.
2. K. Polanyi, "Our Obsolete Market Mentality," *Commentary*, 3, Feb. 1947, p. 117; now in George Dalton (ed.), *Primitive, Archaic and Modern Economies*, New York: Doubleday & Company, 1968.
3. K. Polanyi, "England Überlegt," *Der Österreichische Volkswirt*, XXVI, 1934, pp. 1000-1001.
4. See K. Polanyi, "T. V. A. Ein amerikanisches Wirtschaftsexperiment," *Öst. Volksw.*, XXVIII, 1936, pp. 408-411, pp. 427-430, pp. 448-450.
5. See R. H. Tawney, *The Acquisitive Society*. New York: Harcourt, Brace & Co., 1920.
6. See J. L. Fischer, *La crisi della democrazia* [*The Crisis of Democracy*]. Torino: Einaudi, 1977 (first published in Czech, 1933).
7. O. Bauer, *Zwischen zwei Weltkriegen? Der Krise der Weltwirtschaft, der Demokratie und des Sozialismus*. Prague: Eugen Prager, 1936; Italian transl. *Tra due guerre mondiali?* Torino: Einaudi, 1979, p. 101.
8. H. J. Laski, "Le tournant de la démocratie," *Archives de Philosophie du droit et de Sociologie juridique*, IV, 1934, n. 3-4, pp. 156-168; see also *Democracy in Crisis*. London: George Allen & Unwin, 1933.
9. K. Polanyi, *Europe To-day*. London: W. E. T. U. C., 1937, p. 56.
10. K. Polanyi, *The Great Transformation*. Boston: Beacon Press, 1957, pp. 131 and 145.
11. K. Polanyi, *The Livelihood of Man*, edited by H. W. Pearson. New York: Academic Press, 1977, p. XLVI.
12. *The Great Transformation*, p. 172.
13. K. Polanyi, "Neue Erwägungen zu unserer Theorie und Praxis," *Der Kampf*, XVIII, no. 1, Jan. 1925, pp. 23-24.
14. K. Polanyi, "Die funktionelle Theorie der Gesellschaft und das Problem der sozialistischen Rechnungslegung," *Archiv für Sozialwissenschaft und Sozialpolitik*, LII, 1924, p. 223.

15. See Max Weber, *Economy and Society*, edited by G. Roth and C. Wittich, 3 vols. New York: Bedminster Press, 1968, vol. I, chap. 2, § 9.
16. K. Mannheim, *Man and Society in an Age of Reconstruction*. London: Routledge & Kegan Paul, 1954, I, chap. 2; first German edition 1935.
17. *The Great Transformation*, p. 154.
18. Polanyi's concept of the market—in its broader and narrower sense and in its connection with the capitalist organization of production—concerns the most general features of *capitalist society* and its historical phases. Therefore, this concept of the market appears to have a very different meaning from that employed in the contrast between the market and (capitalist) productive organization which we find in some more or less "institutionalist" economists (from Coase to Simon, from Chandler to Williamson). I could never imagine this specification would be necessary, until I found the opposite opinion in John Adams, "The Corporation Versus the Market," *Journal of Economic Issues*, XXVI, No. 2, 1992, 397-405. Moreover, Adams's idea of the corporation as affording "protection" from the market and as a "nonmarket exchange system, combining workers, technicians, and managers in a common entreprise," (405) to the extent that it is near to corporatist ideology, is far from Polanyi's viewpoint.
19. "Our Obsolete Market Mentality," p. 117.
20. K. Polanyi, "The Essence of Fascism," in J. Lewis, K. Polanyi, D. K. Kitchin (eds.), *Christianity and the Social Revolution*. London: Gollancz, 1935, p. 393.
21. K. Polanyi, "Hitler und die Wirtschaft," *Öst. Volksw.*, XXV, 1933, p. 1057.
22. "Probleme des englischen Generalstreiks," *Öst. Volksw.*, XVIII, 1926, pp. 971-974.
23. "Demokratie und Währung in England," *Öst. Volksw.*, XXIII, 1931, p. 1337.
24. "Tory Planwirtschafter," *Öst. Volksw.*, XXVII, 1934, pp. 47-48.
25. See for example, "Gewerkschaftstagung in Weymouth," *Öst. Volksw.*, XXVI, 1934, pp. 1100-1101.
26. See "Liberale Sozialreformer in England," *Öst. Volksw.*, XX, 1928, pp. 597-600.
27. J. A. Schumpeter, *Ökonomie und Psychologie des Unternehmers*. Leipzig: Haberland, 1929.
28. G. D. H. Cole, *Guild Socialism Re-stated*. London: L. Parsons, 1920, p. 58.
29. K. Polanyi, "Fascism and Marxian Terminology," *New Britain*, June 20, 1934, p. 128.
30. J. A. Schumpeter, "Can Capitalism Survive?," a lecture edited by R. Swedberg as "Appendix," to his article "Can Capitalism Survive? Schumpeter's answer and its relevance for new institutional economics," *Archives européennes de sociologie*, XXXIII, 1992, 337.
31. J. A. Schumpeter, "The March into Socialism," *American Economic Review*, XL, 1950, p. 448.
32. J. A. Schumpeter, *Capitalism, Socialism, and Democracy*. London: Allen & Unwin, 1943, pp. 251-52.
33. *Ibid.*, p. 282.
34. *Ibid.*, p. 264.
35. K. Polanyi, "Universal Capitalism or Regional Planning?" *The London Quarterly of World Affairs*, Jan. 1945, pp. 1-6.
36. See A. Janik and S. Toulmin, *Wittgenstein's Vienna*. London: Weidenfeld & Nicholson, 1973; also C.E. Schorske, *Fin-de-Siècle Vienna: Politics and Culture*. Cambridge: Cambridge University Press, 1987.
37. O. Neurath, "Review of *The Road to Serfdom*" by F. A. Hayek, *The London Quarterly of World Affairs*, 1945.
38. See R. Desai, "Second-Hand Dealers in Ideas: Think-Tanks and Thatcherite Hegemony," *New Left Review*, No. 203, Jan.-Feb. 1994, pp. 27-64.
39. "The Essence of Fascism," *op. cit.*, p. 392.
40. *Ibid.*
41. Quoted by F. Neumann, *Behemoth. The Structure and Practice of National Socialism*. New York: Oxford University Press, 1942, p. 66.
42. J. A. Schumpeter, "The March into Socialism," p. 448.
43. "The Essence of Fascism," p. 393.
44. K. Dawkins, "Nafta e Gatt—l'impresa si fa governo mondiale," *Capitalismo Natura Socialismo*, IV, 1994, 2, 21-37; orig. publ. by *Open Magazine Pamphlet Series*, West Side, N. J.
45. "The March into Socialism," pp. 448-450.
46. K. Polanyi, "Arbeitsrecht in U.S.A.," *Öst. Volksw.*, XXIX, 1937, p. 382.
47. C. B. Macpherson, *The Rise and Fall of Economic Justice*. London: Oxford University Press, 1987, pp. 52 and 128.
48. *Ibid.*, p. 127.
49. *Ibid.*, p. 17.
50. See Georges Corm, *Le nouveau désordre économique*. Paris: Éditions La Découverte, 1993.

Chapter Four

THE CASE FOR CONTROL OVER CROSS-BORDER CAPITAL FLOWS
Fred Block

Restoring high levels of global employment was a central issue in the preparations for the Bretton Woods Conference that planned the post-World War II international monetary system. At that time, the view was widely shared that the international financial arrangements that had been in place in the 1920s and 1930s had contributed significantly to the severity of the Great Depression.[1] The two major architects of Bretton Woods—John Maynard Keynes and Harry Dexter White—agreed that it was imperative to create an international financial system that would help nations avoid a return to the mass unemployment of the 1930s.

The linkage between international financial arrangements and unemployment was also of central concern to Karl Polanyi when he wrote *The Great Transformation* during the Second World War. Polanyi hoped to influence debates about post-war reconstruction, and sought to avert a repetition of the disastrous post-World War I rush to restore the international gold standard. He believed that the gold standard was directly responsible both for the mass unemployment of the 1930s and for the rise of fascism.

Today, a little more than fifty years after Bretton Woods, the link between international financial arrangements and employment levels has only recently returned to policy discussions.[2] Global unemployment rose dramatically at the end of the 1970s and has stabilized at levels that are far higher than in the 1960s or 70s. The shift has been particularly visible in a number of European countries, especially France and Germany, that have had double-digit unemployment levels for most of the past fifteen years. At the same time, economic growth has slowed for almost all world regions other than East Asia.

This secular and seemingly nonreversible increase in global unemployment is linked to the operation of the international financial system. In particular, two changes in the international financial system that originated in the late 1970s have exacerbated problems of global unemployment. The first is the increased international mobility of capital as a result of the relaxation of previous controls. The second is the very dramatic increase in trading in global markets for currencies, currency futures, and a wide variety of "derivative" instruments. It follows that reform of the international financial system would again make it possible for the world economy to make significant progress in reducing unemployment.

BRETTON WOODS AND ITS AFTERMATH

The Bretton Woods agreement made a sharp distinction between a nation's international current accounts and its international capital accounts. Under the Articles of Agreement for the International Monetary Fund countries were expected to eliminate controls over current account transactions—trade in goods and services—as quickly as possible. The volume of a nation's international trade was supposed to be determined by market forces or tariffs, not by the elaborate systems of governmental controls over currency and direct import restrictions that had proliferated during World War II.

However, the IMF Articles were far more permissive in regard to controls over capital transactions. Both Keynes and White were acutely aware of the disruptive role played by capital flight in the interwar period when nations were often prevented from pursuing policies to put people back to work because of either the threat or the reality of huge speculative capital outflows. As a consequence, the Articles of Agreement state explicitly that the Fund can require nations to impose capital controls in exchange for the continued right to draw on IMF credits.

While many of the developed market economies retained significant capital controls into the late 1970s, the Bretton Woods view of capital controls as relatively benign was challenged on several fronts with increasing intensity as the postwar period progressed. U.S. policy makers came to favor the dismantling of capital controls since such controls were seen as a major interference with the development of an integrated world economy. Corporations would be understandably reluctant to invest in foreign countries where systems of capital controls might interfere with their repatriation of profits or their ability to freely liquidate their holdings. Similarly, the opportunities for international expansion of financial institutions would also be limited by continued capital controls.

This emphasis of American foreign policy was also echoed by many academic economists who argued that capital controls were likely to be both futile and destructive to economic efficiency: futile because they were likely to be evaded as individuals and firms found increasingly sophisticated means to circumvent the regulations, and destructive because the greater the degree of integration of global capital markets, the more efficient will be the allocation of resources. In this view, efforts by national governments to segregate national capital markets will only result in a less than optimal pattern of capital investment.

Most importantly, the steady expansion of global business activity from the 1950s through the 1970s created an expanding constituency for the elimination of capital controls which were seen as an annoying relic of a bygone era. These interests pressured governments to dismantle the controls and to allow their national economies to be fully integrated with global capital markets. As a result, virtually all of the developed market economies dismantled their remaining capital controls in the period from 1979 to 1987. With their elimination, both short-term and long-term real interest rates have increasingly converged across countries.

PERIODIZING THE CHANGES IN INTERNATIONAL FINANCE

To understand the connection between international finance and employment, it is useful to divide the post-war period. During the first period (1945-58), the reconstruction years, the United States was the only country to play a significant role in exporting capital. Most other countries retained extensive systems of exchange controls that restricted the movement of capital. The majority of countries in Western Europe did not restore full currency convertibility until 1958.

The second period (1959-1973) was one of fixed exchange rates and limited capital mobility. As envisioned at Bretton Woods, countries fixed their exchange rates in relation to the dollar or gold, creating a relatively high degree of predictability in foreign exchange transactions. While the extent of capital movements expanded, especially with the advent of off-shore dollar accounts, most countries in Europe retained some controls over capital transactions. According to one study, between 1961 and 1972 France's system of capital controls produced interest rates that were 105 base points below those of the U.S.[3]

The third period (1974-79) was one of floating exchange rates and limited capital mobility. With the breakdown of the Bretton Woods system, the world moved in 1973 to a floating rate system that involved much greater volatility in exchange rates. According to theory, a floating-rate system was supposed to reduce volatility because exchange rates would be able to adjust continuously, thus avoiding the occasional large adjustments that occur in a fixed-rate system. But in practice, the large amount of activity in the foreign exchange markets created a pattern of swings as large as 8% over periods as short as several months, even between such major currencies as the dollar and the mark.

This increased volatility led to renewed pressures for the elimination of capital controls, as economic actors within countries moved to protect themselves against any depreciation of their national currencies. When, for example, the franc was perceived to be heading down relative to the mark, asset holders in France would shift a portion of their portfolios towards the mark and other strong currencies. This tended to further intensify the volatility of the foreign exchange markets because of the added sums changing hands. However, because of the added pressure of the oil shocks, many countries retained their capital controls. Therefore, although there was a steady increase in the extent of capital mobility across this period, there was still not the convergence of global interest rates that occurs in the following decade.

In the fourth period (from 1980 to the present), most of the remaining controls over capital mobility were dismantled as the logic of a floating-rate system played itself out. The result has been not only a dramatic expansion in the level of activity in foreign exchange and capital markets, but a change in the nature of the activity. As the economist John Eatwell noted:

> In 1971, just before the collapse of the Bretton Woods fixed exchange rate system, about 90 percent of all foreign exchange transactions were for the finance of trade and long-term investment, and only about 10 percent were speculative. Today those percentages are reversed, with well over 90 percent of all transactions being speculative. Daily speculative flows now regularly exceed the combined foreign exchange reserves of all the G-7 governments.[4]

Standardized data on unemployment rates are available for most of the developed market economies from 1964 to the present. These data make it possible to see the trends in unemployment rates for the U.S. and for Western Europe for three of these four periods. As indicated in the table, the recent period of floating rates and expanding capital mobility has involved higher levels of unemployment than the previous periods. The results are particularly striking for Western Europe that has experienced unemployment rates in period four that are twice as high as in period three.

UNEMPLOYMENT

	Western Europe	United States
PERIOD II 1964-73	2.7%	4.4%
PERIOD III 1974-79	4.6%	6.4%
PERIOD IV 1980-1995	9.4%	6.8%

U.S. unemployment in 1995 and 1996 has been low compared to trends since 1974, but it is still high compared to the 1960s. This is not simply an academic point, since unemployment rates among minority youths remain at catastrophically high levels. Moreover, the current U.S. figures understate the severity of the jobs problem because of the dramatic rise in the number of people who are involuntarily working at part-time jobs. In mid-1996, in addition to 7.3 million unemployed in the United States, there were another 4.4 million working part-time who would prefer a full-time job.

For many developing countries, the unemployment rate is not a particularly significant indicator both because of limitations in the available data and chronic problems of rural and urban underemployment. A far better indicator of the way that global forces are impinging on developing countries is to examine changes in GDP growth. With the exception of South Asia and East Asia, all the major regions experienced a dramatic slowdown of economic growth in the 1980s with both Sub-Saharan Africa and Latin America slipping into negative growth rates.[5] While there has been some improvement in the 1990s, growth rates for the period from 1980 to 1993 still lag behind those of earlier decades.[6] My argument is that the rising unemployment and declining GDP growth are not the result of coincidence. Rather, it is the changes in the international financial regime that have led directly to these higher unemployment rates and slower growth rates.

FINANCIAL CHANGES AND HIGHER LONGER TERM INTEREST RATES

The first step in understanding this connection is to look at how changes in the global financial system have affected long-term interest rates which are high by post-war standards. Figure 1 shows real long-term interest rates for the U.S. based on the rates for ten-year Treasury Bonds. Even the most credit worthy private borrowers pay a higher rate than this, but the ten-year bond is a useful benchmark. These rates rose dramatically at the beginning of the 1980s, and in the period 1982-85 real interest rates averaged 7.2%—more than three hundred base points above the previous highest levels in the post-World War II period.

And even though rates have moved somewhat lower since 1987, the average in the period 1988 to 1996 was much higher than the average real rate of .5% that prevailed during the 1970s and considerably higher than the 2% average for the 1960s. There was hope in the first year of the Clinton Administration that these long-term rates were finally trending downward, but this downward movement has not been sustained despite the considerable progress that has been made in shrinking the Federal budget deficit.

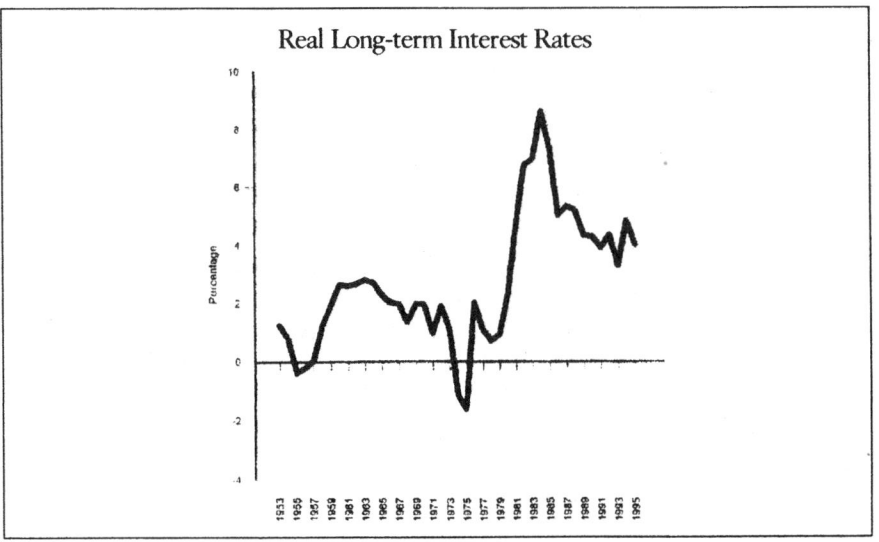

Real long-term rates are the average yeild on U.S. 10-year Treasury Bonds minus the GDP deflator for the same year as reported in *Economic Report to the President*.

It is a puzzle why real long-term interest rates have been so much higher in the 1980s and 1990s than in previous post-war decades. In the 1930s Keynes imagined that over time, as the amount of physical capital expanded, the long-term interest rate would decline to zero. And, in fact, technological advances have led to dramatic processes of capital savings: a million dollars of capital buys far more productive power today than it did ten years ago.[7] One would think that this would reinforce the Keynesian dynamic by reducing the scarcity of money capital, but we have instead a situation where bondholders are assured of returns that are generous in historical terms.

The problem is not just that real interest rates are high, but that with the elimination of capital controls very few countries have been able to insulate themselves from these high rates.[8] Governments that attempt to lower domestic interest rates to stimulate employment are likely to experience crippling outflows of capital in pursuit of higher interest rates elsewhere. This is especially true when either of the world's dominant economies—the U.S. and the German—raise interest rates.

In theory, countries have another choice: they can simply let their currency float downward relative to the currency of the high interest rate countries. But as France learned, during its brief experiment with expansionary policies in the early 1980s, devaluations are a problematic instrument for stemming capital outflows. When French investors saw the dollar value of their French portfolios falling as a result of the devaluation of the franc, they redoubled their efforts to shift into harder currency assets and the country hemorrhaged reserves. Devaluations stopped the speculative pressure on the franc only very briefly. It was finally only a reversal of government policy that ended the crisis.

In short, high levels of capital mobility provide a strong bias towards restrictive monetary policies in the world economy. Countries that fail to align their interest rates with those of the large economy with the highest interest rate risk substantial capital outflows and intense speculative pressures on their currencies. Moreover, even the largest economies can be pushed towards monetary tightening by the pressures of international financial flows.

When governments raise short-term interest rates, it is not inevitable that long-term rates will also rise, although this has been the case in recent years in the United States. Moreover, as Figure 2 indicates, the spread between short-term and long-term rates in the U.S. has been trending upwards, although the pattern is marked by sharp downward spikes during episodes of serious monetary tightening. In 1973, 1979, 1989, and again in 1995 when the Federal Reserve raised short-term rates dramatically, the spread temporarily became either negative or very small. But each time, the tendency for the spread to grow has reasserted itself. While the size of this spread averaged only 92 base points from 1953 to 1972, it averaged 202 base points between 1980 and 1994. This is an extremely important development because the size of the spread in the U.S. is a major determinant of global long-term rates. Hence, if the spread widens to 300 base points, even relatively low nominal short-term rates of 5% in the U.S. would mean that the world economy has to cope with nominal long-term rates of 8% and higher.

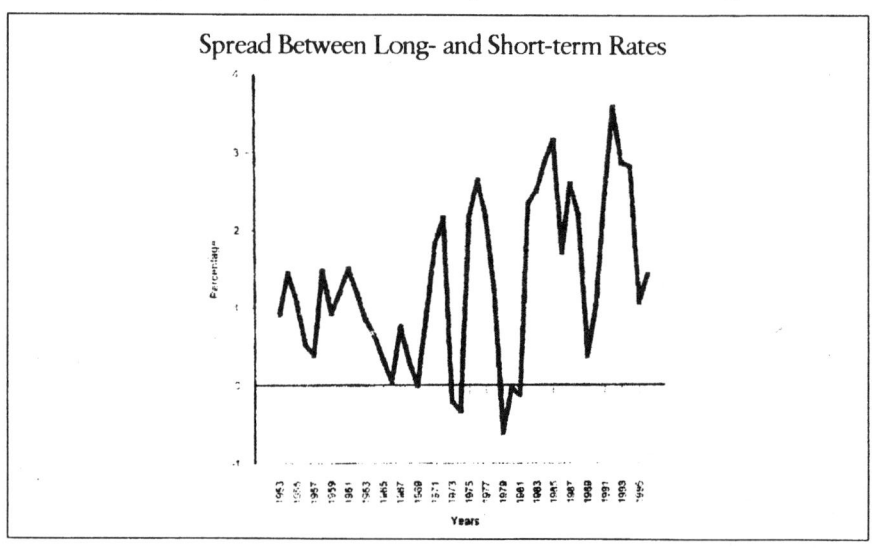

The spread is the difference between interest rates on 3-month and 10-year U.S. Treasury securities as reported in *Economic Report to the President.*

This growth in the spread, or the greater steepness of the yield curve, has been a major topic of scholarly and policy debate. The conventional explanation for the phenomenon is that the large spread between short- and long-term rates reflects an inflation premium. Long-term investors, for whom the persistently high U.S. budget deficit spells the danger of a resurgence of inflation, have been able to insist that they be paid substantially higher nominal rates of interest to protect them from rapid price rises in the future. Nor does this argument depend on the existence of significant actual inflation. Consumer price increases in the U.S. have been in the 2.5-3.5% per year range for most of the past decade,[9] but this is judged irrelevant, and it is in anticipation of the danger that inflationary pressures will suddenly accelerate that the inflation premium is required.

The major problem with this explanation is that it fails to elucidate why investors are able to extract an inflation premium now when they were not able to do so in the past when inflationary pressures were far stronger. After all, investors are a large and diverse group who are ostensibly in competition with each other for the best returns. How do they mobilize collectively to force borrowers to pay them a higher rate of interest?

In the past, if investors did not like the long-term rate of interest, they would commit their funds only for the short term. This increased flow into short-term instruments would, in turn, push down short-term interest rates until long-term rates began to appear attractive by comparison. The gap between long-term rates and short-term rates thus remained relatively small. But since this gap has trended upward since 1980, it would appear that something new is happening in these markets.

What is new is the explosive growth of forms of investment that are neither short-term nor long-term. The most important of these are speculative investments in the foreign exchange markets and purchases of a wide variety of derivatives, instruments whose value is derived from some other instrument or variable, such as the popular Eurodollar interest-rate futures.

Daily trading volume on the foreign exchange markets is now estimated at $1.2 trillion a day; since more than 90% of those transactions are speculative, hundreds of billions of dollars are devoted full-time to currency arbitrage. The nominal dollar value of contracts in the derivative markets reached $12 trillion dollars back in 1994, and although such contracts are purchased for only 5 or 10% of the nominal value, this still represents very large sums of money.

The most visible group of investors in these markets are the "hedge funds," which pool capital from wealthy investors and institutions to pursue complex speculative strategies. It is estimated that these hedge funds have between $50 and $75 billion of paid-in capital, and this, combined with their ability to draw on bank credit, means they are able to mobilize as much as $500 billion. But hedge funds are only the most visible of the speculators; institutions and wealthy individuals pursuing similar investment strategies account for tens of billions of additional dollars. Based on U.S. commercial bank reports to the Federal Deposit Insurance Corporation, it is apparent that there has been explosive growth in such speculative trading accounts in recent years. As recently as 1988, the banks reported $35 billion in trading accounts, but by September of 1995 this figure had risen to $224 billion.

The largest investors now have a real alternative to investing their money either long-term or short-term. When they find both short-term and long-term rates unattractively low, the flow of funds into more speculative investments is likely to increase. As a consequence, long-term investors as a group are now able to extract an inflation premium that was not available before the explosive growth of these speculative markets. In short, the hedge fund operators and their ilk, by redirecting some significant portion of global savings into routinized speculation, have created a permanent tendency towards high long-term interest rates across the entire world economy.

Moreover, this problem will only intensify. As the popularity of these new investment strategies spreads, a larger share of global savings will pursue these alternatives to either short-term or long-term investing. A number of U.S. pension funds have already placed a share of their capital with investment companies that specialize in "managed futures." There is an estimated $25 billion in managed derivatives at present, and as this amount increases purchasers of long-term bonds will be able to extract even higher premiums.

THE CONSEQUENCES OF HIGH LONG-TERM INTEREST RATES

Higher long-term interest rates lead directly to higher rates of unemployment and slower rates of global growth. Since there is empirical evidence showing that the impact of real interest rates on the level of business investment in the U.S. is relatively weak, it is important to be clear on the precise mechanisms through which higher rates have their effect. The argument here is that higher real interest rates tend to dampen global demand, and that it is primarily through slower sales growth and reduced cash flow that business investment is reduced. Three key mechanisms—the contraction of demand in developing countries, the contraction of public sector spending, and the slower growth of consumer credit—are at work in dampening global demand.

During the 1970s, both developing countries and the countries of Eastern Europe borrowed heavily in the international capital markets. The rapid expansion of borrowing helped finance an import boom—which was one of the major factors in the dramatic growth in global trade in that decade. However, with the sudden increase in real interest rates at the beginning of the 1980s, the debt explosion turned into a debt crisis. Countries that had borrowed well beyond their capacity to repay suddenly had to face repayment schemes based on high real interest rates that contrasted with the low or negative rates at which they had initially borrowed.

The consequence of the ensuing debt renegotiations was an extended period of austerity, leading to a sharp reduction in developing country imports from the developed countries. In the last years of the 1970s, industrial country exports to the non-oil producing developing countries were increasing by more than 20% a year, as measured in current dollars. But such exports contracted in the early 1980s, and when growth in these exports resumed, it was at a far slower pace than in the 1970s.

There is good reason to think that the increase in long-term interest rates since 1994 will again dampen growth in the developing countries. With the developing countries' accumulated private debt being more than $500 billion, each 1 point increase in the effective long-term interest rate means that another $5 billion goes to debt servicing. Some developing economies have been successful in attracting capital from the developed countries to their equity markets; but the experience of Mexico, in which the flight of investor capital brought about a financial crisis that threatened the stability of the state, has shown the danger of relying on such fickle capital flows for financing economic growth.

In the current economic climate, most governments have found it difficult to think seriously of using expansionary fiscal policies to combat unemployment. With floating exchange rates and high levels of capital mobility, a country that followed such policies would likely bring about massive capital flight and depreciation of its currency.

But additional complexity lies in the fact that high interest rates actually intensify the pressures on governments to limit deficits even during periods of recession. When real interest rates are higher than real growth rates, governments find that the financing of deficits requires expanding resources. Hence, between 1977 and 1985 debt service as a percentage of total government expenditures rose from 8% to 15% in the U.S. and from 5% to 23% in Sweden.[10] In order to free resources for debt service, governments have to cut other types of spending, and generally the most expendable items are investments in the physical infrastructure of the country: roads, bridges, railways, airports, and dams. This becomes another element in the dampening of demand.

Data on government surpluses or deficits as a percentage of GDP for the major European countries show that even though unemployment rates were at historically high levels between 1983 and 1988, budget deficits actually contracted: France's deficit was 3.2% of GDP in 1983 and 1.3% in 1989. Germany went from a 2.6% deficit in 1983 to a .1% surplus in 1989. The United Kingdom also shifted from a 3.3% deficit to a .9% surplus in that same period. This is in sharp contrast with fiscal policy in earlier periods of high unemployment.

Finally, higher real interest rates tend to dampen consumer purchases, because of limits on the amount of credit that households can service. This has a dramatic impact on the housing market in particular, where each 1-point increase in the mortgage interest rate tends to price a significant percentage of households out of the market for a house. Similar dynamics apply to other consumer durables; higher real interest rates tend to reduce purchases of new cars. The softening of demand in the housing and automobile markets generally slows activity across the entire economy. The weakening of these three forms of demand translates into slower sales growth and slower growth in profits. This means that firms are less able to finance investment projects out of retained earnings. Moreover, when they look at the capital markets to evaluate the costs of raising funds through debt or equity, high real interest rates tend to discourage firms from investing in new projects.

Many major corporations in the U.S., and increasingly overseas, have adopted "hurdle rates" for approving new investment projects, which tend to rise along with real long-term interest rates. For example, when Treasury Bills were paying 8%, the hurdle rate for a large U.S. corporation could be as high as 16%. This means that only capital investment plans that promise to return more than 16% per year were funded. Hence, it is hardly surprising that "lean and mean" corporations have significantly reduced investment spending on physical capital over the past decade.[11]

In Western Europe, higher interest rates produced lagging levels of business investment in the 1980-86 period. Gross Capital Formation as a percentage of GDP fell from 22.7% in 1980 to 19.5% in 1986 in Germany, and from 23% to 19.3% in France.[12] While investment recovered somewhat when interest rates were lower between 1986 and 1989, capital formation has been anemic in much of Europe in the 1990s. The danger is acute that high real interest rates will continue to dampen global investment levels.

COSTS OF HIGH REAL INTEREST RATES

It would be a useful exercise to construct a model to show how much global output is lost with each 100 base point increase in long-term real interest rates. The cumulative loss of output for the entire period from 1982 to the present would be staggering. Some would argue that had the major nations sought unwisely to keep interest rates down to facilitate faster global growth, the only result would have been an intensification of inflation that would ultimately have led to a more dramatic global contraction. In short, this argument goes, any so-called estimate of the output lost from historically high real interest rates is purely illusory because the global economy genuinely lacked the capacity to sustain higher rates of noninflationary growth in the period since 1982.

But such reasoning is strangely circular. In the U.S., for example, high real interest rates have contributed to declining levels of new business investment which means that overall productive capacity of the economy has grown relatively slowly. This in turn has led to the belief that even a modest economic expansion would overtax economic capacity and rekindle inflation. The solution to this perceived threat has been to impose higher interest rates to slow the rate of economic expansion; but this has only depressed new investment. In short, this logic locks the economy into a permanent pattern of slow growth, slow investment, and low capacity utilization.

Moreover, the inflation objection flies in the face of historical evidence. The world economy has experienced periods of faster economic growth without inflation in the past, and even today a number of East Asian economies have combined rapid growth with low rates of inflation. It can reasonably be argued that many countries are now more vulnerable to inflationary pressures because some of the institutional arrangements that had earlier kept inflation in check have eroded. For example, until recently governments were under less pressure to balance budgets, and systems of centralized wage bargaining have broken down. However, there are also important counter-tendencies that make it easier to control inflation. For example, the growing internationalization of trade places severe constraints on domestic producers who might be inclined to pass higher prices on to consumers.

Most importantly, societies have the capacity to develop new institutional mechanisms to hold inflation in check. The idea that monetary restraint and slow growth together form the only effective tool to control inflation is unnecessarily pessimistic. Since even monetarists' accounts acknowledge that inflation has roots in distributive conflicts—too much money chasing too few goods—it seems only logical that if societies can find ways to expand the pie faster, these distributive conflicts can be brought under control.

REFORMING THE SYSTEM

As this analysis suggests, there are two critical steps that are necessary to expand global employment. The first is to lower global interest rates, so that both the private and the public sector can finance new initiatives. The second is to expand the availability of financing to noncorporate borrowers in both the developed and the developing worlds.

Significant progress towards lower interest rates will require international action to reform the international financial system. Three types of reform are necessary. The first is a return to more stable exchange rates. The experiment with floating rates has been a failure. Currency markets were supposed to get exchange rates "right," but this has simply not happened. The markets have a strong tendency to overshoot—to push rates either higher or lower than any analysis of fundamentals would suggest were appropriate. Moreover, the high levels of volatility that have come with floating rates have further intensified the attractiveness of currency speculation and intensified destabilizing capital flows. There are a number of attractive models of a system of fixed exchange rates that would be more flexible than the Bretton Woods system, such as systems that allow currencies to float within a narrow but adjustable band. However, no reform of the exchange rate regime will work as long as $1 trillion or more changes hands every day in the foreign exchange markets.

The second set of necessary reforms are measures to increase the transaction costs in the foreign exchange markets and in the markets for various kinds of derivatives. Some version of the transaction tax, initially proposed by James Tobin in 1978, could make currency arbitrage and derivative transactions far less attractive investment opportunities. Tobin proposed that a very small tax be imposed on all foreign exchange transactions.[13] While such a tax would also raise the transaction costs for those participating in the markets for non-speculative purposes, the burden of the tax would be offset by the far greater predictability of exchange rates. Firms engaged in international trade would be able to devote far fewer resources to protecting themselves from future exchange rate changes. The idea of these transaction taxes is not to eliminate market activity but to discourage speculation. A transaction tax would have to be imposed simultaneously in all the relevant countries or trading activity would simply shift to some location where there was no tax. Governments could also agree to prevent their citizens and firms from engaging in transactions in "outlaw" financial centers.

The third needed reform involves international agreement on the legitimacy of national or regional capital controls as a tool for dampening speculative capital movements. Such international agreement would ensure that governments would help each other recover capital that flees in defiance of their national controls. Otherwise, governments will find that individuals and firms have too many opportunities to circumvent national controls. Moreover, if defiance of capital controls were treated on a par with circumventing national taxes, such controls would be far more likely to be effective.

Together, these three steps should eliminate the bias towards high interest rates in the current world economy. Individual nations would have considerably more autonomy to pursue expansionary policies without the threat of immediate capital outflows and speculative attacks on their currencies. To be sure, even under such a regime, if a particular national economy became dangerously overheated, there would be strong pressures to slow the level of economic activity. But the point is that the threshold would be far higher, so that countries could make considerably more progress in reducing unemployment before they had to worry about the threat of capital outflows. Equally importantly, the higher transaction costs would drive large amounts of funds out of speculative activity in foreign exchange and derivative markets. Lenders would have to settle for more historically normal rates of return on long-term investments, and the large gap between short-term and long-term rates should disappear.

REALLOCATING FINANCIAL FLOWS

If these were the only reforms made, however, there would still be serious danger that the supply of long-term capital would exceed demand by such traditional borrowers as central governments and large firms. It was such an imbalance in the market in the 1970s that led to the explosive growth of developing country debts; banks were so desperate to recycle petrodollars that they pushed loans on countries with little regard for their ability to make effective use of the funds. While another imbalance would be unlikely to play out in exactly the same way, the results would probably be extremely wasteful. One possible scenario would be an explosive runup in asset values in real estate that would be followed by a crash and widespread default on real estate loans.

This danger can be averted by challenging the assumption that corporations will do most of the investing in society's productive capacity. The evidence from the U.S. is that nonfinancial corporations account for a declining share of total new capital formation. In the 1960s, capital expenditures by nonfarm, nonfinancial corporations accounted for more than 80% of all nonresidential fixed investment, but in the early 1990s this figure had dropped to 70%. Moreover, if the calculation were to include investment in intangibles such as research and development and human capital, the corporate share would shrink further.

This downward trend will continue because corporations face strong market pressures to restrict both tangible and intangible forms of investment. The likelihood is that corporate demands on the credit market to finance real investments will continue to be weak. Noncorporate entities, including households, nonprofits, small businesses, employee cooperatives, local governments, and alliances among these different entities, will necessarily have greater responsibility to undertake society's productive investment.

If these groups are not provided with financing, then both investment and employment will fall far below economically optimal levels. But the capital markets have traditionally been reluctant to provide finance to many of these categories of nontraditional borrowers.[14] As recent work on asymmetric markets has shown, the credit market is not balanced by the interest rate but by rationing decisions made by financial institutions. Part of this rationing has been to place these nontraditional borrowers at the end of the credit queue. Hence, our existing financial intermediaries have very little experience in making money by lending to these nontraditional types of borrower.

It is urgent that we develop far more effective mechanisms to make capital available to households and other noncorporate borrowers. Channeling capital does not simply mean opening the tap, but rather developing effective techniques to select and monitor creditworthy borrowers. In both the developed and the developing world, there are successful and financially sound instances of intermediaries that have contributed significantly to community development by providing small and extremely small loans, such as the Grameen Bank in Bangladesh. With substantially lower long-term rates, these successes could be multiplied many times over.

One important part of this effort must involve facilitating investment in human capital. It is impractical to expect either corporations or the public sector to bear all of the costs of providing adults with ongoing education and retraining. But there will be a continuing need for adults to enroll in intensive educational programs that will require significant reductions in their working time. Households should be able to finance these periods of investment in education with mortgage-type loans, which is currently rarely possible. But just as the market for housing finance only emerged after government action, so similar reforms are required to facilitate capital flows to finance household investments in human capital.

But whether the issue is financing human capital or tangible investments, reallocating capital will require major changes in national financial systems. The overriding problem is that today it is far more economical for financial intermediaries to lend huge amounts of money to a handful of large borrowers than to find ways to lend the same amount of money to hundreds of thousands of smaller borrowers. But the future health of the world economy depends on expanding capital flows to those smaller borrowers. If the U.S. and other national economies are to make real progress in reducing unemployment and poverty, both of these types of financial reform are indispensable. We need to reverse the costly growth of speculative financial activity and to redirect available capital to millions of new borrowers. Without these changes, governments will find it increasingly difficult to secure prosperity for their citizens.

NOTES

An earlier version of this essay was presented with support from the World Employment Report of the International Labour Office in Geneva. A subsequent version was published as "Controlling Global Finance,"in *World Policy Journal*, Fall 1996. Karl Beitel provided valuable research assistance.

1. Karl Polanyi, *The Great Transformation*. Boston: Beacon Press, 1957. This work was originally published in the same year as Bretton Woods.
2. By 1977, this linkage was an increasingly important topic of political debate as European nations were being forced to make substantial sacrifices in the quest for a common European currency. For example, in June 1997, a Socialist government unexpectedly came to power in France as voters protested the Conservative government's lack of progress in reducing unemployment.
3. This study is cited in Gerald Epstein and Juliet Schor, "Structural Determinants and Economic Effects of Capital Controls in OECD Countries," pp. 136-161 in Tariq Banuri and Juliet Schor, eds., *Financial Openness and National Autonomy*. Oxford: Clarendon Press, 1992.
4. See p. 120 in John Eatwell, "The Global Money Trap: Can Clinton Master the Markets," *The American Prospect* 12 (Winter 1993), pp. 118-126.
5. John Walton and David Seddon, *Free Markets and Food Riots: The Politics of Global Adjustment*. Oxford: Blackwell, 1994, p. 12. Trends in the East Asian economies appear not to be particularly sensitive to changes in international interest rates. Hence, the argument of this essay should be taken to apply only to other global regions.
6. World Bank, *World Development Report 1995*, p. 165.
7. This argument is elaborated in Fred Block, *Postindustrial Possibilities*. Berkeley: University of California Press, 1990, ch.5.
8. The major exception has been Japan that has tried to revive its economy in the 1990s with extremely low interest rates.
9. Moreover, there is increasing evidence that the Consumer Price Index overstates the actual rate of inflation. See Advisory Commission to Study the Consumer Price Index, *Toward a More Accurate Measure of the Cost of Living*. Report to the Senate Finance Committee, November 1996.
10. Fritz Scharpf, *Crisis and Choice in European Social Democracy*. Ithaca: Cornell University Press, 1991, p. 146.
11. This pattern also helps to explain the dramatic gains in U.S. stock markets during the 1990s. Because of their reluctance to invest in new projects, corporations have—in the aggregate—been repurchasing stock from shareholders. An expanding pool of funds chasing a diminishing supply of stocks has contributed to dramatic increases in share prices.
12. OECD, *Historical Statistics 1960-1989*.
13. For valuable discussions of the Tobin tax proposal, see Mahbub ul Haq, Inge Kaul, and Isabelle Grunberg, *The Tobin Tax: Coping with Financial Volatility*. New York: Oxford Univ Press, 1996.
14. To be sure, much depends on the purposes of these borrowers. Financial intermediaries are very enthusiastic about extending consumer loans to households, but they are extremely reluctant to provide the same household with money to start a small business. A local government might have an enthusiastic response to its desire to float school bonds, but it might get the cold shoulder if it sought to raise money to finance low income housing.

Chapter Five

RE-READING POLANYI: TOWARD A SECOND GREAT TRANSFORMATION?
Björn Hettne

Judging from the current debate in international relations theory, we live in a period of "transformation" or "transition." Of historical transitions we have some record, whereas concerning contemporary transitions we do not know the outcome. Therefore it is advisable to use the concept of transformation, particularly as this revives the Polanyian approach to large-scale structural change, in which modern society is understood both as a result of market expansion and as the self-protection of society against the disruptive and destabilizing effects of the market. The qualitative societal change in Europe, called by Polanyi the Great Transformation, was caused by the expansion of the market system during British hegemony, the Gold Standard, and the Balance of Power era. Various societal and political responses to social turbulence—such as the welfare state, the fascist state, and the communist state—were not compatible. The result was the second world war. Whatever would come after that was a matter for speculation.

Writing in 1944, Polanyi identified three dangerous "universalisms" or social orders with ambitions to become world orders: Hitler's principle of racial domination, liberal capitalism on a global scale, and world revolutionary socialism.[1] Half a century after the publication of *The Great Transformation*, we may now write off revolutionary socialism, hopefully also together with fascism. However, "global liberalism" is still on the agenda, and so is in my view Polanyi's regionalist scenario. In this paper I shall return to Polanyi's concern with the outcome of the struggle between universalism and regionalism, but phrased in the contemporary terms of globalism and regionalism while presenting the arguments in favour of regionalism today.[2]

THE REGIONALIST ARGUMENT
When Polanyi made his analysis of the potential of regionalism, the Third Reich had been crushed on the battlefield, revolutionary socialism on a global scale was replaced by Stalin's "socialism in one country," and liberal capitalism was badly hurt by the collapse of the gold standard. The latter might, however, start breathing again, and therefore the thrust of Polanyi's argument was that it should be left to die. Against the utopian project of recreating liberal capitalism on a world scale, he posed the, at least in his view, more realistic project of regionalism and planning: "The new permanent pattern of world affairs is one of regional systems coexisting side by side."[3] Polanyi developed this regionalist scenario

against what he at the time feared was going to be a new hegemonic world order of universal capitalism, this time under the leadership of the U.S. rather than Great Britain. He underestimated the realism of this hegemonic project, calling it "an attempt doomed to failure." After the war, a new hegemonic structure took shape. The Commonwealth disintegrated and Britain joined the U.S. in creating the Atlantic Community, which provided the framework for the postwar period.

Polanyi used to warn against what he called the "hazards of planetary interdependence" associated with global market expansion.[4] His skeptical view of interdependence based on the market corresponds to that of contemporary neomercantilists who conceive of a market system as a fragile arrangement in need of control. The postwar world economy was in fact a historic compromise between international economic *laissez-faire* and a certain level of domestic control. This essentially Keynesian approach was abandoned during the 1970s. Instead in the subsequent decade dogmatic liberal principles became increasingly dominant, a trend that culminated when the socialist world began to disintegrate towards the end of the decade.

The conclusion of the Cold War led to a hegemonic position for the market, which would indicate that the stage is set for the second phase of Polanyi's famous double movement, i.e., when the self-protection of society is activated. As we know, Polanyi argued that for societies to be completely dominated by the market principle—implying that also land, capital and labour have been commodified—is a recent phenomenon. Historically there have been two other possible economic integration mechanisms: reciprocity and redistribution. The former refers to the socially embedded forms of exchange in small-scale symmetric communities; the latter to politically determined distribution in stratified societies marked by a centre–periphery structure. Both modes of distribution in their historical forms were undermined by the growth of market exchange. However, as the market principle penetrated all spheres of human activity, thereby eroding social structures, redistribution had to be reinvented in order to provide people with the necessary social protection. Polanyi called this type of reaction on the part of society the "double movement." Thus, protectionism was seen as not inherently bad as the conventional wisdom of today makes it out to be.

Even today we can use Polanyi's argument for a regionalized world system as a possible form that tomorrow's protectionism could take. It is different from the classical Listian argument in favour of a coherent national economy. List argued for a strong state in order to better compete on the world market. Polanyi argued against an unregulated liberal world order, and saw the solution to the world order problem in the end of universalism and in an emerging pattern of regionalism. The "regions" explicitly discussed were the British Commonwealth and the Soviet Union. Neither of them has proved viable. The Soviet Union did not try to become a post-Westphalian structure, but rather a nation-state built on an old imperial political structure. This was bound to fail, partly because of the external pressure which formed part of the Cold War order, partly because of the internal heterogeneity of the Soviet state. Today, the CIS is making another attempt at creating regionalism of a new kind but under enormous difficulties and with uncertain prospects. It seems, however, as if the structure of opportunity for regionalism has returned. The postwar hegemonic world order is now in a process of transformation towards some kind of "post-Westphalian," "post-hegemonic," or "post-Cold War" world order. Hence the concept of region again assumes a new importance as a possible mode of organizing the world. World system logic is pointing towards further regionalization, at least in the shorter perspective. Ultimately, the two processes of globalization and regionalization may prove complementary, but in the shorter term they seem to be in conflict, since globalization is an expression of the economic (market) logic, whereas regionalism is an expression of the political (territorial) logic.

There is a difference between the new form of protectionism and the traditional mercantilist concern with state-building and national power. The neo-mercantilists argue in favour of the regionalization of the world into more or less self-sufficient blocs. These blocs would be more introverted than trade blocs and would maintain symmetric relations between themselves. This is the "benign" type. The "malign" type is offensive and aggressive and at the same time introverted, an "extended economic nationalism." The "benign view" of mercantilism coincides with what I call "the new regionalism." It must be emphasized that such a "neo-mercantilist" vision faces serious problems of acceptance due to the strong historical association of mercantilist thinking with extremist nationalism, and because of its periodical revivals (in the form of protectionism) in connection with economic crises. This guilt by association argument can, however, be rejected, since no real efforts have in fact been made to construct a world order on the basis of Polanyi's regionalist recommendations.

Regionalism is perhaps the best world order the world can hope for in the middle run. Introverted rather than aggressively competing regions may provide some urgently needed stability in world politics. In the long run, it may turn out to be a step towards a more unitary world order without losing the stability achieved through regionalization. We will then speak about "transregionalization" as we today speak of "transnationalization," and about interregional relations rather than international relations. In the short run the regions may serve as protective shields against an enforced global culture of middle-class consumerism and mass poverty, that is what we usually refer to as "globalization." A global civilization, where the historical civilizations have become extinguished, would really be "the end of history."

Mercantilism is the ideological expression of the nation-state logic, operating in the economic arena and violating the liberal principle that free trade in the long run is for the benefit of all. Neo-mercantilism retains a similar suspicion of free trade, but transcends the nation-state logic in arguing for a segmented world system consisting of largely self-sufficient blocs big enough to provide "domestic" markets.

In terms of confict resolution, the region may represent a possibility to transcend historical conflicts entrenched in the current state formations, since a more extensive political system introduces a more distant political authority beyond the parties in conflict. The regions may in some respect be functionally similar to nation states but they are not based on the nationalist principle that each people must have its own state. Region states are (like the empires used to be) multi-ethnic. A regionalized world system would therefore in several respects be more stable and peaceful than a liberal world order which historically has revealed an inherent tendency towards collapse. Regions are large enough to have a reasonable degree of economic efficiency, in accordance with the principles of comparative costs, economies of scale and other conventional economic efficiency arguments. On the other hand, perversions generated by excessive specialization and an overly elaborated and therefore vulnerable division of labour could be avoided.

Inter-regional trade will of course continue to take place, but subordinated to the "territorial" principle of the New Regionalism rather than the "functional" principle of the world market. The New Regionalism is thus based on a logic different from the competing trade blocs, which have a centre from which their economic power spreads outwards. It is, in contrast, fundamentally territorial, and takes on political, social and military responsibility throughout the regional territory. Regionalism is "real," since there are visible signs of "regionalism from below," albeit of a highly different strength and orientation. The accusation of utopianism can thus be refuted. Rather the "utopian market," to use Polanyi's term, will lead to political and social problems which ultimately will call for some kind of political intervention. This constitutes the essence of "the double movement" in the contemporary context. Thus, one way of looking at the relationship between globalization and regionalization is to apply Polanyi's concept as follows: globalization implies market expansion. Regionalism is neo-mercantilist regulation of this emerging global market, which is far from being the end of history, but rather the beginning of a period of turbulence. The nation states cannot handle this crisis the way they did in the 1930s, but the regulation of capitalism will manifest itself on the regional level this time. The eruption of "black holes" and the ensuing security crises further underline the imperative for regionalism as world order.

In the debate on the still nebulous "new world order," two concepts have gained a certain pre-eminence: globalization and regionalization. The two processes are going on simultaneously, they deeply affect the Westphalian system, paving the way for a post-Westphalian system. By "Westphalian" is implied an interstate system characterized by the sovereign independence of states; each state is motivated in its international behaviour by a consistent national interest; the interstate system is regulated by a balance of power among the principal powers. Necessarily, there is a particular political rationality underlying this behaviour. The Westphalian rationality takes a particular state as the given guarantee for security as well as welfare. What is outside the state borders is chaos and anarchy. The disorder and turbulence people experience today comes with the realization that this guarantee can no longer be taken for granted, and the confusion is only increased when the two rationalities of Westphalianism and post-Westphalianism coexist.

The post-Westphalian logic implies that the nation-state has lost its usefulness and that solutions to the problems of security and welfare must therefore be found in transnational structures, global or regional. The confusion is sometimes increased even further by the presence of "pre-Westphalian" attitudes and behaviour in areas where the nation-state always was weak and superficial and where it now breaks down. But the main cause of conflict and turbulence is probably the antagonistic coexistence of Westphalian and post-Westphalian rationality, to which I consider the New Regionalism as a possible solution.

The question is how globalization and regionalization actually relate. Are they distinct processes, are they mutually supporting and reinforcing each other, or are they contradictory? The answer to this question of course depends on how the two processes of concern are defined, what empirical phenomena are singled out, and what kind of theoretical framework we use to interpret them. Thus the relationship as such is perhaps not the most interesting issue, since the nature of this relationship follows from the characteristics according to which we define globalization and regionalization. These characteristics cannot depend merely on our theoretical inclinations, but must also be derived from empirical observations of actual economic and political processes going on in many parts of the world. Many of these parts are increasingly acting as "regions," a group of countries with a more or less explicitly shared political project.

Regions are emerging phenomena, ambiguously forming part of the process of globalization, supporting it according to some, opposing it according to others. My hypothesis is that the two processes of globalization and regionalization are articulated within the same larger process of global structural change. The outcome in the form of a new world order depends on this dialectic rather than linear development and can therefore not be extrapolated or easily foreseen.

THE GLOBALIST CHALLENGE

Since it probably is correct to say that regionalization relates to globalization as antithesis to thesis, we should first agree upon the meaning of globalization. Nobody denies its existence but one could read many things, good as well as bad, into it. "Global" is a recent concept in social science, gradually replacing "international," both for the reason of its being more appropriate than the rather misleading concept of "international" and for indicating a qualitative deepening of the internationalization process. "Global" refers to objective (the compression of the world) as well as subjective (the planetary consciousness) processes. A global consciousness may also include negative expectations and, following from this, a wish to halt the process of globalization and initiate a process of "deglobalization."[5] One way of achieving this can be through the New Regionalism, to be explained below. This would facilitate a process of deglobalization by means of an increasing territorial control over transnational transactions. The New Regionalism can also, intentionally or unintentionally, be a road to globalism. If so, the question arises whether this would imply a different globalism than the "direct route" from the state-centred Westphalian system. The argument of this paper is that this is the case.

The contemporary concern with interdependence, world order or the global system is to a large extent a cognitive phenomenon: i.e., it is a matter of how the world is conceived. If interdependence implies a tendency towards a global social system, its origins may be traced far back in history. However, one could argue that this process reached a qualitatively new stage in the post-Second World War era, when many forms of human interconnectedness across state boundaries were doubling every ten years, a tendency which later was to be further reinforced through the revolution in information technology. This is what makes the global system "compressed." The subjective feeling of geographical distance is dramatically changed, some even speak of "the end of geography."

Globalization would not have been possible were it not for the relative political stability of the American world order, which lasted from the end of the Second World War until the late 60s. Since then, however, the world has, if not lacking a world order, at least tried to get along with a defective one. "The old is dying and the new is not yet born." To make sense of this imperceptible transformation is the great challenge for social science.

In spite of its obvious importance for our future world, we lack a consistent theoretical framework explaining what globalization is all about. One possible candidate for such a framework with the advantage of not making the concept of globalization overly abstract is the long tradition of materialist theories concerned with the changing international division of labour. James Mittelman[6] identifies three subsequent modes: the Old Division of Labour, as analyzed by classical political economy; the New International Division of Labour, concerned with the spatial reorganization of production starting in the 1960s;[7] and, finally, the Global Division of Labour, where domestic economies are penetrated by global phenomena to such an extent as to signify a qualitative deepening of the process of internationalization.

If one economic dimension of globalization has to do with the organization of production, another equally important and largely autonomous one is the financial system. The recycling of petrodollars through commercial banks fueled economic transformation by providing the financial base for Third World industrialization. At the same time, this flow of money paved the way for the debt crisis in countries where industrialization strategy failed to catch on, or where investment was simply unproductive due to lack of competence (market realism) in economic planning. In the so-called "most affected countries" the easy credit was used up in paying the oil bill, resulting in an intensified differentiation of the Third World, often referred to as "the end of the Third World." The centre-periphery model became irrelevant as the periphery entered the core, thus making the "new" division of labour increasingly dated.

Trade is of course the classical form of internationalization. The stable growth in world trade during the post-war decades was unique and will not be repeated. It can be explained by unprecedented economic growth in the OECD area, and a significant reduction in trade barriers, two conditions which underwent changes as the 70s wore on.[8] The 80s were marked by the "new protectionism" which avoids open violation of GATT rules, but nevertheless finds other ways to create "non-tariff barriers." The long drawn-out Uruguay round showed that the forces against free trade have considerable weight, something which is conveniently neglected in economic theory.

Societies are not only economic systems but contain people who for good reasons refuse to disappear when they become superfluous, either as producers or "consumers" (normally defined as those who can afford to buy the goods they need). The possible reactions to being unwanted are according to a classic study: loyalty, protest and exit.[9] There is, however, little left to be loyal to as successful protests presuppose an accountable counterpart, something that is very hard to find in a globalized capitalism. This leaves exit as the only rational option. What this concretely means is migration: within the country, into neighbouring countries within the region, or internationally. This will further change the global division of labour in significant ways, but is also often seen as having severe security implications.[10] As is now increasingly evident in Europe, it will have a deep impact on the nature of the pattern of regional integration itself (A "Fortress Europe" or a "European House," that is the question).

It must be emphasized that the changes pointing towards a global division of labour are intertwined and reinforce each other in a most complicated fashion, at the same time as the globalization process itself contains its own contradictions.

It also follows that many of these changes are subject to different interpretations depending on theoretical assumptions and ideological preferences.

THE REGIONALIST RESPONSE

If we look back a decade or so, regional integration was not a very fashionable subject, having declined from a rather prominent position in the 50s and 60s. Why is it that regionalism again attracts the curiosity and interest of the social science community? Either the content or the context of regionalization must have changed. My argument is that both have changed.

Regionalization is, for obvious reasons, a more varied phenomenon than globalization. It takes different forms both over time and between different cultural areas of the world. The crucial issue in relating the two processes, I submit, is the development logic which in a regionalization process is captured and subsumed under a territorial as distinct from a functional logic.

The New Regionalism has been differently defined but usually refers to a second wave of regional cooperation and integration that started already in the early 1980s but took off after 1989. The decline of the earlier interest in regionalism was due both to the previous slow-down in Western European integration, leading to the Euro-pessimism of the 1970s, and the almost universal failure of Third World free trade areas. Rather than leading to development in the sense of generating core-like activities, these free trade areas reproduced the global centre-periphery structure polarizing the partners within the regions. This led to inter-state conflicts and, of course, disillusion as far as regional cooperation was concerned. Today there are again optimistic expectations about the usefulness of regionalism in different respects. However, since old and new forms of regionalism coexist in time, I find the identification of new patterns of regionalization more relevant than identifying a new era of regionalization.[11]

The New Regionalism differs from the "old" in five main respects:

(1) Whereas the old regionalism was formed in a bipolar Cold War context, the new is taking shape in a multipolar world order. In spite of their military superiority, and of course in varying degrees, the former superpowers are being degraded to regional powers competing with other emerging regional powers.

(2) Whereas the old regionalism was created "from above" (i.e., by the superpowers), the new is a more spontaneous process from within the region and also "from below" in the sense that the constituent states themselves, but increasingly also other actors, are the main proponents of regional integration.

(3) Whereas the old regionalism, as far as economic integration is concerned, was inward-oriented and protectionist, the new is often described as "open," and thus compatible with an interdependent world economy. However, the idea of a certain degree of preferential treatment with the region is indicated or implied. How this somewhat contradictory balance between universal GATT regulations and specific regional concerns shall be kept is left open. In my definition of the new regionalism, I stress rather this amibiguity between "opened" and "closed" regionalism.

(4) Whereas the old regionalism was specific with regard to objectives—some organizations were security-oriented and others were economically oriented—the new is a more comprehensive, multidimensional process. This includes trade and economic integration, but also environment, social policy, security and democracy, including the whole issue of accountability and legitimacy.

(5) Whereas the old regionalism only concerned relations between formally sovereign states, the new forms part of a global structural transformation in which non-state actors are active and manifest themselves at several levels of the global system. It can therefore not be understood only from the point of view of the single region. It should rather be defined as a world order concept, since any particular regionalization process has systemic repercussions within and between single regions throughout the world, thus shaping the way in which the world is organized.

We are dealing with an emergent phenomenon and it is therefore difficult to work with very precise definitions. We cannot define regions *a priori*, because they define themselves by evolving from an objective, but dormant, to a subjective, active existence. By region in this context I refer to "macroregions." This concept forms part of a theoretical framework in which the emergence of smaller (subnational or transnational) microregions is causally linked to a macroprocess of regionalization.

We could speak of degrees of "regionness" in analogy with concepts such as stateness and nationness. A higher degree of regionness implies a higher degree of economic interdependence, communication, cultural homogeneity, coherence, capacity to act and, in particular, capacity to resolve conflicts. Regionalization is the process of increasing regionness, and this concept can refer to a single region as well as to the world system.

The process of regionalization from within can be compared with the historical formation of nation states, with the important difference that a coercive centre, or at least the open use of force, is lacking in processes of regionalization. This presupposes a shared, non-coercive project among the potential members of the region in the process of formation. But this is not a sufficiently clear criterion. The difference between regionalism and the infinite process of economic integration is that there is a politically defined limit to the former process. This is the historical outcome of attempts to find a transnational level of governance which reinforces certain shared values and minimizes certain shared perceptions of danger. Like the formation of ethnic and national identities, the regional identity is dependent on historical context and is often shaped by conflicts.

The assumption is thus that despite structural, and contextual differences, there is an underlying logic behind contemporary processes of regionalization. This logic does not refer to a single dimension. Some key dimensions are cultural identity, degree of economic and political homogeneity, and security, in particular a relative capability for conflict resolution: i.e., handling and resolving regional conflicts without extraterritorial intervention.

The New Regionalism also presupposes the growth of a regional civil society, opting for regional solutions to some local, national and global problems. The implication of this is that not only economic, but also social and cultural networks are developing more quickly than formal political cooperation at the regional level. One rather clear example of a regional civil society is the Nordic subregion, where security policies during the Cold War differed to a high degree among the respective national societies over a long period while they themselves converged towards a Nordic community. Europe is of course more diverse, but there is, nevertheless, a unity in the diversity. The same can be said about other world regions.

REGIONALISM AS WORLD ORDER

Does regionalism provide a possible world order? Again, it is important how we define the concepts. In international political economy theory, world order is usually referred to as an arrangement which provides the necessary framework for transactions in the world economy. It is important to distinguish the theoretical meaning of the concept from its historically varying real life content: i.e., specific solutions to the problem of world order at a particular point in time. Thus, world orders are historical, and there are presumably alternative future world orders, more or less attractive, depending on our perspective and values.

We are concerned with the potentials and possibilities of a regionalized world order which implies that to some extent the territorial logic of the state (mercantilism) is applied to the emerging regional systems (neo-mercantilism), albeit in a post-Westphalian context. It should be remembered, however, that real development depends on the dialectical relationship between the two logics, the forces of market expansion and the need for political control, as well as on the context in which these political forces meet. The one constitutes a reaction to the other, but neither of them can be seen as a final solution or "the end of history." If regionalism can be seen as a counterforce to globalization, the process of globalization will nevertheless continue, albeit with the preconditions fundamentally changed.

In order to function, a market presupposes some kind of social order. This premise holds for the past as well as for the present. It was the historical function of mercantilism to create "national economies" out of localized "natural economies." The crucial issue is how economic exchange can take place under the conditions of anarchy supposedly characterizing the international system. This constitutes a world order problem.

Theoretically at least this problem can be solved in more than one way. Recent debate has focussed on the importance of hegemonic stability for the functioning of the international economy and, to the extent that this role is considered essential, the consequent implications of hegemonic decline. These are, on the economic level, a fragmentation of the world economy, and, on the political level, an increased rivalry between leading capitalist countries, or more theoretically between carriers of the predominant model and social projects with the purpose of replacing it with some qualitatively different model.

Hegemony on the level of the world order can thus be described as a form of world governance, a set of rules backed by the authority (and credibility) of the hegemon. Hegemony is thus a special kind of power, based on different but mutually supportive dimensions, fulfilling certain functions (providing public goods) in a larger system which lacks a formal authority structure, and is consequently more or less voluntarily accepted by other actors. Thus, coercion implies dominance rather than hegemony.

The same distinction between hegemony and dominance can of course be applied to regional systems; but here the compatibility of regional hegemonies and a particular world order becomes an issue. The Cold War order was in fact dualistic, in the sense that a socialist subsystem existed as a challenge to the capitalist world order, providing rebellious states with a safe haven. In 1989 this subsystem broke down under the military burden, lagging technological capability, and exhaustion of the various dimensions of hegemonic power. In this bipolar system regionalism had been subsumed under the Cold War logic, which implied a linkage also between regional organizations and fundamental cleavage within the system (hegemonic regionalism). A new world order thus also implies a new type of regionalism. Regional powers are no longer "subimperialist" but driven by their own ambitions which very well could be hegemonic, if not on the global level then on the regional. "Regional hegemonism," which is coercive and therefore rather should be called dominance, is a "malign" form of neomercantilism—the New Regionalism, which is non-coercive, a "benign" form. The great task in creating a post-hegemonic future is thus to promote benign rather than malign neomercantilism, and make regional hegemonies compatible with an overall world order.

THE VALUE OF REGIONALISM

Arguing on Polanyian lines, the New Regionalism can be seen as a reaction to and a modifier of globalization, which seems to imply that global is "bad" whereas regional is "good." Such a position of course needs some nuancing. The New Regionalism can be defined as a multidimensional process of regional integration which includes economic, political, social and cultural aspects. It is a package rather than a single policy and goes beyond the free trade market idea: i.e., the interlinkage of previously more or less secluded national markets into one functional economic unit. Rather, the political ambition of establishing territorial control and regional coherence cum identity (in Polanyi's terms, protecting regional civil society) is the primary regionalist goal.

For other than committed neo-mercantilists, the question whether a regionalist world order is a positive or negative development can, however, only be answered in relation to alternative world orders and with reference to specific values.[12] In this section we will focus on three "world order values": peace and security, development, and ecological sustainability. Can regionalism promote these values better than globalism?

(1) In the case of inter-state and intra-state security problems, the predominance of the nation state and a Westphalian political rationality prevents rational solutions, whereas the regional level opens up previously untapped possibilities to solve conflicts built into the state formation. The UN system, as we so far have known it, is operating in an international context which is becoming ever more different from the world in which the UN originally was born. The emerging world system permits and even enforces a process of regionalization in different parts of the world, at the same time as the increase in regional activity itself constitutes structural change on the world level. The larger region can absorb tensions that have become institutionalized in the historical state formations. Under the umbrella of multilateralism, the regional actor can, with lesser risk of provoking bilateral hostilities, intervene in intrastate conflicts which threaten to become destructive. The outcome is by no means uniform. Rather it would be correct to say that incidents of national disintegration can make or break regional organizations.

Looking at the nature of the conflict itself, we can distinguish between relatively stable and controlled conflict, on the one hand, and those which are explosive and non-controllable on the other. The former are stable in the sense that they do not constitute a threat to regional security but, rather, are used as a pretext for intervention, which then has other causes, such as regional power ambitions. Here the UN has played a peace-keeping role, stabilizing but perhaps also making permanent the situation. The explosive and non-controllable conflicts are either a direct threat to regional security or raise very strong human rights concerns (or both). Here a large number of actors tend to be involved showing the legal uncertainties and the lack of established routines. The type of intervention tends to be (or become) peace-enforcing, rather than peace-keeping.

Concerning the form of intervention, we can first make a distinction between unilateral and multilateral operations. The former can either be carried out by a concerned neighbor, or by a regional/super power. The interventions of the USA in Guatemala, Panama and Grenada, of Tanzania in Uganda, of Vietnam in Cambodia, and of India (albeit "invited") in Sri Lanka are cases in point. The latter can be either regionally confined (for instance carried out by a regional organization as in the Liberian case) or international (for instance the UN system as in the Somalian case). The distinction is not very clearcut, and in real world situations several actors at different levels are involved, the number increasing with the complexity of the conflict itself. The issue of legitimacy becomes confused, which makes it more difficult to identify the intervenor with one or other of the parties; but as such identifications are nevertheless made, more actors feel inclined to intervene. The typical case here is Bosnia.

A third point of comparison is the pattern of conflict resolution, to the extent that there is any. Few conflicts are resolved in a definite way, and it is not at all certain that even a very successful case of conflict resolution will be of a permanent character. It is not the permanence, but the type of conflict resolution attempted which is of interest here. Nicaragua exemplifies the old regionalism of an hegemonic kind, whereas Liberia shows the way future regional conflicts may be resolved: i.e., conflict resolution under the New Regionalism.

(2) If by development we mean long-term development beyond macroeconomic stabilization, what is the difference between the "old" and the "new" regionalism from a developmental perspective? First, the old regionalism was often imposed from outside for geopolitical reasons, and in such cases there were few incentives for economic cooperation, particularly if the "natural" economic region was divided Cold War lines. Second, the attempts at regional cooperation/integration that actually took place were often inherited from colonial times and did not go far beyond the signing of free trade treaties. The outcome was rarely encouraging as the global pattern of uneven development more often than not was reproduced within the region, creating political tensions as a result. In contrast, the New Regionalism is more political. Its approach to free trade is cautious, far from autarkic, more selective in its external relations, and careful to see to the interests of the region as a whole.

Developmental regionalism may provide solutions to many development problems for the South, and of these we may identify five.

i) Self-reliance was never viable on the national level (at least for most countries) but may be a feasible development strategy on the regional (collective self-reliance). This is the viable economy argument. It could be further extended to the "societal viability" argument (or social sustainability argument). Emphasis on the soundness of the artificially isolated economic system, separated from society, has created a new social dualism. The purpose of the new regionalism is to prevent such cases of national disintegration by including social security concerns, whereas neoliberal "market regionalism" reinforces processes of transnational integration and national disintegration.

ii) The viable economy argument is particularly relevant in the case of micro states, which either have to cooperate, or become client states of the "core countries" or tourist resorts for the richer states. This is the argument of sufficient size. This argument which has been elaborated in the Caribbean context has lost some of its force but cannot be neglected.

iii) Collective bargaining on the level of the region could improve the economic position of marginalized Third World countries in the world system, or protect the structural position of successful export countries. This is the argument of effective articulation in the world economy.

iv) Regional conflict resolution will eliminate distorted investment patterns as the security fund could be tapped for more productive use. This is the peace dividend argument.

v) The issues of development, security and peace, and ecological sustainability form one integrated complex, at the same time as they constitute as many imperatives for deepening regional cooperation, if not regional integration. This is the sustainability argument.

(3) Sustainability links the issue of development to the larger issue of ecological management. In the industrialized world, the "national economies" were built with little regard to the pollution problem in the larger region, and regional management of the problem of pollution has become a strong motive force in regional integration. In developing areas the issue is rather how to exploit natural resources in a way that is not only sustainable over time but also fair with regard to various conflicting interests on the national level.

Few serious ecological problems can be solved within the framework of the nation state. Some are bilateral, some are global, quite a few are regional. The most important problems should be solved on a global level, but there are few operative global institutions for resource management and for the handling of ecological crises. The regional are often related to water: coastal waters, rivers, and ground water. Examples are the South Chinese Sea, Barents Sea, the South Asian river systems, the Mekong River system, the Nile, Euphrates-Tigris, and the uneven exploitation of ground water resources in the areas around Jordan. As is evident, these issues cannot be studied in isolation from the issues of development and regional security.

CONCLUSION

In this essay I have essentially applied Polanyi's ideas of regionalism to the current situation which shows certain similarities to the time when Polanyi was writing. The basic recurring question is—where do we situate the regulative function necessary to protect society, the reembedding of the economy in a situation when market forces are stronger than ever and operating in a global context?

My use of the term New Regionalism has both a positive meaning (there are empirically documented new features in most of the current regionalization trends) and a normative one (these trends contain latent possibilities for a "preferred" world order). The argument can be summarized as follows. The dialectics of market expansion on the one hand, and attempts at political intervention in defence of civil society on the other, constitute the basic forces in societal change. In the future post-Westphalian world this takes place in a transnational space, in which the New Regionalism represents "the return of" the political: i.e., interventions in favour of crucial values, among which development, security and peace, and ecological sustainability are the most fundamental.

In fact these issues form one integrated complex, at the same time as they constitute as many imperatives for deepening regional cooperation, if not regional integration. The levels of "regionness" between regions in the process of being formed will continue to be uneven. As Samir Amin has suggested, the world economy will therefore be the outcome of negotiations between regions. Only the future will decide where the levels will be and, consequently, where the balance between regionalization and globalization will be struck.

The issue of peace can of course not be avoided and this issue was for natural reasons central to Polanyi's regionalist argument. In the language of classical realism a regionalized world order would rather be a conflictual structure of hostile "civilizations": for instance the West, Islam and the Confucian cultural areas.[13] This dark vision is strikingly similar to the scenario in George Orwell's *1984*. It even contains the classical type of "unholy" alliances (the Islamic-Confucian connection). My objection to Orwell is the same as my objection to Huntington. They both apply a Westphalian logic to a post-Westphalian context.

NOTES

1. During the First Polanyi conference in 1986, I further developed my newborn interest in the wave of regionalism that had started as our continent turned from Euro-pessimism to Euro-optimism. I am grateful to Abraham Rotstein for mentioning that Karl Polanyi had written an article on precisely this theme around the time of the publication of *The Great Transformation*. The article was not easily accessible, but when I finally could get hold of it, I understood Polanyi's argument as a recommendation as to what kind of world order should emerge from the turbulence of depression and war. I also discerned a basic similarity between the global structural situation at that time and the one existing today. Three of my works are relevant to the present discussion: B. Hettne, "Europe and the Crisis: The Regionalist Scenario Revisited," in Marguerite Mendel and Daniel Salée (eds.), *The Legacy of Karl Polanyi. Market, State and Society at the End of the Twentieth Century*. London: Macmillan, 1991. B. Hettne, "The Concept of Neomercantilism," in Lars Magnusson (ed.), *Mercantilist Economies*. Boston: Kluwer, 1993. B. Hettne, *Development Theory and the Three Worlds. Towards an International Political Economy of Development*. London: Longman, 1995.
2. It is important to keep in mind that "global" is different from "universal." Global interests do not necessarily express globally shared concerns but rather interests which are strong enough to penetrate (and transform) all parts of the globe. This may in a linear fashion lead to a universalization of values, but more likely to countermovements and more dialectical processes. It is at this stage that regionalization enters the picture.
3. "Universal Capitalism," p. 87.
4. *The Great Transformation*, p. 181.
5. R. Robertson, *Globalization. Social Theory and Global Culture*. London: SAGE, 1992.
6. James H. Mittelman, "Global Restructuring of Production and Migration," in Yoshikazu Sakamoto (ed.), *Global Transformation*. Tokyo: United Nations University Press, 1994.
7. F. Fröbel, J. Heinrichs and O. Kreye, *The New International Division of Labour*. Cambridge: Cambridge University Press, 1980.
8. R. Kaplinsky, *Third World Industrialization in the 1980s. Open Economies in a Closing World*. London: Frank Cass, 1984, p. 77.
9. A. Hirschman, *Exit, Voice and Loyalty: Responses to Decline in Firms. Organizations and States*. Cambridge, Mass.: Harvard University Press, 1970.
10. Kimberley A. Hamilton (ed.), *Migration and the New Europe*. Washington: Centre for Strategic and International Studies, 1994.
11. N.D. Palmer, *The New Regionalism in Asia and the Pacific*. Lexington: Lexington Books, 1991.
12. Richard Falk and Saul Mendlovitz (eds.), *Regional Politics and World Order*. San Francisco: W.H.Freeman, 1973.
13. S. P. Huntington, "The Clash of Civilizations?" *Foreign Affairs*, 3/1993, pp. 22-49.

Chapter Six

CONDITIONS FOR RE-LAUNCHING DEVELOPMENT
Samir Amin

I

Development[1] is no longer on the agenda: the governments of the West are pre-occupied with "crisis management"; the countries of the former "East" are converting to market capitalism; and Latin America, Africa and the Arab world are primarily concerned with the servicing of external debt. Only the developing countries of Asia continue to be preoccupied with sustaining an accelerated rate of economic growth—China, East (Taiwan, Korea) and South East Asia, and more modestly India.

For the first three decades after 1945, development was the major preoccupation of all regimes. Three major projects were implemented with considerable success: i) the welfare state in the developed West; (ii) sovietism in the East; (iii) accelerated modernization in the non-aligned countries of the Bandung group of Asia and Africa, and Latin America ("developmentalism"). All three projects either unfolded within the framework of autocentric national economies or—in the case of the countries of the East and the South—aspired to construct such economies. They differed in their relationship ("interdependence") with the world economy: Atlanticism, the construction of Europe, in the case of the developed countries of the West; "negotiated" openings to the world economy in the case of the countries of the South; quasi-autarchy for the countries of the East. There were differences also in the nature of the social forces driving the project in question: historic social democratic compromise between capital and labour within the national states of the West; populism with Marxist or socialist pretensions; neo-colonial bourgeois in the South. There were also differences with respect to political systems: electoral pluralism, one-party states, etc. The diversity of differences, due to the incontestable variety of historical legacies and the fact that some countries were more while others were less egalitarian in terms of income distribution, should not detract from the profound similarity of objectives—to increase material welfare by economic development, and the strengthening of the Nation within the world.

In the course of the thirty "golden years" of post-war growth, the internationalization of the world economy—whether encouraged or resisted—progressively eroded the capacity of the state to manage modernization, while new dimensions of the problem asserted themselves such as environmental degradation on a planetary scale. Then in 1968-71 the world system entered a phase of structural crisis which continues to this day. The crisis manifests itself in the return of high and persistent unemployment accompanied by a slowing down of growth in the West, the collapse of sovietism, and serious regression in some regions of the Third World accompanied by unsustainable levels of external indebtedness. In contrast, East Asia took off into accelerated economic growth.

The post-war era (1945-90) has been characterized by serious conflicts between different parts of the world: the West-East Cold War, and conflicts between the West bloc and the Bandung powers. Nevertheless, despite these conflicts, there was generalized economic development, in some ways more rapid in the East and the South, giving rise to the idea that it was possible to "catch up" with the developed countries.

In fact, strong growth in the world economy was the product of political developments which favoured "poor" nations and the popular classes in a general way to the detriment of the "unilateral logic of capital." I stress this particularly since it is overlooked or ignored in (partial) explanations of the "boom" (or booms). The defeat of fascism contained and limited power relations within all the societies of the world, and between them. In the West it created relations of power significantly more favourable to the working classes than ever before in the entire history of capitalism. These new power relations are the key to the understanding of the so-called welfare state, a historic compromise between capital and labour which the French regulation school has called "fordism" (a questionable designation, since "fordism" was introduced in the United States before, and in opposition to, Roosevelt's New Deal). I stress the fundamental importance of this political factor, underestimated in the dominant analyses which suggest that capital sought—naturally, so to speak—a compromise with labour. The victory of the Soviet Union and the Chinese revolution created internal and international conditions favouring the development of the countries of the East, and also those of the West, insofar as they contributed to pressures exerted on capital to engage in the historic social democratic compromise. Debates concerning the social nature of these developments—to become socialist, or not?—and the role of the internal contradictions resulting in its exhaustion and eventual collapse, should not deflect attention from the positive effects of West-East political competition, reinforced by United States military expenditures (whose decisive role in the compromise of the welfare state I have stressed in previous writings). The simultaneous rise of national liberation movements in the Third World, resulting decolonization, and the ability of post-colonial regimes to harness the benefits of East-West competition, favoured economic growth in the South in a number of ways.

The three pillars erected on the basis of the victory against fascism, which sustained development in the thirty golden years, have progressively been eroded by the limitations inherent in the class relations upon which they rested: the restrictions of the social democratic compromise, the ambitions of the "soviet" bourgeoisies, and those of the Third World. These internal contraditions, manifested in policies which undermined the "logic of national economic development," and fed by trends of ever increasing globalization, lie at the root of the brutal reversal of the political conjuncture of the 1980s. The collapse of the western welfare state, the Soviet model, and Third World national developmentalism have terminated what I call "the post-war anti-fascist era" in which capital was constrained to operate within structures relatively favourable to the peoples of the world.

Over the past three decades, conditions favourable to the re-construction of the logic of unilateral capital were re-created. But the logic of unilateral capital cannot, by and of itself, generate growth—much less development (strong growth, accompanied by full employment and income distribution favouring the popular classes). Based exclusively on a search for the highest financial returns, capital tends to produce an unequal distribution of income between social classes, domestically and internationally, which contributes to relative economic stagnation. Marx and Keynes stand alone in having understood the deflationist logic of unilateral capital, a lesson forgotten during the progressive eradication of the anti-fascist spirit in the post war years.

II

Contemporary society is manifestly in crisis, if we define crisis as a situation in which the expectations of the majority cannot be satisfied by the logic (rules of the game) of the system. People want full employment, improvement in social services, opportunities for social mobility, etc. The unilateral logic of capital produces unemployment, impoverishment, and marginalization. Nations want independence and dignity. But the logic of global capital produces the opposite. In this process, states and governments have lost the legitimacy which enabled them to intervene in regulating social relations in favour of the popular classes, and to defend their national interests on the international scene. Western democracy, sovietism (vulgarly called "communism" by its opponents), and the national populism of Bandung—all three are in crisis. To speak of the "crisis of capitalism," however, is something else. The expression has no meaning until such time as the popular social forces opposed to the logic of capital have coherent and feasible counter-projects, as was the case in the anti-fascist post-war years. The projects of the post-war era, now dépassé, have not given way to new directions but to regression which benefits the logic of unilateral capital. Our period is thus very far from being a "crisis of capitalism" and will remain so, as long as political reactions to the dramatic social consequences of the deployment of global capital remain incoherent and ineffective.

The political forces which have arisen in the wake of the collapse of the post-war order have been placed almost entirely at the service of the logic of the deployment of capital. I have analysed in some detail policies of what may be called "crisis mananagement." Capitalism and crisis are not incompatible: far from it, because the unilateral logic of capital necessarily generates crisis. However, left to itself capital can manage the crisis, though it cannot resolve it. Crisis occurs due to the fact that the profits of capitalist exploitation cannot find enough financially profitable new outlets capable of expanding productive capacity. "Management" of the crisis consists in finding alternative new investments for excess short-term financial capital, in order to avert massive and brutal collapse of financial values such as happened in the 1930s. The "solution" by contrast implies a modification of the rules of the game affecting income distribution, consumption, and investment decisions—in other words, an alternative social project to that founded exclusively on profitability criteria. There will be no solution to the crisis unless and until the "anti-systemic" social forces impose constraints on capital which are exterior to and independent of the logic of pure capital.

Crisis management by national governments proceeds by policies of "de-regulation" designed to weaken "rigidities" of trade unionism, dismantle and liberalize prices and wages, reduce public expenditures (principally subsidies and social services), and privatize and liberalize external transactions. The recipe is the same for all governments, and its justification is based on the same vague and excessive dogmatisms: liberalization "liberates" potential initiatives "victimized by interventionism" and puts the engine of economic growth back on the rails: those who liberalize fastest and most completely will gain "competitivity" in open world markets. But as Marx and Keynes clearly understood, the liberalization in question will ensnare the economy in "deflationist" spirals of stagnation, unmanageable at the international level, multiplying conflicts which cannot be mediated, stuck with repetitive incantations to the effect that liberalization will—some time in the future—bring "healthy" development. On what basis, by what criteria can such policies be judged or evaluated? Nobody knows. At the same time, the legitimation of choice is reinforced by political and ideological propositions which are as equally vague—and false—as those advanced concerning economic mechanisms. Economic liberalization is presented as synonymous with political democracy, and all critiques of these policies are held to be inadmissible in the name of the defense of democracy. The merits of economic liberalism are praised in the name of "transparency"; the state is considered *a priori* as the locus of opacity (ignoring the fact that the democratic state provides the best conditions for transparency), while in fact the—very real—opacity of private business protected by "business confidentiality" escapes even a passing mention. In contrast, the social and economic realities of oligopolies, privileged relations of the private with the public sector, and corruption are never the object of scientific analysis. Rarely have we witnessed an ideological discourse, "pur et simple," as extreme as that of any dogmatic fundamentalism, repeated incessantly by the media as the dominant discourse, as if it were based on established evidence.

The globalization of capital requires a regime of crisis management, such as we have here described. Enormous volumes of short-term capital require the subordination of economic mechanisms to unadulterated private profitability criteria. Liberalization of international capital movement, floating exchange rates, high rates of interest, American balance of payments deficits, Third World indebtedness, and privatization constitute a perfectly rational set of conditions which offer global capital the possibility of speculative financial profits, to avoid the danger of a massive devaluation of the hypertrophic volume of global financial capital. To gain some idea of the enormity of the excess volume of financial capital, we may compare the annual value of world trade (in the region of 3000 billion dollars) with international capital flows (about 80,000 to 100,000 billion dollars) which are 30 times larger. I have elsewhere analyzed the presumed rationality of this set of crisis management policies; they are perfectly rational and efficient from this point of view. This is because the literature critiquing liberalization policies, more often than not treating each measure in isolation, finds them to be apparently absurd.

In the perspective of crisis management, leading international institutions are instruments in the service of the regulation of West-South and new West-East relations. In this context, the function of the IMF and the World Bank (through imposition of liberalization, floating of exchange rates, subordination of the economies of South and East to the absolute imperatives of debt service) and also of the GATT, masquerading behind the discourse of free trade, is the protection of market control by the dominant transnational oligopolies. The G7 countries attempt to co-ordinate these crisis management policies, without attempting to attack either the basic problems of the crisis, or the conflict of interest between the principal partners which contribute to the crisis.

III

The priority accorded the demands of crisis management created by the uncontested triumph of the rule of private profit brings us no closer to a solution. On the contrary. The crisis which is now 20 years old commenced at the end of the 1960s and the opening of the 1970s (before the first "oil shock") with a progressive decline in the level of productive investment, and the growth of a mass of excess financial capital which has not ceased to increase ever since. Ignoring the persistence and tenacity of economic stagnation, successive governments continue to use the language of conjunctural "recessions" and "recoveries," when in fact we have a fundamental structural disequilibrium due to the triumph of ecomomic liberalism. The latter, however, is never put in question. The social catastrophe has ravaged every region of the world. In the developed centers, it is manifested in permanent unemployment; in the peripheries, in the blocking of economic growth, the aggravation of impoverishment, and tragic societal regression. At the global level, the priorities of crisis management have sacrificed measures which should rationally have been deployed to save the environment at a planetary level. The ideology of the dominant discourse presents all these "sacrifices" as temporary measures required to rebuild efficient structures from which to re-launch development. In reality, unilateral subordination to the laws of profit fatally entraps countries into deflationary spirals with no possibility of existing on their own. Reversal, when it comes, is always the product of an "external shock" in the sense of one external to the unilateral logic of capital. The modification of social relations in favour of redistribution of income, preparation for war, war itself, or the geographic opening of colonial expansion, create conditions favourable to renewed ecomomic expansion, and are thus able to sustain a wave of technological renewal. It was in this way that the strengthening of the position of the working classes which accompanied the victory over fascism created the conditions for the expansion of mass production industries after the war. Popular interpretations which explain the post-war fordist regime in terms of a wave of technological innovations invert the direction of causality. In this I side with Paul Sweezy and others who argue the (minority) view that it is in this manner that capitalism historically overcame its natural tendency to stagnation.

We cannot escape the crisis by following policies of "liberalism without borders." This is a utopia, tenaciously held throughout the history of capitalism, because it expresses in extreme form the hard-core ideological vision of a "pure" capitalism reduced to the laws of accumulation guided exclusively by the strict logic of capital. Total liberalism has never existed, and historical moments which approximate to the political condition for its institutions have always been brief. This is because extreme liberalism necessarily produces a political reaction seeking to check, limit, or modify resulting political and social relations, thus creating conditions either for a new phase of expansion or war. The ideologues of liberalism are viscerally incapable of understanding the fact that expansion has always been associated with the setting of limits to total liberalism, not by chance but from necessity. This is why these ideologues for ever condemn history, states, bourgeoisies, and peoples, who refuse to bow down to the requirements of "economic laws" of an imaginary capitalism which exists only in the texts of conventional economics. The post-war expansion lasted four decades before exhausting the possibilities presented by the social systems constructed on the basis of the anti-fascist victory. The project of the liberal utopia has brought catastrophe in a far shorter time. Attempts to institute utopian liberal projects have always provoked political reactions of rejection. But these reactions rarely take the form of a systematic counter-project, of coherent and potentially effective means of solving the crisis. In the first instance, they are almost always spontaneous, partial, contradictory, and even conflictual. Today, in a global system characterized by profound internationalization, these reactions may be described as "protectionist," in the form of the partial closure of borders, control of capital movement, measures to defend domestic industries and the property of nationals, in some cases the return to the social contract of labour and capital, and restoration of state intervention. These reactions find legitimation in the renewel of the discourse of nationalism, which passes easily into chauvinism—aggressive in the case of the relatively strong, defensive in the case of the weak.

Nationalist policies are not necessarily inefficent, as claimed by the liberal theoretical discourse. If Asia has until now escaped general crisis, and high rates of growth have prevailed in Japan, Korea and Taiwan, with accelerated growth in China and, albeit at lower rates, also in South East Asia and India, how do we explain this "exception"? The reasons are undoubtedly many and complex, and vary from one country to another in this region which comprises over half of humanity—if only because social systems and historic legacies in terms of levels of development are different in different countries. All manner of possible explanations have been offered, including some which accord pride of place to cultural factors, real or imaginary, as illustrated by the debate concerning Confucianism. I shall simply draw attention to the fact that all the countries in question have adopted, in varying degrees, policies marked by strong economic nationalism, in the protectionist and statist sense noted above. They have not, like the countries of the European Community and the United States, Latin America or Africa, followed, more or less, the policy prescriptions of liberalism. Rather, the Asian countries have done the opposite, whether it is Japan—an advanced capitalist country—Korea in process of rapid construction, the market socialism of Deng Xiaoping's China, or the more integrated Third World capitalist countries of South East Asia and India. In terms of the level of development, which was more or less the same at the start, impressive results have been achieved in accordance with the degree to which nationalist polices of protectionism and statism were systematic and coherent. Why were these countries able to choose such policies, and to implement them? The reasons are complex and connected with the geo-strategic preoccupations of the United States in the region (exceptional support extended to Japan, Korea, Taiwan and South East Asia in exchange for their participation in the anti-communist crusade, resulting in a tolerance for nationalism not permitted elsewhere); the sheer size of the continental countries of China and India where the expansion of internal markets is always an option in the event of export problems (although other large countries such as Brazil and the new Russia appear either unwilling or unable to mobilize their large domestic markets to their advantage); the particularities of social structures (if China does better than India, it is surely because Maoism set in motion a gigantic social transformation which formed the base on which later economic growth could be instituted); and there are perhaps also cultural reasons. We may also note that none of the countries of the region, with the qualified exception of India, is particularly respectful of democracy. Japan resembles a one-party political model rather than the pluralist western one, and all the regimes of East and South-East Asia are "authoritarian" as far as one can tell.

Are these nationalistic practices capable of protecting the Asian region indefinitely? It is difficult to answer this question. Japan might be threatened, and perhaps also the medium-size countries of East and South East Asia. India is undergoing political crisis which threatens its economic stability. China remains a potential exception, as long as that country can prevent the southern provinces—attracted by the Korea-Taiwan-Hong Kong "model"—from endangering national unity. (An alternative policy would be to direct the growth of these provinces toward the development of the interior of the country.) But the growing economic inter-penetration within the entire region gives Asia a relative measure of autonomy with respect to the "rest of the world." This constitutes a factor favourable to the continued health of the "Asian Miracle." But if nationalism in Asia has produced positive results in terms of economic growth (though not in social justice or democratization), this is not the case in other regions of the world hit by the crisis. In Latin America, Sub-Sahara Africa and the Arab world, developmental nationalism as practiced by populist regimes in the Bandung era is a matter of the past. The retreat has not opened a way to go beyond these policies; on the contrary, it has resulted in serious regression. In my view we should interpret the "ethnic assault on the nation" (here, as well as in East Europe and the former USSR), and the illusions of religious fundamentalism (principally Islamic, but also Hindu) as manifestations of this regression. Far from opening the way to the democratization of states and societies, with a renewal of a positive nationalism and regional cooperation, these involutions raise the possibility of a kind of neo-fascism of weak countries. In Latin America, the reactions are possibly less negative, in so far as democratic forces there appear to be more solid. But can they articulate a coherent project of social progress, which must necessarily embrace, here as elsewhere, a healthy dose of nationalism (in the sense of the rejection of the polarizing capitalist globalization of the liberal utopia) along with a commitment to regional cooperation?

In Europe, we cannot exclude the possibility of a return to nationalism, in reaction to the European liberal project which, reduced to the concept of the common market, carries within it a contradiction which threatens to be fatal to the project. European economic integration cannot be regarded as irreversible until it is accompanied by political integration based on a new social contract between capital and labour, something which can only be brought into being by a coherent Left on an pan-European scale. Implemented by the right, the European project is today visibly in danger of sinking, if not actually exploding under the impact of nationalist backfire—and the "second best" of a "German Europe" offers no way out of the problem. But such right-wing nationalisms which encourage the rehabilitation of fascism will in the course of time generate a renewal of progressive social reaction. Within a system which remains largely based on the principles of liberalism, there is the likelihood of a continuing cycle of action-reaction encasing the continent in a regressive economic, political, and ideological spiral. This cannot constitute an effective response to the crisis, given the degree of globalization attained by the economies of the region. In East Europe and in the former Soviet Union, the impasses within which the rise of nationalisms, and sub-nationalisms, have enmeshed those societies are even more dramatic.

Established powers here and there, in the United States, in Europe, in the former East Europe and the Soviet Union, in Latin America, Africa and the Middle East, are first and foremost pre-occupied with the management of the political crisis, produced by the economic crisis. But political crisis management is no more effective in bringing about solutions than is economic crisis management. I have characterized the political crisis as "chaos" involving impasse within the European Union with the possibility of involutions, dramatic chaos and disarticulation in East Europe and the former USSR, and collapse of a number of societies in the Third World. The political management of this chaos is based on the cynical practice of a *Real-politik* short view, the manipulation of nationalisms, culturalisms, racisms and ethnicities leading to fascism. In East Europe, Latin America, Africa and the Middle East, these policies consist of throwing oil on the fire, in the hope of gaining a short-term advantage by weakening regional powers and reducing the chances of a progressive renaissance of the societies in question. It is in this spirit that I have suggested a critical re-reading of the record of the policies of crisis management in terms of both their military (low intensity warfare) and political dimensions, in particular as they have affected Yugoslavia, Ethiopia, East Europe, Africa, and the Middle East.

Far from serving the objectives of the dominant discourse which claims that "democratization is on the rise," the economic and political forms of crisis management have everywhere reinforced the danger of anti-democratic regression. Liberalism engenders the risk of fascism, as Karl Polanyi showed in his analysis in *The Great Transformation* (1944) where he invited his contemporaries to understand that victory over fascism and rejection of utopian liberal policies which characterized the era following the end of the First World War would create the conditions for new economic expansion. The lesson, now forgotten, must be urgently recalled. We cannot escape the crisis—and the risk of regressing into fascism—without breaking categorically with the logic of neo-liberal globalization.

History does not repeat itself, at least not in the same manner. The term "fascism" carries abusive connotations from experiences of another era which is different from our own. Nevertheless neo-fascism—as I will call it—shares anti-democratic characteristics and common methods with its fascist ancestor. In the developed countries of the centre it does not have to take the form of the "big stick" as advocated by fringe rightist minorities (such as racism), or the unilateral imposition of policies favouring big capital (in this manner it would perpetuate the crisis and the management of marginalization in the form of an "economy of multiple speeds" as it is naively described). But even here, slippage toward the old model of nationalist fascism and chauvinism is not excluded, though masked by the preservation of forms of electoral democracy, manipulated and void of all real content. The danger of the rehabilitation of fascism should not be underestimated. In the countries of the periphery, situated in what P.G.Casanova so well described as "global colonialism," neo-fascism is the more brutal—the weaker and more hopelessness are the societies in which it operates. Ethnic cleansing and the carving up of states into terrorist dictatorships in the name of regionalism such as are already apparent, are among the forms taken by local powers unable to resist the subordination of their societies as small cogs in the globalized economy which is the source of their tragedies and catastrophes. These practices may perpetuate the appearance of the maintenance of "order" favourable to the exploitation of these peoples by dominant world capital, and will for this reason be supported by external powers.

IV

Neither the prescription of the liberal, nor the logic of the neo-fascist rejection, offers escape from the infernal circle of crisis and chaos. An effective response to these challenges is not possible until the lessons of *The Great Transformation* have been learned. History is not shaped by the infallible laws of pure economics, as believed by some university professors. It is the product of social reactions to the effects of these laws, which in turn define the social relations of the framework within which such laws operate. It is the "anti-systemic" forces of organized, coherent, and effective refusal to subordinate society to the unilateral and total needs of economic laws (in this context the laws of profit under the capitalist system) which in reality gives shape to history, rather than any "pure" logic regarding the accumulation of capital. Such forces determine the possibilities and the forms of expansion deployed within the institutional framework which they impose on economic and social organization.

The method advocated here does not permit us to formulate ready-made recipes of how to escape from the crisis. Solutions can come only as a result of transformation of the relations of social and political forces resulting from struggles whose outcome cannot be known in advance. We can however offer some reflections by way of contributing to the crystallization of coherent and feasible counter projects. In this way we may prevent social movements from becoming sidetracked into the impasse of false (neo-fascist) solutions.

Although the world cannot be managed as a single "world market," and ideological and political intervention cannot be eliminated in favour of unilateral submission to the supposed laws of the market (as believed by anti-statist ideologues *de tous azimuts*), the fact of globalization cannot simply be ignored or denied. It is not possible to turn back the clock in the course of history. A return to the post-war model of economic expansion, based on the central position occupied by the autocentric nation state in economic, political and cultural affairs implies economic and other untenable regressions. This is why backward-looking ideologies which deny the irreversible nature of the trajectory of evolution will inevitably be called upon to function like fascisms—that is to say, they will serve the needs of the new conditions of globalization, while pretending to offer escape and liberation. They are based on deception and lies, and this is why they cannot function without authoritarian negation of democracy. They are constrained to mobilize societies on the basis of false problems—ethnic purity, submission to supposed laws of religion—and to use these false causes as instruments to impose their dictatorships by terror.

The challenge thus consists in reconciling the interdependence implied by globalization and the inequalities of power of the "social partners" (workers in different sectors of the economy, some more "competitive" than others) and the "national partners" (dominant centers, middle powers, industrialized peripheries, the marginalized fourth world) in relation to global capital. Let us start with some self-evident banalities: the world as both unified and diverse. But diversity is not exclusively—or even principally—cultural. Emphasis on cultural diversity serves to relegate to secondary importance the major diversities of position in the economic hierarchy of world capitalism. It is at the level of the latter that we must begin to attack the problems. These are manifested not only in inequalities between peoples (culturally different or not, according to circumstance) but also in internal inequalities between classes and social groups. There is no solution to the crisis except by reinforcment of the position of the poor and the powerless of the world: the peoples of the peripheries, and the subordinated social classes of all countries of centers and peripheries. In other words, escape from "global colonialism" and liberal myths implies the rejection of temptations to fall back on neo-fascist illusions. These are the principles which form the point of departure for meaningful reflection on the construction of a counter project which is humanist, universalist, democratic, and respectful of diversities—but not of inequalities.

I have elsewhere proposed the "construction of a polycentric world" as a framework within which negotiated interdependence can be organized in a way which offers dominated peoples and classes improvement in the conditions of their participation in production, and access to better conditions of life. This project implies that we pass beyond action at the level of the nation state—above all in the case of small and medium-sized states—in order to benefit from political and economic organization at the regional level, with collective negotiation between regions. I refer the reader to the more detailed arguments I have developed in support of this proposition. We are here concerned with a new conception of regionalization, different from that conceived in the present framework of power relations. The latter are constructed like transmission belts of polarizing modernization, whereby peripheral zones are attached to dominant centers which share responsibilities for "global colonialism." NAFTA (North American Free Trade Area, attaching Mexico to the United States and Canada), the Lomé Agreements (Association of the European Union with Africa, the Caribbean and the Pacific), a yen zone (Japan and South East Asia), and the proposed "Pacific Zone" (United States, Japan, Australia and the Pacific Rim countries), are neo imperialist concepts inadequate for the purposes of addressing the desired objective of reducing the development gap. Regional "common markets" (like Mercosur in Latin America, ECOWAS in West Africa, the PTA in

East and Southern Africa), and political organizations inherited from the cold war (ASEAN in South East Asia), have likewise been the object of serious critiques, elaborated elsewhere.

In contrast to these inadequate visions of regionalization, I have developed arguments in favour of reconstruction carried out simultaneous at both regional and global levels, particularly in the area of capital markets and monetary systems. I refer the reader to these, and here shall limit myself to a summary of some of my conclusions.

(i) It will be necessary to conceive a new World Trade Organization, not as a successor of the GATT but as an institution charged with planning (dare I use the term?) access to the use of the major natural resources of the planet and also the prices of raw materials, without which the environmental discourse remains demagogic rhetoric, manipulated against the interests of humanity in general, and the peoples of the periphery in particular. Such a World Trade Organization should also take responsibility for planning targets for inter-regional trade in industrial products, reconciling general competitiveness, devising distributional criteria favouring the disadvantaged regions, and creating conditions permitting the improvement of incomes of disadvantaged workers.

(ii) Equally necessary will be the devising of mechanisms of organized capital markets to channel excess finance toward productive investment in the peripheries—taking into account that the global market now favours financial transfers from the poorest to the richest countries and channels excess savings to the United States, thus enabling the U.S. to perpetuate its external payments deficits.

(iii) Finally, it is necessary to rethink the international monetary system which has become non-functional, and replace floating exchange rates and the dollar standard with a system which articulates regional monetary systems—including the European monetary unit, the regional moneys of each of the large regions of the Third World, and that of the ex-USSR—in a way which will guarantee relative stability of exchange rates and reinforce the functioning of capital markets as suggested above. I propose this as an alternative to the transformation of the IMF into a world central bank, on the grounds that this is utopian and dangerous, given the polarizing tendencies of global capital markets.

The functions and purposes of the regions suggested are not limited to spaces of preferential economic integration. They should equally serve as political spaces favouring the collective re-inforcement of the social position of disadvantaged classes and sub-regions. This regionalization is not intended to be confined to the continents of the Third World (Latin America, the Arab world, sub-Saharan Africa, South-East Asia and the two continental countries, India and China) but also to serve the European spaces (the European Union, East Europe, and the former USSR).

The perspective of such a compromise between globalization and local and regional autonomy (which I have termed a "coherent de-linking" in response to the new challenges) would call for a serious revision of the concept of "development assistance," and for the democratization of the United Nations System which could then be employed to implement the objectives of disarmament (facilitated by measures of regional and national security within the framework of regional reconstruction). The United Nations would be able to put in place a system of world taxation (closely related to the management of the world's natural resources); it would be complemented by a system of inter-state relations with a "world parliament" able to reconcile the requirements of universalism (individual rights, collective rights of peoples, political and social rights, etc.) with the diversity of our historic and cultural heritage.

It will be appreciated that the totality of this "project" has no chance of realization unless social forces able to carry out the necessary reforms first crystallize at the level of the nation state, because there is no possibility of reform within the structures imposed by global liberalization and polarization. Reform at the sectoral level (reorganization of administration, taxation, education, support for participatory development), and a more general vision of the democratization of societies and their political and economic management, are preliminary steps and stages which cannot be short-circuited or circumvented. Without them the vision of a reorganized planetary order able to save the world from chaos and crisis and "re-launch development" remains fatally and absolutely utopian.

NOTES

The original title was "Actualité de 'la Grand Transformation': Les conditions d'une relance du développement (Mondialization et Particularisme)." This English-language version was translated by Kari Polanyi Levitt.

1. In order to avoid unnecessary repetition, the above text summarized the conclusions of reflections which I have developed more fully elsewhere.

(i) The nature of the post-war "cycle."

S.Amin (ed.), *Mondialisation et Accumulation*. Harmatten, 1994. See pp. 10-19 for the "three pillars" which constitute the base of post-war expansion and the reasons for their erosion. S. Amin, *Itinéraire intellectuel*. Harmattan, 1993. See chapter VIII for the collapse of the mechanisms of capitalist regulation.

(ii) New forms of the exploitation of labour and forms of global polarization (with emphasis on what I have called the "five monopolies" which reproduce polarization in the new conditions and corresponding forms of the globalized law of value).

S.Amin, *The Future of Global Polarization*. University of Nagoya, 1994 (forthcoming in *Review*, Binghampton, New York).

(iii) Political management of the Crisis.

S.Amin, *Empire of Chaos*. New York: Monthly Review Press, 1993. Chapter 1 Empire of Chaos; chapter 2, The New Capitalist Globalization; chapter 5, Regional Conflicts. S. Amin, "Les stratégies militaires de l'hégémonie américaine," in S.Amin(ed.), *Les enjeux stratégique en Mediterranée*. Harmattan, 1992, see pp. 11-105. S. Amin, *l'Ethnie à l'assaut des Nations*. Harmattan, 1994.

(iv) Critiques of the Bretton Woods Order, and arguments in favour of proposed reforms.

S. Amin, "Replacing the International Monetary System," *Monthly Review*, Vol 5, October 1993. S. Amin, "Le cinquième anniversaire de Bretton Woods," *Cahiers du CEAD*, Montréal, 1994. S. Amin, *Regionalization in the Third World in response to the challenge of polarizing globalization*. WIDER, forthcoming.

Chapter Seven

VISION AND EXPRESSION: LITERATURE AND *THE GREAT TRANSFORMATION*
Kenneth McRobbie

I

Karl Polanyi's *The Great Transformation*[1] attracted but little attention when first published towards the end of World War Two. That initial neglect perhaps stemmed from the nature of the work. For it represents less a body of research which subsequent scholarship may supercede, than a synthesizing prophetic vision.[2] It was, of course, the wrong vision for the times, when renewed market-driven consumption was eagerly awaited after wartime austerity. Polanyi's masterpiece looks not just to a part—the economy—but to the whole; embodying an interpretation of the past, it looks towards a future that, for the sake of human survival, must accord priority to culture and society. Moreover it does so, and this will be our focus here, with passion and insight that could hardly derive from the study of economic phenomena alone. It provided both an interpretation of a century of cataclysmic events which had overwhelmed the most educated and advanced countries, and a vision of the future.

In this a work that is concerned ultimately with the future of human culture in an industrialized world, Polanyi deploys strategies derived from literature: particularly in summoning up images both of mankind's deprivation and of a possible future fullness of being. For it was society's travail, during "the origins of our time" (the alternate title of Polanyi's work) which inspired his deeply felt account of the degradation of the working class during the establishing of industrial market capitalism. It was the unsuspected continued prevalence of this which shocked him on first setting foot in England in 1933, visible (and auditory) proof of "the cultural catastrophe" that continental workers had escaped. (pp. 166-175) In contrast, Vienna, his previous place of exile, although ironically presented as a Mecca for liberal economists, is with discernible pride held up as the place of the working class's "unexampled moral and intellectual achievements."[3] Polanyi's residence there had accustomed him to the growing reaction, on the part of both socialists and fascists, to the deficiencies of the market system which he found confirmed in England. His formidable powers of expression were accordingly employed in presenting the case for spiritual and cultural renewal, convinced that with the abolition of man's "right to live" it follows that "the true nature of man rebels against Capitalism."[4]

Although the book consists principally of a sustained critique of developments during the past two hundred years in Great Britain, one may well wonder whether Polanyi's manuscript would find a major American commercial publisher today, amid the regressive triumphalism of market capitalism's drive to monolithic uniformity. Essentially everything that Polanyi wrote proclaimed that the "myth" of the market was founded on a mistaken notion of human motivation, and thus rightly provoked increasing opposition that was not to be denied. In 1944, though, the full significance of twentieth-century capitalist world power had not registered upon most American and English intellectuals who in effect were the beneficiaries of liberal capitalism's world conquest. (pp.5-6) In contrast, the great generation of Central European intellectuals had felt the earth shifting virtually underfoot into totally new patterns in 1917-19, that were to become even more ominously rearranged in the 1930s. But while Polanyi registered the experience of his time and place, he transcends it in order to take a world-historical view. Thus he criticizes the capitalist market "utopia" as being infinitely more radical than either of the two reactions to it, fascism or communism, of which he says little. In his view, all that needed to be said of the war then raging was that it was the result of the prevailing system: "the origins of the cataclysm lay in the utopian endeavour of economic liberalism to set up a self-regulating market." (p.29) The consequences, if unchecked, would go even beyond what the world was witnessing at that time. "Our thesis is that the idea of a self-adjusting market implied a stark utopia. Such an institution could not exist for any length of time without annihilating the human and natural substance of society."[5] The danger lay in complacency. Despite the comforting illusion that society was being shaped "by men's will and wish alone," (pp.257-8) in fact it had been handed over to "a definite number of concrete institutions the mechanisms of which ruled the day." (p.211)

That the book initially gained little notice may have something to do both with the author's declaration, right at the start, that it will "trace the institutional downfall of a civilization," (p.4) and his conclusion that "out of the ruins of the Old World, cornerstones of the New can be seen to emerge." (pp.253-4) Such ringing statements must have grated upon not a few readers' ears. Just when Allied armies were breaching the Atlantic Wall of Hitler's Europe, making unconditional surrender of the enemy an imminent reality, here was a voice proclaiming that the real enemy was the system which the Allies themselves claimed to represent—more, that Berlin and Rome along with London and New York belonged together in one world system which had "lost" even before the war had begun. This was the man who stood in his garden in the quiet Kentish countryside, on a sunny afternoon during which the blue sky was slowly darkening from smoke clouds drifting over from Dunkirk in 1940, "patiently entertaining" one of his evening class students, and showing him things "which lesser men never do."[6] The war was the consequence: Polanyi would concern himself only with origins. On the opening page he implies that the market system—for which, in effect, the Allies were fighting against an ideology that imposed constraints upon it—would wreak indiscriminate wholesale destruction such as Hitler's military might had been unable to accomplish.[7] While an American audience may have looked forward with anticipation—and no little satisfaction—to the downfall of the British Empire, it would have stared uncomprehendingly at the opening pages of a work which foretold the end of its own branch of the same civilization. Even one of Polanyi's closest younger American associates felt moved to record that there were those, doubtless Americans, who felt uneasy at his master's forceful mode of written expression.[8] But this could only have been written by one to whom the European and English tradition of criticism of one's country's failings was alien. By contrast, the young Polanyi and his generation had admired the Hungarian poet and critic Endre Ady for both his poetry and his journalism: in which he wielded his famous "whip" against his homeland—"This disordered and decaying Hungary...If there is any flesh at all to tear from her body, it will certainly be torn away by the implacable bloodhounds of History!"[9]

In the last decade of his life, Polanyi turned increasingly to literature. The economic origins of the spiritual and cultural predicament of the West was the subject of his essay on a poem that may be the second oldest in Western literature, Hesiod's *Works and Days*. The title of Polanyi's posthumously published volume *The Livelihood of Man*[10] is taken from a line of the poem, which spells out the ominous message that characterizes Polanyi's *oeuvre*: "the Gods have hidden the livelihood of man"—a complaint then, even more so one now. For in Hesiod's epoch was initiated a new social relationship which Polanyi declares has "endured unchanged to the present." Gone was the Homeric world of communality, solidarity, and mutuality which formerly provided security. In its place was one where hunger had become "a part of the human condition." It offers a totally different perspective on that entity—the individual—whose "rise" is so often extolled in modern historical texts. For Polanyi views the poem as revealing of a sea-change in moral standards, as "a documentary manifestation of the birth of the isolated individual" with whom "a new kind of uncertainty is born."

The essay on Hesiod appears in a context which guaranteed that it would become widely read. In comparison, relatively few know of those of Karl Polanyi's editorial activities, translations and correspondence concerned with his long-standing interest in literature, particularly poetry. Of this area of commitment, one of profound interest to him, the most substantial item of evidence is his (and his wife's, jointly edited) out-of-print anthology of Hungarian populist literature, *The Plough and the Pen* published one year before his death.[11] Yet literature had always been an integral part of his life. His literary sensibilities found public expression when he was a boy. At school, he wrote a poem for the Ferenc Deák centenary, and recited one by Petöfi at his graduation ceremony. As a University student, he published an article pointing out contradictions between G.B.Shaw's essays and his dramas ("The Drama of Historical Materialism"). As president and long time member of the Budapest university students' Galilei Circle, he corresponded with the great innovative lyric poet (and revolutionary social critic) Endre Ady. The poet contributed to the Circle's annual March 15th celebration, and was duly eulogized by Karl Polanyi who delivered an address at the University in 1919 on the occasion of his funeral obsequies.[12] When serving in the army in 1915-17, Polanyi took with him two books: the Bible, and the Globe Edition of Shakespeare's works. He drew on his recollections of the latter when writing about his feelings of pesonal crisis at that time, in his later article "Hamlet."[13] Some of Polanyi's own poems have survived, those written to his wife and daughter. His later correspondence includes many references to literature; so far, the best known is the letter entitled "Notes on Premature Resignation," in which "Art and poetry" heads the list of the tasks set himself by "creative man."[14]

Between these earliest and latest engagements with literature, Polanyi wrote *The Great Transformation*. In one sense, it is a work which breaks down barriers between the social sciences and the arts. For if the former are concerned with aspects of collective human behaviour, in terms of what has existed or exists now, the arts—above all, literature—are concerned with personal fulfilment, in the sense of what human beings might have been and may yet become.

Karl Polanyi was of that generation for whom appreciation of artistic culture was a natural accompaniment of specialized scholarship in other areas. He brought to his writings on economics the fruits of his reading in literature and philosophy. Thus not only could he describe—he could also evaluate and query—the results of industrialism and relate them to ultimate questions of human destiny: noting, for example, that "it was in relation to the problem of poverty that people began to explore the meaning of life in a complex society." (p.85) That Polanyi's approach was a cultural one is indicated by his critique of "blind improvement": "the new creed [that] was utterly materialistic and believed that all human problems could be resolved given an unlimited amount of material commodities."[15] To economic analysis Polanyi added social, cultural, and spiritual dimensions. In particular, as we shall see, he argued that the economy is not a phenomenon of nature but is man-made, and for that reason must be subordinated to the needs of the whole man.

In Karl Polanyi's background there were at least four crucial encounters with literature, particularly poetry. First, there were the classics—particularly the Icelandic Sagas, Shakespeare, and Goethe—in which exemplary embattled protagonists freely choose to risk everything rather than compromise cherished principles of ethical and moral conduct. Second, there was the Hungarian poetry associated with the revolutions of 1848 and 1918-19, with its commitment to the nation, independence, and a redefined freedom of the person. Third, there was the impact of Polanyi's stay in England—in some respects a positive one, particularly in terms of his response to its literary tradition. Years before in Hungary, he may have been aware of the impact even there of the career and example of the socialist artist-craftsman William Morris, he who wrote that "the study of history and the love and practice of art forced me into a hatred of civilization which...would turn history into inconsequential nonsense, and make art a collection of the curiosities of the past, which would have no serious relation to the life of the present"[16]—for "civilization" read "capitalism." Also there were the critiques by leading English poets of the 1920s and 1930s: W.H. Auden (with whom Polanyi was on familiar terms) and T.S. Eliot whose long poem *The Waste Land* in some ways confirmed Polanyi's view of the degradation wrought by industrial market society. Fourth, there was the Hungarian Populist literary tradition which in Polanyi's view culminated in the revolution of 1956, embodying the humanistic essence of socialism and signifying what he termed "the third way."[17]

II

Economics and literature may be considered opposite poles of humanity's totality of production. They embody contrasting dimensions of our species's encounter with the natural world: that of the calculable material necessities of life, and that of those no less basic yet incommensurable human needs (social, emotional, psychological) where life is experienced most deeply. Two earlier contrasting examples of the combining of economics and literature, with which Karl Polanyi must have been familiar, come to mind. First, there is William Morris whose views on the arts in later years took on wider social dimensions following his decision to embrace socialism. Second, there is Karl Marx whose economic writings reveal virtually on every page his need to give emphasis and even legitimation to his arguments by quoting from and referring to the whole range of world literature.[18] But whereas Marx drew openly upon—indeed, often drew *into* his text—the literature of several cultures and periods, Karl Polanyi's direct references to authors and their works in *The Great Transformation* are surprisingly few. Thus, its Authors' Index reveals that there is no mention of any playwright—unlike Marx who frequently cited Shakespeare among others—not even Shaw. In the case of the latter this is curious, inasmuch as Polanyi always insisted on the Irish writer's greatness, pointing to his high status in the European theatre—"second only to Shakespeare"—and asserting that his relative neglect in England was due to his scathing criticism of society. At the end of his life Polanyi conceived his "New West Project," in one form of which Shaw was to have figured prominently; in another, he appears in a long list of prominent writers and artists (to be discussed later).[19]

The Great Transformation focuses on economic developments almost entirely in England. Thus, it would not be surprising were Polanyi to look to that nation's writers whose work, as others have shown, in many cases corroborates his thesis.[20] However, only six major figures are represented, and that by name only: William Blake, Daniel Defoe, Charles Dickens, Charles Kingsley, and D.H. Lawrence (the latter only for his "erotic vitalism," along with Stephan George [sic] in the context of a discussion of fascism and "irrationalististic philosophies").[21] Of these, three are simply listed together in the context of "outbursts of pain and anger that came from poets and philanthropists." (p.98) By contrast, the third-rate Hannah More is accorded several times the space allotted the others. The only work of a writer referred to is a didactic poem of hers entitled "The Riot, or, half a loaf is better than no bread" (to be sung to the tune of "A Cobbler there was"), written for housewives in 1795, criticizing "orderly rioting" as a *cause* of scarcity and economic danger.[22] Finally, there is an equally lengthy reference to a series of stories written by Harriet Martineau, *Illustrations of Political Economy*, whose "sumptuous volumes," "in which she undertook to enlighten the poor about the inevitability of their misery," Polanyi notes, were financed by two banking houses. (p.281)

We must therefore look elsewhere for literature in *The Great Transformation*—not for its presence, but its *influence*. Thus, from the very first page the reader is confronted with heightened language, its tone that of prophetic denunciation, while at the work's conclusion one is offered equally prophetic encouragement. Indeed, throughout Polanyi's master work we are presented with a redeeming vision of man's place in the realm of necessity, one transforming the hitherto "dismal science" into radiant science.

III

Polanyi's familiarity with the strategies of literature enlivens every page of *The Great Transformation*. He even shows, though it is a minor point here, that he shared with the novelist an interest in character—introducing representative figures in order to show their fate as "more directly determined" by the decisions of institutions than by personal choice[23]—while an often witty appreciation of the significance of detail[24] in contrasting images helps to focus the mind of the reader. However, most striking is the way Polanyi deploys all the resources of metaphor—with irony, contrast, paradox and contradiction—to express what he considers to be nothing less than the life and death drama being played out following the Industrial Revolution's entry upon the world stage and its resulting subordinating of human beings to the rule of things.

Polanyi's use of metaphor works in two ways. First, it assigns human significance to what would otherwise remain impersonal economic processes; second, it can constitute a reversing of the signs, giving negative signification to what conventional wisdom otherwise approves. Thus Polanyi presents the birth and development of the market economy not in terms of objective process but through depicting its impact upon human beings. Of that momentous epoch—elsewhere variously interpreted as Prometheus Unbound, storybook inventiveness, and heroic transformations of scale—Polanyi asks but one question: what has it meant for mankind? His answer is that not only has the quality of the life of the individual suffered in ways previously unimaginable, social life too has suffered—that is, where it has not been eradicated.

It is in order to express the enormity of such repercussions upon human beings—upon even nature itself—that Polanyi deploys a battery of no fewer than seventy-five epithets (nouns and adjectives) which fall into several groups. Most prominent are thirteen related terms expressing the destructiveness and catastrophic nature of the industrial system.[25] Such ills visited upon a helpless humanity caused the individual to be ground down—the metaphor of the "mill" predominating (though without acknowledgement to William Blake)—into the masses.[26] The resultant abuse, moral debasement, paralysis and psychological unease are represented by no fewer than fifteen terms [27]; sickness, decay and gross horror by some four others.[28] The single most elaborated metaphor is that of water, signifying instability, liquidity, ungovernable force, and the engulfing of society within "the maelstrom of the market"—extending over the Seven Seas—wherein swim "financial sharks": some twenty terms,[29] several occuring as early as the second page of the book in an extended passage elsewhere unequalled in intensity.

> No explanation can satisfy which does not account for the suddenness of the cataclysm. As if the forces of change had been pent up for a century, a torrent of events is pouring down on mankind. A social transformation of planetary range is being topped by wars of an unprecedented type in which a score of states crashed, and the contours of new empires are emerging out of a sea of blood. But this fact of demoniac violence is merely superimposed on a swift, silent current of change which swallows up the past often without so much as a ripple on the surface! A reasoned analysis of the catastrophe must account for both the tempestuous action and the quiet dissolution. (p. 4)

Land, in its turn, is invoked in eight terms representing it as a shifting earthquake-prone entity.[30] Warfare and its correlatives constitute the ultimate image of such a transformation's violent change, as market practices transmute human relationships into a "struggle for survival."(p.28) The organizing of "almost" every colonial war had become the responsibility of financiers.(p.16) In the wider context of competition, now the guiding principle of economic relations, Polanyi deploys some ten or more metaphors of aggression and conquest including annihilation[31]; death (and "living death"), torture and slavery (some seven terms) are humanity's past and present fate.[32] All this had been brought about by money embodied in grotesque forms: ranging from the "metaphysical extraterritoriality" of *haute finance*, to the gold standard's "shores" which are metamorphosed into a pillar (that broke), then a golden thread (that snapped), then "an elastic band of amazing strength" or "thread in the international monetary network."[33]

Polanyi's use of metaphor elaborates on the theme of disintegration, through emphasizing the human cost of innovation in the production and exchange process. It follows then that dehumanization is Polanyi's most serious charge against the market system. Here the underlying literary inspiration seems most strong, for, as Polanyi revealing observes, the "icy silence" maintained by economists on the system's fateful consequences contrasts with literary writers' views "that the very image of man had been defiled." (p.98) From the very first page Polanyi writes as one who, looking back across human history, sees a falling off in the values guiding conduct. Capitalism had degraded the working class—though not without the "owning classes" themselves having thereby become morally degraded. He saw dehumanization as overwhelmingly the fate of the labouring classes, those who were rendered scarcely human any more, "specters that might haunt a nightmare," "detribalized, degraded natives of their time."[34] Polanyi even constructs an image to represent market-mutated man: "We might as well imagine his being born without hands and feet as carrying on his life without land." (p.178)

Far from being hyperbole, Polanyi's use of metaphor is in accordance with the strategy employed by great writers to reveal dimensions of signification behind what otherwise might pass for the ordinary. Thus, he broke through the screen of convention, the shell of technical language, the veil of "icy silence" of those who ignored or tolerated the abuses of the market system. Some of Polanyi's references have a distinctly up-to-date relevance, in relation say to our globally oriented epoch[35] and business ideology's concern for balanced budgets.[36] He is particularly effective in exposing the contradictions that abounded, all stemming from that much-heralded "improvement" which nevertheless generated such unexpected and harmful (yet accepted) by-products during the Industrial Revolution[37]: the view that conflict (even though it might destroy the individual) coexisted with inherent harmony (pp.85,102), the belief that pauperism and progress were inseparable (pp.103,93), the conviction that increasing unemployment went hand-in-hand with increasing wealth (which leading theorists were quick to regard as inevitable[38], although the wealthiest were afforded protection denied the poor[39]), the identifying of "freedom" with "free enterprise" (despite "the hard reality" of great trusts and monopolies). (p.257)

IV

In one sense it is drama that characterizes Polanyi's account of the grim conflict unfolding from the Agricultural Revolution up until World War Two. The successive stages of the action are presented dramatically, as is also the conflict of principle—represented by the individual apparently set against society—upon which hinges what is made to seem the plot. But conspicuous by its absence is any allusion to what unfolds as amounting to tragedy. This is no story of "the lights going out all over Europe" nor funeral dirge for "the world we have lost" such as have decorated so many pages over the past century. Polanyi's account is not a threnody, but a downright good riddance. That is why, despite the variety of epithets expressing the destructiveness of the process, Polanyi never refers to what occurred as tragedy.[40] Nor does he characterize his account as drama, though he does identify certain episodes as scenes and scenarios. (pp. 4, 23) Still, against a backdrop of contradictions, Polanyi can refer to actors on the stage of history as puppets, in what at times seems to be some monstrous theatre of the absurd.[41]

In what amounts to a great drama of transformation, Polanyi presents for the most part an extended final act, one of climax and promised resolution. Not, however, without a rivetting Prologue, flashbacks and comments by the author as Chorus that keep the audience on the edge of their seats. The curtain rises on the opening sentence that rings out like a pistol shot: "Nineteenth century civilization has collapsed"! Thereafter in quick succession follow four similar references on the first two pages to civilization's downfall or self-destruction. (pp.3-4) These set the stage in starkly dramatic terms. If there is no tragedy, no noble-souled protagonist to engage our sympathies, nevertheless we encounter in due course the art of tragedy's device of the fatal flaw—disintegration from internal strains and stresses resulting from the "all too simple" precarious foundations of a system overcome by "the awful suddenness" which took the world "completely by surprise."[42] It is a process that is anything but ennobling, certainly not cathartic. We may conclude that we are witnessing Grand Guignol rather than Greek Tragedy, complete with the spectacle of "new empires [that] are emerging out of a sea of blood." (p.4)

V

Polanyi's book describes a transformation in which humanity has been atomized and subordinated to material imperatives as never before, and he argues for a counterbalancing transformational return to mankind's homeland of the social. In so doing he adduces perspectives more appropriate to the art of literature with its human dimensions of self-realization as yet unknown or at least untried. Such a sensibility is of course almost always profoundly subversive of the existing order. To this extent Polanyi's strategy and style—confronting the negative effects of the commodification of labour, land, and money—combine to work for its negation. Such a procedure opposes an alternative vision or way of seeing to the flawed conventional view. Accordingly, Polanyi depicts looming civilizational breakdown as the consequence of the prevailing view that is "limited" by the market that has "fragmented life," one operating blindly on the basis of "fictions" (a term often repeated), fallacy, and false psychology.[43]

In Polanyi's view the post-Christian era of Western civilization has long begun, man's condition now being an "awful revelation that transcended the New Testament," littered with the "empty husks" of faith. (pp.258A, 171) It is in connection with conventional wisdom's faulty vision—resulting from "economic superstition"—that the majority of Polanyi's religious references occur. They express, as we may expect, self-limiting material fixation, rather than spiritual exaltation.[44] *Laissez-faire* was now the fervently held "militant creed" with its drive of uncompromising ferocity, a secular religion of secular salvation. Faith was invested in international free trade. (p.138) Like a new deity, the gold standard is also "the faith of the age," "the invisible reality," (p.25) even a satanistic creed, engendering "war between heaven and hell." It is Polanyi's conviction that the market system had been elevated to a realm beyond debate; it had become economic superstition embraced with the "fanaticism of sectarians" exhibiting "evangelical fervour" for "soulless institutions" whose blind action disrupted civilization.[45]

The notion of appplying the terminology of religion to the prevailing acceptance of the market system was of course Polanyi's. Yet conventional discourse went even further—thus incurring the full force of Polanyi's irony—by dignifying the operation of the market with the authority of law, of nature itself even. In previous ages, he observes, while it is true that thinkers had sought to discern some law underlying human existence, the point is that "they thought of it as a human law." (p.114) However, in the industrial market era "society was subjected to laws that were not human laws." (p.125) The ultimate contradiction was that "law and order" were regarded as being ensured by *laissez-faire*! (p.117) Such laws destroyed human solidarity, because "compassion was removed from the hearts" of men.(p.102) Bentham thought that he had discovered a new social science, that of morals and legislation (p.120); the law in this context was a "link," as of a chain constituting the "iron regularities" of the law of wages and the law of population.[46] The very different views of Godwin and Owen related to the issue with which Polanyi closes his work, that of the limits confronting man.[47] It is to Owen that Polanyi gives credit for deducing that, though there are indeed laws of the market, their applicability to society must be limited, for the "market economy if left to evolve according to its own laws would create great and permanent evils." (p.130)

To substantiate supposed economic laws, the conventional wisdom felt it could count on the support of an authority by then more prestigious than religion—namely, through science, that of nature itself. For Burke and Bentham "the laws of commerce were the laws of nature and consequently the laws of God." (p.117) Contemporary enthusiam at the apparent discovery of laws "governing a complex society" generated both hope and despair. (p.84) For it was one thing to appeal to the calm authority of science—concerning which, as Ricardo said, within the economy "the principle of gravitation is not more certain"—but quite another to accept that nature's laws were brutish, inexorable, and condemning of mankind to "the sanction of the jungle."[48]

This is far indeed from literature's traditional view of Nature as sylvan paradise, abode of spirits, exemplar and wise teacher. Philosophical materialism lay close beneath the surface of the market system's conception of life. Science too came under its sign, as "naturalism haunted the science of man." (p.126) And for good reason. Policies which were assumed to be natural could thus be accorded the authority of science, absolving their human practitioners—the class of owners who provided work (and therefore the means of life itself) to the people—from any personal, social, or economic responsibility. Such a science was of the natural, not the social, world. Thus, "the law of wages could ... be deduced from the naturalistic facts of the fertility of man and soil"; (p.123) poverty itself could thereby be justified by market society's claim to embody the laws of nature.[49] Of course, this was yet another illusion. The conventional wisdom that markets "were natural institutions, that they would spontaneously arise," because "grounded in the immutable characteristics of the race" was totally unfounded. (pp.249-50) Polanyi shows that "there is nothing natural about *laissez-faire*," that it was "enforced by the state," and maintained by centrally-organized interventionism."[50]

The corollary of the market system's claim to be immanent in natural law was its thrust—virtually accomplished, in Polanyi's view—towards what today is called globalization. In *The Great Transformation* Polanyi repeatedly refers to "mankind," the race, even unborn generations[51] as being entangled in "the financial web" overlaying the planet.[52] The result was that—in contradiction of the proudly individualist assumptions of capitalist ideology—uniformity overlay the globe.[53] First to be affected were those countries most directly responsible for initiating and developing the Industrial Revolution "irrespective of national mentality and history." (p.217) The "pernicious" nineteenth-century dogma of the "necessary uniformity" of domestic regimes and systems within the orbit of the world economy resulted in a situation in which by the end of the century "the peoples of the world were institutionally standardized to a degree unknown before." (p.253)

VI

It is when referring to the phenomenon of work that Polanyi is most incisive in his cultural critique of capitalism. "Unheard of material welfare" was brought about by "an almost miraculous improvement" in the instruments of production and economic resources. (p.3) Though it was an essentially "blind" process according with no conceivably human design, it was ominously "destined to become a new form of life."[54] It was blind to its origins also—as Polanyi points out in a famous concluding passage—for the market was created not by autonomous processes but by conscious government intervention.[55] Polanyi's objections follow from his insistence that it must be society that should define the economy's goals in distinctively human terms. Thus he rejects the conventional view that "improvement" by itself will solve not only whatever problems the growth of material wealth might bring—but *all* human problems.[56] The issue of waste through overproduction in the industrial process is but touched on, for his emphasis is upon the greater evil: namely, that human life, persons, values, mankind itself are being reduced to the status of commodities.[57] This theme is made more explicit in his all-embracing concern lest market mechanisms "dispose of the physical, psychological, and moral entity 'man.'" (p.73) The danger stemmed from misinterpretation, where misbegotten fiction—not that of literature, in which authentic human experience was central—reduced human nature to one or more mechanical drives. Thus Polanyi accuses classical economists of basing their view of human behaviour upon "a system of crude fictions" at the level of unsupported, yet sheltering generalities—whether it was the broad optimism of Smith, or Townsend's belief that men "were *actually* beasts" for whom failure would simply result in their paying "the debt to nature." (pp.73, 113-4)

What does it mean to be human, to experience one's humanity, to have the means truly to experience fullness of being? These Polanyi defines in terms of what has been lost. He recounts how Speenhamland was the first attempt to guarantee "the right to live," one soon negated by the counter-right of the newly empowered middle class to inflict "scientific methods of mental torture." (pp.78, 225) Only state action, he declares, can guarantee the right of the individual to a job.[58] Only through the redemption of working people—now victims, but also harbingers of liberated humanity's future—can the industrial system be made responsible.[59] But how far there was—there is, still—to go! During the rise of the market economy, workers existed in conditions reminiscent of Dante's *Inferno* to which there even appears to be a reference (p.156). Condemned to life in darkness, like animals in the mire, lacking humanity in any shape or form—Polanyi's opinions bring to mind William Morris's condemnation of the worker's lot: "to expend all the divine energy of man in competing for something less than a dog's lodging and a dog's food."[60] It was as if workers were without a country, homeless, degraded to the level of colonial peoples, to that of the animal kingdom even.[61] That Polanyi's concern was with the fate of ordinary human beings is confirmed by his original choice of title for his masterwork, "The Common Man's Master Plan."[62]

The passion of Polanyi's thorough-going indictment comes close to submerging the second part of his thesis: namely, the double movement, in which humanity displays innate powers of resistance to the market system. Such resistance took two forms. On the one hand there was the phenomenon of the Chartist Movement, and in particular Robert Owen whose motives were based on an appreciation of man "as a whole," which confirmed the resilience of human creative vigour. On the other, there was that twentieth-century revolutionary (*and* counter-revolutionary) *élan vital* pressing impatiently towards new solutions, even at the risk of totalitarianism.[63] Such creative responses were not, and could not have been, economic in essence, but rather cultural. Polanyi returns repeatedly to his cultural point of departure, insisting that the degradation of the masses was not economic in essence, but "primarily" due to the disintegration of cultural institutions and practices.[64]

If redemption will come through security of work, it is at this basic level of man's encounter with the material world that Polanyi's account draws closest to the realm of art, and to William Morris's indictment: "what a hideous injustice it must be for society to compel most men to labour without pleasure!"[65] Thus, at the close Polanyi touches on the issue of work, not in terms of the making of an artefact, but as an activity undertaken out of motives other than monetary, whose rewards are "emotional."[66] In his "Notes on Sources" under the revealing sub-heading "Joy," Polanyi shows how close he is to Morris's view—and that of Marx—as to the potentially fulfilling nature of the labour process: "The usual incentives to labour are not gain but reciprocity, competition, joy of work, and social approbation." (p.271) In support of this vision Polanyi quotes from Malinowski concerning how tribal peoples devote much time and labour to "aesthetic purposes," far beyond the limits of the purely necessary, with no concern for payment. (pp. 46-7, 270-1)

In view of Polanyi's effective deployment of literary techniques and expression, it comes as less of a surprise that—as his literary anthology *The Plough and the Pen* makes clear—he viewed the imagination along with the aesthetic faculty as man's most valued creative attributes. However, he distinguished between, on the one hand aesthetic values—that may be exploited both in the contemplative sphere of individual refinement and (as in our time) by commercial interests—and on the other the broad range of moral and spiritual values which had application in a given culture. Thus, in his unpublished "New West Project," he wrote:

> There are signs of a barrenness of the Cultural West in its encounters with the world at large. What matters here is not the level of its achievements in literature and the arts, which flourish as only rarely before, but the weight and influence of its life values.[67]

Polanyi closes his masterwork with an implicit summons to creatively apply strategies of imagination to redefine values. Above all, he warned against persisting in capitalism's too narrow concept of freedom. As he put it, in an article written three years after the publication of *The Great Transformation*, we are lacking that inner freedom for which we are ill-equipped, being endowed with a social imagination that shows fatigue."[68] Yet Polanyi's thesis emphasises that there do exist "inner" resources which may be drawn upon. During the course of his book, he points to a countervailing vision. Contrary to the assertion that the free market is natural for humanity, Polanyi argues that, welling up from deep within man's nature, was a spontaneous movement of self-protection on the part of society.[69] Humanity thus demonstrated the existence of innate, unconscious reserves with which to resist the destruction of society and the impoverishment of motive.[70] Such reserves, he declares, will restore the priority of politics which will reintegrate economics within "institutions [which] are embodiments of meaning and purpose." (pp.195, 254-5) This will constitute a human society to which man ultimately must submit, for the sake of "man as a whole" without (as Owen put it) "childish unavailing complaints." (pp.167, 127) Polanyi's optimism was such that he could write, in 1944, of the recent past as one of transition in which "much of the massive suffering…is already behind us." (p.251)

The Great Transformation sets freedom within the context of realizable human culture in a literary connotation. Hitherto, Polanyi concludes, freedom had been "tainted at the source" through being the privilege of the propertied classes.[71] The sort of freedom that can now be had was that "which favoured moral freedom and independence of mind," in which the "republic of letters" would guarantee freedom of enquiry.[72] Thus, while asserting that man must be free to conceive of the need to expand freedom, he must resign himself to such limitations as are inevitable. Indeed, some may be of his own devising; being in the realm of the practical and desirable, they will be guarantees of the restoration and continuity of culture and society. It may be suggested that Karl Polanyi derived inspiration for such pronouncements from his lifelong association with literature. As a young man in Budapest, in his funeral speech on the death of the Endre Ady, he spoke of the responsibility of the individual to conceive of the possibility of change, and to implement it.

> The believer says—I shall change, and everything is changed. If I change just a little, then my world has already changed; and if everyone else also changes, then the whole world has changed. I measure action on the basis of the extent to which it serves my changing.[73]

Later, perhaps when the final pages of his great work were being written, after his return to London in 1943, Karl Polanyi discovered the work of the Hungarian proletarian lyric poet Attila József. One of the poet's most often quoted lines entirely accords with the sentiments expressed in Polanyi's closing pages: "Come freedom! Give birth to a new order."[74] The tradition of world art was another influence. Rejecting the notion of Art for Art's sake—as he did that of freedom for freedom's sake—in his concluding "Note," Polanyi observed that the achievement of Gothic architecture was compatible with economic regulation in the cities of the Middle Ages.[75] Almost thirty years would pass, before Karl Polanyi turned again to the Hungarian proletarian poet, this time to a verse on the degradation of working people, which concludes with lines which may be taken as reflecting Polanyi's view of the limits of freedom: "It illumines our power / for order and reality by which the mind will know / the finite frontiers of infinity."[76]

VII

Looking back on *The Great Transformation* at the end of his life, Karl Polanyi saw that the agenda he had outlined in its closing pages had still to be accomplished. In the intervening years he had confirmed its validity in two crucial areas. First, from his researches into ancient cultures he had deduced his theory of "embeddedness," the necessary subordinating of the economy to society. Second, with his increasing interest in literature, he found evidence of unsuspected dimensions of the human spirit which provided new perspectives on his conception of society.

For Karl Polanyi those were years of remarkable achievement. Ilona Duczynska described him as "glowing, productive, such as I cannot ever remember him before. [He is] so dynamic, that everyone around him is set in motion."[77] Polanyi himself wrote of his projects, "explosive growth lights up the landscape."[78] There was also retrospective self-evaluation in long, brooding letters. In one, a revealing image is suggestive both of his struggles with "embeddedness" and of more general personal striving, when he describes his task as having been "an uphill grind, to hurl at last the slippery stone of economistic prejudice over the summit into the abyss, only to have it hurtle back again and settle unharmed complacently on the ground floor, that shameless stone, as Homer calls it—!"[79]

This invocation of the founder of the Western poetic tradition, at around the time of his study of his successor Hesiod, serves to remind us of the breadth of Karl Polanyi's interest in that literary form. The image of the stone brings to mind not only the myth of Sisyphus, not only the Biblical injunction to give unto the needy bread rather than a stone, but also the notion that stones may best serve human ends when set in place, embedded as foundations for human habitation. In Polanyi's agenda there was more than one stone. He applied the same image to his and his wife's projected anthology of Hungarian literature, one that will "present the world with half a dozen granite blocks," which Ilona Duczynska herself described as "a monument."[80]

In these last years, Polanyi's new links with literature were little short of remarkable. There was the 1958 "New West" Project for what might be called cultural renewal. Undoubtedly, like others at that time, he was strongly influenced by the public role of writers in Eastern Europe and the Soviet Union. Polanyi criticizes the marginalization of writers and artists in the West, and in large measure looks to them in what he considers the main task lying ahead: "the subordination of science and technology, as well as economic organization to our will to human progress and to the fulfilment of personality has become a requirement of survival." As possible participants in this Project, he listed several authors from each of Britain, France, Germany, the Soviet Union and the United States, in addition to some from other countries (plus scientists, a film-maker, a painter, an actress and a dancer): in all a shrewdly judged sample that will repay further study.[81] More significant was Polanyi's continuing long-established contact with the eminent contemporary English poet W.H. Auden (who in 1935 contributed an essay to his *Christianity and the Social Revolution*, and in 1963 the Foreword to the Hungarian Anthology).[82] Polanyi's closest association with a poet was with the leading younger Hungarian poet Ferenc Juhász whose work was represented in the Anthology. Finally, there was the brief but admiring contact established in 1959 by the American poet Charles Olson, an inspirational figure for the avantgarde.[83] Karl Polanyi's increased emphasis upon literature stems from what he considered to be its ability to present a vision of the whole—the more necessary at a time when, as he wrote to Peter Drucker, one looked elsewhere in vain for a world-picture or world-perspective in any way associated with "the growing point of morality"; even the demands of "merely intellectual integrity" have little effect; instead, transitoriness and irrelevance rule, fear "excoriating our hearts and minds."[84]

For the achieving of Polanyi's goal of building a habitation for the livelihood of man, two things were necessary: form and vision. The first includes aesthetics of style and effectiveness of expression for the task at hand.[85] Polanyi rejected the current one-dimensional market-system discourse which claimed to speak for human motivation and social relations too. As Polanyi put it: "I am engaged in clearing up one small corner of the field" in the sense of trying to "relativize again the economic concern, and subordinate it to the greater concerns that are looming ahead."[86] His sensitivity to stylistic expression and willigness to deploy its resources were reflected, as has been shown above, in his own writing. Western culture's oft-remarked formalism suggested a poverty of both expression and vision, to remedy which became the main thrust of Karl Polanyi's work. As he put it in 1958, "New ground [is] to be broken in everything. (That's good 'New West')."[87] Polanyi's expectation as to the visionary potential of works of literature was forcefully expressed by the friend of his youth György Lukács who—coincidentally, in an essay composed one year prior to the publication of Polanyi's master work—wrote: "For this was and is the mission of poetry and fiction: to put questions, to raise problems in the form of new men and new fates of men," in "anticipation of the spiritual and moral development of the civilized world."[88] Not only did Polanyi look to literature for confirmation that a vision-creating capacity resided within man, some of his student-collaborators did likewise. Thus, George Dalton commented in a letter that he was "vastly moved" by the novels of Romain Gary and Isak Dinesen, and Paul Medow (to whom Polanyi wrote about Pasternak, Pushkin, and Tolstoy) declared his determination to devote part of his time to poetry and music, on the grounds—an interesting commentary on their association—that these were compatible with what he termed "the general sphere that now engages us both."[89]

That such interest was not misplaced was born out, for Karl Polanyi, by what he deemed to be the ability of works of literature to envision the future. Thus he declared—with typical panache and breadth of reference—that credit for initial moral insight into the coming doom of the competitive market economy should be given not to Marx, but Hegel—who, in turn, had derived it "more importantly" from Denis Diderot's then still unpublished novel *Rameau's Nephew*, as translated by the German poet Goethe![90] In the same context, Polanyi suggested that a key conversation, in Dostoyevsky's *The Brothers Karamazov* between Alyosha and Ivan, was revealing of the dialectic of pre-revolutionary Russia.

That literature can envision new possibilities as conceived by and for human beings, expressing the socially significant in terms of the personal, is what attracted Polanyi to the poetry of contemporary Hungary. Literature's strategy is to express such a vision in terms of the personal. He confessed to coming to it with a sense of relief, "having moved from the general to the particular," while regarding the latter as related to the social.[91] Some of the poems he could respond to with an intensity that seems to have surprised even him. He read, pondered, discussed, interpreted; some poems he translated, others he helped his wife to translate. He described the experience, speaking as one who had long been "listening to the breathing of mankind."

> I find myself straining to distinguish *one* people's moaning. Hence the anthology, the seeking for the mot juste in the sleepless hours, the epic of penetrating the meaning of poems, to decipher the patterns of lives—the inner lives—of their authors whose stutterings and hopes revealed reborn souls, the raw material of history still to be.[92]

Literature is uniquely expressive of human needs and capacities which find virtually no other public form of representation or outlet in present-day life. In arguing against what he saw as the repressive dominance of the market, Polanyi denounced its warping of human consciousness: externalizing those capacities which serve it, trivializing or suppressing those which do not. His response, in part, was to emphasis the importance of the countervailing "inner life." Far from being some sort of retreat for the privileged, this was a redoubt in which to devise strategies aiming at some second great transformation. However, the "inner life" requires expression, and this, Polanyi seemed to think, was most effectively achieved within the sphere of literature—or rather, great literature. Artistic expression is not immune from the grasp of the all too-solid fist of the "invisible hand." The commercialized culture of our time, Polanyi declared, "relegates the Muses to the status of the victims of the Marquis de Sade."[93] Accordingly, Polanyi looked for the most part to that least public—least marketable—art form, the one that has traditionally been the vehicle of the inner voice, lyric poetry. The poets' exclusion from market society might enable them to retain relative independence of conception and expression. (Though they too must beware of absolutizing freedom through "art for art's sake.") Among such poets Polanyi valued most those whose vision went beyond the present, combining a sense of the person with a consciousness of history.

In contrast, novelists tend to draw rather upon the present, and to subordinate the inner to outer life. This may explain why, on the few occasions when Polanyi expresses criticism, it is directed against certain novels—including the most famous—on account of their less than truthful vision of society. Thus Polanyi regretted that Pasternak, whom he admired, had in *Dr. Zhivago* omitted key aspects of social reality in the evolving Soviet Union; thus, since his work lacked "moral balance," he "cannot be accepted as the national poet as Pushkin or Tolstoy were."[94] George Orwell's *1984* struck Polanyi as representing an "absence of ideological preparedness [which] caused defensiveness" in a West consumed by a horror of communism, a "calumny of mankind," it expressed "a dangerous intolerance and a growing nihilistic defeatism."[95] No such charge could be laid against Karl Polanyi whose remarkable last phase commenced with the declaration: "I was always conscious of working for the future, only I never suspected it to be so near." What he proposed seems a direct response to *1984*: "my program was to prepare superior [ideological] positions." The commitment seemed timely for, as he wrote: "the end of Western-Americo-Russian materialism is in sight. The world is turning back from the so-called 'economic' to its 'moral and political' axis. Peace and freedom are the dominant concerns for the future."[96] It was a concern which would find expression in the "Co-existence" Project.

This turning towards the future was well expressed in the 4-line verse of Hegel which Karl Polanyi and Ilona Duczynska often cited, with its injunction to "Break with the values of the world"[97]—by extension, breaking the superimposed stone slab of the economy. Thus Polanyi wrote to his brother of the West's "true weakness" being "its lack of moral orientation," adding that "Unless we re-humanize how, we will survive for another few centuries without knowing what for."[98] A new calculus was required, replacing conventionally defined "efficiency" through "costing the ideal requirements of a humanly conceived society."[99]

That such a break with the present was both necessary *and* possible stemmed from Polanyi's faith in humanity's vision-creating capacity. It was also based upon his own experience in writing *The Great Transformation* of which he said: "the growing point of that book [was] that it was an embodiment of a *vision* of man's life in a definite *historical* period."[100] This reference to envisioning the past, through intensive study, confirms that Polanyi's notion of "vision" was grounded in reality. So it would be when applied to the future: the outwards-seeking dimensions and intensity of vision, on the part of a dynamic "inner life," being confirmed by observation of signifying phenomena. In a key letter (1959) Polanyi speaks of his method, as having

> ...an intuitive direction in which meaning is sought (that's the need of inner life, and hence justified)...The real question is what familiar inner experience is pivotal to the new vision? I believe that can emerge only out of those actual curiosities [sic] which drive us to empirical knowledge. Seeking such factual enlightenment the underlying drive defines itself, gets identified, life then has a voice to speak.[101]

Inasmuch as this vision of the future was that of a new world, a necessary one, it was "good," through being based upon—and answering to mankind's need for—moral worth. As Polanyi put it: "The world is turning back...to its 'moral and political' axis."[102] It was "its lack of moral orientation" that had been the West's "true weakness."[103]

We may now appreciate why it was the moral dimension in particular, in Hungarian poetry of the period 1930-56, that spoke so strongly to Karl Polanyi at this time. This was a poetry that had commenced by addressing what Polanyi calls "the human condition of the submerged peasant classes"—"from the Danube,

Jordan and Nile to the Pacific Ocean"—whose condition represented "as much, or more, of a moral vacuum" than "that of the urban West."[104] Then, in the 1950s, the poets strove to restore socialist practice to its moral foundations. Further, they did so despite deadly personal risk—inspiring Polanyi'a comment: "what ails me is not of a literary, nor of any aesthetic purport...My interest is in the moral values represented by the martyrs of the populist and revisionist cause."[105]

The resulting poetry gave passionate expression to values to which Polanyi had always appealed. "To my knowledge," he wrote, "there is no parallel in the history of Letters to the poetry of this period. (The better known Polish poets remain essentially on the political plane, they do not reach the level of personal lyricism."[106] In these poets the "inner life" had found its social voice. In an unpublished short speech, delivered in Toronto in 1959, when he participated in a public Poetry Reading, Polanyi declared that in Hungary "the poet became the living conscience of his country." The role of conscience is to acknowledge hitherto suppressed or ignored truths; it represents also consciousness of personal responsibility for error, and for remedying it. This Polanyi finds in the poetry of that time. As he put it in the course of his speech: "the most powerful strain in the poets' witness[ing] was self-accusation and remorse," culminating in "a passionate rededication to truth, to freedom of creative expression, to the motherland." The strength of this poetry was that it stood for restoration of the significance of the individual as responsible agent of history: it was "the voice of the Hungarian October, a voice in which lyrical poems and history are one."

Thus Karl Polanyi's interest in poetry culminated in the editing (with his wife Ilona Duczynska) of the Hungarian Anthology. Among the distinguished authors included there, he felt especially drawn to Ferenc Juhász (whose work was singled out for praise by W.H. Auden and George Steiner). He tape-recorded readings (with his wife) of some of Juhász's longer poems, one of which they read at the Poetry Reading in Toronto. He played a major part in translating much of the verse included in the volume.

One poem stands out as being of particular relevance to the present discussion. Of this an English version has survived in Polanyi's handwriting, together with some of his explanatory notes. In these Polanyi states that the poem recalls Marx's "Theses on Feuerbach" with its ideal of "human society"; but more particularly, that it represents "the crisis of 'Socialist Humanism' in a soul engulfed by a personal tragedy." Yet the poem concludes on an inspired, if sombre, note of confidence in the future. Its message, as indicated by its title, makes it of special relevance for Karl Polanyi's last years. That title is "Dreams Made to a Human Pattern"—which, in a note, Polanyi comments "is here certainly used to denote our dreams for the future."[107] Indeed, he could just as well have been speaking of his faith in the sort of future—based on personal reconciliation to the need to abandon dreams made to an inhuman pattern—presented in *The Great Transformation*.

NOTES

1. Karl Polanyi, *The Great Transformation: the Political and Economic Origins of our Time*. New York: Rinehart, 1944. Hereafter, page references only to the paperback edition: Boston: Beacon Press, 1957. Subsequent reference to the study as Polanyi's "masterpiece" is justified in view of the increasing attention that has been paid, since publication, to a work which in 1977 was numbered among "The Great Books" (*Time* magazine, 7 March), and in 1995 among "The hundred most influential books since the war" (*Times Literary Supplement*, 6 October).

2. In this, we are reminded of Polanyi's admiration for Hungary's greatest proletarian poet who, in 1933, wrote "Say what is true, not merely what is factual." Attila József, *Osszes versei* (Collected Poems). Budapest: Szépirodalmi könyvkiadó, 1975, p.351 "az igazat mondd, ne csak a valódit," from the poem "Thomas Mann üdvözlése" (Greetings for Thomas Mann"). Polanyi became aware of József's work only towards the end of the war in London.
3. "Vienna became the Mecca of liberal economists on account of a brilliantly successful operation on Austria's *krone* which the patient, unfortunately, did not survive," pp.23-4; for the common people "Vienna achieved one of the most spectacular cultural triumphs of Western history," being "a socialist municipality," pp.287-88.
4. The first reference is to the implications of the Poor Law Reform of 1834, p.82. And see Karl Polanyi, "The Essence of Fascism," pp.359-394 in John Lewis, Karl Polanyi & Donald K. Kitchin (eds.), *Christianity and the Social Revolution*. London: Gollancz, 1935, p.375.
5. For the utopian springs of the dogms of *laissez-faire* and the market, see pp.3, 141, 178, 250, 257-58.
6. Letter to Ilona Duczynska from Stephen Mummery, 23 August 1964.
7. "Our thesis is that the... self-adjusting market" "could not exist for any length of time without annihilating the human and natural substance of society; it would have physically destroyed man and transformed his surroundings into a wilderness." (p.3)
8. George Dalton, "Introduction" to *Primitive, Archaic and Modern Economies: Essays of Karl Polanyi*. New York: Doubleday, 1968, pp.ix-x. "The qualities that made him a brilliant lecturer also made him a difficult writer...what was forceful, lucid, and articulate in the lecture hall sometimes became hyperbole and polemic in print." Of the implications of such a pedestrian attitude, Ilona Polanyi commented, in a letter to Irene Grant, 1 December 1955, on a forthcoming book containing "Some 20 good-sized contributions, many from young scholars—born and bred at Columbia. God forgive them the language they (as they would say) utilize."
9. From "The Road to St.Petersburg" (1914), pp.279-81, in *Endre Ady. The Explosive Country. A Selection of Articles and Studies, 1898-1916*. Selection by Erzsébet Vezér. Introduction, essay, translation and annotation by G.F. Cushing. Budapest: Corvina Press, 1977.
10. Karl Polanyi, *The Livelihood of Man. Essays*. Edited by H.W. Pearson. New York: Academic Press, 1977, pp.147-57.
11. Ilona Duczynska & Karl Polanyi (eds.), *The Plough and the Pen: Writings from Hungary, 1930-56*. London: Peter Owen; Toronto: McClelland & Stewart, 1963.
12. "Szózat a Galilei Kör ifjúságához Polányi Károlynak Ady Endre emlékére tartott gyászünnepélyen mondott beszéde" (Invocation to the Youth of the Galilei Circle: Karl Polanyi's address at the memorial service of Endre Ady), manuscript. The first English translation is soon to be published.
13. Karl Polanyi, "Hamlet," *Yale Review*, Vol.43, No.3, March 1954, pp. 336-350.
14. Letter from Karl Polanyi to Kari Polanyi Levitt, "Notes on Premature Resignation," 25 April 1960.
15. See pp.249, 33, 40, 219; and p.133 for reference to the "almost sacramental belief in the universal beneficance of profits." The process was driven by "a mystical readiness to accept the social consequences whatever they might be," with "an uncritical reliance on the alleged self-healing virtues of unconscious growth" (p.33); economists ignored Adam Smith's "humanistic foundations." (p.115) More to the point, Polanyi complains, no consideration was given to the "rate of change" which he deemed to be of no less importance than the direction of change itself (p.36); this ought to have been the responsibility of government (p.37); the results made "nonsense of the legend of English gradualism." (p.101)
16. *Political Writings of William Morris*, edited by A.L. Morton. New York: International Publishers, 1973. From "How I Became a Socialist" (1894), p.245.
17. See Kenneth McRobbie, "From the Class Struggle to the 'Clean Spring'," pp. 45-80, in Kenneth McRobbie (ed.), *Humanity, Society and Commitment. On Karl Polanyi*. Montreal: Black Rose Books, 1994.
18. See S.S. Prawer, *Karl Marx and World Literature*. Oxford: Clarendon Press, 1976.
19. There are two handwritten lists, on filing cards. On one titled "NEW WEST" appear in alphabetical order, "Auden, Barbusse, Bártok, Brecht, Camus (?), Chaplin, Duncan [Isadora?], Dreiser, Einstein, France, Gide, József, Koestler, Malraux, Moissi, Lukács, Mann, O'Casey, O'Neill, Orwell, Oppenheimer, Russell, Reed, Rivera, Sartre, Shaw, Silone, Weigel [Helene, Brecht's wife, the actress]." On another card there appears to be a rough preliminary listing, with "Cocteau, Ossjetzky, Pilassov"; crossed out are "Mrs Roosevelt, Seghers." In another hand, on the reverse, occur the names: "Bunyan, D'Annunzio, Ehrenburg, Gorky, Hamsun, Hemingway, Kipling, Maierkowski, Neruda, Nexo (Andersen), Pasternak, Rilke, Sinclair (Upton), Steinbeck, Tagore, Wilson (Edmund)."
20. "Writers of all views...invariably referred to social conditions under the Industrial Revolution as a veritable abyss of human degradation," p.39; "a galaxy of poets, thinkers and writers had branded its cruelties," p.156. By comparison, Polanyi writes of publicists in the inter-war years, "The writers of that period excelled in lack of realism," p.189.

21. William Blake p.98; Daniel Defoe pp. 108ff., 284; Charles Dickens p.98; Charles Kingsley pp.98, 158; D.H. Lawrence p.238; "Stephan George" p.238; Ludwig Klages p.238.
22. See pp.295, 170-1, 186.
23. Thus, the "influence of monetary protectionism" is considered. (p.205) "What the businessman, the organized worker, the housewife pondered, what the farmer who was planning his crop, the parents who were weighing their children's chances, the lovers who were waiting to get married, resolved in their minds when considering the favor of the times, was more directly determined by the monetary policy of the central bank than by any other single factor."
24. Two examples have Polanyi's characteristic ironic edge, and, perhaps by contrasting female fertility with denial, remind one of Polanyi's association with the city of Freud. See "International disequilibrium may occur for innumerable reasons—from a dynastic love affair to the silting up of an estuary," p.9; concerning Malthus, "his tendentious warnings of overpopulation [were not] effective with the brides to whom he delivered them personally," p.288.
25. The word-count here and in succeeding footnotes is representative. "Destruction" pp. 25, 76, 77, 77, 157, 223, 224, 246; "catastrophe" pp.4, 33, 35, 39, 40, 76, 157, 157, 173, 234; "calamity" pp.82, 157, 297, 303; "cataclysm" pp.4, 157, 303; "corrosive" p.33; "liquidation" p.246; "devastating" p.157; "unprecedented havoc" p.39; "peril" pp.39, 76; "ravages" p.76; "collapse" p.234; "desolation" p.224; "dislocation" pp.76, 76, 214.
26. "Terrible injuries inflicted on the substance of the race" by World War One, p.21; "What 'satanic mill' ground men into masses?" pp.33, 39; "the mill of the market which ground the lives of the people" p.226; the "labor mill" p.82.
27. "Moral debasement" p.169; "viciously" p.225; "degradation" pp. 39, 80, 157; "inhuman methods" p.77; "awful beyond description" p.76; "horrors" pp.39,102; "scourge" p.215; "pernicious" p.76; "perdition" p.39; "cruelty" p.224; "penalizing" p.224; "fate" p.224; "paralysis" p.236; "dismal feeeling" p.224; "perversion" p.224.
28. "Vomited forth" p.39; "ghastly" p.80; "rot" p.83.
29. "Maelstrom" p.192; "tempestuous action" p.4; "torrent" p.4; "turbulent waters" p.94; "indomitable surge" p.89; "vortex" p.94; "flux and reflux" p.94; "flood" pp.94, 296; "a dam had to be erected to protect the village from the flood of rising wages... to prevent the draining off of rural labor," p.94; "the dam burst, and the old world was swept away in one indomitable surge" p. 89; "swallow up" p.4; "engulfed" p.219; "swift, silent current" p.4; "unpredictable eddies" p.218; "ripple on the surface" p.4; "awful capsize" p.233; "quiet dissolution" p.4; "dissolved" p.4; "commerce in the Seven Seas" p.89. In profitable waters, there swam "financial sharks" p.24.
30. "Earthquake" pp.157, 213; "avalanche of social dislocation" pp.40, 92; "destructive landslides" p.157; "undermined" p.92; "abyss" p.39; "uprooted" p.92; "crumbling existence" p.25; "chasm" p.24.
31. "Struggle for survival" p.28; "hurled themselves into wars to enslave the world" p.28; "the war" of the Agricultural Revolution p.92; "battle" together with epithets "fought," "lost," and "struggle" p.223 and elsewhere; "demonic forces of aggression and conquest" of fascism in relation to the market" p.251; "annihilation" as threat pp. 42,76; "scourge" p.92; "dangers" p.189; "peril" p.189; "fear" pp.189, 236.
32. "Death" p.83; "living death" p.292; "kill that which is doomed to die" p.246; "psychological torture" p.82; "psychological and moral torture" pp.102, 215; "mental torture" p.225; "enslave the world" p. 28.
33. See pp.10, 14, 20-27, 202, 232.
34. On the very opening page, Polanyi declares that the "self-adjusting market" would have "physically destroyed man" (p.3), he who has been reduced to "the [new] concept of the Economic Man" p.43. Thereafter, it is the masses of the people who undergo, because more passively, the rude transformation. "The Two Nations were taking shape," replacing "the traditional unity of a Christian society"; in the one were "huge masses of the population [who] resembled more the specters that might haunt a nightmare than human beings," "physically dehumanized"; in the other "the owning classes [who] were morally degraded," p.102; "veritable abyss of human degradation" p.39; "Speenhamland was an unfailing instrument of popular demoralization" p.99; "the countryfolk had been dehumanized into slum dwellers" p.39; "the dehumanization of the masses" p.98, represented "unprecedented debasement of the laboring classes" p.288; "so much misery and debasement" p.157; in the factory they were "degraded, and tortured" p.165; for the parallel with tribal peoples, p.290. Their lives having become "contorted" (p.225), the people had become "none too precious beasts" (p.83) who had "almost lost their human shape" p.82.
35. Thus, "for the economist, no nations existed, transactions were carried on not between nations but between individuals, whose political allegiance was as irrelevant as the color of their hair" pp.195-6.
36. "*Laissez-faire* was planned; planning was not" p.141; not omitting the mirage of the balanced budget: "Gladstone had made the budget the conscience of the British nation" p.227.
37. Thus, "it was improvement on the grandest scale which wrought unprecedented havoc" p.39.

38. In Chapter 9, entitled "Pauperism and Utopia": "Adam Smith ... declared that it is not in the richest countries that the wages of labor are highest. M'Farlane was not, therefore, venturing an unusual view when he expressed his belief that as England had now approached the meridian of her greatness, the 'number of poor will continue to increase' " p.103.
39. "Even capitalist business itself had to be sheltered from the unrestricted working of the market mechanism" p.192.
40. Aside from a reference to "the authenticated tragedies of small children" (p.156) only the adjective "tragic" appears, and that but three times, related to particular phenomena, but carrying no overall signification (pp.30, 34, 250). Indeed, Polanyi is critical of Edmund Burke's manipulative use of the term, because he "exalted brute fact into tragedy, and invested sentimentality with the halo of mysticism." p.118.
41. "Nations and peoples were mere puppets in a show utterly beyond their control" within world trade, "this gargantuan automaton." p.217. Reference is made to "the absurd device" of permanent disarmament, p.22; to the "absurdity" of unemployment p.215. And "the common-sense attitude towards change was discarded in favor of mystical readiness to accept the social consequences of economic improvement, whatever they be," p.33.
42. See pp. 249, 4, 20.
43. "Vision was limited to the market," "society as a whole remained invisible" p.258; "the radical illusion," p.258, "moral illusionism" p.258A; "blindly," p.102, is one of many such references, including "blind faith ... the fanaticism of sectarians"; p.76 "fictions," pp.73 (twice), 75, and elsewhere; "fallacy" and "false" psychology (p.44) concern the "concept of the Economic Man." p.43.
44. "Faith" p.25, particularly "blind faith," "mystical" ("mystical Readiness" p.33) and "dogma" are the terms occuring most frequently. The gold standard was "the faith of the age," "the invisible reality," operating "miraculously" p.25.
45. The gold standard was "a satanistic creed" contributing to "war between heaven and hell" p.25. The "awful revelation that transcended the New Testament" (p.171) resembled a "secular religion" p.102; its appearance was "comparable... only to the most violent outburst of religious fervor in history" p.30. "The post-Christian era of Western civilization had begun, in which the Gospels did not any more suffice, and yet remained the basis of our civilization" p.258A. In Europe, capitalist countries proclaimed themselves christian: "Only resignation to the inevitable laws of the market could explain the proud acquiescence with which the cross was borne," p.215.
46. See pp. 28, 36, 38, 39, 57, 85 (3 refs.), 126.
47. "Godwin believed in unlimited possibilities and hence had to deny the laws of the market." In contrast, though for very different reasons, for Ricardo and Malthus "the laws of the market meant ... the limit of human possibilities," while Owen (with whom Polanyi concurs) saw that "human possibilities were limited [only]...by the laws... of society itself." p.85.
48. By 1834 there was awareness of the "inexorable brute laws" (p.84) imposing "awful limitations; "the law of diminishing returns was a law of plant physiology" p.125. Also pp.125-127.
49. Thus "these laws were put under the authority of Nature herself" p.125; "the self-regulating market was now believed to follow from the inexorable laws of Nature" p.127; "Essentially, economic society was founded on the grim realities of Nature" p.125; "the laws of a competitive society were put under the sanction of the jungle" p.125. In sum, as Polanyi indicates at the beginning of Chapter 3 (I. Satanic Mill) a new fate awaited the human race in the industrial age—for the non-industrialized countries were not to be spared—namely: "a new integration of man and nature" was attempted—fortunately "unsuccessfully." p.33.
50. See pp.132, 139-41, 148-49, 189, 192, 201-2, 205-6.
51. "Only a madman would have doubted that the international economic system was the axis of the material existence of the race" p.18; the market system affected "yet unborn generations." p.130.
52. References to mankind begin on p.4; "thus was mankind forced into the paths" p.81; "the whole of mankind" p.104; "worldly civilization" p.209; "every part of the globe" p.130; "planetary range" p.4; "one indomitable surge towards a planetary economy" p.89; "the financial web... entangled... the planet" p.233.
53. Thus "over the greater part of the world, civilization was of the same fabric" p.209; "a new way of life spread over the planet" p.130; "organization of life on the planet" p.217; this civilization had "a claim to universality" p.130, in "its elaborateness and its universality" p.253; it was an "enforced uniformity," p.253; there was a "singularly uniform pattern of history during this period." p.209.
54. There had been "an almost miraculous improvement," together with the "alleged self-healing virtues of unconscious growth" p.33; "a century of blind 'improvement,'" "prosperity of gigantic proportions... destined to become a new form of life" p.104; also pp. 39,73,219.
55. See for "an emotional faith in spontaneity" p.33; "a belief in spontaneous progress must make us blind" p.37; "a blind faith in spontaneous progress" p.76; the national market was "in no way the result of ... gradual and spontaneous action," but "on the contrary, the market has been the

outcome of a conscious and often violent intervention on the part of government which imposed the market on society for non-economic ends" p.250.
56. For the "uncritical reliance on the alleged self-healing virtues of unconscious growth" p.33; it was "a revolution... [whose] new creed was utterly materialistic and believed that all human problems could be resolved given an unlimited amount of material commodities" p.40.
57. Machine production brought about "no less a transformation than that of the natural and human substance of society into commodities" p.42; this was "the commodity fiction" pp.73, 75.
58. "The list should be headed by the right of the individual to a job" p.256; "the worker has no security in his job under a system of private enterprise," being continually under "the threat of mass unemployment." p.231.
59. Thus "the laboring people...became representatives of the common human interests that had become homeless" p.133.
60. The worker has been "transformed into a nondescript animal of the mire," one who was "denied the human shape of life" p.99; one of "the dark mass." p.226. And see Morris, *Political Writings*, "Art under Plutocracy," p.73.
61. The immigrant peasant was "denied the human shape of life" p.99; for the parallel with slaves p.166; in the concluding pages (Notes, p.290) Polanyi likened the labouring people's "analogous dehumanization" to the degraded state of the colonial peoples; "a stoic determination to renounce human solidarity." p.102. "By the 1830s the social catastrophe of the common people was as complete as that of the Kaffir is today." p.294. Owen "rejected the animalistic approach to society" p.127; men as "none too precious beasts," p.83.
62. As it appeared upon an initial contract, dated 13 April 1943.
63. For Owen, pp.167-9. A society which "still possessed the resilience required for a creative effort so imaginative and sustained, must have disposed of almost boundless intellectual and emotional vigour." p.169. But there was also "The élan vital which produced the inscrutable urge in the German and Russian people to claim a greater share in the record of the race." p.29.
64. See pp.157, 163, 290-2.
65. *Political Writings*, "Art under Plutocracy," p.67.
66. "Frank H. Knight's 'no specifically human motive is economic'" p.250; "other motives than those directly involved in money incomes may outweigh by far the financial aspect of labour" p.251; "economic motives *per se* are notoriously much less effective with most people than so-called emotional ones." pp.218-19.
67. Karl Polanyi, "For a New West," manuscript, 21 September 1958.
68. Karl Polanyi, "Our Obsolete Market mentality," *Commentary*, Vol.3, No.2, February 1947, 109, 115.
69. Directed against society being run "as an adjunct of the market," p.57; "man's nature," p.249; "a deep-seated movement" grew up and "unconsciously resisted" in order to protect itself from what was "entirely unnatural" pp.76-77, 249; this was spontaneous p.141. It later took the form of protectionism and fascism, also socialism which "consciously" was "merely the continuation" of the endeavour begun much earlier. pp.200, 234.
70. Thus, Polanyi clebrates the resistance that first occured in response to the growing problem of poverty (p.85)—a cultural phenomenon, he insists (p.157)—prompting discussion ranging from revolution to non-violent resistance. pp.93, 169. The assumption is that society can creatively continue to transform itself in order to contain new challenges—Owen's vision of a new society as being the only way to contain the machine—in order that economics not swallow society. p.170.
71. "The comfortable classes enjoy the freedom provided by leisure and security" p.254; "Freedom not as an appurtenance of privilege, tainted at the source." p.256.
72. "Science and the arts should always be under the guardianship of the republic of letters." p.255.
73. See note 12.
74. Attila József, *op. cit.*, p.325 "Jöjj el, szabadság! Te szülj nekem rendet," from the (1935) poem "Levegöt!" (Air!).
75. In this he followed the great Belgian economic historian Henri Pirenne, p.279. Living in England at that time was another Hungarian and near contemporary, the art historian Arnold Hauser who also wrote that great art was compatible with authority, or in other words limitation upon its freedom. See Arnold Hauser, *The Social History of Art*. London: Routledge & Kegan Paul, 1951, Vol. 1, p.47 "in reality the presuppositions on which the aesthetic quality of a work depends lie beyond the alternative presented by political freedom and compulsion."
76. Attila József, *op.cit.*, p.283 "Míg megvalósúl gyönyörű / képességünk, a rend / mellyel az elme tudomásul veszi / a véges végtelen...," from the (1933) poem "A város peremén" (On the City's Rim).
77. Letter from Ilona Duczynska to Irene Grant, 20 July 1957. She said that she and Karl share the work "in common," that it is "a full-time occupation, a passion, monument."
78. Letter from Karl Polanyi to Hans Zeisel, undated but probably 1958. He concludes with Tolstoy's injunction: "work as if you lived for ever."

79. Letter from Karl Polanyi to Professor Aberle, 30 November 1959.
80. Letter from Karl Polanyi to Hans Zeisel, 1958; letter from Ilona Duczynska to Irene Grant, 9 January 1957.
81. See note 18 for the listing. And see Karl Polanyi, "For a New West" (manuscript), 21 September 1958. "The voice of that cultural entity, the Western mind, the thinkers and writers who were its traditional vehicles, is no longer listened to... because it has nothing of importance to say." "The thinkers, writers and artists, denuded of a substance of their own, shut their eyes to reality."
82. *Christianity and the Social Revolution*. Part I, Chapter 1 "The Good Life," pp.31-50. *The Plough and the Pen*. Foreword, pp.9-11.
83. Olson visited Toronto in 1959 to give a Reading, learned that the Polanyis lived in nearby Pickering, and wrote to Karl Polanyi to express his admiration for the work of his sister, Laura Striker Polanyi, whose research on Captain John Smith (founder of the State of Virginia, and the dominant figure in Olson's great poetic opus "Maximus") demonstrated that Smith's autobiographical accounts (hitherto assumed to be fabrications) of his military exploits in Transylvania, were indeed fact. For details, see Hans Zeisel, "In Memoriam," pp.241-44, in Kari Polanyi Levitt (ed.), *The Life and Work of Karl Polanyi*. Montreal: Black Rose Books, 1990.
84. Letter from Karl Polanyi to Peter Drucker, 14 November 1958.
85. There exists a minor but significant example, in a copy of the *Bennington College Bulletin*, dated September 1942 (a quarterly prospectus amounting to 76 pages), in which the first eleven pages on the aims of the College bear numerous corrections in ink, in Karl Polanyi's hand. See also note 8, for Ilona Duczynska's critical comment on the literary style of Karl's students (letter dated 1 December 1955).
86. Letter from Karl Polanyi to Michael Polanyi, 23 December 1956.
87. Letter from Karl Polanyi to Paul Medow, 11 November 1958.
88. Georg Lukács, "Dostoevsky," pp.146-158, in René Wellek (ed.), *Dostoevsky. A Collection of Critical Essays*. New York: Prentice-Hall, 1962, 1943, pp.146-47.
89. Letter from Paul Medow to Karl Polanyi, 13 November 1958.
90. Letter from Karl Polanyi to "Bob," (perhaps Robert McKenzie, London), 5 December 1957.
91. Letter from Karl Polanyi to Harry Pearson, dated 25 October 1959. "Knowledge is not gained by generalizing, but by a sharpening of one's understanding of what's a social question."
92. Letter from Karl Polanyi to Michael Polanyi, 21 October 1959.
93. *Ibid.*
94. Letter from Karl Polanyi to Paul Medow, 11 November 1958. The novel's omissions were: the National War, the October Revolution, and Stalin's "Inferno."
95. Letter from Karl Polanyi to Michael Polanyi, 23 February 1956.
96. Letter from Karl Polanyi to Michael Polanyi, 23 December 1956.
97. On one piece of paper, Polanyi tried out various Hungarian versions of another verse; on another page, he writes out the first verse in English, and in German (with elaborate initial characters). "Brich mit dem Frieden in Dir,/ Brich mit den Werte der Welt / Besseres nicht, als die Zeit / Aber auf's Beste zu sein."
98. Letter from Karl Polanyi to Michael Polanyi, 5 January 1958. The danger is "loss of freedom in a technological society."
99. Letter from Karl Polanyi to Paul Medow, 11 November 1958.
100. Letter from Karl Polanyi to Irene Grant, 15 March 1963.
101. Letter from Karl Polanyi to Harry Pearson, 25 October 1959. There is a curious passage, relating to Terence Hopkins's "fata morgana, his luminous desert, that cemetery of caravans."
102. Letter from Karl Polanyi to Michael Polanyi, 23 December 1956.
103. Letter from Karl Polanyi to Paul Medow, 5 January 1958.
104. Letter from Karl Polanyi to Thomas Bledsoe, 26 April 1957.
105. Letter from Karl Polanyi to Michael Polanyi, 21 October 1959.
106. Letter from Karl Polanyi to Thomas Bledsoe, 26 April 1957.
107. Polanyi's annotations reflect his enthusiasm for the poetry of Juhász. Following his handwritten translation, there are a series of notes. "From another very long and beautiful poem, we know that his beloved wife was on the brink of suicide. This reflects his philosophy & 'religious' thoughts. His wife may have turned to the Church. Juhász's many mentions of man & human recall Marx's 'Thesis on Feuerbach' with its ideal of 'human society.'" To one side there is a note: "But where to seek human dreams?" Below, Polanyi continues: "The poem was written in the intense heat of a dusty village Sunday. The key word "emberszakasú" means, zoologically, "anthropoid," but literally "on a human pattern," "human shape," and is here certainly used to denote our dreams for the future. On the reverse, there is another note. "Written in 1956, with his wife on the brink of suicide...the crisis of 'Socialist Humanism' (1956) in a soul engulfed by a pesonal tragedy." Then comes more on the poet's wife Erzsike: "her turning away from life, her death-wish, her hopelessness, her yearning for heaven, her fear of love's passion that has gored her.—Her innocence stands for both her purity and naiveté."

TRANSITIONS FROM PLANNED
TO
MARKET ECONOMIES

Chapter Eight

ON THE ECONOMIC IMPLICATIONS OF (MIS)UNDERSTANDING MARKETS IN TRANSITION COUNTRIES

J.A. Kregel

Marx would have been perplexed by the absence of working-class consciousness; Lenin would have been appalled by the failure to act; Hayek would have been baffled by the absence of spontaneous order. Only Karl Polanyi would have been able to provide a logical explanation of the "Great Transformation" that is currently taking place in the former Soviet Union. Indeed, he would probably have predicted what is now occurring. He would also have been able to explain why Jeffrey Sachs and other western advisors to the Russian Federation are unmoved as they witness the spectacle of collapse and disarray from which they deduce the success of their policies for building a democratic market society. The simple explanation is their failure to understand the distinction between the substantive and formal definitions of the market.

> For once man's everyday activities have been organized through markets of various kinds, based on profit motives, determined by competitive attitudes, and governed by a utilitarian value scale, his society becomes an organism that is, in all essential regards, subservient to gainful purposes. Having thus absolutized the motive of economic gain in practice, he loses the capacity of mentally relativizing it again. His imagination is bounded by stultifying limits. The very word *economy* evokes in him not the picture of man's livelihood and the technology that helps to secure it, but recalls instead a particular set of motives, peculiar attitudes, and highly specific purposes, all of which he is used to calling *economic*, even though they are mere accessories to the actual economy...Not the permanent and abiding features of all human economies but the merely transitory and contingent ones appear to him as essentials...In his ignorance, he can grasp neither the true preconditions of survival nor the less obvious ways of attaining the possible. This obsolete market-mentality is, as I see it, the chief impediment to a realistic approach to the economic problems of the oncoming era.[1]

Thus the groups of housewives driven by hunger and despair to selling kittens in underground passageways are identified as exhibiting market behaviour and using capitalist initiative to create markets. The problems of producing "man's livelihood and the technology that helps to secure it" are thus completely ignored by the admiration for the existence of these ladies whose actions are no longer controlled by *Gosplan*, but are now "subservient to gainful purposes."

Polanyi would also have been able to explain to us why the advice based on this conception of the economy has been not only ineffectual but counterproductive: "Nowhere has liberal philosophy failed so conspicuously as in its understanding of the problem of change."[2] He pinpointed as the cause of this failure the presumption that rapid change will lead to rapid economic conversion and adjustment which will redirect individuals and resources displaced by change to alternative occupations, "but—this is the point—only in a market economy can such compensating effects be taken for granted." (p.34) "However natural it may appear to us to make that assumption, it is unjustified." It is precisely this assumption of rapid market-led adjustment which is used by the proponents of shock therapy to justify their introduction of stabilisation policies as necessary first steps to transformation. It is necessary to eliminate the "distortions" caused by price subsidies, inflation, and lack of profit incentives linked to private property to allow the market to produce the desired transformation. Yet they fail to notice that the "market" does not yet exist.

To those who argued in favour of the benefits of rapid change Polanyi cautioned:

> It should need no elaboration that a process of undirected change, the pace of which is deemed too fast, should be slowed down, if possible so as to safeguard the welfare of the community...A belief in spontaneous progress must make us blind to the role of government in economic life. This role consists often in altering the rate of change...For upon this rate, mainly depend[s] whether the dispossessed...adjust themselves to changed conditions without fatally damaging their substance, human and economic, physical and moral; whether they...find new employment in the fields of opportunity indirectly connected with the changes; and whether...those who lost their employment through the change are able to find new sources of sustenance...The time-rate of change compared with the time rate of adjustment will decide what is to be regarded as the net effect of the change. But in no case can we assume the functioning of the market laws unless a self-regulating market is shown to exist. Only in the institutional setting of market economy are market laws relevant...it [is]the modern economists, whose strictures imply the prior existence of a market system...who strayed from the facts. (*loc. cit.*)

In analysing the process of introducing a democratic free-market economy into the former Soviet Union, anyone familiar with the early "stabilisation policies" proposed for the transition to a market economy could not but have been struck by the naive belief manifested in the ability of the market to provide the necessary adjustments. For not only were markets assumed to exist, institutional structures common in the industrialised economies were also assumed to emerge miraculously with the introduction of private property. Plans for reform thus contained recommendations for balanced government budget policies in conditions in which there was no integrated system of taxation or controls on expenditures. Such plans also recommended that monetary policy be conducted so as to produce positive real interest rates, in a system with no money or capital market, no system of commercial bank lending to private enterprise, nor any appreciable private investment.

The modern economist, whether evaluating the impact of changes in a historical context (the passages quoted above refer to revisionist economic historians) or evaluating the impact of the changes required to replace central planning as an organising concept for the economy of the former Soviet Union, thus makes the same error of assuming what has to be proven, of taking for granted the spontaneous creation in the Russian economy of what has only been built up through three hundred years of conscious effort and direct government intervention in the capitalist economies.

The three great pillars of the transition programme recommended by western experts and international institutions—the elimination of price controls, the opening of the economy to foreign trade and capital flows, and the privatisation of state property—have exactly the same intention of turning labour, land and money into commodities freely traded for gain in the market. The Russian economy was to be transformed from one in which economic activity was embedded in the social structure, in which prices were fixed as equivalencies which allowed certainty in exchange, in which reciprocity and redistribution prevailed—to a system based solely on gain from profit.

The direct and indirect influence of Polanyi's *The Great Transformation* on those who drafted *The Market Shock*[3] on behalf of the Agenda Group should be clear and obvious. Polanyi was not in favour of turning back the clock with reference to the introduction of machine production; he appreciated that the machine could not be stopped. He was rather interested in the possibility that it could be introduced without, however, the accompanying "satanic mills." The Agenda group took a similar position to the problem of the transformation of the Central and Eastern European economies: namely, to ensure that the end result would be positive, rather than negative.

It seemed clear that there was a large degree of similarity between Polanyi's "Great Transformation" and the problems faced in converting the former planned economies into market-based economies. The Group followed Polanyi in criticising the tendency of the major reform proposals to accept the "economistic fallacy," of taking not only the operation of supposed laws of the market for granted, but also the existence of appropriate market institutions. A great deal of attention was thus given to the process of creating markets through creating conditions in which market-making could develop, and providing a basis for a more gradual transformation process.

Not only did the policies recommended by the international institutions depend on the operation of markets and market laws which did not exist, the ensuing stabilisation policies precluded the state from playing an active role in the process because this contradicted recommended budgetary policies. Thus our book *The Market Shock* placed emphasis on the necessity for an active role of government in creating markets in a way which avoided the doing of "fatal damage" to the human and social fabric of the country. This meant an active role for the state in both fostering the growth of the market and in putting a brake on the rate of change so as to keep it within the rate of adaptation of the people.

But here there was a fundamental contradiction in the transformation process, for it implied that government should simultaneously have one foot on the accelerator, pushing for "market reform," and the other foot on the brake, defending society from the impact of the market in terms of unemployment, falling living standards, and deprivation. In the transformation taking place in Eastern Europe there is no economic driving force equivalent to the role played by the introduction of machine production in bringing into existence the "satanic mills." The decision to introduce the "market" as well as the decision to do it by means of a "market shock" was not an economic imperative, it was a political decision.

It is most probable that the original idea behind *glasnost* and *perestroika* (which seems to be a forgotten word in market Russia!) was to try to engineer a controlled entry or soft landing in the market economy. But the impediments to change turned out to be stronger than the impetus for change within the government. The "shock therapy" was thus an attempt to use the slogans of the market and economic reform to wrench power from the defenders of the old regime. For the common mortal this shift has turned out to be much more rapid and much more brutal than the introduction of the machine age and the English industrial revolution.

There are many advocates of the free-market reform movement who argue that there *was* no Big Bang, just as revisionist economic historians denied the hardships of the Industrial Revolution. They argue that since there are still parts of the economy which have not been fully and completely given up to re-organisation by means of free markets driven by the profit motive, Russia has not introduced real shock therapy.

Polanyi would say that such advocates have misunderstood the nature of the uprooting experience of passing from a system in which certain fundamental needs were supplied centrally to one in which each individual exists only for himself and his own gain. Somewhat inconsistently, it is these same people who usually point to the relative successes that have so far been achieved in terms of the proportion of total output produced by the private market sector, or to the increase in incomes of individuals operating in the market sector. Again, they have not considered Polanyi's explanation of the fact that the introduction of the market system can at one and the same time bring about an increase in real wages above historical levels, and also lead to widespread "cultural denigration." This is precisely what appears to be taking place in Russia today as prima ballerinas are forced to sell their physical prowess in the market as go-go dancers and prostitutes as they accept efficient allocation of their resources by following the profit motive. There is no disputing that their real incomes are clearly higher than they were under the old system.

Polanyi placed great emphasis on the role of the state as an agent for slowing the rate of change to compatibility with the rate of adjustment. But this counterbalance, which works when pluralistic liberal democracies are developing market systems, does not seem to carry over to oligarchies in the process of being transformed from command to market systems. Since it is the government itself rather than the machine that is the source of the push to the market, any attempt to temper the rate of change appears as obstructionism and draws opprobrium and criticism from abroad. Indeed, it is now the case that the very existence of democracy has been identified with rapid progress toward market reform, so that any action to stem the tide of change is viewed as anti-democratic and subject to condemnation both inside and outside the country. The simple attempt to protect society from the ravages of the market by slowing the rate of change to match the rate of adaptation is branded as revisionist, or worse, communist.

In his explanation of the counterbalancing forces to the thrust of the market, Polanyi places great weight on the role played by the Speenhamland system in delaying the creation of a full-fledged labour market and thus the full introduction of the market system. He also noted that this system was not edifying for labour, but simply indicated its role as the normal response of the system to excessively rapid change.

Despite the difficulties facing the government in playing its dual role of promotor of the market and protector of the people, there are other forces at work in Russia to counter the speed of change. One of them is the system of state enterprises and the power of the enterprise directors (among whom the Prime Minister belongs) to influence the pace of economic reform. Under central planning, state enterprises were akin to small, decentralised regional governments, providing not only employment, but a wide range of social services to their workers and the other residents of the industrial towns in which they were located. These included schooling, health services, enterprise shops, and even could extend to street cleaning. In the period of penury after *perestroika* and before the flood of western imports, enterprise shops provided a first line of defence against starvation for their workers. These amalgamations of social, political and economic functions are just as anachronistic in the new Russia based on free markets as the Speenhamland system was in Britain of the 18th century, but they serve a similar purpose of shielding the population from the ravages of change. This explains the great difficulty in transforming them into "efficient" production units, as well as the difficulty in preparing them for privatisation. It also explains why they have survived the attacks of both *perestroika* and the shock therapy, for they represent the last line of defence of Russian society against the ravages of full and complete introduction of market relations. On grounds of economic efficiency they must be replaced, just as Speenhamland had to be replaced; but this should not blind us to the role they play and the basic needs they represent.

It is interesting to note that Parliament, the seat of democratic decision making, and the Central Bank, seat of independent monetary decision making, have both been willing to risk their sovereignty against the government in order to defend and preserve state enterprises. Members of Parliament understood much more quickly than western economists that privatisation meant that the enterprises would have to shed the very activities which made them a shield to protect the Russian population against the ravages wrought by change in social organisation. They thus fought, not against reform or against the introduction of the democratic free market system, but to save the only institutions which seemed capable of serving as protection from the negative impact of the market. The state enterprises were a tangible representation of the so-called "social safety net" which everyone talks about, but no one seems capable of organising. Responding to the excessively rapid pace of economic change, the democratic voice made itself heard in a Parliament that was bombarded, burned, and disbanded in the name of preserving the rapid pace of "democratic" market reform.

The Central Bank found itself in the same difficulty. It was faced with the choice either of cutting off funding to Parliament for democratically approved government programmes, or of cutting off funding of state enterprises in order to meet the conditions of market-economy monetary control where there were as yet no markets and thus no laws of the market operating to protect the unemployed. The Bank chose to continue to finance Parliamentary measures and the losses of state enterprises rather than risk the massive unemployment and social unrest which might result. The Bank was duly attacked on the one hand as a revisionist saboteur of "democratic market reform" instituted by the government, and on the other by Western "experts" who failed to recognise the significance of the state enterprise system as a defence against the rapidity of social change and increased uncertainty in the economic conditions of the Russian people which were driving this response. Rather than hollow words about "social safety nets" to be provided by a government that cannot organise tax collection, the state enterprises exist and indeed function in this role. If they are to be successfully privatised a solution to this problem must be found.

One possibility would be to try to preserve these social welfare aspects of the enterprises as independent local providers of health and other social services, either under contract with the government or directly with the people. This would avoid having to disband a network of service provisions and create a new system from scratch in conditions in which even the most rudimentary decisions appear difficult.

Polanyi provides a definition of socialism as "the tendency inherent in an industrial civilisation to transcend the self-regulating market by consciously subordinating it to a democratic society." (p. 234) Currently, in the Russian Federation this tendency is branded as anti-reform and thus anti-democratic: it is the Parliament which must be subordinated to the introduction of the self-regulating market; it is the Central Bank which must be subordinated to the self-regulating market, by allowing money to be managed as if it were a commodity determined by the market. Thus, the failure of the Bank to act "independently" against the democratic decisions of Parliament, on the one hand, leads to calls for increased government control, and on the other, to calls for the bank to introduce currency convertibility which would bind its monetary creation activity to the strictures of the market.

It should by now be clear, if it was not so previously, that direct identification of the "democratic" process with market reforms leads to the elimination of any form of democratic expression of dissatisfaction with the pace of transformation, as well as any state action which is not consonant with the destruction of the defence mechanisms protecting the society from an excessively rapid process of change and the enforcement of market measures. It is now the case that those government bureaucrats who formerly defended the Soviet state are the same as are at present defending Russian democracy by imposing free market reform, insisting on rapid privatisation, and promoting the break up and sale of state enterprises. They are also the same persons who have seen their relative position in society solidified through the privatisation of state assets. They have received, gratis, property rights to their exclusive and privileged living quarters which previously depended on their position in the Party hierarchy, and have used their position to appropriate former state property through asset-stripping of state enterprises, all in their role as representatives of the "democratic" interests of the people. Their position of power and dominance now rests on the firmer foundation of the natural law of property and the IMF, rather than the leading role of the Party in the workers' revolution and the support of the military.

There is clearly a struggle going on today in the Russian Federation, but it is not between advocates of alternative programmes for transformation: it is a struggle for political power. There are no machine owners to provide impetus for the introduction of the democratic free market. However, there is a ready supply of candidates from amongst the former *nomenklatura* and state bureaucrats, fighting to preserve their position in society. In this they are aided by western economists who cannot distinguish between the substance of economic activity and market behaviour based solely on personal gain. Democracy, free markets, and property rights appear to constitute a firmer foundation for personal privilege and position than to be among the leaders of the dictatorship of the working class in a Soviet system in which there is no incentive for the rest of the population to provide spoils. The gains to be made from occupying the positions of power in a market system are much greater than under central planning. The former *nomenklatura* have thus adopted the banner of rapid privatisation and free market reform as the best way to preclude any real political change. It is such as these, in the garb of Manchester liberals, who have replaced the "machine" as the driving force for economic change. But it is the sort of change which takes into account only the "mere accessories to the actual economy...Not the permanent and abiding features of all human economies but the merely transitory and contingent ones." They ignore the substance, which is the fact that it was the machine that provided changes which produced the basic means of survival for society. As yet, there is no recovery in domestic investment, or domestic production, and the "substance" of subsistence is primarily imports.

There is an additional point which merits consideration in this regard. A great deal of attention has been paid to control of the economy by the "mafia," as well as to the insistence that this phenomenon is a purely "Russian" affair with no relation to better-known foreign counterparts. But, in a population facing cultural denigration, starvation and unemployment, unwilling to return to a system which had provided safety and security only under intolerable conditions of personal unfreedom, the traditional conception of the mafia as guarantor of minimum personal rights and defender of the common man against the uncaring state, does seem to make a great deal of sense. Had Polanyi known more about the organisation of the mafia he might have categorized it along with Speenhamland as a defence mechanism by which society attempted to protect itself from the ravages of excessively rapid change to a market system.

However one might want to call the Soviet Union, it was a system in which the economy was embedded in a network of socio-economic relations, in which a variety of other incentives were substituted for the profit motive. It was not the antithesis of the market system in the form of, say the Potlatch, but nonetheless it was a structured system which functioned without profit and monetary accumulation as primary goals. In the space of less than five years it has been brought into a market system without any of the positive benefits normally associated with the existence of the full-fledged self-regulating market. The defence mechanisms which have been set in motion, along with the implications of stabilisation policy which deny an active role to the state in providing those institutions, have created a situation of stalemate in which little progress is being made towards the creation of the self-regulating market system, but in which basic democratic freedoms are increasingly infringed in order to make more rapid progress. Popular democracy, if now left to itself in Russia, will deny further market reform. The failure of market reform would lead to what Polanyi has called the "issues of early capitalism," "first and foremost...popular government." (p. 223) "The reform of the market economy achieved at the price of the extirpation of all democratic institutions," which spread in the 1920s, appears as an increasingly possible solution to the current impasse. In the meantime, international institutions continue to bargain about the size of the budget deficit, the level of real interest rates, and to recommend stabilisation of the rouble exchange rate—and Jeffrey Sachs continues to see the formalistic elements of the market on every street corner. Removal of the Speenhamland system was not easy, but it was required to allow passage to the self-regulating market economy. In the short term it created even more misery and dislocation. Elimination of the system of state enterprises is also necessary, and it will cause the same increase in misery and disruption of the normal conduct of life if it is done without recognition of the resultant impact on the basic conditions of the populace. The end of the 18th century was a time of revolution and political upheaval, as was the 1920s. If the "economistic fallacy" continues to be applied to the problems of Russian transformation, one would expect the same for the Russia of the 1990s.

NOTES

1. Karl Polanyi, *The Livelihood of Man*. New York: Harcourt Brace, 1977, p. XIV.
2. Karl Polanyi, *The Great Transformation*. Boston: Beacon Press, 1957, p. 33.
3. J. Kregel, E. Matzner, and G. Grabher (eds.), *The Market Shock*. Ann Arbor: University of Michigan Press, 1992.

Chapter Nine

FROM PLANNED ECONOMY TO MARKET ECONOMY IN THE FORMER EAST BERLIN

Birgit Müller

This article was inspired by talks with staff employed in East Berlin enterprises who, with the end of the GDR, had come to feel further isolated and even less able to act collectively. This came as a surprise, given that the legal status of employees had changed considerably with reunification. Workers had gained new rights, such as the freedom to nominate their representatives within the enterprise and the right to strike, previously denied under Real Existing Socialism. This led me to examine what opportunities were open to workers, under the former planned economy, to determine working conditions and social relations on the shop floor and to develop and express their own views and opinions. I also sought to assess the possibilities open to them today. To what extent were the rights granted to employees under German legislation applied to privatised enterprises in East Berlin since reunification? Did the legal possibilities now open to East German workers correspond to their expectations of a democratic transformation of the workplace? Did they make use of such newly acquired rights? What were the strategies employed by managers in both East and West Germany to restructure the former "people's owned enterprises" (*VEB: volkseigener Betrieb*)?

In this study of three East Berlin enterprises I examined the relationship between economic rationality and the pursuit of power and influence in the workplace. I considered the way in which mechanisms of power had evolved with the change from one economic and political system to another. What freedom and potential for exerting influence had the staffs retained, and what had they lost? Did the democratic system bring more freedom, providing space for new liberties? Foucault regards power as a resource that everybody possesses in their respective fields of action.[1] He distinguishes two forms of power that coexist in modern contemporary society: sovereign power defined by the sovereign-subject relationship, and disciplinary power that emerged with industrial society and is exercised through the disciplinisation of the social actors.[2] Its supreme form is the normalisation of discipline, its internalisation by the social actors.[3] I will apply the distinction between sovereign and disciplinatory power to the operation of East German enterprises after unification, and inquire to what extent disciplinary norms of industrial society have been internalised by social actors in the East.

FIELDWORK IN A PERIOD OF RAPID SOCIAL CHANGE

From May 1990 onwards—that is, before the monetary reform of July 1st and also before the unification of the German states on October 3rd later that year—I witnessed the transformation that took place in three East Berlin enterprises. I spent two one-month periods on the factory floor at each of the enterprises concerned: Stanex[4] July 1990 and May-June 1991, Taghell August 1990 and July 1991, and Hochinauf September-October 1991 and February-March 1993. I also visited the factories regularly during these three years and conducted interviews with employees after working hours, both in the workplace and elsewhere.

In the first factory, Stanex, that in July 1990 still had 2000 employees, I studied a department responsible for the production of automatic machines for electrical parts assembly, with 100 employees. The department had its own administrative structure and functioned, even at the time of the planned economy, almost as a separate enterprise. Stanex had initially been set up by a research institute working on the rationalisation of production methods and the development of the necessary apparatus and machinery. In June 1991 Treuhand (the Privatisation Agency) allowed Stanex to be taken over by a Swiss real estate company, provided that it guaranteed employment to 250 of the 2000 employees. The buyer encouraged management of the various sections to set up independent enterprises and employ some of the 250 workers regarding whom the undertaking had been given. The department I visited became an independent company with 62 employees, whose director went on to become the owner. Today fifteen people are still working there.

The second enterprise, Taghell, had originally been a family business, and underwent the complete process of nationalisation until becoming a VEB in 1972. Until 1989 the brass lamps produced by Taghell were in high demand, despite being priced at a level that the average consumer in the GDR could hardly afford. After a sharp drop in business, activity picked up in 1990 through orders from an old client. However, due to organisational problems and workforce reduction from 110 to 60 employees the enterprise had difficulties delivering orders on time. The director and former manager attempted to acquire the valuable land and factory buildings. Production cutbacks and the decline in orders undermined the economic viability of the enterprise to such an extent that in September 1992 it was put into liquidation by Treuhand.

Study of the third enterprise, Hochinauf, that produced lifts, began in August 1991. The enterprise had been purchased by an international combine in 1990 that went on to restructure it, reducing personnel from 1000 to 500. Managers were brought in from the West to improve the firm's market position. Despite doing improved business in 1991, the manufacturing section was forced to reduce costs while increasing production. In 1992 the enterprise invested heavily in new machinery and premises for production and administration. With the transfer in 1993 of a production unit from West to East Berlin, work organisation underwent drastic changes. However, these changes were ineffective in view of ever-increasing competition from cheaper production units that the combine had built up in Eastern Europe. In the summer of 1996 the decision was taken to shut down production in East Berlin.

My role as researcher was influenced by the important changes taking place in the enterprises concerned, and by the changing attitude of the staff towards me. When in May 1990 I first visited Taghell and Stanex I was received by both management and staff with great openness. I was able to move about freely within the enterprise, carry out long interviews and take detailed notes. Day by day I identified elements making for potential conflict, harmony or antagonism within the enterprise. Naturally, employees as well as management did their best to convince me of the rightness of their opinions; on the other hand, no one prevented me from talking to people with a different point of view. When the enterprises were being privatised managers wondered whether their posts would be secure. The employees, on the other hand, continued to question the political past of their directors as well as the economic decisions they were currently making. At that time, however, they had already given up hope of replacing them. The resulting "stalemate" provided ideal conditions for anthropological research. The past was very significant in determining the views of the parties involved, so much so that staff and managers alike continued to overwhelm me with their impressions and opinions of a planned economy. Their accounts were influenced by a desire to communicate the past to a West German, drawing attention to the cultural characteristics of East German society.

By 1993 the situation had changed drastically. In all three enterprises those who were directors at the time of the planned economy had gone on to become managers in the market economy. Mutual mistrust on the part of managers and staff affected my role as observer. The managers who had been trying, with or without success, to run the enterprises feared that I might turn the employees against them and undermine their authority. When in July 1991 the manager of Taghell refused me entry, he "justified" his decision by explaining that when the employees talked to me they were led to believe that they were cleverer than he. For their part the employees, particularly those I had not known for long, feared that I might be acting as a spy on behalf of management, and that all I was doing was secretly monitoring their performance and betraying their "tricks." Although there remained on both sides some who trusted me during my research, in the final phase at Hochinauf in April 1993 I had the impression that I was being torn between employees and management.

POLITICAL AND ECONOMIC POWER IN "PEOPLE'S OWNED ENTERPRISES"

Although in a planned economy economic considerations were subordinated to political ones, in practise enterprises carried on their business according to their own economic logic. This meant that in the GDR national economic interests often conflicted with the interests of the enterprise. The director of an enterprise was at the center of the resulting tensions, representing the political interest as a high-ranking Party member while having to provide for the success of his enterprise. The most difficult task for a manager of an enterprise was to fulfill the Plan as determined by the state authorities. Precisely how he achieved this was considered to be of only secondary importance and could, in fact, contradict the rules and regulations of a planned economy. Both the manager's political freedom within the enterprise and his position with regard to the political institutions were dependent on his economic success in the face of the cumbersome system. On the other hand, an economic leader who conformed to the ideology would never be dismissed and rarely be demoted even in the case of failure. The worst that could happen to him would be a transfer to another enterprise. "To be a leader was a profession," was an employee's comment on the lack of professional selection.

Reinhart Bendix[5] attributes this retention of power, despite economic failure, to the particular form of legitimation of authority in communist—or, to use his expression, plebiscitarian—regimes. Plebiscitarian regimes tend to link charismatic legitimation with the legal legitimation of authority. Those in power give instructions as if authority in the legal sense lay in their hands, such instructions being made absolute as if imparted by charismatic authority.[6] By issuing commands in absolute terms, the ruling authorities relieve themselves of responsibility and let the burden of failure fall upon the executors, in this case the directors of industries. The directors in turn try to clear themselves of responsibility by pointing out the absolute nature of the instructions they received. However, given that the director is himself a charismatic leader promoting socialist ideals and wielding legitimate authority through the plan as legal instrument, the mechanisms of plebiscitarian authority are extended throughout the enterprise.

In the three enterprises studied I came across two types of director in the planned economy: the pragmatic and the ideological leader. The director of Taghell, who was of the pragmatic kind, declared after the collapse of the communist regime that his only reason for adhering to the Party had been to forward his own career. Furthermore, he was proud to have been able generally to obstruct the influence of the Party Secretary within the enterprise, and to have assigned positions of authority to employees who were not Party members. All the same, Taghell had benefitted from good political relations, in view of the fact that influential polititians showed a liking for its products, particulary the heavy brass lamps. The director never missed an occasion to give such lamps as presents to members of the district council (*Rat des Kreises*), that is to those who could influence the distribution of raw materials and capital goods. Apart from the official plan's obligations, the enterprise often received commissions to furnish ministry and Party buildings with brass lamps. In the second case, that of Stanex, the director of production of its industrial automatic machines was an ideological leader. As a loyal party member, though lacking in any personal charisma, he exercised strict ideological control over his personnel. Work meetings were often accompanied by political lectures that might last for hours. He personally supervised the brigade books and the wall newspapers. He viewed his assisting in the development of components as his personal contribution towards solving the problems of productivity in the GDR. His superiors, however, were less enthusiastic about his project, considering it to be a source of new problems in supply and plan obligations. Despite the pragmatic attitude of his superiors, the department director stuck to his project, as he himself put it, out of idealism. He was convinced that he was making a political contribution to the progress of the GDR.

Although increased productivity and reductions in the labour force were officially recognised as priorities in the development of the GDR, and although, with competition for innovation, employees who contributed by work rationalisation were compensated, individual initiatives on a large scale were not particularly welcome. The bureaucratic structure of the economy in the GDR reproduced itself, the political organs controlling all incentives to improve production and the development of new products. Incentives were transmitted to the production units through strictly defined channels. Sticking to one's own strategy, though it was for the common good, could be regarded as implicit criticism of the official line. The department director at Stanex experienced the consequences of official mistrust in terms of his private life. Although he was finally authorised to produce the automatic machine for electrical parts assembly developed by the department, he was refused permission to spend a holiday in a country whose borders were open to the West, in this case Yugoslavia.

Economic success was measured in terms of meeting the obligations set out in the plan. This could be achieved through manipulation of these obligations on paper, through production destined for export to non-socialist hard currency countries, through the production of a range of products declared priorities by the State, through the development of new products, and above all through new investment. Internally as well as externally such economic success legitimised the power of the socialist director. Alongside and despite the official "code of honour" was another form of morality existing for economic activity operating in the interests of the enterprise and the pragmatic functioning of the socialist economy. Enterprise directors exchanged materials necessary for production and passed on orders that never appeared in the official balance sheets of the plan. Members of the political authorities who influenced favourably investment decisions taken at high political levels, received "small gifts" in return. When political organs placed special orders, the enterprises involved would be allocated all the necessary materials outside of the plan and were authorised to pay overtime. Such forms of parallel economic activity were recognised and tolerated, if only because the planned economy depended on them. Given their informal character they were hard to control and often bordered on illegality. For example, when an exchange of hoarded materials went unrecorded in the accounts, it was very tempting for the partners to pocket part of the proceeds. Employees at Taghell described how an entire order of lamps would disappear overnight, and spoke of party officials helping themselves to warehouse stock. The truthfulness of such reports is hard to assess, as is the extent of the illegal transactions and the personal gain involved. Observation and comment on the part of personnel limited such practices to some extent, while at the same time contributing to the creation of circles of accomplices (in German *Seilschaft*, rope parties), both internal and external to the enterprise.

Successful East German enterprises would aim to limit the obligations fixed by the plan as much as possible and to employ as many people as they could obtain from the state authorities. Such a workforce was not always used to full capacity, but it was necessary to provide for irregularities in the planned economy. Once workers were taken on, it was practically impossible to dismiss them. Even in cases of serious misconduct, such as lengthy absence from work without explanation or theft within the enterprise, the unions could refuse to consent to a person's dismissal and the labour office would send the offender back to the enterprise for "re-education." Employees were well aware of the strength of their position, and they made use of it in negotiating with their superiors for a congenial tempo in the work process. In such enterprises work was therefore characterised by a subtle mixture of resistance and cooperation. It was such a mixture that Voskamp and Wittke[7] referred to as a pact to accomplish the plan. At Taghell for example, long periods when lack of materials or spare parts brought the machinery to a standstill alternated with night shift and weekend work. At times of diminished activity, labourers could dawdle over breakfast or, if they did not want to be disturbed, retire to a spot down by the river through a gate to which a colleague kept the key. Towards the end of the month however, when all departments had to make a concerted effort to achieve the aims of the monthly plan, such workers would play their part. Their commitment extended beyond working overtime. They worked weekends and consecutive shifts, pushing the machinery to its limit, ignoring safety regulations. The foreman told me in confidence that at times during the night shift they utilized a Romanian 63-ton press to rivet the arms of lamps, a high-speed machine that would punch down uncontrollably. The methods was thus dangerous but efficient.

The intensity of the work depended not only on negotiation, but also on discipline and motivation. The consensual nature of the *pact for the accomplishment of the plan* made it difficult to impose complete discipline in GDR enterprises, although foremen always assured me that they managed to maintain discipline in their workshop. Foreman Kaiser at Taghell tried to achieve discipline by taking part himself in the work and by setting a good example. Foreman Fischer at Stanex laid down many strict regulations. At Hochinauf, foreman Spohr monitored his workers via a sort of panopticon resembling that described by Michel Foucault.[8] He had painted the windows of his office over-looking the workshop white, and then scraped off the paint at eye-level—he was approximately 1.90m tall—making three spy-holes the size of a small coin through which he could observe his workers without being noticed. He claimed he hardly needed the spy-holes because he could tell whether a machine was being operated or not from the sound it made. Such a method of surveillance is reminiscent of a primitive model of a "disciplinary society" in which discipline has not yet become normal and interiorised, still having to be continuously imposed by those in power.[9] The workers, for their part, stressed that at the time of the planned economy they did not have to show any great respect for their foremen. The latter might delegate disagreeable tasks or reduce the end-of-year bonus; in extreme cases he might write an unfavourable report when a worker sought to travel to visit family in the West—but all in all, he could do little to require increased effort.

The organisation of production in the planned economy provoked two typical reactions among the workers that were not incompatible. It encouraged them to test the limits of freedom and to work as little as possible; but at the same time they were encouraged to work on their own initiative, to find pleasure in their work and to be proud of what they produced. Even today, workers insist on the pleasure they enjoyed in those moments of "madness" at work. Thus there were,

> ...grilled chickens in the tempering furnace, cooked pork knuckles and whipped cream on the boring mill. But this did no harm to anybody. They all went back to work afterwards. It may sound a bit strange to a Westerner, but this was exactly what made life worth living here...We sat for an eternity in this enterprise, from seven to half past four; this made it bearable. It was really a great bunch of people...the niches to be found here, and that made life agreable, they were also at work, not only in our free time. And they were to some extent pleasant niches, I must say. (Skilled worker, 16.6.1991)

The workers at Stanex who participated in such jokes and pranks were at other times totally immersed in their work. During the final stage of production, when all twelve units of the automatic machine were working flat out, the two labourers in charge together with mechanical and electrical engineers often worked day and night. In these privileged moments, cooperation between skilled workers and engineers, which even at slacker times was intensive and independent of the formal hierarchy, developed almost into a symbiosis. These "niches" also afforded space for serious political debate between staff on the same hierarchical level. Party members were involved in heated debate with non-members, orthodox communists with "Gorbachovists." These working groups created a space of relative autonomy. Such protected space was a precondition for the emergence of hidden alternative discourses about society that questioned the official line.[10] In the course of the 1980s these discussions became more and more passionate and also open. The formerly hidden critical discourse was shifted to larger circles and took place before a growing public.

UPHEAVAL AND RESIGNATION IN THE ENTERPRISE: FROM AUTUMN 1989 TO SUMMER 1991

During the autumn and winter of 1989 employees of the three enterprises began to question the competence and legitimacy of their directors. After the collapse of the wall, when the first general meetings were held for all personnel, directors had to accept questioning as to their capacity to manage an enterprise. At Taghell, at the end of January 1990, on the initiative of the workers and the foreman of the "finishing" workshop, a very frank discussion was held with the director of the enterprise, the party secretary, the president of the relevant trade union, and two managers. According to the minutes of the meeting, drawn up by foreman Kaiser on January 26th, 1990, the workers asked the directors questions about technical and financial management. They wanted to know whether their enterprise was operating profitably; why, even before the collapse of the wall, so many lamps had been produced only to be put into stock; how they were going to fulfil the plan for 1990, and whether the enterprise could leave the "Kombinat." The management's evasive replies did not satisfy the editor of the minutes. The workers complained about the technical standard of equipment in various departments and about working conditions; but they did not call for the dismissal of management; nor, on the political level, did they question the system of a planned economy.

The workers at Hochinauf reacted very differently. The minutes of the meetings held in 1989 and 1990 show that the reaction was above all political. During the first meeting, held on November 17th, 1989, participants agreed to set up a wall newspaper. They decided to forward a written request to the unions asking for a statement about their "opinions concerning the changes necessary in society and industry." Practical questions concerning the management of the enterprise appeared at the time to be of secondary importance. The main priority was to secure help from the higher echelons of the trade union in determining the right way to go. Even the decision taken on May 8th, 1990, regarding "the organisation of a general vote of confidence in the first level of management"—a vote that was postponed in the same session and never subsequently took place—did not in fact question the managerial capacity of the old directors, but merely referred to their political responsibility for the planned economy. In the eyes of the employees, the former directors were unfit to manage the enterprise in a market economy because they had been members of the Party and the *nomenklatura*.

The different reactions on the part of personnel at Taghell and Hochinauf reflect the different forms of management that existed before the collapse of the wall. The director of Taghell who had exercised no ideological control over the enterprise, keeping his staff immune from political pressure, but who in their eyes had derived personal profit, was criticised at the practical level for his handling of the business. On the other hand, the director of Hochinauf was regarded as a communist by his staff and as an ideological leader had lost all credibility since the collapse of the wall. During the staff meetings that took place between November 1989 and April 1990 no radical demands were made; the few decisions that were then taken were not even carried out in a consistent manner. Nevertheless this period remained impressed upon the memory of those who took part, both managers and employees. The employees speaking up against the management expressed openly for the first time those worries and concerns that at the time of the planned economy they had only dared whisper. The simple fact of having expressed openly what they had always thought filled them with pride, though it deeply disturbed the leaders. As Jim Scott would say, when a hidden transcript goes public, the actors enjoy a feeling of fulfillment and satisfaction. They no longer felt obliged to show signs of subservience to those they despised.[11] Afterwards, the employees explained to me that the end of the planned economy would also bring about the fall of the leaders who had been responsible for it, and that in the running of the enterprise a far more important role would be given to staff representatives. Among the activists, however, nobody came forward prepared to take on the role and responsibilities of management or to guide the enterprise into a market economy. The leaders themselves were so troubled by this development that they chose to avoid any direct confrontation with staff. In the spring of 1990, when important decisions for the future of the enterprise had to be taken, the director of the section for automatic components went on sick leave for a couple of weeks. The director of Taghell stopped visiting the workshops. The director of Hochhinauf for his part entered into intense negotiations with potential Western buyers who eventually secured his position for him.

The worries and concerns expressed in early 1990 soon lost their relevance because they were still firmly anchored in the logic of the planned economy. Political and social changes took place faster than could have been imagined. The hidden transcripts now lacked explosive power in this new social reality. The ideas that the most active staff representatives had of their future role, and the leaders' fears of losing their power, bore no relation to the real capacity and willingness of the former to bring down the latter. In fact, the staff itself was unable to elaborate any consistent concept of the future of the enterprise. Even among the most active employees there was nobody ready to assume the role and responsibility of director and lead the enterprise into the market economy. Although communication within the enterprise was now entirely unrestricted, countervailing in the Arendt sense could not develop.[12]

Employees had an ambivalent image of the meaning of "public property" and what might become of it after the "peaceful revolution." They identified themselves with "their" enterprise, to whose development they had contributed. Although they were aware that as individuals they possessed no part of it, they still felt that the enterprise could not belong to anyone other than themselves. Over a brief period the idea that the people should get a share of the "property of the people" was discussed at various "round tables." The union representatives of Hochinauf asked their president to "make a stand against the enterprise director, supporting the view of IG Metall that public property (or property belonging to the people) should become 'jointly owned property'."[13] This decision was never carried out because of the enterprise's rapidly deteriorating economic situation. Also the idea of transforming publicly owned property into individual shares proved a subject for but brief discussion; it was totally ruled out after the enterprise was bought by a large Western concern in the summer of 1990. In the case of Taghell and Stanex that did not find Western buyers, greater willingness to change was expressed among employees than at management level. The commercial departments in both enterprises developed marketing concepts that found no support among management. At Taghell employees took up initiatives, then dropped them again, campaigning for product improvement, and for the introduction of computer information systems to optimise management of client files. At Stanex the employees on their own initiative went to look for new clients, but were stopped by management. Staff in the purchasing departments were enthusiastic about the possibility of introducing new materials and semi-finished products, and thus save on the cost of prefabrication. The employees were generally highly motivated, but they lacked an overall concept for the restructuring of the enterprise.

For many enterprise managers, holding on to power was an end in itself outweighing the economic well-being or performance of the enterprise. The managers of Taghell and Stanex, fearing that their position or influence within the enterprise would be harmed, fended off potential Western investors. In April 1991, Taghell's director took the opportunity to buy a 2.5% share in the business from the widow of the former owner for a total of 5,000DM. In January 1992 he secured from her the right to re-privatize, which enabled him to place a claim with Treuhand for return of the State's shares. His position within the enterprise could not be touched, given that he was now considered the owner; not even Treuhand could replace him. Similarly, the director of the department at Stanex set out in December 1990 to turn his department into an independent enterprise, and take over ownership. In the summer of 1991 he succeeded in putting his plan into action when a Swiss real estate firm took over Stanex. The latter was keen to pass on the burden of keeping 250 employees and offered support to department directors who were willing to become independent entrepreneurs, providing them with the old machinery and renting out the necessary premises. The staff were surprised by the socialist director's sudden transformation into a capitalist entrepreneur; one employee referred to it as "becoming one's own class enemy." The workers council elected in the autumn and summer of 1990 were unaware of the legal possibilities open to them. When decisions were taken that ought to have concerned them they often intervened too late or not at all. This was the case for example in autumn 1990, when the management went ahead with massive redundancies.

When the workers council was to be elected at Taghell, in autumn 1990, the more active members were carefully manoeuvered out of the running by the director. He simply promoted them to management level before the vote took place, thus making it impossible for them to be elected; then, once it was over, he cancelled their nomination. At Stanex, the council composed of former union representatives (BGL) took the side of management when, in summer 1991, some of the staff questioned the legitimacy of the sale of the enterprise to a Swiss real estate agency. With the help of the new owner, the president of the council was himself able to found his own enterprise. The only workers council capable of standing up to management was at Hochinauf, thank to the strong practical and legal support it received from the workers council of its sister enterprise in West Berlin.

Job insecurity undermined the way employees identified with the enterprise, where they had now become interchangeable in the workplace. Instead of being part of the respected working class—the official ideology of the East German state had referred to factory workers as the pillars of the state—they had now been reduced to an anonymous workforce.

DISCIPLINE AND NORMALISATION

The market economy brought with it the new experience of existential insecurity. Employees in all three enterprises had the feeling that they had lost control over their material living conditions. Many of the people I spoke to went so far as to use the term "death" to portray the economic collapse of the enterprise. To express the fear that one of their colleagues might be made redundant they would say: "He probably won't survive." On the one hand, they felt exposed to the "world economy" or "market trends" which lay beyond their control; their superiors supported such fatalistic concepts, referring to the world economy as if it were a metaphysical force and appealing for a joint effort to save the enterprise. On the other hand, employees became increasingly aware that their interests—to ensure the well-being of the enterprise, and thereby protect their job—did not necessarily coincide with the interests of management, and that what sacrifices they made for the enterprise made no sense if management intended to make them redundant anyway.

At Stanex, when orders came in less and less frequently, the enterprise was only able to survive thanks to the extension of the technical unemployment system. The employees were then paid by the labour office and received 70% of their East German wage. When the director succeeded in buying the enterprise and again when the technical unemployment scheme was threatened, he selected employees to stay with the enterprise on political grounds rather than in terms of their qualifications. His comrades from the old industrial militia (*Betriebskampfgruppe*) were authorised to stay, whereas many highly qualified engineers were selected for redundancy. Although the majority of the personnel were indignant at such practices, there was nothing they could do. For most of the staff this exhausted enterprise represented a "blade of straw to which one could cling." Many came to work, although technically their hours had been reduced to zero, simply to counteract depression and not to fall totally out of the habit of working.

The director of Taghell had a very different strategy. He increasingly cut back activity and rid himself of a large proportion of the workforce. He eventually claimed the right at Treuhand to reprivatise not only the business but also the very valuable property. Neglect on the part of management, however, was so blatant that a representative of Treuhand threatened the director with court action for fraudulant bankrupcy, and forced him to sell his shares to Treuhand thus opening up the way for liquidation on September 1st, 1992. Worried by the quantity of letters and invoices back-dated to the month of August and by the sale of all the electronic equipment to the director for just one mark, the employees contacted Treuhand at the end of September and only then found out about the liquidation. The Treuhand put Taghell up for sale. By December 1992 with no potential buyer having been found, the remaining staff decided to make their problem public. They wrote letters to the mayor and talked of their difficulties with local radio stations. Their aim was to secure the sale of Taghell as a productive enterprise in which they themselves could retain their jobs. Until February 1993 it still seemed possible that the production of lamps or other metallic components would continue and that a buyer could be found who would continue to employ the remaining 25 people. In March 1993, however, the case fell into different hands at Treuhand, and the new person responsible decided to sell the enterprise as real estate.

At Hochinauf, a general feeling of insecurity also reigned among personnel. Up until January 1993, management reproached production workers for not meeting the expectations of their West German employers in terms of productivity. Furthermore, widespread insecurity was fueled by rumours of a restructuring of the division of labour within the international combine, and of the reduction of German production capacity, amid uncertainty as to developments in the German construction industry, the main client for lifts. The philosophy of the management at Hochinauf was to convince staff that their success within the enterprise depended on an optimistic attitude to work. Colour posters depicting the ideology of the firm going "from loser to winner" were pinned to walls, or distributed among the offices. Under the heading "The losers are always part of the problem and the winners always part of the solution," six different images of smiling winners confronting grimacing losers appealed to the employees to think positively. When, in January 1993, the production of lift cabins was transferred together with its technical infrastructure from West to East Berlin and merged with local production, two management philosophies clashed. The former production manager, Oswald, was now only responsible for pre-production, while the new production manager, Wolpert, who had been brought in from the West Berlin firm, was made responsible for overall production. Given that the two had totally opposing concepts of work, they found themselves in direct competition with one another. Whilst Oswald felt more and more pushed into a corner, Wolpert made no secret of the fact that he would have preferred to manage the entire production process, including pre-production.

After the collapse of the wall, Oswald had been one of the driving forces behind change in the enterprise. Employed previously in the investment department, he was elected in March 1990 president of the workers council. In this role he negotiated with the Western partner the merger of the two enterprises, along with social conditions for the personnel. He also tried, though without success, to overthrow the old management. On November 1st, 1990, he accepted the post of production manager. It was at this time that redundancies began in his department; thus he found himself having to lay off personnel that he had until recently defended. His relationship with his immediate superior, the former director of the "peoples owned enterprise," was extremely tense; consequently, he turned to the higher levels of management in the West. But there too tensions mounted in spring 1991, because production failed to satisfy demands made by Western management. Oswald shared the opinion of his staff, foremen and labourers who believed that the increase in productivity demanded was utopian and could not be achieved. He considered production as the weak point in the enterprise, hindered on all sides by limitations imposed by the shortcomings of other departments. Fear of being held responsible for problems in production filled him with anxiety; he became increasingly reluctant to discuss problems with his superiors in West Berlin. He felt he was constantly having to struggle and to pay for the mistakes of other departments, such as construction and acquisitions. He tried to cover up delays in his department and hide them from external view. At the same time he found himself ignored by his superiors when decisions were taken concerning his department. Thus, the decision to transfer control of cabin production to Wolpert, leaving him responsible only for pre-production, came as a complete surprise.

Wolpert had left East Germany just before the fall of the wall. After a brief period of unemployment he found work with Hochinauf in West Berlin. In only two and a half years he had been promoted to the post of cabin-production manager. Even before production was transferred, two thirds of the staff were from East Berlin and received Western salaries. When I talked to Wolpert just before the move, he explained how much he appreciated working conditions in the West and insisted that the staff he was responsible for from East Berlin had also adapted to Western conditions.

> When you come over here and when you have worked before in the East, then you simply enjoy the working conditions here. I mean not only the elegant desks and attractive offices, but also the commitment of the staff. If you call somewhere, or if you need the help of others for your work—this happens all the time because you are not working all alone—you find people that help you, to some extent. You are simply aware of a very different response. Maybe there isn't such competition as there was in the East, peculiar as this might sound. So you simply realise that the whole social climate is very motivating for somebody who comes over here. Here you are expected much more to think for yourself. When you work creatively your superiors or your boss will react very positively to it.
> (Wolpert, Production manager, Hochinauf 15.12.1992)

Workers from East Berlin employed in production in the West indeed did seem to feel the same way. They also stressed how different the atmosphere was—that in the West the climate was less competitive. At first I found these statements surprising because I had always heard, in East Berlin enterprises, that since the introduction of the market economy, competition between personnel had intensified and personal relationships had deteriorated. An explanation for this apparant contradiction appears to lie in the fact that both Wolpert and his staff had taken a risk and managed to be integrated into a successful enterprise. Much to their surprise and relief they realised that they could keep pace with Western working practices, thanks to business organisation being geared towards maximum efficiency. What they had experienced as competition in East German enterprises was the effort of each department to close itself off, to disassociate itself from any responsibility for management errors, and to ward off supplementary demands.[14] Wolpert now experienced a sense of relief at having direct responsibility for the cost of orders his section executed, at being able to ask for support from elsewhere in the enterprise, and at having contact with his clients. His work appeared to be more transparent to him, and he developed the conviction that his position was secure as long as his department was successful.

After the move to East Berlin, Wolpert aimed to run cabin-production in the same way from the shop floor. He involved himself personally in production problems, took in hand conflicts between foremen and labourers over authority, and did not hesitate to communicate his concerns and problems to his superiors in West Berlin. He was convinced that the productivity of his staff depended, to a large extent, on self-discipline and the nature of the organisation of their work.

> Now everybody will cry to Sodom and Gomorrah and say: no that's not true, I work much more and I stay at work much longer. But to organise oneself better at work is a difficult thing that really has to be learnt. When you haven't done this over the years, then it may be necessary for somebody else to show you and tell you: now pay attention, you should start to organise your time better, or when you are working on one project then do it more systematically. That's simply work organisation! This doesn't always have something to do with laziness or industriousness. To organise oneself in such a way that something comes out of it, that's the difficult thing. This is the reason why many people in the East have difficulties increasing their productivity. Because they don't know how to organise themselves. (Wolpert, Production Manager, Hochinauf, 15.12.1992)

Wolpert placed a great deal of emphasis on self-discipline in the work place, and was always available when problems arose concerning production or organisation. He often noticed faults or problems even before the foremen did, and was equally willing—tape-measure at the ready—to explain his views to the workers. This active style was appreciated by his superiors, and he was respected by the foremen who found themselves relieved of a measure of responsibility. The workers, on the other hand, who were subjected to his constant presence gritted their teeth and accepted him. The foreman, Bierschenk, comparing his former boss with the new one, did not hide how pleased he was not to have to work for Oswald anymore. Oswald had always "off-loaded work and responsibilities onto his foremen," whilst Wolpert "took the trouble to look after his workforce." Despite his constant criticism of the planned economy and the conviction that he was a victim of East German society, Oswald continued to act along the lines of the old model. He considered responsibility a danger, tried to avoid it, and concealed problems from his superiors. Although he believed himself to be defending the interests of his staff, they in fact had nothing to gain from his attitude. He may have spared them trouble in the short term, but in the long term they were burdened with insecurity, being repeatedly told that their productivity was too low.

Under Wolpert's management production workers in East Berlin in two and a half months achieved a level of productivity equal to that of their colleagues in West Berlin. However, the satisfaction they felt at achieving such a level of productivity was soon dampened by the fact that for this output they were being paid an Eastern wage. In other words they received half the salary of their Western colleagues for the same work. To outside observers, the two groups adopted similar attitudes to work; however, the motivation was different. Workers in East Berlin insisted that Wolpert used fear in order to keep them at their work. They contrasted this to the type of relationship they enjoyed with their superiors before the collapse of the wall. In those days, they claimed, they could be on familiar terms with their superiors without feeling anxious. The opposite was the case in the West Berlin enterprise, where workers originating from both East and West confirmed that they did not fear their superiors and that most of the time the latter would be unable to spot their mistakes.

Like their colleagues in the East, the West Berlin staff complained about having to work under extreme pressure; to escape from it they would take more breaks, hide behind half-finished cabins, or disappear for long periods supposedly looking for tools or material. They were however prepared to do extra overtime that had not been agreed to by the workers council. In this way, although efforts to establish discipline had the same effect, the reasons behind the decision to respect such discipline differed. For the East Berlin workers, the new organisational structure lay somehow super-imposed over their former enterprise structure. As a result they found it hard to integrate the new discipline fully: they respected it out of fear of losing their jobs. The East Berlin workers who had gone to find work in the West considered the organisational structure they found there to be correct in principle and in the nature of a market economy. They consequently accepted the discipline expected of them and were party to a new set of labour relations that Galbraith would have described as submission to *conditioned power*.[15] They were also less afraid of the consequences of negative behaviour; they could stand up for themselves if the pressure became too great or unjustified, or if they felt mistreated.

This difference was also apparent in relations between the workers who had come from the West Berlin enterprise and the members of the workers council elected prior to their arrival by their East Berlin colleagues. Members of the council, who benefited from their position and rarely left their offices to make an appearance on the shop floor, were pleased to discover that their new Western colleagues found it easier to accept them as defenders of their interests than those who had elected them. As soon as they arrived in January 1993, the new employees sent a delegation to the workers council to announce that they would stop working if the gas heating was not fixed immediately, a request that was indeed quickly granted. Since its installation in autumn 1992, the heating system produced a strong smell of gas which I too noticed in December later that year. Although the workers throughout this time had complained about the smell and of the headaches they suffered, they had not dared to make an official complaint, let alone deliver an ultimatum.

All the foremen I managed to talk to in East Berlin enterprises agreed that, since the introduction of the market economy, they were treated with more respect by their staff. The fact that they were consulted on matters concerning redundancy or technical unemployment increased their powers without their resorting to new disciplinary methods. Superiors in the West, however, were less likely to tolerate the authoritarian style practised by such foremen as Spohr at Hochinauf. The panopticon built by Spohr was dismantled in the spring of 1992, and he was moved to an office from where he could no longer observe the production work for which he was responsible. He did not, however, change his ways. He soon came into conflict with four machine operators who had come from West Berlin and were better paid than he. They laid an official complaint with the workers council. When Spohr protested to the director of personnel, the latter took steps to split up his department, nominating a second foreman and thus relieving him of part of his duties.

When questioned about the key differences between a planned and a market economy, in the context of their working environment, employees replied that in addition to job security they had lost a degree of freedom together with those "moments of madness." Whereas in an enterprise governed by a planned economy the workers' principal aim had been to increase their moments of freedom, within the market economy their main concern was to secure their position. Discipline was far less integrated in enterprises in the GDR than in the Federal Republic. Personnel in the GDR had not assimilated the discipline of production to the same extent. This was generally because many of them did not consider the planned economy to be a rational system, and therefore tried to disassociate themselves from their enterprise. Methods of control and surveillance in the GDR were more hierarchical and authoritarian then in the West, but they were also less efficient.

Burawoy and others[16] have demonstrated that staff in Western enterprises have been gradually alloted more and more responsibility in their work over the last twenty years, and that as a result it is persuasion rather that restraint that has lead to improved performance. At Hochinauf a modern Western style of management has prevailed, one designed to encourage personnel to identify with the enterprise by stimulating a sense of responsibility and optimism. The ideology of enterprise harmony veils any divergences of interest between management and workforce. The normalisation of discipline is not due to the common interest of management and workers in "saving" the enterprise. Rather, it is the result of that evolution in modern societies towards increasingly subtle mechanisms of control and punishment that often create a diffused feeling of fear.[17] This may explain why, during training seminars organised for managers, fear is promoted as the key instrument for motivating staff. Nevertheless, what can engender a sense of fear amongst staff is not so much direct repression but rather the creation of a general sense of insecurity regarding the future of the enterprise in the context of the combine and the market.

If a society organised in accordance with the rules of the market is one that is characterized by discipline, by putting an end to free spaces and moments of madness at work—in the words of one employee, "those comfortable nests," then what contrast is offered by a society governed by a planned economy? Despite the *Stasi* (secret police) surveillance, the censorship and the travel limitations in the GDR, there nevertheless were liberties in everyday life, in areas beyond the reach of power, that exist less and less in our perfectly organised society, one marked by existential insecurity.

Does the existence of these liberties confirm, however, Polanyi's view of the compatibility of "freedom" and "the power of planning"?[18] The answer is two-sided. On the one hand, the liberties that the workers in the East German enterprises today think of with nostalgia are not a direct consequence of the efficiency of socialist planning; rather, they are a consequence of its shortcomings. Plans were never executed quite as intended, and resistance against disciplinary methods was successful because management had to rely on the goodwill of the workforce to put in extra effort to meet the plan targets. On the other hand, security of employment was part of the basis of socialist society and it was given to all regardless of performance. The workers under real existing socialism did indeed possess that which Polanyi termed the privilege of the well-off classes in market society: "liberty born out of (a certain) leisure in security."[19] However, other types of employment, those involving liberties other than the liberty of leisure, and those giving access to institutional power, were severely restricted by political ideology and depended to a large extent on agreement with the political system.

NOTES

1. Michel Foucault, *Sexualität und Wahrheit*. 1. Band, *Der Wille zum Wissen*. Frankfurt: Suhkamp Verlag, 1977, p.115.
2. Michel Foucault, "Disciplinary Power and Subjection," in Steven Lukes, (ed.), *Power*. Oxford: Blackwell Publishers, 1986, p.238.
3. Michel Foucault, "Disciplinary Power and Subjection," p.241.
4. Names of all enterprises and persons are pseudonyms.
5. Reinhart Bendix, *Work and Authority in Industry*. Berkeley: University of California Press, 1974.
6. Bendix, *Work*, p.XLI.
7. Ulrich Voskamp und Volker Wittke, "Aus Modernisierungsblockaden werden Abwärtsspiralen—Zur Reorganisation von Betrieben und Kombinaten in der ehemaligen DDR," (Inability to Modernize leads to Increasing Decay. The Reorganization of Enterprises and Combines in the former GDR), in *Berliner Journal für Soziologie*, 1 (1991), 17-39, 31.
9. Michel Foucault, "Disciplinary Power and Subjection," p.241.
10. James Scott, *Domination and the Art of Resistance. Hidden Transcripts*. New Haven: Yale University Press, p.118.
11. James Scott, *Domination and the Art of Resistance*, pp. 208-209.
12. Hannah Arendt, "Communicative Power," in Steven Lukes, (ed.), *Power*, p.64.
13. Hans Merkens, Dagmar Bergs-Winkels u.a., *Die Organisationskultur eines VEB*, (The Organizational Culture of a VEB (People's Owned Enterprise)). Working Paper, Industrial Research Group. Free University of Berlin, 1990.
14. Minutes of the assembly of the workers council of Hochinauf, 20.4.1990.
15. J.K. Galbraith, "Power and Organisation," p.214.
16. Michael Burawoy, *Manufacturing Consent*. Chicago: Chicago University Press, 1979, p.182. Horst Kern and Michael Schumann, *Das Ende der Arbeitteilung?: Rationalisierung in der industriellen Produktion: Bestandsaufnahme*. (The End of the Division of Labour? Rationalizing of Industrial Production. The State of the Art). München: C.H. Beck, 1990. Ulrich Voskamp and Volker Wittke, "Junge Facharbeiter in der Produktion—eine Herausforderung für betriebliche Arbeitspolitik," (Young Qualified Workers in Production—A Challenge for the Politics of Labour in the Enterprise), in *SoFi-Mitteilungen*, 19, 1992.
17. Michel Foucault, "Disciplinary Power and Subjection," p. 241.
18. Karl Polanyi, *The Great Transformation*. Frankfurt: Suhrkamp, 1990, pp. 342-344.
19. Karl Polanyi, *The Great Transformation*, p. 336.

Chapter Ten

SURVIVAL STRATEGIES IN POST-1989 BULGARIA
Yulian Konstantinov

New problems of economic survival faced the great majority of Bulgarians during the last five years of change from "Socialism" to "Capitalism." The discussion that follows will deal specifically with the options which are available for two distinct groups in Bulgarian society: on the one hand, white-collar workers and officials from the lower levels of the previous state economic and administrative structure; on the other, ethnic minority groups. Of these latter the focus will be primarily on two: the nearly half million strong *Roma* (Gypsy) component (in a population of 8.4 m), and the Bulgarian Muslims (*Pomaks*) who number around 220,000. In addition to these comparatively low-level actors, the newly forming class of what may be called "real agents of reform" (or the "enfranchised *nomenklatura*")[1] will be briefly described from the point of view of their present and expected future courses of action. The linkage comes from the fact that survival strategies realised by low-level actors are to be seen mainly as a function of orientations in the higher economic and political echelons of power.

Although the general discourse that describes the "process of transition" in a country such as Bulgaria presents it almost exclusively in terms of movement from a previously centralised economy and authoritarianism to a "free market economy" and democracy, empirical investigation of survival-strategies does not seem to indicate a tendency towards the "formalisation" of economic life. By examining the economic behaviour of both low- and high-level actors I shall try to argue that there is continuity in the embeddedness (in a Polanyian sense)[2] of economic activity as a function of aspects of the social, cultural and ethnic life of majority and minority communities. By observing economic activity, we are able to redefine social, cultural, and ethnic identities and reinterpret their boundaries. Thus the empirical material gathered, mainly through investigating the massive survival-strategy of "trader-tourism,"[3] strengthens the case for culturally specific behaviour in an extreme situation (and, consequently, the case for cultural relativism) side by side with "substantivist" orientations (again in a Polanyian sense) exhibited by the actors. It may be too early to come to any more general conclusions at the present stage of investigating transitional phenomena in Eastern Europe, but I shall tentatively propose that the chances of economic life becoming "disembedded" from social, cultural, and ethnic constraints in this area do not appear to be high. Direct transference of Western expertise as to how to achieve a "free market economy" is beginning to ring increasingly hollow, and there is growing dissatisfaction with the workings of the consultantship industry and Western "relief-programs." From this point of view a suggestion will be made as to the value of spontaneously developing survival-strategies "from below" as they evolve and are being tried out.

TRADER-TOURISM

The phenomenon of trader-tourism, in spite of its massive proportions, has remained virtually unnoticed in recent economic anthropological research.[4] Briefly, trader-tourism is a form of trading activity under the guise of tourism without payment of customs duty; as we shall see below, the trader-tourist also avoids entirely or to a large extent the paying of taxes. In this way trader-tourism forms part of the informal economic activities that create a predominantly "invisible income" for the participants.

Bulgarian trader-tourists travel mainly to Istanbul where they buy merchandise from wholesalers at close to production cost. Each buys goods (predominantly clothes) for an average of 1000-2000 USD and returns with them to Bulgaria, where they are subsequently offered for sale in the numerous open-air markets in towns and villages (*bitaks*), or in the tens of thousands of small shops (*boutiques*) which have almost entirely replaced the previous state shops. Many of these goods are sold simply from stalls in the street, thus giving the town-scene a new "free market" appearance somewhat like a village fair.[5]

The trader-tourists travel in bus-parties of 40-45 persons, the trading trip (of 2-3 days) being organised by a travel agency whose owner is usually the guide during the trip. This person (the "organiser") is usually a woman, an ex-employee of the previous State Tourist Company (*Balkantourist*) or a similar state organisation. Her role is pivotal for she sees to it that the customs officials at the Bulgarian-Turkish border do not become too particular about the obviously commercial look of the "tourist" bus. The latter, on the home-bound journey, is jampacked with merchandise to such an extent that there is barely room to sit or move. The delicate operation of "passing for" tourists is carried out by the simple expedient of the bribe. This is contributed collectively and usually amounts to 200-400 USD per bus. The latter may carry anything from 20,000 to 80,000 USD worth of goods. Thus for any given year since 1991 the annual amount of imported goods would be no less than 100 million USD, with bribe-money given in the region of 0.5 million. Trader-tourists travel usually not less than twice a month, so that the annual number of trips may be put at 50,000 roughly for the whole of the country. If one takes into account the fact that trader-tourism is practised over the whole territory of the former Soviet Bloc—from Sofia to Murmansk to Vladivostok—one may end up with millions of people engaged in this huge survival operation.

BULGARIANS, ROMA, AND MUSLIMS

Trader-tourism, under present conditions, is open to anyone who can put together a minimal starting sum (at least 400 USD), take a couple of holdalls, and be prepared to face the hardships on the road to Istanbul and back, and the subsequent setting up of a stall in the market. The money is collected within the family or kin, and often in a "joint-venture" with friends. In many cases the friends tend to be former colleagues from a state office or enterprise. From this perspective the money put together very much resembles former mutual support funds at places of state-employment, the VSKs (*vzaimo-spomagatelna kasa*, mutual support funds). These VSKs accumulated capital from participating employees, earned minimal interest, and helped out in major personal economic projects of the previous period—primarily the acquiring of a flat, a small country cottage, or a car.

It is to be emphasized that at present the small entrepreneur cannot seriously hope to find support for economic activities outside the kinship and former colleagues network. Interest rates of commercial banks are prohibitive (up to and even above 100%); foreign relief-programs (like PHARE) have become quickly bureaucratised on a local level and are out of reach for those who are not personally connected with the bureaucrats on a client-patron basis. With national unemployment reaching well over 20% (1997), a rate of inflation of over 200% a month, and crumbling social security provisions, the greater mass of the population is hard-pressed to find ways out of their present predicament. Initial orientation to the service sector (e.g., opening small grocery shops, restaurants and cafes) has been dampened by the combined factors of the initial capital required and crushing racketeering activities directed towards such new entrepreneurs. Against this background trader-tourism offers a viable option. It requires a relatively small starting capital, offers quick returns, and with its low-prestige profile and mobility is less prone to suffer from the attention of racketeers. Most importantly, however, it offers profits of 40% or more on the money invested in a trip and subsequent avoidance of taxation as a result of clearing customs by bribing the officials. To the importance of corruption as the mainstay of this survival strategy I shall return later.

While the pressure of the economic crisis bears down upon the whole of society (with the exception of a tiny percentage towards the top of the pyramid), the burden is not equally distributed. Thus for the Bulgarian majority unemployment figures are considerably lower than for the principal minority groups. These latter are the Bulgarian Turks (around 600,000), the already mentioned *Roma* (around 500,000), and the Bulgarian Muslims (220,000). For the mainly agricultural communities of the Turks and Bulgarian Muslims, as well as for the largely marginalised urban and village *Roma*, unemployment tends to reach over 80%. Especially hard-hit are the Bulgarian Muslims as a result of their dependance on tobacco-growing, and on the now lost jobs on cooperative farms. They have also suffered due to the dismantling of the village workshop system, and the closing down of big industrial and mining enterprises, which used to provide employment on a daily and seasonal labour-migration basis. The peasant-worker type of Islamic economy depended for its "worker"-part on salaried jobs provided by co-operative farms, workshops as extensions of cooperative farms and bigger industrial enterprises (mainly the textile and armament industries), as well as on daily migration to mining and flotation sites in the Rhodopes.[6] All of these sources of employment are now mostly memories of the past.

The *Roma* are in a very similar situation and may be discussed in comparison with the Bulgarian Muslims (the *Pomaks*). Within such a comparison, however, two radically different attitudes and orientations seem to appear in respect of one and the same economic cause—the economic crisis and the plight of the minorities. More specifically, these radically different attitudes concern primarily one of the few popularly available survival strategies, that of trader-tourism as described above. The distinction may be seen as stemming from the difference between the strategies for preserving cultural identity that the two groups employ, and thus a case could be made for cultural dominance over economic action even in an existentially critical situation. Three years of investigating the market and participating both in its "stall" and "trading-trip" components have convincingly shown that attitudes range from swift and massive inclusion into trader-tourism as with the *Roma*, to almost total exclusion as with the Bulgarian Muslims. On the intermediate side, the pattern exhibited by the Bulgarian Turks points to partial inclusion, exercised mainly by the urban Turkish population, and Turkish family and kinship networks who have members in both Bulgaria and Turkey. Of the *Roma* and their participation in trader-tourism it can be said that both in the town markets and in the bus-parties to regional trading hubs, the *Roma* comprise more than half the total number of traders. By the general public—i.e., the Bulgarian majority—they are perceived, however, as the characterizing participants, for, although the other half of the market population is comprised of Bulgarians, trader-tourism is referred to as "Gypsy trading" (*tsiganska turgoviya*). Another characterizing component is made up of foreign traders, among them citizens of the CIS, Chinese, Vietnamese and Middle Easterners. CIS citizens are the most prominent here; thus, in Turkey for instance, trader-tourist activity has come to be associated mainly with them, under the blanket term *Russian trading*.

Returning to the specifics of the Bulgarian case, it could be said that not only are the *Roma* the characterizing protagonists of trader-tourism—it is the *Roma women* who perform this role. On the whole the structure of the merchandise in trader-tourism is largely oriented toward the needs of women and children, and women are prominent in both the buying and selling population of the market. It is thus the case that trader-tourism, in the Bulgarian context, has a strongly marked ethnic and gender aspect, both of these features defining a cultural sphere of operations which presents problems for newcomers from the majority population. To a terrain of informal economic activities which the *Roma* perceive as "theirs," Bulgarian members of the impoverished previously state-employed population come as mere novices. They have then to accept the leadership role of the marginalized *Roma* community with which previously only the most superficial contact would have existed. Moreover, male former state-officials have to cooperate—in trader-tourism—with the *Romni*, the Gypsy women. This is a marked reversal of social roles, for in the previous scheme of things a *Romni* would be employed mainly in lowly menial jobs such as cleaning. The distance between a male administrator and a *Romni* cleaner would be so great that the two would be hardly able to register each other's existence, let alone cooperate on equal terms.

And yet such cooperation does now take place, as has been established through field-research conducted since 1992. While this is so, there are serious differences between the two groups in their attitude to the trader-tourism economic activity they mutually participate in. The most pronounced of these can be seen in the fact that the Bulgarian traders treat the market and trader-tourism mainly as a transitional stage, a necessary "excursion" into the Gypsy world, one which they try to get out of as quickly as possible. In spite of the dangers of racketeering, the next desired stage is the *boutique* (shop) in the "centre of town." From there on, orientations are modelled along the lines set by the "enfranchised *nomenklatura*" and symbolized by glitzy offices, BMW cars, and dazzling life-styles. In contrast, the *Roma* exhibit every sign of intending to permanently occupy the niche so timely opened up by transitional events. There is no room for ethnographic detail here, but let it be mentioned that while *Roma* traders have occupied the same stalls in the market for several years now, Bulgarian vendors tend to appear for much shorter periods and then to be replaced by newcomers. During field work in 1994 many tour-organisers told us proudly that they were no longer travelling with the Gypsies—that was a past phase—they were on to "bigger things now" (i.e., trading in gold). On the strength of observation of the structural dynamics of trader-tourism it can be concluded, therefore, that cooperation and constructive interaction do not extend beyond the domain of the market, and instead of eroding ethnic and social boundaries, seem to maintain and—if anything—strengthen them. The massive inclusion of *Roma* in trader-tourism may be expected to compensate to a considerable extent for the disintegration of social security provisions and loss of employment. As one Evangelical *Romni* of the Turkish Gypsy group told us in the Sofia *bitak* of Malashevtsi: "God has thought of us and has given us this trading."

It was no accident that the *Roma* were the first to see and use the opportunities offered by transitional phenomena in the direction of trader-tourism. Generally marginalised by host communities during their migrations, they have always sought to preserve cultural independence homogeneity through economic activities ignored or spurned by the majority populations. During the decades of "socialism" in Bulgaria (1944-1989), in spite of drastic measures to include the *Roma* in the state-planned economy they continued to predominate in marginalized economic niches of an informal character. *Roma* traders bought and sold used clothes in the streets all through the socialist period—the cry of the *vehtoshar* (used clothes trader): *"Stari drehi koupouvam!"* (I'm buying old clothes!) is known to generations of Bulgarians down to the present period. As has been well-described in the literature, market activities—especially live-stock trading[7]—have become so ingrained in the *Roma* culture that the men would call themselves *forroske save* (boys of the market). In an earlier field-trip to the markets, I visited in 1979 the one for live-stock accompanying the June village fair in the village of Kamen (NE Bulgaria) which boasted for sale not only domestic animals and poultry, but also second-hand Soviet-made cars as well as all sorts of household appliances and electronic equipment, the traders being almost exclusively *Roma*.

Without going further either into the vast literature on the subject or into local empirical data, it may confidently be suggested that informal economic activities in town-markets are deeply embedded in *Roma* social relationships. Of particular interest here are studies of various cultural manifestations of such embeddedness, as for instance the already-mentioned description by Stewart of *Roma* horse-traders in Hungary. There he portrays in fine anthropological detail the intriguing metaphorization of relations between the sexes ("wife-swapping") using an economic activity (horse-trading) as symbolic material. In a similar way trader-tourism can be seen—from the point of view of the traders themselves—as symbolizing the spirit of the community in its search for imaginative loopholes ignored by the *Gadzhe* (the Non-*Roma*, the "fools"). The ability to withstand the difficulties of the present economic crisis by finding such loopholes through boundaries (mainly by the expedient of bribery), to face the difficulties of the road, to overcome fears and apprehensions, to face the risks of the market—all these contribute to the self-realization of the participant as a *culturally-successful* being. From this point of view, the member of the enfranchised *nomenklatura*, the "new businessman," is in a less advantageous position. Irrespective of dazzling economic success, his achievement cannot at present count towards cultural reinforcement, except via increasingly dubious forays into conspicuous consumerism. This point—the search for cultural support and legitimacy—is of great significance when we examine orientations in the development of the newly forming class of the "enfranchised *nomenklatura*" to which I shall return below. The *Roma* may be said to represent the pole of positive inclusion into the informal economic activity of trader-tourism, which functions as a cultural booster for them. At the same time, the other minority community in this comparison, the Bulgarian Muslims, represent the other extreme in the orientation toward trader-tourism as an available survival strategy: an orientation of exclusion. In contrast to the *Roma*, trader-tourism (or informal market activities of this type) may be said to be perceived by most *Pomaks* as detrimental to the cultural stability and preservation of their community.

The reasons for such a contrasting treatment of economic activity can be but briefly sketched here. They seem to be mainly connected with the evolving strategies employed by the community of Bulgarian Muslims for the sake of preserving their cultural integrity. The basic task the Bulgarian Muslims have to confront in this regard stems from their openness to speculation as to who they ethnically are, in a nation-state type of discourse. Living in four regional nation-states (Bulgaria, Greece, Turkey, and Macedonia (FYROM)), they have become an object of nation-state conflict[8] as each of these states claims that ethnically they are connected with the majority population. That they are ethnic Bulgarians, Islamized during the period from the 15th to the 17th century, is academically widely accepted;[9] but this does not improve matters much, in fact quite the contrary. It prompted the regime of Todor Zhivkov to undertake the so-called campaign of "Rebirth," forcing the Bulgarian Muslims to become "born again" Bulgarians (1972-1974). The same assimilation campaign was subsequently tried out on the Bulgarian Turks (1984-1989) and became one of the major propellants of change in November 1989 and the ousting of the Zhivkov regime.[10] To withstand assimilatory pressures the Bulgarian Muslim community has relied mainly on demographic strategies, such as retaining the compactness of the community, preserving a tightly-knit family and kinship network, sustaining a high birth-rate (especially when compared to Bulgarian families), and developing a peasant-worker type of economy. One of the most striking representations of this endocentric strategy of community insulation can be seen in the fact that Bulgarian Muslims (as well as Bulgarian Turks) did not participate in the large-scale migration from village to town so characteristic of the whole period of socialism, but most spectacular between the mid-50s and the early 80s. As a result more than 90% of the Bulgarian Muslim population today live in one area of the country, the Rhodopes, while more than 80% of the Bulgarian Turkish population occupy the

North-east and South-east of the country, i.e., eastwards of a line from Rousse on the Danube to Kurdzhali close to the border with Greece.

The village to town migration of the previous period and the trader-tourism phenomenon of the present transitional period may be compared as massive survival strategies employed by the majority of the Bulgarian population. As such they are typical of the whole territory of the former Soviet Bloc. Initially triggered by collectivization and the emphasis on heavy industrial production, now with the present destruction of this type of economy there is a shift in direction—one hopes only temporarily—to trading and providing services as the shortest and easiest route to acquiring start-up capital. The rhetoric of state socialism described the strategy of migration as part of the "modernization" of the country; now the strategy of mass "free-market" engagement is described in similarly positive terms at home and abroad as representing the transition to a free market economy. That first "transition" to modernity proved to be largely mythical, however, and one may expect that the inner logic of the present one also differs from its depiction in official discourse. Another similarity between previous and present survival strategies "of the masses," and the continuity between them, is to be seen in the nature of non-participatory reactions as much as in participatory ones. Thus both the Bulgarian Turks and Bulgarian Muslims—numbering nearly one million people at the time—did not participate in the migration to towns, but, conversely, increased the compactness of the agricultural areas they had traditionally inhabited. Such migration as occurred was in the direction of Turkey in successive officially sanctioned ways.[11] Similar practices increased the compactness of Islamic populations. Reliance on demographic and economic means for community preservation can be found in neighbouring former Yugoslavia, especially in Bosnia, Kossovo, and Western Macedonia (FYROM).

This community strategy for cultural preservation is, in economic terms at least, extremely unfavourable at present. The case of the Bulgarian Muslims is perhaps most pronounced in this context. As mentioned above, the Bulgarian Muslims have lost heavily on all economic fronts—due to the precarious state of tobacco production, the dismantling of industrial enterprises and cooperative farms, and the closing down of village workshops. To these set-backs we may add the increasing difficulty in finding productive employment in neighbouring Turkey, and also the growing rigidity of borders—with Turkey[12] and Greece in the first place, and with other Middle Eastern and European countries as well. And yet, even in compact Bulgarian Muslim populated areas, Muslims do not participate in market activities, the main actors there being again the *Roma*, Bulgarians, and foreign groups such as Russians, Ukrainians and Romanians. It is difficult not to observe, in view of such a situation, that the Bulgarian Muslims are deliberately declining to avail themselves of a survival strategy at a time of crisis (i.e., they refuse to "see economic sense") irrespective of powerful "push" factors. In the current situation, grim as it is, Bulgarian Muslims continue to focus on agriculture and mountain pastoralism as principal forms of employment—with some seasonal migration to construction sites in Bulgarian towns—in which, however, only the male population is engaged. In some cases such labour migration extends along now traditional *gastarbeiter* routes to Islamic countries such as Libya or Kuwait.

In vernacular texts, the reluctance to venture beyond the confines of the community enclave—except for the younger male population—is transmitted by a self-definition in which the *Pomaks* describe themselves as "simple people" who, if they were to go to towns and other traditional domains of expected deception like the market, "would be cheated, robbed, perhaps even killed." This form of control extends especially over the young women who "would get spoiled," if they went to town, "would be abducted as sex-slaves" and "generally ruined." This type of rhetoric is in marked contrast to that of "self-realization" as employed by the *Roma*: one which promotes skills in market-dealings as an ability to gain the upper hand in respect of the non-*Roma* ("the fools"). Thus the two cultures treat one and the same economic material as an instrument for drawing different cultural boundaries and sustaining separate identities. In this sense, both village-to-town migration of the previous period and the trader-tourism of today present cases of economic embeddedness in the dominant social and cultural fabric of identity-sustaining systems.

THE "ENFRANCHISED *NOMENKLATURA*"

Where do the Bulgarian majority stand in all this? The target-group focussed on here is comprised of members of the previous amorphous class of *slouzhashti* (literally, civil servants): i.e., low-echelon state employees in administrative offices or branches of the economy, at the bottom of the hierarchy, and middle to top echelons of administrators. In a country predominantly rural prior to the great migratory movement of the mid-1950s, the *slouzhashti* of the socialist period represented first generation urban dwellers who still retained strong ties with the villages. Educated in the initial decades of the period, the civil servant class pursued *slouzhashti* careers and demonstrated demographic shifts in a direction diametrically opposite to those of the Bulgarian Turks and Muslims, associating their urban existence with the values of a centrally planned economy deeply embedded in ideological precepts. This ideological use of economic activity was largely experienced as being on the side of progress, modernity and humanity. From this particular perspective remnants of previous free market activities could be observed only as practised by the low-prestige, marginalized *Roma* population, and were considered as curiously preserved but dying out.

The ideological use of the economy proved, however, to be heavily detrimental to the general quality of life; one may say that as early as 1956 cyclical campaigns were initiated for improving economic efficiency. These culminated in the introduction of the "new economic mechanism" in 1978 (long before the Soviet *perestroyka* started), so that by the beginning of 1989 there were already more than 10,000 private enterprises in Bulgaria, representing those that had been moderately liberated from state control. In the process of the creation of such enterprises and the campaigns introducing new economic mechanisms we can see the engendering of the new class of the enfranchised *nomenklatura*, now largely branded as the "mafia," "money-launderers," "cops" (*tchengeta*), KGB-agents (*kagebisti*), etc. The label used in the West before 1989 was mainly "technocrats" which had a positive ring to it, but after the reforms of '89 was replaced by negative terms of the mafioso-type. With the changes of November 1989 the paths of the lower and higher echelons of the previous *nomenklatura* diverged sharply. It must be said, however, that a great deal of divergence existed already in the previous period.

Thus education for the higher echelons was obtained at elite schools and exclusive colleges—primarily foreign (English) language schools in Bulgaria, and, at the level of higher education, at the trade and diplomatic schools in Moscow and Sofia. Subsequently the alumni of such colleges were quickly propelled into foreign-trade representation and embassies, with strong Secret Service connections. Foreign experience and contacts were later to prove extremely advantageous for this economic *nomenklatura* class (*stopanska nomenklatura*), leading them to a role which can rightly be called that of prinicipal agents of reform. The whole point and propellant of the 1989-changes, from this point of view, had to do much more with the liberation of this younger and able class of state officials from the stifling control of the geriatric Politbureau than with anything dissidents ever did in the country.

Still, the new class was liberated "from above" by, paradoxically, a self-subversive strategy of the previous generation of Communist Party cadres, the "fathers." It was they who had created educational possibilities for the new class of the "sons," they who had propelled them into Western-connected careers, and ultimately they who gave them possibilities to become Western-style millionaires as they now are in a substantial majority. The absurdities of this development are often revealed in one and the same family by the different generations: a previously powerful Party administrator may be now an impoverished state old age pensioner, while the son is president of the local branch of a Western company, exclusive representative of its products in Bulgaria, a wealthy "new businessman." The absurdity of the situation increases further when the impoverished parents demonstrate in the streets for "the rights of the common people," reliving their revolutionary youth of the 1930s and 1940s, while the children enjoy sybaritic life-styles. And yet there is a consistent logic in all this. Under the previous semi-feudal system the children could never rise above the ranks of grey officialdom, living in a prefabricated high-rise, and driving a Soviet-made car—and the parents certainly wanted a better future for them.

This was realized during the course of rapid change, following the ousting of Todor Zhivkov after 33 years of authoritarian rule (November 10, 1989). During 1990-91 with a still largely Communist ("Socialist") government in power, the order of the day was to save Party funds from the eager hands of the newly emerged Democratic Opposition (UDF, Union of Democratic Forces). The typical scenario was to start a privately-owned business as an extension of a state enterprise with one of the enfranchised *nomenklatura* often being simultaneously Director of the state enterprise and President of the private company. This naturally gives immense opportunities for quick enrichment—mainly by selling expensive Western products to the state enterprise, while selling cheaply its products or raw materials abroad. In this way the state enterprise is driven slowly into bankruptcy, but is kept hovering on the brink by credits (so-called "bad credits") coming ultimately from the National Bank. This latter, in turn, is supported by the help of international monetary institutions, first and foremost the IMF. Periodic injections by the IMF are all the more necessary in view of the huge foreign debt of the country (in the region of 11 b.USD). When, in the fall of 1996, the IMF refused to subsidize the enrichment of the enfranchised *nomenklatura* in this way any further, economic catastrophy descended swiftly during the following winter months.

The activities of the enfranchised *nomenklatura*, although bringing desired wealth, quickly undermined the state economy, and thus threw out onto the street the lower *nomenklatura* echelons, the "citizen-clients."[13] These, consequently, had either to engage in available survival strategies led by the *Roma* (trader-tourism), emigrate to more affluent countries (an increasingly impossible option), go back to the villages, or wait for a job to emerge miraculously. If one is to extrapolate on the basis of the *Roma* participation in trader-tourism, involving no less than half of the *Roma* population, and knowing that home trader-tourism is almost equally divided between the *Roma* and the Bulgarians, we may expect that around 250,000 Bulgarians have chosen the trader-tourist option, or around 11% of the working population. In the countries of the CIS (especially Russia, Belarus and Ukraine) this percentage is probably even higher.

FUTURE ORIENTATIONS
The shift in emphasis from production to trading in the last seven years has made possible the survival-strategy of trader-tourism. The disappearance of cheap home products has created a demand for imported cheap goods, and the regional economies—primarily the Turkish and Greek—have responded instantly to this demand, experiencing a current minor boom as a result. In Istanbul such developments are especially visible, as whole streets in its commercial section have shop-signs and advertisements in almost all languages of the former Soviet Bloc countries. The trader-tourists are the suppliers of such goods for the home public, but the success of their enterprise depends largely on the possibility of smuggling goods into their home countries. In the case of a country like Bulgaria, this is possible—given the scale and continuity of the operation—by the almost institutionalised corruption of customs officials at all levels. Thus the success of trader-tourism is due to not paying customs duties, nor taxes (as the goods smuggled into the country do not officially exist). The overall "grey economy" of this type may amount to as much as 0.9% of the current Bulgarian GNP. This figure, although extrapolated by crude methods, may be surprisingly close to the truth. In a recent survey conducted by the Labour Office (*Arbeiterkammer*) in Austria, the overall informal economic activities in Bulgaria were estimated at 38 b. Austrian schillings (3.4 b. USD), or 1.9% of the country's GNP. Austria, one may add, is in the forefront of Western countries affected by informal economic activities coming largely from countries of the ex-Soviet Bloc.

With the blocking of foreign aid in September 1996, the country spiralled into hyperinflation. In a situation of virtual anomie, the original idea of transforming the political power of the previous regime into economic power seemed to be forgotten. The very symbol of this strategy—the leading pre-1989 "technocrat" and supreme "mafia-leader," ex-prime minister Andrei Loukanov—was brutally shot dead on the steps of his home (2 October 1996). Wholesale plundering of the country ensued, leading to sky-high prices of food and energy, as well as the disappearance of grain and petrol by January and February. Finally, a massive wave of demonstrations, culminating in an attack on the Parliament building, blocked the path of a second Socialist government and necessitated early Parliamentary elections in April 1997.

CONTROL AND ORGANIZATIONAL INFRASTRUCTURE
Against such a background, it is of primary importance to consider the future course of action of the real agents of reform, the enfranchised *nomenklatura*. At least two aspects of the situation seem to be of primary relevance here. The

enfranchisement of the *nomenklatura* and particularly the first period of the transferring of Party funds into private businesses (1990-1991), the "money-laundering period," seemed to operate on two false assumptions. The first was an assumption of continuing control "from above." Conceived within the tightly controllable *nomenklatura* atmosphere of the previous period, the expectation was that the "new businessmen" will continue to operate as trusted Party cadres, to whom is delegated a responsibility equal to their competence and experience. This proved to be largely erroneous. Once liberated, "the sons" no longer wished to be controlled by their parents or grandparents. Since however the "reformed" Communist Party chose to preserve the continuity of its development and most of all its massive grass-roots support, serious conflicts began to develop between a very much impoverished "red" grass-roots electorate, belonging generally to the older age-bracket (over 55) and the "young musketeers," the enfranchised economic cadres of the younger generation (35-55). The conspicuous consumerism of "the sons," their celebration of new wealth in a macho-culture atmosphere with heavily erotic overtones, provoked the ire of the Communist parent and grandparent generation who still remember (and are now painfully reminded of) the poverty of their humble backgrounds and the Stalinist sentiments they built careers on. These are essentially the participants in Socialist Party-organized rallies. Because of the predominance in these of elderly women, often banging empty pots and pans, they are popularly known as the rallies of the "red grandmothers" (*cherveni babichki*). Conflict was growing between these elderly grass-root members and the elitist circles of the liberated "sons" and "grandsons," a conflict popularly known as the "red grandmothers" versus the "red mobiphones" (the *mobifon*, a cellular phone being one of the status-symbols of the enfranchised *nomenklatura*, together with the BMW car, the fashion-model lover, and the Rolex wrist-watch).

More important than the dissatisfaction with the "hooliganism of the children," on the part of the "red (grand-)parents," is the fact that the whole point of the exercise was beginning to be lost. After all, the reformed Socialist Party was supposed to take advantage of the transformed wealth—it had not been created to be squandered in Great Gatsby style, but to strengthen the Party's economic muscle. Most important, however, was that there existed a vast reserve of political capital for the Party to draw upon, if—in the likely event of its being elected to govern again (in the late fall of 1994)—it could rewaken production in the country, reduce inflation and unemployment, decrease corruption, and battle successfully with rampant criminality. For these reasons there existed growing motivation for control to be resumed by the Party elite, and the "young musketeers" brought to heel. In economic terms this difficult operation was to be linked with the coming of privatization to the country. Once former state assets became productive again, and sole responsibility for that was assumed by the enfranchised *nomenklatura*, the whole pattern was supposed to change. This would have been felt most acutely by the trader-tourists: their particular survival strategy would lose its viability, and the years 1991-1994 would be nostalgically looked back upon as the golden age of trader-tourism in Bulgaria. However, two years of Socialist government (1994-1996) patently proved that the "red mobiphones" had seized power with the sole intent of quick enrichment on an individual basis. The "red (grand-)parents" and their ideological reflexes had been sacrificed and discarded, the political capital to be gained was ignored, and thus trader-tourism and the whole informal economy received an additional breathing space for its operation.

The second false assumption made in the initial period after November 1989 was that the new businessmen would be able to negotiate in an atmosphere resembling the orderly and unproblematic Party meetings of the previous era. This proved not to be so. No serious structure for the developing of common strategies and negotiation of interests was created. The single main effort in this direction—the creation of the *Confederation of Large Industrialists*, popularly known as the G-13—performed miserably. Loudly proclaimed in 1995, it disintegrated soon after, giving way to unabashed gang-wars.

For while the failure to establish an organizational infrastructure was obvious, the need to negotiate interests still remained. The atmosphere of near anomie was—and still is—characterized by private armies of ex-sportsmen and Secret Service officers fighting it out in the streets, as well as by the bombing of cars and offices, assassinations and all forms of violent extortion. The resulting atmosphere of increased criminality and pervasive corruption connected with the disintegration of state institutions is conducive to semi-legal survival strategies of the trader-tourism type, but, again, imposes a crushing burden of unprecedented criminality on the lower layers of the population who are defenceless. An additional grim feature of the situation is that the *Roma* have become seriously implicated as marked participants in criminal activities, and this is conducive to violent reactions often of a racist nature.

PSYCHOLOGICAL FACTORS

The sharp separation of the enfranchised *nomenklatura* from the rest of society can be expected to pose serious psychological problems for this type of actor, actually the most decisive agent in the current processes. This part of the picture has remained clouded by moral condemnation and value-judgements of a generally negative character and, to my knowledge, has remained completely uninvestigated. Material churned out by both the home and international press has tended to mystify the whole scene and create an image of unmitigated villainy in respect of the enfranchised *nomenklatura*. Labels such as "mafia," "KGB-agents," etc. have become commonplace not only in popular language and the media, but also in more serious academic discussion. Texts produced by members of the enfranchised *nomenklatura* themselves suggest several main problematic motifs. As noted by other researchers, notably Sampson,[14] the actors try to promote an image of themselves as patriotic citizens, working selflessly for the national economy and the country. Hence for instance the label *industrialists* for the Bulgarian "confederation" of the (originally) G-13, while in actual fact it represents mainly trading and speculative finance, in fact trader-tourism writ large. Promoting a desired image of themselves as responsible captains of industry and finance, the actors present "self-made men" biographies to the public. According to these they have made their wealth on the strength of their individual talent, industriousness, flexibility, daring, courage, and similar virtues. The desire to forget about the true reality of the operation and replace it with stories of personal heroism is palpably obvious.

This type of narrative reaches a crescendo when it comes to the issue of their previous Secret Service related past. A good example is provided by the almost hysterical reaction to a short article which appeared a few years ago in the *Financial Times*.[15] Presenting the liberation of the economic *nomenklatura* as a carefully planned operation set in motion as early as 1982 by the Politbureau and the State Security apparatus (*DS*), the article targeted specifically Mr. Iliya Pavlov, the President of *Multigroup*, the most powerful enfranchised *nomenklatura* concern in the country. The Bulgarian public wouldn't have been aware of the appearance of the article had it not been for the vehement denunciation of its content on the pages of the *Multigroup* controlled daily *24 Chasa* and its Sunday edition (*168 Chasa*). The rhetoric employed in the denunciation of Virginia Marsh's article is worthy of being quoted:

> Recently an article from the Financial Times has been used by *interested persons and groups* to increase malicious propaganda against *honest private businessmen*, and primarily against the more visible among them. The politically involved press and state electronic media *literally crawl out of their skins* to popularize the lies and fabrications piled up high in this article. (Italics mine, Y.K.)

Anyone acquainted with the style of official pre-1989 denunciations of "Western propaganda's malicious attempts to denigrate the achievement of mature Socialism" would instantly recognise it in the above quotation, complete with the Russian journalese expression "crawl out of their skins" (*vilezayut iz shkouri*). Now the "malicious propaganda" is directed against "honest private businessmen" and seems to come again from the mysterious "interested persons and groups" of the Cold War years.

Ironic as all this is, it contains strong signals regarding future orientations on the part of the real agents of reform. Just as Bulgarian trader-tourists in the market regard this occupation as temporary, so the enfranchised *nomenklatura* may be said to occupy a "mafia"-like position only for the time being. In spite of the failed attempts to regularise relationships and negotiate interests in a more civilised way than is currently practised, the desire manifests itself in the overall discourse directed towards regaining legitimacy and public trust. The present deficit of praise for the achievements of the "new businessmen" and the enveloping public rhetoric of distrust, fear and derision, are in sharp contrast to the legitimate positions these actors enjoyed till very recently and the nature of the contact they had with other social groups. The mafia label is especially misleading. The enfranchised *nomenklatura* certainly do not come from poverty-stricken Sicilian villages, nor from the immigrant ghettoes of American cities. This is a second generation urban *nomenklatura*, accustomed to a position of responsibility and authority. It is to be expected that it will attempt to use further economic developments—primarily privatisation—to regain such a position, much in the same way as has happened in the more transitionally advanced countries in Eastern Europe, particularly the Czech Republic, Hungary, and Poland.

NOTES

The original version of this text was read to the Fifth International Karl Polanyi Conference, Vienna, 10-13 November 1994, organised by the Karl Polanyi Institute of Political Economy in Montreal and the Research Unit for Socio-Economics at the Austrian Academy of Sciences. During the three years after the Conference the tendency set by the enfranchised *nomenklatura* to transform previous political into present economic power, degenerated into wholesale looting of the national wealth of the country. A total impoverishment of the majority of the population followed, becoming especially acute in the fall of 1996 and winter of 1997. This catastrophic collapse modified in some respects the role of trade-tourism, but the basic tendencies and orientations, as outlined in the paper, still apply in the most critical period (October 1996-February 1997).

1. Ryszard Bugaj and Tadeusz Kowalik, "The privatization debate in Poland," in *Privatization in Eastern Europe*. Wien: Renner Institut, 1992, pp. 140-157.
2. Karl Polanyi, *The Great Transformation. Politische und ökonomische Ursprunge von Gesellschaften und Wirtschaftssystemen*. Wien: Europa Verlag, 1977.
3. For the term and phenomenon, see Chris Hann and Ildiko Hann, "Samovars and sex on Turkey's Russian markets," *Anthropology Today*. 1992, Vol. 8, No 4, August 1992, p. 3-6.
4. But see the description of the so-called "Russian markets" in Turkey in Hann and Hann, 1992, 3-6. See also note 11.
5. For a more extensive presentation of the points touched upon here, cf. Konstantinov, 1996 (note 11).
6. See specially Gerald W. Creed, "Agriculture and the Domestication of Industry in Rural Bulgaria," *American Ethnologist*, 1995, Vol. 22, No.3, 528-548. For a similar type of economy in former Yugoslavia (Bosnia), cf. William G. Lockwood, "The Peasant-worker in Yugoslavia," *Studies in European Society*, 1973, Vol.1, No.1,pp. 91-111.
7. See Michael Stewart, "Gypsies at the horse-market," in Roy Dilley (ed.), *Contesting Markets*. Edinburgh: University Press, 1992, pp. 97-115.
8. Emmanuel Sarides, *Ethnische Monderheit und zwischenstaatliches Streiobjekt; Die Pomaken in Nordgriechenland*. Berlin: Free University of Berlin, 1987. See also Yulian Konstastinov, "Strategies for Sustaining a Vulnerable Identity: The Case of the Bulgarian Pomaks," in Hugh Poutton and Suha Taji-Farouki (eds.), *Muslim Identity and the Balkan State*. London: Hurst & Company in association with the Islamic Council, 1997, pp. 33-54.
9. See Hugh Poulton, *The Balkans. Minorities and States in Conflict*. London: Minority Rights Publications, 1991, pp. 105-173.
10. See Yulian Konstantinov, "An account of Pomak conversions in Bulgaria (1912-1990)," pp. 96-113 in Gerhard Seewann, (ed.), *Minderheitenfragen in Südosteuropa*. Südost Institut. Munchen: R. Oldenbourg Verlag, 1992. Yulian Konstantinov, "Patterns of Reinterpretation: Trader-Tourism in the Balkans (Bulgaria) as a Picaresque Metaphorical Enactment of Post-Totalitarianism," *American Ethnologist* 1996 23 (4),pp.1-21. Yulian Konstantinov and Gulbrand Alhaug, *Names, Ethnicity, and Politics. Islamic Names in Bulgaria 1912-1992*. Tromso Studies in Linguistics 15. Oslo: Novus Press, 1995. Yulian Konstantinov and Trond Thuen, *Boundaries as a Resource: Regional Small-Scale Trading in the Balkans*. Occasional Papers (Stensilserie) A, No 84, Institute of Social Science, University of Tromsø, 1996. Yulian Konstantinov, Gideon Kressel, and Trond Thuen (eds.), *Working Papers on Trader-Tourism*. Vol. I. Sofia/Sede Boquer/ Tromso, 1996. Daniel N. Nelson, *Balkan Imbroglio. Politics and Security in Southeastern Europe*. Boulder, Co.: Westview Press, 1991, pp. 55ff.
11. See Wolfgang Höpken, "Die Integration bulgarischer Türken in der Türkei nach dem Zweiten Weltkrieg," pp. 359-377 in Gerhard Seewann (ed.), *Minderheitenfragen in Südosteuropa. Südost-Institut*. München: R. Oldenbourg Verlag, 1992.
12. By February 1997 the Turkish Government intervened to stop the growing labour immigration from Bulgaria, and threatened to evict and send back immigrants who had arrived illegally in Turkey after 1994, about 70,000 people.
13. For the term and concept evolved in reference to developments in the former Soviet Union cf. Anderson, "Hunters, Herders, and Heavy Metals in Arctic Siberia," *Cambridge Anthropology*, 1995, pp.38-39. Judith Palloit, "Rural depopulation and the restoration of the Russian village under Gorbachev," *Soviet Studies*, 1990, 42(4), pp.655-674.
14. Stephen L. Sampson, "Money without culture, culture without money: Eastern Europe's nouveaux riches," *Anthropological Journal of European Cultures*, 1993, Vol. 2, Spring.
15. Virginia Marsh, "Ex-communists embrace a half-capitalist Bulgaria," *Financial Times*, May 10, 1994.

Chapter Eleven

CHANGING MODES OF ECONOMIC INTEGRATION IN BULGARIAN HISTORY
Tanya Chavdarova

At present the various Central and East European societies have in common numerous socio-economic problems. Nonetheless, the ways in which they have tried to solve them and to move away from the command economy are different. This demonstrates that their diverse historical premises should be examined in order to explain the specifics of ongoing market developments in each country. This paper aims to highlight the changing relationship between basic patterns of economic integration in modern Bulgarian history, in accordance with Polanyi's formulations. The analysis addresses historically established and habituated patterns of relationships between reciprocity, redistribution and market exchange in specific periods of dramatic socioeconomic change. The most important issue is whether redistribution and reciprocity exert a powerful influence on the institutionalization of the market, and what kind of balance between those forms of economic integration can be observed at present. It is from this perspective that a historically determined political and cultural impetus for or against the consolidation of a market economy in Bulgaria can be evaluated.

THEORETICAL BACKGROUND

This paper draws heavily on Karl Polanyi's theory of economy and society. The first part of the analysis is concerned with the fundamental characteristics of economic systems. In describing them, Polanyi's theoretical differentiation between basic patterns of economic integration—reciprocity, redistribution and market exchange—is followed.[1] It is these modes that are the major determinants of the specific forms of economic organization and their historical changes.[2] The second part focuses on the relation of these integrative forms to the social, command and market economies. These economies are considered from a social-structural perspective that could provide knowledge about the dominant socio-economic structures embedded in the economic institutions. The social economy, as linked to reciprocity, is dominated by the principle of adequate response and has validity within community structures: family, neighbourhoods, relatives, friends and colleagues. The command economy implies the dominance of political authority, administrative decision-making, and application of political criteria to economic activities which results in the parallel existence of forcibly created formal structures and informal institutions. The market economy is the background for the flourishing of formal organizations, individuals and free associations. All these types of economy have their place and could be found in each society. The socio-economic specifics come from the way they are combined and relate to each other in a particular historical period.

The third part of the analysis stresses the socio-economic dependence ensuing from the social, command and market economies. The social economy creates a specific communal dependence among actors. Dependence stemming from a command economy takes various forms. While pre-capitalist societies have been characterized by institutionalization of the individual, the family and the kin, in the socialist command economy there is a strong personification of the central redistributive institutions. Under socialism personal dependence (Marx) had been replaced by a kind of institutional dependence. Its essence is expressed in terms of political dominance and subordination, since economic had not been separated from political power. A new type of total impersonal dependence has come into being through the dominance of free market exchange. It is defined as indirect interaction among economic actors with money being the sole mediator between the bargaining profit maximizers. In this third aspect the dominant economic actors are in focus. The main question concerns the kind of rational action on the part of the individual which stems from each pattern of social dependence. Economic action is thought of as stimulated and/or limited by the circumstances of socio-economic structures in which they have historically been placed.

The theoretical framework, as related to three levels of analysis—economic system, social structure and the individual—is presented in Table 1.

Table 1. Theoretical Framework.

Characteristics of the Economic system:

Pattern of economic integration	Dominant patterns of economic organization
Reciprocity	Networks
Redistribution	Forcibly created formal institutions, informal networks
Market exchange	Formal organizations

Characteristics of Social structure of economic institutions:

Types of economy	Dominant social structures
Social economy	Kinship
Command economy	Clans, bureaucracy
Market economy	Associations of free individuals

Characteristics of Individuals' economic action and behavior:

Types of socio-economic dependence	Dominant economic actors
Communal	Community
Institutional/personal	State, other central authorities
Impersonal	Individual

On a more general theoretical level, this paper is based on path dependence theory.[3] Its central assumption from the sociological point of view is the concept of bricolage (first developed by C. L. Strauss). In David Stark's summary of it: "The introduction of new elements most typically combines with adaptation, rearrangements, permutations, and reconfigurations of existing organizational forms."[4] Thus in order to understand ongoing socio-economic developments, we need to examine the historical background and identify those traditional organizational forms and modes of economic action whose reshaping contributes to bringing about the new order.

RADICAL CHANGE IN MODERN BULGARIAN HISTORY

There have been three dramatic socioeconomic changes in the modern history of the country. The first capitalist period marked the beginning of Bulgarian modern history. Following liberation from the Turkish yoke, it ended with World War II. The second, the Socialist period, lasted till 1989, during which time rapid political change brought about substantial socioeconomic transformation. The third period of change began in 1989 with the overthrow of communist political power.

THE PERIOD OF THE OTTOMAN EMPIRE (1396-1878)

The classical period of the Ottoman Empire (1300-1600) is a distinct entity characterized by an autocratic centralist government and a command economy. The "decline" period of the seventeenth century was a period of transition, following which the eighteenth century witnessed a radically changed Ottoman Empire that followed "liberal" policies not only in its administration but also in land holding and the economy in general. A radical change in the attitudes of the Ottomans toward European civilization occurred during that period. For the first time they started admitting Europeans' superiority and began imitating and borrowing Western models. The results were the radical "Westernizing" reforms of the nineteenth century.[5]

Though part of the Ottoman Empire, Bulgarian society was of a traditional peasant non-market type, marked above all by insecurity. As Polanyi points out, in non-market societies reciprocity and redistribution in reality coexist. Reciprocity is the most powerful mode of integration when it subjugates redistribution and the market. (Polanyi, 1992, p. 37) In the period under consideration, reciprocity and redistribution coexisted without being subordinated to each other.

The redistributive mode of economic integration was the core of the Ottoman Empire. It manifested itself most clearly in the property and taxation systems. There was no private property in the Ottoman Empire. The Sultan was the owner of all landed property which he distributed on the basis of standardized holdings (the size varying in accordance with the three grades of land) via the courts in each territorial commune. The candidate for land of low rank (raja)—head of a family or non-married male adult—had to pay money for the issuing of a document (*tapija*) certifying the transaction. The Sultan could take back the land at any time, thus creating a great source of insecurity for the peasants. Regulations decreed that if the land was not cultivated within three years, it had to be taken away.

The upper ranks (*asceri*) which included no Bulgarians were granted either a salary or the right to collect part of the taxes due from a particular area (usually a village) in recompense for their services, before retiring with a pension. The only private property recognized (*mujlk*) were the houses and gardens. Later, in the 17th century, the Sultan started distributing plots of land to some members of the *asceri* as a reward for special services rendered. Nonetheless, he retained the right to take them away whenever he wished. In order to preserve these as their private property, subjects took advantage of a specific Ottoman regulation. According to this, if the land given as a reward was made over as a charitable donation to a religious or other kind of institution, these could claim property rights over it. The *asceri* thus rewarded accordingly gifted the land under the condition that they would govern it on behalf of the institution, and that after their death this right would pass to their offspring. Thus, a kind of hidden private property system was created in the 17th century. This was the only way land could be inherited. The lack of inheritance rights was a specific feature of the Ottoman Empire (the prebend system) which was the main reason for the absence of an aristocracy in the later period.

The taxation system was organized on the basis of the numbers of plots of land distributed and not on the social unit (individual or family). As a rule, the plots were in the name of the head of the nuclear, not of the extended family. Each family and even each single male were given a plot of land for cultivation. Usually, after satisfying their own needs, and after paying taxes, the family traded the rest of its agricultural produce and/or exchanged it in the town market for artisan products. Thus, the family also had the option to "pay for a document" and receive an additional plot of land. The taxes were in kind, in money and in labor. Since the 14th and 15th centuries wage labor was imposed upon peasants whose land had been taken away because of debt. There was also relatively high temporary labor migration due to obligatory labor service in different parts of the huge Ottoman Empire.

The Ottoman command economy was accompanied by a social one which was essential for the Bulgarian peasant population. Although the taxation system made the nuclear family and even the individual responsible for achieving certain economic results, all economic activities were shared within the framework of the extended family which was patriarchally organized on a household basis.

There was another social unit existing not only in that period but also earlier in medieval Bulgaria, the *zadruga*. The *zadruga* or kin commune was a typical unit of Slavonic tribes. In the period under consideration, on the land of the Bulgarians it was comparatively weaker and was concerned with stockbreeding. The *zadruga* was distinct by virtue of involving collective ownership, collective property disposal, collective work and consumption, and collective responsibility for all its members.[6] Collectivism, solidarity and economic uniformity are its basic features. The ruler of the *zadruga* was the father or the eldest brother. He had mainly a representative function (he represented the *zadruga* in the village commune) and was not so much a ruler as a leader. It was only his age and not some personal quality that accorded him the leading position. In contrast with the *zadruga*, in the extended family, organized on a household basis, the leader (*starejshina*, literally *the oldest man*) was sole owner of the household's property and his role in making economic decisions was much stronger than in the *zadruga*. (*Rechnik po Soziologija*, 1996) In both cases—the *zadruga* and the extended household-based family—there was strict differentiation of the social roles of the members.

Under the dominant social economy extended families reciprocally exchanged labor which was both an existential and an ethical imperative in the peasant community.[7] Even poor peasants shared their resources with their neighbors and other communities, knowing that help from them is likely to be needed at any time. "Non-maximizing" patterns of action and non-individualistic rationality were enforced through socially institutionalized "norms of reciprocity" and social sanctions. Reciprocal exchanges were effected with relatives, kinsmen, friends, and patrons. Communal interdependence became normative social dependence together with the personal dependence handed down by official Ottoman authorities. Communal interdependence defined the collective action as governed by the values of social and economic sameness. Here the concept of sameness replaces that of equality. Equality, following the Western perspective, is related to a way of treating differentiated individuals. The concept of sameness more adequately reflects the historical situation in which the primary definition of the individual is that of being a community member.

In order to appreciate the basic principles of the peasant's economic commitment to his kinship community, the extreme insecurity of life under religiously hostile foreign dominance should be underlined. Because of such insecurity, Scott shows, the peasants operated according to the "safety-first principle."

> For those peasants with very low incomes, little land, large families, highly variable yields, and few outside opportunities, the pattern of safety-first ...should hold quite consistently.[8]

There are no reliable historical data on degrees of economic inequality within the Bulgarian peasantry. As some authors argue, the notion that all Bulgarian peasants lived close to the subsistence level would be erroneous (see for example Hadgijski).[9] Although Scott's criteria in this respect are not met, his theoretical speculations on peasants' economic behavior could be relevant to our peasantry too.

Scott develops the concept of a subsistence economy which in its Bulgarian variant could be seen as an economy of insecurity. Those peasants who share a common existential dilemma follow the "safety-first" principle when making economic decisions: i.e., they tend to avoid risks in favor of what is familiar.[10] Traditionally, the individual is activated to the degree that his subsistence is threatened. And even in such cases survival strategies have been elaborated by the extended family and not by the individual himself. Accumulation has not been brought about by the individual, but through the collective strategy of the extended family. It is accumulation in the form of decision-making regarding cultivation of additional plots of land. Such a solution just requires harder work. There is minimum risk because the only consequence of not paying the taxes when due would be that the plot would be taken away, and thus the money paid for getting the document would be lost.

A typical feature of any peasant society is its moral economy. This does not imply a community governed by ethics alone, but one whose material conditions produce values which attempt to sustain and legitimate their continuation. They provide standards of justice which are applicable not only among peasants but between peasants and the elite. That power would be considered legitimate which conforms to the concept of justice held by the peasant. The underpinnings of such a concept are the norms of reciprocity and the right to subsistence.[11] Subsistence, which is often culturally defined, operates along a continuum between surplus-giving peasantry and surplus-appropriating elite. It is only at times when this exchange threatens subsistence routines that social explosions are to be expected.

There is further specificity of rational action which stems from this type of relationship with the elite. The peasant, as Scott shows, does not calculate how much (in taxation) has been taken from him but how much has been left to him and whether this is enough for living. Thus the Bulgarian peasant has a historically developed specific non-maximizing safety rationality. Activism is only related exclusively to the community—the extended family and the *zadruga*—not to the individual as he is perceived in the Western tradition. The line between activism and passivity passes through the point of threat to the security of subsistence and nowhere else.

Bulgarian economic life was deeply embedded in community structures and followed customary law. Ottoman legislation provided a formal economic framework, but everyday economic life was determined by the informal rules of Bulgarian habits. It seems that formal and informal rules did not coincide. They operated at different levels, at those of command and social economy; they reflected different integration forms, those of redistribution and reciprocity.

THE FIRST CAPITALIST PERIOD

Prior to the Liberation some market development had already taken place. Bulgarian producers had begun taking advantage of the huge market of the Ottoman Empire. There were definite signs of the diminishing role of the economy of barter and the increase of money transactions through the strengthening and spread of artisans and trading activities.[12] While the extended household community maintained its role as the main production and social unit, a trend towards community disintegration and the advent of private appropriation became noticeable. The fact of Liberation resulting from the Russian-Turkish war of 1878 and the establishment of a new state radically interrupted this smooth process of shaping market mechanisms and capital accumulation. Reciprocity and redistribution as modes of integration forms were intensified but on a different level and in a different way. Instead of being excluded and separated from the market, they became assimilated into market exchange, so that the latter could hardly be defined as a free market.

Economic development was stimulated in inherently contradictory directions. On the one hand, it became so strained, that money became, as Hadzhijski wrote, a measure "even for things that have no price." (Hadzhijski, p. 417) The sharp renunciation of traditional values was accompanied by the detachment of the nuclear family as an economic community from the extended family. It was carried out "through ambition being provoked because of uneven enrichment." (Hadzhijski, p. 419) The moral degradation of the patriarchal ethos which stemmed from the economic boom was defined by Hadzhijski as a transformation of the survival strategy into one of prosperity. On the other hand, he argues, the interruption of the smooth development of the market disturbed the process of early capital accumulation. Given the scarcity of private capital in the context of the economic backwardness and poverty of the country as a whole, private capital could rely only on state capital.[13] When analyzing this period, Avramov points out that "private capital was...formed from that of the state; it expected (and was given) its goals by the state."[14] Thus, at the very beginning of capitalist development in Bulgaria, the state was able to occupy a strategic redistributive position in the economy.

The economic actors' personal dependence on the political factor was revived in a modified form in that period, fostered by economic backwardness and poverty. To take advantage of informal networks for broadening economic opportunity was an important element of the new prosperity strategy. Conditions were created for owners' (mainly landlords') dependence on the ruling political class. Though the owners and the ruling class could be distinguished as formal socio-structural units, the power of the latter was substantially greater. This was due to the circumstance that political commitment was deemed to be the main source of economic prosperity. The relations between those two groups gradually crystallized into a patron-client relationship. The new economic ethics of prosperity allowed, tolerated, and even required informal contacts and connections with political figures.

Because of the weakness of private capital the cooperative form of ownership expanded substantially. From the Liberation up until World War II a vast network of cooperatives was established in Bulgaria. These were mainly agricultural cooperatives with more than 150 years of history behind them, but also there were artisan and credit cooperatives. Their growth specifically contributed to the development of a patron-client relationship. By serving as lobbying centers, the cooperatives "provided the substance of penetration of political and economic structures." It was on the basis of these that the largest state banks came into existence and they thereafter demonstrated their "gratitude" by giving credits to their founders, the cooperatives. Thus the cooperatives turned out to be a machine for bad debts.

Various techniques of patron-client relations were implemented. (1) Some mutually contradictory rules and norms for private business were introduced so that the private entrepreneur would be continuously forced to rely on the good will of the civil servant. (2) In other cases the rules were quite unacceptable to businessmen who as a result felt they had to transfer their business (or part of it) to the informal sector. This consequently made them even more vulnerable. (3) Some civil servants required a commission for permitting some activity or transaction that was essentially legal. Businessmen had to be familiar with the unwritten regulations if they wanted to keep doing business. Thus a "socio-political concubine" between politicians and/or civil servants and private businessmen came to exist. (4) Another even stronger form of merging the social figures of owner and ruler was abuse of political power for the benefit of promoting one's own business.

Political patronage during the first capitalist period channeled state resources towards marginal peasants in return for their votes. Conceiving of the state as something "foreign," business strategy consisted of devising means for "clandestinely improving the terms of exchange...while avoiding open confrontations." (Scott, p. 231) Pilfering was encouraged. The patron-client relationship was also a reaction to the absence of any conditions for replacing the personalized trust between contracting parties with systemic trust[15] or faceless commitments.[16] Given the unstable and to a certain degree contradictory nature of legislative reforms, some special measures to ensure a contract's execution and avoid fraud had to be taken. When the market is imperfect the entrepreneur must be able to compensate for its shortcomings, remedy its deficiencies, and establish connections among the different markets. Thus the entrepreneur was defined by his ability to reduce the risks caused by the market's imperfections in order to lower the cost of a contract's negotiations and ensure its execution.[17]

This required the development of an outlook different from that of Western rationality,[18] one which presupposed that actors decline to enter into impersonal economic transactions. This gave birth to specific, community-like economic groupings where social proximity and common cultural identity were used as social capital for building norms of cooperation, trust and loyalty. Information about potential trade-partners' identity was exchanged within that context. Thus, the kin-based networks were gradually enriched and complemented with friendship, neighbours, and colleagues-based networks. In sum, all possible informal networks were mobilized as part of the strategy for prosperity.

The safety-first type of rationality in the pre-Liberation period could be traced in the form of building trust for doing business.[19] Now competition took the shape of group competition.[20] Reciprocal transactions were carried out between separate networks because this was the way to lower transaction costs. So far as economic institutions come into existence in order to lower transaction costs, reciprocity was institutionalized in this way.[21]

It is the market that generates the differentiation between public and private and thus generates individualism.[22] "The market's emancipation presupposes that public and private are two autonomous spaces but are equally a person's 'own' in which he/she is equally integrated and equally distant from the roles performed." (Bahrdt, pp. 63-66) In Bulgaria after the Liberation the subordination of the market to the political sphere gave birth to another type of integrity and social behavior. Instead of equal treatment being accorded to all economic actors in the market (i.e., the dispersion of economic power), protectionism and informal power relations (patron-client relationship) dominated. That was why the domain of formal relations was hostile to the individual. It did not bring forth identity and integrity but "acquired such values only after being validated by the institutions of informality."[23] A public economic role could be "owned" only after it had interacted with informal networks. In its turn, the domination of informality determined the weakness of the official sector. These were the two realities, and the individual was totally included ("owned") in the first but had only a token role in the second. What to the Western mind was not conceivable (the mixture of the public and private), to a Bulgarian was quite natural. For Bulgarians the public and formal became "foreign," and the only way for it to be "owned" by them was through the private, the informal. Individualism and utilitarianism became an important feature of economic activity, but these were associated with traditional network behavior rather than with formal institutionalized activity.

Even in the best periods for private capital, the state maintained its extraordinary role in the economy, especially with regard to its institutional structure. The 70 years of capitalist development could not consolidate free market exchange as the dominant mode of economic integration, and as a consequence the impersonal form of social interdependence could not be imposed as a total form. The infiltration of redistribution and reciprocity into the market mechanisms did not permit this.

The specific features of the first capitalist period are concentrated in the overlapping processes of the official institutionalization of market exchange and the unofficial re-institutionalization of reciprocity and redistribution. If the formal approach to economic life is followed,[24] this is a contradiction in terms, insofar as institutionalization is defined by the process of formalization. In terms of the substantivist approach, this means that reciprocity and redistribution are forms of exchange alongside that of the free market. The difference between the formal and substantive aspects of those three modes imposed a duality upon economic life as a permanent feature in the subsequent economic development of the country. This contrasts with society's stimulation of the economy through promotion of self-regulated market mechanisms so typical of Western pre-capitalist societies. According to the Western "logic" of economic development, "state intervention in the economy" comes later, in order to level down the social tensions created by free market exchange. It is reasonable to assume that if the economic and social processes in Bulgaria had been left to follow their own evolutionary logic, they would have reached the point of the economy's separation from politics. Private capital would have become strong enough to relieve the market of the pitfalls of reciprocity and redistribution.

SOCIALISM
Socialism has been traditionally interpreted as a period of breakdown. The focus has been primarily on its opposition to the advanced capitalist societies. In this paper socialism is considered as a period of historic mediation between the first capitalist period in Bulgaria and its rebirth. In the context of the broader historical process of change in the dominant integration mode (from reciprocity through redistribution towards free market exchange) state socialism represents a sort of turning back to redistribution. Here it is the interpenetrating state and communist party's institutions that build up the redistributive center. Whereas in pre-capitalist societies market exchange had a naturally limited scope, under state socialism it was compulsorily entrenched. The highly developed division of labor naturally requires complete dominance of the market. The compulsory destruction of the latter via the totality of redistribution principles turned the former relatively sovereign economy into politicized territory.

One of the consequences is the changing nature of reciprocity under state socialism. For instance, in tribal societies dominated by reciprocal exchange, the social and economic meanings of reciprocity could not be distinguished because of the embeddedness of the economy in society. With the decline of tribal society reciprocity became a complementary form of economic integration. Under state socialism it was subordinated to redistribution. Yet it developed not as a complementary but as a compensatory form. Two closely-bound factors actively contributed to this: the socialist economy as an "economy of shortage" (Kornai) and the negation of market mechanisms. Production deficit was unavoidable given the claim of the state to centrally command the enormous variety of labor and goods. Reciprocity was to compensate partially for the deficits which the redistributive command economy constantly produced. Market exchange principles that were not permitted, but that were "naturally" required by the level of industrialization and division of labor, infiltrated the area of reciprocity and forced social recognition and loyalty to become mainly a subject of instrumental economic interest.

Were market exchange principles totally demolished under socialism? Was it not the case that "driven from the door, they came in through the window"? Some authors, Kosminski and Aslund among others, argue that within the framework of socialist structures market mechanisms were functioning as informal structures. The officially forbidden market shaped its own "second economy," which was parallel to the official one and had multidimensional relations with it. While informal economies in the advanced capitalist states basically aimed at profit maximization, thus complementing the official economy, the second economy under socialism had compensatory functions. It oiled the wheels of an "economy of shortage."[25] The two economies needed each other to survive. While being only compensatory, the second economy actually enabled and lubricated the official one. Viewed from the opposite direction, endless bureaucratic obstacles to the production processes made the second economy more flourishing. The greater the number of regulations, the greater the opportunity for the second economy.

Another argument that could support the view that the second economy acted as a lubricant for the command economy comes from the nature of private appropriation under socialism. This was only possible through the channels of the second economy because of the contradiction between the officially proclaimed socialist principles of labor reward and private appropriation. The latter took place in the form of abuses of economic and political power on the part of top members of the economic and political *nomenklatura*. Private accumulation could be realized only with the help of high-level participants in the second economy. Those at lower levels needed to maintain personal ties with the economic and political elite in order to avoid normative regulation.

A market of personal connections was developed. In this way the informal network became more strongly commercialized than in previous periods. Personal ties were exchanged and accumulated as capital that produced profit. The state's domination in the public sphere generated a market in the private sphere. The interpersonal relations in which economic activity was embedded created a specific kind of social dependence. On one hand, commercialized networks brought about the development of personal dependence, this time not just within the kin-group but within a broader framework. On the other hand, the command economy produced an institutional dependence which was strongly personified because of the total interlocking of formality and informality in all economic institutions. Under the conditions of social dependence that could be characterized on the basis of the personification of institutions, the social integrity of economic man came from preserving the norms of representation. Legitimate institutional behavior is a "token," a "symbolic" one. Its meaning shifted from "redemption of the sin" against the power authority to a demonstration of compliance with it and recognition of its merits. (Bahrdt, pp. 79-83) The leading feature of this token behavior was evasion, the outwitting of the formal institutions as a prosperity strategy. Such behavior legitimized the informal network of human relations as a vehicle and a real regulator of social life.

THE TRANSFORMATION PERIOD SINCE 1989

The irrationality of socialist planning was becoming more and more obvious, and this brought about in the 1970s the official introduction of certain market mechanisms. "Market developments" manifested themselves through the formal sanction of some private activities in the 1980s which transformed a number of second economy activities into legal ones.[26] However, these developments took the form of capital export. Capital started to be exported in the legal form of joint-stock companies, with foreign participation, which had been under the control of the secret services.[27] In 1989, the process of capital export gained legitimacy and was intensified. From this standpoint, the events of 1989 did not interrupt the previous developments. They also did not bring interruption, in as much as redistribution in harmony with reciprocity played the predominant role. Yet, in another sense, a critical discontinuity took place: the former redistributive institutions disintegrated and an institutional gap was created that has not yet been filled.

Reciprocity and redistribution ceased to act as forms of economic integration and began functioning as disintegrative forms. Reciprocity preserved its cohesive strength at a micro-level within the frame of particular groupings. The personal bonds, social obligations and loyalties that had been shaped and passed on for generations led to a situation in which "an economic civil war is being carried out within the ruling party" for the taking over of particular economic institutions.[28] It is hard to carry out this "war" without active reciprocal exchanges among some symmetrical groupings. The former political and economic *nomenklatura* and its offspring, the secret service networks, those of "newcomers" in the power elite, and certain criminal networks ("wrestlers") could be deemed the most vital reciprocal groupings. Yet it is the uniting of particular symmetrical groupings that is causing the disintegration of the economy at large. An explanation could be looked for in the link between reciprocity and redistribution. As was already stressed, those two integrative modes are generally complementary. At present, reciprocity complements a redistributive process which does not integrate with the economy in either a formal or a substantive sense. Redistribution that has been carried out as hidden privatization has been essentially criminal. The core of privatization that has been taking place in this country is "capitalization of the private sector through decapitalization of the state." (Avramov)

The informalization of social life at large, combined with decapitalization of the state under the conditions of a weak civil society, leads to the gradual disintegration of statesmanship. One of the symptoms is the lack of a consistently implemented program for introducing market principles. Another is the extraordinarily high crime rate, especially among teenagers. It has something to do with the lumpenization of hired labor given the officially recognized 12% unemployment rate and a distorted labor market. The high crime rates mark a desire to share in the on-going redistribution. In this sense, it is an important part of the redistribution process. Also, the introduction of a currency board is an emblematic symptom and symbol of the current tendencies. This measure was taken after the total collapse of the financial sector with 14 banks going bankrupt within a couple of months in 1996 and hyper-inflation during the first two months of 1997.

For the new political anti-communist elite which emerged from socialism, as poor as everybody else and unable to take advantage of the restitution law (passed prior to the privatization law), political power has become the only source of individual enrichment. It is in the interest of this political elite that the state functions as a "political capitalist." The new private entrepreneur who does not come from the *nomenklatura* depends on the political administration and bureaucracy. As in the first capitalist period, this is the case because of the obvious necessity for the production funds to be raised. And again, as in the former capitalist period, the main source turns out to be the state. This specific reproduction of historical circumstances brings about reproduction of the old cultural codes of economic relations. Now the new entrepreneurs are defined by their ability to develop a perfect sense of recognizing legislative imperfections and to making use of them. These tendencies reveal that though there are new actors on the economic scene, no *new* type of economic actor has appeared. Clan relations[29] reappear and infect private business at its birth. Thus the reproduction of capitalism is at the same time a recreation of modes of socio-economic action which are genetically imprinted in the Bulgarian economy.

CONCLUSION

Modern Bulgarian history has been marked by constant disruption of organic societal development. Bulgarian society did not go through a natural and idiosyncratic form of modernization, and suffered from externally imposed models. The process of the market economy's establishment and expansion, which proceeded alongside the disintegration of traditional society, has been interrupted. Economic development in the first capitalist period was discontinued by the communist invasion. Again, market developments that occurred within the framework of socialism in the 1970s were not allowed to reach the highest point of development.[30] Each time there is discontinuation in economic development, there is reversion to specific traditional institutional structures of the economy and to patterns of economic activity which are imprinted on the nation's memory. The repeated discontinuation of societal organic development could be considered a very powerful mechanism for strengthening and reinforcing cultural-historical specifics.[31]

This could explain to a large extent why the on-going transformation is "backward-looking" and why it is marked by "desire to return to lost traditions" (Borucha-Arctowa, 1994). In this perspective, redistribution and reciprocity have always come to life again in varied balance. At present, they preserve their place in a paradoxical way: they reject themselves by giving up their sense of integrative form. Their strengthening in a period of dramatic change has brought about erosion of statesmanship and disintegration of the economy. Their traditional implantation at all levels of social life has disturbed, and will also in the future, the market mechanisms in order to acquire a real integrative significance in society.

The market economy in Bulgaria during the first capitalist period existed through being specifically embedded in redistributive and reciprocity mechanisms. Redistribution as the main integrative form in communist society led to the complete penetration of the economy by politics. Under the circumstances of deep social anomie that we witness today, there is no pattern of economic integration. The important role of reciprocity is manifested through relationships among some symmetrical groupings, in which both the mechanisms of kinship and those of a shared past and culture, social obligation, and loyalty function. But this is "negative" integration. At present redistribution and reciprocity preserve their role in a paradoxical way: they reject themselves by giving up their function as *integrative* forces. Their strengthening in the period of dramatic changes has made particular social groups winners; but, on the other side, it has brought about erosion of statesmanship and economic deregulation.

The traditional implantation of reciprocity and redistribution at all levels of social life has disturbed the introduction of market mechanisms which could help to overcome the anomic situation in the economy. But, precisely because of the traditional significance of reciprocity and redistribution, it could be expected in the future that they would support the process of embedding the economy in society.

The communist merger of political and economic power is gradually being replaced by new forms of a non-legal "dirty relationship" between political and economic actors, that resemble the "patron-client" relationship. In the sphere of politics this will condition a new power oligarchy; and in the sphere of the economy it will stimulate hidden economic acts of privatization of profits and nationalization of losses (Stark).

One of the gravest problems for Bulgarian development is the country's constant disembeddedness from all formal normative regulation. Historically, formal legislation has never had a chance to be gradually developed from the indigenous customary law. The legal system has always been either borrowed or imposed. In this respect, the hypothesis of mainstream economists—that what we find today in Eastern Europe is an institutional vacuum—is doubly right: in the absence of workable formal institutions, and in the total crisis of customary law.

NOTES

1. According to Polanyi, reciprocity indicates the relationship between certain symmetrical groups, where mechanisms of social obligation, loyalty and acknowledgement apply. Reciprocity is the basis of a social economy which is embedded in certain traditions and social norms and which cannot be subjected to theoretical analysis outside of their context. Whereas reciprocity implies symmetry, redistribution is confined to centricity. (K. Polanyi, *The Great Transformation: The Political and Economic Origins of our Time*. Boston: Beacon Press, 1957 [first 1944], pp. 48-49). This is when economic processes flow towards or from a center. Here economic interaction is characterized by the dominance of distant authority. Market exchange ensures the dispersion of economic power among all the participants in a transaction. Typically they are profit maximizers and exchange between them is governed by price-dominated bargaining. "The market economy implies a self-regulating system of markets...capable of organizing the whole of economic life without outside help or interference." The institutionalization of any of those forms, Polanyi stresses, does not stem from and is not a generalization of individual interactions. So reciprocity supposes a symmetric system of grouping; redistribution, some form of centricity; free market exchange, a system of market price formation. Polanyi's emphasis is on the process of expropriation of material resources—whether as social exchange, as disposed of from the resourses by a particular centre, as a transaction by virtue of law and custom, or as transactions between equal actors.

2. It is the institutionalization of one or other of these integrative forms that guarantees an economy's unity and stability. K. Polanyi, "The Economy as Instituted Process," in K. Polanyi, H. Arensberg, and H. Pearson (eds.), *Trade and Market in the Early Empires*. New York: The Free Press, 1957, in M. Granovetter and R. Swedberg (eds.) *The Sociology of Economic Life*. Oxford: Westview Press, 1992, p. 33.

3. The model of path-dependence is formulated by D. North as follows: "Path-dependence means that history matters. We cannot understand today's choices without tracing the incremental evolution of institutions. If, however, the foregoing story sounds like an inevitable foreordained account, it should not. At every step along the way there were choices—political and economic—that provided real alternatives." (D.C. North, *Institutions, Institutional Change and Economic Performance*. Cambridge: Cambridge University Press, 1990, p. 98.)

4. D. Stark, "From System Identity to Organizational Diversity—Analyzing Social Change in Eastern Europe," *Contemporary Sociology*, 1992, p.21, pp.299-304, p.300.

5. H. Inalcik and D. Quataert, "General Introduction," in H. Inalcik and D. Quataert (eds.), *An Economic and Social History of the Ottoman Empire, 1300-1914*. Cambridge: Cambridge University Press, 1994, p. 11.

6. E. Grosdanowa, *Bulgaskata Selska Obshtina Pres XV - XVIII Wek (The Bulgarian Rural Commune during the XV - XVIII Centuries)*. Sofia: Bulgarian Academy of Sciences, 1979.
7. M. Andreev, *Bulgarskoto Obichajno Prawo (Bulgarian Customary Law)*. Sofia: Nauka i Iskustwo, 1979.
8. J. Scott, *The Moral Economy of the Peasant. Rebellion and Subsistence in Southeast Asia*. New Haven and London: Yale University Press, 1976, p.25.
9. I. Hadgijski, *Bit I Dushewnost na Bulgarskija Narod (Mode of Life and Spirituality of the Bulgarian People)*, Vol. 2. Sofia: Bulgarski Pisatel, 1974.
10. "What safety-first does imply, however, is that there is a defense perimeter around subsistence routines within which risks are avoided as potentially catastrophic and outside of which a more bourgeois calculus of profit prevails." (Scott, 1976, p. 24)
11. "This subsistence claim is morally based on the common notion of a hierarchy of human needs, with the means for physical survival naturally taking priority over other claims to village wealth. In a purely logical sense, it is difficult to imagine how any disparities in wealth and resources can be legitimated unless the right to subsistence is given priority." (Scott, 1976, pp. 176-7)
12. L. Berow, *Ikonomicheskoto Raswitie na Bulgaria pres Wekowete (The Economic Development of Bulgaria over the Centuries)*. Sofia: Profisdat, 1974.
13. A. Gerschenkron, *Economic Backwardness in Historical Perspective*. New York: Frederick A. Praeger Publishers, 1965.
14. R. Avramov, " W Uprawljawastata Partija se Wodi Ikonomicheska Wojna" ("There is an Economic War Going on in the Ruling Party"), in the newspaper *Capital*, March 18-24, 1996 No. 11.
15. N. Luhmann, *The Differentiation of Society*. New York: Columbia University Press, 1982.
16. A. Giddens, *The Consequences of Modernity*. Cambridge: Polity Press, 1990.
17. H. Leibenstein, "Entrepreneurship and Development," *American Economic Review* 1968, p.58, pp.72-83.
18. R. Munch, *Die Kultur der Moderne*. Frankfurt: Suhrkamp, 1993, (first 1986).
19. J. Landa, "Culture and Entrepreneurship in the Developing Countries," in B. Berger, (ed.), *The Culture of Entrepreneurship*. San Francisco: Institute for Contemporary Studies, 1991.
20. J. Hirschleifer, "Evolutionary Models in Economics and Law: Cooperation versus Conflict Strategies," *Research in Law and Economics*, 1982, p.4, pp.1-60.
21. O. Williamson, *The Economic Institutions of Capitalism*. New York: Free Press, 1985.
22. H. P. Bahrdt, *Die Moderne Grossstadt. Soziologische Ueberlegungen zum Staedtebau*. Muenchen: Nymphenburger Verlagshandlung, 1974.
23. S. Stanoev, *Bulgarskata Gradska Kultura Predi I Sled Demokratichnata Promjana (Bulgarian Urban Culture before and after the Democratic Change)*, 1996, Manuscript, p.4.
24. For the difference between "formal" and "substantive" meanings of the economy and the concept of "economic," see Polanyi, 1992, pp. 31-4.
25. On this issue, see M. Los (ed.). *The Second Economy in Marxist States*. New York: Collier Macmillan, 1990; S. Sampson, "The Second Economy of the Soviet Union and Eastern Europe," in L. Ferman, S. Henry and M. Hoyman (eds.), *The Informal Economy. The Annals of the American Academy of Political and Social Science*, September, 1987. W. Gaertner and A. Wenig (ed.), *Economics of the Shadow Economy*. New York: Springer Verlag, 1985.
26. For instance, the DCM 35 of 1987 permitted for the first time part-time private activity for those employed in the state sector, full-time private businesses, pensioners and housewives. DMC 17 of 1987 allowed leasing in the service sector.
27. According to data published in the mass media, capital exports amounted to USD 15 billion which is more than the foreign debt of the country.
28. "The fight" is about positions in the governing bodies of large state enterprises, i.e., about control over their plundering. (Avramov).
29. The concept that the transformation period was one of transition from "plan to clan" was first elaborated by for Hungary, see D. Stark, "Privatization in Hungary: from Plan to Market or from Plan to Clan," *East European Politics and Society*, 1990, 4, 351-392. The term "uncivil economy" was formulated by R. Rose and is essentially the same: R. Rose, "Toward a Civil Economy?" *Studies in Public Policy*, No. 200. Glasgow: CSPP-University of Strathclyde, 1992.
30. V. Naishul, "Liberalism, Customary Rights and Economic Reforms," *Communist Economies & Economic Transformation*, 1993, p.5, p.1, pp.29-44.
31. It seems the "discontinuation" phenomenon is characteristic also for some other ex-communist societies. This could shed light on the reasons why the on-going transformation is "backward-looking" and why it is marked by a "desire to return to lost traditions." M. Borucha-Arctowa, "Social Consciousness in Transition: Toward a New Economic and Political System," in G. Alexander and G. Skapska (eds.), *A Fourth Way? Privatization, Property and the Emergence of New Market Economies*. London: Routledge, 1994.

Chapter Twelve

FINANCIAL STABILIZATION AND SOCIAL DESTABILIZATION IN HUNGARY

László Andor

The European Union has much to gain from stability in eastern Europe—and much to lose if things turn sour.[1]

During the past decade in Eastern Europe, we have witnessed a series of unexpected events of global importance. Most observers were taken by surprise by the emergence of Mikhail Gorbachov, *glasnost* and *perestroika*. Just one year before the event, no analyst had anticipated the domino effect that brought down the Communist governments between the Baltic and the Black Sea. More importantly and most sadly, the international political community was totally unprepared to handle the emerging crisis and tragedy of Yugoslavia.

If such a succession of surprises could happen, there surely is no guarantee that we can even now be any more sure in our forecasts and expectations; sudden changes on a similar scale cannot be ruled out. Until a comprehensive and rationalistic explanation can be found for our previous experience, and adequate decision-making mechanisms applied, insecurity remains an inherent part of regional politics.

Unexpected and massive political changes, particularly the emergence of general insecurity at considerable cost, have been the experience in Eastern Europe in recent years. These costs have been and will be borne not only by the peoples concerned, but by the wider international community. Economically speaking, many of the human and material costs involved could have been spared by wiser thinking and more determined action.

In order to find out how meaningless sacrifice could have been prevented and how further destruction may be avoided, researchers and policy-makers will have to re-examine the entire security context of the region. The conventional approach is to ask what forms of international integration can secure and guarantee stability in a region, or what level of military expenditures should be set for the new democracies. However, the main question this paper intends to address is the scope of security policies. Which areas of political and social life should be taken into account when thinking about and acting for a more stable environment? What was forgotten, or ignored, when governments were unable to prevent various military conflicts in and between the post-Soviet states, the collapse of the Yugoslav state, and the slide of its successor state into a war unprecedented in post-war European history? Our hypothesis is that the failure to anticipate certain political events, and make adequate strategic decisions in the economic, social, political and military spheres, can largely be explained by the separating of economic issues from the other areas.

SECURITY AND STABILITY: ECONOMIC VERSUS POLITICAL

The relationship between security and the economy can be approached from either direction. We can speak about the economic aspects of security, and the security aspects of the economy. The latter is the case when political instability plays an important intermediate role, since it is usually a consequence of some kind of economic disturbance and can spill over into more serious international conflicts.

There are several examples in history when security problems were deliberately addressed by economic measures. A most revealing example is the creation of the EEC and its predecessors, which was a typical instance when the role of economic prosperity in maintaining political stability and peace was recognised.

The various commodity price shocks of the 1970s played a major role in the developing of a new concept of economic security appropriate to a world in which economic links create a high degree of interdependence between previously independent nation states. However late and uncertain necessary policy responses have been, it has become widely recognised that "the economy is taking on strategic dimensions,"[2] and that effective security policies must have a broad interest in economic affairs.

Two major linkages between the economy and security are much in evidence, and can be applied in the East European context as a basis for further analysis. The first linkage is the capacity of economic crises to undermine political stability; the second is the impact of economic policies on social and political structures. While the former linkage is widely recognised, the latter has been much less discussed, mainly because of ignorance and lack of interest on the part of mainstream economists in anything outside their models, including the intended and unintended consequences of their policies on political and social stability.

Based on the two linkages, we have developed a model which enables us to analyse the transition process in three phases. Phase one was the period when a deepening economic crisis undermined the stability of the Communist regimes (linkage one). Phase two was the period when democratically elected governments attempted to restructure their economies by mainstream neo-liberal policies (linkage two in operation). Phase three is when the prolonged economic crisis of the mid-1990s becomes a source of further instability in the region (the return of linkage one).

PHASE ONE: THE COLLAPSE OF THE SOVIET SYSTEM

The first phase in our transition model is when the economic crisis undermines the political stability of the Soviet system both as a domestic social, economic and political structure, and as an international bloc of states.

There were two major sources of the economic crisis emerging in the 1980s. Internally, the end of extensive industrialisation exhausted the development capacities of the centrally planned economic system. The centralised structures proved unable to accommodate a transition to intensive development, i.e., an enhancement of productivity within the same economic structure.[3] The result was a slow-down in macroeconomic growth, stagnation of incomes, and, with some variation, increasing foreign indebtedness. The second source of the crisis was external: economic warfare[4] between the two military blocs, with a new round in the arms race in the early 1980s which stretched the economic capacities of the Soviet Union to the limit.

The East Central European (ECE) states were weakened by their own economic stagnation, but the weakening of the Soviet Union (SU) caused further uncertainty for them. True, it was seen as a new opportunity to redefine their roles between East and West, but such a redefinition would have required a greater degree of certainty about the future too. The deepening economic crisis and the accelerating disintegration of the Eastern bloc represented a double driving force behind the domestic political reforms[5] in the region.

The emerging crisis of the ECE-SU relationship caused a problem first of all in a material sense. The advantage of the Soviet military alliance for small states in the ECE was that they could behave as free-riders[6] on common, largely Soviet military expenditures. We should not underestimate the amount of resources devoted to defence purposes in the ECE states, but their proportion of the total GDP was significantly smaller than corresponding figures in the USSR.

In principle, the ratio of defence expenditures should increase once a state cannot enjoy free-riding any longer. National military self-reliance, *ceteris paribus*, is more expensive than collective security. The economic crisis, however, prevented ECE countries from increasing or even maintaining the real value of their defence budgets.[7] The financial crisis, whether temporary or not, emerged as a source of the security problems in the region.

Quite apart from material problems, the crisis and collapse of the ECE-SU relationship caused uncertainty in military doctrines as well. Soviet hegemony obviously was not simply about shared expenditures, but common principles and objectives. The loss of leadership was, again, understood as a gain of independence and sovereignty, but with the inevitable danger of creating a Hobbesian set of frustrated small states.

Following the rise of democratically elected governments in the region, the double problem of collective insecurity was addressed. First, economic reconstruction, and thus strengthening of the material basis of security, was expected from the implementation of mainstream neo-liberal policies. Second, a new security alliance, and thus new leadership, was expected to emerge from the integration of ECE into NATO. Phase two of our analysis is the period of this double experiment.

PHASE TWO: THE FREE MARKET EXPERIMENT

Mainstream neo-liberal economists entered the East European theatre with experience in the Third World debt crisis behind them. Their expertise in foreign debt management was expected to prove useful in guiding comprehensive reform of socialist economic systems. However, some aspects of both the debt crisis as well as the East European transition were not fully appreciated by these economists.[8]

LESSONS FROM THE DEBT CRISIS

The origin of the global debt crisis in the 1980s was in many ways related to armaments, although this aspect of the crisis was never properly addressed by debt manager institutions and individuals. The oil price shock, a form of economic warfare itself, was the event that gave rise to the massive funds available for borrowing in the 1970s. The shock was triggered by war between Israel and Egypt in 1973. A large proportion, sometimes up to one third, of the money borrowed by LDC governments was spent on military purposes. The accumulation of foreign debts turned into a raging financial crisis in the early 1980s, following the decision of the U.S. government to launch a new arms build-up. The U.S. needed funds to finance the new military-industrial build-up, so it increased interest rates after 1979 to suck in overseas capital from Japan, Germany and other countries. The funding requirements of the U.S. budget deficit[9] in the 1980s crowded out indebted LDCs from the capital markets.

The adjustment programme prescribed by the Bretton Woods Institutions (BWIs) amounted to complex public sector reform. Adjustment did not only mean that expenditures had to be brought in line with revenues, it was also designed to secure efficient public sector management for the future. Thus, it was not simply about cutting public spending, but also about penetration by private enterprise into all areas of the state. For economists employed by BWIs, defence spending was "just another type of public expenditure to be reduced." Accordingly, the real value of defence budgets started to decrease significantly after 1985. The reduction in military expenditures would have been good news in general, but the consequences of BWI policies were as controversial here as in other areas.

BWI policies have been widely criticised by academic experts as well as various NGOs. Focusing on political stability, we shall highlight two major consequences of the adjustment exercise. One is the rise of sub-national forces, as a result of the weakening of the integrity of the nation-state. The nation-states, however problematic their borders were in Africa, Asia and Latin-America, have provided a framework for integrating society and the economy, and, following the Weberian definition of the state, monopolising legitimate violence. The overall assault on the public sector therefore undermined this capacity, leading to the emergence of new socio-military patterns that cannot be accommodated within existing international law.

The other consequence, not unrelated to the first, was the repression of the developmental role of the state in LDCs. It had been a matter of consensus in previous decades that the role of the state in assuring basic human needs, and accelerating economic development by education and industrial policies, was vital for social and political progress in the Third World. In the 1980s, BWI policies turned diametrically against this common-sense opinion, and urged indebted governments to get rid of all those "wasteful" expenditures. Debt service, of course, was not considered to be wasteful, while governments were reluctant to cut defence budgets. This created a situation where many LDCs spend as much as 60-85 per cent of their public expenditures on defence and debt financing only. This required them to cut other areas, primarily social spending, with the associated permanent threat of social unrest and domestic instability. The number of food riots in LDCs soared in the 1980s, and the instability of one country often threatened the security of her neighbours as well.

Some students of security affairs and of Eastern Europe were aware of the security implications of the economic crisis[10] when the transition proper began, but their voice was not strong enough to influence decision-makers. BWI economists arrived in Eastern Europe determined to prove the virtues of their policies. They saw new frontiers opening up for them, just like they were for

Western multinational companies. It was, however, not only the LDC debt crisis that they failed to comprehend, but also the economic and political conditions of Eastern Europe. Inadequate analysis of the role of the defence sector in the economy and society proved to be a much greater mistake in the case of the Soviet Union than in that of Peru or Malawi.

Improper handling of the defence sector by crisis managers raised the risk that the defence establishment would be antagonised by economic reform, a form of which was inevitable given the circumstances of crisis. Market reforms have also threatened the defence sector by the penetration of various forms of dangerous entrepreneurialism.

RATIONAL EXPECTATIONS

It is not only the content of economic policies but also the style of economic policy-making which can be criticised within the security context. The role of the BWIs has been fairly contradictory in this sense. On the one hand, they had a strategy since the middle of the 1980s to create an ever improving domestic environment for their policies, previously seen as forced upon benevolent governments from outside. This required governments to present adjustment programmes as their own policies. On the other hand, however, BWIs have not been too eager to develop a democratic debate on the making of economic policies. Theoretical justification for this practice was provided by the theory of rational expectations, which advises governments to give practically no information, or even misinformation, about their activities to the public in order to avoid public hedging of required sacrifices.

One might have expected that the detaching of economic policy making from the democratic process was meant to last only for the early period of transition, when committees under the names "Blue Ribbon" and "Bridge" were established to provide economic policies for the fledgling democracies regardless of the outcome of general elections. This practice, however, continued to operate in the later years as well.[11] The coup-like economic policy making is obviously a major threat to the respectability of democratic institutions, but it is also a temptation to political and economic leaders to invite non-democratic forces to support the implementation of these policies.

The undemocratic features and other shortcomings of reform programmes might have been forgiven, if they had been able to resolve the original problems as was expected of them. By the mid-1990s, however, neither answers produced sufficient results. Although Partnership for Peace was invented to establish formal links between NATO and former WTO countries, membership in NATO proper was denied them. No serious political force in the region considers Partnership for Peace a long-term solution, so until NATO membership arrives, ECE governments will not consider their security framework as settled.

Similarly, the economic transition has resulted also in a half-baked market economy. It is true that six former COMECON countries have accomplished a co-operation agreement with the EC/EU, but this falls far short of the "final target" ECE countries find justified for themselves, i.e., real membership in the European Union. One could argue that ECE states have by now the toughest part of the transition behind them, but this does not mean that they have reached a position where economic growth is sustainable. With the possible exception of the Czech Republic, macroeconomic instability is a common feature, and pressure from BWIs for further public sector reform is a permanent feature. The scale of economic difficulties is by no means smaller than in 1989, and many of these difficulties have been created by the transition itself.

PHASE THREE: UNCERTAINTY PROLONGED

In the international political discourse, the year 1989 has emerged as a major dividing line in human history. With the destruction of the Berlin Wall, it was not only the communist regimes of a region ("Eastern Europe") that fell, but, according to Francis Fukuyama, the last significant challenge to western civilisation[12] was eliminated.

Half a decade after the emergence of the new political structures, it is clear that the economic crisis is not the only factor that represents continuity with the old regimes. The economic elite of the new systems is to a large extent (60-80 percent) based upon the elite of the previous systems, now representing themselves as private entrepreneurs instead of party or state bureaucrats. This factor, along with popular discontent directed against the hardships of the transition, also brought back to power large sections of the previous political elite in various countries of the region.

DEMOCRACY AND STABILITY

The political crisis of the late 1980s in ECE was predominantly driven by the demise of the Soviet system—as a social system and as an international block—in the East, and the international debt crisis in the West. With the introduction of the multi-party parliamentary system, the political crisis seemed to be resolved. The economic crisis, however, remains, not least because both major external circumstances of the late 1980s—instability in the East and debt crisis in the West—have not been removed. This state of affairs rendered the solution of the political crisis temporary and relative, challenging the claims about the capacity of democratic institutions themselves to maintain peace.

Theories of democratic stability, which have been popular in the West, would allow us to expect that the introduction of parliamentary democracy in the former socialist countries can by itself play the role of regional stabiliser. Some advocates of democratic stability, however, like Strobe Talbott,[13] add to their argument a kind of "safety clause," saying that Western help must play an important role in stabilising Eastern Europe even after democratic institutions have been introduced.

Others, like Moses[14] suggest that democratisation has only played a role within a broader project of "bourgeois revolution," which, based on historic experience, questions the durability of democratic institutions. Using Marx's analysis of French developments in 1848-52, Moses argues that "democratic and capitalist development do not necessarily go hand in hand" in Eastern Europe either.

Democratic institutions were obviously welcomed by the peoples of Eastern Europe, but for them "struggle" played a secondary role in bringing those changes about. Western pressure for democratisation in ECE was a major factor, highlighted by political scientists employed by the World Bank. Haggard and Kaufman[15] as well as others argued that adjustment policies can be much more successfully implemented in "democratic" circumstances, where economic and social distress questions the legitimacy of the government only instead of the legitimacy of the entire regime.

The financial argument for pluralism, however, can easily turn out to be self-destructive. The political institutions of the Western democracies were surely not designed to handle economic crises eliminating one-fourth or an even larger share of production in a country. In OECD countries, even a minor drop in GDP can create significant political distress, and a U-turn on just one single policy issue can bring into question the credibility of an established political force.

Both economic and political distress have been much greater in most East European countries than in any country in Western Europe since World War Two. Poland, while pioneering economic shock policies in the region, went through five governments within the space of three years, which is indeed an indicator of serious political instability. Since the general elections of September 1993, intra-parliamentary relations have settled down, although conflicts between different branches of power, i.e., the government and the president, have often appeared very sharp.

In other countries, the instability of democratic institutions can be measured by high electoral volatility and shifting political sympathies. The possibility of peaceful and continuous change is, of course, one of the advantages of the mechanisms of competitive democracy as we know it. However, we have to face the fact that in Western democracies which have displayed decades-long periods of continuity, even if governments or political blocks have been tested in elections every four or five years, a fundamental change between such blocks in power has usually been caused by a major economic crisis or rearrangement of external conditions. If, in the former socialist countries, economic stabilisation cannot be achieved and external conditions cannot be relied upon, the stability of the political power may become based either on repression or on apathy and non-participation. Neither solution delivers sufficient accountability and transparency of power, the presence of which would be vital to prevent governments from turning towards adventurism and hazardous strategies.

RE-INTEGRATION DELAYED

Prolonged uncertainty about the destination of change defies most of the *ad hoc* theorising about the new world that has emerged since 1989, introducing the term "transition" into the world of economic science. Ideologues of the new era, often the same persons as those of the old, distinguished between transition and transformation by claiming that transition is a long process towards a situation clear to the rulers, while transformation is longer and no one has a coherent vision of the place of destination. Having spent more than half a decade muddling through without reaching solid ground, while any coherent vision of the new world is fading, it now seems that we are more in a period of transformation.

The single most important cause of uncertainty for long-term development prospects has been the lack of clarity about the real possibilities of Euro-Atlantic re-integration. More than half a decade after the fall of the Berlin Wall, it would require recognition of misconceptions on both sides to re-route political rhetoric and policy-making in the direction of real possibilities and intentions.

On the Western side, more and more comments emerge concerning how profoundly "experts" misunderstood the situation in the East. After the event, even the most ardent supporters of the neo-liberal policies acknowledge that during the first period, i.e., until 1992-3, the BWIs got practically everything wrong.[16] Their forecasts hardly ever proved correct, and their policies hardly ever produced the promised outcomes.

Learning from the mistakes of the past years, however, is not enough. Gowan[17] explains that a major source of instability is the disunity of Western powers concerning policies towards Eastern Europe. Following the decline of Soviet influence in ECE, a hegemonic oligopoly emerged towards the region. Macroeconomic adjustment is guided by BWIs, while the trade regime, i.e., microeconomic conditions, is determined by the EU. From this perspective, the disunity on economic policies on the regional scale reproduces the disunity of Western powers on military policies within the context of former Yugoslavia. Of course, the war in the Balkans is conditioned by local contexts, but politicians and analysts of the region are aware that lessons to be drawn from the fate of Yugoslavia are of more general application precisely because of the capacity of economic crises to undermine political stability.[18]

The governments of the transition countries intend to address the prolonged uncertainty by increasing their efforts to gain admission into the Euro-Atlantic organisations. First of all, they have done their best to get the EU to elaborate an agenda for integration. Having accomplished the enlargement of the Union with the former EFTA countries, this seemed to be a logical step forward. However, as the Essen summit showed very clearly, such expectations had little basis, and the intensive diplomatic efforts were in vain.

Economic and political scientists in ECE countries have stood united behind the aspirations of their political leaders. In an article in the *Financial Times*, for instance, Csaba[19] argued that reluctant EU members must be convinced that granting membership to the Visegrád countries "would not be exorbitantly expensive and would be in the EU's interest, since it would represent a powerful contribution to the continent's stability." The costs of entry would fall very far below those of German unification. According to Attila Agh, the process of integration imposes tasks on both East and West.

> We in East Central Europe have a major job to relieve Europeanization of its ideological burden and to replace it with a pragmatic programme for European integration, for the structural accommodation of our countries within the fields of the economy, politics and social structures of the EU. The Westerners also have an urgent task, which is to provide East Central Europe with a clear perspective in the form of a Grand Design for joining Europe.[20]

This scenario gives the role of the legislative to the West and the executive to the East, which is imbalanced, but obviously better than no co-operation at all.

In June 1995, however, puzzled governments received an unusual message from Sir Leon Brittan, the EU commissioner responsible for "extension" affairs. The commissioner said the Easterners should not pressure the EU in order to get a deadline for entry, because any attempt to define a deadline would itself postpone the entry. Not speaking about when membership cards will be issued, according to the commissioner, can accelerate the integration process. (Formal logic would lead us to conclude that entry will be achieved quickest by not even thinking about it.) It thus comes as no surprise that ECE politicians currently in office have started to change their rhetoric, and attempt to shift the blame for failure on ignorant Westerners.[21]

Instead of a steady course of integration, we have thus witnessed the pursuit of individual and national fortunes rather than a collective effort to strengthen co-operation among the ECE states. They have been competing with each other for Western aid, investment, and verbal appraisal. The lack of regional co-operation made it inevitable that competitive devaluation encouraged by BWIs was not obstructed by any forceful policy. Without a new development framework, short-term sacrifices have turned out to have led to long-term losses.[22]

THE DE-LEGITIMATION OF THE STATE

Incapable of tackling their vast economic problems, governments have been forced to find scapegoats for the failure of the transition. Possible candidates are: the communists ("they spoiled everything in the previous decades and they still hang on to real power despite apparent changes in power"); external actors (the West or neighbouring countries); the black economy ("figures are bad because economic activity is performed in the shadow sector," or "tax fraud and corruption derail transition that otherwise would be formidable"). The choice or rather the actual mix of these and other factors depends on the character of the dominant forces in each country.

While none of these tactics can resolve the fundamental problems of transition economies, some of them, primarily the second, can raise concerns from the national security point of view. The first and third, although not directly connected with the system of international security, can lead to the violation of human rights by governments, which is an indirect capacity to create distress and instability.

What is even more interesting, however, is that the mainstream "transitionist" intelligentsia have started to speak out against attempts to implement the law and to tackle the black economy. Leading liberal writers and journalists tend to rehabilitate economic crime, saying that if the government launches an investigation into every suspicious privatisation deal, we will never have the "Rockefellers" who would be able to make post-communist capitalism great.[23] While only a few years ago they argued, following Hayek, that capitalism goes hand in hand with the rule of law, now they claim that it is inevitable that various—even illegal—forms of private accumulation must be tolerated for at least a generation.

Similarly, Schleifer[24] argues that although a slower pace of reform would mean less corruption in ex-socialist countries, nevertheless market reforms should be accelerated if we want to defeat corruption, since a state in which fair competition rules would be reached sooner. Less regulation, then, not more is the road to the promised land. Leitzel et al.[25] conclude their analysis of the criminalisation of the Russian economy on the note that crime is still the lesser evil as compared with other options.

The theoretical basis in political economy for these judgements is the recognition that the market system in itself is not stable, and that other mechanisms are required to stabilise an economy and society operating on the basis of the market. The build-up of the "mafia," as an artificial and extended version of the family, does play such a stabilizing role even if it does operate largely outside the legal system. Its rise is inevitable, in as much as dominant ideological tendencies reject previously used mechanisms such as planning, regulation and redistribution.

We thus find ourselves in a situation in which one has to choose between the illegitimate and the illegal. Economists and other ideologues accepting the BWI's neo-classical orthodoxy must conclude that the illegal is still better, while those opposed to street violence, gun rule and patriarchy would opt for the currently illegitimate but definitely more peaceful mechanisms.

Addressing crime but not its roots can be counter-productive, while a tolerant attitude may lead to its escalation not only domestically, but on an international scale. It is obviously not only private companies and individuals that can be driven into violating international law or norms under the impact of great economic hardship such as was experienced during the transition, but states also. It is, for example, understandable, even if it is not acceptable, that certain countries in desperate need of foreign exchange decline to follow the international community in discriminating against or outright sanctioning of particular states,[26] like Serbia, Chechnya or Iran.

The notion of crime, however, has not properly been elaborated in the context of regional disintegration. The Western community has several times condemned Serb leaders for committing "war crimes," while very similar acts perpetrated by the other side in the same war have not been mentioned. The selectivity of the human rights agenda of the international community has been widely commented on (China, East Timor, etc.), which significantly weakens the implementability of any kind of international decision that tries to supersede national divisions.

A major reason for the lack of respect for international law on the part of certain countries is the sharp detachment of that law from morality. The loss of a guiding paradigm for international relations with the end of the Cold War has been embedded in the general decline of rationality, which started with various post-modernist fashions, and culminated in the rise of Newt Gingrich and those of his persuasion who openly questioned the meaning of rights and social relations as understood not just since the time of Franklin D. Roosevelt but since Abraham Lincoln, and in some aspects since Thomas Jefferson.

One cannot forget that Western governments rejoiced when Yeltsin's troops were bombarding the building of the democratically elected parliament, and that the Constitutional Court was dissolved by the President. The international community accepted that these institutions were symbols of tyranny and bolshevism. Clearly, this was an encouragement to Yeltsin, signalling that he is free to use any means necessary against his political rivals, and that in the event that he has to choose between democratic procedures and market reforms, he should opt for the second without hesitation. Messages from the West were similar when the war in Chechnya began; the IMF did not hesitate long in putting together a more than 6 billion dollar loan package when the possibility of using financial leverage to orient the Russian government towards more peaceful solutions presented itself.

Of course, these are events in Russia which, even in the event of a worst case scenario[27] becoming reality, need not necessarily affect national security in the ECE. (In fact, they probably would.) But there are two reasons for concern.

First, these cases reveal the preferences of Western governments and multilateral institutions, and we cannot be sure that these will not be the same in the case of the ECE. Second, if prolonged crisis and uncertainty create widespread popular opinion to the effect that life is impossible under conditions of legality within the prevailing ideological framework, individuals will cease to respect the state, and governments will violate laws domestically as well as internationally.

CONCLUSION: BRINGING THE ECONOMY BACK IN

The veteran of American political ideology, Samuel Huntington, pioneered the guiding theory for the 1990, according to which it is ethnicity and cultural differences that determine all major conflicts in the post-communist era. The tragedies of Yugoslavia and Rwanda have been explained away as "tribal wars," incompatible with Western civilisation. Most of the Western press have tended to blame irrational factors (e.g., the emergence of evil persons) for these human disasters, suggesting that only the elimination of those irrational factors can lead to lasting solutions. It could be concluded then that those conflicts are actually cultural specificities of those nations, and are natural for them, without the perspectives of a more peaceful society.

Another type of semi-scientific argument has suggested, for example, that the "rise of nationalism is inseparably linked to the absence of a democratic tradition within communism."[28] Such a view must leave us puzzled then as to why extreme right-wing nationalist political forces gained much stronger influence in the first half of the 1990s in Western Europe rather than in East Central Europe.

The profound failure of the "irrationalist" school to explain the social conflicts of the 1990s, and to provide a basis for coherent and workable policies, defines an immediate task for social scientists. This task is to deconstruct the "ethno-nationality" discourse, and to discover the politics of nationalism, i.e., explaining nationalist sentiment as a means to material and political power.[29] Analysis of the East European transformation provides ample evidence that any attempt to explain the changes and conflicts by primarily cultural differences and ethnicity is wrong and misleading. Economic contradictions continue to create social and political instability, and potential military conflicts in Eastern Europe and elsewhere.

Therefore, the experience of ex-communist countries underlines the need for the political economy of national or international security to become a major field of research. That there are linkages between areas that are treated quite separately from each other—such as social matters, environmental questions, and national security—must be made clear and explicit, on the basis of a general concept of security. Policy-makers should realise that pursuit of national security is pointless without taking into account certain objectives in social security, while social security cannot be achieved without addressing issues of national security.

The first steps towards new East-West security co-operation within the framework of Partnership for Peace must be welcomed. Conventional thinking, however, is only suggesting making further steps towards NATO, whereas this paper argues that a military partnership for peace must not simply be deepened but also widened in the direction of an economic partnership for peace. Decisions concerning economic co-operation should be made with respect to their possible consequences on human relations within and between countries.

Among those who do recognise the linkage between economic hardship and political instability, there are nevertheless many who adopt an escapist position and suggest that "much of the pain of the transition has past." This may be correct to some extent, but it can just as well be misleading. Political and social history demonstrate a number of comparable cases that give cause for concern. Analogies with bourgeois revolutions allow us to draw parallels with Bonapartes, others with post-war exploitation and humiliation suggest comparisons with the rise of Hitler, and the structural adjustment context justifies fears of Pinochets. The post-communist transition in Eastern Europe seems to combine all three fearful experiences, which strengthens the case for economic action to forestall political instability and military insecurity.

NOTES

This paper was written when the author was senior visiting fellow at King's College, London, Department of War Studies. An earlier version was published in *Security Dialogue*.

1. Edward Balls, *The Guardian*, May 8, 1995.
2. Judit Balázs, "Economics At Risk: Security Options Towards The End Of The Century," *Development and Socio-Economic Progress*, No.58, 1993, p.167.
3. The distinction between extensive and intensive phases of socialist economic development is based on the work of the eminent Hungarian economist Ferenc Jánossy.
4. For an assessment of the impact of Western economic warfare on the East see Philip Hanson, "Western Economic Statecraft in East-West Relations: Embargoes, Sanctions, Linkage, Economic Warfare, and Detente," *Chatham House Papers 40*. London: Routledge, 1988.
5. An attempt to explain the link between political and economic reforms in Eastern Europe is provided by Lawrence L. Whetten. *Interaction of Political and Economic Reforms within the East Bloc*. New York: Crane Russak, 1989.
6. Free-riding has been a pet theory of neo-conservative economists in the public choice school. The concept is based on the image of someone who can actually use public transportation without paying the fare, because the vehicle, financed by tax-payers and other passengers, will run anyway. You become a free rider also when sitting in a bus and reading the newspaper of a person sitting next to you, even if you have paid your fare.
7. Amid acute financial crisis, Hungary carried out the largest military expenditure reduction in 1989 (17 per cent). Figures show a decline of the defence expenditure component of the GDP from 3.3 per cent in 1987 to 2.7 per cent in 1989, and a further decline to 2 per cent in 1992. This means a reduction in both operational costs and investments, with longer term technological impacts because of the latter. Since procurement expenditures fell even in nominal terms—as opposed to operational costs—military infrastructure suffered a general decline in this period.
8. We are speaking about the circle of economic advisors in and around the International Monetary Fund and the World Bank whose mental horizon does not extend beyond neo-classical economics, and who mostly divide their time between academia and practical policy-making. The prime example is Jeffrey D. Sachs of Harvard University, who has been an advisor of governments in Bolivia, Poland and Russia, but he is far from being the only one in the business.
9. According to Deger and Sen, "the single most important factor in exacerbating world debt has been governmental budgetary policy in the USA. The financing of defence spending under the Reagan Administration, through excessive reliance on borrowing, has made the USA the largest debtor country in the world." See Saadet Deger and Somnath Sen, *Military Expenditure: The Political Economy of International Security*. New York: Oxford University Press, 1990, p. 134.
10. Deger and Sen, for example, phrased their warning in the following terms (*Military Expenditure*, p. 147): "Unless the recent trends of economic crisis are reversed, conflicts will continue. Their underlying causes, however, will increasingly be developmental failures rather than political actions. The catalyst will be the difference between actual growth and expected growth, and the inability of debtor governments to meet the aspirations of major sections of their populations. Unless the security implications of the debt crisis are fully understood, and political solutions take precedence over technicalities, the recent dawn of peace may be darkened by new clouds of conflict."

11. A very clear example of the continuing separation of economic policy from democratic institutions is the March 1995 austerity programme of the Socialist-Liberal government of Hungary, which was produced in consultation between only the Prime Minister, the newly appointed Minister of Finance, and the Governor of the National Bank.
12. Western civilisation in this context is defined as the free market economy plus liberal/representative democracy: see Francis Fukuyama, *The End of History and the Last Man*. London: Hamish Hamilton, 1992. Usually, we refer to this combination as the "capitalist system."
13. Strobe Talbott, "The New Geopolitics: Defending Democracy in the Post-Cold War Era," *The World Today*, January 1995.
14. Jonathan W. Moses. "The Eighteenth Brumaire of Boris Yeltsin," *Security Dialogue*, Vol.25, No.3, 1994.
15. Stephen Haggard and Robert Kaufman (eds.), *The Politics of Economic Adjustment*. Princeton: Princeton University Press, 1992.
16. László Csaba, "A nemzetközi pénzügyi szervezetek és a kelet-európai rendszerátalakító politika," *Közgazdasági Szemle*, Vol.XLII, No.2, 1995.
17. Peter Gowan, "East Central Europe's Headless Hegemon," *Labour Focus on Eastern Europe*, No.50, 1995.
18. Michael Barratt Brown—in his article "Debt and War in Yugoslavia," *European Labour Forum*, 1992/3 Winter—explains how the debt crisis turned out to be the single most important source of first economic, then military warfare between the federal republics of the Yugoslav state.
19. László Csaba, "Time for a wider Union," *Financial Times*, May 9, 1995, p.18.
20. Attila Ágh, "From Competition to Co-operation: the Europeanization and Regionalization of Central Europe," *Budapest Papers on Democratic Transition* No.98. Budapest: Hungarian Centre for Democracy Studies Foundation, 1994.
21. In political circles in Hungary, voices critical of the role of the West were seldom raised before 1995. But Prime Minister Gyula Horn came out with a forceful critique of the EU, two months after he was forced into the most serious budget reform of the entire transition process. He accused the EU countries of being too wrapped up in their own problems and not paying sufficient attention to Central and Eastern Europe. Regional market reforms were producing too many losers, generating serious social tension, and could not be carried through without western help. "The countries of the EU have become too introverted, they are submerged in their own problems," he said. Mr. Horn observed that after the euphoria died down following the collapse of communism, he saw little evidence that the EU was seriously tackling the problems of eastern Europe. "West European countries do not sense what challenges we have to face," he said. See "EU countries are too introverted, says Horn," in *The Financial Times*, 1 May 1995, p.2.
22. Leading intellectuals have started to criticise the damaging aspects of national rivalry in the region. The writer György Konrád has complained about the "childish competition" between nations who should be friends, and Attila Ágh has explained how "overcompetition" between ECE states has turned into a negative sum game in recent years. See Attila Ágh, "From Competition to Cooperation."
23. György Bolgár, "Döntsd a tőkét, és siránkozz!" *Népszabadság*, 15 April 1995.
24. Andrei Schleifer, "Korrupció elleni harc a kommunista világban," *Népszabadság*, 2 May 1995, p.8.
25. Jim Leitzel, Clifford Gaddy, and Michael Alexeev, "Mafiosi and Matrioshki: Organised Crime and Russian Reform," *The Brookings Review*, Winter Vol.13, No.1, 1995.
26. It is no surprise that Russia was not prepared to abandon its nuclear deal with Iran. Similarly, it is hard to condemn Uzbekistan for providing tank reparing facilities to Chechnya, or Hungary for selling certain glass instruments to Iran which can be used to produce chemical weapons (as alleged by the Panorama programme of BBC/TV).
27. Historically conscious analysts often point out similarities between contemporary Russia and Weimar Germany. A wise warning by Ian Kershaw is a notable example: "However terrible, the past can be regarded as over and done with. But if Hitler will not recur, similar forces to those that created him might. This will not be in Germany, where, without any complacency about the resurgence of neo-Nazism, conditions are simply not comparable with those of the Weimar Republic...But in former Yugoslavia we see the annihilatory force of a potent mix of racial nationalism and war to attain 'ethnically cleansed' territory. And looming problems in the crisis-ridden former Soviet Union threaten to turn Bosnia into a side-show. While history never repeats itself, it can produce similar or analogous developments." See Ian Kershaw, "Herr Hitler Man of the Volk," *The Guardian*, 22 April 1995, p.21.
28. Gerard Delanty, "The Revolutions in Eastern Europe and the Redefinition of Europe: a New Social Contract?" *Contemporary Politics*, Vol.1, No.1, Spring 1995, 85.
29. Several students of the Yugoslav drama have already gone far beyond the the "ethno-nationality" discourse. Gagnon, for example, argues that it is "purposeful and strategic policies rather than irrational acts of masses" that has fuelled events in the Balkans. See V.P. Gagnon, "Ethnic Nationalism and International Conflict: The Case of Serbia," *International Security*, Vol.19, No.3, Winter 1994/5, p.164.

Chapter Thirteen

THE PRIVATIZATION OF THE STATE: THE BRITISH EXPERIENCE

Alan Scott

> Viewed social scientifically, the modern state is just as much a 'business' [*Betrieb*] as a factory is. Precisely herein lies its historical specificity. The relations of domination are similarly determined in each case.[1]

The quotation is from "*Parlament und Regierung im neugeordneten Deutschland.*" It comes in a passage in which Weber appears to be doing more than merely drawing a parallel between the modern mass bureaucratic states and modern, increasingly bureaucratic, private enterprises. He is claiming that private and state "*Betriebe*" (which here may be translated as "businesses" or "enterprises" as an alternative to the more neutral "organizations") are mutually interdependent to such an extent that they come to mirror one another. The point becomes more explicit where Weber goes on to discuss the dependence of the emergence of capitalism upon modern juridical and administrative systems:

> Historically too, the "progress" towards the bureaucratic state, towards rationally codified rights and rationally thought-out juridical and administrative rules, is now closely connected with modern capitalist development. The modern capitalist enterprise rest essentially on *calculation*. It requires for its existence a judiciary and administration whose workings can at least in principle be *rationally calculated* according to fixed general norms in the same way as the expected performance of a machine can be calculated. (Weber, "*Parlament und Regierung,*" pp. 322)

In these two quotations we have the suggestion of a reciprocal relationship between commerce and the modern bureaucratic state: the former is dependent upon the latter for the creation of a stable legal-administrative environment while the state comes to mirror, or mimic, the organizational forms which commercial activity has created. We also have the suggestion that in both cases standardization is a necessary condition for predictability of outcome; that, in other words, politics and economics share a common developmental logic: the logic of bureaucratic domination and rationalization.

Two broad questions arise from this entwinement of the forms of economic and political power. First, and most obviously, how should we conceptualize the relationship between forms of political rule and economic relations? Second, how should we analyze this relationship *now*—i.e., after the apparent shift away from the kinds of centralized bureaucratic management Weber famously analyzed? It is with this second question that I shall primarily be concerned. It breaks down into the following further questions: (i) How should we analyze *sociologically* the effects of recent innovations in the running of private enterprises—"flatter" management structures, spreadsheet accounting, devolved cost centres, etc.? (ii) Have these innovations in the private sector in their turn had the kinds of effects on the contemporary state form that Weber describes? (iii) To what extent do these changes require us to modify the arguments we have inherited from Marx and Weber in analysing relations of sub- and superordination within organizational structures and in the relation of state to civil society?

At first glance, it would appear that a quite radical revision of the "classical" analysis is necessary. In the age of the vanishing state and balkanizing bureaucracies, the sociological tools which we have inherited, in particular Weber's near obsession with bureaucratization and the political preconditions of market relations, would seem to miss the point. In this paper I want to pursue the hunch that this is not in fact the case. That, in other words, the basic Weberian assumption that politics precedes markets—but that the state in its turn comes to mimic capitalist enterprise—is still valid. "Relations of domination," I shall argue, continue to be "similarly determined." This is not to say that no revisions are necessary—at the end I try to identify some that are—but rather that important aspects of recent innovations in both the public and the private sectors have not, as their official ideology sometimes suggests, fundamentally challenged the power of centralized bureaucracies whether at state or intra-organizational level. I shall also argue that it is by re-examining aspects of Karl Polanyi's work rather than that of more mainstream figures in sociology that we gain the best leverage upon the issues raised above. Irrespective of differences of political stance, Marx, Polanyi and (even) Weber can all be read as critics of liberalism, but it is Polanyi who takes us deepest into areas of liberalism's contemporary manifestations. I shall initiate the discussion by comparing and contrasting Polanyi's analysis with that of Marx and shall go on to examine these differences in the light of Britain's experience and specifically with brief reference to the organizational and political innovations of the post-1979 Conservative Government.

MARX AND POLANYI ON THE PRECONDITIONS OF THE "FREE" MARKET

Karl Polanyi's *The Great Transformation* contains a critique of economic liberalism both as a political creed and as an account of the nature of industrial society. His critical analysis of market society via a critique of economic liberalism closely parallels Marx's critical analysis of capitalism via a critique of political economy. But Polanyi wanted to break even more thoroughly with the assumptions of economic liberalism than Marx had. His dispute with economic liberalism focuses on the issue of whether one should in any sense accord primacy to the economic over the social and political. Thus he writes "economic liberalism misread the history of the Industrial Revolution because it insisted on judging social events from the economic viewpoint."[2]

If we want to show that Polanyi's analysis is an advance over the Marxist critique of political economy then we need to show, first, that no matter how systematically Marx criticised liberalism's assumptions, he shared its tendency to judge social events from an "economic viewpoint"; second, that a more complete break with the economic viewpoint produces a better understanding of the nature of market societies. I shall argue that we can plausibly make both claims for a Polanyian over a Marxist interpretation. It should first be noted that Polanyi's critique of economic liberalism has much in common with that of Marx (which no doubt influenced it). Specifically, both are concerned to counter the assumption that rational egotism is "natural" by showing that there are particular historical preconditions for its emergence and operation which rational egotism cannot itself bring about. Both adopt the broadly Hegelian strategy of showing that while liberalism does offer an adequate account of the actions of subjects in markets it cannot account for the conditions of the possibility of such action which are, of course, at the same time liberalism's truth conditions.[3] But whereas Marx wants to identify the *economic* and *political* parameters of market activity, Polanyi wants to push the argument further by identifying its political and *social* parameters. This has two important implications for the substantive analysis of capitalism: (i) it accords an even greater significance to the role of the state as setter and manipulator of the parameters of market behaviour; (ii) it focuses on the social and behavioural preconditions of a market society in addition to the legislative and ideological. With respect to the second point, the reformation of society along free market lines entails more than a mixture of legislative restrictions and a successful hegemonic project; it entails a bringing into line (a *"Gleichschaltung"*) not merely of institutions but also of the way in which actors orientate their actions.

An economic liberal interpretation of the new free-market utopia of the Reagan/Thatcher era might issue in the following assessment:

> Reagan's victory dealt a fatal blow to state theories of reproduction. Neo-liberals campaigned to reduce state intervention, to deregulate, to lower protection, to suppress unions, to dismantle the welfare state; in sum to *leave the market to itself.*[4]

Adam Przeworski, who perhaps more than anyone else has demonstrated the analytical power of rational choice theory in analysing political processes and who is himself critical of neo-liberalism, offers here an analysis which immediately raises the question: can a market ever be "left to itself"? The central claim implicit in both the Marxist critique of political economy and in Polanyi's insistence that the free market is a utopia is that the market is not, never was, nor can be, autonomous and self-regulating. Both would argue that Przeworski's "error" stems from the adoption of an economic viewpoint; from taking rational self-interest as a given rather than as a social construct. They would further argue that such an analysis can lead one to take the New Right's political project at face value. How might such an argument against rational choice theory, and economic liberalism more generally, be applied to the substantive analysis of markets? Essentially, through the attempt to shift the analysis one stage back.

This attempt to move the level of analysis back behind the assumption of economic liberalism to a previous layer of preconditions is a common sociological response to methodological individualism. It is the technique Marx adopts in his historical move against political economy where he looks for the prior historical conditions of the possibility of capitalist accumulation:

> The whole movement [of capital]...seems to turn around in a never-ending circle, which we can only get out of by assuming a primitive accumulation ...which precedes capitalist accumulation; an accumulation which is not the result of the capitalist mode of production but its point of departure.[5]

What prior conditions must pertain in order for capitalist activity to occur and be profitable and how are these conditions brought about? Marx's answer is, of course, that primitive accumulation (which requires massive state sponsorship and intervention) is the point of departure, the necessary precondition, for the emergence of "free" markets in commodities. It is this argument which Marxian analysts continue to use, often to great effect. For example, Logan and Molotch in their celebrated work on the American city (1987) identify state largesse in "giving away" primitively accumulated land as the key to the emergence of free markets, and they go on to identify two key economic aspects of the state's necessary continuing contribution to what appears to be a "free" market: subsidy and regulation.[6]

How might such an analysis be applied to contemporary British capitalism and what would be its limits?[7] Most obviously, we can point to the continued role of the state both as regulator and subsidizer of economic activities even, or perhaps especially, in those cases where it claims to be withdrawing from intervention. Thus, for example, in the case of privatization the state creates new opportunities for investment and speculation. The privatization of telecommunications, gas, electricity, water, and more recently coal, plus the ongoing privatization of British Rail can be viewed as an attempt to bring about in an advanced capitalist society a new wave of "primitive accumulation" (though without physical force) and the opportunities for the speculative profit this brings with it. There may no longer be a West to win (and thus land to give away) but the scale of public property sale has in some respects recreated the conditions Logan and Molotch describe in the case of the early American city; conditions in which labour is weak(ened) and profits are high.

One might even in such an analysis characterize post-1979 British economic policy as "corporatism without labour." There has been a close collaboration between the state and at least some sections of business around a new "growth coalition" on a national level. But while business, or some areas of business, have clearly benefitted it is the state which has determined, and (insofar as it is currently able to control events) continues to determine, the pace, and to a degree the direction, of change.

But the economic role of the state is not restricted to the recreation of conditions analogous to those of early capitalism. It also uses its largesse, and particularly its continued regulatory role, to determine who should benefit from this "new bonanza." British energy policy illustrates this well enough. On the one hand nuclear energy is sheltered by legislation from the chill winds of market forces (it has a guaranteed share of the market for electricity production) while gas and coal are exposed to the market's full force. The latter are set up in competition against each other for that part of the market not reserved for British Nuclear Fuels (gas wins). In such cases the market can appear to be itself an arm of policy.

Even in cases where privatization is difficult or will take perhaps a further legislative period the state still actively prepares the way. Thus the commercial activities of the postal service (the nationalized "Royal Mail") are highly restricted while those of their private competitors are less so. The latter can then build up their strength to act as real competition if and when the full privatization of the postal service becomes politically viable.

In these cases the state is employing its legislative power to act more-or-less overtly as a regulator of the market. But it acts no less as its subisidizer. This can be done either explicitly (e.g., through the continued subsidy as well as protection of British Nuclear Fuels) or indirectly through selling state property at "attractive" prices—i.e., below their market value (as was the case, for example, with the sale of British Gas). Occasionally these implicit subsidies have themselves infringed EU regulations, the sale of Rover to British Aerospace being the best known example.

All this analysis is pretty standard, even obvious. By pointing to the regulatory and subsidizing role of the state and by mobilizing a modified form of Marx's historical account of primitive accumulation we can provide an analysis of the political determinants of market parameters and this can be used to counter economic liberalism's self-understanding. However, I want to argue that this is not sufficient. The Marxist critique of liberalism encounters its limitation when it shifts its focus away from the *political* and towards the *social* preconditions of the market economy. In particular I shall use Polanyi's analysis to show that to counter the self-image of economic liberalism we need not only to show that the state provides both the point of departure for the market and continuing regulation plus subsidy, but also that it assists in bringing about the type of *society* and *economic subject* without which the market cannot operate. Because Marxism ultimately shares liberalism's "economic viewpoint," it has not fully appreciated the role of the state in the management of action and the regulation of social relations, and it ultimately slips into an instrumental interpretation of the state against the grain of its own attempt to find the "point of departure."

We can see this by returning to Logan and Molotch's otherwise powerful analysis of markets in place. When they speak of the social role of the state in growth coalitions, Logan and Molotch do so with respect to (i) social order, and (ii) ideology. For example, they note that the maintenance of social order is a vital precondition for a working market in urban land:

> While a good opera or ballet company may subtly enhance the growth potential of some cities, other cultural ingredients are crucial for a good business climate. There should be no violent or ethnic conflict. (Logan and Moltosch, *Urban Fortunes*, p. 60)

But as an account of the social dimension of growth coalitions, such an analysis remains too narrowly economic. Even sophisticated neo-Marxism, such as Logan and Moltosch or regulation theory, has tended to reduce the social aspects of a market society to these two dimensions: social order and ideology. But this neither captures the full social significance of the new free market utopia nor breaks sufficiently with economic liberalism's tendency to view developments from an "economic view point." Let us examine these limitations more closely.

(i) *Social Order*. With respect to social order, when those whose analysis issues from a neo-Marxist political economy come to look at the social aspects of the New Right's project they tend to focus on work and on industrial legislation, and particularly on the so-called "juridification" of industrial relations (e.g., on legislation introducing strike ballots, outlawing secondary picketing, etc.), or they focus on legislative restrictions more generally.[8] In the UK at least, there is evidence enough of the importance of these factors (the recent Criminal Justice Act being one of them). But there is nevertheless a danger in the over-application of a "social order" model because there is more to the creation of a market society than restrictions on behaviour. By over-emphasizing the role of *legislative restriction* we loose sight of the way in which the process of creating a new market order entails the reconstitution of action; the constitution of new subjects, not merely the constraining of the old. This over-emphasis on restriction has been reinforced by the fascination of recent social theory with "discipline," stimulated by Foucault's earlier work. But to secure their co-operation actors (or some actors) must also be empowered by being released from previous constraints. In brief, sociological analysis of markets needs to examine both their constraining and enabling characteristics.

(ii) *Ideology*. Similarly, with respect to ideology, where the positive support for the Thatcherite project has been examined it has tended to take the form of a broadly Gramscian perspective, emphasizing its democratic popularism: for example, its mobilization of popular nationalistic sentiments or popular anxieties about law and order. The application of Gramsci's analysis of hegemony to Thatcherism has produced many insightful findings.[9] But such analysis has tended to focus upon explicit beliefs, on cultural practices which are, in Durkheim's sense, "sacred" (e.g., rituals of nationalism or monarchy), or on the ideological mobilization around exceptional events (e.g., the Falklands Crisis/War), rather than on the reproduction of the social order in action on a routine basis. We need to account not only for the political support which can be mobilized for the New Right's project, but also for the ways in which it has altered actors' orientations in their everyday lives—even, or crucially, for those actors who do not lend it support at a political or ideological level. Unless we do so we will not understand the full power of the political changes which have occurred in Britain over the last fifteen years or so, and which may yet engulf its more corporatist European partners.

A vital clue to an alternative interpretation of the social changes wrought by the shift towards market relations lies in the following observation:

> Bureaucratic rationalization can also, as we have seen, be a revolutionary force of the first order against tradition. And it has often been such. But it revolutionizes by *technical* means (as do all transformation of the economy), in principle "from outside": first things and structures then, on that basis, people; the latter by altering the conditions to which they must adapt and perhaps by increasing their possibilities of adaptation to the outside world by setting rational ends and means.[10]

Weber contrasts this "bureaucratic revolution" which changes people *"'von außen' her"* by altering their *"Anpassungsbedingungen"* (conditions to which they must adapt) and possibly increasing their *"Anpassungsmöglichkeiten"* (possibilities of adaptation) with charismatic revolutions which alter people *"von innen heraus"* (from the inside).

This characterization of a bureaucratic revolution is, even by Weber's standards, remarkably blunt not to say brutal. But it also offers a much better characterization of, and basis upon which to analyze, change than do those so far discussed. Specifically, it points to the need to examine the following: (i) the character of *institutional* changes and their effects on actors' orientations; (ii) the enabling features of market relations (e.g., in rationally setting ends and means); (iii) institutions and markets as *social* structures of domination and obedience; (iv) the manifestations of altered actor orientations *within* organizations in their everyday routine actions. In other words, it plays down the role of politics, ideology, and belief, and plays up the importance of institutional transformation. Changes in orientation follow institutional change, and institutional change is the consequence of bureaucratic command. Whereas accounts of changes in orientation which emphasise hegemony portray actors as offering positive support to some new "project," Weber's figures are merely *"Anpassungsfähig,"* capable of adaptation to new circumstances.

It is in understanding these "positive" and "routine" social characteristics of market societies where, I want now to argue, Polanyi's analysis can be of help. Such an analysis, I shall suggest, also points to the importance of examining power at the micro level within organizations moulded on market lines. Here Polanyi appears closer to Weber than to Marx.

THE MAKING OF A NEW FREE MARKET UTOPIA

The point of departure for understanding the complexity of the process of the making of a market society might be the following three thoughts which are central to Polanyi's argument in *The Great Transformation*. The first thought is that "a market economy can exist only in a market society" (p.71); the second, that market societies are not natural, they are made; the third, that they are made by states. The "free" market, Polanyi argues, is an "institutional structure" (p. 37) which does not emerge spontaneously from our proclivity to "trade and truck" but is planned and state-sponsored, hence the paradoxical observation: *"Laissez-fair* was planned; planning was not." (p. 141)

But what is a "market society" and how is it made? The general anthropological argument underlying Polanyi's critique of economic liberalism is that *Homo Economicus* is a product of the market society, not the other way round. A market society is not merely one in which resistance to the market principle is disabled through legislation or in which the free market project is politically hegemonic, but one in which most institutions and the everyday orientation of social actors are brought into line with the principles of the market: individualism, competition, self-interest. The market subject not only lends ideological support to these principles, but comes to embody the new order in everyday action. Indeed it is possible to embody this "ethic" without lending it explicit intellectual support. Polanyi's analysis of market *societies* suggests the need to develop a sociological account of this process of *"Gleichschaltung."* Moreover, such an account has to identify the mechanisms which make this realignment possible.

In the rest of the paper I shall make some provisional attempts to develop such an account of this process of bringing a society into line with a new market order and of the role of the state in this process. The implicit model will again be that of contemporary Britain, but the mechanisms I seek to identify are to be found more widely.

THE CREATION OF A MARKET SUBJECT THROUGH INSECURITY AND UNPREDICTABILITY

Central to the constitution of an economic subject is the structure of rewards through which the social order seeks to assure its maintenance and reproduction. Perhaps this can be seen most clearly if we compare Weber's characterization of bureaucratic domination with a Polanyian account of the nature of a free market order.

Both types of social order must secure their stability by creating a structure of rewards which guarantees a degree of predictability at the level of social action. I shall argue that these two social orders are to be distinguished by, first, the *techniques* employed for assuring predictability of outcome; second, the *media* through which control is exercised. The conclusion I hope to draw from the following discussion is that both Weber and Polanyi are right to argue that, despite the different logics of the bureaucracy and the market, these are in fact *compatible* and *complementary* forms of social organization.

Polanyi's argument that a market economy can only exist in a market society is essentially an extension of Weber's argument to which I referred at the start: market economies require specific juridical forms. But Polanyi, perhaps even more than Weber, is aware that juridical predictability is an insufficient guarantee of the stability of a modern market order. In his account of bureaucracy Weber famously argues that control is exercised in the form of the (usually written) command, and that such commands flow down through the official hierarchy. His analysis further suggests that there is one form of action orientation particularly suited to such corporate structures, namely one of instrumental rationality (*Zweckrationalität*). But it might be useful for our purposes to make a further distinction between kinds of instrumental rationality. Weber gives us a powerful characterization of the instrumentalism of the civil servant whose honour, he argues, lies in a particular form of *Sachlichkeit* (matter-of-factness): namely, in the ability to obey a command as if one believed it oneself, whether or not one does, and as though it issued from one's own volition. At its most extreme Weber appears to be describing a subject who subordinates his/her will to the command. How might the loyalty of such a subject be secured other than through the mechanisms of surveillance which have been the ubiquitous companions of bureaucratic domination?

Bismarck's famous observation that the prospect of a pension secures loyalty for life gives us a clue to the nature of the reward principle of bureaucratic or corporate structures: they offer stability and predictability in return for loyalty. Where loyalty is systematically rewarded, actors can then be *commanded* and *obedience* required and expected. I think we can read Weber as saying that *stability* and *predictability* are key mechanism for securing loyalty—and hence predictability of outcome—from those directly subjected to bureaucratic domination. But, as he is acutely aware, the bureaucratic subject is not suitable to the unstable environment in which innovation and leadership are possible. Stability may induce predictability of outcome, but it is anathema to the principles of the market itself. While fully aware of this, Weber's analysis of the "relations of domination" does not explain fully how stability may be maintained within social orders which, at least superficially, resemble the conditions of the "anarchy of production" rather than the order of the corporation.

The principle underlying the market is not one of obedience to command, but individual pursuit of self-interest. There are fewer direct "commands" and thus less need for either obedience or loyalty. This poses quite different problems of social stability. In the case of the bureaucracy the problem is one of inherent conservatism, the inability to adapt. Weber is thus worried, in the context of bureaucratic domination, about the possibility of entrepreneurialism, initiative and leadership among its loyal and obedient subjects. The problem of the free market, on the other hand, is not the management of stability but the control of change; to secure predictability of the outcome of actions in conditions where actors are not bound by loyalty to a stable and predictable environment.

As the starting point for the discussion of the nature of market subjects I shall assume at least the significance, if not the validity, of two further central arguments in *The Great Transformation*. The first is that a pure market society is a utopian project because the market poses insurmountable problems to social stability which can only be addressed by recourse to non-market mechanisms. In other words, extra-market sources of social cohesion are necessary in order to sustain contractual relations.[11] The second argument, which assumes the validity of the first, is one Polanyi and Weber share: namely, that market relations do not of themselves necessarily disturb hierarchical relations of power and authority; indeed they may assume and reinforce them.

This concern with social stability and hierarchy leads us to pose the following questions when we come to compare bureaucratic domination with markets. (i) Does action freed from direct command give rise to a new form of predictability at the level of behaviour which is necessary for social stability? (If so, must such stability be secured by a particular *structure of reward*?) (ii) How is the power of local and state administrations maintained in the face of newly autonomous and self-interested actors? In other words, what, if any, mechanism replaces the command as the mechanism for transmitting the will of centralized power? I shall address these question with reference to a further major innovation of the "new free market utopia," namely "internal markets" in the public sector.

A strong state is necessary both to discipline and reward an existing workforce into accepting their new conditions of employment and the new "ethic" and "ethics" under which they must work (described, in somewhat chauvinistic language, as the elimination of "Spanish practices"). The basic aim of internal markets in the provision of public goods is neatly captured in Polanyi's description of the purpose of Bentham's Panopticon: "not only a 'mill to grind rogues honest, and idle men industrious'; it would also pay dividends like those of the Bank of England." (p. 121) The quote captures the dual purpose of this political project: the reformation of work practices and the establishment of a system for the provision of public goods modelled on a market and thus having the production of profit (however artificial) as its basic organizing principle.

The idea of the internal market as the principle for governing large organizations is quite simple. One replaces a centralized bureaucratic hierarchy in which commands flow downwards but never up with "flatter" less tightly controlled organizations. The chief mechanism used to achieve this is the devolved budget. Each section of the organization becomes its own "budget holder" and buys services from other parts of the organization or, crucially, can go outside the organization where comparable services can be found more cheaply in the wider market. Each unit is, of course, also a supplier of services to other parts of the organization, and, again crucially, can sell its services in the wider market if these in their turn are competitive. The technical innovation which makes this organizational principle workable is the computerized spreadsheet which can show on a continuous basis the income and expenditure, and thus the profitability, of each section of an organization independently from the profitability of the entire corporation. The computerized spreadsheet may turn out to have the kind of significance for contemporary society as that ascribed by Weber to double-entry bookkeeping in early capitalism. If a "cost centre" cannot offer its internal (or external) clientele competitive rates and appealing goods or services, it will not survive. It is thus motivated to try to maximize its profit to ensure survival. There is then no need to command a unit to modernize or to be more efficient. Unit members themselves will have a personal motive to modernize (e.g., to retrain) and adapt—rogues will have been ground honest and idle men industrious. The flow of commands downwards has been replaced by the working of the market's hidden hand, or so at least it would seem. All this is well-known, but how does it work as a *social* organization?

The devolved budget and the cost/service centre are the organizational embodiment of the political beliefs of the Thatcher/Reagan era. The technique promises to provide precisely the mechanism to realize the new free market utopia. It breaks down the hierarchical and bureaucratic structures which promote a "dependency culture" not only within a paternalistic welfare state, but also in all those micro welfare states—those private as well as state organizations which promise workers a job for life (or at least a reasonably stable post) and a pension in return for loyalty, but which also induce an attitude of complacency and conservatism among the weak and frustration in the strong. The new worker serves his/her employer not through loyalty but through initiative motivated by the inducements provided by a loosened organizational structure. Security, for example of employment, may have been lost, but freedom has been won. In these organizations of the quick and the dead, the life of the quick is heady, exciting and potentially rewarding. The quick may in the medium or long term be too quick to stay with the organization, but as long as they do so the organization will profit from their energy; its interest will be served—just as classical liberalism had it—as a byproduct of the individual's "enlightened self-interest." Nature dictates that the quick will, of course, one day in their turn become the dead. So here too disloyalty can have positive organizational advantages: individuals rather than organizations carry the financial burden of physical and mental decline. The free market thus works in part precisely because it does not require either obedience or loyalty—i.e., because it is a sphere free of direct bureaucratic domination. It emancipates the worker from command and may yet secure a new predictability of response by empowering him or her, or by appearing to do so. Even a critical analysis of the new free market utopia must recognize the "emancipatory" implications of these changes for actors who were previously the subjects of direct bureaucratic domination.

How then is a degree of hierarchical control maintained? The internal market works by changing the actors' orientation and ethic through altering the environment within which they act. In Weber's terms, it sets them rational goals by changing the conditions in which they must act, and to which they thus must adapt. It does so in part by influencing their speed of response and time horizons. We can illustrate this point by comparing contemporary market culture with an older form. Stefan Zweig's autobiography *Die Welt von Gestern*[12] opens with an account of the effects of long-term social and economic stability on the psyche of the pre-First World War Viennese middle class. No-one rushes, nothing is rushed. Zweig claims that even as a young child, when his father was still relatively youthful, he does not recall seeing him run up or down stairs or make an inelegant hasty gesture. The cycle of entrepreneurs, of which Zweig's father was a highly successful member, could have made their fortune quickly through speculation, through venture capital. But in an atmosphere of economic stability there was no need to hurry. If we are to believe Zweig, they chose to build up their businesses slowly and on a firm footing. Not sloth, but caution and persistence would be rewarded. Furthermore, as in a bureaucracy, the recipient of such reward was not to be the individual as he/she is now, but the not yet existing older man or woman, or that material representation of posterity "the family." Economic stability dictated the tempo both of action and of capitalist enterprise.

In contrast to the Vienna of Zweig's childhood, the chief technique of rule now is the creation of an environment of instability. If Zweig is right that stability induces a slow tempo, then the tempo can be increased either by uncontrolled events of the type that destroyed the world of the *fin-de-siècle* businessman, or by the controlled instability induced by the intentional and constant rearrangement of the parameters within which decisions have to be made and action taken. To increase speed through the constant rearrangement of parameters is to rob the actor of that calming force on which Zweig Senior knew he could rely: strategy. Without strategy we can only respond; we can only manage stairs by rushing at them. Instability induces both speed and uncertainty, conditions in which our time-horizons are foreshortened. The "short-termism" of which the new capitalism is so often accused is a rational response to circumstances, or perhaps it is the only response of those who seek to remain in the game. But it also provides a powerful lever for central nodes of power within organizations and society.

In brief, the power of bureaucratic hierarchy (whether at the local level of a particular organization or at the level of the nation state) is maintained through the mobilization of the remaining regulative authority which is deployed to manipulate opportunity structures by shifting resources and centrally determined pricing. This induces uncertainty and instability into the environment of those released from the kinds of direct bureaucratic domination Weber described. The new autonomy is real but its beneficiaries find themselves in shifting opportunity structures within which they must operate and over which they do not have direct control. Of course, as economic liberalism has taught us, markets always have such "externalities" (e.g., consumers' preferences) over which the entrepreneur has no direct influence. The point here, however, is that these parameters are not those of fate (or of the fate-like workings of a market) alone, but are in part manipulable through bureaucratic decision. Furthermore, these parameters are not sufficiently stable for actors to develop longer term strategic responses which would enable them to challenge such centralized constitution of the environment. Combined with other factors inhibiting collective action—discussed below—their newly won *autonomy* is unlikely to translate into effective *control*.

It is this combination of *autonomy without control* which is the underlying source of stability of both social and hierarchical relations with internal markets. Centralized bureaucracy, whether local or state, does not give up its power by constituting newly autonomous subjects as long as it retains control of the environment in which the actors operate autonomously. What appears to have changed is not the fact but the mechanism of control; the substitution of ever shifting environmental parameters for the direct bureaucratic command; or rather it is the formation of the parameters rather than routine daily decision which is the object of direct bureaucratic manipulation (this distinguishes a contemporary bureaucracy from those Weber described). Indeed in the public sector there is nothing particularly subtle about this new form of control at a distance. For example, in the provision of health and educational services, where the state is still paymaster, it sets centrally the price of the "units of resource" (patients or students). By altering these nominal prices (in effect by increasing or—more often—decreasing subsidy) the state retains enormous power over those very bodies which have been promised greater autonomy.

In the following section I shall examine some of Polanyi's arguments which suggest that individuals acting as rational egotists in these quasi-markets[13] are in an even weaker position to challenge central authority than are Weber's loyal *sachliche Beamte*.

CONTROL AND THE DESTRUCTION OF SOCIAL RELATIONS

I shall say less about this aspect of the new free market forms not least because Polanyi has so much to say about it. *The Great Transformation* emphasizes over and over that the market displaces social relations with contractual and instrumental ones.[14]

For the sake of our concern here with the stability and sustainability of the free market, the central point is a simple one. By enabling actors to act effectively only if they do so as rational egotists the market's institutional structures destroy the normative basis of collective action; they manufacture conditions in which prisoners' dilemmas are sure to arise at any point where a collective response might be appropriate. The key point here is that power is not exercised merely through the continual manipulation of parameters but through the initial role of bureaucratic organization in *constituting* those parameters. This again echoes Marx's arguments concerning the "point of departure." Markets can be constituted in such a way as to give a high probability of predictability of outcome even, or precisely, in the actions of rational egotists.

Again the internal market illustrates this point. It sets up "units" in competition for scarce resources (controlled centrally) which make it unlikely actors will combine to challenge the criteria which determine the level and distribution. More than this, it removes these issues from the sphere of explicit discussion and makes distribution seem a side-effect of a combination of individual/unit activity and fate—i.e., the market. In bureaucratic organizations it may be difficult, as Weber argues, for those lower down to challenge the decisions which are passed down to them. But in modern flatter organizations there are in many cases no overt decisions to challenge. In a sense, and partly as a result of Foucault's influence, too much emphasis has been placed on surveillance as a mechanism of control and too little on mechanisms which inhibit the very possibility of public disorder in the form of collective responses.

The mechanisms which inhibit the emergence of collective action among suppliers of services within an organization organized along the lines of the internal market have analogous effects on those who use those services and who become "consumers." The point has been made polemically ("consumers" versus "citizens," etc.), but Weber already made the point clearly enough:

> ...it is extraordinarily difficult to persuade people to join together when they have nothing more in common with each other that a desire or intention to buy something or to provide for their needs, since the whole situation of the consumer stands in the way of socialisation. Even starvation, in Germany at least, has not persuaded (or has hardly persuaded) the great mass of ordinary housewives [sic] to accept the meals prepared in the special wartime kitchens in place of their own amateurish individual cooking.[15]

The "whole situation" of both the supplier and consumer of public services "stands in the way" of their socialization. We may have won the freedom to associate only to loose the desire. This again suggests that however important judicial restrictions on action may be, it is more efficient to preempt the possibility of collective action through the substitution of the institutions with the market and thus remove the cultural and communicative conditions of its possibility (or at least likelihood).[16] I shall return to this point in the conclusion. Here I shall conclude by examining an aspect of the new arrangements which could well be interpreted in Gramscian terms as "hegemonic."

Once authority is thus stabilized, the hierarchy of these new flatter structures can reintroduce command mechanisms in the form of organizational projects. This is a major innovation in the art of governance. In traditional bureaucracies there is a cascading structure of authority through which organizational decisions run, as Weber constantly repeats, on a routine and day-to-day basis. What has occurred in these new organizations is that routine decisions are removed from the command structure and reallocated to "autonomous" groups, with bureaucratic decisions in the old form restricted to key organizational *strategies and projects* as set out in "mission statements," etc. Actors act autonomously, and thus bear a higher burden of responsibility for the outcomes of their actions, but the framework in which they and the projects for which they work are no more under their control than they would have been in a traditional organizational structure. Indeed by reinterpreting many key organizational decisions as the outcome of the fate-like workings of a market or as technical issues, many aspects of these new organizations are harder to challenge at a discursive level. The spreadsheet's "bottom line" holds trumps at least as long as it corresponds to the aims the organization has set "itself."

It thus becomes possible to run direct commands alongside quasi-markets and to reintroduce the non-market language of production targets, quality control, directives, etc. Polanyi's insistence on the inevitability of planning would suggest that what we have here is not, as Weberian analysis implies, a hybrid of two ideal types (the corporation and the free market), but rather that markets are necessarily characterized by such a mix of market mechanism and centralized direction (i.e., that they are necessarily "sociologically ambivalent," to use Merton's phrase). The newly freed actors, whether individuals or organizations, find themselves responding to bureaucratic decisions just as before. As in traditional organizations, actors as subordinates have little influence over strategy, but as entrepreneurs within their unity they nevertheless shoulder a greater direct responsibility for the success or failure of outcomes. In other words, policy and its implementation ("operation") become decoupled. Under these conditions actors are no longer *servants of* but, paradoxically, *entrepreneurs for* an institution. They can, in other words, only pursue their self-interest so long as it accords with the interests of the organization they serve. This is because their actions are oriented towards entrepreneurialism, though rewards stem not directly from the success or failure of their action, or even the fate-like character of the market but, as for the civil servant, from the institution's assessment of their worth.

Freed from the necessity of constant participation in the flow of commands on a routine daily basis, the top of the hierarchy can focus its energies on the development of the strategies and plans whose implementation they do not have to directly supervise. Thus, paradoxically, while responsibility becomes devolved power shifts to the centre. The system is—in Weber's sense—more "efficient" than a traditional hierarchical organizational structure because expensive supervision (surveillance) of day-to-day running is redundant, having been replaced by market mechanisms and the quasi-technical accounting tools. Supervision and surveillance may then themselves be more selectively—"efficiently"—deployed.

NATURALIZATION

The importation of new management models from the private into the public sector provides one clue to the central paradox of contemporary British life. At a time when the ideological underpinning of the new utopian project appears to be crumbling, its power over our lives grows. What has of course happened is precisely what Weber describes in the *Protestant Ethic*. Once a new pattern of belief has been translated into habitual behaviour and becomes embodied and embedded in institutional arrangements, the original beliefs and values which sustained that behaviour and those institutions can fall away. Just as we can have a Protestant ethic without Protestantism, so too can we have what I would like to call the "accelerated Thatcherism of institutions" without Thatcherism as a popular and populist political ideology.

What was once a political ideology of the New Right becomes a seemingly neutral organizational *technique*. It is no longer anyone's exclusive intellectual property. What is more, it can then be imported by Social or Christian democracy—where these have overcome anxieties about its potential social destructiveness (see above)—and exported geographically minus its original political/ideological baggage. It can take as firm a hold on the minds of socially aware leftists as it can on those of market zealots. Furthermore, as a technique of rule it then becomes highly resistant to reversal even were there to be the political will to attempt it. It is perhaps the dim, or not so dim, recognition of this that has led the British Labour Party towards an accommodation with these new but by now deeply rooted structures.

Removed from its original intellectual and ideological context and retranslated as technique, the new management can also become an ideal, a utopia. We can come to focus exclusively on its empowering ability, believing that if only the environment remained stable, if only government or local bureaucracy would "leave the market to itself," then it would deliver on its promise to liberate us from the all too obvious constraints of bureaucratic domination. But it follows, from Polanyi's central claim that the market is a constructed institution, that the manipulation of its parameters is not an accidental "externality" but a necessary condition of its stability, maintenance and its employability as a mechanism for ensuring predictability of outcome.

CONCLUSION

I want to suggest two possible conclusions which might be drawn from the developments in Britain over the last fifteen or so years. The first concerns the appropriateness of the notions of "disorganized capitalism"[17] versus Weber's and Polanyi's argument that capitalist enterprise and the "enterprise" of states are compatible, the second concerns the need for a new conceptualization of power.

The British case at least suggests that analysing contemporary capitalism by contrasting Karl Renner's "organized capitalism" with the new "disorganized capitalism" is misleading. The notion of "disorganization" suffices to capture elements of deregulation (especially in the labour market) and the social disruption of modern techniques, but it fails totally to comprehend the continuity in the state's role. The areas which are "disorganized" remain tightly controlled and selective. Nor is the choice necessarily between "corporatism" and "dualism" as Goldthorpe has argued.[18] What Britain exemplifies is a kind of dual track policy in which some areas remain organized and others are disorganized, and where even the disorganized sector remains tightly circumscribed. Nor does privatization necessarily decrease the power of the state through its displacement by the market. It can make the state in some respects more powerful not only because it becomes a key source of high profit in the market through deploying its new largesse, but also because it acquires new powers of regulation and direction.

We need another concept or metaphor to capture this duality. The anthropologist Ernest Gellner[19] makes a distinction between "wild" and "cultivated" cultures. We might adapt this useful metaphor to talk of "wild" and "cultivated" capitalism. The creation of areas of "wild capitalism" has the advantage of reproducing in a controlled and regulated fashion something like the conditions of early capitalism without (and here is the contrast with "disorganized capitalism") the state losing the ability to regulate these processes while at the same time enabling the state to distance itself from the "failure" (though rarely the "success") of its outcomes and hence to minimize the likelihood of crises of legitimation. It is possible to create wild capitalism even in the context of a neo-corporatist state (the activities of *Treuhand* in the former GDR must be one of the most vivid examples of such a strategy of controlled chaos). Extending the agricultural metaphor, contemporary Anglo-American capitalism looks something like the EU's "set aside" policy in farming where areas of land are left uncultivated. The key point here is that farmers have to apply for the right to set aside land to the EU Agricultural Commission; they receive subsidies for doing so, and the land might at any time, were there a change in policy, be returned to the plough. The point I am making with this, perhaps over-elaborated metaphor, is that modern states in which labour is (or was) organized do not have to choose between dualism and corporatism, but must merely decide on the balance between the two. Britain, like America, has chosen a balance leaning towards wilderness rather than cultivation. Conflicts between Britain and its EU partners can to a degree be interpreted as disputes about the *degree* of deregulation that is desirable—e.g., about the social costs.[20] The suggestion might be extended further by arguing that capitalism was never either fully organized or disorganized, but always some mix of the two, and that it is the state which determines this mix.

There is also the related issue of the balance between centralized bureaucratic power and the apparent anarchy of the market. Like Weber, Polanyi is aware that a free market is compatible with rule through administration. There is a remarkable passage in *The Great Transformation* which not only echoes Weber but appears also to anticipate Foucault's later work on "governmentality" where Foucault argues that the market economy is but itself a new mode of state control "at a distance." Ironically, the passage even uses one of Foucault's most favoured examples to demonstrate the proximity of liberalism to rule through administration.

> This growth of administration reflected the spirit of utilitarianism. Bentham's fabulous Panopticon, his most personal utopia, was a star-shaped building from the centre of which prison wardens could keep the greatest number of jailbirds under the most effective supervision at the smallest cost to the public. Similarly, in the utilitarian state his favourite principle of "inspectability" ensured that the Minister at the top should keep effective control over all local administration.

> The road to the free market was opened and kept open by an enormous increase in continuous, centrally organized and controlled interventionism. (p. 140)

The constant changing and manipulation of environmental parameters, in which newly "emancipated" subjects act, ensure that these power relations are not disturbed by the shift back to the market. "Local administration," even down to the level of individual action, remains under "effective control." Subjects acting within uncertain and shifting parameters replace command as the chief mechanism, but still secure predictability of outcome and enable bureaucracy to maintain a degree of control. Emancipated actors behaving as rational egotists can and do act in ways which can be predictable, and hence controllable, so long as the environment within which they must operate can itself be an object of bureaucratic *decision*. Though we need to reassess the nature of the mechanisms through which restrictions are imposed, the new free market utopia does not require us to revise Polanyi's assessment of earlier free market society:

> Social history in the nineteenth century was thus the result of a double movement: the extension of the market organization in respect of genuine commodities was accompanied by its restriction in respect to fictitious ones. (p.76)

Similarly, the new free market utopia does not falsify Weber's claim that capitalist enterprise and bureaucratic domination are compatible, nor Polanyi's argument that planning is inevitable; it confirms them. It vindicates too Marx's magisterial observation on bureaucracy:

> The highest point entrusts the understanding of details to the lower echelons, whereas these, on the other hand, credit the highest point with an understanding of the universal, and thus they deceive one another. (*Contribution to the Critique of Hegel's Philosophy of Law*)[21]

Nevertheless, my final point is that the change in the art of governance is such that we need to rethink our sociological conceptualization of power. Weber's famous definition of power as the likelihood that one agent will submit to the will of another is not a universally valid definition, but rather one appropriate to a particular form of domination, namely bureaucratic domination. It is not exportable to the modern forms of governance which I have sought to describe. We can retain Weber's emphasis on likelihood of outcome, but under conditions where many "decisions" are retranslated as technical outcomes the notions of *will* and *submission* seem redundant. Here too we need a new metaphor to account for the possibility of predictability of outcome in the absence of the direct command. We need, in other words, to conceptualize relations of power where the powerful is not a willing subject and where those upon whom power is exercised are not just or always submissive. Power here seems to be no more, but crucially no less, than the power to control the parameters within which actors act autonomously.[22]

NOTES

This article first appeared as an article in *Economy and Society*. I would like to thank the Journal's editors and publisher for permission to republish it here.

1. M. Weber, "*Parlament und Regierung im neugeordneten Deutschland*" in J. Winkelmann (ed.), *Max Weber: Gesammelte politische Schriften*. Tübingen: J.C.B. Mohr, 5th edition 1988 [1918a], p. 321.
2. K. Polanyi, *The Great Transformation*. Boston: Beacon Press, 1957 [1944].
3. Precisely this Hegelian argument has been made by J. Berger and C. Offe ("Functionalism vs. rational choice: some questions concerning the rationality of choosing one or the other," *Theory and Society*, 11, 1982, 521-26) in an astute critique of rational choice theory. The more usual line of sociological critique is to appeal to norms (e.g., of solidarity). Elster in particular seems to have conceded considerable ground in the face of this type of criticism. Thus he has recently written: "Much of the social choice and public choice literature, with its assumption of universally opportunistic behaviour, simply seems out of touch with the real world, in which there is a great deal of honesty and sense of duty. If people always engaged in opportunistic behaviour when they could get away with it, civilization as we know it would not exist." (J. Elster, *The Cement of Society*. Cambridge: CUP, 1991, p. 120.) Or in even more Durkheimian language: "Society is indeed a joint venture, but the bond among its members is not simply one of mutual advantage, but also one of mutual respect and tolerance." (Elster, p. 137) This seems to cede too much to rational choice theory's critics and loses the hard edge and potential explanatory power of a theory which can reduce action to a common and simple basic principle of self-interested calculation. It confirms the observation of one sociologist critic of action theories inspired by utilitarianism: "But when the utilitarian model also tries to include wider psychological and cultural dimensions it loses its identity and becomes more and more like other theoretical approaches." (F. Crespi. *Social Action and Power*. Oxford: Blackwell, 1992, p. 10.) Nevertheless, the direct appeal to solidary norms seems a less effective move against economic decision-making models than the strategy adopted by Marx, Polanyi, and latterly by Berger and Offe which seeks to identify the parameters within which is does have validity.
4. A. Przeworski, *The State and the Economy Under Capitalism*. Chur, Switzerland: Harwood Academic Publishers, 1990. [Emphasis added].
5. K. Marx. *Capital*. Vol. 1. London: Penguin, 1976, p. 874.
6. With respect to subsidy, they argue that "In more recent times, the mammoth federal interstate highway system, hammered out by a 'hoard of special interests representing towns and cities'...

has similarly made and unmade urban fortunes." (J.R. Logan and H.L. Molotch. *Urban Fortunes*. Berkeley: University of California Press, 1987, p. 57.) Once the transport infrastructures are in place, the continual pursuit of urban fortunes drives urban entrepreneurs to develop more sophisticated strategies to maintain the strategic advantages of their localities *vis-à-vie* their competitors. These strategies are no less dependent upon state sponsorship than were earlier calls for state highways to be built here rather than there.

7. The discussion of Britain here is brief and illustrative. For more detailed analysis see, for example, A. Gamble, *The Free Economy and the Strong State*. London: Macmillan, 1988; also W. Hutton, *The State We're In*. London: Jonathan Cape, 1995. On privatization and regulation see the articles in M. Moran and T. Prosser (eds.), *Privatization and Regulatory Change in Europe*. Milton Keynes: Open University Press, 1994.

8. This is one of the points at issue between Werner Bonefeld and Bob Jessop. Bonefeld criticizes regulation theory for underestimating the role of the political, including the role of class struggle. (W. Bonefeld, "'Reformation of State Theory," *Capital & Class*, 33, 1987, pp.96-127.) Though from a different perspective, the argument here is that it is an insufficient response to such criticism to merely allow the political sphere a degree of "relative autonomy." See, B. Jessop, "Regulation Theory, Post-Fordism, and the State: more than a reply to Werner Bonefeld," *Capital & Class*, 34, 1988, pp.164-168.

9. The work of Stuart Hall has been the most influential application of Gramscian ideas to the analysis of "Thatcherism." See, for example, S. Hall, *The Hard Road to Renewal*. London: Lawrence and Wishart, 1988, especially chapter 10. In terms of the Weberian distinction between charismatic and bureaucratic revolution discussed below, the danger of a Gramscian analysis is that it can mistake the latter for the former.

10. M. Weber, *Wirtschaft und Gesellschaft: Grundriss der verstehenden Soziologie*. Vol. 2. Cologne & Berlin: Kiepenheuer and Witsch, 1956, p. 836.

11. Habermas has developed this line of argument in some detail, that modern forms of instrumentalism rest upon the very traditional ethic which they systematically destroy. See J. Habermas, *The Theory of Communicative Action*, vol. 2. Cambridge: Polity Press, 1987. But the point is quite clear from Polanyi's analysis of the destructive nature of the market for social relations (see the discussion below).

12. S. Zweig, *Die Welt von Gestern: Erinnerungen eines Europäers*. Frankfurt am Main: Fischer Verlag, 1992 [1944].

13. I use the term "quasi-market" with some caution as one of Polanyi's central arguments is that markets can only be "quasi."

14. The argument is reminiscent not only of Marx on the contract or Simmel on money, but also again of Habermas's more recent analysis of modernity as the "colonization of the life world" by the "systems logic" of power and money. But Polanyi's version of the reification argument is less abstract than that of Habermas, because in focusing on the market he identifies the socially destructive force as an institutional mechanism rather than an abstract "system." See Habermas, *The Theory of Communicative Action*.

15. M. Weber, "*Der Sozialismus*," in Marianne Weber (ed.), *Gesammelte Aufsätze zur Sozialpolitik*. Tübingen: J.C.B. More, 2nd edition 1988 [1918b], p. 504.

16. This seems to be the thought behind the shift in Foucault's work from his early concern with discipline to his later concern with "governmentality." (M. Foucault, "Governmentality," in G. Burchell, C. Gordon and P. Miller, (eds.), *The Foucault Effect: Studies in Governmentality*. London: Harvester Wheatsheaf, 1991.) In a sense, discipline appears partially redundant where the chain of command is disrupted and overt mechanisms of control have been replaced by indirect ones.

17. C. Offe, *Disorganized Capitalism*. Cambridge: Polity Press, 1985.

18. J. Goldthorpe, "The end of convergence," in Goldthorpe (ed.), *Order and Conflict in Contemporary Capitalism*. Oxford: OUP, 1984.

19. E. Gellner, *Nations and Nationalism*. Cambridge: CUP, 1983.

20. P. Hirst and G. Thompson, "The problem of 'globalization': international economic relations, national economic management and the formation of trading blocs," *Economy and Society*, 21:4, 1982, pp.357-396.

21. Quoted in C. Lafort, *The Political Forms of Modern Society*. Cambridge: CUP, 1986.

22. Throughout this analysis I have treated "the state" as though it were a unity. In analysing the reformation of society into a market society this seems legitimate. But the state too is, of course, a set of institutions, and indeed institutions which have themselves been exposed to the processes described (for example, the quasi-privatization of the British civil service). If the general analysis outlined here is useful, it would be necessary also to apply it to the state itself.

IDENTITIES, CULTURE, CITIZENSHIP,
AND
DEMOCRACY

Chapter Fourteen

OF SOCIAL SPACES, CITIZENSHIP, AND THE NATURE OF POWER IN THE WORLD ECONOMY
André C. Drainville

> Le vrai sens du mot [citoyen] s'est presque entièrement effacé chez les modernes: la plupart prennent une ville pour une cité et un bourgeois pour un citoyen. Ils ne savent pas que les maisons font la ville mais que les citoyens font la cité.[1]
> —Jean-Jacques Rousseau

In the last decade or so, the critique of historical essentialism that had hitherto been carried out primarily by social and cultural theorists, literary critics, and urban materialist geographers has yielded broad explorations of the spatial dynamics of power.[2] Everywhere in the social sciences, spatial metaphors are gaining in currency, and talk is increasingly of boundaries, locations, positions, situations, place-images and mapping. As a result, power has appeared less and less as a moment in time, and more as a territory, a site-specific logic of organization and displacement.

In the field of international political economy as well, concerns for what Edward W. Soja has called the "socio-spatial dialectic of capitalism" have caused an avalanche of studies interested in the world economy as a structured "field of practice," which have cut across a broad spectrum of theoretical literature, encouraged a reassessment of past contributions to the study of the world economy, and helped shape on-going assessments of political possibilities.[3] In the midst of a profound crisis which has broken the sense of historical continuity provided in the post-war period by U.S. hegemony, when the *Pax Americana* appeared to analysts of global accumulation as yet another chapter in the history of great hegemonies, and New York seemed to have succeeded Genoa, Bruges, Amsterdam and London as great cities at the centers of world economies, global accumulation has been increasingly conceptualized as a distinct and relatively coherent social experience; a space, to use a phrase from Michel Foucault, "in which we live, which draws us out of ourselves, in which the erosion of our lives, our time and our history occurs, the space that claws and gnaws at us."[4] This conceptualization of the world economy as a distinct space—a site of struggle with a history and a spatial coherence of its own, with specific constraints and possibilities—is (already) well enough established to have commanded review articles of its own, and to have made important reference points of authors like Manuel Castells, Anthony Giddens, David Harvey, Frederic Jameson, Henri Lefebvre and Edward Soja.[5]

Thinking about the world economy as a space unto itself has served international political economists well. From Charles-Albert Michalet's critique of liberal conceptualizations of the world economy as but a collection of national economies and Christian Palloix's influential study of global circuits of social capital to Kees Van Der Pijl's analysis of the process of transnational bourgeois class formation in the Atlantic area and Robert Cox's exploration of the making of hegemonies in the capitalist world economies, the contemporary literature on the world economy has been able to go beyond nationally-rooted analyses of power and see world-level processes at work, and new world orders in the making.

However, spatially informed analyses of the world economy have remained incomplete. Indeed, as I have argued elsewhere, they have continuously focused on transnational capital itself, and they have assumed that where it exists as a class for itself, a corresponding social space also exists.[6] In fact, these analyses have looked at the space of the world economy very much like Rousseau's *modernes* have looked at cities: where the latter took the *cité* for granted the moment they spotted a few bourgeois and a few buildings, the former looks at the Trilateral Commission and the IMF in New York, the BIS in Basle or the OECD in Paris, and discovers both citizens of the world, and the global social space they desire to create. Neither inquire how, or indeed if, bourgeois have become citizens, and neither asks how social spaces, be they cities or world economies, are constructed. In both cases, taking for granted that capital is able to create social spaces in its image wherever it appears has led critical analysis to both exaggerate the social embeddedness of bourgeois rule and underestimate possibilities of transforming it.

This article is an attempt to think through more thoroughly, and more politically, what may constitute the space of the world economy. Because, like cities, world economies are political constructions defined primarily by the moving relationship between social forces and political orders in the making, this is, in fact an exploration of a broad notion of citizenship taking shape in the world economy that attempts to determine both who has access to the global *cité* in the age of the New World Order, and the terms of what Étienne Balibar called the "rights to politics."[7]

The first part of the article presents a short review of the literature documenting the conceptualization of the world economy as a distinct social space. The second part will explore the workings of what Robert Cox has called the *nébuleuse* of international organizations managing the world economy,[8] in an attempt to learn more about the transformation of political participation in the post-Bretton Woods period. More specifically, it will look at the efforts of the *nébuleuse* to solve three problems that have raised important challenges to the political organization of the world economy: the transition in Eastern Europe to what the IMF, the OECD and other organs of management of the world economy have called "market democracy," the crisis in the post-war international migration regime, and the third phase of the debt crisis. Looking at the attempts of the *nébuleuse* to solve these problems will help us discern the political invention of a *cité*—and thus of a *droit de cité* and a citizenship—in the world economy.

SPACE AND THE STUDY OF THE WORLD ECONOMY

Spatial concerns have remained on the margins of the academic discipline of international relations until very recently. This has had much to do with the hegemony of realism as a governing paradigm of international relations.[9]

The analytical tradition of realism is founded on the refusal of space. The familiar realist world is composed of states, conceptualized as exclusive centers of rationality and individualized vectors of power moving in an unconstraining and untheorized milieu. Just as in the physical sciences the movement of bodies in a vacuum is measured by the equation F=MA (Force = a Mass set in motion by its Acceleration), the realist tradition proposes to measure the movements of states, their relative influence and their trajectories, by an equation (P=RM: Power [and influence] = Resources Mobilized) that incorporates spatial dynamics only as afterthought, regarded as disturbances, noises and interferences exogenous to the rational process of inter-state relations. Even in the last decade, when regime analysis emerged as a central organizing concept, realism allowed no room for the autonomy of informal codes of inter-state behavior or inter-subjective meaning, which in spatially informed analyses constitute essential elements of global coherence.

Of course, even in the midst of realist hegemony, some critical conceptualizations of the world economy (dependency, world systems and unequal exchange theories, or the *école de la régulation*, for example), did share with more recent spatially informed analyses the critical insight that capital in the world economy as elsewhere is not the play-thing of capitalists, but a historically and spatially specific social relation. These analyses, however, remained firmly anchored in national social spaces. For example, in world systems' and dependency theories, which relied heavily on spatial and architectural metaphors, the world economy was not conceptualized as a place where material struggles were specifically played out, but simply as a bridge between the national social formations, the more significant milieu in which classes and fractions of classes make history. In the words of Immanuel Wallerstein: "[to] be 'social' [is] to be 'national'."[10] As a result, the world economy was understood, very much in the realist fashion, as a mere grid of exchange relationships, a plane for the expansion of capital populated by capitalists but not in and of itself a capitalist space.

This was most strongly expressed by the Parisian *école de la régulation* whose realist ontology engendered a most familiar *realpolitik* analysis.[11] In a statement that defined the *école*'s approach, Alain Lipietz proposed that, considering the national framework of class struggle and institutionalized social compromises, the analysis of accumulation should give priority to the *causes internes* and banish the world economy to a mere condition of social formations.[12] Regulationist realism was predicated upon a particular definition of social reality and social processes: for regulation analysis, social processes became real *when and if they were concretized in state institutions*.[13] The configuration of the world economy itself was understood as the space between regimes of accumulation, a mere "system of interacting national social formations."[14]

Thus, for dependency, world systems, and unequal exchange theories, and for the *école de la régulation*, there existed between national social formations and the world economy a relationship somewhat similar to that between peasants and a pre-capitalist market. Market-day was, of course, a social event taking place within given spatial boundaries, and the goings-on at the marketplace shaped, to a certain extent and in certain circumstances, social relationships. However, this did not make exchange relations at the market more than the outcome of a social process of production organized elsewhere: it was but a relatively unconstraining environment, a meeting point but not a social space, that is to say a relatively coherent *milieu* of social life which both frames and conditions social relations.[15]

Starting in the first part of the 1980s, the literature on "global cities" offered a first expression of the contemporary interest in conceptualizing the word economy as a social space in the making. This literature was inspired both by authors like Manuel Castells, David Harvey, Henri Lefebvre, Edward Soja and Peter Hall, who were at the heart of the urban-centered revival of materialist geography through the 1970s and 1980s, and, more generally, by Fernand Braudel's emphasis on the role played by great cities at the center of world economies. From Mike Davis' examination of spatial disarticulation in Los Angeles to Anthony King's analysis of London's "big bang buildings" and Saskia Sassen's look at New York, London and Tokyo, this literature has sought to present global cities as condensations of all that is dynamic in the world economy.[16] Echoing René Descartes's portrayal of Amsterdam as an "inventory of the possible," the literature on global cities has attempted to map social dynamics in the world economy through a reading of urban social relations. With this literature, McLuhan's global village was replaced in the writings on international political economy by a web of global cities acting as moorings for the space of a world economy.

Furthermore, the emergence in the last decade or so of "transnational historical materialism" as a central paradigm of international political economy has lead to concerns for the spatial interplay of ideas, institutions and material capabilities being placed at the heart of contemporary analyses of the world economy.[17] In the spirit of *Annales* historians, who emphasized the spatial and temporal specificity of social and ideological structures, this literature has displayed a growing preoccupation with a much more abstract understanding of space as a distinctive constellation of practices, techniques and modes of organizations.[18] It has stressed that the space of the world economy is unlike more concrete and geographically specific spaces, such as classrooms, manufactures, households, cities and townships, that have traditionally preoccupied social and materialist geographers, in that it is not constructed directly out of what David Harvey called the "built and administrative environments," the transportation, legal, financial, educational and administrative systems necessary for the reproduction and organization of daily life.[19] The real, concrete spatiality of these environments, their organic nature, is absent from the discontinuous space of the world economy. The world economy is a space without a territory, or rather a space occupying a diversity of territories; it is an "espace-vitesse" created out of the global integration of production and the movement of hot money in the casino atmosphere of the world economy.[20]

In effect, the attempt made by transnational historical materialism to "conceptually arrest movement [and examine] the points of stress and conflicts that exist within any social practice," and explore world orders as specific "modes of social relations of production" (that is to say "self-contained structures each with its own development potential and its own distinct perspective on the world"), issued an invitation to take spatial dynamics in the analysis of the world economy seriously. Answers to this invitation can be seen in many recent efforts to come to terms with the on-going restructuring of power in the world economy. In the 1992 *Socialist Register*, for example, Stephen Gill investigated the creation of a European "integrated economic space" and its relationship to the construction, specifically in the world economy, of a neo-liberal code of discipline defining the terms of political participation and imposing boundaries on national democracies.[21] Also in the 1992 *Register*, Leo Panitch and Ralph Miliband based their exploration of socialist possibilities in the new world order on a distinctively spatial conceptualization of the world economy as a specific site for the construction of a discourse of inter-capitalist solidarity.[22]

In the wake of spatially informed analyses, Lenin, Bukharin, Trotsky and Luxemburg have been recast as "key figures" in the historical analysis of the spatial dialectics of capital,[23] and the venerable realist distinction between national and international politics, conceptualized hitherto in terms of order and anarchy, has been recast as "a spatial demarcation between authentic politics and mere relations."[24] Crises of accumulation are now apprehended as "a period of time-space compression," and the Gulf War as a signal of "...the problems of Space and Time in socio-political and economic transformation."[25] Undergraduate textbooks have begun reflecting new concerns for spatial dynamics, and theoretical debates have become quests for "thinking space" and for new "political spaces other than those bounded by the parameters of the nation-state."[26]

Of late, even the *école de la régulation* has become rooted in a global spatial analysis. Alain Lipietz and Danièle Leborgne, for example, have proposed that, where fordism was built on a "territorial" division of labour lending itself well to a nationally-centered analysis, post-fordist production is more flexible, and depends for its integrity on the creation of *espace[s] maîtrisés*, which are the spatial forms of social compromises in the contemporary period.[27]

In his exegesis of Marx's writing, Althusser had noted that the use of spatial imagery in theoretical writings was not simply a rhetorical device, but an indication of new problematics in the making.[28] Indeed, in the international political economy literature, references to space represent a new concern for the specificity and autonomy of the world economy as a realm of accumulation. Thinking about spatial dynamics in the world economy has allowed international political economists to break free from analyses of global processes of accumulation still grounded in national social formations, and begin exploring what is specific about global accumulation.

Such an exploration, however, has remained lacking. Taking transnational capital as its starting point, it has tended to project its class coherence unto the whole of the world economy and thus assume that the world economy was constituted as a distinct and complete social space, a finished *cité*. It has consecrated bourgeois citizens without looking into the political making of citizenship in the world economy.

CITIZENSHIP IN THE WORLD ECONOMY

Political citizenship, in the world economy or wherever else capitalism lives as a mode of social and political organization, is not invented *ex cathedra*, from pontificating edicts issued from above. Rather, it is made and remade from the bottom up, it is woven from discrete, partial and sometimes contradictory attempts by institutionalized political power to assemble a social order complementing and validating the private ventures of the *bourgeoisie*. This is the essence of what Nicos Poulantzas called the political task of transformation.[29] Through this political process, bourgeois become citizens and social spaces are assembled.

Thus, meaningful indicators of the construction of citizenship in the world economy will not be garnered from, for example, the World Social Charter proposed in the 1994 United Nations' Human Development Report, or from the cosmopolitan declarations that inevitably followed the Summit for Social Development held in 1995 to celebrate the fiftieth anniversary of the UN. We have to look elsewhere for clues revealing the making of citizenship in the space of the world economy: in the way in which organs of management of the world economy (Cox's *nébuleuse*) have tried to find solutions to specific problems confronting global accumulation.

In the post-Bretton Woods period, the *nébuleuse* has formed an informal and fluid regulatory network seemingly autonomous in the task of political transformation. The *nébuleuse* does not simply attempt to manage the world economy as a foreman would a production line, it also, as the chief economist of the European Bank for Reconstruction and Development said, tries "to foster particular forms of economic and social change."[30]

The studied economism of published material coming out of the *nébuleuse* often makes it difficult to see the political process of transformation at work in the ordinary management of the world economy.[31] However, occasionally problems arise that present consequential challenges to the social and political organization of the world economy. In these circumstances, analyzing the problem-solving efforts of the *nébuleuse* can reveal much about political transformation. In the post-Bretton Woods period, three issues have raised particularly consequential challenges to the political organization of the world economy: the transition in Eastern Europe to "market democracy," the crisis in the post-war international migration regime, and the third phase of the debt crisis. A we shall see, a cursory glance at these recent problem-solving efforts of the *nébuleuse* will reveal that political transformation in the world economy entails a double process whereby political relationships within national social formations are transformed, and the position of states as privileged sites of political attachment is reinforced.

Already, this suggestion prompts a rethinking of spatially inspired writings reviewed in the previous section. As these writings emphasized the relatively autonomous regulation of the world economy by the *nébuleuse* and the globalization of everyday life, the politics of capitalist accumulation appear to have either by-passed states altogether, or to have reduced them to mere "transmission belt[s] for globalizing forces," administrative sub-spaces of the world economy.³² If anyone was still looking for an executive committee of the modern bourgeoisie, it would seem from these writings that it could only be found at the seat of the Transnational Commission in New York, or in the quiet and discreet meeting rooms of the "big doughnut in Basle" (as the Bank for International Settlements headquarters is affectionately referred to by central bankers).³³ In fact, globalization and the making of a social space of the world economy do not so much by-pass states as they pass through them, and depend on them for their political organization.

Spatial coherence depends not on the effacement of specificities but in their organization, the arrangement of differences. Social spaces, whether the concrete space of cities and factories, or the abstract space of the world economy, are always the result of timely and evanescent compromises between spatial integration and spatial differentiation and confinement. In the space of the world economy, both of these processes are organized by states, which have historically been pivoting points of this spatial dialectic of integration/fracturation, serving to institutionalize and define both coherence and difference. On the one hand is the process of spatial integration ("the tendency for each place to become rigorously equivalent").³⁴ As Sol Picciotto has pointed out, states have historically served as points of organization and diffusion for globally defined terms of accumulation, forms of wage relations and private ownership.³⁵ On the other hand is the process of spatial differentiation (the spatial fix that limits the leveling of local specificities and anchors the process of integration).³⁶ As the position of states as "bounded power containers," and their place as centers of class struggle engenders what Wallerstein called "institutional proclivities" that distort, re-shape and absorb the dynamic tensions of global accumulation, the process of spatial confinement also passes through states, and to an extent is subject to the veto of states.³⁷

In a recent article, David Harvey gave a good example of this double process of integration and differentiation when he wrote that money simultaneously possessed "universal properties as a measure of value and medium of exchange," and permitted "a high range of decentralized and particularistic decision-making in the realm of market behaviors [feeding] back to define what the universality of money is all about."³⁸ In the contemporary period, monetarism—the first expression of transnational neo-liberalism in action—offered another good example of this double process at work in the world economy. From the collapse of the Bretton Woods monetary system to the beginning of the eighties, monetarism was both shaped by a global consensus that "the health of free societies depends upon them restoring stable money," and organized politically as a collection of national attempts to control monetary growth.³⁹ Thus, monetarism represented at once spatial integration (an unwavering global code of discipline that sought to stabilize monetary relationships in the immediate post-Bretton Woods period), and organized difference (a collection of nationally confined, and nationally specific, policies of monetary targeting).

The making of citizenship in the world economy also entails a double process of integration and differentiation. The former process is an attempt at establishing transnational social equivalences; a relatively coherent political cadre on which to hang the globalization of production. More specifically, the shaping of citizenship in the contemporary world economy is accompanied by a two-fold transformation of the structures of political participation: at once, national citizens are increasingly cast as bearers of economic rationality whose primary function is to bring to states claims for greater efficiency in the management of economic resources, and lead the assault on what Desmond King called the social rights of citizenship,[40] and their relationship to the state is increasingly contingent on their position as minority shareholders in the running of the affairs of the state. As we shall see, this is a part of the process of political integration in the world economy that passes through states and is reliant on the ability of states to structure political participation, either through consensus-building or coercive measures.

As for spatial differentiation, it rests on the confinement, indeed the ostracization, of citizens to national territories. There are, in the age of the New World Order, no citizens *of* the world economy, only national citizens *in* the world economy.

The restoration and strengthening of national ties of citizenship are central to the political management of the contemporary world economy. Contrary to what Claude Julien had observed two decades ago in *Le suicide des démocraties*, national democracies are not "mortally wounded" by the internationalization of accumulation.[41] They are reinforced and transformed by the political difficulties of the managing of global accumulation. The growing transnational segmentation of production, the liberalization of international exchanges, the integration and growing self-sufficiency of global credit, and the increasing political cohesiveness of transnational capital, have both augmented the social and political autonomy—and isolation—of transnational accumulation, *and* increased the political importance of states-bound democracies as centers of political validation for the imperatives of global accumulation. Though truly organized globally as a productive venture, the world economy remains socially rooted in the space of the nation state, and politically dependent on the ability of states to strike social compromises.

STATES AND SPATIAL INTEGRATION/DIFFERENTIATION IN THE WORLD ECONOMY

a) The Transition in Eastern Europe

That states occupy a central position as functionally specialized political units of the world economy is first manifest in the way in which the *nébuleuse* has had to deal with the transition in Eastern Europe. In the problem-solving vernacular of the *nébuleuse*, the transition is about the "human conversion" of mathematical theoreticians into bankers and consultants; it is about establishing pricing mechanisms, capital markets and market-based social safety nets, liberalizing exchange rates, and putting into place the paraphernalia of managed free markets: contract laws, private property, a functioning labour market, anti-cartel laws, an independently-set monetary policy, responsible monetary growth, and a restrictive fiscal policy designed to "progressively hand over to the market its role as the central allocator of resources."[42]

Above and beyond the objective installation in the East of all the accoutrements of post-Keynesian capitalism, the *nébuleuse*'s management of the transition in Eastern Europe is also a regulatory experiment with the double ambition to bring lessons for the regulation of capital accumulation (both in the

East and the West), and to set social foundations for global capitalism in the post-Bretton Woods period. Through its management of the transition, the *nébuleuse*'s ambition is to nurture the "silent revolution" that IMF Managing Director Michel Camdessus observed, and thus define "the widespread acceptance of a set of general propositions about the most effective way of achieving sustainable growth [and] good governance."[43]

The transition has mobilized the whole of the *nébuleuse*, from highly visible trans-governmental organizations, which have taken the operational side of the transition as the starting point of their labors, to organic intellectuals of transnational capital whose interventions have been more personal, and more directly political (George Soros, for example, who actively campaigned for direct transfers of hard currencies to Eastern Europe.)[44] The start-up call of this mobilization was issued at the Houston G7 Economic summit of July 1990, when G7 heads of states requested that the IMF, the World Bank, the OECD, the EBRD and the Commission on European Communities "undertake a detailed study of the Soviet Economy, make recommendations for its reform, and establish the criteria under which western economic assistance could effectively support such reforms."[45] The following December, the OECD launched a program called "Partners in Transition," administered by its "Center for Cooperation with the European Economies in Transition." While its immediate task was to provide technical advice to Eastern European countries engaged in economic reform, its broader aim is to make a long-term contribution to state policy in the West as well, for example in applying to western state-owned enterprises the lessons learned in the process of privatization in the East.[46] In the same double-edge spirit, the BIS has talked about the unity of economic reforms everywhere, and has argued that "...not just the former socialist countries but *all* countries should embark on a transition to free and more open market economies."[47]

This says much about the role of states in the process of spatial integration in the world economy. In his preface to the French edition of *Underwriting Democracy*, George Soros compared what he called the revolutionary process now taking place in Eastern Europe to the popular European revolutions of 1848.[48] Inasmuch as both represent attempts at transforming political relationships between states and citizens, Soros is justified in making this comparison. The uprisings of 1848 were, however, social movements seeking to defend and broaden collective rights to politics, where the transition to market democracy in Eastern Europe is guided from above, by the *nébuleuse*'s attempts to adapt the structures of political participation to the exigencies of global accumulation. Unlike 1848, 1989 and after is about defining citizens in the narrowest sense of the term, as individual actors in a depoliticized process of influence-peddling where, as the Trilateral Commission understood it a decade ago, the building of "working democracies" is a necessary prerequisite to a more efficient market-based allocation of resources.[49]

At the center of the *nébuleuse*'s blueprint for transition in Eastern Europe is the desire to make states more responsive to market forces. As World Bank chief economist Lawrence H. Summers put it, the problem that must be resolved through the transition is "a combination of [state] plans without controls and markets without incentives."⁵⁰ In this context, where the arbitrariness of the state must be kept in check and the disintegration of the "administrative-command system" begun under *perestroika* accelerated and radicalized, programs for "controlled spontaneous privatization" (the *nébuleuse*'s code word for coupon privatization) and the establishment of market-based social safety nets constructed and managed by state privatization agencies like Russia's GKI in collaboration with international organizations, are aimed at creating new interest groups centered on firms and shareholders. For the *nébuleuse*, these groups would both bring to states different claims than those brought under state socialism by political organizations like worker's councils, and serve to discipline state plans.⁵¹ As the World Bank recently phrased it in its salute to Romania's 1993 privatization plan, the creation of responsible "nations of shareholders," is a means through which states are made responsive to the demands of global economic restructuring.⁵²

In the *nébuleuse*'s plans for market democracy, reconstructed citizens of Eastern Europe become anchoring points for market discipline. In effect, they play the role assumed by published monetary aggregates in the monetarist phase of the crisis in the late 1970s, or more recently by fixed targets for budget reduction: they de-politicize the state, and discipline it for the good of the world economy. By giving "unstoppable political momentum" to reforms, state-led privatization also insures the social entrenchment of market discipline, and effectively forbids a return to state socialism.⁵³ As the IMF wrote, states in Eastern Europe have braided through privatization the rope with which they will "tie their own hands."⁵⁴

The linking of markets and citizens is, of course, not an invention of the *nébuleuse*. Indeed, what C.B. Macpherson called the "market maketh citizens" assumption⁵⁵ has been at the heart of every liberal redefinition of citizenship, from physiocrat-inspired attempts to tie citizenship with land ownership in the post-revolutionary period in France to Thatcher's neo-liberal Citizens Charter, which regarded British citizens exclusively as consumers of state services. The *nébuleuse*'s emphasis on making nations of shareholders in Eastern Europe is thus but a variation on a familiar liberal theme.

Still, it is a variation that reveals something of political dynamics in the contemporary world economy: the limited transformative capabilities of the *nébuleuse*. In attempting to further spatial integration in the world economy by creating nations of citizen-shareholders, the *nébuleuse* does not so much rise above states as it acts as a bridge between states that alone have the ability to structure political participation and fashion nations of shareholders.

In the same vein, what Stephen Gill called "neo-constitutionalism" ("the move towards the construction of legal and constitutional devices to remove or insulate substantially the new economic institutions from popular scrutiny or democratic accountability"),⁵⁶ or even more generally, the New Right's assault on civil, political and social rights, can be thought of as part of a transnational neo-liberal concept of control guiding global restructuring. However, these plans are only actualized politically as state creations. Again, the *nébuleuse*'s political power to transform appears limited.

The transition in Eastern Europe also reveals something of the process of spatial differentiation in the world economy. In the first phase of the transition, the period when what Michael Bruno of the World Bank called *big bang moves* were launched in Bulgaria, Czechoslovakia, Hungary, Poland, Romania and Russia, maverick ideologues of neo-liberalism attempted to impose reforms from above.[57] These ideologues are perhaps best represented by the group of expert assembled under the aegis of Georges Soros Open Society Fund that initiated the Sachs plan in Russia.[58] Everywhere, they invented strict conversion programs involving uncompromising targets for monetary growth, the marketization of social security, inflexible wage ceilings and rigid schedules for the privatization of state enterprises. These programs brought about declining growth almost everywhere and, more politically important, widespread dissent threatening the whole of the transition process.[59] In this context, those agencies of the *nébuleuse* responsible for orchestrating the transition have had to concern themselves much more with its political and social sustainability. In the last year or two, this has become the principal preoccupation of the *nébuleuse*: "...what, if anything, can ensure the maintenance of the social consensus over the reform programs and its political sustainability in the near future?"[60] These agencies have emphasized that, in order to be sustainable, transition programs had to emerge from national negotiations dealing with the content and the cadence of the conversion to market economy. Contrary to what first-wave ideologues had thought then, the political difficulties of the transition have showed the *nébuleuse* that "...there may not be one best way of resolving the privatization issue, and [that] each country must choose the one that fits its political and social framework best."[61] Thus, the political difficulties of the transition have made the *nébuleuse*'s task of political transformation much more reliant on states of former socialist countries—which are increasingly becoming integrated in the family of agencies managing the world economy. These states have had an essential role to play, both in promoting transition programs to their citizens and in constructing the political structures needed to anchor reforms deeply in national civil societies.

b)The Third Phase of the Debt Crisis

The centrality of state-bound political affiliation to the management of global accumulation is also evident in the *nébuleuse*'s handling of the third phase of the debt crisis. The first phase of the debt crisis began in August 1982, when Mexico became the first large debtor country to suspend its debt servicing, and reached its political zenith in the summer of 1985. In May of that year, Fidel Castro convened a conference of debtor countries in Cuba which attempted to assemble a debtors' cartel; in June, Peruvian president Alan Garcia denounced the dictatorship of the IMF and declared that Peruvian debt servicing would be limited to 10% of export earnings. In December, Nigeria followed suit with a similar declaration limiting debt-servicing to 30% of export earnings. In the same year, the Carthagene club was established to give debtor countries a forum similar to the "Paris Club" of major creditors.

This first phase of the crisis presented an immediate, and unavoidable, political threat to the international monetary system, that forced the IMF and the World Bank to negotiate politically the terms of insertion of debtor countries in the international credit economy. In this first phase, the IMF and the World Bank approached the debt crisis very much like Soros's mavericks addressed the transition. Their main concern was to safeguard existing mechanisms of market-based credit regulation, and their policies were intent on forcing the necessary adjustments onto debtor countries. In this period, the IMF acted very much as a debt collector would, and conditionality was applied coercively to secure debt repayment. This was a period during which the IMF unfailingly followed the guidance offered by the monetary approach to the balance of payments and sought to re-establish external equilibrium of debtor countries by contracting internal demand.

As the growth of international credit in the 1980s put debtor countries even further beyond the reach of IMF conditionality than had the 1976 breakdown of the par-value system, the *nébuleuse* faced a double crisis of authority and legitimacy.[62] The IMF has reacted to this much as it did in trying to make the transition in Eastern Europe more sustainable: it has attempted, in the vernacular of both the World Bank and the IMF, to work "alongside host countries" to secure politically viable adjustments.[63] The IMF (especially since the appointment in 1987 of Michel Camdessus as Managing Director), and the World Bank (after the Preston report written in the late 1980s), which had up till then dealt with debt crises through bi- and trans-national political negotiation, have emphasized more and more the necessity for low-income debtor countries—that have been the most vulnerable in an increasingly privatized global credit economy—to establish more responsive national and regional political structures and concentrate on procuring basic services for their citizens.[64] In so doing, the IMF and the World Bank have increasingly by-passed transnational negotiations, and concentrated on reforming national structures of political participation and strengthening national political and social capabilities, thus attempting to solve the debt problem by reinforcing national ties of citizenship.[65] This has been especially clear in the IMF's involvement in the management of the debt crisis in low income countries (where the Fund has retained a greater influence). In sub-Saharan Africa in particular, the IMF in line with the 1989 Brady proposal has sought to link debt repackaging with the improvement of political prospects for reform and, in the words of IMF managing director Michel Camdessus, has increasingly sought to involve states in "a complex process to marshal a consensus behind a coherent medium-term strategy."[66] Furthermore, administrative reforms to make aid packages more growth inducing, and thus more politically viable, have, according to the IMF itself, relied more on increasing state capabilities.[67]

Similarly, since the latter part of the 1980s, the World Bank's handling of the debt crisis in sub-Saharan Africa has also increasingly relied on the ability of states to manage adjustment programs efficiently and build social consensus. This has become particularly clear with the World Bank Action Plan (July 1993), which is the result of a broad review of Bank procedures that took place in the late 1980s as creditors and debtors alike were increasingly questioning the usefulness of Bank aid. It has emphasized the necessity of a "country-by-country approach," and the need for states, as well as local non-governmental organizations, to be involved directly in all phases of Bank projects.[68] Furthermore, the World Bank has increasingly made its aid contingent on the ability of recipient states to secure broad popular coalitions in favor of reform.[69]

The increasing importance of states in the political management of the debt crisis has been underscored as well by the creation of new credit facilities by the IMF. The first special facility opened by the Fund was the 1963 Compensatory Financing Facility, which was designed solely to offset exceptional imbalances in export earning, and included no provisions for social and political sustainability.[70] The 1974 Extended Fund Facility, introduced in the context of the OPEC crisis, spoke of structural adjustment in a manner that presaged later preoccupations of the Fund, but was limited to correcting imbalances in production trade and prices.[71] In contrast, the 1986 Structural Adjustment Facility, which was the first Fund window opened exclusively to low-income developing countries, was explicitly designed to facilitate politically sustainable adjustment, and linked growth-inductive policies in low-income debtor countries with debt re-negotiation.[72] Similarly, the 1987 Enhanced Structural Adjustment Facility emphasized the Fund's new preoccupation with "soft-track conditionality," designed to "...bring some of the poor (and the not so poor) into coalitions...broad enough to provide sustained support for adjustment policies" and thus to secure broader, deeper and politically more viable adjustment.[73]

Thus, even in the exceptional circumstances of the debt crisis, when the political authority of the *nébuleuse*, and therefore its transformative capabilities, are at their peak, its ability to entrench socially a global imperative of accumulation is limited. Though the IMF has been, and continues to be (as the recent re-negotiation of Brazilian debt indicates), able to force through measures of structural adjustment, political transformation in the world economy remains contingent on the ability of states to negotiate "country-by-country" settlements with national social forces. Furthermore, as was made clear again at the recent Gaborone (Botswana) seminar on third world debt, the reduction of debt overhang depends more than ever on state-bound micro-policies of financial surveillance, and on strengthening financial discipline in the public sector.[74]

As with the transition in Eastern Europe, then, problem-solving efforts of the *nébuleuse*, and spatial integration/differentiation in the world economy, depend on states tying their own hands.

c) The Migration Crisis
The management of transnational migration flows provides a final recent example of the central role played by state-bound political allegiances in the *nébuleuse*'s effort at political transformation in the world economy. On the face of it, the virtual absence of a functioning international migration regime in the post-Bretton Woods period and the persistence—indeed the reinforcement—of national barriers to population movements between countries, appear either as anomalies or as indications that states have continued, even in the age of transnational liberalism, to resist the setting up of international codes of conduct encroaching on their sovereign power.[75] In either case, it seems that contemporary regulation of migration movements has eluded the *nébuleuse*'s grasp, and therefore says little about the construction of citizenship in the

contemporary world economy. However, the weakness of international migration regimes speaks eloquently of the *nébuleuse*'s refusal to manage transnational migration flows as a global reality, and of its efforts to define the global refugee crisis as a crisis of national standards. By attempting to reinforce national control over migration flows and to bolster the principle of national sovereignty, the *nébuleuse* has actively worked to imprison social and political relations within national social formations, and thus restrict the political possibilities of citizenship in the world economy.

After World War II, there existed minimal coherence in the treatment of transnational economic migrants, at least among countries at the centre of the world economy. The operative migration regime was, in effect, a variation on what John Gerard Ruggie labeled "the regime of embedded liberalism" (that is to say the political and economic form of the post-war compromise that predicated multilateralism and global growth upon domestic interventionism, and gave states the responsibility of negotiating the terms of their insertion in the international economy).[76] As Aristide Zolberg pointed out, national migration policies in this period shared a single overriding objective: "...to procure a limited supply of cheap and disposable foreign labour to facilitate the structural adjustment that participation in the world economy entailed."[77] With regionally based migration movements feeding dual labour markets serving at once to feed growth, facilitate adjustment to global markets and protect the indigenous labour force on whose co-optation the Fordist social compromise was built, there was little need for transnational political concertation, and little room for autonomous political interventions of the *nébuleuse*.[78] The United States drew foreign labour principally from Mexico; Germany and Switzerland from southern Europe; the Netherlands from Surinam and Curaçao; France from the Maghreb, and the task of international agencies like the ILO and the OEEC (later the OECD) was limited to "persuad[ing] reluctant European countries [the United Kingdom, Belgium and Scandinavian countries] to go along with the proposed importation of guest-workers."[79]

In the post-Bretton Woods period, slow growth in the world economy, the crisis of Fordism, the increasing transnational segmentation of production, the deepening liberalization of exchanges and the rupture of regional migration systems, have all contributed to a crisis of the "embedded liberalism" migration regime. Consequently, there has been a renewed interest in developing more comprehensive transnational codes of conduct and more efficient ways of handling migration flows. To a large extent, the regional rationalization of the processing of refugees in the EEC (which has brought about the "one-demand policy," European-wide data banks and visa requirements), is a predictable response to this crisis of authority in the management of transnational migration. More surprising though, and more revealing of the limits of political transformation in the world economy, is the reaction of transnational agencies. Far from working to develop world-wide codes of behaviour, or seeking a "managed *laissez-faire*" migration regime akin to that which operated in gold standard countries at the end of the nineteenth century,[80] the *nébuleuse* has sought to solve the migration crisis by supporting the increasing authority of states to discipline migration flows. The OECD, for example, has looked upon the crisis simply as a crisis of national standards, and has tried through its Continuous Reporting System on Migration (established in 1973) to encourage the signing of bilateral treaties and the reinforcement of national capabilities to regulate migration movements.[81] By seeking the reinforcement of state capacities, the *nébuleuse* has not only played on the historic will of modern states to make national citizens out of (in this case transnational) nomads, it has also installed state sovereignty as an essential prop to the political management of global accumulation.

Of late, the OECD has also worked to emphasize the link between transnational migrations and international development. This linkage was particularly evident at the OECD's conference on migration held in Rome in March 1991. Here again, the clear division of labour established between states and the *nébuleuse* is most revealing of the position occupied by the former in the political management of the world economy. While the Rome conference stressed that global development policies were essential to stem the flow of migrants at the source, it a) designated states as political managers of the migration crisis by assigning to them sole responsibility for controlling borders and establishing national migration programs, and b) assigned to transnational agencies the more narrowly economic task of managing the liberalization of investments and exchanges, the liberal answer to development programs. This division of labour not only renders, as Zolberg recognized, the adoption of global codes of conduct in the sphere of labour migration "as unlikely as the institutionalization of a New International Economic Order more generally";[82] it also entrenches the position of states as specialized political units of the world system. Turning Barrington Moore's classic "no bourgeois, no democracy" formula upside down, we could say then, that as far as the *nébuleuse* is concerned, there is no sustainable transnational bourgeoisie without working national democracies.

CONCLUSION

Spatial analyses of social relations often offer little more than descriptive compendia of actors present in one place, with little thought as to how these actors came to be assembled and how their relationships were constructed, or could be transformed.[83] In the study of the world economy, attempts to take space seriously have thus far generated little more than exhortations to reconstruct, re-imagine, or re-map world politics. Talk of space has produced nebulous strategies of reading, of cognitive mapping of the world, or ritualized invocations of Marx's "insistence that modern social, economic, and political processes must be seen as a totality at the level of the globe."[84] At best, thinking about space in analyzing the world economy has been an invitation for contemporary academics to make their own academic discipline the center of their political activities and "transgress the boundaries" (of gender, class, race and ethnicity) drawn by the discipline of international relations.[85] Yet, because it serves as a way to focus the analysis of social relations, and to capture power relationships where they are constructed, there is something radically important about conceptualizing the world economy as a social space in the making. It encourages us to question assumptions of transnational hegemony that have increasingly accompanied writings of critical international political economists. These assumptions are, in fact, the way in which the left has internalized the discourse of the New World Order. Whereas the triumphalist mainstream liberal literature speaks of the triumph of order and presents the rational bourgeois *conquérant* as the last man, the critical literature speaks of a deeply embedded transnational hegemony for now and for the envisionable future and consecrates the bourgeoisie as citizens of the world economy.

This brief look at selected problem-solving efforts of the *nébuleuse* suggests that assumptions of transnational *bourgeois* hegemony should be subjected to better empirical scrutiny. Indeed, it appears from looking at the *nébuleuse*'s attempt to manage the transition in Eastern Europe, and to solve the debt and migration crises, that political transformation in the world economy is not only incomplete, but that it relies both on the confinement of political and social relationships to the space of national social formations, and on the capacity of states to structure political participation.

In attempting to solve the problems of the transition in Eastern Europe, and the on-going debt and migration crises, the *nébuleuse* has in effect build a wall around the space it is attempting to manage. What Gramsci called the superstructures of civil society, the earthworks of capitalist hegemony, remain national constructions, and citizenship-making in the world economy appears primarily as an exclusionary process whereby citizens, those with the "right to politics," are defined first by whom they exclude. Just as Athenian citizenship took as its starting point the exclusion from politics of women and slaves as well as the ostracization of dangerously powerful or unpopular citizens, and just as the rationality and the political legitimacy of French *citoyens* after the Revolution was secured by the exclusion of less rational beings (madmen, women and slaves in the West Indies), so the construction of citizenship in the world economy relies on banishing citizens from the space of the world economy, and on curtailing transnational political possibilities.

This, of course, is not to say that the world economy is but the *fantôme* that Alain Lipietz spoke of, that international political economists who conceptualize it as a social space are letting fashionable metaphors get ahead of social and political realities, or that the "day of reckoning" for transnational capital foreseen by Davidson L. Budhoo in his famous letter of resignation from the IMF, is close at hand.[86] Rather, it means that, as a social space, the world economy appears to be constructed like those Los Angeles gated communities that Mike Davis talks about in *City of Quartz*: it is build as a private preserve of the *bourgeoisie*, a walled enclave with no political points of access. The world economy, in fact appears no more a *cité* than those private enclaves, and transnational capital is no more hegemonical than Orange County suburban house owners hiding behind electrified fences and protected by private security guards.

This conclusion invites a course of political action centered on immediate issues that have an urgency of their own beyond the discourse of states, and that present specific organizational prospects, concrete points of entry into the space of the world economy. In this sense, concern for the world economy as a social space represents the political revival of a broad anti-authoritarian tradition of marxism. It is the theoretical expression of a renewed internationalism of resistance that, as I have argued elsewhere, has increasingly challenged the hegemonical pretensions of the New World Order.[87]

NOTES

1. Jean-Jacques Rousseau, *Du contrat social*. Paris: Éditions du Seuil, 1977, p. 184.
2. For a review of the increasing use of spatial imagery in contemporary social theory, see Scott Lash and Jonathan Friedman, *Modernity and Identity*. Oxford: Blackwell, 1992.
3. Edward W. Soja, *Postmodern Geographies. The Reassertion of Space in Critical Social Theory*. London: Verso, 1989, p. 6. On the world economy as a "structured coherence of production and consumption within a given space...," see David Harvey, "The Geopolitics of Capitalism," in Derek Gregory and John Urry (eds.), *Social Relations and Spatial Structures*. London: Macmillan, 1985, p. 146. On the world economy as a "field of practice": a social formation as well as a distinct and relatively coherent historical experience, see Richard Ashley, "The Geopolitics of Geopolitical Space: Towards a Critical Social Theory of International Politics," *Alternatives*, 12:4, October 1987, pp. 403-43. In the same spirit, James Der Derian set out to find in the "scripted representations of international relations," indications that the meeting place of states is also a theater where identities are constructed, and political meanings assembled. For Der Derian, world politics is a special terrain, a hyper-real world of war-play and modeling and strategic fantasies, an arena of modern panopticism, telemetric and photo-intelligence. See James Der Derian, "The Space of International Relations: Simulation, Surveillance, and Speed," *International Studies Quarterly*, 1990, 34, pp. 295-310. See also Der Derian, "Spy Versus Spy: the Intertextual Power of International Intrigue," in James Der Derian and Michael Shapiro (eds.), *International/Intertextual Relations: Post Modern Readings of World Politics*. Lexington: Lexington Books, 1989, p. 163.
4. Michel Foucault, "Of Other Spaces," quoted in Soja, note 3, p. 17.
5. See for example Anthony Giddens, "Time, Space and Regionalisation," in Gregory and Urry (eds.), note 3, pp. 265-295. See also R. Pett and N. Thrift (eds.), *New Models in Geography*. London: Unwin Hyman, 1989, reviewed in *Antipode: A Radical Journal of Geography* 24, 2 (April 1992), pp. 157-159; Iver B. Neumann and Jennifer M. Velsh, "The Other European Self-Definition: An Addendum to the Literature on International Society," *Review of International Studies* 17, 4 (October 1991), pp. 327-348.
6. André C. Drainville, "International Political Economy in the Age of Open Marxism," *Review of International Political Economy*, I,1 (Spring 1994), pp. 105-132.
7. On citizenship as *le droit universel à la politique*, see Étienne Balibar, "Liberté, égalité, citoyenneté," in Kaïssa Titous, *L'Europe au mirroir de ses immigrés*, special issue of *Cosmopolitiques*, (1990).
8. Robert W. Cox, "Global Perestroika," in Ralph Miliband and Leo Panitch (eds.), *Socialist Register 1992: New World Order?* London: Merlin Press, 1992, p. 27.
9. On this subject, John Agnew wrote of the "territorial trap" of conventional thinking in international relations theory, which relies on the assumption of states as territorially-bounded power containers and privileges a territorial conception of space. See John Agnew, "The Territorial Trap: The Geographical Assumptions of International Relations Theory," in *Review of International Political Economy*, vol.1, no.1 (Spring 1994), pp. 53-80.
10. Immanuel Wallerstein, *The Capitalist World Economy*. Cambridge: Cambridge University Press, 1980, p. 230. In the same spirit, see Giovanni Arrighi, *Geometry of Imperialism*. London: NLB, 1978, p. 113.
11. On the realist ontology of the *école de la régulation*, see Bob Jessop, "Regulation Theories in Retrospect and Prospect," *University of Amsterdam, Research on Capital & Strategy in the Faculty of Political and Social Sciences*, nos 5/6, Amsterdam, May 1989. Alain Lipietz, "Les transformations dans la division internationale du travail," in Duncan Cameron, François Houle (eds.), *Canada and the New International Division of Labour*. Ottawa: University of Ottawa Press, 1985, p. 39. On the "primacy of the national dimension" in Aglietta's analysis, see Hugo Radice, "The National Economy: A Keynesian Myth?" *Capital and Class*, 22 (Spring 1984), p. 113.
12. Alain Lipietz, *Mirages et miracles. Problèmes de l'industrialisation dans le tiers-monde*. Paris: La Découverte, 1985, p. 21. On the regulation approach and the study of the world economy, see

M. Gottdiener and Nicos Komninos (eds.), *Accumulation, Regulation and Spatial Restructuring*. New York: St. Martin's Press, 1989.

13. On regulation analysis at the intersection of marxist analysis and systems analysis, and on the special preoccupation of regulation with state institutions, see Robert Boyer, *La théorie de la régulation: une analyse critique*. Paris: Agalma/La Découverte, 1986, especially part III: "Entre critique de l'othodoxie et rénovation marxienne," pp. 21-25.

14. Michel Aglietta, "World Capitalism in the Eighties," *New Left Review* 136 (November-December 1982), p.6.

15. On spatial forms as social forms, see for example "Critical Notes: Social Science, History and Geography," in Anthony Giddens, *The Constitution of Society*. Berkley: University of California Press, 1984, pp. 355-373.

16. Anthony D. King documented the growing interest in "globally-oriented urban research" in the second chapter of *Global Cities: Post-Imperialism and the Internationalisation of London*. London: Routledge, The International Library of Sociology, 1990. "Global cities" are defined by Jan G. Lambooy as cities "with functions that have a worldwide importance." See *Global Cities and the World-Wide Economic System: Rivalry and Decision-Making*," Research Memorandum no. 8803, Department of Economics, University of Amsterdam 1987. Mike Davis, *City of Quartz: Excavating the Future In Los Angeles*. New York: Vintage 1992; Anthony D. King, *Urbanism, Colonialism and the World Economy: Cultural and Spatial Foundations of the World Urban System*. London: Routledge, 1990, p. 2; Saskia Sassen, *The Global City: New York, London, Tokyo*. Princeton: Princeton University Press, 1993.

17. Drainville, note 6. On transnational historical materialism as a coherent approach to the world economy, see Stephen Gill, *American Hegemony and the Trilateral Commission*. Cambridge: Cambridge University Press, 1990, pp. 46-51.

18. On the world economy as a distinctive constellation of discrete practices, techniques and modes of organizations, see Philip Cooke, "Spatial Development Processes: Organized or Disorganized," in Nigel Thrift and Peter Williams, *Class and Space: The Making of Urban Society*. London: Routledge & Kegan Paul, 1987, p. 327. The notion of space corresponds at this level to what Fernand Braudel called *la vie matérielle (l'habitude...la routine...mille gestes qui fleurissent, s'achèvent d'eux mêmes...hors de notre pleine conscience...des incitations, des pulsions...des façons ou des obligations d'agir)*. Fernand Braudel, *La Dynamique du Capitalisme*. Paris: Flammarion Champs, 1985, pp. 12-13. On the importance of spatial imagery in Braudel's analysis, for example, see Michel Aglietta, "Le Schumpeter de l'histoire" and Jacques Le Goff, "Le Changement dans la Continuité," both in *Espaces Temps* 34/35 (1986).

19. Harvey, note 3, p. 129.

20. On "espaces-vitesse," see Paul Virilio, *L'espace critique*. Paris: Christian Bourgeois Editeur, 1984, pp. 120-121. On the social geography of space-time and on "chrono-politics," see also chapter 1 of P. Virilio and S. Lotringer, *Pure War*. New York: Semiotext(e), 1983. This is related to what John Agnew called a "structural understanding of space" as a dynamic relationship between regions, nodes, districts, etc. See John Agnew, note 9. On the decontextualization of space as a feature of the contemporary geography of class formation, see Nigel Thrift, "The Geography of Late Twentieth-Century Class Formation," in Nigel Thrift and Peter Williams, *Class and Space: The Making of Urban Society*. London: Routledge & Keagan Paul, 1987, pp. 207-253.

21. Stephen Gill, "The Emerging World Order and European Change: The Political Economy of European Union," in Miliband and Panitch (eds.), note 8, pp. 157-196.

22. Leo Panitch and Ralph Miliband, "The New World Order and the Socialist Agenda," in Miliband and Panitch (eds.), note 8, pp. 1-25.

23. Lawrence Birken, "Lenin's Revolution in Time, Space and Economics and Its Implications: An Analysis of *Imperialism*'," *History of Political Economy* 23, 4 (1991), pp. 613-623.

24. R.B.J. Walker, "Security, Sovereignty, and the Challenge of World Politics," *Alternatives* XV, 1 (Winter 1990), p. 11.

25. David Ruccio, Stephen Resnick and Richard Wolff, "Class Beyond the Nation State?," *Capital and Class*, 43 (Spring 1991), 26. Stephen Gill, "Reflections of Global Order and Socio-Historical Time," *Alternatives*, 16 (1991), p. 275.

26. See for example Marie-Francoise Durand, Jacques Lévy and Denis Retaillé, *Le Monde: Espaces et Systèmes*. Paris: Dalloz, 1992. Jim George, "International Relations and the Search For Thinking Space," *International Studies Quarterly* 33, p. 3 (September 1989), 269-279. Ronnie D. Lipschutz, "Reconstructing World Politics: The Emergence of Global Civil Society," *Millennium* 21,3 (Winter 1992), pp. 389-420.

27. Danièle Leborgne and Alain Lipietz, "Idées fausses et questions ouvertes de l'après-fordisme," *Espaces et Sociétés*, 66-67 (1992), 39-68.
28. "Du 'Capital' à la philosophie de Marx," in Louis Althusser, Jacques Rancière and Pierre Macherey, *Lire le Capital*, tome I. Paris: Francois Maspero, 1965, pp. 28-31. On the relationship between structuralism, post-structuralism and spatial analysis, see Neil Smith and Cindi Katz's excellent article "Grounding Metaphor: Towards a Spatialized Politics," in Michael Keith and Steve Pile (eds.), *Place and the Politics of Identity*. London: Routledge, 1993, pp. 67-83.
29. See for example Nicos Poulantzas, "La fonction générale de l'État," in *Pouvoir politique et classes sociales*. Paris: Francois Maspero, 1982, pp. 43-50.
30. "Interview with John Fleming of the EBRD," in *Transition: the Newsletter About Reforming Economies*, 4,4 (May 1993), 4. The EBRD, which was created in April 1991, is the most recently born international organisation, and the one which defines its social mandate most broadly. According to Jacques Attali, the EBRD is in fact the first international organisation to put forth an explicit social and political doctrine (of human rights and multiparty democracy). Jacques Attali is quoted in Ibrahim Warde, "Les faiseurs de la révolution libérale," in *Le Monde Diplomatique*, May 1992, p. 3.
31. For IMF economist Jacques Polak: "The proprieties of the [International Monetary] Fund contain an unwritten rule that political arguments should be dressed up in economic garb whenever possible." J. Polak, *The Changing Nature of IMF Conditionality*. Princeton University Essays in International Finance, no 184. September 1991. Princeton: Princeton University Press, p. 32.
32. Stephen Gill, Robert Cox, and Kees Van Der Pijl. "Structural Change and Globalizing Elites: Political Economy Perspectives in the Emerging World Order." Paper presented at the international conference on "Changing World Order and the United Nations System," Yokohama, Japan, March 24-27, 1992.
33. In this spirit, A. F. W. Plumptre refers to the B.I.S. as "a club of the world's central bankers," in A.F.W. Plumptre, *Three Decades of Decision: Canada and the World Monetary System, 1944-1975*. Toronto: McClelland and Stewart Limited, 1977, p. 262. In the Bretton Woods period, Fred Hirsch spoke of the B.I.S. as a "refuge" for central bankers, in *Money International*. London: Penguin Press, 1967, p. 239.
34. Virilio and Lotringer, note 20, p. 74. The double process of integration and differentiation corresponds to what Marshall Berman called the paradoxical "unity of disunity" in modernity. See *All that is Solid Melts Into Air*. New York: Simon and Schuster, 1982, p. 15. As Stefan Kipfer argues, this duality is also present in the "world city" paradigm, S. Kipfer, "Social Forces in the Making of World Cities: The Case of Local Politics in Zurich, Switzerland." Unpublished paper presented at the XVIII Annual Conference of the Political Economy of the World System (PEWS) section of the American Sociological Association; University of California at Irvine, April 7-9, 1994.
35. Sol Picciotto, "The Internationalisation of the State," *Capital and Class*, 43, Spring 1991, 48. On the historical importance of state forms in disseminating modes of social relations defined in the world economy, see also Robert Cox, *Production, Power and World Order: Social Forces in the Making of History*. New York: Columbia University Press, 1987, pp. 112-150.
36. On spatial fixes, see Harvey, note 3. Harvey's spatial fixes are akin to T. Hägerstrand's "stations," presented by Giddens as "stopping places" in which the physical mobility of an agent's trajectories is arrested or curtailed for the duration of encounters or social occasions." See Giddens, note 15, p. 119.
37. Wallerstein, note 11, p. 223. On states as bounded power containers, see also Anthony Giddens, *The Nation State and Violence*, quoted in Christopher Dandeker, *Surveillance, Power and Modernity; Bureaucracy and Discipline from 1700 to the Present*. Cambridge: Polity Press, 1990, p. 34.
38. David Harvey, "Class Relations, Social Justice and the Politics of Difference," in Keith & Pile, note 28, pp. 41-66.
39. Bank of Canada, *Annual Report of the Governor to the Minister of Finance and Statements of Account for the Year 1981*. Ottawa, 1981, p. 6.
40. Desmond S. King, *The New Right: Politics, Markets and Citizenship*. Chicago: The Dorsey Press, 1987.
41. Claude Julien, *Le suicide des démocraties*. Paris: Grasset, 1972.
42. Alan Geld and I.J. Singh, "Fact-Finding Tour at Russia's Industrial Firms," *Transition: The Newsletter About Reforming Economies*, pp. 3,11 (December 1992/January 1993), p. 5.

43. Michel Camdessus, "Opening Adddress," in *Central and Eastern Europe: Roads to Growth*. Washington: International Monetary Fund and the Austrian National Bank, 1992, p. 16. With this address, Camdessus opened a seminar on "Central and Eastern Europe: Roads to Growth" jointly organized by the Austrian National Bank and the IMF. The seminar was held at Baden, Austria, in April 1991.
44. Soros first introduced his proposal in the *Wall Street Journal*, on December 7, 1989. See also by Soros, "An EC Gift for the Hungarian Economy," *Wall Street Journal*, April 4, 1991, and *Sauver la démocratie à l'est*. Paris: Alban Michel, 1993. On George Soros's proposals, see also Abdul G. Khan, "A Case for Direct Hard Currency Transfers to Russia's Needy—A Comment on George Soros's Recent Proposal," in *Transition: The Newsletter About Reforming Economies* 3,11 (December 1992-January 1993), pp.8-9.
45. A summary of the findings from this study can be found in: International Monetary Fund, World Bank, OECD, EBRD, *The Economy of the USSR*. Washington: The World Bank, 1991. For the full report in 3 volumes: IMF, IBRD, The World Bank, OECD, *A Study of the Soviet Economy*. Paris: OECD, 1991.
46. Jozef M. van Brabant, "Property Rights' Reform, Macroeconomic Performance, and Welfare," in Hans. J. Blommestein, Michael Marrese, Centre for Co-operation with European Economies in Transition, *Transformation of Planned Economies: Property Rights Reform and Macroeconomic Stability*. Paris: OECD, 1991, pp. 29-50.
47. Bank for International Settlements, *62nd Annual Report*. Basle: B.I.S. June 1992, p. 6.
48. Soros, *Sauver*, note 44, p. 10.
49. David Owen, Zbigniew Brezinski and Sabuto Okita, *Democracy Must Work: A Trilateral Agenda for the Decade*. The Triangle Papers, no. 28. New York: New York University Press, 1984, p. 4. On halting "the downward spiral of governmental collapse" as a necessary "prelude to changes on a more fundamental level" in the context of the transition in Eastern Europe, see Jeffrey D. Sachs, "Russia's Struggle with Stabilization," in *Transition: The Newsletter About Reforming Economies*, 5, 5 (May-June 1994), pp.7-9.
50. Lawrence H. Summers cited in Mario I. Blejer et al., *Eastern Europe in Transition: From Recession to Growth?* Washington: World Bank Disussion Papers, no 196, 1993, p. iii.
51. Harvey B. Feigenbaum and Jeffrey R. Hening, "Privatization and Democracy," *Governance: An International Journal of Policy and Administration*. 6, 3 (July 1993), 440. The expression "administrative-command system" is from Simon Clarke, "Privatisation and the Development of Capitalism in Russia" in Simon Clarke, Peter Fairbrother, Michael Buraway and Pavel Krotov, *What About the Workers? Workers and the Transition to Capitalism in Russia*. London: Verso, 1993.
52. *Transition: The Newsletter About Reforming Economies*, 4/3 (April 1993), p. 12.
53. International Monetary Fund, World Bank, OECD, EBRD, note 44, p. 20.
54. Guillermo A. Calvo and Jacob A. Frenkel, "Transformation of Centrally Planned Economies: Credit Markets and Sustainable Growth," in IMF, *Roads*, note 43, pp. 111-137. On this subject, see also: World Bank, *Poland: Income Support and the Social Safety Net During the Transition*. Washington, World Bank, 1993; Zeljko Bogetic and Louise Fox, *Income Policy During Stabilization: A Review of Lessons from Bulgaria and Romania*. Washington: World Bank: Europe and Central Asia Region Discussion Paper 123, 1993, p.19.
55. C.B. Macpherson, *The Life and Times of Liberal Democracy*. Oxford: Oxford University Press, 1977.
56. Gill, note 21.
57. Michael Bruno, "Stabilization and Reform in Eastern Europe: Preliminary Evaluation," *World Bank Discussion Paper*, no. 196, p.16.
58. Soros, *Sauver*, note 44, pp. 133ff.
59. Mario J. Blejer and Alan H. Gelb, "The Contractions of Eastern Europe's Economies," in *World Bank Discussion Paper*, no. 196, pp.1-7.
60. Bruno, note 57, 33-35.
61. Bruno, note 57, 30. On the essential role played by state agencies in regulating the process of privatization and avoiding the political risks of spontaneous privatisation plans, see Clarke, note 51, p. 216.
62. On the crisis of the IMF, see Richard E. Feinberg and Catherine Gwin, "Reforming the Fund," in Catherine Gwin et al. (eds.), *The International Monetary Fund in a Multipolar World: Pulling*

Together. Washington: Overseas Development Council, 1989. See also Richard E. Feinberg, *Between Two Worlds: The World Bank's Next Decade.* New York, 1986.
63. Feinberg and Gwin, note 62, p.9. On the IMF's "country-by-country" approach, in the quest for an optimal approach to reforms, see John T. (Jack) Boorman, "A View from the IMF," in I.G. Patel (ed.), *Policies for African Development.* Washington: IMF, 1992, p.62.
64. On the changing relationship between the World Bank and developing countries, and on the new SDA (Social Dimensions of Adjustment) program, administered by the Bank with the United Nations Development Program, see Banque Mondiale, *Obtenir des résultats: ce que la Banque Mondiale veut faire pour mieux agir sur le développement.* Washington: World Bank, 1993. On SDA, see also *Making Adjustment Work for the Poor.* Washington: World Bank, 1990.
65. Polak, note 31, p. 3.
66. M. Camdessus, "Opening Remarks," in *Ibid,* pp. 21-22. See also Peter B. Kenen, "The Use of IMF Credit," in Gwin *et al.*, note 62, p. 69; and Polak, note 31, especially section 2: "Institutional Features of conditionality," pp. 6-16. The Brady proposal was launched in March 1989 at the IMF Interim Committee meeting by Nicholas Brady, U.S. Secretary of the Treasury. See Patrick Lenain, *Le FMI.* Paris: La Découverte, 1993, p. 67.
67. *Ibid.*, pp. 53-60.
68. Banque Mondiale, note 64, p. 8.
69. Boorman, note 63, p. 10.
70. Kenen, note 67, p. 74.
71. *Ibid.*, p. 75. On the growth of a more structural approach by the IMF in the 1970s, see Azizali Mohammed, "Recent Evolution of Fund Conditionality," in J.A. Frenkel and M. Goldstein (eds.), *International Financial Policy. Essays in Honor of Jacques Polak.* Washington: IMF, 1991.
72. Kenen, note 66, p. 76.
73. Polak, note 31, pp. 7-8. See also Joan M. Nelson, "The Politics of Pro-Poor Adjustment," in Joan M. Nelson, *Fragile Coalitions: The Politics of Economic Adjustment.* Washington, D.C.: Overseas Development Council, 1989.
74. Boorman, note 63, pp.48-68. The Gabon seminar, held in February 1991, was co-sponsored by the Association of African Central Banks and the IMF.
75. Aristide R. Zolberg, "Labour Migration and International Economic Regimes: Bretton Woods and After," in Mary M. Kritz, *International Migration Systems: A Global Approach.* Oxford: Clarendon Press, 1992, p. 315.
76. John Gerard Ruggie, "International Regimes, Transactions, and Change," in Stephen Krasner (ed.), *International Regimes.* Ithaca: Cornell University Press 1983, pp. 198-214.
77. Zolberg, note 75, p. 318.
78. J.N. Bhagwati, "Incentives and Disincentives: International Migration," *Review of the World Economy,* cited in *Ibid*, p. 331. See also James F. Hollifield, "Immigration et logiques d'États dans les relations internationales," *Études Internationales* XXIV, 1 (March 1993).
79. Zolberg, note 75, pp. 324-325.
80. *Ibid.*, p. 321.
81. See for example Organisation for Economic Cooperation and Development, *Tendances des migrations internationales.* Paris: OECD, 1992, part B.
82. Zolberg, note 75, p. 331.
83. Doreen Massey, "Politics and Space/Time," in Keith & Pile, note 28, p. 142. This article was first published in the *New Left Review* 196, (November/December 1992), pp.65-84.
84. Walker, note 24, p. 23. On strategies of reading, see Richard Ashley and R.B.J. Walker, "Reading Dissidence/Writing the Discipline: Crisis and the Question of Sovereignty in International Studies," *International Studies Quarterly* 34 (1990), 364-416. On reconstructing and re-mapping, see Lipschutz, note 26, p. 391.
85. See for example V. Spike Peterson, "Transgressing Boundaries: Theories of Knowledge, Gender, and International Relations," *Millennium,* 21,2 Summer 1992, pp.183-206.
86. Davidson L. Budhoo, *Enough is Enough. Dear Mr. Camdessus...Open Letter of Resignation to the Managing Director of the International Monetary Fund.* New York: New Horizons Press, in the collection "Documentary Sources for Social Change," 1990, p. x.
87. André C. Drainville, "Left Internationalism and the Politics of Resistance in the New World Order," in David Smith and Josef Borocz, *A New World Order: Global Transformation in the Late Twentieth Century.* Westport: Praeger, 1995, pp. 217-238.

Chapter Fifteen

INDIVIDUALISM, IDENTITIES, AND INCLUSIONARY CITIZENSHIP IN WESTERN POLITICAL CULTURE
Gregor Matjan

Individualism as a result of social dynamics is deeply rooted in the development of the capitalist market economy. Along with the "free market," individualism today has become a dominant force in Western societies. As a result, Western culture in general and political culture in particular have undergone rapid changes within the last 20 years. Political institutions, parties as well as bureaucracies—in short, all components of the state apparatus—are confronted with a crisis of legitimation, an increasingly fluctuating electorate, and strong demands on their regulatory power. The more freedom there is in the (globalized) economy and private relationships (e.g., in the shaping of one's own lifestyle), the more states react with institutional closure, strict immigration laws, and a policy of cutting welfare programs in order to consolidate their budgets. These politics of boundary-drawing directed towards migrants and all kinds of peripheral groups within societies lead us to Polanyi's problem of "freedom in a complex society." What is meant by freedom, and who is able to enjoy its benefits? How can freedom and the need for security be balanced? Is it merely utopian to envisage the creation of a free society that includes not only the unrestricted right to buy and sell but also to live a life according to one's own envisioning and together with others who share those visions? I believe that Karl Polanyi's work can provide some answers to the burning problem of the individual and collective freedom, not only in terms of how freedom can be defended, maintained and preserved, but also concerning how freedom needs to be established permanently and dynamically in Western societies. Contrary to other contemporary scholars of capitalism and the Enlightenment such as Horkheimer and Adorno (in their *Dialectic of Enlightenment*),[1] *The Great Transformation*[2] reflects a moderate optimism with regard to the future development of our society. In what follows I will try to point out in which respect Polanyi's writings can be interpreted optimistically and which dynamics within the political culture of Western states support this view.

INDIVIDUALISM AND FREEDOM IN A COMPLEX SOCIETY
In the concluding chapter of *The Great Transformation* entitled "Freedom in a Complex Society," Karl Polanyi wrote:

> The individual must be free to follow his conscience without fear of the powers that happen to be entrusted with administrative tasks in some fields

of social life...Compulsion should never be absolute; the 'objector' should be offered a niche to which he can retire, the choice of a 'second best' that leaves him a life to live. Thus will be secured the right to nonconformity as the hallmark of a free society. (Polanyi, p. 255)

In accordance with the classic view of the history of ideas, we can distinguish two closely interconnected views of freedom. One is the liberal notion of individual freedom as the right to private enterprise and the "pursuit of happiness" that resulted from the institutional separation of politics and economy. This notion became the dominant ideology of the 19th century. As a "by-product" of this differentiation, a second, rather more collective notion of freedom brought forth republicanism, civil rights, and the idea of Enlightenment. In concrete terms, these modernist ideas of freedom became institutionalized in the liberal welfare state with its balance of power between public interest and the market. However, what Polanyi highlights here refers to a third meaning of freedom that is not covered by either liberalism or republicanism. It is the right to nonconformity, the right to defend one's way of life *against* the systemic powers of market and state.

These views of freedom correspond with two variations of individualism: utilitarian and expressive individualism.[3] Polanyi argues against the first, and is in favor of the second. For him, the right to nonconformity is the hallmark of a free society. It clearly implies the right of self-expression, the protection of (not just ethnic) minorities in a general sense, and a "requisite variety" of ways of life or pluralism. According to Polanyi's work, pluralism may not be understood simply as a plurality of elites or institutions in a Schumpeterian sense. Essentially, pluralism requires a cultural multiplicity of groups and ways of life expressing themselves within a sphere that we would nowadays call "civil society," a place where deviant and oppositional positions can exist without interference by the state and without following the imperative of economic efficiency, its critical potential serving as a political corrective to the dominant institutions and powers.

For Polanyi this right to nonconformity is endangered mainly by two dominant or hegemonic institutions: the market and bureaucracy. Markets create welfare and profit, not freedom and peace. Bureaucracies are characterized by Polanyi as a constant source of abuse of power. Therefore, personal freedom, civil rights, and the right to work have to be institutionalized in such a way that they stand above all the imperatives, be it economic efficiency or bureaucratic rationality. A massive obstacle to the priority of these principles is embodied in liberalism's view of freedom of enterprise and freedom of personal expression as inseparably intertwined. For Polanyi, the libertarian ideal of a stateless society where everybody participates equally in the market represents a dangerous illusion. A regulating and political state power (not just a technocratic bureaucracy) will always be needed to protect public interests when they become endangered by an ever-expanding market. Following the same argument, he turns against the communist view of a stateless society which additionally neglected market forces in favor of universal cooperation. Consequently, the liberal negation of power as a paradigm of social reality led to fascism, just as the socialist negation of economic values resulted in authoritarian communism.

Acceptance of the necessity of planning and controlling the economy on the one hand, and acceptance of the necessity of individual expression, personal freedom, and pluralism on the other, represent the main features of the sort of society imagined by Polanyi. To reach that goal, three premises have to be fulfilled: the factors of "work," "land," and "control of money" have to be removed from the market and subordinated to societal governance. (Polanyi, pp. 251f.) The type of political and economic crisis between World Wars, inflation, unemployment, political instability, and civil wars that finally led to fascism, turned out to be a result of lack control over the three factors mentioned above.

Since Polanyi's time, control over money has been practised more or less successfully in most developed countries. Today, states have become players amongst others in the global financial system that operates almost without any restriction. Financial markets not only determine all other productive sectors of the economy but also political decision-making. The Maastricht criteria for reaching a common currency standard among the EU countries additionally enforce this process of "monetarization" of the economy. From that it follows that non-economic rationality has been restricted to very small niches. From the end of World War II up until today, work has been strongly regulated by corporatist systems in many Western European countries, although neoconservative and neoliberal policies during the 1980s have more or less reduced the density of regulation. Nowadays, the widespread use of flexible, computer-based technologies also allows for both further flexibility and more individual influence in the organization of work as well. Land has become of major importance in a wider sense. With the rise of ecological movements during the 1980s, land and natural resources in general have become an issue involving regulation. Although the legislation and implementation of environmental laws sometimes seem to progress too slowly, quite a lot has been done during the last years to remove natural resources from the unrestricted grasp of the market and to protect nature as a common good.

To sum up, the three decisive factors to be subordinated to societal control appear neither strictly regulated nor simply uncontrolled these days. What we face is a complex, overdetermined system in which regulation or deregulation of each factor has pronounced results on the others, but—as Althusser puts is—economy dominates in the final instance. The balance appears to be stable at the moment, but—as chaos theory suggests—in a dynamic system small causes can have unforeseeable effects, as happened with the "Big Bang" of October 1987. According to Polanyi's premises, we live, at least in Western Europe, in a relatively free society where political power and economic performance are said to be under democratic control to a certain extent. Nevertheless, individual freedom seems to be endangered by several strong tendencies towards what Frank Parkin (influenced by Max Weber) called societal "closure."[4] In the closing paragraph of his book, Polanyi emphasises the "indomitable courage and strength" that will be necessary to remove injustice and unfreedom. (Polanyi, p.258B) For him, political power and planning are by no means general obstacles in this struggle, but the means to create more freedom and justice against the overarching dominance of market principles. Obviously, Polanyi did not have a static notion of justice and freedom, but rather a dynamic one. The struggle for both has to go on, and there will be no opportunity to lean back and live in the best of all societies. Although the modern welfare state has proved capable of combining a high level of control over the market with a relatively high level of individual freedom and justice, it is by no means perfect. Just at the present moment, for example, we are witnessing a constant but self-induced pressure to negate social and ecological achievements in the context of economic crisis.

INDIVIDUALISM: EXPRESSIVE AND UTILITARIAN

Today we realize that different dangers are compelling us to think of ways to maintain and extend safeguards for personal liberty. If we look, for example, at the history of the United States, freedom of expression and freedom of enterprise, together with expressive and utilitarian individualism have been the central motives of development since the early times of colonization. Its beginning was represented by the flight of the Pilgrim Fathers from the hierarchical Church of England in pursuit of their utopian vision of equality within a religious community. A secularized, politicized version was later formulated in the republican tradition of Enlightenment philosophy, originally by Rousseau, and then by the American federalists during the period of the Revolution. A critical review of the ideal and practice of liberal individualism was undertaken by Alexis de Tocqueville, who introduced the term individualism for the first time in the middle of the 19th century. At the present time, the republican issue reappears in the light of communitarianism with its strong emphasis on recognition of differences.[5] Community, civil society, and "moral economy" represent core elements of republican thinking. As against culturally "unembedded" liberalism, they present an alternative model for organizing a complex modern society after the breakdown of communism.

If we identify utilitarian individualism mainly with the liberal notion of free enterprise, expressive individualism can be located within the republican-communitarian tradition of thought outlined above. Expressive individualism is not so much based on the individual self as on the idea of the equality of all individuals.[6] In utilitarianism, equality does not stand as a goal in itself, whereas expressive individualism regards equality as a prerequisite for individual freedom. Its egalitarian component appears much stronger than its individualist component in the sense of atomized, freely-acting individuals. Expressive individualism is socially rooted in manifest or latent groups, voluntary associations or communities of people who share common attributes such as political ideology, religious belief, or way of life. They express their way of life by using a variety of shared "condensational" symbols with which they identify.[7] Each individual uses or refers to symbols which are legitimized by the group as signs of recognition. In doing so, the symbols fulfil two functions. On the one hand, they are means of integration and identification for the group itself, especially when it is still latent. On the other hand, their function is symbolic representation towards the "outer" world: ie., distinctiveness.[8] Identification and distinction mark the common symbolic dimensions of life-styles as well as social movements or political parties. In this respect, these social arrangements follow a homologous combination of social structure and symbolic expression.

Utilitarian individualism, on the contrary, has nothing to do with civil associations of this kind. Its basic social relations are markets or loose networks of single individuals ("elites"), each pursuing his or her own goal with an almost unrestricted range of means. Collective action may occur when it seems strategically useful, but is nevertheless the exception to the rule.[9] Even if collective action emerges out of the individualistic structure, it is supposed to be accidental, temporary, and to follow the utilitarian principles of the actors taking part in it. The utilitarian's time horizon extends to only short—or medium—range projections. No tradition or moral obligation limits individual action, other than personal conscience or regulative laws according to which the actors select their range of possible alternatives. The utilitarian individual appears "unencumbered"[10] in the sense that no particular societal structure connected to this kind of attitude seems to exist. Unlike in a class society, one cannot simply associate liberalism with the bourgeoisie and socialism with the working class. It is almost the other way around: societally conscious movements develop mostly out of intellectual middle-class backgrounds, reestablishing a discourse on poverty and "welfare" in a world that is dominated by the belief in achievement, in the efficiency of markets and the perspective of consuming—an ideology that is widely shared among those that once formed the core of the working class.

The formulation of this ideal type of individualism which has become dominant in England and the United States started with liberal and utilitarian philosophy and was implemented at the beginning of modern industrialism. In the United States it was most prominently represented by Benjamin Franklin and later by the classical and neoclassical economists. With Thatcherism and Reaganomics, utilitarianism and "individualization" became the most significant features of the "dominant ideology." However, contradictory versions of this story do exist. According to the conservative cultural critic Daniel Bell,[11] the affluence of Western societies based on utilitarian individualism has nowadays given rise to a radicalized and postmodern version of expressive individualism ("psychedelic bazaar") that now undermines such fundamental props of the market economy as the work ethic and unrestricted growth. I wish to argue here that these "Cultural Contradictions of Capitalism," such as Bell describes them, may turn out to be essential prerequisites for a "re-embedding" of the market economy within a pluralistic culture.

WAYS OF LIFE: A DYNAMIC CULTURAL SETTING
How can these two variations of individualism connected with the ideal of Karl Polanyi manage to bring the economic sphere under societal control? Along with Polanyi, I think that the classic, unrestricted and unembedded sort of utilitarian individualism as described here actually does not exist. As an ideal type it has been perpetuated in classic economic theory as "homo oeconomicus" and, with the rise of neoliberal discourse, from there made its way into the minds of ordinary people. The anthropology that backed this model has been sharply critized by Karl Polanyi:

> Actually, as we know, the behavior of man both in his primitive state and right through the course of history has been almost the opposite from that implied in this view [that markets are natural institutions]. Frank H. Knight's 'no specifically human motive is economic' applies not only to social life in general, but even to economic life itself. (Polanyi, p. 250)

Utilitarian theories with their focus on individual rationality pay no attention to where preferences derive from.[12] Only if markets were natural institutions and individual's preferences would be internally generated could we assume an abstract, rational course of action based simply on maximizing one's utility. However, utilitarian "meta-preferences" (the preference for a utilitarian course of action) are no more "natural" than any other kind of "meta-preferences" (e.g., altruism or equality).[13] Thus utilitarian individualism is rooted, in (historical) tradition as well as today's Western (political) culture, in a particular individualist way of life. Its rationality turns out to be not as general, abstract or value-free as the calculations of economists might suggest. If we assume that institutions are cultures made manifest, this way of life establishes a very strong and dominant institution which basically consists of personal networks (elites as well as markets in a broad sense) but is inseparably tied to a bureaucracy that regulates its activities—the modern liberal welfare state. In this sense it is a compound self-regulating regime or "system" which Habermas analyses in opposition to the so-called life-world.

Nevertheless, I tend to reject Habermas's[14] dualism of "system" and "life-world" because my aim is to show that both are to some degree institutionalized and functional elements for the integration of society. However, both also contain spheres of personal freedom and expression. To me, this ambiguity is better captured by the terms "establishment" or "center." If we think of the establishment, we might imagine a combination of functional (systemic) and personal (socio-cultural) interactions. For instance, we might think of a manager in his representative office (as part of a systemic power structure) or of an upper-class garden party (as part of informal social "networking" based on "high culture"). Turning to the opposite interpretation, there is no life-world as such, no intimate privacy which has to be defended against the intruding agencies of state and economy. The assumption of a life-world (or privacy) has been criticized by two diverging currents in the social sciences: feminists like Nancy Fraser[15] show that border-drawing between privacy or life-world and the public system is ideological because it reproduces the male order by dividing the social world into male and female spheres. On the other hand, economic rationalists like Gary Becker[16] suggest that many private or familial transactions are based on economic rationality as well as on systemic processes.

What is of interest here are not so much the economic and political implications of the liberal welfare state as the socio-cultural arrangements in which it is embedded. Therefore, I would like to refer to it as the "establishment" or, with Karl Polanyi and Mary Douglas[17] as the "center," as opposed to the "periphery" or "border" of society. The center included a symbiotic arrangement of networks and hierarchies designed to stabilize and control society on the one hand, and to facilitate innovation, growth, and progress on the other. Power, knowledge, and wealth are accumulated at the center so as to enable the state/economy to be a competitive player in the world market. As Polanyi writes: "For, however generously devolution of power is practised, there will be strengthening of power at the center, and, therefore, danger to individual freedom." (Polanyi, p. 255) What he points out here may be called the paradox of dynamic individualization: the more individualized a society and the more "devolution of power is practised," the less can individual freedom be admitted by the central institutions for reasons of "functionality" or "integration." This paradox was discussed in a similar way by two of Polanyi's fellow emigrants, Horkheimer and Adorno in their famous *Dialectic of Enlightenment*. For them, capitalism brings forth individualism as an ideology of freedom to legitimize simultaneous processes of standardization and subjection of the masses under the laws of commodification.

Following the "Cultural Theory" of Thompson,[18] Ellis, and Wildavsky[19] which rests upon the work of the British anthropologist Mary Douglas, I would propose a pluralistic approach to resolve this paradox. The authors distinguish between five "ways of life"—of which one, the "hermit," has no central relevance for modern society. The other four are characterized as follows: individualism, hierarchy, egalitarianism, and fatalism. Individualism here stands for utilitarian individualism or achieved status; hierarchy relates to ascribed status or bureaucratic structures; egalitarianism is equivalent to expressive individualism and face-to-face groups; and fatalists can be described as atomized individuals with little group solidarity. Fatalism also reflects a form of utilitarian individualism, but at a different level. Individualists, in the sense of Cultural Theory, are acting largely independently of prescriptions by others and with little or no obligation to self-imposed group or community standards. Fatalists, however, are acting under severe constraints from outside, while also lacking reference to a community.

These four ways of life may help us to understand the inseparable connection between social relations that can or cannot be institutionalized and cultures as their legitimizing worldviews ("cosmologies") or ideologies. As the authors of Cultural Theory pursue their functional argument, they regard a plurality of ways of life as essential to (macro)stability. What turns out to be decisive (and unusual, for functional explanations) is not just the existence of pluralism itself, but the dynamic interchange and fluctuation between the ways of life: i.e., "macro-stability by micro-variability."[20] This point of view is very much influenced by the latest findings in chaos or catastrophe theory which is grounded on the assumption of a dynamic imbalance deemed necessary for the adaptability of society as a whole. Chaotic transitions occur when the dynamics of interchange between ways of life become disturbed, when institutional closure becomes too rigid. Then, learning processes are blocked in a way that MacIntyre called an "epistemological crisis."[21] The social arrangement remains unstable until it collapses and renews itself, as happened with the socialist countries of Eastern Europe in 1989 or during the days of 1968 in most Western countries. Although chaotic transitions are exceptions to the rule, we have to accept that they belong among the inherent cultural dynamics of complex societies. This in no way means that we are helplessly exposed to the forces of such sociocultural dynamics. As mentioned above, the crucial point is the extent of closure in social spheres or ways of life. Closure can be avoided, but, as Polanyi tells us, openness or "freedom in a complex society" is not self-evident—it has permanently to be fought for.

INSTITUTIONAL CLOSURE
In modern Western European societies the power of market individualism has—at least to some extent—been mitigated by strong social democratic parties and the political and cultural integration of most sections of the working class. In

terms of Cultural Theory we could state that individualism has been limited by a strong hierarchy represented by the clientelistic organization of trade unions and social democratic parties. With the growth of affluence, these limiting institutions have transformed themselves from agents of class struggle into integral parts of a technocratic symbiosis of hierarchy and individualism, into what we call the "center" or "establishment." In this setting, hierarchy guarantees law enforcement, stability, and safety; for its part individualism brings the innovative and adaptive capacity of the market and allows people to achieve a higher social position (vertical mobility). Therefore, I would not agree that in Western European societies control of markets is too weak. The main problem arises from institutional closure of bureaucracies and markets. As we may observe today, the greater the symbiosis of the two ways of life, the more they try to restrict access to their benefits.

Although GNPs continue to grow, welfare states become more and more exclusive. Policies of budgetary consolidation combine higher taxes on lower income groups with restricted claims on, and tighter control of, welfare expenditures. Restrictions are directed not only towards foreigners and immigrants, but also towards all other peripheral groups and even towards such a numerical majority as represented by women. These restrictions affect material living conditions as well as access to and production of cultural goods and rights of political or public representation. For those living on the "periphery," job markets, welfare services, and also information (e.g., the internet, to give a modern example of the increasing "knowledge gap") become less accessible. The establishment discourse (and even social science itself) defines these groups somewhat cynically as "losers out in modernization" who are said to be prone to anomic tendencies or right-wing extremism. Reversing the argument, the German sociologist Wolf-Dietrich Bukow[22] named this material and sociocultural closure on the part of the establishment a "project of a community based on the solidarity of beneficiaries."

Beyond the "socio-democratic consensus," the cultural impact of the establishment turns into a dominant ideology or "bourgeois consensus" to secure its base of legitimation. Its "symbolic politics" become hegemonic and ideological, in the sense that people who are actually excluded are made to believe that they are included. This ideology of symbolic integration which is opposed to the political symbolism of expressive individualists, is established by a consensus among the "power elite"[23] consisting of mass media journalists, politicians, and representatives of the economy (that mostly share a common utilitarian individualistic way of life). This dominant ideology relies mainly on nationalist language and symbols, even if opposed to extreme right-wing rhetoric. In order to maintain Germany's or Britain's position as a relevant factor in the world economy not everybody can benefit, runs the argument.

The excluded communities and groups are now themselves forced into a process of closure. Out of a need of self-maintenance, the expressive individualism of subcultures together with the cultural traditionalism of migrant communities grow more and more radical. Youth gangs and radical subcultures who are not averse to violence take over suburban ghettos, while religious and national fundamentalisms win more and more adherents among ethnic minorities. Fatalism is blooming and gives further rise to anomie, crime and violence that again serve as justification for a "radicalization of the center," such as tougher punishment for criminals and an extension of "precautionary measures."

This process of mutual closure can be found all over Europe. Perhaps the most prominent example is Italy, where the chaotic transformation process is almost finished. The process of closure started with the constitution of a "Lombardian" identity and tradition by the *Lega Nord*[24] to secure Northern Italy's economic standards against a corrupt and morally decaying political center. The political ideology and rhetoric of the League are thoroughly individualistic as opposed to the clientelistic "amoral familialism"[25] of the South. Its jealous exclusiveness is obvious and can hardly be ignored. The *Lega Nord* recruits its partisans from the middle classes who are the bearers of the region's excellent economic performance. With the breakdown of the old establishment, the oppositional and particularistic ideology of the League affords an obvious contrast to the national ideology of Berlusconi and the modernized neofascists of Gianfranco Fini. Peripheral groups such as people in the suburbs from Southern Italian cities or African and Albanian immigrants see themselves excluded. The establishment did not vanish, it just reappeared in a different guise. With Berlusconi's attempts to bring the national TV-Station RAI under his control, closure became too tight and led to massive resistance by civil society. This has brought forth a renewal of the Left. For the time being, the process of closure has come to an end, and the functionality of the system has been widely reestablished after the surprising electoral victory of the Left.

That in Germany, France, Great Britain, and Austria, this process of closure did not require systematic transformation was due to their different starting positions. Regional differences in affluence and culture are nowhere as extreme as in Italy—except perhaps in reunified Germany where we can observe similar processes at the extreme Left (PDS) and extreme Right of the political spectrum ("Republikaner"). What is happening in almost all Western European societies is the identifying of new differences and cleavages along the lines of race, gender, and age. Immigrants and people of foreign origin who have been living in a country for generations find themselves excluded from the national "community of beneficiaries."[26]

Nevertheless, this dynamic of exclusion and institutional rigidity does not follow directly from individualization. Though utilitarian individualism plays an important role in this closure of societies, it is not the dominant factor. Economic rationality does not *per se* exclude people (some economists and managers arguing in favour of immigrant rights), but the closure of bureaucratic hierarchies does. The positivist belief in the effectiveness of law as a means to regulate society—Max Weber's "iron cage of rationalism"—seems to me the more dangerous development. An explanation for that can be found in the homology of bureaucratic structures (and also of police and military forces) and the structure of authoritarian and nationalist parties and organizations. Nationalists and right-wing parties are very much in favor of a strong hierarchical organization of society following in more or less modernized fashion the fascist model of the militarily organized state where if everything is kept under control all insecurities will be minimized.

USING THE "CULTURAL CONTRADICTIONS OF CAPITALISM"

As Karl Polanyi believed and also experienced personally, the anti-individualistic character of both fascism and communist bureaucracy was a source of danger to personal freedom and justice. But utilitarian individualists espouse moral standards that are too modest and themselves act too opportunistically to be able to be a directing force of resistance. Markets are flexible enough to cope with a variety of regulations, and they function as an innovative counterpart to the inflexible structures of bureaucracy. Only a strongly expressive individualist culture can exert a positive influence on the openness of society. With its distinctive emphasis on personal freedom and equality, and its principle of voluntary association, such a culture could act as a pluralist countermodel for market and bureaucracy, neither reducing man to the status of simple rationalist economic actor not taking hierarchies as given.

In my view, the "rise of radical egalitarianism" (or expressive individualism), such as is feared by conservative critics such as Daniel Bell and Aaron Wildavsky, can have a positive effect on the cultural plurality of society and help to reduce the dominance and rigidity of established institutions. The "Cultural Contradictions of Capitalism" have to be utilized as a potential for change, in order to control globalized capitalism and national bureaucracy. Liberal utilitarianism ought to be recognized as one way of life amongst others, not as a universal ideal. As such it would play a limited functional—not a dominant—role. To conclude on an optimistic note, I am convinced that the current nationalistic and neopopulist counterreaction against individualism in either form represents no more than a counterreaction against a slow but steady process of "reflexive modernization."[27]

To return to Polanyi again, the "ultimate resignation" we may observe nowadays in political apathy and general disenchantment with established politics, and with the inability of the market to stabilize societies, can pave the way for positive, if perhaps chaotic development, once its critical potential towards markets and bureaucracies can be articulated and channelled in politically effective ways. Nevertheless, it could end disastrously if we forget Polanyi's word to the effect that the constant struggle for the removal of unfreedom and injustice will require "indomitable courage and strength."

NOTES

1. Max Horkheimer and Theodor W. Adorno, *Dialectic of Enlightenment*. New York: Seabury Press, 1972; originally published in 1944.
2. Karl Polanyi, *The Great Transformation: Political And Economic Origins of our Times*. Boston: Beacon Press, 1957; originally published in 1944.
3. Robert N. Bellah, *et al.*, *Habits of the Heart. Individualism and Commitment in American Life*. Berkeley: University of California Press, 1985. Bellah identifies the manager and the psychotherapist as the ideal types of utilitarian and expressive individualism.
4. Frank Parkin, "Strategies of Social Closure and Class Formation," in Frank Parkin, (ed.), *The Social Analysis of Class Structure*. London: Tavistock, 1974, pp. 1-18.
5. Charles Taylor, (ed.), *Multiculturalism and the Politics of Recognition*. Princeton: Princeton University Press, 1992.
6. Alexis de Tocqueville, *Democracy in America*. New York: Alfred A. Knopf, 1969.
7. Edward Sapir, "Symbolism," in *Encyclopedia of the Social Sciences*. New York: The Macmillan Company, 1930, pp. 492-495.
8. Murray Edelman, *Politics as Symbolic Action. Mass Arousal and Quiescence*. Chicago: Marham, 1971.

9. Mancur Olson, *The Logic of Collective Action. Public Goods and the Theory of Groups.* Cambridge: Harvard University Press, 1965.
10. Michael J. Sandel, "The Procedural Republic and the Unencumbered Self," *Political Theory*, 1, 1984, pp.81-96.
11. Daniel Bell, *The Cultural Contradictions of Capitalism.* New York: Basic Books, 1976.
12. Aaron Wildavsky, "Choosing Preferences by Constructing Institutions: A Cultural Theory of Preference Formation," *American Political Science Review*, 1, 1987, pp.3-21.
13. Cf. Harry G. Frankfurt, "Freedom of Will and the Concept of a Person," *The Journal of Philosophy*, 1, 1971, 5-20. Amartya Sen, "Choice, Orderings and Morality," in S. Körner, (ed.), *Practical Reason.* Oxford: Oxford University Press, 1974, pp.54-67.
14. Jürgen Habermas, *Theorie des kommunikativen Handelns.* 2 vols. Frankfurt/Main: Suhrkamp, 1981.
15. Nancy Fraser, *Widerspenstige Praktiken. Macht, Diskurs, Geschlecht.* Frankfurt/Main: Suhrkamp, 1994.
16. Gary S. Becker, *A Treatise on the Family.* Cambridge, Mass. & London: Harvard University Press, 1981.
17. Mary Douglas and Aaron Wildavsky, *Risk and Culture. An Essay on the Selection of Technical and Environmental Dangers.* Berkeley, Los Angeles & London: University of California Press, 1982, p. 83.
18. Michael Thompson, *Rubbish Theory: The Creation and Destruction of Value.* Oxford: Oxford University Press, 1979.
19. Aaron Wildavsky, *The Rise of Radical Egalitarianism.* Washington: American University Press, 1991.
20. Walter L. Bühl, *Kulturwandel. Für eine dynamische Kultursoziologie.* Darmstadt: Wissenschaftliche Buchgesellschaft, 1987, p.70.
21. Alasdair MacIntyre, *Whose Justice? Which Rationality?* Notre Dame: University of Notre Dame Press, 1988, p. 361.
22. Wolf-Dietrich Bukow. *Leben in der multikuturellen Gesellschaft. Die Entstehung kleiner Unternehmer und der Umgang mit ethnischen Minderheiten.* Opladen: Westdeutscher Verlag, 1993.
23. C. Wright Mills, *The Power Elite.* New York: Oxford University Press, 1959.
24. Cf. Oliver Schmidtke and Carlo E. Ruzza, "Regionalistischer Protest als 'Life Politics.' Die Formierung einer sozialen Bewegung: die Lega Lombarda," *Soziale Welt*, 1, 1993, pp.5-29.
25. Edward C. Banfield, *The Moral Basis of a Backward Society.* New York: Free Press, 1958.
26. Rainer Bauböck, *Transitional Citizenship: Membership and Rights in International Migration.* Aldershot: Edward Elgar, 1995.
27. Ulrich Beck, *Risikogesellschaft. Auf dem Weg in eine andere Moderne.* Frankfurt/Main: Suhrkamp, 1986.

Chapter Sixteen

THE CONSTITUTION OF WORK TIME
Reinhard Pirker

At first glance the concept of work time would not seem to merit further elucidation. Everybody knows—if nothing else—that work time is that part of one's life which is used to earn one's living. Yet in the literature on economic and social history the attentive reader will find indications that those socio-structural conditions which make work time possible are found only in modern societies. We will look at the literature on pre-modern traditional societies in order to show that the concept of disposable time—which people can use for different purposes and which can be classed as leisure or work time—is the result of a historical development which has led to the establishment of modern society. Following a historical section containing some basic considerations about the constitution of work time, there will come a discussion of methodological individualism. From the perspective that work time is a structural characteristic of modern society we reject the claim that methodological individualism ought to be the predominant explanation of social phenomena. The shortcomings of this approach will be demonstrated with reference to three central issues which always emerge when methodologically individualist concepts are employed.

TIME AND ECONOMY IN THE TRADITIONAL WORLD
A poem of the 12th century says that everything which is changing loses its value.[1] One might wonder in what kind of world such a statement would be meaningful.

Obviously, this statement is nonsense in our contemporary modern world given the change in our understanding of time. In the religiously inspired conception of time of the Middle Ages there existed an identity of present and eternity. The present did not have an independent existence in people's awareness of time. There was no difference between experienced duration (history) and action itself. Thus the crusaders believed that they were not punishing the descendants of the executioners of Christ, but the executioners themselves.[2] The past event was held to determine the present to such a degree that the idea did not even occur to them that time has elapsed in the meantime, suggesting that there was no sharp distinction between past, present and future.

According to the Christian view of "Genesis," time does not belong to human beings but to God who created it and with this act invested His time in every creation.[3] In this sense time was the God-given substance of nature and humanity. Thus it would be pointless and impossible to measure the time of objects (whether human or natural) by a third, for instance, a clock.

Similarly it was sinful not to use one's time for the God-given purposes which were defined by the Church. It was a still worse offence to use the time of others for that. This substantialist interpretation of time did not allow for notions of time as something man disposes of; quite consistently then, the economic use of time was banned, the taking of interest and commerce being regarded as illicit activities. "Time is merely a moment of eternity, it belongs to God alone and human beings may only live in it. It is a sin to grasp or measure it, to derive advantage or gain from it; it is theft to weigh even the smallest moment."[4] Again and again clerical and theological treatises inveigh against commerce and merchants. It was a dogmatic certainty that merchants could not enter the heavenly kingdom because they violated the sacral norms: usury is a "sin against time (*contra tempus*), for what is being sold is the time that must be shared by all."[5] The Church dubbed as "usury" credit which was granted only with interest.

The religiously founded conceptions of order which were controlled and transmitted by the Church managed to bind together in a spiritual community the most diverse activities and institutions; they provided both social position and natural location which were not to be altered. It followed that traders moving from one locality to another were not accorded a natural place, and thus their activity could not but violate traditional principles of order. Christian dogma could refer to conceptions of order in antiquity, because Aristotle had been opposed to trade which he regarded as dangerous for the *oikos* and the polis.[6] After all, the leading Christian dogmatist Thomas Aquinas was an interpreter of Aristotle.

Returning to the conception of time, which of its specific relations supported the prohibition of interest to the medieval traditional ways of householding? The medieval European *oikos* economies in kind encompassed, in addition to several generations of blood relations, also all the male and female servants. This social form of *oikos* was virtually the only one in existence; even the nobility practised only a further expanded, larger variant of this household system.[7] Production and consumption were not separated in the *oikos*. Distribution was regulated by a hierarchical social structure. The father or head of the *oikos* (despot) had absolute power over its members, but he also had to care for them. He is not to be understood as a rational planner of the production and consumption of goods, but as ruler of the members of the *oikos* and its land.[8] His power to dispose of them was not regulated in the spirit of a private right of ownership. Private appropriation played no part in the *oikos* as a solidary and protectionist association. The social relations of the entire household were not secured by contracts between the members either, but rested upon ceremonial acts, upon reciprocity.[9]

In its central areas of functioning, the *oikos* was subordinated to sacral norms. It did not engage in trade intentionally; when it did engage in trade, it did so in order to exchange unplanned surpluses with the result that ultimately the self-sufficiency of the *oikos* would be strengthened. Time was not used economically. Once a level of subsistence was reached, labour was not expanded. In the absence of any separating of production from consumption within the *oikos*, the amount of labour required of each was defined culturally via the principle of just subsistence which guaranteed a livelihood differentiated according to one's social station. Collective work was geared towards concrete, temporally discontinuous tasks. It was not directed according to chronometric sections of time, nor was the beginning or the end of such work fixed chronologically. There existed no separation of work from leisure time, since work was not structurally distinguished as a distinct, independent part of life.[10] The beginning and the end of work were embedded in ceremonial acts which differed in accordance with local customs.

Work and life in the *oikos* required neither an exact chronology nor exact chronometrics. Sufficient for this form of social life was an awareness of time characterized by the cycles of planting and harvest. Waiting for the cyclical return of natural events as an integral part of the labour process pointed to the special meaning of planning behaviour in traditional economies. Planning in the sense of establishing stocks that would last until the next harvest did not amount to planning a future which was open in principle. It did not topicalize the future at all, since only past events were being repeated and traditions imitated. For this reason one must sharply distinguish between planning by keeping goods to be physical consumed from saving in modern societies which accumulates commodities for future production processes. In traditional societies the farming population experienced time cyclically and as bound to natural events. The Church integrated cyclical time within a sacral context. The natural rhythm of the passing year was adjusted to Christian liturgy. The year of the Church symbolized the periodical return of the birth, suffering, death and resurrection of Christ. By means of holidays (almost every third day was a holiday), work prohibitions or fasting prescriptions the sacral character of time was evoked and re-evoked, the history of salvation being symbolized in the yearly cycle. In this sense the farmer's life was geared towards the sacral frame of reference.[11]

THE LINEARIZATION OF THE SOCIAL TIME STRUCTURE AND THE DISCOVERY OF WORK TIME: WORK TIME AS A STRUCTURAL CHARACTERISTIC OF MODERN SOCIETY

The influence of the cyclical conception of time that traditional economies made do with was weakened by the dualization of the concept of time in the Christian doctrine, especially by St. Augustine. Yet there are reasons to believe that the problems which occupied him were not those which concerned the farming population of the *oikos*. In discussing the conception of time in antiquity St. Augustine was led to the conclusion that time is also the creation of God. God himself is timeless (eternal); He created the world from nothing, and thus determined its beginning (and end). The cyclical conception of time in antiquity was still connected with a certain independent trend of the world for cyclical and thus aimless renewal; thus St. Augustine's conception of teleological history was directed against this old idea of the independence of the world. According to him, all events strive towards the kingdom of God. The cyclical conception of time in antiquity with its aimless renewal of the world was opposed by St. Augustine's postulation of dual time, earthly and divine. Eternity and time were qualitatively different for him, since he was interested in history as a process: "For how could uncounted centuries pass which You did not create, You being the author and creator of all centuries."[12] Thus no "then" could have existed when there was as yet no time.

With the construction of such a dual notion of time, the essential step towards the linearization of time[13] was taken. This can be demonstrated as well by reference to the problem of sin, of individual accountability. Sin presupposes the idea of the temporal direction of past and present. It can be forgiven after confession, but it cannot be undone. What is past must here be understood in a sense of time separate from the present which establishes guilty behaviour. This indicates that it was imperative to date the lapse. The problem of sin is thus shifted away from the concreteness of matters of fact to the dimension of time.[14] Even this religious foundation of time remains an obstacle to thinking of time as something human beings can dispose of, however, since earthly time was still subordinated, as with St. Augustine, to the end of time which brings salvation.

History became open for earthly problems from the 12th century onwards. To mention only one theoretician, Joachim of Fiore, it may seem that with him the decisive point consisted in a new way of viewing the future: namely, not by denial of earthly conditions, but by focussing on perfecting them. Such perfection does not take place in the beyond which transcends time (and space) as St. Augustine still taught, but in a future of earthly time. By allowing for an earthly future of the world, the sacral reference to eternity was suspended and thus lost its normative role. The disembeddedness of time from the teleology of the history of salvation is thus theoretically postulated.[15] The concept of purgatory as a place of purification was also introduced in the 12th century, thus integrating historically datable and measurable segments of time into the eschatological time of the beyond. It can be shown by reference to medieval texts that the time to be spent in purgatory could be calculated according to how grievous the sins were. Thus even in the beyond there was developing a kind of time as the object of estimation and comparison, a bookkeeping of the beyond.[16]

The religious foundation of medieval culture had given to the old traditional social forms the function of safeguarding the present. The life of the *oikos* was culturally buttressed by the temporal cycle. But the traditional social form of the *oikos* with its cyclical time orientation increasingly yielded to another form, namely that of commerce.[17] The establishment of markets demanded greater coordination, and the dimension of time thus gained a central ordering function. Activities had to be sequentialized and synchronized. The professional orientation of the trader pointed to a linearized understanding of time, because term-oriented activity can only be identified if the course of time is thought of as an irreversible linear axis on which points in time can be marked.[18] Markets constantly topicalize the future for the agents (the merchants). This presupposes an experience of the divergence of past and future which is incomprehensible given a cyclical understanding of time focussed on the return of the same. The functioning of markets demands a radical revision of the traditional orientation in time. The old, the traditional can no longer be assumed to safeguard the present, for with the discovery of space and the importance of the length of trade routes for the speed of turnover on capital invested, the merchant needs a way of precisely calculating time, as well as a clear separation of the temporal horizons of past, present and future. The merchant's activity in the clear and true sense is characterized by great foresight.[19] The linearized time consciousness of the merchant had emancipated itself from St. Augustine's perspective of history as salvation according to which all events find teleological fulfilment in the kingdom of God. The most reliable indicator of this emancipation was the calculation with which business was conducted. Historically it was the merchant who dicovered the disposability of time and thus opened the future for earthly purposes. Since then, modern society can be distinguished from traditional society by the discovery of objectifiable, datable, measurable, divisible time in a dimension differentiated from that of objects or social facts.

The merchant discovered the disposability of time—but not only that. He also became aware of the time of others: to be precise, the work time of others. Basic to the constitution of work time is a process which has entered into the literature under the heading of proto-industrialization[20] or industrialization before industrialization.[21] Proto-industrialization refers to the rapid increase of commercial commodity production in rural areas which was central to the process of the transformation of traditional European agrarian societies into industrial capitalist ones.

In spite of the fact that the proto-industrial work force was bound to the household, its integration into supra-regional labour markets being thus prevented—so that one cannot yet speak of fully formed labour markets and real wage-labour systems—proto-industrialization nevertheless destroyed the *oikos* as such. The proto-industrial household no longer produced only for its own use but for intermediate merchants who sent its products to the market. While the proto-industrial family remained partly bound to agrarian subsistence forms, it nevertheless lost its self-sufficiency through the establishment of a rural division of labour between farming and a cottage industry.[22] Under the new system the producers no longer operated according to the traditional mode. "They say in their own language that we must tie the threads for others."[23]

By the determination of pay and delivery dates through the system of cottage industry there was established a work week that was independent of the yearly cycle. Such a work week was distinguished from the work rhythm of the farmer; but traditional task-oriented time consciousness did not completely yield to the new date-oriented time consciousness in the minds of the producers, because it was still within the power of those who worked in the proto-industrial household to determine the amount of labour power they expended. Even though the rhythm of work had to follow pay and delivery dates, determining the duration and the temporal location of the workday were left to the producers themselves. Periods of very intensive work were followed by periods of great leisure. Criteria from the traditional culture continued to partially determine the basic work pattern (Monday absenteeism) and task-oriented labour continued to dominate.[24] All the same, the destruction of the *oikos* during proto-industrialization created the decisive socio-structural conditions for subsequent changes: labour power could become a commodity due to its being uncoupled from its traditional basis of reproduction, therewith also leading to the isolation of work time from the unified conduct of life in the household. This means at the same time that at the basis of the constitution of work time there is a social process which concerns the disposition of others' labour and the time of which others' lives are composed.

The use of life time as work time was finally accomplished by the process of real industrialization which broke resistance on the part of the traditional work force against the constituting of their life time as work time. This required the educational impact of work houses, schools, the military, manufacture and factories. Historically, this learning process has to be viewed as comprehensive disciplining which enforced a new work ethic (punctuality and hard work) as well as new standards of movement, behaviour and effort.[25] This learning process was stimulated by the fact that labour power had become a commodity, which presupposed that the life time of an individual could be divided and part of it placed at the disposition of a buyer. The apportioning of life time required a sharp distinction between work time and leisure time which reflected the concentration of work forces in the unit of the company quite apart from the household. Fully developed modern society which depends on labour markets is characterized by strict time keeping and the separation of work and life.[26] Given the existence of labour markets and firms, the linearization of time can be considered complete and finally dominant due to its role for modern social structures: work time can be viewed as a structural characteristic of modern society.

THE CONSTITUTION OF WORK TIME: SOME METHODOLOGICAL CONCLUSIONS
Work time is not an a-historical category. It did not evolve until the process of the Great Transformation[27] which marks the shift from the agrarian societies of the Middle Ages to modern society. In the traditional *oikos* economy, work time was not an independent category, working and living were not separated. It was only possible to think meaningfully of work time once labour markets were established: this may be taken as a structural characteristic of modern society. The process of the constitution of work time as described above will now serve as a point of departure for some considerations in which the claim to primacy of methodological individualism is critically examined. The concept of methodological individualism seems to have been coined by Schumpeter,[28] as is confirmed by Machlup[29] and Blaug.[30] It only became commonly used after Ludwig von Mises based a general study of economic behaviour on the implications of this concept.[31] Three central issues surface again and again, though weighted differently, in connection with methodologically individualist concepts. In dealing with these issues the point here is to reject the supposedly general and exclusive validity of such concepts for theory construction in social science.[32]

SOCIAL ATOMISM AS COMMONPLACE
At issue here is the idea that it is virtually a matter of course to explain social phenomena exclusively by reference to the behaviour of individuals, since it is not possible to understand them other than by understanding the actions of individuals.[33] Thus methodological individualism is said to express the principle and irrevocable insight that "all actions are performed by individuals" and that "a social collective has no existence and reality outside of the individual members' actions."[34] Von Mises also presupposes that analysis of social phenomena requires that every action be undertaken consciously and purposively.

This thesis is actually a commonplace, a banality even. Generalizations in the social sciences probably always presuppose the intentional activity of human agents and must refer to it at least implicitly. Yet theories in the social sciences which claim general validity and never ascend to the level of action must be regarded with scepticism. For instance, Thompson accused the structuralist Althusser that he dealt wholly inadequately with human behaviour by interpreting human beings only as bearers of modes of production and denying a role to their conscious purposes.[35] Similarly, I would not wish to insist that my interpretation of work time as a structural characteristic of modern society renders wholly determinate or even obsolete individual actions. Within certain limits, labour markets still allow for alternatives, for intentional decisions as to how to divide time between labour and leisure. Nevertheless, it certainly does make sense to speak of a social structure, as will be shown below.

THE REDUCTION OF ALL STATEMENTS ABOUT SOCIAL PHENOMENA TO GIVEN CHARACTERISTICS OF INDIVIDUALS

This point of view denies that talk of social structure makes any sense at all, given that it does little more than group together the characteristics of individuals. Methodological individualists describe their method as composite or synthetic. Social wholes can only be constructed or reconstructed from the known properties of their elements.[36] It is a method of theory construction which starts from given elements (individuals) and explains the structure of social institutions in terms of a pyramidal structure. Every element is determined by those on which it depends. Once some of the elements have been put together, their characters cannot be changed when the structures building on them are expanded. Research proceeds in but one direction: the macrostructure can only be explained by the individual micro-elements, the whole only by its parts. There is no feedback. The composite method is used not only by the Austrian School, but is of great importance for the whole of mainstream economics which accepts macro-economic statements only if they rest on micro-economic foundations.[37] Indeed, there are demands that macro-economics should be reduced entirely to micro-economics, which would make it a mere epiphenomenon of the latter.

This game can be played in the opposed direction too, of course. One might mention the methodological imperative to build micro-economics on macro-economic foundations, including social institutions and culture as well, such as some post-Keynesians subscribe to.[38] Instead, one might follow Arthur Koestler, for whom parts and wholes exist nowhere in an absolute sense, neither in the realm of living organisms nor in the domain of social organizations: "What we find are intermediary structures on a series of levels in an ascending order of complexity: sub-wholes which display, depending on the way you look at them, some of the characteristics commonly attributed to wholes and some of the characteristics commonly attributed to parts."[39]

Returning to the topic of work time, we may observe that when, for example, a certain division of work and leisure time is selected, and analysis refers exclusively to this (rational) act of choice, then it would not be possible to take into consideration what this choice presupposes: namely, not only an individual preference but also a social structure which makes the division of life time into work and leisure time possible at all. That this was not possible in traditional society and was not a requirement for the reproduction of the *oikos* is well established by socio-historical research (see section 2 above). It was only in modern market-based society that time became a measurable and divisible quantity, socio-structurally differentiated and accessible as a commodity to trade on labour markets. This presupposes a social process of the linearization of time which is historically connected to the destruction of the *oikos* and the establishment of labour markets (see section 3 above). This means that actions related to work time can only be interpreted as individual and intentional once there exists such a modern social structure in which time has become available as a parameter. The individual act of choosing a particular work time cannot socially produce work time as such. In this sense it is plausible to speak of a social structure which precedes the individual agents.

THE EXOGENEITY OF PREFERENCES AND THE EXPLANATION OF SPONTANEOUS FORMATION OF PURPOSES

Even though methodological individualists do not go so far as to claim that external factors do not figure in an explanation of human behaviour, they nevertheless treat them in a peculiar fashion. They take it as given that individuals confront the external world and react to it by perceiving their limitations and possibilities. They do not systematically take into account the process of perception as being influenced through cultural and socio-psychological mechanisms, and of the genesis of the individual as such. The question of how an individual's taste evolves is commonly neglected by assuming that it does not in fact change. An individual's utility functions are considered invariable and are thus not discussed. Methodological individualists assume explicitly or implicitly that all discernible changes in taste rest on simple and fundamental utility functions. Individual purposes and preferences are basic and all statements must refer exclusively to these supposed constants. Stigler and Becker fortunately formulated this with inimitable audacity: "De gustibus non est disputandum."[40]

Due to the continuing tendency on the part of orthodox economists especially to take the preferences and purposes of individuals as givens, it cannot be stressed too much that institutions are not only important as limitations upon individual action but that one cannot assume that it is only individuals that act upon institutions through the pursuit of their goals. For institutions are also important for individual action in that they influence the formation of goals. Factors like institutional structure or routine, given norms, and general culture influence not only individual actions themselves but also the interpretation of the world and the goals according to which human beings orient themselves.

Von Mises and Hayek explicitly reject psychological explanations of set purposes within the framework of economic theory. In keeping with their a priori construct of the rational individual, goal-oriented action need not be explained—in the economic domain it simply happens.[41] L.M. Lachmann, a scholarly interpreter of Hayek, has entered the discussion by arguing that the explanation of action need not go beyond von Mises and Hayek. He distinguishes between goals and plans on the one hand, and motives on the other, and accepts that motives may be determined by psychological processes. Yet he also grants that plans often emerge spontaneously and thus could not be the outgrowth of something preexisting.[42] It is of course acceptable in social science analyses to assume a certain level of spontaneity and indeterminacy in the formation of expectations and plans.[43] But for Lachmann this is reason enough to exclude consideration of any systemic influence on the part of the external world on the formation of individual purposes and plans.

J. Elster is a leading social scientific methodologist who in "Sour Grapes" convincingly attacks the basic conceptual structure of the utilitarian ends-means framework.[44] His arguments focus on the formation of goals—in Elster's terms, adaptive preference formation. The fox who cannot reach the tempting grapes which hang too high for him declares them to be unripe. Elster interprets this as a means-dependent preference change in the direction of an attainable final state as a consequence of a futile attempt to attain gratification. The reduction of all behaviour to a decisive preference function which determines all acts of choice in the course of time is in any case an extreme claim, since the assumption must also be upheld that this preference function is conceived as individually immanent. If, however, the possibility of adaptive preference formation or endogenously imposed preference change is allowed for, then the individual can no longer be considered as autonomous and inviolable. The orthodox credo that the individual constitutes the given and irreducible unit of analysis should be abandoned, since the occurrance of adaptive preferences could result in a trade-off between autonomy and welfare.[45] It is obvious that the linear structure of time with its irreversible processes so characteristic of modern society (see section 3) constantly demands such a preference adaption. The assumption of exogenous preferences must therefore be rejected as most implausible.[46]

NOTES

1. A.J. Gurjewitsch, *Das Weltbild des mittelalterlichen Menschen*. Munich: Bech, 1978, p. 128.
2. J. Le Goff, *Kultur des europaeischen Mittelalters*. Munich, 1970, p. 293.
3. G. Dux, *Strukturwandel der Legitimation*. Freiburg, 1976, p. 121.
4. Le Goff, 1970, p. 281.
5. W. Forster, "Der Heilige Johannes von Capestrano und die soziale Frage," *Franziskanische Studien* 35, 1953, p.8.
6. In this sense Aristotle defined every object twice according to its use. "The first use is unique to the thing, the other is not. An example of uses is the wearing of a shoe and its being used as an object of exchange. On both occasions the shoe is being used. Even he uses the shoe, but not for its unique qualities, who trades it for money or food with someone who needs it, since it was not made for trading." (Aristotle, *Politics* I, Hamburg: Felix Meiner Verlag, 1978, 1257a, pp.5-13). A shoe is manufactured for a certain purpose (*telos*): namely, to be worn. This de-termination is immanent to the shoe, it alone differentiates it as such from other objects. That a thing can be exchanged for another does not follow from the determination of the essence of the shoe; rather, the imposition of a purpose from without (trade) runs against the intrinsic purpose of the shoe. Thus Aristotle declares such behaviour to be incompatible with the natural order of things and unethical, threatening the order of the *oikos* and the *polis*.
7. O. Brunner, "Das 'ganze Haus' und die alteuropaeische 'Oekonomik'," in O. Brunner, Vendenhoek and Ruprecht, *Neue Wege der Sozialgeschichte*. Goettingen, 1956, p. 40.
8. L. Bauer and H. Matis, *Geburt der Neuzeit. Vom Feudalsystem zur Marktgesellschaft*. Munich: Deutscher Taschenbuch Verlag, 1988, p. 44.
9. C. Meillassoux, "Versuch einer Interpretation des Oekonomischen in den archaischen Subsistenzgesellschaften," in K. Eder, *Seminar: Die Entstehung von Klassen-gesellschaften*. Frankfurt/Main: Surhrkamp, 1973, pp. 35ff.
10. H.W. Hohn, *Die Zerstoerung der Zeit. Wie aus einem goettlichen Gut eine Handelsware wurde*. Frankfurt/Main: Fischer Alternativ Taschenbuch, 1984, pp. 38f.
11. Hohn, 1984, pp. 43 ff.
12. St. Augustine, *Confessions*, XI, 13. Stuttgart: Reclam, 1977.
13. Hohn, 1984, pp. 49 ff.
14. N. Luhmann, *Funktion der Religion*. Frankfurt/Main: Suhrkamp, 1977, p. 164.
15. H. Grundmann, *Studien ueber Joachim von Fiore*. Darmstadt: Wissenschaftliche Buchgesellschaft, 1966.
16. J. Le Goff, *Die Geburt des Fegefeuers*. Stuttgart: Klett-Cotta, 1984, p. 278.
17. Bauer and Matis, 1988, pp. 99 ff. and 232 ff.
18. Hohn, 1984, p.90.
19. E. Maschke, "Das Bewusstsein des mittelalterlichen Fernkaufmanns," in P. Wilpert, *Beitraege zum Berufsbewusstsein des mittelalterlichen Menschen*. Berlin: de Gruyter, 1964, p. 315.
20. F.F. Mendels, "Proto-Industrialization. The First Phase of the Industrialization Process," *Journal of Economic History* 32, 1972, pp.241-261.
21. P. Kriedte, H. Medick, and J. Schlumbohm, *Industrialisierung vor der Industrialisierung. Gewerbliche Warenproduktion auf dem Land in der Formationsperiode des Kapitalismus*. Goettingen: Vandenhoek & Ruprecht, 1978.
22. W. Sombart, "Die Hausindustrie in Deutschland," *Archiv fuer soziale Gesetzgebung und Statistik* 4, 1891, pp.103-156.
23. Schwerz, 1836, p. 110, quoted in Hohn, 1984, p. 116.
24. E.P. Thompson, "Zeit, Arbeitsdisziplin und Industriekapitalismus," in E.P. Thompson, *Plebeische Kultur und moralische Oekonomie*. Frankfurt/Main: Ullstein, 1980, pp.44ff.
25. Bauer and Matis, 1988, pp. 315 ff.
26. Thompson, 1980, p. 61.
27. K. Polanyi, *The Great Transformation. Politische und oekonomische Urspruenge von Gesellschaften und Wirtschaftssystemen*. Wien: Suhrkamp, 1977.

28. J.A. Schumpeter, *Das Wesen und der Hauptinhalt der theoretischen Nationaloekonomie*. Leipzig: Duncker & Humblot, 1908, pp. 88ff.
29. F. Machlup, *Methodology of Economics and Other Social Sciences*. London: Academic Press, 1978, p. 454.
30. M. Blaug, *The Methodology of Economics. Or How Economists Explain*. Cambridge: Cambridge University Press, 1980, p. 49.
31. L. von Mises, *Human Action. A Treatise on Economics*. New Haven: Yale University Press, 1949.
32. *Cf*. S. Lukes, "Methodological Individualism Reconsidered," in S. Lukes, *Essays in Social Theory*. London: Routledge and Kegan, 1977; A. Giddens, *Die Konstitution der Gesellschaft. Grundzuege einer Theorie der Strukturierung*. Frankfurt/Main, New York: Campus, 1988, pp.271 ff.; G.M. Hodgson, *Economics and Institutions. A Manifesto for a Modern Institutional Economics*. Cambridge: Polity Press, 1988, pp. 53 ff.
33. F.A. Hayek, *Individualismus und wirtschaftliche Ordnung*. Salzburg: Neugebauer, 1976; M. Weber, *Wirtschaft und Gesellschaft*. Tuebingen: Mohr, 1985.
34. *Cf*. von Mises, 1949, p. 42.
35. E.P. Thompson, *Das Elend der Theorie. Zur Produktion geschichtlicher Erfahrung*. Frankfurt/Main, New York: Campus, 1980, p. 207.
36. F.A. Hayek, *The Counter-Revolution of Science*. Glencoe: Free Press, 1952, p. 39.
37. Blaug, 1980.
38. See S.C. Dow, *Macroeconomic Thought. A Methodological Approach*. Oxford: Basil Blackwell, 1985.
39. A. Koestler, *The Ghost in the Machine*. London: Hutchinson, 1967, p. 65.
40. G.J. Stigler and G.S. Becker, "De gustibus non est disputandum," *The American Economic Review* 67, 1977, 76-90.
41. *Cf*. von Mises, 1949, pp. 11ff.; Hayek, 1952, p. 39.
42. L. M. Lachmann, "Methodological Individualism and the Market Economy," in E. Streissler, *Roads to Freedom. Essays in Honour of Friedrich A. von Hayek*. London: Routledge and Kegan, 1969, pp. 93f.
43. It is interesting in this context to note that the validity of a certain level of spontaneity for the formation of grounds of action was also demanded by the unorthodox Left. Rosa Luxemburg, for instance, attacked the Leninist model of organization for its "socialism of decrees," for underestimating the political force of spontaneous strikes. R. Luxemburg, *Politische Schriften II*. Frankfurt/Main, New York: Suhrkamp, 1969, p. 190.
44. J. Elster, *Subversion der Rationalitaet*. Frankfurt/Main, New York: Campus, 1987, pp. 211ff.
45. Elster, 1987, p. 240. To be fair, we must stress that Elster would not agree with the conclusion that individualism as a methodological motive must be given up. Elster discusses the possibility of evading the trade-off between autonomy and welfare by having recourse to learning and being informed. Does the new situation lead to the revelation of true preferences, or is there a forced fundamental change of the preference function which violates autonomy? If a person who previously preferred city life to country life decides to live in the country after she has learnt about that life, then one could say that the preference change rests on a foundation of information and experience and need not be related to meta-preferences. The problem would seem to be Elster's undeveloped concept of experience-based preference change. (For a critique of Elster's retention of methodological individualism and his rejection of functionalism in social science. See R. Pirker, *Zeit, Macht und Oekonomie. Zur Konstitution und Gestaltbarkeit von Arbeitszeit*. Frankfurt/Main, New York: Campus, 1992, pp. 17ff.
46. In this connection one should point also to the attempt made by the German sociologist Luhmann to interpret actions as counter-movements to the "self-annihilation of time" (N. Luhmann, "Zeit und Handlung. Eine vergessene Theorie," *Zeitschrift für Soziologie* 8,1979, 63-81). He in turn builds partly on the forgotten theory of the Marquis de Vauvenargues. For Vauvenargues it is not the motivational situation of an agent that explains the action in causal terms. Instead, action is deduced from the necessity to reproduce the present at every moment: it would not be without consequence to ignore the demand of time to escape the disappearance of the present moment, for otherwise one would suffer "ennui," boredom. This relativizes the dominant view which strongly influences the sociological and economic theories of action, namely, that action has to be viewed primarily in relation to a personal bearer or agent. By accepting the primacy of the duality of agent and action, the theory of action is forced to give primary consideration to individual motivation and rationality. The relation between action and time is analyzed as being of only secondary importance: for instance, as the problem of deferred gratification or of decision under conditions of uncertainty or risk. Following the agent/action framework, if the agent acts according to his intentions, then his action is also determined by his temporal horizon, his readiness to take risks and to defer gratification. Nobody would seriously want to dispute that the agent acts according to his intentions, or that only persons could act; but we must also ask whether the necessity to act in order to separate the present from the flow of time does not itself create intentions. A conception which derives action from temporal pressures cannot presuppose motivational situations and preferences as individually given and stable in all cases. Instead, such a conception must postulate the existence of endogenously alterable preferences which can be adapted to the different presents which change with the course of time.

Chapter Seventeen

DEMOCRATIZING CAPITAL: ALTERNATIVES TO MARKET-LED TRANSITION
Marguerite Mendell

The 1980s witnessed critical changes in the Western industrialized economies. The ideological shift to the right which began towards the end of the 1970s and global economic restructuring severely challenged the policy regime of the post-war period. Economic decline and high rates of inflation were largely disassociated from the structural changes underway and misinterpreted as the outcome of an adherence to state intervention and its alleged inherent inefficiencies.

The 1980s were a decade of ideological rectitude and confusion—of rigid commitment to *laissez-faire* combined with poorly conceived improvisations on the part of states forced to respond to crises generated by the new policy regime. One recalls Karl Polanyi's analysis of 19th century liberalism which required legislation, regulation and the development of new institutions to install or impose the free market. These responses, Polanyi's "double movement," were predictable, wrote Polanyi in *The Great Transformation* in 1944.[1] The market economy cannot function without the appropriate institutional framework to prevent social dislocation *and* market failure. The lessons of the 19th century were forgotten in the 1920s and, once again, in the 1980s when the attempt to impose the free market in developed industrial economies resulted in erratic and drastic ad hoc responses. The evangelical commitment to restore a free-market system (as though it had ever existed outside the imagination of its believers) deepened the economic crisis and led to severe distortions, misinterpretation of socio-economic phenomena and inappropriate policy implementation throughout the West. Paradoxically, a period of approximately six years of economic growth, as measured by increasing GNP from 1983-1988 in the U.S., for example, concealed a swelling undercurrent of structural economic decline. Unbridled speculation assisted by the deregulation of financial markets, girded by high interest rates and an ever more precarious service economy produced this hollow growth. Policy makers were unprepared for the catastrophe they had helped to create by dogmatically adhering to a conservative monetarist agenda.

Despite the overwhelmingly negative results—and even some recanting among influential economists and public figures—the schism between this stark reality and the continued belief in the principles underlying conservative economic policy continues. The values, the moral philosophy of the 1980s, have been universally adopted, even by its detractors. The enshrinement of individualism in economics and in contemporary moral philosophy continues to dominate the policy agenda. An economic scorecard is kept principally to track inflation. Although interest rates have come down, the real rate of interest in Canada, for example, remains very high. Economic growth is constrained by this perceived looming threat of unleashed inflation. Chronically high rates of unemployment have become normalized at least in so far as discretionary economic policy is concerned. The result is a combination of structural and endogenous policy-generated unemployment. Cyclical unemployment has virtually disappeared as a phenomenon as have the availability of discretionary tools to cope with this. As governments unravel the post-war social safety net, automatic stabilizers—unemployment insurance, social programs, income maintenance—are also slated to disappear. Not merely the welfare state but also the policy apparatus to mitigate the business cycle are now considered obsolete, part of a supposedly profligate period of prosperity now associated with waste and inefficiency.

It is in this climate that various uncoordinated and seemingly alternative economic strategies have emerged in regions and localities in the West to cope with economic and social decline. In Polanyi's formulation, we are observing several counter-movements—or, we could say, the double movement has been disaggregated to include new forms of intervention which, in many cases, are not state led but may include national, regional or local government as partners in these coping strategies. I deliberately use the term "coping" to distinguish these responses from genuinely alternative means to govern social and economic life which are also emerging and gaining political legitimacy, no doubt because of the repeated failure of governments to reverse economic decline and social decay rather than their genuine endorsement of these alternatives. I believe that this is above all a period of political expediency and that the need to build and consolidate new institutions to firmly ground these alternatives is urgent. They will otherwise remain fragile, marginal and vulnerable whenever their challenge to economic and political orthodoxy will be no longer tolerated.

For the time being, there seems to be an attitude that whatever works, works, and must be supported, if even reluctantly. This is especially true if states are let off the hook and are able to disengage fiscally, as these alternatives seek autonomy to develop democratic economic initiatives based within civil society. I believe it is critical to inject this observation into any analysis of what are otherwise salutary initiatives, which are nevertheless, in many ways, effectively undermining the prevailing approach to social and economic policy. Still, there is great danger in assuming that the alternatives which have emerged and are, indeed, multiplying, represent a transition to a new social order. This is most commonly expressed by those who were influenced by the French Regulation School and its analysis of the transition from Fordism to post-Fordism.[2] By assuming that a new and homogeneous social order is emerging, this analysis not only ignores the unbroken power of central governments, but, worse still, it implies that attention need not be focussed on the national agenda.

I will argue that the struggle to implement alternative economic strategies must be embedded within a sound macroeconomic framework which provides the appropriate economic environment for these initiatives to flourish. This means a continued and vigorous challenge to the prevailing economic agenda. To think globally and act locally as so many have advocated, is implicitly to condemn any democratic, decentralized alternative socio-economic strategies to being no more than an intermediate resolution of the crisis. But if these initiatives are rather viewed as part of a long transition process which will produce new social and economic relationships, they require institutional legitimacy going far beyond their current crisis management role.

FROM SOCIAL ENGINEERING TO NEO-CORPORATISM OR CONCERTATION

The economic crisis of the 1980s produced many important responses within cities and regions throughout the West. Ironically, the promotion of free trade internationally was accompanied by many regionally based partnerships between the private sector, local or regional governments and trade unions, to rescue areas hard hit by deindustrialization and the absence of any coordinated industrial strategy. Many of these experiences were extensively documented both for their success as well as for the unprecedented cooperation between labour and business. Better known examples in the U.S. were the effective bail out of New York City through the sale of municipal bonds, which involved the civic administration and city employees; a social pact (so to speak, since this basically involved the agreement by workers to a wage freeze) reached between Chrysler, the autoworkers and the municipality in Detroit to rescue the auto-maker and protect jobs. In Québec the largest trade union, the Québec Federation of Labour, established a solidarity fund in 1983 (*Fonds de solidarité des travailleurs (euses) de Québec*) to invest in firms located in Québec to create jobs. It was established to provide a needed source of risk capital for small and medium size enterprises. To protect its investors, however, only 40% of the fund was designated as venture capital. It also provided attractive tax incentives for investors. In 1993 the assets of the fund totalled $797.1 million of which approximately one half is invested in small and medium firms in Québec.

This initiative is significant because it marked a new epoch in capital-labour relations in the province of Québec. In contrast with the class antagonisms of the 1960s and 70s which included the imprisonment of the leaders of the three major unions in the province, we were now witnessing "concertation"—a new dialogue between labour, capital and the state at the provincial level, to revitalize the Québec economy.

Although it is beyond the scope of this paper to enter into a detailed discussion of Québec, a few comments are necessary to situate these more current events in context. Unlike the U.S., Canada has a history of state-initiated development programs. Its better known marketing boards, for example, were established to protect the agricultural sector from price fluctuations, this being part of a panoply of income maintenance programs established in the post-war period. As is well known, even unemployment insurance has served to maintain income in many regions of the country where employment is largely seasonal. In Québec, as elsewhere in the country, regional development programs existed. To establish an industrial base in Québec, following the "Quiet Revolution" of the 1960s, the government established a series of programs to promote Québec based enterprises.[3]

Before we discuss the 1980s, the programs and events of the earlier period must be put in relief: when, at the same time that this government maintained a hands-off market image, it was actively engaged in economic development in the province. There was, of course, a difference from the government's previous position. These new programs were part of an industrial "supply side" strategy to create business opportunities which would then, it was assumed, help to reduce unemployment in the province. Moreover, it was also part of a punitive strategy consistent with the dominant neo-liberal agenda which viewed the unemployed as welfare dependents rather than as victims of the downturn. To be fair, personalities in the Québec government, certainly in the latter part of the 1980s, came to distance themselves from free-market discourse and practice, and moved more towards a neo-corporatist program. Still, the central focus was on the need to revitalize the private sector.

This brief background will contribute to an understanding of the current policy agenda in Québec. On the surface, it appears highly complex and fragmented, but is, in reality, a continuation of a coordinated strategy to promote small and medium sized enterprises. To attain this objective, the Québec government has initiated and/or supported the almost exponential growth of investment funds in the province. These have largely been established by key players in the Québec economy, including local and/or provincial governments.[4] What is interesting, from the perspective of this discussion, is the implementation of a credit-driven economic development strategy in which the state, the Québec government, plays a vital role both by contributing finance capital and in determining its allocation. However, an in-depth analysis of these funds reveals that, in many instances, the criteria for access to these funds—whether as equity, grants, loans or participating loans—in some cases are conventional estimates of rates of return without allowing for social benefits which may underestimate the projected return in some cases, or result in a positive estimate where a purely cost/profit calculation does not. Moreover, many of these funds provide additional opportunities for speculation, profit and tax breaks. As such, they cannot be distinguished from conventional investment instruments, even if their stated objectives are otherwise. What is also clear is that an inflexible approach to economic recovery, whatever form it takes, is destined to produce losses as well as gains. The brief history of these funds established to provide risk capital exclusively to small and medium business has documented many losses.[5] Despite this, a credit-driven economic strategy based on partnership between the private and public sectors and the trade union movement has become a significant economic policy tool in Québec.

This particular relationship based on a "concertation" model in Québec is part of the differentiated intervention strategy which is increasingly to be seen in other regions and countries. As Egon Matzner and Wolfgang Streek point out in their Introduction to *Beyond Keynesianism*, current studies show that today different capitalisms are distinguished by the,

> ...role and structure of the *state* and the way in which it intervenes in the economy. Not only do some states intervene more than others, but, perhaps more importantly, the styles and tools, if not the targets of intervention differ greatly, and so do the capacities of states with different institutional

equipment to conduct particular policies and attain specific objectives...Moreover the social networks with which effective institutional, or socio-economic intervention must link up are mostly located on the supply-side, or in the production sphere, where they typically generate and enforce social or communitarian obligations that constrain market individualism.[6]

I quote this at length to situate Québec in this larger context. Each case, of course, will produce different institutional relations grounded in particular cultures and histories. What is common, however, is an overwhelming commitment to the free market and competition despite the awareness that remedial institutional relationships are essential to guide the market, for better or for worse.

There are, however, other social networks which have emerged in the West during this period. This represents further disaggregation at the community or local level. In some cases, we simply observe an expanded role for existing community organisations now actively involved in economic issues. In other cases, new institutional relations have been created similar to the "concertation" model above but at an even more decentralized level. There is a significant difference here, however. Unlike the neo-corporatist relations observed in Québec and elsewhere, which have by and large replaced conflict with conciliation and cooperation, the economic agenda of communities, which are also examples of new partnerships, are, I believe, more vulnerable if the state assumes too prominent a role. In these cases, the struggle to build autonomous institutions becomes greater since the state regards itself as beneficent and, therefore, more prominent than in the concertation model where it more generally serves the private sector and its initiatives.

I turn to this now because the struggle for democratizing the market is being waged here. The issue is more than one of embedding the market in a new set of social relations which are basically market driven. It represents an economic strategy from below, determined and shaped by the needs and aspirations of communities and built on the capacities of their citizens. It is these experiences which, I believe, are relevant to economies in transition in Eastern Europe where market-driven economic strategies continue to produce severe hardship for many and risk destroying the creative potential of people discouraged by an approach which is prepared to accept deep economic and social insecurity as a necessary and inevitable cost of economic transformation.

WHAT IS THE LINK?

In a recent article, János Simon presents the results of a survey conducted in 1989, 1990 and 1993 in Hungary on the meaning of democracy to the population.[7] In 1993, in addition to freedom, respondents added material well-being and a right to employment to their definition of democracy. Thus the meaning of democracy now includes a significant material dimension. The author concludes that without the implementation of a comprehensive social policy to improve the lives of Hungarians, social tensions will mount. This is certainly true. However, there are also possibilities within civil society which are rarely considered and which must be explored and encouraged, as well as relevant experiences in the West which may serve as helpful guides. The blueprint for democracy has thus far failed because it has been equated solely with the establishment of the free market. Similar failures abound in the West, witness rising rates of unemployment and poverty throughout the industrialized economies. The social damage has, to some extent, been contained because it is not easy to quickly dismantle the welfare state, thereby leaving a measure of social protection in place even if it is under attack. However, as the assault on these institutions in the West deepens, the number of disenfranchised individuals grows.

The West has spawned a new underclass, excluded from productive economic life. Neo-corporatist or industrial strategies will not reach this community in an environment committed to punitive social legislation at worst or to ad hoc labour market policies at best. The events of 1989 across Eastern Europe and the former Soviet Union were to have resulted in the convergence of both East and West towards a free market economy. Instead, there has been convergence of a different kind: in neither the East nor the West are markets free; social engineering has yielded to managed economies; both societies are faced with increasingly disenfranchised populations.

COMMUNITY ECONOMIC DEVELOPMENT: A DEMOCRATIC ALTERNATIVE TO "THE GRIM HYDRAULICS OF TRICKLE-DOWN ECONOMICS"[8]

I would like to return to the "whatever works, works" aphorism—the politics of expediency to which I referred earlier. I do so to explain why alternative economic development strategies are enjoying a new and widespread legitimacy throughout the West. However, even this must not be exaggerated. Community economic development in its various manifestations is receiving a great deal of attention, it is true. At the political level, it is being accommodated, at best. In this regard, the state does not act as a social partner; its role varies from providing beneficent ad hoc support—financial and/or institutional—to legislating new community-based institutions. I refer here especially to the recent establishment of community banks in the U.S. and government backed community investment funds in Canada (in the form of bonds or government guaranteed loans, for example). These are, indeed, significant initiatives on the part of governments which are recognizing the discrimination faced by communities unable to secure finance either through conventional bank loans or through the many new financial intermediaries (in Québec, for example) which are not available for small projects. In fact, a very interesting question arises in a comparative analysis of what we may call differentiated state intervention. Why would one region in Canada, for example, follow a neo-corporatist industrial strategy which largely ignores micro initiatives at the community level, while another develops the appropriate legal apparatus to serve these types of economic initiatives?

I believe the answer lies in what Matzner and Streek refer to as the "different institutional equipment" of regions, or what might be more broadly seen as different political cultures. Such a comparative analysis would assist in understanding why, in this environment of "whatever works, works," there remain priorities that can only be explained through culture and established institutions. The role of the state in regions embarking on new initiatives could then, to at least a limited extent, be predicted. Similarly, cohesive communities with a shared history would be more likely to develop a common economic development strategy. However, recent events have shown that this is not essential. The word "community" has been used rather loosely to mean many things. For example, community economic development is often interpreted as local economic development; community is used to spatially designate a geographic neighborhood. The sense in which I wish to speak of community does not necessarily imply a shared past or a common culture, though, of course, it includes these as basic and fundamental to what communities were in the past, perhaps still are in some cases and might become in the future.

The community we speak of emerges from a recognition that it can be constructed through a common strategy to revitalize neighborhoods, create employment and develop alternative economic institutions and programs. Of the many differentiated socio-economic interventions observable today, community-based economic development succeeds only by re-embedding the economy into society, by developing a social economy in which non-market criteria determine the allocation of economic resources. This is no longer an ideal or limited to a few rather well-known examples—Mondragon in Spain or New Dawn Enterprises in Cape Breton, Nova Scotia, for example. In fact, the examples are too numerous and scattered to document but sufficiently visible for it to be concluded that they are significant.

DEMOCRATIZING CAPITAL: EMPOWERMENT OR CRISIS MANAGEMENT?
LESSONS FOR EASTERN EUROPE

There is a very large and growing community investment movement in the West. It includes the establishment of social and ethical investment funds, community banking and revolving loan funds. I wish to focus on the latter for two reasons: first, unlike other financial innovations, revolving loan funds are democratically established and provide the greatest potential for community lenders. Second, I believe that there is an adequate enough social and economic base in Hungary for consideration to be given to the establishment of revolving loan funds as a much needed source of micro capital.

Revolving loan funds may be called social banks or quasi banks. They operate on the same principles of lending and borrowing; however, interest rates for both borrowers and lenders are negotiated. What distinguishes these from conventional banks, is their base in communities, low income communities, specifically. The growing disenfranchised population referred to earlier has been severely punished by job losses due to economic restructuring and the current political environment which considers the unemployed as a social burden. Because the skills and talents of laid off workers are not validated, there is no attempt to create an institutional framework which recognizes their potential input into an economic development strategy. Instead, they are considered an undifferentiated mass of trainable workers. Nor can they approach the banks for loans to establish small independent initiatives. They face the double burden of economic marginalization and the "redlining" practices of the commercial banks. The lives of a growing number of marginalized workers have become more contingent in this environment. The so-called "jobless recovery" has altered the attitudes of workers and policy-makers alike who were conditioned to expect jobs as the economy moved out of a slump.

Revolving loan funds provide micro credit to those who cannot re-enter the economy as productive workers. The fund defines economic development in socio-economic terms. Loans are made to individuals and/or groups for start-up capital, housing projects, or to assist projects underway which are considered high risk by the banks. They include loans to create new forms of social ownership such as community owned enterprise and community land trusts.[9] Revolving loan funds have been referred to in the literature as part of a growing social economy movement. They are not only contributing to a re-embedding of the economy in the community but are, in significant ways, transforming property relations.

There is a history of alternative investment funds in the West. These include small credit unions and the more recent development of loan circles based on the highly successful Grameen Bank model in Bangladesh as well as barter networks such as the LETS system in Canada. Each of these, in varying ways, is built on social collateral. Each of these has emerged to fill an urgently needed source of risk capital. These funds are not created by governments; they are generated by loans made by individual lenders who support its socio-economic objectives. Since borrowers cannot, in general, guarantee their loans, their objectives and plans are very carefully evaluated. All projects which receive support are provided with extensive follow-up and technical assistance. There is an active movement to develop niche markets for local enterprises to break up global markets, for example. More than monitoring loans and repayment, this intervention reflects the underlying philosophy of these funds which actively participate as partners in the projects they support. The details of the operations of these funds are well documented.[10] What is relevant to this discussion is that the establishment of alternative investment funds is crucial to a community economic development strategy which, to use the jargon, is "empowering." There is ample evidence to show that a top down strategy, even if it is earmarked for low income communities, is precarious. In other words, community development organizations which focus on feasibility studies, training programs and economic development, and are unable to establish autonomous community based investment funds but rely instead on government grants or subsidies, will be part of a government crisis management strategy which may shift its priorities and withdraw financial assistance or not renew it. A pool of community controlled risk capital is essential.

In fact, these independent funds are flourishing. In the U.S., for example, over 50 revolving loan funds exist and are coordinated by the National Association of Community Loan Funds in Washington. Such funds currently represent approximately $125 million. The success of these funds and the establishment of community banks in the U.S. led to the recent adoption of legislation to increase available capital for community banking. Of great significance, in this period of successive business failures and defaulting on bank loans, is the overwhelming success of the projects supported by these funds; they boast a loan loss ratio of just under 1%. This is in sharp contrast to commercial lending and to the many bankruptcies among small and medium size enterprises eligible for the usual sources of funding—state, para-state and private.

Also of great interest is the emergence of networks of social investment funds and community economic development organizations—both national and international—to exchange experiences and share resources. As these are basically micro experiences, it is difficult to compile an inventory. However, the recent addition of electronic networks in Canada and the U.S. will assist greatly in developing "strategic alliances" within the alternative sector. In Europe, INAISE provides a network of European social investment. INAISE now collaborates with IRED, an international network of community/local economic development organisations. IRED representatives recently met with representatives in Eastern Europe who expressed great interest in learning more about these alternative financial instruments developed in other countries.

Another interesting development is the recent recommendation by the Bretton Woods Commission, a private U.S.-based multinational group of academics, business representatives and former government officials to the World Bank Group[11] to shift its funds to subnational governments and directly to private companies. Subsidiarity or decentralization has, of course, been an important part of the EEC (EU) agenda. Although our focus is on community based economic development funds, movement in this direction by international agencies is highly significant since it will open up opportunities to local governments which can participate as partners in these initiatives.[12] As long as community lending institutions are built on a democratic base, the participation of local governments is welcome. This differs from the neo-corporatist developments described above. We do not speak here of the establishment of a "development fund"; community-based revolving loan funds represent new socio-economic institutions.

LESSONS FROM EASTERN EUROPE

This section of the paper can be but speculative. I wish to pose several questions regarding the possibility to develop alternative community based economic programs in Eastern Europe. I refer to Hungary, in particular, although the same questions may be raised for other countries in the region. The first point to be made is that "the generalization of the market contract is not appropriate for all economic life." (*Towards a New Sector*, p.9). This is true for the West which has not been able to deal with growing poverty, unemployment and economic decline. These difficult conditions have led to a reconsideration and legitimation of alternative economic strategies. The situation is even more acute within transition economies which do not have the social infrastructure to assist in the radical social transformation underway.

The question raised here is whether factors in the present situation—the pre-communist social relations upon which successful small enterprises were established during the communist period, the legalized second economy (since 1982), the former active local councils and the current existence of nearly 20,000 associations mobilized around social, cultural, economic and political issues in this post-communist period—provide a social basis upon which community based finance can be established. Despite the introduction of new instruments of credit and low interest rates for small enterprises, these continue to "redline" small borrowers. Banks resist long term repayment schedules. In fact, banks are more interested in equity investment, where the risks are lower. For small enterprise start-up capital, friends and families are relied upon. Social collateral from friends, family, co-workers, or "love money" is a key source of capital.

One asks where all the "private" initiative in rural communities and in the second economy under communism disappeared to. These experiences can surely be considered a foundation for new democratic initiatives today. Indeed, then as now, village economies were based on reciprocity, work sharing arrangements, borrowing and lending within the community. Have these social networks collapsed or is there an overwhelming cynicism which blocks any possibility to use these networks "against the market" so to speak, to mobilize capital? How useful would it be to actively engage in discussions of alternative economic strategies by illustrating their role in the West? I believe this is being done. Are these exchanges productive?

Iván Szelenyi wrote about "parking orbits" to refer to the embourgeoisement of the rural economy during communism. These entrepreneurs parked in villages to create productive local economies and became a "relatively autonomous civil society" within communist Hungary.[13] Endre Sik[14] wrote likewise about networks of independent "social economies" with a developed accumulation strategy as the "institutional solutions to organize the market itself" during the communist period. These networks were founded on mutual trust and a shared hostility towards the state. This distrust has grown in the current period as communities try to cope with economic crisis and economic insecurity. Might these defensive coping mechanisms which effectively mobilized communities not be transformed into autonomous development strategies today?

Trust and shared cultural identity have not been destroyed in the transition. Quite the contrary: these ties have deepened in the face of growing insecurity. Can new meaning be given to these social networks which acknowledges their potential to be self-determining and active economic agents in society? This question is not rhetorical. We spoke earlier of the absence of community in the West, in the sense of "a shared identity" and the challenge to establish a community regulated economy instead around a common socio-economic definition of community. In Hungary, a more traditionally defined community is already present in many areas which succeeded in establishing independent socio-economic institutions. Thus the social base which has to be constructed in the West is to be found there.

One hears of the wealth accumulated in the second economy, little of which has been reinvested in enterprises. Much of this wealth has instead gone into conspicuous consumption and personal savings. The distrust of the previous regime and the current transition crisis have discouraged reinvestment and have resulted in short-term planning. And so the second economy has played a passive and cautious role in the transition. Can this behaviour now be converted into a long-term investment strategy if the appropriate institutions are created, including, first and foremost, of course, the availability of credit? Can this behaviour be transformed with the introduction of an industrial strategy at the local level by autonomous local authorities? This is distinct from the international financial assistance which is currently available primarily through PHARE (EU) which supports Local Enterprise Agencies and the Hungarian Foundation for Enterprise Promotion. They neither provide micro credit nor are they widespread. There are only a few LEAs in the country and their availability is limited to their specific location. Economists had already proposed the establishment of community-based local financial institutions in response to inadequate state provision in the previous period.

Recent studies of villages and small towns and of new private enterprises confirm the persistence of social networks in the current economy. In fact, they suggest that these are as integral to the operations within enterprises, between enterprises and within communities today, as they were in the past. They emphasize the social endowments of today's entrepreneurs and the importance of "contact capital." These people were socialized under conditions of shortage and created these important links to struggle against economic constraints imposed by the system, with both borrowing and lending. So called "industrial districts" have been identified in Hungary which engage in the social regulation of economic processes. This includes the establishment of local funds and the retention of profits in the district.

There appears to exist a potential source of micro credit which may be built upon the strength of social solidarity present in many regions and communities. More comprehensive documentation is needed on "previously existing social networks," industrial districts, and new social formations. For example, when asking if informal finance existed within communities, I was told that there is no clear evidence of this, but that such arrangements surely do exist within the interstices of social networks. As noted above, there are attempts to compile an inventory of alternative savings and lending practices in the West. A comprehensive survey is needed here as well. Meaningless aggregates are inadequate to evaluate social and economic life; we need new tools of analysis.

CONCLUSION

There is growing awareness of and support for what might be called an alternative third sector. This differs fundamentally from previous references to a "third way." We are speaking here of the development and consolidation of new socio-economic institutions referred to as the "social economy." The focus has been on the question of finance and the democratization of capital. I believe this is central to a strategy which is otherwise contingent and vulnerable. The new focus on "managed economies" is, in fact, more often than not, devolution rather than genuine decentralization and democratization. Moreover, micro credit remains unavailable. However, there is growing evidence of successful community initiatives with access to community finance. These are not marginal; they are situated within those very localities hardest hit by irreversible structural changes. That they are gaining support is significant; that they are gaining autonomy is even more so. These lessons must be shared with economies in transition. In some cases, there exists a social base upon which these initiatives may be built. In others, the betrayal of the market may provide the foundation upon which to consider these alternatives.

NOTES

1. Karl Polanyi, *The Great Transformation*. New York: Rinehart, 1944.
2. See M. Mendell, "New Social Partners: Crisis Management or a New Social Contract? in *Urban Fields: Subject, Locality and Practice*, Vered Amit-Talai and Henri Lustiger-Thaler, (eds.), McLelland Stuart: 1994, pp. 71-92 for a detailed critique of this.
3. For example, the *Société générale de financement* (SGF) was created in 1962 followed by the *Caisse de dépot et de placement* in 1966, which consists of public sector pension funds. The *Société de développement industriel* (SDI) was established in 1971, the *Société de développement des entreprises québecoises* (SODEQ) in 1976, the *Régime d'épargne-action du Québec* (REAQ) in 1979, the *Sociétés de placement dans l'entreprise québecoise* (SPEC) in 1985 and the *Coopératives des travailleurs actionnaires* in 1985.
4. The key players in Québec are the *Caisse de dépot et placements* noted above, the *Mouvement Desjardins* (a cooperative federation of financial cooperatives in Quebec), the *Banque Nationale*, the *Fonds de solidarité* (see above) and the Québec government.
5. See Mendell, Levesque and Van Kemenade, 1994, "Les fonds régionaux et locaux de développement au Québec: des institutions financieres relevant principalement de l'économie sociale." Chaire du CRISES. No. 9610, p.34. In a recent study in Québec, Jean Desrochers notes that the failure rate of new small and medium size enterprises is 80%. Jean Desrochers, "La gestion financière," in Pierre-André Julien (ed.), *Les PME, bilan et perspectives*. Québec et Paris: Presses Inter Universitaires et Economica, 1994, pp. 253-269.
6. Egon Matzner and Wolfgang Streek, *Beyond Keynesianism: The Socio-Economics of Production and Full Employment*. Egon Matzner and Wolfgang Streeck, (eds.), Aldershot: Elgar, 1991, Introduction, pp. 7-8.
7. János Simon, "The Meaning of Democracy." (Hungary). Draft document presented to the author, 1994.
8. I borrow this phrase from Robert Fitch's "Explaining New York City's Aberrant Economy," *New Left Review*, No. 207, September/October 1994, 23. It seems we need a new metaphor. Or perhaps it is still appropriate since a trickle is insignificant anyway!
9. See Tim Crabtree, George McRobie and Andy Roberts, *Towards a New Sector. Macro Politics for Community Enterprise*. London: New Economics Foundation, 1992, for the extensive literature on community enterprise in the U.K. and Scotland. Community enterprises have emerged in the U.S. and in Canada as well.
10. See M. Mendell and L. Evoy (eds.), *Community Economic Development. In Search of Empowerment and Alternatives*. 2nd edition. Montreal: Black Rose Books, 1997, pp. 110-129 for one example of a revolving loan fund in Montreal.
11. The World Bank Group includes the World Bank, the International Development Association, the Industrial Finance Corporation and the Multilateral Investment Guarantee Agency. Only the World Bank is obliged to lend through central governments.
12. See David Gisselquist, "How to Encourage Government Decentralization. Interesting Ideas for Redirecting Lending," *Transition*. Transition Economics Division. Policy Research Department. The World Bank. Vol.5, No.7, September 1994, pp.7-8.
13. Ivan Szelenyi, *Socialist Enterprises: Embourgeoisement in Rural Hungary*. Madison: University of Wisconsin Press, 1988.
14. Endre Sik and Agnes Czako, "The Role of the Network as a Resource in Economic Transactions in Post-Communism," in M. Mendell and K. Nielsen (eds.), *Europe. Central and East*. Montreal: Black Rose Books, 1995, pp. 224-247.

Chapter Eighteen

RECIPROCITY AND THE INFORMAL ECONOMY IN LATIN AMERICA
Larissa Adler Lomnitz

The importance has been recognized of reciprocal exchange networks for economic survival in complex modern societies. The types of exchange encountered within these networks can be compared to those proposed by Polanyi:[1] that is, reciprocity, redistribution and householding. However, Polanyi regarded reciprocal exchanges as the basic form of exchange within primitive egalitarian peoples. The case was different in modern complex societies, where redistribution and market exchange represented the dominant forms of exchange. Although reciprocity is encountered in modern societies in the form of certain archaic customs (such as Christmas gift-giving) it is generally unimportant in the economy as a whole.

On the basis of ethnographic studies in urban Mexico and Chile,[2] I shall discuss how in those societies reciprocity is an important form of exchange—providing an informal social security system, which allows the poor to survive physically, the middle classes to maintain their social status, and the rich to keep their economic privileges. It may also serve as the basis of productive units which complement and support formal organizations. Thus, I hope to show that reciprocity is today a vital and important form of exchange which complements market and state redistributive mechanisms.

A social network is a social field of relationships between individuals as defined by some underlying variable.[3] This may refer to any specific item of exchange such as goods, services, or information. In spite of considerable variations in structure, functions, and other important factors, for these networks to be able to function, a psycho-social variable, *confianza*, is required. This *confianza* or trust may be defined as a shared perception of the effective social closeness that promotes, induces, or maintains the desired exchange. We consider the concept of *confianza* as the equivalent of the condition of "embeddedness in social relations" which Polanyi deemed necessary for reciprocal relations to exist. (Polanyi, p.46) In other words, where *confianza* exists, embeddedness of the exchange relationship in social life has to be a precondition.

THE INFORMAL SECTOR OF THE URBAN ECONOMIES
Since the 1980s, the term "informal sector" has referred to the urban poor of the Latin American cities who were originally known as *marginados*. In a previous study, I defined "marginality" as applying to that sector of the working class

characterized by a chronic state of economic insecurity, both in terms of income and lack of permanence of employment. The informal sector was then composed of urban workers not incorporated into the formal, modern sector of the economy, thus lacking job stability together with the benefits of modern labor legislation and welfare. (Lomnitz 1977, p.13) Other definitions include that proposed by the International Labour Organization which viewed the informal sector as related to the persistence, in a formal urban market economy, of certain traditional practices which characteristically involve a "tendency toward affiliations, utilization of local resources, family business, small-scale operations...in non-regulated competitive markets."[4] Thus, the ILO regarded the mode of the organization of production as the main defining characteristic of the sector. The unit of production (family enterprise or self-employed individuals) became the focus of analysis, as did the ways in which informally produced goods and services articulate with the "formal sector."[5] On the other hand, what also characterized the informal sector and its economy was "the persistence of the importance of family, traditional rural activities, and rural ways in the cities."

As the field of study developed, the term "informal sector" became detached from what is now termed "the informal economy." According to Castells and Portes, it is no longer a euphemism for poverty,[6] but a term denoting a type or "process of income-generation characterized by one central feature: it is unregulated by the institutions of society, in a legal and social environment in which similar activities are regulated."[7] For De Soto, who also uses the same definition, the informal economy is one that, aiming at achieving goals which in themselves are legal, uses illegal or deregulated forms to reach those ends. According to another approach, the informal economy relates to "production relationships through the articulation of formal and informal activities." (Castells and Portes, p.12) In other words, "informality" is linked with formality, as in fact there is an interdependence between the two sorts of "economies" that tends to make one dependent on the other. The growing literature on centrally planned and modern capitalist economies shows this to be the case.[8] In fact, as modern states develop, the increasing volume of regulations leads people to find informal ways to by-pass them.

There are three areas of informality in which social networks are essential. First, among the urban poor, social networks are substitutes for security of income and lack of access to formal security systems. Second, in small family enterprises, the use of unpaid family labour as generalized reciprocity[9] guarantees a unit of production that requires little or no capital while giving security. Third, the use of social networks, where a substratum of trust has been built among its members, allows deregulated or illegal activities to take place.

To be able to survive during recurrent periods of unemployment, members of the informal sector in Latin American cities make full and varied use of their social resources. This stratum is typically composed of migrants and descendants of migrants from the landless peasantry. These have congregated in large cities where they occupy a characteristic economic position whose most relevant aspect is constant insecurity of income, due to structural lack of articulation with the urban industrial economy. The informal sector is generally unprotected by state-regulated social security systems or other formal programs; its members' economic activities often become unregulated or illegal due to legislation that tends to regulate health, housing, and also educational and labor norms.

In my 1977 study I showed the way in which this stratum generates its members' own security mechanisms by means of reciprocity networks, mainly among neighbors and kin. For example, to complement the head of the household's wages, wives make tortillas to sell, children shine shoes or beg, and the old people raise animals or become water carriers. On the other hand, there is also inter-family and inter-household cooperation within a network. A network typically consists of four or five nuclear families who dwell in adjoining quarters or under the same roof. Non-kin neighbors may be incorporated into such informal networks by means of an intense exchange of goods and services, which usually leads to the ritualized formalization of the relationship through fictive kinship (*compadrazgo*).

As pointed out earlier, along with physical and social proximity one key variable governing membership in networks is *confianza*. *Confianza* is born first of all out of sociability; it is generally kinship among extended grand families in which this trust appears as part of a cultural norm. However, it develops when exchanges are performed often, as is the case when partners in the exchange suffer similar fates of economic deprivation at different times. For example, in the shanty town studied, women call daily to request cooperation from among neighbors, such as the frequent borrowing of small amounts of food, or money, or for baby-sitting. Hence, these women were the basic agents in the formation of the network structure. I found that all the networks were organized around a female figure who set the tone for mutual assistance, such as a mother, older sister, or neighbor with a forceful personality who cared for others. Without such a female figure as moral leader the network tended to disintegrate.

THE HOUSEHOLD ECONOMY

The basis of an individual's "social capital" (or networks) is the family as culturally defined. In Mexico, the family as the basic unit of solidarity is a three-generational group, the "grand family." (Lomnitz and Perez Lizaur, 1987) This culturally recognized solidarity group should not be equated with the "household," in which the element of residence and sharing of domestic functions is combined in the social group living together. The residential pattern in the shanty town studied was determined by property conditions; its formation was a dynamic process involving many random factors, including availability of vacant houses. According to the combination of certain variables (residential arrangements, structure of the social group, and domestic functions) I found three different types of households: 1) according to the type of family living in a unit, the household may be either nuclear or extended; 2) according to residence, it may be under a single roof, in a single plot, or joined; 3) according to domestic functions, it may be classified as either sharing or not sharing expenses and cooking. (Lomnitz, 1977, pp.102-103) The majority of households encountered in my study lived in extended families under a single roof, single plot, or joined. They usually contained both or one of the grandparents, many of them sharing expenses and food preparation.

The household within this informal sector represents not only a unit of consumption, but also a unit of production and internal cooperation ensuring security and survival. Census data which only take into account the income generated by the family head(s) will only yield part of the total economic activities which take place within the domestic unit. Children shine shoes, carry water, watch cars, sell chewing gum under street lights, collect food. They also help to take care of animals raised in the households, deliver *tortillas* made for sale by their mothers, and take care of their brothers and sisters when their mothers go out to work. Women help their husbands in their small family enterprises as unpaid family laborers, have their own food preparation enterprises, do washing for middle-class people, pick up scrap metal or paper to resell, and raise animals such as pigs or bird stock. Old people carry water, sit long hours in front of tables selling peanuts or candies, and help women take care of children. What we have here is the informal economy of subsistence that adds to the declared economic activity of the household. Again, it is largely the responsibility of a centralizing woman to keep this social group running harmoniously as an economic unit.

THE STRUCTURE OF NETWORKS IN THE SHANTY TOWN
In my case study, networks could be classified according to the intensity of reciprocal exchange among their members. These ranged from networks with a high intensity of exchange, where physical, social and economic distances were minimal, and trust was maximal (as in the case of the intra-household networks previously described)—to networks where the intensity of exchange was minimal (consisting of families that were neighbors but were not related by kinship or fictive kinship). In intermediary situations, networks were composed of relatives and non-related neighbors. Finally, each individual also possesses social resources spread out within the city (workmates, in-law relatives, friends) as also in the rural areas where the migrants originate. These networks (similar to the ones described in the middle-class section of this paper) could eventually be mobilized for services needed on special occasions: to move to another part of the city if a shanty town is razed, to get special loans, to return to the village if one's luck has not been good.

The goods and services exchanged within the reciprocity networks may be classified as follows: 1) information, including instruction for migration, tips on residential opportunities and jobs, general or specific orientations for urban living; 2) job assistance, both in finding employment, as well as training newcomers or younger members of the family in skills to be sold in the labor market; 3) loans of all sorts; 4) services, including accommodation of migrants from the countryside, feeding and providing for the primary needs of families during the initial period of urban adaptation or unemployment, assistance to friends and relatives in need, and a host of minor but not unimportant services such as shopping, and taking care of children; 5) moral support: here networks are mechanisms that generate solidarity which extends to all the events in the life cycle.

Women play a major role in creating and maintaining the social networks that form the underpinning of the exchange system. Not only are they crucial to maintaining the family unity, they are continually meeting with female neighbors and creating new ties. As trust is basic for exchanges to occur, the role of women is essential in creating a basis of solidarity among participants, and maintaining an adequate flow of goods and services circulating within the network. On the other hand, men get together with other men from the many different places where they work; this creates external networks which are reinforced by joint drinking bouts and playing football. Such bonds, however, do not include the female family members: they represent an individual's male network, one that is useful, perhaps for introducing men into the labor market, but remains restricted to male activities.

MIDDLE CLASS NETWORKS

The middle class in Latin America comprise a social category which can be better characterized by what they are not, than by what they are.[10] They do not own the "means of production," but they differ from the lower classes by their rejection of manual labor. The social survival of this group has come to depend largely on its access to, and intimate knowledge of, the bureaucracy. Social resources are used for economic ends. In the study done in Chile in 1970 and also later in 1988, I found an informal system of reciprocal exchanges of economically valuable services within a network of relatives and friends. These networks operate a system of reciprocity which consists of a continuous exchange of favors. An ideology of friendship and social closeness motivates the exchanges. The favors tend to be bureaucratic in nature, and usually consist of preferential treatment in dealing with red tape and/or priority access to one of the services offered by the state, often involving setting aside the rights and priorities of third parties. This system consists of a tacit dyadic contract or chain of such contracts between persons linked by mutual friends or relatives who act as intermediaries. The initial favour is usually granted without any specific idea of how it would be returned: the required reciprocity is held in reserve for future use, should need arise.

This social institution, called in Chile *compadrazgo* in the 1970s or today *pitutos* (in Mexico *palanca*), operates among social equals, both men and women: people who have attended the same school, undergone similar political experiences, occupy similar positions in the economy, move in the same social circles, and are typically members of this exchange system. The services rendered are called *favores* and are motivated and justified by means of an ideology of friendship. The most typical *favor* obtained through such social relationships is getting a job (normally in the public sector), which entails a mental survey of all personal relationships until hitting upon a friend with some link to the personnel department of the specific agency where employment is sought. In the same way, when a candidate to fill some vacancy is required, a list of friends is gone over until the appropriate person is found. Other typical favours include the expediting of certificates, licenses, permits, passports and numerous other types of documents normally involving a considerable expenditure of time and bothersome red-tape procedures. Most of these services entail economic advantages for the individuals that receive them, as they guarantee a higher level of material life. A typical characteristic of the salaried middle-class is the absence of savings and the recurrence of economic difficulties in a situation of chronic inflation. Middle-class people live in economic insecurity, although their outward standard of living is patterned after the life style of the middle classes of more prosperous societies. Money may be scarce, but a well-placed friend in a loan company or bank is able to facilitate the getting of a loan by providing information, or by guiding his or her friend's application to the top of the pile. Another friend might be helpful in getting one's children admitted to a public but prestigious school where they can meet other children who will become life members of their networks. Friends may give advice on job openings, scholarships, medical services in public hospitals, licenses, tax problems, political patronage, customs facilities, and public housing. The opportunities for being helpful to one's friends are endless. The ideal of the middle class is to have always the "right friend at the right place at the right time." (Lomnitz, 1971, p.96)

Since the key to having friends is being sociable, an attitude of sociability is encouraged from early childhood on. In each family there are overlapping networks around the wife and husband, indeed around both. In each of these networks there are relatives and friends of both sexes. The degree of friendship is continually reassessed and, consciously or not, rated in a scale of *confianza*, which in this case may mean their approachability and readiness to exchange favours. Close friends are people who see each other regularly, who socialize frequently at each other's homes, and who may drop in unannounced. They are treated as relatives and may be entrusted with more confidential information than most relatives. A readiness to request and perform services among such friends is considered a duty—for, as the Chilean saying goes: "What else are friends for?"

Hence the Chilean middle class contains a structure of open, flexible reciprocity networks featuring a continuous exchange of services among social equals. These services are economically valuable, though in themselves they are not available for money. Typically such favours are bestowed within the culture of sociability, without any overt expectations of reciprocity; thus, they are absolutely incompatible with money transactions of any kind. Women have a special role in keeping the reciprocity networks active because of the central importance of hospitality involving the home, not only for family rituals and gatherings (as is the case in Mexico), but also, and very specially, as the place where friends meet all the time. Women who are able to create an informal atmosphere of welcome, or who surround themselves with highly placed friends and like to introduce them to one another, are particularly valued. A social invitation may represent a favor in the context of reciprocal exchange; thus, hospitality received is felt as an obligation to be returned in various ways.

CONCLUSIONS

I have presented ethnographic material from two different Latin American urban strata to show the persistence, or rather the adaptation to urban conditions, of certain features commonly associated with traditional economies that have definite survival value and help to explain the pattern of socio-economic response based on reciprocal networks in different social strata. In each case, a complementary system of informal exchange emerges parallel with the formal economy. These informal systems are embedded in long-term social relations (primarily kinship, but also fictive kinship, neighborliness, personal friendship, "and old school-tie" solidarity). The characteristic feature of such systems is a tendency towards the formation of networks that can be converted into economic assets: security, status, and power. The "informal sector" for the poor means sheer physical survival; for the middle class it means the maintenance of a perpetually threatened economic status. In his model of economic exchanges Polanyi identifies three types of exchange: reciprocity, redistribution, and market exchange. However, he considers only the latter two forms as important in contemporary society; reciprocity he would view as characteristic of primitive stages of social development. The aim of this paper, and of my previous work upon which it is based, is to show that, even in capitalist systems today, reciprocal exchanges play a vital role in the economy.

NOTES

1. Karl Polanyi, *The Great Transformation*. Boston: Beacon Press, 1968, pp. 46-48, 53.
2. L. Lomnitz, "Reciprocity of Favors in the Chilean Middle Class," in George Dalton, (ed.), *Studies in Economic Anthropology*. Washington DC. AAA, 1977, pp. 93-106; L. Lomnitz, *Network and Marginality*. San Francisco: Academic Press, 1977; L. Lomnitz and Lizaur Perez, *An Elite Family in Mexico*. Princeton: Princeton University Press, 1987; L. Lomnitz and A. Melnick, *The Chilean Middle Class*. Boulder: Lynn Reinhart, 1991; Adrián Mayer, "The significance of quasi-groups in the study of complex societies," in M. Banton (ed.), *The Social Anthropology of Complex Societies*. ASA Monograph No. 4. London: Tavistock, 1968.
3. J.A. Barnes, "Class committee in a Norwegian island parish," *Human Relations*, 1954, 7:39-58, 98-99; J. Coleman, *Foundations of Social Theory*. Cambridge, Mass.: The Belknap Press of Harvard University, 1990; J.C. Mitchell, *Social Networks in Urban Situations*. Manchester: Manchester University Press, 1969; Stanley Wasserman and K. Faust, *Social Network Analysis. Methods and Applications*. New York: Cambridge University Press, 1994, pp. 3-27; A. Wolfe, "On Structural Comparisons of Network Situations and Social Networks in Cities," *Review of Sociology and Anthropology*, 1970,7:4.
4. International Labor Organization (ILO) PREALC. "La politica del empleo en America Latina: Lecciones de la Experiencia de PREALC." Santiago: ILO, 1974, p.9.
5. Bryan Roberts, "The Provincial Urban System and the Process of Dependency." Mimeograph, 1974, p.1; P. Souza and V. Tokman, *El Sector Informal Urbano*. Santiago: CLACSO, 1975; V. Tokman, "The Informal Sector: Fifteen Years later." Paper presented at the Conference on the Comparative Study of the Informal Sector. Harper's Ferry, West Virginia. October 2-6, 1986.
6. Manuel Castells and A. Portes, "World Underneath: The Origins, Dynamics, and Effects of the Informal Economy," in A. Portes, M. Castells, and L. Benton (eds.), *The Informal Economy*. Baltimore: John Hopkins University Press, 1989.
7. H. De Soto, *El Otro Sendero*. Buenos Aires: Sudamericana, 1987.
8. Jochanan Altman and G. Mars, "The cultural basis of Soviet Georgia's second economy," *Soviet Studies*, 1983, Vol. 35, No. 4, pp. 546-560; Gregory Grossman, "The 'Shadow Economy' in the socialist sector of the USSR," in *CMEA Five Year Plans (1981-1985) in a New Perspective. Colloquium 1982*. OTAN, Economic and Information Directorates, 1983, pp. 99-115.
9. Marshall Sahlins, "On the sociology of primitive exchange," in M. Banton (ed.), *The Relevance of Models for Social Anthropology*. Monographs No. 1. London: Tavistock, 1968.
10. Susana García Salord, *Estudio Socio-Antropológico de la Clase Media en México: el capital social y el capital cultural como espacios de constitución simbólica de las clases sociales*. Doctoral Dissertation, 1997.

PART TWO

KARL POLANYI AND ILONA DUCZYNSKA

ILONA DUCZYNSKA POLANYI

Chapter Nineteen

ILONA DUCZYNSKA: SOVEREIGN REVOLUTIONARY
Kenneth McRobbie

*Si la verité nous met le couteau à la gorge,
il faut embrasser sa main blanche.*

—The Huguenot poet Agrippa d'Aubigné
(one of Ilona Duczynska's favourite quotations)

Polanyi family history in English has so far focused on the intellectual achievements and scholarly careers of the two eminent brothers, Karl and Michael, who achieved world reputations in their respective fields.[1] But in view of the fact that Karl's masterwork *The Great Transformation* has recently again been singled out, this time as one of "the hundred most influential books since the war,"[2] it is more than time to do justice to the woman to whom its author paid tribute in these unambiguous terms: "To my beloved wife Ilona Duczynska I dedicate this book which owes all to her help and criticism."[3] Confirmation came in a letter from Michael Polanyi to his brother Karl, concerning "Ilona, whose share is scarcely less than yours." (March 30, 1944) A detailed study[4] of Duczynska's life and thought is long overdue, in order to retrieve from the past the image of a remarkable woman, many of whose passionately held concerns are relevant today, to account for Karl's admiration and gratitude, and to establish her place within a distinguished family whose horizons she must be credited with having widened.

The family backgrounds of husband and wife were dissimilar. Karl Polanyi was born into an industrious and cultured bourgeois family; Ilona Duczynska came from gentry stock in which, on both her father's and her mother's side, there was nevertheless creative flair and artistic achievement. She was born on March 11, 1897 in Maria Enzersdorf, Lower Austria, and died on April 24, 1978, in the cottage in Canada which had been her most permanent home.[5] Her father, grandly styled Alfred Justus Ritter von Duczynski, was descended from a noble Polish military family. His ancestors had emigrated to Austria, and, ironically enough, served in the army which helped to suppress the Hungarians in the 1848-49 War of Liberation. A self-educated minor railway functionary,[6] he was at heart an inventor. Design drawings for a powered navigable airship, on which he had collaborated with his father, were viewed by his then young daughter when on display in the Vienna Museum of Technology. The vivid memory may have inspired her later study of aeronautics and her determination to get a pilot's licence. On her mother's side, among the Hungarian landed gentry relatives there was poetic talent in the person of Duczynska's much loved cousin, Ferenc Békássy, friend of Rupert Brooke and John Maynard Keynes at Cambridge, who was killed in the First World War. His poems were published posthumously in translation, by Virginia Woolf.

What distinguished Ilona Duczynska from most of the Polanyi family, into which she married when in her mid-twenties, is immediately apparent. The lives of Karl and Michael Polanyi were essentially confined to the study and university lecture hall. But she on three different occasions broke off her education—and consequently never earned a degree—to devote herself to causes that demanded action and collaboration with others. Hers would be a life less of the study than of conspiratorial gatherings in upper rooms, streets, even the Vienna woods.

A socialist while still at school, it was out of a sense of hopelessness and desperation engendered by the war that she immersed herself in scientific studies. In 1916, at the age of eighteen, while attending the *Technische Hochschule* (the "Poly") in Zürich—women being excluded from studying engineering in Budapest and Vienna—overwork and hunger resulting from poverty brought on the first of two bouts of tuberculosis within the space of two years. Previously, she had witnessed, in Zurich, a street demonstration signaling the rebirth of the international socialist movement in favour of peace. While convalescing from September 1916 to March 1917, she read of the outbreak of revolution in Russia, and was inspired to make contact with socialists in the Poly and in the city. She met Karl Radek, worked with Angelika Balabanoff—and recalls receiving a disapproving stare from Lenin himself (whom then she did not yet recognize) for her choice of reading matter in the *Bibliothek für soziale Literatur* in Zürich.

Duczynska abandoned her studies and acted as a courier to smuggle the Zimmerwald anti-war manifesto into Hungary. There she enrolled at the University in Budapest, joined the Galilei Circle, and became a close friend of the eminent scholarly anarchist-idealist theoretician Ervin Szabó. However, she considered that the times called for immediate action. Convinced like so many others that Hungary should leave the war, she planned to assassinate the main advocate of the war policy, Prime Minister István Tisza. She had previously owned a Browning pistol in Zürich; now she purloined one from the desk drawer of József Madzsar, a relative of Oscar Jászi, with whom she was staying. She was well aware of precedents. A short time before, Friedrich Adler, son of the Austrian socialist leader, was lionized by the population of Vienna in massive street demonstrations, for his successful attempt on the life of the Austrian Prime Minister. She was probably also influenced by her familiarity with Russian culture, including the activities of the *Narodnaja Volja* (The People's Will). However, her plan was forestalled by Tisza's sudden resignation. Thereupon she formed a radical youth group for the purpose of propagandizing and distributing leaflets among workers in munition factories and soldiers in the Budapest barracks in an attempt to persuade them to oppose the war effort. Together with her first husband (of a short-lived "student marriage") Tivadar Sugár, she was arrested, detained for several months (during which time her illness returned), was convicted of high treason, and sentenced to a lengthy prison term.

Rescue from prison came for Duczynska with the Károlyi "White Aster" revolution in Budapest which put an end to the war. In 1919, she served in the People's Commissariat for Foreign Affairs of the equally short-lived 1919

Republic of Councils. Duczynska was sent back to Zürich under the false identity of Marguerite Mercier, supposedly a French governess from Lyon, on a mission to consolidate press connections, but soon went underground under yet another false name following the counter-revolution in Budapest. In April 1920 she travelled for twenty days as a deaf-and-dumb cousin of a Russian family, on a Red Cross train from Basle returning Russian emigrés of the 1905 revolution to their homeland. In Moscow "in the full radiance of its heroic age,"[7] as she would describe it towards the end of her life, she worked for a few months with Karl Radek on preparations for the 1920 Second World Congress of the Comintern in Petrograd. Subsequently, at her own request she traveled to Vienna on another mission—carrying a toothpaste tube filled with diamonds intended to subsidize the Hungarian Communist Party whose leaders were in emigration. Her instructions were to give the stones to György Lukács who—according to one of her accounts—as the son of a banker was deemed more financially responsible, by the Soviet comrades, than Béla Kun head of the former government.

Within a few months she met Karl Polanyi who, following serious illness and hospitalization towards the end of the war, was convalescing in a hostel for Hungarian refugees on the outskirts of Vienna in Mödling. They married on February 25, 1923. By then Duczynska had been expelled from the Hungarian Party, on account of an article she wrote that was critical of the authoritarian basis of the party.[8] Thereafter she contributed to other left-wing journals, and was editor of *Der Linke Sozialdemokrat* from 1927 to 1929. She resumed her studies, this time at the *Technische Hochschule* in Vienna, during the period 1930-34. It was here that she met a group of younger Hungarian students; together they organized a short-lived clandestine radio station, an account of which was presented at the Vienna Conference by Barbara Striker, one of three young women involved.

Karl Polanyi left Vienna for England in 1933, and their daughter Kari followed one year later. Duczynska was now embarked upon her longest period of clandestine political activity. From 1934 to 1936, she was charged with editorial responsibility for *Der Sprecher*, the organ of the autonomous (now communist) *Schutzbund*, the remnants of the workers defence militia deserted by their previous (social democratic) leaders after the events of February 1934. These were the heroic days of working-class opposition to fascism in Austria. In 1936, ill health caused Duczynska to join Polanyi in England, where, to her surprise, she was informed that she had been expelled from the Austrian Communist Party—on instructions from Moscow. It marked the advent of xenophobic Stalinist terror directed against Russian and foreign Communists of her generation.

When she moved to England she secured employment in positions in which she could utilize her mathematics background, before joining her husband in the United States at Bennington College, Vermont, in September 1941. She lectured in physics and mathematics until January 1943, while also providing what Karl Polanyi acknowledged as indispensable assistance during the writing of *The Great Transformation*. It was at this time that she learned to fly, at Troy Municipal Airport (New York State); also, she worked in the Department of Aeronautics at the nearby Rennselaer Polytechnic Institute, where she was offered a position for the duration of the war. In the summer of 1943 she wrote the examination for the Associate Fellowship of the Royal Aeronautical Society of Great Britain (to which she was elected in early 1947). By then she felt that she should use her skills to contribute to the war effort in England. Accordingly, the Polanyis returned to London.

In England Duczynska obtained positions with the Miles Aircraft Company, the Ministry of Aircraft Production, and finally—for an eight month period, which she remembered as one of the happiest of her life—with a team of brilliant eccentrics in the Aerodynamics Department of the legendary Royal Aircraft Establishment (Farnborough, Hampshire), where her duties included research and translating German texts on jet propulsion.[9] It was at this time that she and Polanyi became associated in London with a group of Hungarians around Count Mihály Károlyi (who in 1918 had been President of the first Republic of Hungary); these formed a potential democratic administration ready to return home after the war. However, these plans were not realizable. Duczynska's political activities now consisted of writing articles for several newspapers and journals.[10] For a time it seemed that a new career might open up when she joined the staff of London's Imperial College of Science and Technology. But she resigned in mid-1947 to follow her husband to New York where he was appointed Visiting Professor at Columbia University. Then came the blow. Both of them were shocked to find that, under the provisions of the McCarran Act, Duczynska was denied an entry visa "for all time" due to her communist past.

It was this set-back that brought Duczynska to the more tranquil society of Canada, where her daughter had settled following marriage to Joseph Levitt. She accepted an invitation to stay with David and Barbara Cass-Beggs in Toronto, because it was the city to which Polanyi could most easily commute. However, the uncertainties of wartime, and now postwar separation, imposed a strain on their personal lives. Duczynska chafed at the unaccustomed idleness in what struck her as uncongenial surroundings, and her thoughts turned increasingly to Hungary. Indeed, both of them had entertained thoughts of going to live there; Polanyi even received an invitation from the Péter Pázmán University (soon to be renamed) in Budapest. Not surprisingly, in view of her initial involvement in Hungarian political life, Duczynska was intensely interested in the socio-economic programme of the new regime. For background she read what she could find in the Toronto Public Library on the Hungarian Populist movement and its writers, particularly their associations with the peasantry, to which she had been introduced by Endre Havas—whose memory she always honoured—in London during the latter part of the war. Accordingly, in 1948 she returned to Hungary to study the epoch-making land reform which had resulted in the transformation of the countryside. She traveled from village to village, including some on estates where she had resided as a girl. She subsequently compiled a manuscript, "Hungary: An Essay in Land Tenure and Nationhood." However, all she ever published were two articles, the reason apparently being that she was deeply disturbed by the first signs of totalitarianism which she would have been obliged to criticize in a more comprehensive study. This she felt reluctant to do in the context of the Cold War. So she took the plunge and emigrated to Canada in 1950, a step she viewed with mixed feelings.

Karl Polanyi's professional career, despite serious discontinuities, culminated in scholarly acclaim; Duczynska's was interrupted, and finally abandoned shortly after coming to Canada. Polanyi easily adapted to life in North America; but for Duczynska the change came as a profound shock, bringing for a time a stifling sense of isolation. She obtained minor posts in Physics and Aeronautics at the University of Toronto, but abandoned these out of apprehension that projects she was engaged in might have application for weapons development. She wrote articles on a variety of topics for a communist Hungarian paper published in Toronto.[11] However, for the most part she had little choice but to devote herself to essentially practical tasks: making fully habitable the tiny cottage perched on the crest of a steep river bank,[12] and assisting Polanyi in his research and correspondence with typing, helping to prepare manuscripts, and obtaining books from the University of Toronto Library.

The 1956 Hungarian Revolution, and the dramatic events leading up to it, had the effect of spiritually repatriating husband and wife to Hungary. It united them intellectually and emotionally as perhaps never before, and caused them to embark with great enthusiasm on their one and only shared project, the English-language anthology *The Plough and the Pen: Writings from Hungary 1930-1956*.[13] For a while, it seems, influential emigrés in London impeded its acceptance by publishers, until it finally appeared in 1963 in London and Toronto. It contained a foreword by the leading English poet W. H. Auden with whom Duczynska would later consult when preparing a volume of poetry in 1970. The anthology was unique in that its selection was made only from among the work of those Hungarian writers—and they happened to be the most eminent—who had refused to leave the country after 1956. Especially original, given the revived cold war atmosphere, was the Introduction which maintained that it was the indigenous Hungarian populist tradition (to some extent taken over by the Communists) that had inspired a revisionist revolutionary commitment to a socialism free from Russian domination, a "Third Way" between the existing ideological polarities and power blocs.

The emphasis on independence from both blocs was represented in Karl Polanyi's final undertaking, the founding of the journal *Co-existence*,[14] the early issues of which were published from Pickering. Proofs of the first number were delivered on the day of his funeral. World-famous scholars, friends and colleagues old and new were involved in the ambitious project which Duczynska together with Kari Polanyi Levitt endeavoured to keep alive for two more years, before being persuaded to entrust it, not without profound apprehension—as events proved, fully justified—to Robert Maxwell's Pergamon Press.

Thereafter Duczynska lived a life of extraordinary activity, dedicated partly to overseeing her husband's literary legacy, partly to implementing new projects of her own, dividing her time between Canada, Vienna, and Budapest. Canada meant for her the Montreal home of her daughter and two grandsons whom she cared for in Vienna for a year, introducing them to European educational and cultural life. But it also meant her beloved cottage near Toronto, surrounded by trees, with a lake on one side, a river on the other. It was a retreat where she was able to work in relative peace, where the world beat a path to her door in the volume of mail brought by the postal delivery Jeep which drew up daily at the edge of her precipitous and often snowed-in driveway. It was to this retreat that she brought back from Europe the materials—and inspiration—to go on working. She collaborated on a volume of the *Selected Poems* of Ferenc Juhász, whose work had so impressed both her and Polanyi when they were preparing the 1963 Anthology.[15] Together, they had read at a public poetry reading (and tape-recorded) the volume's 300-line title poem (based on an ancient Rumanian folk-song corpus earlier utilized by Béla Bartók).

To the day of her death, Ilona Duczynska corresponded tirelessly with those of her husband's former students who had undertaken to edit or otherwise prepare for publication his numerous and often uncollected works—a task in which she felt it incumbent upon her to intervene, courteously but *very* firmly—when interpretations of his ideas were in question. She corresponded with publishing houses in the United States and several other countries where translations of his works were beginning to appear. When Hungarian editions began to be published, largely at her instigation, she personally checked the translations before they went to press.

The circumstances of Duczynska's life, and her talent for perceiving connections, never allowed her for any length of time to concentrate uninterruptedly upon a single task. She looked both forward and back. Thus, in Hungary, while accepting responsibility for the future of Polanyi's legacy, she became increasingly involved in the fate of the youthful intellectual opposition. At the same time, she began to look back to her roots, to the great period of revolutionary optimism of the early decades of the century, and to the clear-cut issues of the struggle against militarism and fascism. Writers and editors in Hungary prevailed upon her to give interviews on TV, radio and in periodicals, and to write articles about her early activities. Indeed, Duczynska herself came to feel the need to tell what she knew, what she had lived by, and above all how she had been drawn to socialism. She sought out and interviewed survivors of the old days, and undertook research in Budapest and Vienna where she had access to the State Archives. Though she did not live to complete more than the first chapter of her memoirs, there are numerous fragmentary drafts and notes. However, the chapter on her childhood and youth published in Hungary[16] will have a place in the canon of the nation's literature. With its outstanding quality, its sensitive interweaving of the dawning consciousness of youth, family background and socio-political change, "Early Morning" is an intensely personal document of value for the cultural history of the first two decades of the century.

Her project of retracing her Hungarian past was born of her friendship with the eminent Hungarian novelist József Lengyel, the "Hungarian Solzhenitsyn" as English critics called him—though they should have added that he stubbornly remained a reformist Communist. To Duczynska's places of residence was now added the peasant cottage which she shared with Lengyel and his wife in Monoszló, a village tucked away behind hills on the north shore of Lake Balaton which, as she used to say, the Mongols had failed to find. Lengyel too had taken part in the 1919 Budapest Republic of Councils; again, like Duczynska he had become an emigré in Vienna; later he too traveled to Moscow. However, in 1937 he was arrested, and spent the next eighteen years in Siberia, returning to Budapest only in 1955. There he began to write of his experiences. Duczynska translated no fewer than five of Lengyel's novels and short story collections, which recounted the careers of characters who participated in the 1919 revolution, the resistance to fascism, and their fate in both German and Russian prison camps. The final novel *Confrontation* in some respects bears an uncanny resemblance to Arthur Koestler's *Darkness at Noon*, to which of course Lengyel had no access. Duczynska translated it after having smuggled the manuscript out of Hungary where it was available only in a restricted edition for selected Party members. In order not to prejudice her continued ability to re-enter Hungary, she was identified on the title page as "Anna Novotny".[17]

The assumed name was the *nom de guerre* Duczynska had used during her illegal political activity in Vienna in 1934-36 when she was active in the *Schutzbund*. It must have suggested itself in the early 1970s when she was close to finishing the first draft of her book-length manuscript on the period 1918-36 in Austria, with emphasis upon the momentous events commencing on February 12, 1934, when the *Schutzbund* defended Vienna's socialist public housing projects against the overwhelming might of Austria's armed forces in a week of civil war. As early as 1963 Duczynska had conceived the notion of writing of that great period in the history of the Austrian working class movement. As Karl Polanyi put it in the closing pages of *The Great Transformation*, the workers of "Red" Vienna could be regarded as having "achieved one of the most spectacular cultural triumphs of Western history."[18] But if Duczynska looked back to the years 1934-36, she also looked forward in her book[19] to the lessons that street-fighting in Vienna could give to "modern guerrilla warfare within the worldwide framework of American imperialism," and to the idea of an autonomous communist movement. She describes in some detail the theories of the distinguished retired Austrian General Theodor Körner, who had developed a concept of guerrilla tactics in civil war in the late 1920s. He had made recommendations to the leadership of the Austrian Social Democratic Party—which were fatally ignored—based on the writings of the German military theorist Clausewitz,[20] concerning the tactics that armed worker battalions should adopt against regular military forces. Hence Duczynska's dedication at the beginning of her book: "In Memory of all who worked and died true to social and national revolution—socialists, communists, guerrillas of all countries, believers in all faiths." The reference is fully in keeping with her lifelong interest in contemporary oppositional groups and popular movements.

Duczynska's papers contain many related items: a copy of her early article on Emiliano Zapata,[21] photographs of peasant insurgents while visiting her Viennese comrade-in-arms and fellow engineering student Trude Kurz de Lara in Mexico, newspaper clippings on the Cuban Revolution, the Paris student demonstrations of 1968, and the growing movement for an independent Québec. This continuing commitment accounts for her explanation as to why she gave the title *Acta Sanctorum* to her 1970 collection of József Lengyel's short stories:

> Personally, I should not be surprised, if the Old Professor and the carpenter's daughter and those others who suffered and did not let go of the *Prinzip Hoffnung* felt ill at ease among the Saints Established and long for a home among the Saints Outcast, for the company of St. George who killed the dragon, of Jan, and of Che.[22]

When Duczynska was young she lived, debated and worked among those of her own age. When she was old, she lived for and among the young in Budapest who held her in affectionate awe and welcomed her with open arms. In Hungary today, eminent former members of the intellectual opposition—the novelist György Konrád, the historian György Litván, the literary scholar Erzsébet Vezér, former students of György Lukács, philosophers, sociologists, poets and writers—testify to her inspiration, resolve, tolerance even. She demanded and was granted audience at official levels, more than once by the Minister of Culture György Aczél, former cell-mate in Spain of Robert Graves, on behalf of dissidents and in the name of reforms to achieve socialism with a human face. An image is still invoked in Budapest, as if from some Arthurian legend of the Three Queens, the widows of three great men—Ilona Duczynska, Júlia Rajk, and Countess Catherine Károlyi—intimidatingly occupying front seats at the Budapest trial of a young dissident, who subsequently received a suspended sentence.[23] It was at this time that she was presented with a high state decoration by the President of the Republic in the Parliament building. In accordance with protocol, Duczynska was instructed, by "a very official" lady: "No speeches! Just shake hands, and say thank you." Irrepressibly in character, she delivered herself of the following (in Hungarian):

> I am greatly impressed to have been presented with this honour, all the more so because I believe that my standpoint is well known. I am a believer in a socialism with a more human face, which lies beyond the socialism that has come into existence historically. And I am ready to side with all those who take their stand with it.

In the last year of her life, in addition to continuing her support of dissidents and *szamizdat* publications in Hungary, Duczynska took up the cause of a young West German poet and printer, Peter-Paul Zahl, who had been imprisoned following the shooting of a policeman. In custody since 1972, a re-trial in 1976 resulted in his sentence being increased from four to fifteen years, in the context of repressive federal legislation. In addition to trying to organize assistance for a committee of support for Zahl, Duczynska campaigned to get him moved to a more humane prison environment and to have his case reviewed. To this end she attempted to mobilize prominent personalities including leading churchmen in several countries as well as the Bertrand Russell Foundation. Accordingly, she circulated some of Zahl's writings, among which was the following passage that well expresses her own outlook: "More and more the sole criterion becomes the disposition of mind and the convictions (*Gesinnung*) of the other person, more and more concepts like 'deviant behaviour, deviance' become operative."[24]

In assessing a person's life, account must be taken of the subtle drives and needs of personality. The challenges confronting Ilona Duczynska were the product of the times; those she sought out she rightly identified as of prime importance, and made them lifelong causes. At quite an early age she seems to have become convinced of the reality of good and evil. She sought that which was not yet; she strove to fully realize a half-intimated purity, the freshness of morning (such as haunted her childhood memories). She was all too aware of loss, at a personal level: her father murdered in distant Chicago when she was only ten, her cousin Ferenc killed on the Eastern Front when she was seventeen. Of loss too, at the social level, was the shattering of her first experience of community when her German classmates volunteered for service in 1914. With the outbreak of war, she wrote, "my heaven and earth had collapsed...What I'd believed in with all my faith, the world of workers' solidarity, their active internationalism—was a world of paper gone up in flames, its ashes scattered on the wind." ("Early Morning") The Zimmerwald Movement gave her an opportunity to rebuild that world on surer foundations, one at which she never ceased to labour.

Along with her studies of mathematical true and false Duczynska developed an awareness that between black and white—polarities she would never abandon—there was a broad terrain of shifting shades of grey where human beings must make moral choices. It was here that she took issue with dogmatic marxists' insistence on "inevitable" because "historically determined" courses of action as stated by a party leadership remote from the rank and file. She always considered herself to be of the rank and file, on whose behalf she demanded the right to share in decision making and to choose. But choosing has its consequences and its price. A sense of the tragic was never far from her view of life, particularly when she reflected on the fate of her generation.

If later in life Duczynska frequently looked back, it was in order to clarify her vision of the present and the future. For she looked forward with confidence, trusting in the younger generation, trusting that it could not be prevented from calling into existence a social order worthy of humanity's still unrealized potential. Any such social order, she believed, must be rooted in a more completely realized socialist conception of human needs and relationships. She felt strongly what her friend József Lengyel had termed "the incommensurability of life." This she viewed as the meeting point of the best—if, thus far, unrealized—qualities of individual human beings. Among Duczynska's many talents was a genius for working with others, with persons in all walks of life whom she could charm and whose loyalty and admiration she won by treating them as equals. Many of those she encountered she invested with something of herself and her own powers, and flattered by seeing them as how she herself wished them to be.

In his "Hamlet" essay in which he recalled an experience as a cavalry officer amid the cold and mud of the Austro-Hungarian campaign in Galicia in the winter of 1915,[25] Karl Polanyi wrote of a black despair which had brought him close to death. Ilona Duczynska knew despair, and more than once. But she never doubted that she had the strength to go on, under no matter what conditions. In her heart she did not feel she was alone. She viewed life as an endless campaign, in which one is continually called upon to choose. And this has consequences for others far more important than whether one lives or dies.

NOTES

1. Karl Polanyi was professor of economics at Columbia University. His younger brother Michael was professor of chemistry and thereafter of philosophy at Manchester University before going to Oxford; Michael's son John was professor of chemistry at the University of Toronto, and co-recipient of the Nobel Prize. Kari Polanyi Levitt was professor of economics at McGill University and visiting professor at the University of the West Indies.
2. *The Times Literary Supplement*, October 6, 1995, 14.
3. Karl Polanyi, *The Great Transformation*. New York: Rinehart, 1944, p.v. A quarter of a century later, one of Karl's former students, George Dalton, dedicated to Ilona his edition of *Primitive, Archaic, and Modern Economies. Essays of Karl Polanyi*. New York: Doubleday & Co., 1968.
4. For a useful introduction, which emphasizes context, by one who was personally acquainted with Duczynska in her last years, see György Dalos, *A cselekvés szerelmese* (The Lover of Action). Budapest: Kossuth, 1984, 165pp.
5. She died fourteen years after Karl Polanyi (the anniversary of whose death is April 23rd).
6. Karl Polanyi's father had been a millionaire railway builder, but went bankrupt.
7. "Beszélgetés Duczynska Ilonával" (Conversation with Ilona Duczynska), *Valóság* (Reality), 74, 7, 1974, 50-60; 56.

8. Ilona Duczynska, "Zum Zerfall der K.P.U." (On the Disintegration of the Communist Party of Hungary), *Unser Weg* (Our Way), Berlin, March 1922.
9. For example, *Concerning the Light Path in a Mach-Zehnder Interferometer*. From the German (1941). Mimeograph. Royal Aircraft Establishment, Farnborough, Hants., January 1946.
10. Among others, see Ilona Polanyi, "The Hungarian Revolution," *The London Quarterly of World Affairs*, January 1946.
11. There is even one Canadian article: Ilona Duczynska, "A prérik szabadságharca" (The Prairies' Fight for Freedom. Outline of the Lives of Louis Riel and Gabriel Dumont). *Kanadai magyar naptár* (Canadian Hungarian Almanach). Toronto, 1954.
12. The address of which became affectionately known as "Skunk's Hollow," Rosebank, Pickering, Ontario.
13. *The Plough and the Pen: Writings from Hungary 1930-1956*, edited by Ilona Duczynska and Karl Polanyi. London: Peter Owen; Toronto: McClelland & Stewart, 1963.
14. *Co-existence. A Journal for the comparative study of economics, sociology and politics in a changing world*. No.1, April 1964. Publisher: Co-existence, Box 429, Pickering, Ontario, Canada. Editor: Rudolf Schlesinger, Glascow University, with an Editorial Board of twelve scholars of international repute.
15. *The Boy Changed into a Stag Cries out at the Gate of Secrets. Selected Poems of Ferenc Juhász 1949-67*. Translated, and with an Introduction by Kenneth McRobbie, with Ilona Duczynska. Toronto: Oxford University Press, 1970. In his Foreword to *The Plough and the Pen* (p. 11), W.H.Auden referred to the title poem as "one of the greatest poems written in my time".
16. She completed several short items which exist in manuscript, several others which appeared in Hungarian journals, and one major piece which represents the first chapter of her autobiography, "Korán reggel" (Early Morning), *Uj Irás* (New Writing). Budapest, No.3 March 1973, 6-25; it has an Introduction by József Lengyel.
17. József Lengyel, *Confrontation* (Szembesités), translated by Anna Novotny (Ilona Duczynska and Kenneth McRobbie). London: Peter Owen, 1973. The confrontation of the title takes place between two old communists who are former comrades in the Hungarian Embassy in Moscow: one the First Secretary (who had been imprisoned by the nazis), the other a prisoner recently released from Siberia.
18. See pp.287-8.
19. Ilona Duczynska, *Workers in Arms. The Austrian Schutzbund and the Civil War of 1934*. With an Introduction by E.J.Hobsbawm. New York: Monthly Review Press, 1978, Preface pp.11-12. The book is an abridged version of *Der demokratische Bolschewik*. Munich: List Verlag, 1975. In the "Acknowledgements," after expressing gratitude to her translator, Ilona's first words concern Karl Polanyi: "I thank my late husband, Karl Polanyi, for the first incentive to this work, for his wish that the facts and experiences it may offer should not go unrecorded".
20. Carl von Clausewitz, *Vom Kriege* (On War), 3 vols. Berlin, 1832.
21. Ilona Duczynska, "Emiliano Zapata, mexikói agrárforradalmár, 1879-1919" (Emiliano Zapata, Mexican Agrarian Revolutionary, 1879-1919). *Kanadai magyar naptár*. Toronto, 1957.
22. József Lengyel, *Acta Sanctorum*. Translated and with an Introduction by Ilona Duczynska. London: Peter Owen, 1966. See the "Translator's Note." Lengyel originally gave the title to just one of the stories. The references are, of course, to the young Czech student martyr Jan Palach and Che Guevara.
23. The young philosophy student and poet, Miklós Haraszti, had among other things organized an unauthorized demonstration against the Vietnam war, and written a sarcastic poem "The Mistakes of Che [Guevara]".
24. Peter-Paul Zahl, *Am Beispiel Peter-Paul Zahl. Eine Dokumentation*. Frankfurt am Main, 1977, "Schlusswort" (Final words before the Court, 1 March 1976), p.105.
25. Karl Polanyi, "Hamlet," *The Yale Review*, Vol.XLII, No.3, March 1954, 336-350.

Chapter Twenty

ILONA DUCZYNSKA AND AUSTRO-MARXISM
Alfred Pfabigan

In the course of an autobiographical interview[1] Ilona Duczynska told the author that her early experience of Hungary from 1917 to 1921 was decisive in giving shape to the rest of her life. Although her Austrian period extended over three decades, Austria was a "second choice" for her. A contributing factor in the devaluation of Austria was a Duczynski family tradition which drew Ilona and her mother towards Germany where she attended secondary school. Early negative sentiments towards Austria were reinforced when Ilona failed in an attempt in 1917 to develop contacts with the Austrian Left on behalf of the international socialist anti-war movement. As a young political activist she was disappointed by the apparent lack of interest on the part of the Viennese comrades. These early reactions lent emotive precognition to her later critique of bureaucratic mass parties.

Notwithstanding this, Ilona's book *Der demokratische Bolschevik*[2] addressed in considerable detail important aspects of the Austrian working-class movement. In this comprehensive study of a crucial part of the history of the First Republic, "Austria" mutated into an avant-garde location, where avant-garde questions were discussed and put into practice by avant-garde protagonists. As in many other studies of Austrian history, Austria appeared as a laboratory of modernity; it was a place where the central question found societal solutions. This question was the relationship between democracy and political power: in Duczynska's words, a synthesis of *Macht und Menschlichkeit* (literally "Power and Humanism"; in 1990s language perhaps, "Power with a Human Face.") (p. 291) Ilona considered that working on the book had extinguished her "guilt" and repaid her debt to the Austrian working-class movement. Red Vienna was a happy experience: "Our experiences of Red Vienna were lived through the child [her daughter]. It was a time of tranquillity in terms of political activism and intellectual production, thanks to the strength of the working class in Red Vienna." (Interview with Pfabigan) Ilona reported that she was politically "totally inactive" until 1927. She qualified as a primary-school teacher and "the spirit of the educational reforms awakened in me a sense of contentment such as I had never previously known. This had nothing at all to do with politics. It was something quite different—children...it was a period of experiencing a totally different kind of life. But it was short lived." (Interview)

On the morning of July 15, 1927, the radio broadcast news of the burning of the *Justizpalast*. Ilona was on holiday in Klosterneuburg, a summer resort near Vienna. She hurried back to the city where a press pass enabled her to cross police barriers. Here she witnessed the total collapse of the Social Democratic Party leadership and their "non policies." It was clear, she reflected, that political "neutrality" was over.

What followed was an episode in the history of the SD Party which constituted a further link in the chain of Ilona's long intellectual preoccupation. She edited and personally signed a leaflet in the name of Party loyalists opposed to the leadership. This action was intended to be a rallying cry for an organized left-wing opposition within the Party. Sympathizers who turned up at her apartment in the Vorgartenstrasse formed a "political working-class association" which published a small journal called *Der Linke Sozialdemokrat* financed out of Ilona's modest income from editorial services performed for the *Osterreichische Volkswirt*. Organized opposition within the Party, as distinct from communist disruption tactics, was at that time unknown in the Social Democratic Party of Austria (SDAPO). The left within the party called for more energetic opposition to the rise of fascism. This was perceived as a threat to party unity. The call for a demonstration to counter a proposed march by the *Heimwehr* (a right-wing para-military force) provided the excuse for disciplinary action against Ilona. A committee chaired by Bruno Marek, later mayor of Vienna, banned her from party activities for five years. The years which followed were characterized by persistent political retreat on the part of the Austrian Social Democratic Party in the face of the rising power of domestic clerical fascism. The experience was traumatic for Ilona: "There was no comfort to be taken from the fact that events unfolded as predicted."

Shortly before the outbreak of hostilities on February 12, 1934, Ilona sought a meeting with Otto Bauer, leader of the SDAPO. His home was already under strict military party security. Her appeal for a last minute change of policy fell on deaf ears; Bauer dismissed her as a "communist" although Ilona did not join the communist party until later, after the workers' defeat in February 1934.

On February 12th Ilona was in her laboratory of the physics department of the University of Vienna, desperately trying to contact the fighters of the *Schutzbund*. Her failure to establish contact with them was shattering: "The depressing experience of being excluded from the centre of the action has haunted me ever since." She gathered together the remnants of the group which years earlier had put out the *Linke Sozialdemokrat*. A poster was produced and put up in the Karl Marx Hof, to announce publicly to those in the armed resistance the existence of an independent left political grouping. Having established contact with the autonomous *Schutzbund* Ilona took on two important assignments. She became editor of an *Information Bulletin*, and she worked with a small group in establishing a miniature portable radio transmitter which could send a weak signal for short distances in working-class neighbourhoods to sustain the morale of those still representing an opposition to fascism.

Her experiences of the impotence of the numerically powerful Social Democratic Party, the struggle of a left minority in February, and her participation in the activities of the autonomous *Schutzbund* all provided material for several decades of research in England and in Canada. Eventually it led to the establishment of a second home in Vienna.

The fruits of these labours are contained in *Der demokratische Bolschewik*—"regrettably" published not in Austria but in Germany in 1975. The work reflects the circumstances of Ilona's political activities in Vienna and corrects previously accepted certainties in a way that is both surprising and original. Irreconcilable contradictions—which previously seemed self-evident to Duczynska (and apparently also to Karl Polanyi)—were reconciled in this work. Revolution and order, self-determination and discipline, force and political accountability were mediated in a text which could have served as an initial draft of an autobiography—which remained unwritten.

Ilona Duczynska's book is both an historical account of a social experiment of world significance (see Friedrich Heer's Introduction) and a well-developed foundation for a "project" in an existential sense. Although Austria was her "second choice," the book is a patriotic work. The Austrians have long had a habit of forgetting episodes of heroism, to the point of denying its existence. But no political community—not to speak of a nation—can afford to turn its back on the past or suppress the tragic and heroic episodes in its history without incurring serious loss. To transcend the past requires closure. No taboo, officially sanctioned or self imposed, can dispel this trauma. Only historical retrospect independent of organized political interests, can give back to a people the dignity and proud traditions which are theirs by right. The struggle of the Austrian *Schutzbund* was the first armed resistance to fascism, the initial combat which preceded the Spanish Civil War and the full-scale military engagement of the fascist powers in the Second World War.

The perspective from which Ilona Duczynska's account of the events preceding February 1934 was written is that of the familiar critique of the political left. According to this, the defeat of social democracy was due neither to accidental "breakdown," nor to a chain reaction of unavoidable events, nor yet to the inevitable unfolding of history since the foundation of the First Republic. It was unavoidable due ultimately to the passivity and policies of retreat practised by the Party leadership. The events which led up to the February outbreak are presented in the form of an accusation, a story of treachery, an indictment of irresponsible trust in the imagined goodwill of political opponents, a critique of the grandiose rhetoric that gave the impression of unassailable strength, and a description of the resulting disillusion of party activists and followers.

The Social Democratic Party Programme of 1926 (known as the "Linzer Program") was fundamentally ambivalent, being both "an expression of the hopes of a conscious working class" AND the "effective instrument of their defeat." (p.90). It provided justification for the use of force in defence, though the key question was whether the political leadership was prepared to use it. Thus far Duczynska's critique had followed the general lines of numerous other studies of the period. What was new was her systematic research into social democratic policies of national defence,—in particular, the existence, within the party elite, of carefully crafted alternatives to the party leadership's strategies of passivity and fatalism, associated with the name of Theodor Körner von

Siegringen, former chief-of-staff of the Austro-Hungarian army, later President of the Austrian Republic, and the party's leading theoretician on the military use of force. General Körner developed an ingenious synthesis of Clausewitz, Engels and Lenin in applying modern military technology to the special circumstances of Austria. Although Körner hated war, the master theoretician was convinced of its inevitability; from this premise, his analysis proceeded with a greater sense of realism than those of his competitors. With reference to Clausewitz, he cited the obligatory imperative that a Marxist must "think everything through to its conclusion before speaking of force."(p. 168) While seemingly banal, this sentence really sums up the opposition to the unyielding scholasticism of austromarxist verbalization about force.

Following the 1968 discovery by Norbert Leser of an unpublished manuscript written by Körner in 1928 entitled "Principles of Armed Force and Civil War," Duczynska located a large number of similar writings. These are reproduced in a selection of Körner's writings, accompanied by Ilona's presentation of Körner's ideas as forerunners of the guerilla tactics of 20th century liberation movements. As a democratic loyalist, Körner was faithful to the principles of the Linzer Programme: proletarian force was justified and legitimated only in reactive defence against massive violations of civil rights by the political forces of the Right. Körner was not a theoretician of military coups. He regarded "lawfulness" as a psychologically important source of strength for the working class. Following Clausewitz, he drew a clear distinction between the primary role and responsibility of the political leadership, and the implementing role of the technical executive. This formulation of the division of roles between the political directorate and the technical military executive was an implied criticism of the Austromarxist practice of conflating these two spheres. Körner insisted on the independence of the military leadership within the framework of the programme set and directed by the political leadership. He repeatedly polemicised against imitation by the *Schutzbund* of conventional army procedures with its military drills, marches, parades, and preparation for eventual military engagement in similar style. Körner's words clearly spoke to Ilona's heart. Later, she described how, at a *Schutzbund* Conference she had attended with Angelica Balabanoff, a model *Schutzbund* uniform was exhibited in a glass case. "This represents everything we are opposed to," commented Balabanoff.

Körner's organizational conception was the dissolving of the *Schutzbund* into small autonomously acting groups. In contrast to the party leadership's concept of a decisive final battle between the might of the armed state and that of the proletariat, he posited a series of sorties which could inflict maximal damage on the opponent with minimum losses.

> The first rule is never gather in large numbers! Keep to small groups of three or four, never more. There should be many such groups, each able to attack swiftly, and disappear again swiftly. The police will be searching together with a hundred cossacks for a crowd of thousands to massacre. But if you confront a force of one hundred police with one or two sharpshooters, they are more likely to hit a target than if they were aiming at a single individual—especially if they fire unexpectedly, and disappear without being identified.

Moreover, comrades, avoid fortress-like positions such as houses or barricades. Eventually the military will overpower you and blow you to pieces with their firepower. Our fortresses are buildings with many courtyards, entries and exits and such places where one can take aim, shoot and vanish. If they capture such a building, having suffered large casualties, they will find nobody there." (p. 153)

The account of the years of struggle by Körner against the "crude schematic militarism" of his arch-opponent Alexander Eifler who conceptualised the *Schutzbund* as an "inferior pseudo-army," make sad reading. (pp. 159,162) But Körner was isolated. He found no support. Duczynska drew the conclusion that the *Schutzbund* was not intended to be a fighting force, but "a threatening gesture." (p. 222) It was not until February 5, 1934, that Friedrich Adler, Otto Bauer and Julius Deutsch invited Körner to assume the role of military chief of the *Schutzbund*. Following a brief assessment of the situation, Körner informed Otto Bauer that he would not support a military engagement. "In my opinion the use of force is now hopeless and I decline leadership and responsibility." (p. 180) By this time, Otto Bauer had effectively lost control of the situation to autonomous regional initiatives. According to Duczynska, the retreat of the party leadership resulted in radicalisation and also apathy.

Körner's critique is convincing. Without question, the strength of the paramilitary arm of the party had passed its peak. But whether Theodor Körner really presented an alternative to Austromarxism is questionable. Eifler's plan of action, characterized by Duczynska as "essentially military *putsch* tactics" (p. 186) presented the party with a clearer orientation than the basically perverse reflections of Körner. Eifler's plan had a compactness and predictability lacking in Körner's call for the autonomy of paramilitary fighters. Eifler's imitation of conventional militarism accorded with the social democratic idea of "counter institutions" resembling those of the bourgeoisie, yet new and different due to their purposes and objectives. The most important of these was, of course, the much vaunted "Red Vienna."

The historic necessity of the victory of the working class and the attempt to embody proletarian force into the forward movement of history was an empowering idea. Eifler's concept of the *Schutzbund* as a mass organization numbering some 80,000 members at the height of its strength, based on the model of a regular army, lent credibility to the hope that victory of the working class was achievable within a lifetime. Körner's conception devalued the social-psychological factors essential to the effectiveness of an army. The symbolic value of a *Schutzbund* organized according to his principles would have been much smaller. Körner's orientation was really very different. Based on the autonomy of small groups, it was alien to the organizational character of Austromarxism, and put its entire organizational culture in question. It is difficult to imagine how a bureaucratic, oligarchistically led mass party like the Austrian Social Democratic Party, which was engaged primarily in parliamentary activity, could have supported a guerilla-style paramilitary organization. Several characteristics of the Party were paralleled in the *Schutzbund*. The bureaucracy of the Party corresponded to the militarization of the *Schutzbund*. The creation of a substitute world of essentially non-political sub-organizations affiliated to the

Party corresponded to the depoliticization of the *Schutzbund*. The belief in the magic of a large dues paying party membership corresponded to the belief in the effectiveness of amassing the largest quantity of arms, etc.

This raises the question as to whether the political directorate was really interested in the deployment of an efficient proletarian armed paramilitary organization. The adoption of Körner's proposals would have implied a revision of social democratic policies of the legendary ambivalence of "*Sowohl—also auch.*" A guerilla organization with an autonomous organizational life would sooner or later have challenged the party leadership. But division within the party, and the destruction of the apparent unity of the working-class movement — according to Duczynska, a mechanism for self-disempowerment through ambivalence in action—was surely not Körner's intention.

Although Körner's critique is convincing and his alternative was definitively articulated, it was alien to the milieu which gave rise to it. Ilona Duczynska exaggerated this alienation by her concentration on Ernst Fischer's thoroughly unreliable portrait of Körner as a "democratic bolshevik"—with the minor aside that if Karl Renner had been in Russia in 1917 he would also have declared his sympathy with the Bolsheviks. Eric Kollman's biography of Körner[3] suggests that the existential break in the life of the former general was less than was suggested by Duczynska. The "leftist" Körner who plays the principal role in Duczynska's book is not in evidence there. Kollman paints a picture of one who situated himself on the left wing of the movement for a greater Germany, and whose acquaintance with marxist theory derived from Adolf Schaerf (not exactly the intellectual source for the formation of "democratic bolsheviks").

What Körner conceptualized, according to Duczynska, was a *Lebensgefuehl* whose realization she found in the exponents of the "autonomous *Schutzbund.*" Although such an ideology was not based on Körner, and rejected the leading role of the Party, each individual had, according to Duczynska, a sense of empowerment derived from freely chosen conscious participation in a group. The context of this existential state of being (*Lebensgefuehl*) was reconstructed uncritically; the sketches are skimpy and evidence the difficulties in communicating such an exclusive historical experience. The author suggests that it is probably impossible for subsequent generations to comprehend the liberating effect of the Seventh World Congress of the Comintern, and the new forces set free. For the author, the autonomous *Schutzbund* represented a break with the past, something basically new, which could not be described in terms of conventional categories of analysis: "Their ideas were free of all orthodoxies; reproducible only in a spirit which itself rejects all orthodoxy." (p. 249)

A confrontation of the "really existing" historical figure of Körner, in all his complexity, with the historically ambivalent figure of the *Schutzbündler* does not do justice to Duczynska's methodology. Her approach to the writing of history accords with the *Prinzip Hoffnung* of Ernst Bloch: Körner and the *Schutzbündler* personify, if only partially, Bloch's "anticipatory consciousness."[4] The reconstruction of the existential world of the *Schutzbündler* is to be understood as "an allegory of happenings belonging to other spaces and realities."(p. 289) Finally, a synthesis of "Power and Humanism," underpinned by a "Philosophy of Liberation," was the source of Ilona's "eternal dissent."

The sphere of power comprises organization, tactics, strategy and all institutional social formations. The sphere of humanism comprises direct democracy concerned with its inner purposes; the community of fighters who, from the earliest hours of the foundation of the state penetrate its institutions as an anti-body in the corpus of bureaucracy; and spontaneous initiative in all areas of public life. (p. 290)

This certainly transcends the narrow spatial and personal circumstances of the First Republic. Without question, Duczynska has described a "historical moment," an apparently marginal contradictory phenomenon whose influence was brief in terms of time and space. But the same could be said about the legendary Paris Commune.

NOTES
Translated by Kari Polanyi Levitt, February 1998.
1. The interview was conducted in Semmering, Austria on April 1-3, 1977 in a convalescent home of the *"Bundesversicherungsanstalt für Arbeiter und Angestellte,"* which is the state-run health insurance institution for workers and employees.
2. *Der demokratische Bolchewik Zur Theorie und Praxis der Gewalt.* Mit einem Vorwort von Friedrich Heer. München: List Verlag, 1975. The English (abridged) verion is *Workers in Arms. The Austrian Schutzbund and the Civil War of 1934.* With an Introduction by E.J. Hobsbawm. New York: Monthly Review Press, 1978.
3. Eric C. Kollman, *Theodor Körner. Militär und Politik.* Wien: Verlag für Geschichte und Politik, 1973.
4. Ernst Bloch, *Prinzip Hoffnung.* Vol. 1, Frankfurt am Main: Suhrkamp-Verlag, 1959, pp. 49ff.

Chapter Twenty-One

"THIS IS THE VOICE OF RADIO SCHUTZBUND!"
Barbara Striker

A MEMOIR

In the latter part of 1934, Ilona Duczynska (who had taken to using her underground name Anna Novotny) had a mission. As propagandist for the Vienna workers militia, she had to prove that, despite the defeat of the *Schutzbund* in February 1934, the movement was still alive and relatively well. But how to prove it? Of course, there was *Der Sprecher*, the Newsletter of the *Schutzbund*, and it was possible to have recourse to leaflets. But that was not enough. Ilona had a vision—one that embodied more up-to-date means of propaganda, which could reach a large number of people with absolute certainty—and thus she hit on radio as the means.

Her vision would become reality, in the shape of a long-wave radio transmitter broadcasting on the official wave-length of Radio Wien! The transmitter would have to be specially designed and built. For obvious reasons of secrecy it must be small and also must be able to function as a conventional radio receiver. It would be able to serve as a transmitter only after the insertion of a transmission tube. To build such a device, it was necessary to enlist the help of others.

Fortunately, a young relative was available and more than willing. This was Otto-George (son of Laura Polanyi Striker, Karl Polanyi's sister), twenty-one years of age, the nephew of Ilona (then thirty-seven). He had come from Berlin and was a student of applied physics at the Technical University of Vienna. Furthermore, he had been interested in radio since the age of eleven, and, more to the point, was imbued with socialist ideology. Ilona met him due to the fact that her mother Helene, who was still occupying the Polanyi apartment in the Vorgartenstrasse, had sub-let a room to Otto-George's mother. After Karl and Kari went to England, Ilona no longer lived there in view of her underground work.

I first met Otto-George Striker in 1933, at a Hungarian students club in Vienna. It was a four-room establishment which was popular because it was *warm*—rented rooms having no heat!—and with provision for study, lectures, trips, and free lunches and dinners (but no politics); it was supported from the proceeds of the *Fasching* (Carnival) Ball sponsored by well-to-do Hungarian businessmen. I too was a student, initially of Pharmacy, though soon I switched to Chemistry. It was through Otto-George that I first met Ilona.

Otto-George occupied a large sublet room close to the University which he used for study purposes; he called it his workshop. In addition there was a small apartment where he and I—by then his student wife—lived in the first district, near the Kohlmarkt, in premises made available by the collapse of the Anglo-Austrian bank. It was here that Ilona came to visit, in the course of seemingly innocent meetings between relatives. The house in which we lived was well-situated for conspiratorial purposes, with two entrances, no *hausmeister*, and with access to many rooftops. From around September 1934, however, such visits were really planning sessions in which very soon several other equally young fellow-students were involved. There was Käthe Schiff, a young Austrian instructor in physics (who later became a professor of crystallography in Germany), Trude Kurz (who remained a long-time friend of Ilona's and became a professor of cybernetics at the National University of Mexico), Péter Erdös who was a Hungarian student of electrical engineering (later, a professor of economics at the Technical University of Budapest, strange as it may seem this was the case), Karl Remi a young radio technician (who later occupied a high position in Sweden), and Otto-George who did the main work on converting the radio into a transmitter (later in life, the main initiator of post-war Hungary's instrument industry and measurement sciences).

The meetings usually took place at night. It took four months of hard work before the vision became a reality. Rooftops were scaled in order to erect an antenna to prove to the satisfaction of the group that the newly constructed transmitter actually worked. The preparations were lengthy, though, because the device would have to function without an antenna, the whole purpose of the plan being mobility and thus portability. It was not until one year after the February 1934 rising of the Schutzbund that everything was declared ready. The radio's casing was that of one of the most popular domestic brands, a Eumig, but what was inside the receiver was home-made. To this, of course, could be added the all-important tube. It would then be able to broadcast on the wave length of none other than Radio Wien.

Ilona's vision—unlike most—was extremely practical. Radio Wien's daily programming was interrupted at midday. Precisely at 11.55 a.m. there was a five minute intermission during which was to be heard only the ticking of a metronome. This was the time selected for the radio group's message. The range of the radio transmitter was too limited for the broadcast to be heard throughout the city, let alone the outlying districts. Thus it was necessary for the apparatus to be moved after every transmission to a new location. In workers' districts, which were the target of the messages, there was no lack of apartments offered to the group.

The procedure was simple. Ilona selected the location of each transmission. One person was responsible for bringing the radio to the appointed place: that is, to one or other of the flats available. My job was to carry the large transmission tube which I had tucked away in a two-pound box of absorbent cotton and sanitary pads inside a briefcase full of chemistry notes. The announcer was the last to come, always a young Viennese worker. The text of the message was written by Ilona. After the transmission, the text was torn into pieces and flushed down the WC; then the speaker left; next, the tube was removed from the set, handed to me, and I left. Finally, the receiver was taken out by two of the men, and deposited in Otto-George's sublet room. Then, quite soon, Ilona announced that there would be no more broadcasts. Apparently, the vision had served its purpose within some larger plan.

If I remember correctly, there were five transmissions in all, perhaps all in the course of a single month, each lasting only three or four minutes (so as to avoid detection). But they certainly had results. On the one hand, the police authorities were quite desperate, because they were unable to locate the transmitter. Some newspapers in Vienna reported the messages. Ilona declared that they were good for morale, bringing new courage and strength to the many who received them. And, of course, for all of us young people who felt privileged to participate in this mission, it was an exciting experience. For me, that was the end of the adventure. As for Ilona, she disappeared from view, as far as I was concerned. Life must have been difficult; she had no income; her mother (widowed since 1907) had only a small pension which she supplemented by letting rooms.

The decades passed, bringing many new challenges for Ilona and all those who had collaborated on realizing her vision. The old friends were scattered. Otto-George and I went to the USA during the war; afterwards, we returned to Hungary. I met Ilona again during her first return visit to Budapest in 1948 and from 1963 on quite regularly; I met Trude Kurz (de Lara) again in 1967 and 1986 also in Budapest.

In the course of our last meeting, Ilona presented a copy of her book on the *Schutzbund* to Otto-George and me. I am proud—and deeply moved—to cite here the dedication that Ilona inscribed in the copy of the Hungarian edition that she gave us:

A tribute to bygone days:

In remembrance of the low ticking of the Rawag metronome, and the strong voice of the speaker:

'Hallo, hallo, hier spricht der Sender des Schutzbundes,'

and in memory of the ever-miraculous transformation of the transmitter into receiver, and of the helpless and unhappy Viennese Police Force, and of the many other wonderful common experiences, I present this belated writing

With all my love, Anna.[1]

NOTES

Translated by Kenneth and Zita McRobbie.
1. Ilona Duczynska's illegal name was 'Anna Novotny'.

Chapter Twenty-Two

FROM GIRL REVOLUTIONARY TO OLD DISSIDENT
György Konrád

I glimpse behind the steering wheel of the venerable old June bug of a Volkswagen a pair of glasses, and behind them a fine little old face, grey hair boyishly combed back, eyes that were blinking, and the smile nourished from within lingering at the corners of the mouth of this eighty-year-old girlishly idealistic soul. The car that sometimes takes a knock, a scratch, that signals when parking with a bang just how far it can go forward or backward, because it and its driver have been used to each other for a long time, already knows by itself, the way between Vienna and Budapest, like a cow finding its own way to pasture and homeward again.

In die alte Heimat?—the Austrian border guard jocularly asked Ilona, and now I am proud that, in the old country, it was natural that her address then, in the 1970s, was our apartment, where she got along splendidly with my mother, wife and children, just being there in the kitchen, because the leisurely exchange of thoughts, the flow of talk woven from stories, humour and ideas that Ilona Duczynska liked so much, saying it's what we've a right to, we aren't dogs, although the word dog coming from her was not in any sense depracatory, because she had a huge old friend of a dog at the edge of the wood on the precipitous riverbank in Pickering, near Toronto, where she lived all alone, surrounded by the kind attentions of neighbours, though I was aware that she had more exchanges with people of a different sort in the old country.

She liked these get-togethers. She was always on a tight schedule, with knee-length stockings, hair combed back, always in the same suit, the old machine carrying her from one apartment to another, from friend to friend, resigned to its owner who despite being bent with age was able to make new friendships, and hold new long conversations, because that also gave life to the June bug's respected years, this inextinguishable sympathy, and a curiosity emotional rather than spiritual, which within the whole circle of our friends made Ilona into a fairytale-like little elf granny.

This picture is almost twenty years old, dating from around the time when we started protesting openly against various censorship authorities, which called for conspiracy, whisperings on benches beside the Danube which couldn't be overheard, forwarding of messages, occasional smugglings of letters or manuscripts, in all of these mischiefs Ilona was unsurpassably professional. It was the profession she had learned fifty-five years earlier during the First World War, when she sought to end that war.

The girl of impoverished gentry background had come home from Switzerland where she had been acquainted with revolutionary pacifists, Zimmerwaldists and Angelika Balabanova, discussing with them how she might start an anti-war movement in Budapest too. On coming home she suffered a minor disappointment in her Vas County lord-lieutenant relatives, because she found the County Hall guarded by gendarmes, while inside a ball was in progress, with a tableau in which her adored aunt, who in their country house had taught Spinoza and Kant to the children, was to be seen *horribile dictu* in a costume holding a parasol on the flood-lit stage. From such frivolity the nineteen-year-old Ilona forthwith left for Badacsony where, in a small wine-press house belonging to the family, she composed on hand-made rag paper the peace manifesto, and in solitude above the lake thought things through.

She found a helper in the Galilei Circle, a young man who "was like a flame" leaping high, who radiated light around him. This was reason enough for the two of them to make a start on the historic task, and on married life too for the time being. They threw leaflets over high fences into factory courtyards. They also organized a union of shop stewards, one of whom, as used to happen in those times, was pressured into becoming a police informer. Although she had already in January 1918 succeeded in organizing a workers peace demonstration in the Andrássy út, she was soon, together with the radiant young man, sitting on the bench of the accused, and afterwards only as a favour from the nice prison guard could they meet in the prison corridor.

The practice of power was alien to Ilona's unshakeable but mild soul, therefore she did not like to talk about the Republic of Councils; she left Moscow in 1921 when the revolution had already created its bastard, the new autocracy decorated with red flags. Ilona was more interested in saving, in helping, in mediating, for example in acting as courier in the matter of a tube of toothpaste from Moscow to Vienna. It had been filled with Czarist diamonds, and the Comintern was sending it to the Hungarian Communists in emigration; if I remember well it was given to her by Radek and Rakosi who said that she should deliver it to György Lukács, not Béla Kun, because the philosopher was the son of a rich banker and as such not tempted to steal, whereas a petit bourgeois journalist would be more likely to lose his head over precious stones. Well, in smuggling, as I have mentioned, Ilona was a true artist. Who would have thought that a sweet, frail old granny would get up to such a thing? She was expelled from the communist party, shortly after the toothpaste tube escapade, at the very same philosopher's suggestion because while Lukács did indeed manage the business of the gems very well, Ilona's natural inclination to ideological deviation was more than he could tolerate.

Who was friend and who enemy was something Ilona deduced not from theory, nor from a membership card, but rather from a handshake or the directness of a stare, from listening to the voice, almost as if repeating silently the words within; that is to say, she could decide at the first moment of meeting. Before I got to know her I had already heard about Ilona from János Pilinszky, that saint of twentieth-century Hungarian poetry who inclined to heresy. It was as a reader of poetry that she became János's friend, and I very much appreciated that it was my novel *Látogató* [The Case-Worker] which lead her to me and the family. This was a great coup for me because, among other things, through her I got to know some splendid people. For example, Mrs Mihály Károlyi, countess Katalin Andrássy, with whom the revolutionary Ilona was connected not only by the thoroughness and refinement of their education, not only by certain similarities in childhood upbringing, the déclassée would-be assassin with the red countess, but also by their wonderful ability to laugh at the world and at themselves, thus demolishing liars so gracefully. They defended with the full weight of their presence a certain accused who told the truth in a court of law, together with a third, a lioness of a woman whose husband László Rajk the former revolutionary French teacher, fighter in Spain, illegal party leader in Budapest, was minister of internal affairs after the war. Then at the beginning of his fall, demoted to minister of external affairs, this adventurous young man was hanged in 1949 after a show trial, so she was imprisoned, and their son placed in an institution under another name.

The boy has grown up, become an architect and a dissident, and the authorities gave cause for lady Júlia to go to the head of the country, to Kádár who had been a pupil of her husband's and later at the time of the hanging was minister of internal affairs. In her deep hoarse voice she declared that this won't do, they should not touch her son; and Kádár, who had himself spent five years in prison and been tortured to the same degree as Rajk, said that there would not be another Rajk trial, and kept his word. And Júlia the grande dame of the former communists of multiple prison sentences, with her broad-shouldered stature like a man's, with her frank no beating about the bush directness, naturally sat beside Ilona and Katinka in the first row of the big courtroom in the law building where the accused Miklós Haraszti a young writer was of course another friend of Ilona's.

The entrance made by the women, all three of them widows of extraordinary men, was a demonstration that impressed the court, spectators, and the highest government authorities. Karl Polanyi (probably the most original modern Hungarian thinker in the social sciences) deserved Ilona. Countess Károlyi was likewise deserved by Count Mihály Károlyi, President of the First Hungarian Republic in 1918, one of the few modern Hungarian politicians whose moral dignity, in glory and in failure, in richness and in poverty, remains incontrovertible. Of Rajk I have already spoken. So behind the three Graces were the impressive profiles of their three men; but I still maintain that it was the husbands who deserved these magnificent, daring personalities.

To shoot someone would not have been appropriate for Ilona, for she could never have raised a weapon against simple people, or those in uniform. It was a different matter though, were Count István Tisza to have been shot, the Hungarian prime minister towards the end of the First World War, a tall upright man of iron, who did not want to enter the war, but once having entered into something would see it through to the end, like folk from the Bihar region where he had his estates. It was impossible to convince Tisza, to try to argue with him was a waste of breath, so people had to wrestle with him in their own way. Count Károlyi challenged him to a duel. His widow would tell of that terrible night, biting her nails, while they fenced all night long in the wing of his palace which today houses the Literary Museum. The peace-party's Károlyi, the worse fencer of the two, seeking to wound the war-party Tisza, he who was concerned only that no blood should be shed, and all night long knocked away Károlyi's sword, without injuring his opponent in the least. Then Ilona also was looking towards the other wing of the palace, in such a way that in her eyes I saw the two men in their white shirts compelled by honour to clash their blades together until dawn, dancing around in the large reception hall, the one from which the Countess was barred during the course of the duel.

Of that sportsman with the charmed life Ilona also had other memories from 1918, and in 1975 after the passage of fifty-seven years there still welled up a tear which stayed glistening in her eye when she recalled the history of those times. It was Tisza who was the obstacle to the peace in which the young girl believed as in a saint, just as so many did at that time; to sweep aside the one who blocked the path, Ilona believed, was her mission determined by destiny, although she knew that whoever raised a hand against the country's prime minister would surely die. All the same, she acquired a pistol, from none other than a friend of the pale scholarly director of the capital's library, who was the eminent theoretician of social anarchism. Just as the novels of that time prescribed, the place where assasination was discussed was Buda's Németvölgy Cemetery. There, while the death bell tolled high above, beneath the willows on top of the mountain, the historian with the slim hands spoke long and often with Ilona. She walked out of the cemetery gate, alone now, and took the streetcar down to the city centre; she paced up and down under the row of plane trees in the Andrássy út, in front of the Tisza mansion to which a carriage usually returned the prime minister for lunch. Mademoiselle assassin grasped the butt of the pistol in her handbag as security personnel began leaping out from a police car. Then the door of the carriage opened at the very moment when, right behind Ilona, a newsvendor shouted out to the whole world that Tisza had resigned! That very morning he had thrown in his hand, the situation thus was transformed in the twinkling of an eye. An assassin of noble birth was not about to execute, in the name of the universal desire for peace, a man going into retirement. Ilona did not draw the pistol from her handbag, but just stared at the man of iron's drooping shoulders, head hanging, as he entered the portal of his house having come straight from Parliament.

The pistol was returned on the afternoon of that day. During that same period Ervin Szabó had also lived through some anxious hours, picturing Ilona in a hundred different ways, caked with blood or in handcuffs. Then he also heard a newsvendor in the city centre, and nothing being said about any assassination he at first felt happy, then this changed to sadness, and when Ilona asked him "What did you feel as you listened to the news?" the scholar's reply was "I felt sorry for you." And fifty-seven years later that tear appeared again in the corner of Ilona's eye, only I suspected that her sorrow was at having been denied the opportunity for such a splendid trophy, which circumstance incidentally also removed the rope from around her neck. Someone chosen by destiny, who with one pistol shot can open the road leading homewards for millions of soldiers, to be a tragic heroine prepared for a tragic ending, had that role taken away from her by the great director. As compensation he cast her for an uncertain future, one burdening this young lady with all of six decades, marriage, a daughter, grandchildren, and with persons among whom are some to be helped and some to be loved.

Among her other attainments there was the study of mathematical science at university in Zurich, knowledge which helped her while in England, the country to which she emigrated, when working on a supersonic fighter aircraft, its development requiring an enormous number of thermodynamic calculations and experiments. Let us locate then the beautiful young assassin in London a quarter of a century later, in a garage on the city's outskirts, in which experiments vital to the very existence of the air force were being undertaken in great secrecy. Whoever possesses jet-propulsion aircraft will also have possession of the sky, and earth besides. Thus competition was waged between German and English-American researchers. German scientists were supplied with every possible convenience and item of equipment in palatial underground establishments, as Ilona was able to verify with her own eyes after the war. She and her colleagues had only this garage-like building which even had a hole in the roof, beneath which a wash basin was needed to catch the dripping rain. Otherwise the atmosphere was friendly, strange figures were brought together, a Hindu physicist would from time to time take up the yoga sitting position on the floor, an American would pick up his saxophone when he got tired and start playing, but they worked away, continuing even during periods of bombing, and they beat the Germans to it with consequences which are well known.

Her friend, then close to fifty, wife of the emigré President of the Republic, trained as a fighter pilot, though prime minister Churchill, with whom she was on friendly terms, did not allow the countess to enter the fray. Everyone is deprived in a different way by fate from having a tragic obituary, and it was decreed that we should sit together in a room overflowing with papers and old letters amid which the countess is radiant as she presents her discoveries following days of archival research. Her grandmother, wife of a count Andrássy, and the young Lajos Kossuth, the future great Hungarian republican, at the time when he was still estate steward, developed mutual ties of poetic friendship. They exchanged letters that were spirited yet melancholic, while from Paris her grandfather was entertaining his wife with the latest news of society's doings and of card games right about the time when conception must have taken place. Thus her presentiment was not entirely without foundation that the rebel Kossuth was her secret grandfather, which complements her well and explains why as a girl she had been attracted to count Károlyi who, even though he gambled away fortunes at cards, settled down at Katalin's side, being the one who became the other rebel republican president.

You can imagine how enthusiastic Ilona was at this thought. She had no particularly interesting things to say about her ancestors, about Polish aristocrats successfully gambling away their estates at cards, although her Hungarian grandfather was a curious character. As he became increasingly impoverished, he sold his country houses, moving into ever smaller premises, until he ended up with but a single room, one surrounded with doric columns, its windows protected with iron sheeting; in the middle of the room there was a well, so that in the event of enraged peasants laying siege, he would be able to hold out for weeks without suffering thirst. Below the windows there were guns leaning against the wall, so that single-handedly he could effectively defend himself, keeping going on toast and water, no besieger able to get to him.

If there was something strange in this behaviour, the same can be said of her father's as well. Assured of becoming a brilliant officer in the engineers, he ended up as a railway official in Vienna on a modest salary, scraping to make ends meet for his family in an apartment with two rooms and a kitchen. However, he was unable to do without being served in a manner worthy of his origins, and every evening the porridge and milk was brought in by a servant wearing white gloves from the kitchen where he slept in a chest. The father was attracted to nature medicine, and wanted his family to take sun therapy, air therapy, and so during summers in grandfather's shrinking garden, among flowerbeds, as naked as the day they were born, they had to walk round and round in single file so that sunlight and fresh air could come into contact with their private parts. Finally, papa disappeared in America, where he had gone with his inventions to get fantastic wealth, but his companions stole his inventions, and did away with him under suspicious circumstances. Thus early in her youth Ilona had to learn the ways of poverty, though there were wealthy relatives in whose country houses a guest-room awaited her.

Poverty would remain, however, her life-long true companion. In her one-room kitchen apartment in Vienna I saw no sign of luxury. Here the aging June bug also was at home transporting her to a woman friend, one who was also a storehouse of the most curious tales. I can report that Ilona enjoyed all of them, even when hearing them not for the first time. Good stories, in parts somewhat grotesque, mature like wine over the course of the years. These can be told well only by one who herself enjoys the telling, at the corner of whose mouth, as she stares before her, a tiny breath-like smile almost never vanishes, which by the winter fireplace, because even the thought of central heating in Ilona's room was strange, in the red pile of ash, accords human dimensions to every figure equally, good and bad, for the heroes of her stories are no longer alive, have vanished totally, until we summon them forward from out of the shadows.

Translated by Kenneth and Zita McRobbie.
This essay by the eminent novelist, sociologist, and former dissident György Konrád originally appeared in the Budapest weekly *Elet és Irodalom (Life and Literature)*, 23 December 1994.

Chapter Twenty-Three

FROM CENTRAL EUROPE, THREE FRIENDS REMEMBER
Eva Czjzek, Erzsébét Vezér, and György Litván

EVA CZJZEK: MEMORIES OF A FELLOW TRANSLATOR

Ilona's memory lives within me as vitally as if it was only yesterday that I accompanied her down to the garden gate. I see her before me in her short sheepskin coat and Basque beret, getting into her ancient little car. The motor starts with difficulty, and as it backfires she waves goodbye with a heart-warming smile. I did not know then that it was for the last time. The almost life-threatening little Volkswagen, the worn overcoat and the beret were just as organically a part of her as the single room plus kitchen flat where the WC was out in the corridor in the "Bassena Haus" in Vienna, the building in which Trotsky was thought to have lived at one time. I am convinced that Ilona would have remained faithful to this puritan style of life even had fate blessed her with more money. For she was obsessed with an idea which, in spite of many painful disappointments, she never betrayed. She considered herself to be a communist, but this ideal communism of hers was different from what real communism had degenerated into. She had been expelled from the Party at the age of 25.

Ilona was a fighter for truth, frequently at the risk of her life. A profound humanity determined her actions. She always took the side of the losers, the weak, whom she protected with all the resources of her personality. There was nothing she hated more than hypocrisy and falsehood. Despite her excellently trained mind—surely in those days there was a higher level of mathematics and physics teaching in the university—she was completely without intellectual arrogance. She was infinitely modest, mind and heart together within her agreeing in wonderful symbiosis.

Was she a marxist? To this question, I would like to reply in the words of the eminent blind Austrian philosopher, Ernst Bloch: "Only a good marxist can be a good christian, only a good christian can be a good marxist." These words best confirm the truth of Ilona's life.

I see before me in the little room in the Rodlergasse on December 24th parcels stowed away in a basket. She was preparing to give them as presents to the children living in the house. I have an unforgettable memory of a chilly, raw Good Friday. Despite the sleet, Ilona had come round to fetch me; we were going to hear the St. Matthew Passion. I see her before me wrapped in a travelling rug seated in the auditorium, eyes shut, her face transfigured, giving herself completely to the spell of Bach's unequalled masterpiece.

It is to her that I owed my acquaintance with the distinguished writer László Németh in the mid-1960s. When I succeeded in publishing in the *Neues Forum* his essay entitled "Small People, Great Soul," his wife Ella travelled to see me in Vienna in the hope that I would translate more of his work. He would receive his acquaintances and friends, among them Ilona Duczynska, at my place.

At the time of our first meeting I already felt close to her. She was the same age as my mother, and her cultured, archaic, pungent Hungarian expressions recalled in me "old inhabitants of the old country," the atmosphere in which I grew up and which is now gone forever. We became friends and met often.

Of course, the main link between us was literature. We became fellow translators. She translating from Hungarian to English, I from Hungarian to German; we considered this occupation as a mission on behalf of the old country. As the elder, she followed my work with touching interest and attentiveness. With her exceptional sensitivity and with the excellent sense of language that she owed to her Polish ancestors, she could put her finger on the smallest misunderstanding in terms of meaning and shade of difference between words. That was how she became the ablest publisher's reader I could ever wish for. Her command of German was at the same level as that of her Hungarian mother tongue. She spoke English and French equally as well as Hungarian, and was conversant with Slavic languages.

Without prejudice she would approach different sorts of people without hesitation and with sympathy; what was most important, she knew how to listen. She was the complete "outsider," and found the right tone for everybody. The fascination of her character resided in the fact that she never assumed a mask; she was always herself, and thus totally convincing. She was acknowledged for her authenticity even within the circle of her political adversaries. Young people she conquered with her liveliness of spirit and exquisite sense of humour. My children and grandchildren were enthusiastic about her too.

One could learn a great deal from her. She was one for essentials, she never wasted time on unnecessary things. She always kept to her scale of values, making time for what to her seemed important...even when she was coming to the end of her strength. I see her before me propped up among pillows in a hospital bed, bent over a mass of manuscripts. On seeing her pale, transparent small features I can scarcely conceal my dismay—she on the other hand radiated pleasure, informing me how that very day she had already translated thirty pages! (And feeling ashamed, I thought of how I could never manage more than four or five.)

However, when she succeeded in completing some piece of work, she liked "to celebrate." At such times she would come round in her car to my place on the hillside at Grinzing and bear me off to Sievering, among the vineyards, to Mitterwurzerweg. That is to say, to where there was an intimate though well-known little *Heuriger* (an inn where you could buy a measure of new wine) where too one could feel very much at home. In the spacious garden, set out on the green lawn, wooden benches and tables awaited the guests. Beside the entrance gate the owner's rabbits gambolled in a cage, on the threshold a cat lay peacefully sleeping, while the watchdog took no notice of our arrival and did not consider us worth so much as a yelp. So there we were, Ilona and I, forgetting cares and illness, in the relaxed atmosphere sitting at our ease, a jug of red wine before us. It was such a treat to listen to Ilona's stories.

With her death, something went out of my life.

Vienna, March 1998[1]

ERZSÉBET VEZÉR: AN ANNIVERSARY TRIBUTE

The woman loved and admired by everyone who knew her would have been one hundred years old on March 11 of this year. It certainly wasn't because Ilona Duczynska had been forgotten that this commemorative article is appearing somewhat later, for no one can ever forget her, only the exact date of her birth. With her death we lost not only an exception human being—a revolutionary flame flickered out, a flame which in her alone had burned with the faith of the 1920s.

She was born a revolutionary: a brave, wise, sovereign revolutionary who would have sacrificed life itself against war and poverty. Yet her distinguished family and admirable education would have predestined her for something different. On her mother's side she was descended from the Békássy family who were of the gentry and owned the Zsennye estate among others, and from a noble Polish family on the side of her father who died early but from whom she inherited her technical scholarly ambition. In Zsennye there is a memorial plaque commemorating her dearly beloved cousin the poet Ferenc Békássy who fell in the First World War, of whom Babits, Kosztolányi and Árpád Tóth make mention. But there is a memorial plaque also in England, in Cambridge, preserving his memory, even though he fought against that country in the army of the Monarchy, for he had been a university student there. Ilona's anti-war sentiment must have been nourished by her cousin's death.

In the circle of her family's country gentry, she felt restless even as a little girl. When she reached the age of seventeen, in the first year of World War One, in a letter to her friend Edit Gömrói she complained of how terrible it was that she can only sit knitting socks, though there is so much more she would like to do against the war. But soon she found the framework within which she could work to greater purpose against it, in the Galilei Circle organized by progressive students. From Switzerland, where she had gone to study, she had brought back to her homeland in 1917 the anti-war declaration of the Zimmerwald Conference, and along with a few Galilei companions she distributed leaflets among the workers and soldiers.

She was brought up in Austria, but her first field of battle was to be in Budapest in association with the Galileo Circle of the youth of Hungary. Her master and—as she used to call him—"our spiritual father" was Ervin Szabó. It was from him that she learned the basic law of the revolutionary movement's unity of thought and deed. Her other great model was the revolutionary lyric poet Endre Ady. I once asked her what her generation had to thank Ady for. She replied, in that spirited girl student's voice of hers: "For everything."

She was arrested, in January 1918, for her anti-war activities and was the principal accused, together with her first husband Tivadar Sugár. At one point, the defence lawyer sought to put words into her mouth to the effect that she was not a revolutionary, but a reformer; she would not accept that, being unwilling to catch hold of the lifebelt thrown her way. She rather accepted the two and a half years prison sentence. The process commenced in September 1918. In the closed main session it was she who was interrogated first. On September 24 the verdict was handed down, and stated:

> The accused Ilona Duczynska, in addition to the six months pre-trial detention which occurred through no fault of hers, is condemned to a further two years during which, every second week she shall be for one day on only bread and water, on which day she shall also have a hard bed, and

during the first month of each six month period she shall spend fifteen days in solitary confinement. (József Halmi, "Files of the Galileo Trial," January 1919)

Ilona was not long in prison. On the night of October 30th, with the declaration of the National Council, the cells were opened one after another. Ilona and her companions were borne on the shoulders of the crowd in front of the National Council. It was the revolution that set her free, and from then on her life was inseparable from the workers movement.

During the short-lived regime of the Republic of Councils she worked on the People's Committee for Foreign Affairs. This body sent her on an official mission to Switzerland; from there, after the fall of the Republic of Councils, together with old Russian revolutionaries she went to Moscow where she took part in the Second Congress of the Comintern in 1920. But she found conditions there unfavourable, and therefore at her own request she was sent to Vienna where the Hungarian revolutionary emigrés were established. This is where she met Karl Polanyi, and friendship soon grew into love.

However, Ilona was still interested in politics. She was shocked by the internal disagreements within the Hungarian Communist Party, by the dissensions and factions within the emigrant party with none of which she could associate herself. Thus she wrote her article "Comments on the Disintegration of the KMP" which resulted in her expulsion from the Party. As György Dalos writes, in his book on Ilona (*Lover of Action*, 1984): "Ilona was a private revolutionary; she did not want to be a soldier recruited for battle, but rather a partisan. Such persons are unable to belong to any party."[2]

Subsequently she joined the Hungarian emigré liberal wing of the Social Democrats in which Karl Polanyi also participated; they married, and had a daughter. Later, while Polanyi was preparing to write his great works on economics, Ilona followed the struggles within the parties and joined the left opposition in the Social Democratic Party. As a sovereign revolutionary she became a militant in the *Schutzbund* (the defence association of the workers of the Austrian Republic). In 1927 she launched a paper entitled *Der linke Sozialdemokrat*. She took part in the activities of the Austrian workers movement; right up until—and even after—its defeat in February 1934, as propagandist by means of the press and radio on behalf of the *Schutzbund*. Her book, *Workers in Arms* (1978), published also in Hungarian, constitutes a fine memorial to one of the movement's leaders, Theodor Körner, "the theoretician of violence," who—like Ervin Szabó before him—successfully united within himself theory and action.

Meanwhile Karl Polanyi and their daughter had moved to England, and later Ilona was to follow. During the Second World War we find the Polanyis on the same side as Michael Károlyi. Together they fought for the New Democratic Hungary in the English Hungarian Council. Ilona had qualified as a pilot while teaching briefly in America. After the war, because of Ilona's communist past, she was not allowed to join her husband in the USA, so the couple settled in Canada, in Pickering near Toronto.

Ilona went home for a brief period in 1948. She studied the land reform in Hungary, and for that purpose travelled across the entire country together with People's College students. She even wrote an article about this for an English newspaper in Canada, and an article for an important English journal, but nothing more, having become alienated by Rákosi's policy. But she never severed ties with the motherland.

After the 1956 revolution, in 1959 and again in 1963 she went home, accompanied by Karl Polanyi. In 1963 appeared their jointly edited Hungarian Anthology of Populist literature, *The Plough and the Pen: Writings from Hungary, 1930-56*, which introduced modern Hungarian literature to the English-speaking world for the first time. In the second half of the 1960s her connection with Hungary became more close when she resided part of each year in Monoszló with her old comrade-in-arms and friend József Lengyel. Soon this friendship was extended to the Hungarian democratic opposition which was being organized at that time. She smuggled abroad József Lengyel's novel *Confrontation*, which could be published at home only years later.

It was at that time, in the course of her regular visits to Hungary, that Ilona Duczynska would become known to us as a living person. Scurrying between Pickering, Vienna and Budapest, she appeared wherever democratic rights and revolutionary thought had to be defended. She protested against everything that represented lawlessness, no matter in what part of the world it took place; her protests and stands carried all the more weight because her past served as backdrop. She conquered everyone with her capacity for loving, with the absence of any show of intellectual superiority. This was because she was wise, too, and had that quality, which is rare in passionate people, of being able to argue calmly and without anger, even with a certain charm, while yet being very determined. To be praised by her was like being awarding a medal, while her scolding always made you stop and think. Never for a moment did her interest diminish in anything in which she discoved stirrings of the new. It can be understood, then, that closest to her were the young. When she came to Pest, and in her last years she came almost yearly for a longer or shorter time, she was surrounded by dozens of young people. She did not sit among them like some curiosity which the past had left behind, but as someone of experience, a friend who has something of consequence to say about their present and their future.

It is impossible to list all her other wickedly provocative deeds in such a short article. Yet it must be mentioned that she used her influence with György Aczel, then the all-powerful Minister of Culture, in the interests of the anarchist oppositional poet Miklós Haraszti; today it is perhaps common knowledge that at opening of the trial Ilona Duczynska, Katherine Károlyi and Júlia Rajk appeared together, by way of a demonstration, and thus were able to have the process suspended. She agreed with the democratic opposition's manifestation of solidarity with Charter 77, and this she expressed with gracious and clear understanding when she accepted a high order from the President of the Presidential Council.

Now for a few personal memories of mine about her. Once, perhaps it was in 1977, I succeeded in drawing her away for a week to the Writers' Vacation House at Szigliget. Naturally, even there she was surrounded by followers of the democratic opposition. At a table close to ours sat János Pilinszky, the eminent lyric poet, who—though not particularly sociable by nature—overhearing what Ilona was saying, came to sit at our table, and for the rest of the time that Ilona was there they had long conversations, drinking in each others words. The Catholic poet and the world revolutionary.

On another occasion I took her to visit Valéria Dienes, for they were bound together by their pasts. By then Valéria was already very old and was confined to her bed by illness. They started to speak about the past: "My dear Ervin..." was how Valéria remembered Ervin Szabó. Then she started to sing religious songs that she had composed in an old but enchanting voice. Ilona just sat there, listening raptly, sometimes saying: "Beautiful...beautiful."

Thus it is from her that we can learn tolerance, the sovereignty of thought, courage, and humanity.

GYÖRGY LITVÁN: WANDERER AMID REVOLUTIONS, ILONA DUCZYNSKA 1897-1978

"Gods die, man lives": these words of Babits[3] were quoted by an old friend of mine, on hearing the news of the death of our mutual friend Ilona Duczynska. Truly she was ageless, unchanging, tireless, as are the gods. And anyway, her age seemed unreal, and still seems so today. "Only" eighty-one years old? From "ancient times" no less, she would play an active part in history for all of six decades. More, through her association with Ervin Szabó, the Madzsars, the Polanyis and Angelika Balabanova, old masters and friends, she effectively commanded the experience of a far longer period, the whole century. Arriving year after year in her antiquated Volkswagen, it was as if she came to us in a time machine from out of the infinite past. In her worn grey costume, with her short grey hair, in her there stood before us in mind and body a real turn-of-the-century Russian revolutionary.

Eighty-one, really? Up to the very last day, she lived like a student. She was making one new friend after another in Canada, Berlin, Vienna and Budapest, and it was with those who were twenty that she was always on the best of terms. Each year, more and more people awaited her return to Hungary, and she regarded the latest friendship to be just as sacred as those hallowed by half a century.

What made her so irresistible? Was it the inquisitive and artful gleam in her eye, her smile's girlish charm which made her almost beautiful? You only had to meet her once, to know that this was part of it. But the gleam in her eye and hidden smile expressed something more: a spirit unbroken and unbreakable. Among the witnesses to and participants in great events, I never knew any in whom there burned so brightly the flame kindled in their youth. There was nothing about her of the "veteran." She couldn't be pensioned off. She simply remained what she was at the age of twenty, on the threshold of her revolutionary career. But that was secondary. Her real secret was that she never became an anachronism.

The paradox of our history is that, while it is rich in revolutions it is poor in genuinely revolutionary personalities. Our revolutions were mostly led by reformers. Duczynska belongs among the greatest Hungarian revolutionary personalities of the century.

In 1917, when everyone was sick and tired of the war, and every honourable and courageous man of the left *meditated* and *conferred* about what could be done—she all on her own, this student coming from a gentry background, belonging to no organization, newly returned from Switzerland, was the first who started to *act*, and attracted to herself the most resolute revolutionary elements. A few months later, she courageously faced a court martial. She was freed from prison by the White Aster Revolution.

She showed the same initiating power in Austria, during the 1920s and 1930s, where she organized Left-wing groups, took part in the struggles of the

Vienna workers' *Schutzbund* and edited their paper, even after the defeat of February 1934. There would be no opportunity for a spectacular revolutionary role in the second half of her life. It was as a physicist that she assisted the British war effort against fascism. In the early 1960s she readily put her literary interests at the service of the early stages of *detente* and international rapprochement. Together with her husband Karl Polanyi, a man of many parts, she compiled an English-language anthology of the newer Hungarian prose and poetry. She never sought to play a "role" or to create a stir. As a disciple of the old anarchists and Ervin Szabó, she was most truly in her element as persistent weaver of threads in everyday quiet conspiracy.

Only in her last years did she reveal—and even then with shy modesty—that in the spring of 1917, armed with a pistol, she was quite prepared to make an attempt on the life of István Tisza, which at the last moment was rendered unnecessary by the Prime Minister's sudden fall from office. It is certain, though, that her aim would not have wavered.

Not long ago, in the Vienna State Archives, I came across a confidential report of July 1919, from the Austrian consul in Budapest, about a certain Ilona Duczynska who was sending considerable amounts of money by couriers to Austria and Switzerland, to foment socialist revolution there. (She was greatly amused, when I presented her with the text last year.) Who knows how many such "wiles" she was involved in or attempted over the decades? By nature, she was not one to talk about herself.

Nor, by nature, was she at all irresponsible. She was no adventurer, but a tireless wanderer through revolutions. She evaluated what had, and had not, to be done, with a rigorous moral sense derived from her inner self and from her masters. Only that judgement coming from within did she heed; to external discipline or restriction she never would submit, and in the same way she never sought to judge others. She showed infinite tolerance of every conviction that was sincerely held. From this it followed that she felt at home only in opposition, in the role of militant revolutionary, not of victor. She always sided with those who were oppressed and persecuted. This is what gave meaning to her free, wandering life: assisting ever more people, in ever more parts of the world.

These sympathies, like her opinions, were at time controversial, even strange; but her moral sense and personality set the stamp of authenticity upon whatever she said or did. She was an institution all by herself, representative of a great generation who still lived among us, for ever a mark to steer by. Perhaps that is why we felt she was immortal, and will remain with us always. And when she finally had to take her leave, she did not ask that, in all respects, we follow her path and continue her work. With an apologetic, modest smile, she bequeathed to her children and grandchildren just one thing: a sense of duty.

NOTES

Translated by Kenneth and Zita McRobbie.
1. This article was written expressly for the volume.
2. György Dalos, *A cselekvés szerelmese*. Budapest: Kossuth, 1984.
3. Mihály Babits (1883-1941), one of the two most important figures in the Hungarian poetic revival of the early twentieth century.

Sources: *The Hungarian News*, Budapest, May 20, 1978; *Népszabadság, Hétvége* July 12, 1997.

Chapter Twenty-Four

THE POLANYIS DISCOVER A POET
György Bodnár, Ferenc Juhász

GYÖRGY BODNÁR: THE POLANYIS AND THE NEW HUNGARIAN POETRY OF FERENC JUHÁSZ

The publication in 1957 of the Collected Works of the poet Ferenc Juhász was a revelation to Karl Polanyi and Ilona Duczynska. They had already conceived of a literary anthology which would present the crucial role of writers in the reform movement culminating in the 1956 Revolution. Now they would decide to present Juhász as leading representative of the new generation of poets in the literary anthology which they jointly edited *The Plough and the Pen* (1963). The ideals of Hungarian populist literature served as the guiding principle of the editors' selection of both poetry and prose. Although Juhász was a follower of folk tradition only at the beginning of his career, having by 1963 achieved his own revolution in poetry, his work could still be harmoniously accomodated to the central theme of the anthology. The Polanyis certainly regarded the populist movement as more than a matter of literary style and tradition. For them, populism represented the cause of the people, standing in opposition to both conservatism and communism's voluntarist notion of popular culture. Consequently, the editors' conception of popularism reveals the impact of the 1956 Revolution. Their selection of several of the poems of Ferenc Juhász as climax of the anthology was appropriate because during the immediately preceding years the author had struggled with the totalitarian regime and the straitjacket of its literary dogmas in order to achieve a personal poetic revival. It may be helpful to provide some indication of the poet's work in order to show why the Polanyis were so attracted to him.

It must be remembered that in the early 1950s Hungarian literature, which had a notable past of great achievement and openness to the modern world, was severely restricted by political and aesthetic dogmas. As its condition was determined by external forces, so its liberation was dependent on relaxation in the political arena. The direction it took, however, was not a direct continuation of its earlier evolution; some change of course was due to its temporarily disoriented logic. All at once, poets felt an inner compulsion to give utterance to what hitherto had not been permitted, to criticism and self-criticism, and the drawing of conclusions suggested by the inevitable inner struggle of their poetic selves. From the mid-1950s this dual internal and external struggle became the source of renewal for Hungarian poetry, along with self-correction and reconstruction of the self.

This process found its most dramatic expression in the *oeuvre* of Ferenc Juhász who belongs to the post-war generation of poets. Within a short period of time, his life and career spanned two poles of political and literary history. In 1945 he was seventeen, a poor peasant youth who commuted daily to study in Budapest. Of mixed Hungarian-Swabian parentage, he came from a very restricted milieu, but soon became a friend—indeed "disciple"—of the future surrealist painter Simon Hantai. Because he was genuinely enchanted by the popular nationalistic and realistic ideal of 19th century Hungarian poetry, he did not experience any significant internal conflict when realism was made a norm in the 1950s. But in 1952 and 1953 he was the first to utter sombre words of grave dissatisfaction, and in 1954 he composed "The Prodigal Country" ("*A tékozló ország*"), a long poem which proved bewildering to a self-complacent socialist establishment's understanding of literature.

The poem recalls the historical past, the peasant revolution of György Dózsa in 1514, one that is far more than an incidental episode in the history of Hungary, and remains for Hungarians a constant reminder in times of great national turmoil. Those critics were correct who detected, in the historical references, the perturbation of the poet as he witnessed the crisis of socialism as expressed in the laments of the poem whose title was also that of his Collected Poems.

There was undoubtedly a parallel between the contemporary social dilemma and the stream of images depicting destruction. The macrostructure of the poem is in the form of the lament; yet it is in turn shaped by the content which transcends historical boundaries. The verses echo colloquial intonations, yet are shaped by distinct rhyme patterns. They conform to the flow of the lament of the unknown bard, but also to his meditations and his distracted, disintegrating chronicle. The laments and meditations recall the perennial intonation of lyric poetry, while the chronicle assumes an epic character. The form of the chronicle is the chronological order of references to past events, but it depends on the structure of emotions and memories going beyond time and thus is embedded in the framework of infinite space and time created by microscopic description and the chain reaction of images.

After 1954 the national, historical and social imperatives and the desire for personal, human and poetical self-examination received powerful emphasis in Juhász's poetry. Experience and meaning, issuing from widely different sources, found expression in the polyphonic verse-structure which suggests that the poet had gone beyond his obsession with extensive enumeration. Along with parallelisms, he mastered reticence, spacing and the presentation of relations, modes which were unattainable in a linear structure.

The greatest poem that Juhasz wrote at this time, "The Boy Changed Into a Stag Cries out at the Gate of Secrets" was written for the 1955 Bartók Anniversary. But even without knowing the historical circumstances of its composition, it is obvious that the poem is a companion to the "Cantata Profana" of Béla Bartók, because both works constitute a retelling of the same ancient folk ballad. Both the traditional folk song and the poem embody three parts: a description of the parents and son, the mother's appeals to him to return home, and the son's transformation into a stag which causes him to resist all entreaties. The balladic dialogue provides an answer to the highest question of poetic existence: the son can no longer return to the world of simplicity and harmony, for he is subject to new laws of existence. However, the reason for his estrangement, the nature of the new laws, as well as the poet's adopted universe, are more complex and mysterious. At first, the mother summons her son by reminding him of the simple pleasures of everyday life which formerly had contented him; later, she trusts in the attractive power of his memories of home, family and friends. Finally, she offers him peace and shelter from the trials of the urban-industrial world. The conclusion of the son's response is a virtual word-for-word repetition of the closing line of the traditional ballad: "I can no longer drink from the flowered cup you bring / only from a clear spring, only from a clear spring." Thus the poet testifies simultaneously to the breakdown of the old harmony, and to his strong belief in the truth of his new verse. He rejects the appeal to memories of home by pointing to their darker side: "Where is my youth? Do not mention my father, because he will rise up from the grave." The son's memories of home also include the presence of destructiveness, and the absurdity of being, which is death. He replies with Whitmanesque pathos to his mother's phantasm of the ruinous modern city. His answer combines the individual, the man-made mechanical world, the earth and the universe in a monumental tableau. Thus, the poet responds not only with his *ars poetica* but also with his *story*. His answer cannot be reduced to the boy's arguments. The love with which Ferenc Juhász describes his origins in poverty emerges in the entreaties of the mother, and cannot be separated from the pain and emotion of his alienation. His chosen path takes him ever further from home, but his fidelity might also give hope for the unification of both the *mystery* and everyday life. This inner purification and ephemeral polemic is elevated by Ferenc Juhász into the mythical world, which constitutes in the words of Thomas Mann, "return, timelessness, ever presence."

The poem "Verse, for Four Voices" in its origins is a love poem set within the context of the guilt that is a strong component of poetic experience at this time. The poet's wife has lapsed into destructive silence; she seems to have given up on life. The husband is overwhelmed by this tragedy and also by his own sense of guilt and sin. The poem describes his efforts to reclaim both love and life, culminating in the struggle against the "white lamb" which is death. His power of reason likewise struggles against the irrationality of annihilation. Only at the conclusion does thought triumph over emotion, when the poet integrates the end of life with the order of existence. At first, personal emotion gains general expression. Later, it widens into a moral code which takes into account the entire chaotic era. Against dissolution and destruction he posits struggle. Against the immobile mass he juxtaposes individuality. Against the alternative of self, he proposes the recognition that "to live only for oneself is not a virtue." And the poet appears amid the hail of arguments, not merely searching for responses to polemics but desirous of answers to the mysteries of the widening world. The poem oscillates between stability and collapse.

The combination of polyphonic structure and message of these two poems emerges in "Thursday, the Day of Superstition: When Things are Most Difficult." (1963) The poet's inner condition of struggle with loneliness and death as expressed in 1956 has not changed; on the other hand, the surrounding world, that of seven years later, has. The later poem, in its strength, tension and richness—along with poetic emotion—contains the historical experience of 1956. But it is simultaneously a love poem and an expression of patriotism. In the background looms the atmosphere of the defeated uprising and the contemplation of tragic alternatives. The poet gives even broader perspective to his confession. In his vision of the rainy neon-lit Octogon, one of the chief intersections in downtown Budapest, the poem expands through metaphor into visionary associations, a world of vivid myth, in which the microcosm is just as present as the macrocosm. For Juhász the homeland is a part of eternal life. In this world of emotion and thought, the poet seems to be saying, the only possibility for man is ceaseless effort; victory comes through knowledge achieved in survival and expression of the anxiety of being.

FERENC JUHÁSZ: THE BLUE TWIN-STAR
Once upon a time, just as in a fairy tale, one starry clear night, in the Piszkéstetö observatory, an astronomer friend asked: "Would you like to see your own star, Lyra?" "Yes," I answered, "yes. Show me my far away self." And with both hands the astronomer turned pages of the star arithmetic coffin-thick book on a dining-room table wide surface as if folding freshly-ironed linen sheets, he found the letter-number fog-mark line of Lyra's point in space, then programmed the calculator of his star-telescope, and then the abdomen segmental tower cupola opened, the telescope silently at an angle turning towards infinity. "Now, look into it," said the astronomer.

And I looked not upwards but downwards with one eye, in a kaleidoscope-like periscope mirror, and there was my star, Lyra, in the depths of the mirror's centre: a tiny, radiating blue spot, ringed around with a fine blue sparkling circle, a pupil of the hundred milliard times quadruple-eyed god, the blue sparkle of fairy loneliness.

From the tower of my solitude now I look with memory's telescope into the cosmic hollow of the far away past, and there within the depth of dark and icy time, as if a blue twin-star of my youth, is the blue flame speckle of the blue haloed Siamese twins speck ray, so clear a blue their blueness is almost white: Karl Polanyi and Ilona Duczynska. Like hope, faith, the double love-drop of wholeness like twins grown together breastwards in an eternal blue ray wreath. But the two bodies have one heart, and one heart serves the blood's circulation within vein foliage of both bodies, from the heart to the water seaweed hatchery of the capillaries, up to the eyeballs' capillary foliage cathedral, to the three dimensional millicron bushworld.

I met them only a few times. Karl once in Budapest, in an antique János Arany suite in the Grand Hotel on the Margaret Island. Invited to an early evening tea and sandwich. Two old people, two love stars. Like my father and mother in a beginner's poem of mine. Karl sitting in a wheelchair, I couldn't quite make out whether it was Ilona who pushed him in from the other room, or whether it was he who propelled himself, turning the spoked rubber bicycle wheels with strong arms, with delicate hands.

Already at the first cup of tea he told me his Theory of Chance, that ball of possibility which bounces mysteriously, with weaving network movements, and gleams in sudden scurryings, then evaporates with its ray-point fact in the entity of social existence like electrons inside the curving peel of power space. And if just once it happens, brightening your existence, in this entanglement of the point, if then you catch the point, like a body, if you hold it and swallow it, like an isotope, then the isotope of your existence becomes your inspiration point: a graph-peak map of your outstandingness and expanding use is being created, like the fineness and shining of the three dimensional bar-cube-cone of computer graphics. If not, you fall into the nothing, you fall out from yourself as from possibility, with infinite inward falling.

Why did Karl Polanyi tell me this? So that he would speak about himself like this, as an Introduction? I don't think so. He was more modest and more wise than that. And he was elegant and simple, like an autumn silver furry velvet flower. But perhaps so that he might help me in my great fear, in my great misery. So that with his moving theory he would encourage, encourage, so that I wouldn't let myself go, so that I would be in forever readiness, so that I would always catch the inspiration point, the finished product consciousness-making fermentation moment, with the net-bucket of my reverie and mourning, like a butterfly, into the air with palm curving, like a flying light insect, twilight June beetle, the brown happy segmented horned handled book-foreheaded, armour-stripe covering droning in the grassy hills of the May lake shore.

Ilona always came unexpectedly. Like someone who would appear out of the earth, round, thick wrinkle-line map, with forrows-netted face, with woollen hat pulled down to her eyebrows, in thick heavy ankle boots, in thick woollen socks pulled over trousers up to the knee, in short thigh-length coat. "Servusz," she said, and smiled, whether she arrived at midnight or in the afternoon or from Vienna or directly from Canada, as if just from the Galilei Circle, from the magic ring of youth she would step into my apartment, as if coming back from the nether world beyond, back to earthly existence, returning to human form from spirit-body, from light-ray shape, back-existentializing...as if from two lidded star-motored aeroplane...with pilot's goggles, in leather pilot's helmet covering ears, leather coat...provoking the elegant anger of Bernat Aurel, and then she told me how the toy dwarf watermill of the garden's little stream operates, how it works, the turning Vörösmarty poem miniature watermill, destiny mill's hopelessness hope.

And right after that started to talk about the translation. About the meaning of a couple of words, word-compounds, word-mosaic poem line, what she thought, about whether she thought well in English—how is it in Hungarian? Tiny earth elf, earth spirit, elf woman. The consolation, magic, assistance, little saint earthwoman of love. With deeply thundering voice, just like a golden striped blue-belted green vested beautiful plump bumblebee in a fur coat. Can we shine and love, the way they could? The way he and she could, Ilona Duczynska and Karl Polanyi? Do we have within us that much humility, helping discipline, attentiveness, the certainty and faithfulness of giving ourselves to the other? Do we have inside us that much service—honour, rescuing—desire, enough to redeem the other from hell? Even a whole literature? Is there in us as much faith in the Enlightenment, and let me say it love of country, a world-view, human, political honour and because faith—power, as in Ilona and Karl?

Who perhaps would wave away this celebration (because the day is a celebration in whatever coat) and who are shining as a twin-star with blue sparkle wreath glory in the present of our memory and in our heart and not in the telescope of our loyalty. Who were not only separate in living together. But who were the uplifting and helping apostles of love, the preachers of the word of Hungarian literature in Canada, because in their heart is Hungary.

They loved with action! Because what else was it, like a lifebelt thown from an airplane into the surging sea, after the Revolution of '56, its blood, its war, what else was it than the beautiful book dropped on tense and shocked, shamed Hungary, the *Plough and the Pen*, this anthology which indicated but also demonstrated who for them in literature is Hungary. Lifebelt, asbestos helmet, asbestos coat, asbestos boots, this book in the firestorm. Ours. So that they could show to the more shining, more less-secretive world, what kind of spiritual raft floats on the passion, on depression, catatonic silence in the middle of Europe, on the fragments.

People had not yet been split into origins and black-white tense emotion. For them the people still meant what originally it was: a common language, and a common morality of self-realizing intense emotion. Serving together for life and the visual organ of trust, like the compound eye of a bee. So many millions viewing together many million prisms' facets: space, spread out happenings in space, thus history. And now, thrusting aside my bashfulness, coming out from behind the poetry shield, as the snail climbs out of his tiny house, let me confess with happy impudence, existence naked, what gratitude I feel to Ilona and Karl who with world flaming faith and trust did, performed magic, make my poetry known in the world (perhaps the *Plough and the Pen*'s title is also the inspiration of one of the poems of my youth).

My God! With what out-pouring goodness and love, with what attention and devotion they worked for me, with worries and joy to procreate into English my Hungarian words and lines. The two fevered spirits, two old enchanters! The two miracle light star operators! And of course to these two magic-shirt sewing fairy-tale plenomena, there was need for a third one, who resurrected me on the third day: Kenneth McRobbie, the poet, my translator into poems from the rough, living with Ilona and Karl in one geographic space, in one family warmth, in a way I would have liked to. These three, poem-winged people of the magic mountain.

Translated by Kenneth and Zita McRobbie.

MEMORIES
OF KARL POLANYI
IN VIENNA (1920-1936)

Chapter Twenty-Five

THE EARLY FORMATION OF KARL POLANYI'S IDEAS
Éva Gábor

The impression made on two fellow students, later eminent Hungarian scholars, who knew the young Karl Polanyi, may provide a fitting introduction to this brief survey of what the Hungarian intelligentsia owed to him around the turn of the century. Both were associated with Polanyi in the Galilei Circle, that organization of dedicated students from Budapest University, of which he was the founder. Mór Korach, later an Academician, and as a young man Vice-president of the Circle, has described Polanyi's influence upon others in the group:

> He was a genius of a rhapsodic mentality; he could see far into the future. His greatest influence was exerted upon young people. He embodied moral honour, integrity and sincerity. The moral climate of the Galileo Circle radiated from him. He was a person at one with the way we felt.

The other comment I would like to reproduce here, by Zsigmond Kende who was Secretary of the Circle, coincides with the sentiments expressed in Korach's opening words: "His mentality was similar to that of a prophet. He believed himself to be an anachronistic phenomenon, and in 1911 indeed he was."

Now as we approach the end of the twentieth century, we may look back with a certain envy and nostalgia to the past. And never more so than to that almost legendary generation with its outstanding personalities who rose to world prominence—though many would be forced by events to enrich the West with their talents during a long and fruitful maturity—who originated from this region, Hungary in particular.

Much research remains to be done on the significance of family background in relation to the talents and inclination of children, particularly those who went on to achieve outstanding careers. In the case of some, at least, we are fortunate enough to know, from their appreciative accounts, that there existed a close-knit family circle in which they could develop within an atmosphere of profound harmony. There they could inherit talents, cultivate their own distinctive intellectual qualities, and, at least equally important, do so within an environment of high moral standards.

In my view, the Polanyi family at the turn of the century represented the ideal model family, one which achieved remarkably harmonious assimilation within what was a new environment. Moreover, it succeeded in creating for its offspring a secure existence and appropriately high level of culture. All this was achieved within the space of two generations. What was most characteristic of families such as the Polanyis was that their main aim was not to accumulate a fortune, but to increase their intellectual capital. (Here, historians of the family would rightly refer to virtually all the members of the family: from the railway builder who was the father, to the third generation including Karl Polanyi's nephew the Nobel laureate John Polanyi.)

It is to Karl Polanyi that I must return, however, he whom we are celebrating now in 1994, in terms of both the thirtieth anniversary of his death and the fiftieth anniversary of the publication of his masterwork *The Great Transformation*. It is more than appropriate, it is necessary, in this anniversary year when much is being made of Karl Polanyi's work in terms of the influence upon him of his residence in Vienna, to state that, in my view, his career was in large measure determined by his family background, and by the *genius loci* of his native land (despite his being born in Austria) in terms of its historical, political and cultural atmosphere and traditions—which, be it remembered, he himself recognized and heartily embraced in the latter part of his life. Thus, he wrote:

> Whatever I have become has had its origins here in Hungary. My own life has been given meaning by Hungarian lives. Whatever mistakes I made were paid for here. Whatever good I have done, whatever little I have given to the world, should be returned here.

My reason for emphasizing this, in an age when national and family tradition often find little expression in international conferences such as the present one, is that when discussing Karl Polanyi's themes, his mode of selection, his emphases and values, it is essential to bear in mind the effects upon him of his early training, his first imbibing of moral principles, his contacts with warmth of affection: treasured recollections of which he carried with him to his dying day. Without an appreciation of his family background, the researcher is unable fully to appreciate the totality of the intellectual, emotional and spiritual heritage which inspired the writing of much of his work.

Karl Polanyi was born in 1886 in Vienna, third of a family of six children, a family in which mental and moral values were dominant characteristics. His father Mihály Pollacsek was a successful railway engineer, having graduated in Zurich and been employed from the very early age of twenty-two, from 1870, by Swiss Railways. In 1890 he set up in business as a railway entrepreneur in Hungary, building over 1000 kms of track. In the course of his responsibilities he travelled between Vienna and Budapest—taking the family along with him, at least for a while. Thus, from his very early youth, Karl felt at home in both capitals; moreover, he felt it natural to feel so, and open-mindedly valued highly the culture of both centres.

By 1890 the family had become domiciled in Budapest, their first residence being the then rather splendid address of Andrássy út (Street) number 2. It was splendidly located in one of the new upper-class thoroughfares such as were then being erected amid the current building boom to which the present-day city owes much of its glory. It was splendid also in the cultural sense, one that would have an influence upon the young Karl, in as much as he would grow up having experienced—no bad thing for an economist!—the presence of art and artists from his earliest years. This he owed to his mother Cecile Wohl a remarkable figure known to succeeding generations as "Cecile Mama." It was her custom, her passion even, to hold court at home in what amounted to a literary salon. There gathered the greatest figures in Hungarian literary and artistic life, together with other prominent personalities and people in public life such as the idealist-anarchist theoretician Ervin Szabó, the historian Oscar Jászi, and the future Marxist philosopher György Lukács. The distinguished literary historian Erzsébet Vezér even goes so far as to suggest that "Cecile was the originator of the many intellectual and left-wing orientations of her children."[1]

This was the time when Hungary was preparing for the Millennial Celebrations, the 1000th Anniversary of the Conquest and Settlement. National feeling and ambition seemed to know no limits. Among the lighter touches was the "Constantinople in Budapest," an entertainment centre to be erected along the Danube. The architectural activity would lead to striking buildings in a presumed national style and also to a Hungarian variant of *Jugendstil* architecture which to this day enhance the capital and some provincial cities. Great prosperity was evident, among the upper classes at least.

Like the children of other well-to-do families, the Polanyi children began their education at home, under the guidance of private tutors and governesses. Of these experiences, no record has as yet come to light. Presumably, it is to this period of tutelage that the children owe their early mastery of English, German and French—in that order of importance. And here it may be noted that Karl Polanyi's extraordinary mastery of English, which extended to near-perfect idiomatic usage, was what made it possible for him to establish himself in England after 1933. He soon began publishing in English, and invitations to give public lectures before large and critical audiences were almost immediately forthcoming in Great Britain and later in the USA. His success in obtaining work with the Workers Educational Association would have been impossible, had he not been fluent and therefore able to lecture and hold discussions in the native tongue of students from a wide range of non-academic backgrounds. (It may also be mentioned that his wife, Ilona Duczynska, had a similar fluency in English. Indeed, in the course of one of her letters from Vienna, probably dating from early 1936, she switches from Hungarian to English, on the grounds that "it is so much quicker.") During his Vienna years, of course, Polanyi worked and wrote entirely in German. Events beyond their control decreed that all of the Polanyi children, without exception, would have to establish careers for themselves in other countries, where their early training in languages and other cultures stood them in good stead.

The role of Karl's father is difficult to establish during this time. It is clear though that he was close to the children and that his influence was enormous, despite his frequent absences—or perhaps, on account of a possible desire to compensate for them. He is remembered by all of them as a figure of great moral influence. In addition, he apparently insisted that they undergo a Spartan form of physical self-discipline. It appears that both parents shared in what they regarded as the great responsibility of selecting the right grammar school for their sons. In 1898 Karl was duly enrolled in one of the best schools in Budapest, the Trefort Street *Minta Gymnasium* whose teaching staff included some outstanding representatives of the Hungarian intellectual elite who would later teach at the University. The institution was founded in 1872, and it rapidly established its reputation. One of its features was that it embodied what was then termed modern education, providing a firm foundation in mathematics, languages and literature. Among its illustrious graduates were the musician Léo Popper (Karl Polanyi's closest friend), the economists Nicholas Káldor and Thomás Balogh, and the "father" of the H-bomb Edward Teller.

Hardly had Karl been in school a year when the family suffered a grievous blow. In 1899 the father's railway enterprise went bankrupt. Apparently, though not (legally) fully financially liable, he hnourably compensated creditors to such an extent that his expenditures impoverished his family. Thereafter, he sought employment in Germany, but died in 1905. Karl was 13 years of age at the time. From then on, he and the other children assisted the family by contributing financially in any way they could. Karl would continue to win scholarships and awards at school; in addition, he gave private lessons for which he was paid.

In 1904 Karl Polanyi graduated from grammar school. It would seem that financial considerations may have influenced his choice of studies thereafter. Accordingly, he entered the faculty of law and political science of Budapest University. In his first year he studied Roman law, and the history of Hungarian and international law and ethics; his second year was devoted to the study of statistics, the national economy and modern history; in his third year he took Church law, politics and civil law. In 1907 he spent the second semester at the Vienna Law School. It was at the University of Kolozsvár that he obtained the doctorate (the equivalent of an English university Master's) in 1909. Thereafter he returned to Budapest where his studies showed both an enquiring mind and, more to the point, one that was not satisfied with the diet of study for a degree in Law. He studied for a number of semesters in the Faculty of Arts, Budapest Univesity, and participated in a seminar on psychology and philosophy in which Ernst Mach's *Analyse der Empfindungen* played a major role. At that time he translated into Hungarian a selection from this work for which he wrote a Preface.

Perhaps after graduation Karl Polanyi's studies were in part undertaken to supply the requisite student credentials which enabled him to continue to participate in the organization that was far and away the most important experience of his student years, the Galilei Circle. Karl's older brother Adolf, together with other students, had organized in 1902 a socialist student movement with which Karl became associated. It seems that it was the exiled Russian revolutionary Samuel Klatschko, then living in Vienna, who inspired Karl Polanyi to found the progressive student organization, the Galilei Circle. Accordingly, in November 1908 the Circle was organized, with Karl Polanyi elected as its first president. During his final year of law, Polanyi had supported his professor Gyula Pikler against attacks from right-wing students, and this reinforced his determination to found an organization for students within the Association of Free Thinkers. He must have realized that this undertaking was of enormous originality, that its purpose was uniquely progressive—but even he could not foresee that by his actions his name would be forever engraved on the history of Hungarian society at a crucial formative stage. Although there had been a workers educational programme that dated from as early as 1902, the Circle was a unique initiative on the part of free-thinking young people, originally medical students of liberal views, seeking to create an organization whose motto was "To learn and to teach," with the aim of fostering independent thinking and responsible progressive action in the public life of their country. Karl Polanyi would describe, in a 1934 *curriculum vitae*, how the Galilei Circle had "over 2000 members" and delivered "more than 2000 tutorial lectures in one year." Others have put the figures as high as 10,000.

The aims of the Circle included fighting against the illiteracy, lack of education, and ignorance of progressive ideas at that time rife among the masses of the workers; its aims were directed also towards raising the standard of intellectual life among some groups of the educated classes. Some of the topics presented included: problems of modern physics; discussions on chemistry, ethnography and psychoanalysis; the causes of cultural backwardness; reform of the middle schools; the connection between art and morality; the Hungarian tax system; the right to vote. The Galilei Circle kept its distance from politics—a stand that caused some not to join it, and a few within it (like Ilona Duczynska) to form an anti-war group—but this did not mean that its leadership and membership were indifferent to the problems of everyday life. It was open to all progressive ideas, including some relating to socialism. To the Circle, socialism had applications far beyond the economic system. Karl Polanyi regarded it as pertaining to the wider field of knowledge and the realm of moral issues in modern industrial society (as he makes clear in the latter part of *The Great Transformation*).

The Circle thus played an active part in relation to large numbers of working people, intellectuals and students. As president, Karl Polanyi had additional public duties. He gave an address every March 15th for several years, to commemorate the beginning of the 1848 War of Liberation. It was also on this date, which became the principal Hungarian national holiday, that the outstanding revolutionary lyric poet Endre Ady saluted the Galilei Circle with a special poem and thanked its members for their devotion and adherence to their common cause. In due course, Polanyi resigned the presidency, to take over leadership of the Committee for Workers Education. The following will give some indication of his activities. From May 1913 on, together with others he was co-editor of the fortnightly journal *Szabadgondolat* (Free Thought). During the course of the same month he spoke under the auspices of the Hungarian Association of Free Thinkers in commemoration of Ignác Martinovics (executed in 1795 for his radical reform programme). In December 1913 he joined the Archimedes Lodge of the Society of Freemasons where he gave a series of lectures in February 1914 on the relationship of science and morality, and in March and April on the relationship of the Freemasons and Free Thinkers; in all, he gave dozens of lectures in this and other lodges. In May 1914 he participated in the work of the organizing committee of the National Radical Bourgeois Party; in June he acted as recording secretary at the party's organizing session, and was elected to the secretariat. These activities have been interpreted as preparation for what was to be, as things turned out, a political career noteworthy for being extremely short-lived

Following the outbreak of the First World War, Karl Polanyi served in the army as a cavalry officer. He was invalided out in 1917, and after a lengthy spell in hospital returned to Budapest. There in February 1919, in the great hall of the University, he delivered an address on the occasion of the funeral of the great innovative lyric poet and social revolutionary Endre Ady. Later in the same year he was one of the organizers and lecturers of the Free Society of Old Galileans. But the times were out of joint. Defeat in the war, revolution (first liberal, then communist), and foreign invasion created a situation which, followed by conservativism and incipient fascism, was antipathetic to the ideals of the Galilei Circle and to all that Karl Polanyi stood for and would stand for. During a period of acute personal crisis, he left Hungary in June 1919 for Vienna. He would return only in 1959, forty years later.

Looking back on that period, Zoltán Horvath, the prominent cultural historian, has labelled Polanyi's "the second reform generation." The reason was that those belonging to it, particularly the young intellectuals, were not satisfied merely to become acquainted with progressive ideas, or with analyzing social, national, political and cultural phenomena. They wanted to do more. They wanted to promote change, without which the antiquated forms would simply have been self-perpetuating. It was the achievement of this particular generation to recognize that organization is required in order to be able to move forward in pursuit of worthy goals. And, within such an organization, the forward movement of change must also be represented in the personal attitudes of the members. Karl Polanyi found it necessary to create the Galilei Circle because he was conscious of his own willingness to enter into such a commitment, and of the need for a structure in which like-minded persons could meet and work with others. As he said, in his speech on the occasion of the funeral of Endre Ady in 1919:

> The believer says: I shall change, and everything will be changed. If I change just a little, then my world has already changed; and if everyone else also changes, then the whole world has changed. I measure change in others by the extent to which it enables me to change.

The famous saying of Galileo Galilei "eppur si muove" had been adapted by the members of the Circle that bears his name, to their own way of thinking—"learn, and teach." One has to learn unceasingly in order to be able to change, and one has to teach others to be able to contribute to change. The Galilei Circle itself seemed to undergo change. In 1914 it might have reminded the observer of the Girondins; in 1919 it called to mind the Russian student movement. In fact, it bore the positive characteristics of both.

During the 133 days of the Republic of Soviets in early 1919, the Galilei Circle, due to its tradition of free thinking, was closed down. The succeeding right-wing clerical militarist regime of Admiral Horthy proclaimed that neither the Circle nor its members were wanted in Hungary. The majority of its members emigrated in the course of the year and the one following.

Karl Polanyi emigrated to Vienna in mid-1919. There is no surviving record of his feelings at that time, but his later letters make it clear that it was a very difficult period for him. Though born in Vienna, he had moved to Budapest when still quite young; it was there that his deepest friendships lay, along with the roots of his intellectual development, his culture, and his mother tongue. His younger brother Michael left Hungary at around the same time, and continued his studies in Chemistry in Karlsruhe. By contrast, Karl with his doctor of laws degree had no such certainty of a career. However, two experiences contributed to shaping the next part of his life.

First, in 1920 in a Viennese hostel for Hungarian emigrés, he met his future wife, Ilona Duczynska, also an emigrant, also a cultured personality, but, unlike him, a revolutionary. Second, Oscar Jászi, soon to become a world-famous historian, once president of the Civil Radical Party in Hungary, and also an emigré, invited Karl to become his private secretary. He also made him a contributing editor of the *Bécsi Magyar Ujság* (Vienna Hungarian News) on which Polanyi developed the journalistic skills which later enabled him to support himself. The paper was of a high level, and became a trustworthy source of information to emigrant Hungarians among whom it was widely popular. Karl Polanyi published in its pages between 1921 and 1923, and his contributions were characterized by their variety and openmindedness. An idea of his interests at that time may be gathered from a list of some of the topics he wrote on: anthroposophy, guild socialism, the novels of H.G. Wells, the problems of Russia, economic problems of the Ruhr, questions of war and peace, and Freud and psychoanalysis. After the paper ceased publication in 1923, Polanyi became a contributing editor for *Der Oesterreichische Volkswirt*. A reading of his numerous articles for that paper, which are receiving considerable study of late, reveal that he remained true to the ideals of the Galilei Circle.

Later in life, thinking back upon his youth and his reading of the works of Marx, he affirmed that he had never been an uncritical reader—seeing weaknesses, one-sidedness, their utopian character, and dogmatism—yet for a time he cherished the hope that the social reforms implicit therein could be achieved. Social democracy too he would criticize, because of its "lukewarmness" and proneness to compromise. He seems then to have favoured guild socialism as a model for the welfare state based upon principles of democracy, in which personal freedom is preserved wherever possible

In the mid-1920s, Karl Polanyi rethought his experiences in the Galilei Circle. Overall, he considered, there had been one basic mistake: namely, the shunning of politics and parties. Due to this, the Circle had fatally neglected the crucial question of the nationalities which comprised more than fifty per cent of Hungary's pre-war population. Similarly, the Circle had ignored the peasantry and the working class.

The Galilei Circle proclaimed the freedom of the mind. Later, Karl Polanyi would write about this, from the perspective of qualifying the role of freedom, as would be expected by readers of the concluding pages of *The Great Transformation*.

> Freedom of mind is not interpreted by us to mean that we do not acknowledge justice, morals, law and authority. We look to justice to be inexorable, we follow the commandments of morality, we exercise law, and we proclaim authority.

NOTES

1. Erzsébet Vezér, "The Polanyi Family," pp.18-25, in *The Life and Work of Karl Polanyi*, edited by Kari Polanyi Levitt. Montreal: Black Rose Books, 1990. See also Ferenc Múcsi, "The Start of Karl Polanyi's Career," pp.26-29, and György Litván, "Karl Polanyi in Hungarian Politics (1914-64)," pp.30-47, also in *The Life and Work*.

Chapter Twenty-Six

"I FIRST MET KARL POLANYI IN 1920…"
Ilona Duczynska Polanyi

Karl Polanyi was born on October 21st, 1886, in Vienna, where his father, Mihály Pollacsek, a railway engineer and his wife Cecile Wohl were living at the time. Karl was their third child, and there would be three more. Both parents were strong personalities, total opposites in terms of their background, temperament, customs, ethics, and ways of life and thought. In Karl, elements that were unmixable somehow balanced each other—his father's unbending rectitude and strict puritanism; his mother's mental charm, the radiance of her wit, her vitality and disorganized ways: in brief, what went to make "Cecile mama" in her later years a focus of Budapest's literary and intellectual milieu.[1]

At the outset of the liberal era in Hungary, soon after the Austro-Hungarian Compromise of 1867, Karl's father and his sisters—Lujza, Vilma and Teréz—arrived in Budapest from somewhere near Ungvár in Northern Hungary, now part of Ukraine, where the family had owned a moderate-sized steam-driven flour mill, an enterprise which later faded away into a kind of fictitious existence. They set out to rise in the world, aiming for the fuller life of the new urban bourgeoisie of nationally assimilated Jewry. The women of the family stood out, with their keenness of mind, wit, charm and domineering character—Shavian heroines come to life. They all grew to be very old, a generation of great ancients, the mothers of distinguished sons. Their memory lived on in their children. Lujza's son was Ervin Szabó,[2] Vilma's Ernö Seidler,[3] Teréz's Odon Por.[4]

Some time in the early 1870s, young Mihály Pollascek went to Zürich to study engineering at the renowed and venerable *Eidgenössische Technische Hochschule*, the Federal Polytechical Institute (known as the Poly).[5] His career there started with somewhat of a setback. Under the sway of boundless new freedom, the young man thought of joining a troupe of itinerant actors. He was allotted a role, a very minor one of course, in Goethe's "Clavigo." When the corpse was brought in on a bier, and the question was asked "Who are they bringing here?" he was supposed to reply "Marien." But, he forgot his line—and so his acting career was finished. This obvious lack of talent, coupled with the rigorous demands of the Poly—which threatened him with expulsion *"wegen Unfleisses"* [for lack of diligence]—tipped the balance. Mihály accordingly received his degree in civil engineering from Zürich and then went on to continue his studies in Edinburgh.

Along with increased knowledge of civil engineering, the young man brought back with him a lifetime's commitment to the Scottish capital's puritan ethic, something in any case congenial to his character. Edinburgh even more than Zürich made a lasting impact on the young man. It was quite different from the Anglomania which swept Central Europe in successive waves: that admiration for upper-class English education, coupled with complete ignorance of the social facts of English life. When the young engineer and entrepreneur returned to Central Europe he returned as what he understood to be a practising Scotsman. To the image of this mythical personage he remained true to the end of his life. It was one of puritanism and stern rectitude. He was cut out for a high-minded nineteenth-century Liberal, a captain of industry, a member of the rising Jewish bourgeoisie. He carried out his first project for the Federal Swiss Government railways, and designed the Zürich railway station. Towards the end of the 1880s he settled with his family in Budapest. The nineties saw an economic boom in Hungary with incipient industrialization of the country, the rise of an entrepreneurial class, part Jewish, part German, but invariably assimilating and patriotic. Mihály Pollacsek, entrepreneur and railway contractor, saw his fortunes on the ascendant. He was unable to avoid becoming a millionaire. Equally so, as a man of stern principles and unbending rectitude, he was unable to avoid losing every penny soon after.

When and how the young engineer Mihály Pollacsek met Cecile Wohl, the young girl from Vilna who became his wife, I do not know. The earliest photograph of Tsippa Wohl, daughter of a Jewish scholar from Vilna, shows a thoughtful, plain-looking seventeen-year-old in full Victorian attire, the type of woman upon whom the passing years would add beauty layer by layer, so many year-rings on the tree of life. Of the impact she was to make by dint of her intellectual charm on the Hungarian intelligentsia of later decades there was no foreboding. Cecile was not a "Russian student," nor a bluestocking, and not at all a revolutionary. She was an apprentice in a jeweller's shop in the Taborstrasse in the Jewish district of Vienna. Her father was a historian, a rabbinical scholar of some standing, from a well-known Jewish family in Vilna; yet he was a passionate assimilant to Russian society, holder of the Czarist Order of St. Anna, and at the same time an admirer of the civilized Western world and its attitudes. When he lost his wife and married his non-Jewish housekeeper, the seventeen-year-old Cecile (as she would in future be called) was sent away to Vienna, accompanied by another young girl, Anna Lvova (Nyunya), the daughter of the Mayor of Simferopol. The two young women got married at the same time. Their children were of the same ages. For many years, the families spent their vacations together at Klamm on the Semmering. The personal ties never parted, and were maintained even into the next generation.

Meanwhile at the home of Mihály Pollacsek in Budapest, at Andrássy ut 2, a palatial building in which they occupied one entire floor, an upper middle-class style of life was taking shape in the now numerous family, though it did not conform at all with that of the surrounding society. The father, whom all his children adored, was averse to both the Hungarian nobility—in Hungary called "the gentry"—and the *nouveau riche* "gentroid" Jewish bourgeoisie of Budapest, which "assimilated" to all the vices of the historical Magyar ruling class. He had no connection with either one. He lived by his creed of puritanism, positivism, progress, the scientific outlook, democracy, the emancipation of women—the Perfect Puritan on Shavian lines. Personally, he remained Jewish and a Pollacsek.

He refused to magyarize his name, regarding it as beneath his dignity. His childrens' names, however, were changed to the Hungarian Polányi. The religion of his wife and children became Calvinist. He remained formally a member of the Jewish religious community, as a protest against the *arriviste* Jews who changed religion to be *frère et cochon* with the native nobility. He is buried in the Jewish cemetery in Budapest. Only the last born, a retarded child of sweet disposition, little Pál who died young, was permitted to be baptized.

The whole thriving family was highly esteemed in all quarters, but lived in artificial isolation in a social no-man's-land, virtually strangers in their own country. The home was one of high principles and lofty education, where Goethe and Schiller, Racine and Corneille, Shakespeare and Milton were read from ten years and up, where the necessities of life such as food and clothing were of such extraordinary simplicity that no discernible change was brought about when financial catastrophe struck the family. Thus, a visitor on the day in question did not notice the slightest sign of any member of the family being troubled by it.

The transition to poverty was instant and complete. Some time around 1900 there was rain all summer long. Construction work was impossible, day after day. Under the terms of the contract this spelt ruin; the enterprise collapsed, due to a penalty of one thousand pounds payable for every workday lost. Mihály Pollacsek was insistent that the small shareholders be paid back in full. Thus came the switch to poverty. The elder children, including Karl who was then fourteen, took up private tutoring to help out with the family budget. The pattern of life hardly changed. Their hypertrophied will-power and self-discipline now played their part.

The Polanyi children turned out as unlike each other as most brothers and sisters usually do. The oldest, Laura, a radiant beauty and university graduate in history, with whom half the eminent young men of the city were in love, married an undistinguished textile manufacturer, leaving a wound in her father's heart which never healed. Adolf, the eldest son, founded the first socialist students' group in the University—they were eight in all. He was a firebrand, who harangued striking workers. But this had to remain a secret: the Old Man would have none of it. Democracy was fine, but socialism was out. When an octogenarian, Adolf still remembered trudging over twenty miles homeward through the night, after addressing a meeting of striking miners, and slinking into the house at dawn, to avoid a clash, but more perhaps to spare his father's feelings.

Karl, Karli as he was always called, was the father's better loved son. At that time he was the guide and protector, model and tutor to the two little ones whom he loved with the rare true love of the elder brother. They were Michael—Misi—who was to run the course of his own not un-Faustian ventures, and Sophie who grew to truth and sweet goodness personified, and was to die the anonymous death of the assassinated, in the hellfires of the crematoria, ashes scattered by unknown winds over unhallowed ground.

The father believed in Education with a capital "E," and spared no expense in having his children partake of it. The childrens' upbringing was spartan: bodies trained in athletics; European standards of education; early reading of the classics of world literature. Up at seven, a cold shower, one hour of Swedish gymnastics till eight; hot cocoa with one dry bun. After that came the private tutors in Latin, English, French, German and the minor subjects, who took the children in turn. In the pursuit of education and the strengthening of will power, effort was continuous. When Laura, the eldest, brushed her beautiful long hair, she would recite French irregular verbs to the rhythm of her moving arm. The same mental exercises were to accompany—in silence—the brushing of teeth. Each child had his or her own horse or pony. Riding lessons were taken very seriously and given by an army sergeant according to "imperial and royal" [*k. und k.*] army regulations. As the children would reach the age of thirteen, they were handed over to the milder rigours of grammar school, the "gymnasium" which featured studies in classics. Such was the early education of the older children, Laura the beautiful eldest sister, the bright Adolf, and Karli the boy who was "*zu brav*" (too good). I believe that much of the instruction of the younger children—his much loved younger brother Michael and his gentle sister Zsofka—was done by Karli.

The apparently immutable routine of the children's life was broken at times by acts of grace and adventure which could not be earned by good behaviour. They came to one as by predestination. When the father journeyed to inspect a stretch of railway construction or set off for some European capital, the air in the children's school room would be electric with suppressed excitement. Almost out of the door, he would turn back, an awkward little smile playing around his lips, as if trying to remember something, point to one of his bigger children and say "You may come along!" It meant up and away on horseback along the unfinished railway tracks near the Danube—once it was a day-long ride to Esztergom!—or off in a sleeping car to some strange new country, a journey to Denmark, a trip through the Carpathians, explorations on horseback in the Great Plains. The children adored him. He was and remained throughout their lives the image of reigning goodness. As men and women in their seventies they still exchanged letters on each anniversary of his death, letters of filial affection, as limpid as the morning of a summer's day.

In Karl's early memories the image of the mother was much fainter than that of the father. In the formative years, the mother seems to have been there mostly by indirection, as a loosening up of repetitive sequences of ordered existence, a wayward incursion, incalculable whirlwind, life force in action, some flashing radiance, some temper.

How Cecile of the bohemian moods was able to cope with the complexities of the large middle-class household remains a mystery. She was like a book not yet written. She tried to cope with the demanding bourgeois household as best she could—that is, not at all. It was a mixture of mess and miracle, run by chance, high temper, and personal charm. Documents mostly could not be found. When baby Karl was born, they forgot to register him. It may well be that the switch-over to poverty made things easier. Orderliness can hardly have prevailed under either of them.

Cecile was a mother who passionately loved, as well as disapproved. I have often heard Karl say that what children never forgive in a parent is the parent's wish to see them develop not what is good in them but what isn't. Cecile, in her own person, was a *bohéme*, a "*Barfüssler*" [one who goes barefoot, a hippy]; she looked down on worldly goods, status, and standing; but for all that, she wished for her sons brilliant careers and wealthy wives. Her children loved her, from the time they were little and as mature men and women. Their respective husbands and wives were, to her way of thinking, impossible. I personally can recall only one chance meeting with her, at the Café Bauernfeld in Vienna. There, relations between us were far from happy.

Meanwhile, the road to life for the young of the family, which had been set to suit an emerging bourgeois society in the spirit of liberalism and Western thought, had begun to diverge as though under the action of a magnetic field—the ways of the "Zeitgeist" were no less inscrutable than those of Providence. The spirit of the Russian Revolution entered into the lives of the new generation, during those Semmering vacations and the occasional visits to Vienna. It was embodied in the person of Aunt Nyunya's husband Samuel Klatschko. In him Ervin Szabó and Karl Polanyi found a beloved friend and mentor, their first great teacher. It was from here, at the turn of the century, that the first intimations of the Russian revolutionary movements reached Hungary. The two cousins, Ervin Szabó and Karl Polanyi, each following his individual bent, responded to different trends of revolutionary inspiration. Ervin soon learnt the art of underground work and conspiratorial techniques; Karl, fascinated by the high ethic of the Russian student movement, lived with the image of the self-sacrificing, man-of-the-movement pre-formed in his mind, many years before the "Galileo Circle" came into being.

By the turn of the century Samuel Klatschko had been living in Vienna for some twenty years, and had become a non-party envoy of all the underground parties and movements then existing in Russia. A man of sterling character, committed to the cause of the Russian Revolution, belonging to no party yet trusted by all, he soon found himself acting as representative of the Russian revolution's "Red Red Cross." In the course of a stormy life, he learned many trades. In 1865, then a fourteen-year-old grammar school boy and *Narodnik*, he ran away from the rabbinical paternal home and somehow made his way to the United States. There he joined a group of Russian revolutionary emigrés, called *Tschaikovtzes*, after their leader N.V. Tschaikovsky.[6] They founded a utopian communist community in the 1870s which, like many similar efforts, eventually collapsed. Klatschko became a cattle driver and herded some hundred head of cattle as far as (presumably) Chicago. With the money so earned, he returned to Europe. In Paris, where he set up as a photographer, he met his future wife, and they settled down in Vienna. In the course of his wanderings, he came to know not only the literature of Marxism and Russian Populism, but met many of the greats of the early Russian revolutionary movement: such as Plekhanov, Axelrod and Leo Deutsch. In Vienna, he worked as a translator in a Patent Office where, over the course of the years, he became a business partner and a patent-lawyer. Much of his not inconsiderable income he dedicated to the support of revolutionaries and underground activists from Russia, irrespective of their party allegiance. Shortly before his death, Karl Polanyi jotted down a few notes on the life of Samuel Klatschko, to preserve him from oblivion. At the bottom of the page, he wrote: "He was the kindliest man I ever met."[7] While he was growing up, the Klatschkos were like a second family to him. With them Karli spent holidays, knew calf love, and in silent wonder and secret adulation came face to face with a world of men and ideas very different from all he had known previously.

The Russian underground channelled people to Vienna who would report at the Klatschko family's modest three-room flat at Belvederegasse 3. There food, lodging, financial aid, identity papers and railway tickets were provided to transient revolutionaries—whether socialist revolutionaries, bundists, anarchists, trudoviks, bolsheviks, or mensheviks. They were men with no names. It was not done to ask them questions. Some might have thrown bombs in the past, others might do so in the future. The Polanyi home on the Andrássy út in Budapest soon became overnight quarters for revolutionaries on the run. Meanwhile the steam laundry of the Szécsi family became a check point, where Frida Szécsi, the fiancée of Adolf Polanyi, checked the confidential papers the revolutionaries had been given in Vienna: the particular spot where the rubber stamp had been applied most vigorously was an indication of their reliability.

The father's death early in 1906 shattered the family. Karl was then nineteen years old, a first year student in Law. Responsibility for caring for the family now rested heavily on the older brothers and their earnings from private tutoring. The future careers of the three brothers had been mapped out according to the canons of the urban middle class: business, law, medicine. They all graduated as required—then went their own ways soon after. Adolf the businessman ended up an engineer; Karl the lawyer, who was quite unable to tell a fib in the interests of a client, became an economic historian; Michael the physician became a scientist, economist, philosopher and religious thinker.

Karl, when still a grammar school boy, had taken part in the movement of the "Socialist Students," founded in 1908 by his brother Adolf and his cousin Odon Por. Most of his readings in Marxism can be traced back to these times, as can his disillusionment with the Social Democratic Party. The "Socialist Students," operating inside the party, were barely tolerated. The enthusiasm of the energetic leaders of the group—Jenö László, Gyula Mérö, Béla Vágó, Egon Szécsi, József Migray and others—could not prevent their ultimate frustration. Karl Polanyi was about 22 years old when he abandoned the Marxist views he had formerly held.

The lectures of an eminent philosopher of law, Professor Gyula Pikler, opened up new paths for progressive thinking. Polanyi, a student of Pikler's and an athletic young man, participated in repelling attacks on Pikler by reactionary students. Supporting contingents from other departments—medical and engineering students—participated in the fist fights. The students who demonstrated in favour of Professor Pikler's progresssive ideas won the day, and were loath to disband after their victory. Accordingly, in October 1907, "two medical students, Rohonyi and Kende," came to ask Polanyi's advice. That well remembered incident may have been the point at which the movement, dreamt about for so long, that "Russian" one, began to take practical shape in his mind. Let it be free in spirit, let it keep away from party politics, let it be dedicated, decent, let it appeal to the students who live in poverty in their thousands! Let it be a movement aiming to learn and to teach!

Within a year the Galileo Circle was constituted, with Karl Polanyi as its first President. The vision was now to come true. To mobilize against clericalism and corruption; against the privileged, and against bureaucracy—against that ever present and pervasive morass in this semi-feudal country! Individual dedication and ethical commitment demanded built-in safeguards in the institutional structure of the movement. The leadership was to be renewed each year: last year's functionaries were to resign, and the students were to elect new ones every year from among the new students.

If I were to evoke the image of Karl Polanyi in a single word, it would be one that was not infrequently in his mind—the *skandalon*.[8] Throughout his life, he went counter to encrusted notions, relentlessly shaking people into some new awareness: as the fiery young orator in his days of the Galilei Circle; in his apparent withdrawal in early manhood; in his novel approaches to the social sciences in the late decades of his life.[9]

The university in Hungary at the beginning of the century was a backward and reactionary institution which kept students from partaking in the scientific and philosophical renaissance of the times. The progressive student body hungered for the new doctrines. They had outgrown the naive materialism and monism of the nineteenth century. In their thirst for knowledge they turned to the natural philosophy of Ernst Mach and Avenarius, and soon to Einstein and Freud. They taught some ten thousand illiterate workers to read and write. Out of this sweeping cultural movement a new brand of young intellectuals had arisen—dedicated, educated and poor. To the poet Ady, they were the "young brothers of my heart."

Karl Polanyi was first to become a "former Galileist," as the retired leaders of the Circle came to be called. Caring for the family weighed ever harder upon him. He strained his capacity for work beyond endurance. These were also the years when the intellectual élite of Budapest began to gather round the extraordinary personality of Karl's mother Cecile. Karl kept rather aloof. He formed few personal ties. His two close friends were Leo Popper who died young, and György Lukács.

Polanyi was called to the bar and worked for some time at his uncle's Law Office. He was the most improbable lawyer. Sensitive to the call of duty, he would yet turn up late at trials. His detestation of the profession was boundless. Not only could he not tell a lie, he found his true vocation in telling disagreeable truths —*at all times and in all circumstances.*

Military service as an officer in training came almost as a relief. He was called up early in 1915 and served on the Galician front as a lieutenant. Two books were with him at all times, the Bible and the Globe Shakespeare. His study on "Hamlet"[10] which he published late in life gives the only indication of the melancholy which assailed him at that time.

> Nearly forty years ago I was serving as an officer in the old Austro-Hungarian army. The Russian winter and the blackish steppe made me feel sick at heart. It happened that at the time my personal life had taken a turn towards darkness; daylight seemed bounded in a narrowing disk that grew dimmer and dimmer.[11]

Invalided out of the army, Polanyi was brought back to Budapest towards the end of 1917. The revolutionary events that took place towards the end of the war he witnessed only from a hospital bed. His young friend, the Galileist Péter István Tölgy, who was untouched during the first wave of arrests in January 1918, acquainted him with the new shape of things in the Galileo Circle (now officially disbanded and declared illegal). He related the ties formed between students and the shop stewards of the ammunition factories, their political actions carried out against the war,[12] and the first indications of the Workers' Councils in Budapest.

It may have been at this period that Polanyi's self-accusation cropped up for the first time. It was to recur many times over in the next fifty years. Why did he have to establish the foundations of the Galileo Circle and the student movement so exclusively at the level of the cultural? Why did he permit it to live in the rarefied atmosphere of philosophical theories, when the country's real need was for a young generation of intellectuals prepared to face the country's life and death problems—agrarian reform, the nationalities question? Continuous political leadership did not, could not emerge. Four decades later, Polanyi wrote, to his lifelong close friend Oscar Jászi, a letter which is perhaps the most revealing and authentic document on the course of his life.[13] The letter was written on October 27, 1950, at the high point of Polanyi's teaching and research in the social sciences, in economic history. In retrospect he passes harsh judgement on the lack of realism he displayed in the preceding decades of his life "which in the theoretical as in the practical field condemned me to futility. From 1909 to 1935 I achieved nothing. I strained my powers in the futile direction of stark idealism, its soarings lost in the void." In this over-arching self-accusation the first intimations of the later life-work—scattered, yet seminal—are necessarily lost to sight.

After the White Aster Revolution[14]— still from his hospital bed—Polanyi sought to contact the "new Galileists" through his friend Tölgy. He would have liked to meet them. The answer was a rebuff. During the events of the Károlyi Republic Polanyi's all-round outspokenness was more radical than ever before. He attacked with vehemence the idea of a dictatorship of the proletariat, turning passionately against the Communists. But when the Communists *en masse* were arrested and beaten up at the behest of the Social Democratic government, he turned with even greater vehemence against the government in an article published in *Szabadgondolat* (Free Thought). Just for a day, he had been a Communist—on that fateful May 2, 1919, a day of great danger to the Republic of Councils. From the hospital he sent a message to the friend of his youth, György Lukács,[15] again by Tölgy, to say "I'm joining the Party." Whether the message ever got through in the great confusion, he never knew. In later years he pondered it more than once. In June 1919 he was taken to Vienna to undergo a serious operation from which he recovered, in some measure, after many months.

I first met Karl Polanyi in the late Autumn (or November) of 1920, when I arrived in Vienna from the Soviet Union, having been sent by the Hungarian Communist Party. A handful of Hungarian intellectuals, now virtual outlaws, had found sanctuary in the "*Helmstreitmühle*" in the Hinterbrühl near Vienna. The poet Béla Balázs was there and his wife Anna, Karl Polanyi, and a young Communist whom he had taken under his wing—known as Netter in the *Helmstreitmühle*, as János Lékai in Hungarian history.[16] That was where I touched down, too.

Polanyi was thirty-three years old, wasted from his long illness and very lonely. His outlook was deeply influenced by Tolstoy. He was like one who looks back on life, not towards it. The soul's dimming had lifted, giving way to a kindly, deep understanding of the lives of the living, as though he himself hardly belonged among them.

The Karl Polanyi of the Galilei Circle I had not known. Not merely on account of a ten years age difference between us—rather, because of the difference in the age. That newer age—mine—allowed no argument other than that of revolutionary action. Between the small group of activists to which I belonged in 1917-1918 and the group of "former Galileists" there was no common ground. Only in our declining years, in 1963 in Budapest, among Polanyi's contemporaries, was I too touched by the radiance of the Galilei Circle, reflected back over half a century. The image of the young Polanyi remains imprinted on my mind, in the words of his close friends and fellow Galileists

Zsigmond Kende and Maurice (Mór) Korach. Thus Kende: "He had the makings of a prophet, and felt himself to be an anachronism. So he was, in 1911. But not in the years to come." Korach too emphasized this quality: "He was a genius, rhapsodic in his world of thought. He saw far into the future."[17]

What I have been able to relate of his family history, his childhood, the essential influences on his mind in the years of his youth on the road to manhood, is no more than a memory of his memories—of necessity, twice incomplete. Yet these fragments of memory which surfaced, at various times during the more than four decades of our lives together, stand for a life's summation, in all its authenticity.

Around 1921, Karl Polanyi began to draw away from the Tolstoyan philosophy. The reality of human society, man's inalienable interwovenness with society, the impact of all of his actions or non-actions on society, and society's reaction, became central to his thought. The first fruit in the new direction his life had taken was the turning towards socialism on a theoretical plane in 1922. In his study *"Sozialistische Rechnungslegung"* (Socialist Accountancy, 1922)[18] he analysed economic problems encountered in constructing a socialist society. It came at a time when bougeois economists were assiduously proving the impossibility of socialist economic organization and of socialist accountancy, and the counter-arguments had nothing better to point to than the experiences of war communism in Soviet Russia. Needless to say, it drew fire from both sides;[19] its underlying considerations may not be without interest even today—or perhaps more particularly today.

From 1921, he worked in the editorial offices of the Hungarian emigré paper *Bécsi Magyar Ujság* (Vienna Hungarian News), in a very modest capacity, until the paper folded. In 1924, he joined the editorial team of the *Oesterreichischer Volkswirt* (The Austrian Economist) where he worked for nearly ten years as an expert on foreign policy and international problems. The well-known independence of the weekly and the interest he took in the topics made it a congenial task. In the late 1920s he began to take a lively interest in current discussions in the Soviet Union leading up to the first Five Year Plan. He was sympathetic towards Soviet economic experiments in planning the economy.

With the exception of an interval during which Polanyi joined the Citizens Radical Party of Oscar Jászi, largely on account of their personal friendship, he was never an active member of any political party—in my conviction for reasons deeply rooted in his personality. Every and any exercise of power, unavoidable in the life of a party politician, was alien to him. In his work as a publicist at the *Volkswirt* he was the "Red" among the editors. In his personal views he was an enthusiastic admirer of Red Vienna. In our home, in one of Vienna's proletarian districts, our child grew up in the world of proletarian organizations, among the *"Arbeiterturner"* and *"Kinderfreunde."* But Polanyi did not put down roots in Vienna. His well-known Seminar held for the Socialist Students on questions of economic theory, his lectures given at the *"Volkshochschule"* on economic history, were the earliest beginnings of his later teaching life. Yet in the field of creative theoretical work these years remained frustrated.

In the same period of the late Twenties, Polanyi first formulated his philosophical criticism of contemporary religions as well as of contemporary socialism, in a manuscript *"Ueber die Freiheit"* (On Freedom)[20] which fell into oblivion. Here the transcending of the individual Christian ethic, the reality of society, society's final and inescapable nature (*"die Unaufhebbarkeit der Gesellschaft"*), and the awareness of this inescapability are insights which were to become the cornerstones of his future life-work.

In 1933, shortly after the suspension of Parliament and of the Constitution, when the *Volkswirt* intimated that the socialist tendency of Polanyi's writings would make his further participation an embarrassment, he went to England. There his work took a new, productive direction. He found a circle of friends and eminent scholars who, while generally to the left of him, were kindred spirits. They were Christian Leftists who combined their Christian outlook with enthusiastic support, one might even say uncriticial sympathy, towards the Soviet Union. They had a deep impact on Polanyi's world of thought. He became co-editor of a Symposium published in 1935 under the title *Christianity and the Social Revolution* [21] which contained his study "The Essence of Fascism." A number of young Marxists collaborated in this volume—Roy Pascall, John Cornford (killed in action in the Spanish Civil War), Communist ministers of the Church (Father Ireland, Father Noel, and Father Grosser of London's East End), and the great historian of Chinese science Joseph Needham. In front of me lie a few sheets of paper, yellowed and crumbling, with writing in Polanyi's bold hand, preserved by the whims of fate. On one, is written: "There was a time, when the godless, the atheists, were called freethinkers. We have long-since overcome that stage."[22]

But stronger than any intellectual influence was the trauma which was England. It was his encounter with full-fledged capitalism—of which he had imagined that we knew all that is worth knowing! Yet the houses which Engels had described were still standing; people still lived in them. Black hills of slag stood in the green landscape of Wales; from the depressed areas, young men and women who had never seen their parents employed, drifted away to London.

The repression in Vienna, in February 1934, turned the emigrant into an exile. Under difficult material conditions he was making his way, one in which he was able to pursue his cherished vocation. He taught under the auspices of the Workers' Educational Association and the Extramural Delegacies of the Universities of Oxford and London. These brought Polanyi into contact with British working-class life and experience. He was teaching—and he was learning. The weekly classes he held were in small towns and villages of Sussex and Kent (such as Bexhill and Heathfield) and the coal-mining district of East Kent to which he travelled by Green Line bus. There were plenty of opportunities to get to know one another, especially when it was too late to return home at night and the tutor would find hospitality at the home of one of his students. While having come to feel warm affection towards his students, Polanyi developed a hatred of the classic species of class society in its classic homeland. He was teaching economic history, the history of early capitalism in England. And he collected the memories in which his students, by way of oral tradition in their families, were richly endowed. Blake's "dark, satanic mills" lived on through the generations, and the British working class—even after its economic rise, and in spite of it—still bore the stigmata of the crippling events of its inception. It is given to the best among men somewhere to let down the roots of a sacred hatred. This happened to Polanyi in England. At later stages, in the United States it merely grew in intensity. His hatred was directed against market society and its effects, divesting man of his human shape.

The study of England's social and economic history and its teaching in Tutorial Classes formed in his mind the basic ideas which he later came to formulate in *The Great Transformation*.[23] The perspective of the book, its outline and, above all, the experiences from which it stemmed, had been shaped by 1940. The book was published in New York in 1944, in London in 1945. At a sociological congress in England in 1946, Polanyi formulated his thesis in three points, as represented in his article "On Belief in Economic Determinism."[24] In the Summer of 1943, having completed a lecture tour of American Universities and finished the writing of his book, he returned to England and resumed teaching University Extension and Workers Educational Association classes.

In the Autumn of 1943 there occurred our meeting with Mihály Károlyi and his wife Katalin who were living in London as exiles, and the developing of our friendship. It is to the Károlyis that we owed our inner repatriation to Hungary, to them and to our mutual young friend Endre Havas, a pure-in-heart communist who was to perish as a victim of the terror under Rákosi.

Around the beginning of 1947 Columbia University offered Polanyi a Visiting Professorship in Economics to develop a course in General Economic History, based on *The Great Transformation*. His greatest gift—teaching—now found new and as yet untried scope, in the exposition of his own theoretical findings before a mature audience of young scholars, composed mainly of World War Two veterans. "The real surprise," he continued in the 1950 letter to Jászi cited above, "came to me in the last four years." These years he described as being spent "in the fever of one single uninterrupted work-day." "The outcome, whether I conclude my book or not," he wrote, "will be an interpretation of the economics of early societies, especially regarding trade, money and market phenomena, which will lay down the foundations for comparative economic history." After Polanyi retired from his chair in 1953—at the age of sixty-six—research work continued for another five years in the Interdisciplinary Project on Economic Aspects of Institutional Growth, with the active participation of his former students and colleagues. The results were published in 1957 under the title *Trade and Market in the Early Empires*.[25]

The fruitful work of teaching and research at Columbia University was somewhat impeded by the impact of the Cold War on our personal lives. As a former member of the Hungarian Communist Party—I took a proud stand on this point which was fully understood and supported by my husband—I was banned from the United States "for all time" at the U.S. Consulate in London in 1947. Our permanent home set up in Canada in a little house overlooking the Rouge River Valley, near Toronto, was our reply. For Polanyi this implied a shorter academic year (sometimes just one semester), and frequent trips between Toronto and New York. Towards the end, it was the young scholars who came on frequent visits to our house on the river bend. His portrait hangs there still, above the couch.

Our *Weltanschauung* and our activities, in which for several decades we had known mutual understanding while not following identical paths, eventually merged following the Twentieth Congress of the Soviet Communist Party in 1956. Karl Polanyi's last years were among the happiest and most productive of his life. The intensive study of eighteenth-century Dahomey had begun early, around 1949. It was given its final shape in the winter of 1962 under the title *Dahomey and the Slave Trade*, published posthumously.[26] In 1963 we jointly edited a literary anthology entitled *The Plough and the Pen: Writings from Hungary 1930-1956.*[27] In the last few years of his life, his scholarly work merged with his increasingly keen feeling for, and insight into, the predicament of mankind.

A cancerous growth which first became apparent in 1957 required surgical treatment several times a year. To the last day of his life, Polanyi did not lose the will to live, continuing to work with discipline and dedication. His political philosophy in these years was dominated by the stand he took against the Cold War and for the idea of Co-existence.[28] "I am nursing the seeds of sanity in the world..."

The last decade of his life, the breathless pace of his scholarly work and the feel of life opening wide towards the world of man, are perhaps closest reflected in the fragment of a backwards yet also forward looking letter that Polanyi wrote in 1958 to a love of his early youth, Bé (Beatrice) de Waard.[29] "My life was a 'world'-life—I lived the life of the human world...My work is for Asia, for Africa, for the new peoples...The opposition which my world of thought has called forth at last, is a good sign. I should have loved to last and be in at the fight, but man is a mortal thing."[30]

The period of three weeks in the Autumn of 1963, spent in Budapest at Hungary's invitation, were the last in my husband's life that can be said to have been spent in relative health. They were at the same time the fulfillment of his life—his homecoming, in the knowledge of the deadly turn his illness was taking. In his message to the Hungary of the young writers, poets and scholars, he wrote: "My viewpoints now are wholly centred on my homeland, to which one whose youth was shaped by the Magyar fate owes all and everything."[31]

Karl Polanyi died on the 23rd of April, 1964. He worked to the last evening of his life. Over his coffin, lines by Attila József[32] were spoken, lines written to the recondite God he kept hidden away, kept out of all his undertakings:

My God, I love you with all my heart.
Were you a newsboy selling papers
I'd help you cry them in the street.

NOTES

1. This account brings together several of Ilona Duczynska's memoirs on her husband and his family. (1) The larger part consists of "Karl Polanyi (1886-1964). A Family Chronicle and a Short Account of his Life," a 17-page English version (in typescript) made in 1970 by Ilona Duczynska of an "Introduction" she wrote to a selection of Karl Polanyi's writings for *Századok* (Centuries), CV,1,1971, pp.89-95. "I have put them [the biographical notes] into English for Kari, Tom and Harry and for our close friends." (2) Two handwritten manuscripts, one of them a corrected and abbreviated version (4 pages) of the other (10 pages), entitled "Karl Polanyi, his works and days." In an accompanying typewritten note, Ilona states that the original "was written in hospital in Budapest in the autumn of 1966." She adds "Much of the wording is practically identical [with the Hungarian "Introduction"], only I prefer this to the other English text, because it was written in English in the first place." In fact, this document focuses on the early years of the family. The first draft in particular contains many intimate details, and is more representative of the outspokenness of both Karl and Ilona (and, as such, was not intended for publication in Hungary at that time). Indeed, Ilona adds to the typed explanation a handwritten note, dated June 1970, to that effect: "The clear (second) version is not necessarily the better one." (3) A typewritten document of 12 pages, plus one of Notes, dated 1970, entitled "Karl Polanyi, Notes on his Life" which includes lengthy quotations. I have put these items together—the tops of the handwritten pages gnawed by mice, in some places calling for guess-work—in order to create a continuous account of Karl

Polanyi's life and work as viewed by his wife. Except for very few changes (usually stylistic, or involving repetition) and explanatory additions indicated by square brackets, the texts are as Ilona Duczynska wrote them. I have added several footnotes to her originals. (Kenneth McRobbie)

2. Ervin Szabó was a socialist *savant* of great independence of mind and anarcho-syndicalist leanings, an inspiration to every early revolutionary movement in Hungary. He died shortly before the end of the First World War.

3. Ernö Seidler, a prisoner of war in Russia, returned to Hungary in 1918 a Bolshevik, and was co-founder of the Hungarian Communist Party in 1918. He was Military Commander in Budapest during the Hungarian Republic of Councils of 1919. In the course of the Stalinist terror he was murdered in the Soviet Union. His sister was Irma Seidler, who is mentioned frequently in Lukács's correspondence; she was in love with Lukács who refused to commit himself; she committed suicide in 1911. This engendered Lukács's sole literary work, "Von der Armut am Geiste" (On Poverty of Spirit).

4. Odon Por became known in England as a writer on Guild Socialism.

5. These detailed references are explained by the fact that Ilona Duczynska too enrolled at the same institution in 1915.(K.McR.)

6. Ample reference to N.V. Tschaikovsky and the Tschaikovsky group is contained in P.A. Kropotkin's Autobiography.

7. Letter to Ilona Duczynska from L. Furthmüller (Klatschko's grandson): "Trotsky in his Autobiography speaks of him with great admiration. To become an eminent politician, he writes, the only qualities he was lacking in were the bad ones."

8. She adds "*der Stein des Anstosses*," stumbling-block, offence.

9. Here she quotes from the opening page of an article by Kari Levitt, "Karl Polanyi and Co-Existence," *Co-Existence*, No.2, 1964. This article is reproduced (as Annex D) in Kari Polanyi Levitt, ed., *The Life and Work of Karl Polanyi*. Montreal: Black Rose Books, 1990, pp.253-263. "All his life a socialist...[he never gave in] to determinism or fatalism."

10. *The Yale Review*, Vol.43, No.3, March 1954, 336-350; and *Kortárs*, May 1968 (in Hungarian).

11. Letter to Richard Wank, December 1925.

12. This was Ilona Duczynska's role, as she suggests later in the memoir.

13. "In the ethical field the Galilei Circle was a creative success. Probably for the first time since 1848 did the student masses come to know of moral *engagement*, and put it into practice in their personal lives. But politically my omission was past remedy...It was due to the Galilei Circle's failing, that there was not available in 1918 a generation, welded in one with the peasantry and with the national minorities in long-standing, stern battles...Whose responsibility? Mine. I had been leading the Circle in an anti-political direction. Neither with the working class, nor with the peasantry, nor with the national minorities did I try to achieve, or even seek some unity based on action...I have never been a politician, I had no talent that way, no interest even."

14. On October 31, 1918, the soldiers, in revolt, refused to be sent to the front. They tore off the imperial insignia from their hats, and wore instead the white asters which on All Souls' Eve are brought into the cities to be put on the graves.

15. György Lukács (1885-1971) was the son of a Hungarian Jewish banker. He achieved a world reputation as the most eminent Marxist philosopher, literary critic and aesthetician. He was Commissar of Education in the 1919 Hungarian Republic of Soviets, and also acted as "political commissar" for one of the Red Guard companies at the front.

16. Lékai was a young student incurably ill with TB. He had been in the "second set" of young revolutionaries that took over, when the "first set" was arrested in January 1918. Towards the end of the war he made an unsuccessful attempt on the life of Count István Tisza.

17. The quotation continued: "He was not made for giving continuous, political lead. The moral impact he had on the young people was the essential thing—the honesty, veracity and candour. The young ones felt it. He was the fountainhead of the moral climate of the Galilei Circle. Never cold or superior—yet his arguments had a cutting edge. He was the man for us, our hearts were with him...."

18. *Archiv für Sozialwissenschaft und Sozialpolitik*, Band 49, Heft 2, 1922, 377-418.

19. L. von Mises, "Neuere Beiträge zum Problem der sozialistischen Wirtschaftsrechnung," *Archiv*, Band 51, Heft 2, 488-500. F.Weil, "Gildensozialistische Rechnungslegung," *Archiv* Band 52, Heft 1, 196-217. K. Polanyi, "Die funktionelle Theorie der Gesellschaft und das Problem der sozialistischen Rechnungslegung. Eine Erwiderung," *Archiv*, Band 52, Heft 1, 1925a, 218-228.

20. Manuscript in I.D's possession.

21. John Lewis, Karl Polanyi, Donald K. Kitchen, (eds.), *Christianity and the Social Revolution*. London: Gollancz, 1935. Part III Dies Irae. I. "The Essence of Fascism," pp.359-394.
22. The extract continues: "Also among atheists there can be found plenty of narrow-minded, shiftless people, petty-bourgeois in their mentality, who should be regarded as anything rather than freethinkers—while the religious bent may make man fit for the most daring revolt of the spirit, and among those who died in the cause of free thought, the foremost place will ever be held by Jesus from the town of Nazareth. By freedom of the spirit we do not mean a denial of truth, nor of ethics, law or authority. On the contrary, we mean that freedom of the spirit will relentlessly seek truth, abide by the dictates of ethics, act according to the law and respect authority. Relentlessly and consistently. Not calling retreat before any consideration whatsoever, and rousing the human disposition out of its somnolence into ever alert watchfulness. Searching for truth behind and in the face of all and every kind of class-truth and race-truth; following the path of a pure ethic, despite the cut-and-dried precepts of the 'moralists,' and beyond those; taking its stand on the foundations of justice, even in defiance of the law, and bowing but to the authority of goodness and truth, turning against all phoney authority that rests on debauched success and on the display of power. To search, then, for truth, and where the taboos of tradition bar the way, to act by the postulates of ethics, even if this is decried by the compromisers and opportunists as 'super-idealisms,' as a show of 'juvenileism,' as 'Donquixotery,' or simply as being green and immature. To stand for justice, even against the law and to erect an altar to the authority of the heroes of goodness and truth on the ruins of the authority of conventions, cynicism, ignorance and the soul's torpidity." ("Manuscript in I.D's possession.")
23. Karl Polanyi, *The Great Transformation. The Political and Economic Origins of our Time*. New York: Rinehart, 1944. Ilona quotes from the letter from Karl Polanyi to Oscar Jászi, dated October 27, 1950, relating to his teaching and writing. "I was fifty years old when circumstances in England led me to studies in economic history. I earned my living that way, as a teacher. For I was born to be one. I little thought then that yet another vocation was in store for me and that I was preparing myself for it. Some three years later, apparently again under the pressure of circumstances, I wrote a book, once more trying to give an interpretation of recent history... but this time I under-pinned my train of thought with a perspective in economic history."
24. *The Sociological Review*, Vol. XXXIX. Section One, 1947. Ilona reproduces three points by Polanyi: "1. That economic determinism was pre-dominantly a nineteenth-century phenomenon, which has now ceased to operate in the greater part of the world; it was effective only under a market system, which is rapidly disappearing in Europe; 2. that the market system violently distorted our views of man and society; 3. that these distorted views are proving one of the main obstacles to the solution of the problems of our civilization."
25. Karl Polanyi, with C.M. Arensberg and H.W. Pearson, *Trade and Market in the Early Empires*. New York: Free Press, 1957.
26. Karl Polanyi, *Dahomey and the Slave Trade*. Seattle & London: University of Washington, 1966.
27. Ilona Duczynska and Karl Polanyi, eds., *The Plough and the Pen: Writings from Hungary 1930-1956*. Foreword by W.H. Auden. London: Peter Owen; Toronto: McClelland & Stewart, 1963.
28. See Kari Polanyi Levitt, "Karl Polanyi and Co-Existence."
29. Beatrice de Waard (1888-1962). Dutch-born fiancée of Leo Popper (1886-1911), who moved to Paris after his early death. Popper's essays on aesthetics influenced the early work of Lukács. He was Karl Polanyi's best friend.
30. From Karl Polanyi's letter to Bé de Waard, 6 January 1958. Typescript fragment in I.D's possession. Ilona also cites the intervening passage: "But the world had seemed to have stopped living for decades, to catch up a century within a few years. This is how I am only now coming into my own, somewhere on the way I have lost thirty years or so—waiting for Godot—until things were at par again, the world in its course had caught up with me. Looking back, all this seems somehow funny—that martyrdom of isolation was no more than a mirage—in truth I was waiting only for myself. Now the dice are cast against us (against you, against me). One more decade—and I would stand vindicated in my lifetime."
31. Karl Polanyi, "Our Homeland's Duty" (in Hungarian), *Kortárs* (Contemporary), December 1963. Ilona also quotes the following "...in the years of the crisis which is endangering all mankind, I have fully turned towards socialism, which is no longer merely the cause of the working class, but a matter of life and death for all humanity. In this no small part is due to my Hungarian homeland."
32. Attila József (1905-37) was Hungary's greatest proletarian lyric poet, whom Karl and Ilona Polányi discovered together in 1943. The lines constitute the whole poem "Istenem" (My God) (1924): "Dolgaim elol rejtegetlek / Istenem, én nagyon szeretlek. / Ha rikkancs volna mesterséged, / segítnék kiabálni néked." I have retranslated the text. (K.McR.)

Chapter Twenty-Seven

LETTER TO A FRIEND, 1925
Karl Polanyi

Vorgartenstrasse Nr.203/10, Wien
Herrn Richard Wank
Hidegkuti u.115
Budapest

Vienna, Christmas 1925

My dear Rikárdka!

Maybe I have even forgotten Hungarian, but there are things I shall never forget.
    I've become a different Person from the one you knew, my Rikárdka. I don't know whether at that time you knew, I can't remember—impossible to remember such things—whether you knew my secret. Then it was a secret: by now I've as good as forgotten it. But, should you not have known it, I have to tell you. If I had told you about it before (it would only have been in 1917, not before) forgive me for repeating the confession.
    When first we met, I was mortally ill. My mind was sick, I was the victim of a melancholia constantly on the increase since my twentieth year. Nothing more ghastly can be imagined than this illness. Tormenting, incessant senseless *inner excitement*—that is one of its elements. Another: *a poisoned feel to life*, something like inward sickliness, as if it were some infernal retching of the soul's self; the third, *narrowed down consciousness*, obsessed, compulsive thinking, you see only a white spot as large as your hand, space doesn't open up, you cannot be at your ease [on] the level, no third dimension, a flattening out, and what remains is one word in the middle of a patch where everything is clear—suicide. This word does not represent intent, nor something you are scared of, but a fate *already consummated* (that you live is but an illusion, mere accident, suicide is pre-ordained, you are "born to be a suicide," and you haven't much time left). This state of things kept getting steadily worse when I was in the field [on active service], coming on in bouts lasting two to three weeks, increasing in intensity, and never letting up. This feature of the illness went together with a very ugly little trait: it was simply impossible to tell anybody anything about it. If only you would be able to tell about it, you felt, you'd be saved. But to tell about it was just as impossible as to die of it. You *had* to conceal it.

I do not know, I say, when it eventually subsided. For, sure enough, pass it did!!!—did I tell you that? If I did, it could only have been near Laibach, for that was where I noticed for the first time that I was feeling differently, as if it were growing lighter around me. But whether or not I confessed to this, I cannot remember. I don't think I did. (Or maybe in 1919, in the hospital?) This sickness took ten years off my life. Today, I know that it worked the other way round. My wrongly lived life had brought on the trouble; the illness was but the cry of pain of my miserably crippled true life, not the reverse. But at that time, how could I have had any intimation of this?

Then came the turning point. A tremendous transformation. I came out of it, I changed, I understood. I was restored to health. During the time I was laid up in the Jewish hospital, I was indeed already this new Karli. Whether outwardly there was or was not any difference between the two, I cannot say.

Here was the starting point of my later life. Perhaps I can put it this way: my former ego knew duty and the joy of art, passionately, but in isolation, not leading to the building up of the personality. That's how I was when in the field. Forbiddingly, rigidly duty-conscious, yet avidly grasping and delighting in poetry, unwitting constraint. Today all is different. Nine years of illness leached away such intensity; I have become relaxed. I do not know, and don't believe I'll ever understand what then was choking me, as the rope chokes a man being hanged: the problems of pure artistic form. Something else has taken its place, the ethical world; to live and comprehend ethical reality, and thus create it. Duty?—what once was the supreme task is today an imposed, "zwangsläufig" by-product, "Abfall."

I comply with it, stick it out, do not give in—but do so casually. I've changed from being a stickler for duty, into doing my duty out of sheer habit. There's something that's more important—life. Previously, I did not understand. I must have been a slow to develop, somewhat infantile young man. That's to say, it's only now that I have matured into a man. And so it is only now that I begin to understand life. You always used to talk about life with a capital "L," a life of passion, of red miracles.—That I never understood. Nor do I understand it now. But there is another kind of life which I am living—today. Life as closeness, as love, as inner vision, as small-scale fulfilment, the soul-saving life of the microcosm. And I don't mean this only in the idyllic way (although that to) but in the *universal* way. During these years my ideas on social issues have found passionate expression. The social sciences, activity, but above all the possibility of freedom of thought on social issues. *How can we be free, in spite of the fact of society?* And not *in our imagination only*, not by abstracting ourselves from society, denying the fact of our being interwoven with the lives of others, being committed to them, but in *reality*, by aiming at making society as "übersichtlich," as a family's inner life is, so that I may achieve a state of things in which I have done my duty towards *all men*, and so be *free* again, in decency, with a good conscience.

The last five years of my life have meant more and been better than the preceding thirty-five. More meaningful, so happy from minute to minute, so happy beyond words in fulfilment, like the life of my two and a half years old little daughter. If you knew me today, you would love me more, for to a some slight degree at least I would be deserving of it. At that former time I was egotistical, mean, narrow, senseless, opinionated, and vain. Above all, vain. Thank God, now all is *a little* better.

I am working a great deal, in a scholarly, social way. I also earn my living at—fortunately—respectable journalism. And I live in such happiness, so close to the essential, that at least, at Christmas, I have to tell you this, my Rikárdka. If only I could see you again!

Je t'embrasse, Your Karli

You could stay with us, you would have no expenses—could you not come? *Do give it serious thought.*

> The letter appears in a translation by Ilona Duczynska (revised by Kenneth McRobbie). She wrote of it, as follows. "This letter came to me from the widow of Rikárd Wank. It was preserved for 50 years. Mrs. Wank by chance shared a hospital room with my friend Mrs. Júlia Rajk [in Budapest]. In conversation, it turned out that Julia was in touch with me. A letter was handed to her, and from her to me. Richard Wank was a frequent visitor later at our house, also in Klosterneuburg. Of this letter and of what it told I had no knowledge until 50 years later."

Chapter Twenty-Eight

KARL POLANYI AND OSCAR JÁSZI AT THE *BÉCSI MAGYAR ÚJSÁG* (VIENNESE HUNGARIAN NEWS)
János Gyurgyák

The date 1919 marks a stage both in the development of Karl Polanyi's ideas and in the history of Hungary. The organic development of turn-of-the-century Hungary would give way to a succession of dictatorships, utopian solutions, and "third way" ideologies and theories. Those who were dreaming of a democratic Hungary were pushed to the periphery and, indeed, often into inner or external emigration. It was in emigration that Polanyi had to face this reality. It may be that the key to his later works lies in an appreciation of the same faith and resolution with which he gave up the study of national history and political activity and instead turned to research into the past and present in order to see the future more clearly.

Polanyi underwent a profound spiritual and intellectual crisis which was further exacerbated by serious illness. But in a letter to Oscar Jászi he expresses the view that action is "the true precondition for constructing an image of society. Without such an image we are helpless, because we do not know what we are up against." And he goes on: "I have to state that we do not possess such an image of society today. It is to us a dark, threatening, inextricable web." Yet, he continues: "Knowledge is power, because while we do not know anything about some things...even the most anguishing, the most deformed, the most badly conceived image means a thousand times more than nothing at all."[1]

What was the reason for the bankruptcy of so-called liberal socialism? Why did there yawn an unbridgeable chasm between the clarity of theory and political practice? This was the cardinal question both for Polanyi and a whole generation that believed in evolution, reform, and negation of violence, yet were unprepared for the changes that ensued. Accordingly, in his first articles written in emigration Polanyi sought answers to these questions. He considered that:

> ...liberal socialism has come to a dead end...it has cut off forever the rightful place of economics from the newly created society, leaving nothing but liberal economics which incorporates harmoniously 'other' (moral and intellectual) powers and values. This primacy of the economy cannot be remedied with any kind of holy water.

At that time, as in articles he wrote before 1919, the contradiction that most worried Polanyi was that between the primacy of moral aims and deterministic materialism. In the same article, he wrote: "If it is true that the economy alone is the objective structure of society, then in our opinion politics, institutions, public life, etc., also would be merely dependent on it." (*Ibid.*)

Old ideologies were unsuitable for interpreting new facts and events in the world, Polanyi decided. "We have to set a new ideology in place of the old," he writes to Jászi. (1921) The working out of a "direct and constructive" conception of socialism is the most urgent duty. It was on these problems that his writings focused between the years 1921 and 1924. During this period, earlier intellectual influences—Tolstoy, Spengler, and Rudolf Steiner—for a time continued to influence him. Polanyi thought that by combining such influences it would be possible to create a new theory which could serve as a basis for re-interpreting socialism. He accepted Spengler as the critic of existing systems, along with his view that Western European societies had entered upon a period of decline. "The future-living Faust-like (Western European) culture...now seeks realization in the form of socialism." (January 7, 1920) Steiner had discovered the proper representation of the life of human societies: the relative independence of the functions of the organism, and the necessity of the unity and harmony of these functions.[2]

During these early years in emigration an important influence on Polanyi was his friendship with Oscar Jászi. The views they shared, their aims, their work together are to some extent revealed in Jászi's diary entries for those years (Polanyi was for a time Jászi's private secretary). Jászi faithfully presents their daily discussions of theoretical problems—such as Duhring, Endre Ady's importance, the Physiocrats, problems of natural law, guild socialism—as well as of political questions of the day. There was no event of importance in scholarship or politics which escaped their attention. In addition, Jászi introduced Polanyi to the *Bécsi Magyar Újság* (Viennese Hungarian News) and to the technique of writing newspaper articles. They discussed details concerning the structure of Jászi's planned book.[3] "What form should we give to the Anti-Marx plan?" After the completion of the first draft, Jászi's diary contains the entry: "We spent some pleasant hours together; he is sensitive, and has a good sense of humour. I read aloud from a draft of my book; it had quite an effect on him."[4] Jászi's sober, theoretical, practical anti-bolshevism evidently impressed Polanyi. However, despite such evidence of mutual understanding, their differing outlooks began to take them in diverse directions even at that time. Each saw himself in terms of his own ideas as having an individual destiny which constituted both vocation and obligation. Neither was able to separate destiny from vocation. Thus, Polanyi wrote to Jászi,

> I had hoped that we would stay close to each other, because I have learned much from you. I want to know now, though, how we stand, because I know what I want and would like to know what you want...You appear to be interested in general conditions and principles, while I am interested in concrete meaning and the process of transformation. (July 30, 1921)

After the early twenties they drew apart somewhat and their relationship cooled; their correspondence, however, never entirely ceased. Jászi was gratified at Polanyi's scholarly success. In one of his letters, he wrote: "Your success makes me all the more satisfied, because I well remember the hours we spent in that Viennese café when I tried to bring your highflown ideas down from the clouds to earth."(February 23, 1948) In a letter to Polanyi in 1939, Jászi observed that he wanted "to say thanks for the faith with which you can live in our period, that sign of your heroic view of life, which is only possible when one is able to isolate oneself from alien sorrows."(January 7, 1939) On the other hand, he did not accept Polanyi's radical anti-capitalism from which necessarily followed certain consequences, concerning which the latter responded: "I never pretended to be a 'Christian communist,' and nothing can alter my conviction that no one can be called a communist who is not one. I have never in my life thought of myself as a communist, still less as being a 'fellow traveler.' " (February 23, 1948)

Ilona Duczynska identified the year 1921 as that in which Polanyi's life took "a new turn." It was at this time that Polanyi distanced himself from the ideas of Tolstoy. "The reality of society, the indissoluble bonds between human beings and society, the influence of all activity on society, and the reacting of society, became the main lines of his *oeuvre* at this period."[5] In that year one of his most important works was published, "Believing and Unbelieving Politics".[6] According to Polanyi, two types of politics are possible: believing and unbelieving. Unbelieving politics tries to achieve its aim without changing people; believing politics can conceive of general progress only through the development and progress of the individual. Polanyi views the period's leading ideologies as basically mistaken—and thus in need of revision—first and foremost because they failed the test of *liberté, égalité, fraternité*. The essence of socialism is that it represents the more perfect ideal of equality and liberty.

> In that lies its truth and its strength. If we deny the value of those ideals of liberty and equality, then no sociology, economics, statistics or evolutionary theory can in our eyes portray socialist society as preferable to the Indian caste-system...We may desire more real liberty and more general equality simply on the basis of acknowledged ideals of equality and liberty. There is not, nor can be, a socialist who is not socialist in the name of human ideals.

Unbelieving politics, according to Polanyi, includes both reactionary and Marxist types which differ from each other only in their conclusions. The basic idea common to both is that human nature is unchangeable; from this necessarily comes belief in the miraculous effect of institutions. From bodies of organized power, then, would come those material, moral, and intellectual goods which would inspire a greater degree than nowadays of unselfishness, patience, and mutual aid. The idol of this politics is the state. As in the case of reaction, it culminates in pressure and dictatorship which, according to Lenin, makes people accustomed to be good. (*Op.cit.*, p.986) Polanyi did not believe in the enforced law of evolution, and could not imagine socialism without democracy. The entirety of human ideals cannot be replaced with others: "Then new ideals in materialist form may be proclaimed to the people: but all human ideals are born from a common root, and whoever will destroy that can never expect the tree to bear fruit." (*Ibid.*, p.988)

To unbelieving politics Polanyi opposes believing politics; within the latter he underlines the importance of guild socialism and liberal socialism. Believing politics, according to him, believes in the changeability of human nature.

> Believing politics is no more than a politics that knows that without a change in the individual...no institution can assure long-lasting achievement of our common aims—humanistic education, intellectual training and schooling, theoretical conviction, and above all the providing of moral examples: tradition-building equipment which tries to change basically that which is changeable and should be changed as to viewpoint, value judgement, ideas, and ideals.

Polanyi thinks that we need not just changes in form, but basic reforms. "It is not enough to refute the school models of orthodox Marxism," he wrote. In order to erect new economic and historical-philosophical foundations on the teachings of socialism, "we have to banish the last germs of the unbelieving and uncreative ideology which basically despises humankind." (*Ibid.*, p.990) At the end of his paper he bitterly summarizes the aims of existing political trends. "The unbelieving organizers," he wrote, assume that basically man is selfish and bad, assume too "an iron law of the invariability of human nature." Such organizers would say:

> Thus it is to your selfishness and badness that we appeal: do but one of the following trifles, and we sincerely promise that society in its entirety will be transformed into an empire of truth and love. Vote in this or that ballot, on this or that coloured paper, pay this or that sum, shoot whom we point to; we promise that if you do all this...society—which is built upon you—will change fundamentally.

Over the next few years Polanyi saw as his main duty—particularly in articles written for the *Bécsi Magyar Újság*—the working out of a new ideology of socialism, in order to establish socialism on a moral foundation, because for him socialism had "basically a moral purpose which aims at the totality of human liberty and solidarity."[7] He considered that Marxist socialism simplified and dulled the original form's content and meaning. "Marxism, therefore, like all kinds of scientific system building, is transitory," he wrote, "while socialism as the way towards the ultimate fraternity and social perfection of humankind is eternal."(*Ibid.*) The article that Polanyi wrote on the occasion of the publication of Karl Kautsky's "Die proletarische Revolution und ihr Programm" is especially important from this aspect. In Polanyi's view, Kautsky concerns himself only with externals, with the letter of Marxism; his faith in the unquestionable authority of Marx has collapsed. Polanyi does not subscribe to the type of socialism which Kautsky represents (the widening of parliamentary democracy, socialization of the economy, etc.). For him, what are missing are the moral fundamentals, and an explanation of the connection between corporative production and industrial democracy.

There is one sentence in a letter he wrote to Jászi in which Polanyi reveals how attentively he had followed the course of the Russian revolution. "All Moscow's failures signify more than all the successes of Washington; under the ruins in Russia we can find greater treasures than in the plains of Ur and Eridu." The Bolsheviks—he agreed with Bertrand Russell—subscribed to the mission of Peter the Great.[8] On the other hand, Polanyi dissociates himself from this experiment for cultural, economic and above all moral reasons. Ethical reservations compelled Polanyi to face the problems of both socialism and democracy. The issue was defined by György Lukács in 1918 in his "Bolshevism as an Ethical Problem": "Is democracy nothing but a tactic of socialism...or is democracy so integral to socialism that it cannot be omitted until one clarifies its ideological and moral consequences?"[9]

Polanyi's life-work will proclaim that democracy is the *sine qua non* of socialism, and to ignore it means putting into question socialism itself. In another article Polanyi expressed the opinion that for a long time it will be impossible to go beyond democracy: "the idea of democracy has risen again, and no force can stop it now."[10] He rejected the use of violence and all attempts to concentrate power.[11] In this regard his attitude perhaps represents a watershed shared by other members of the "second reform generation", as represented by the poet and artist Anna Lesznai in a letter written to Jászi. Despite these reservations, Polanyi considered that for the Russian revolution to fail would be a set back throughout Europe for all movements on behalf of freedom and emancipation of the working people. He agreed with Jászi that only "the great political withdrawal toward a free and democratic politics as planned by Lenin" would save the situation.[12] In his view just such a great political withdrawal, opening up new perspectives for Russian society, was to be seen in the introduction of the NEP (New Economic Policy), and the abolition of war-communism. For, critiques aside, it clear that Polanyi regarded faith in socialism as integral to Western civilization.

> Democracy confirmed its power for centuries in England. At the same time, when the last wave of the French Revolution reached Moscow...Western European culture wants to exist, to live, and to develop. Therefore it will not die. (February 4, 1924)

Here then Polanyi adheres in an orthodox way to the original Marxist view that the stage of socialism can be reached by surpassing capitalism. At that time Polanyi had great hopes for guild socialism, which he expected to be realized in England. There, as he put it, "the parliamentary majority is omnipotent." "Hence," he went on, "we can find some grounds for the existence of revolutionary theories, and therefore Great Britain has become the school of practical radicalism."[13] The essence of guild socialism for Polanyi is that "it seeks to socialize the instruments of production, not by taking them over through public ownership but though democratic control by trade-unions and corporations." He considers it to be of world-wide importance because it avoids the basic contradictions of both the collectivist-communist and the syndicalist view of society.

> Without seeing the final aims in the far distant future, we can yet say that collectivist socialism aimed at the general collectivization of the state while syndicalism tried to eliminate the state...The producer will become free only when he is his own master. On behalf of the collectivist state it can rightfully be objected that the capitalism of workers' groups is not socialism but just the opposite; it would create group monopolies in place of private monopolies; it would increase anarchy within the economy, and lead to the resurrection of private capitalism. Production is not an end in itself, but must serve consumption; in this only the state and the community can effectively represent the consumer. Therefore we have to place direction in the 'hands' of the state rather than those of the producer who concentrates only on his private interests and not those of the public. (*Ibid.*)

The basic idea of guild socialism is set out in terms of its functional view of society, and its efforts toward autonomy. "There are functions," Polanyi pointed out, "which impel people to ally together: production in common, consumption in common, common neighbourhoods, intellectual bonding." He identified existing "natural communities": trade unions, corporations, municipal boards, ideological and cultural groups, each fulfilling a function in life. "An individual can belong to more than one group," he observed, "depending on which part of his life is served by the organization. In a truly democratic society no manner of violence or privilege of ownership will disturb the natural aggregation of individuals." (*Ibid.*)

The essence of guild socialism is that the interests of the producers are represented by the producers themselves (the trade unions), and the interests of the consumers by the consumers' organisations, the municipalities, and the state.

Producers' societies have to become industrial alliances (organised on the basis of a given industry, not on the basis of a trade), so that the new industrial association is none other than a modern guild. The instruments of production are removed from private ownership and placed not in the hands of the state but in the hands of trade unions now transformed into guilds. Guilds created along these lines, in which both blue- and white-collar workers are united, can take over the direction of factories. But how different structures organised along different lines will exist in harmony with each other is not made clear.

While the outcomes of the period 1919-1923 were mainly ideological and theoretical, those of 1924-1933 were more practical. In 1924 Polanyi joined the editorial board of *Der Oesterreichische Volkswirt* (The Austrian Economist) with special responsibility for international and foreign affairs. His familiarity with and mastery of economic issues stem from this period. We may conclude this brief discussion of Polanyi's early relations with Jászi with mention of his later expression of a viewpoint that reflects their earlier, if relatively short-lived accord. In 1927 Polanyi contributed to *Láthatár* (Horizon) an open letter which stands as an important document in intellectual history. In it he urges the view that democracy is the basic question before Western Europe.[14] Democracy had failed in many places because it had not taken reality into account, because it had been "walking in the clouds." Polanyi continues:

> We sacrificed the reality for the idea of democracy...The abstract form of democracy which ignored the realities of the class struggle, religion, war, and violence deserved to fall; let bygones be bygones. Fascism is not an abstract formula but a concrete reality which can be destroyed—by a very similar, close-to-life, order-maintaining democracy capable of analysing the facts, biding its time, and making decisions.

NOTES

Translated by Andrea Polyák.

1. Letter of Karl Polanyi to Oscar Jászi, January 7, 1920. Columbia University, Butler Library, Jászi Papers. (Photocopy, National Széchenyi Library, Budapest.) Henceforth, references to letters will be made in the text.
2. Karl Polanyi, "Is It Possible to Help Russia?" (Lehet-e Oroszországon segíteni?), *Medvetanc*, 1921, pp. 223-226.
3. Oscar Jászi, *Marxism or Planned Socialism?* Paris, 1983. (Published in Hungarian).
4. Oscar Jászi, "Diary," 1919. National Széchenyi Library, Budapest.
5. Ilona Duczynska, "Karl Polanyi and the Galilei Circle" (Polányi Károly és a Galilei-Kör) *Századok*, 1971, 1, pp. 89-95; 93. [The passage quoted here is presented in the author's original, and previously unpublished, English version, for which see elsewhere in this volume. K.M.]
6. Karl Polanyi, "Believing and Unbelieving Politics," (Hivó és hitetlen politika), *Napkelet* (Sunrise), September 1920, pp. 984-990.
7. Karl Polanyi, "Karl Kautsky and Democracy" (Karl Kautsky és a demokrácia), *Bécsi Magyar Újság*, September 17, 1922, p. 6.
8. Karl Polanyi, "The English Elections" (Az angol választások), *Bécsi Magyar Újság*, 1921, p. 6.
9. György Lukács, "Bolshevism as an Ethical Problem" (A bolsevizmus mint erkölcsi probléma), *Szabadgondolat*, VIII, No. 10, December 1918, pp. 228-232.
10. Karl Polanyi, "The Rebirth of Democracy" (A demokrácia feltamadása), *Bécsi Magyar Újság*, November 26, 1922, p. 4.
11. "Believing and Unbelieving Politics," p. 986.
12. Oszkár Jászi, "Danton or Napoleon?" (Danton vagy napoleon?), *Bécsi Magyar Újság*, July 12, 1921.
13. Karl Polanyi, "The Constitution of Socialist Great Britain" (A szocialista Nagybritannia alkotmánya), *Bécsi Magyar Újság*, April 16, 1922, p. 9.
14. Karl Polanyi, "On the Objectives of Hungarian Democracy" (A magyar demokrácia célkituzéseirol), *Láthatár* (Horizon), May 14, 1927, p. 10.

Chapter Twenty-Nine

EDITORIAL MEETINGS OF THE *OESTERREICHISCHE VOLKSWIRT* (1928)

Richard A. Bermann

The editorial offices of the *Volkswirt* and the residence of its Editor and Publisher Walter Federn are housed in an old building at Porzellangasse 27. The spacious offices are used exclusively for work as is evidenced by their (somewhat chaotic) appearance. The rickety old-fashioned furniture is buried deep under newspapers, magazines, books, and diverse materials pertaining to the state of the economy. On Tuesday mornings an assorted set of wobbly old chairs are excavated and ceremoniously carried into the office of the Editor-in-Chief located far from the clatter of typewriters; there they are arranged around his imposing desk, so that each chair is equidistant from the only ashtray and the large box of officially provided cigarettes which is now opened.

A visiting observer of an editorial meeting of the *Oesterreichische Volkswirt* reported with some amusement that he had the impression he was witnessing a cabinet meeting of the United States of the World. Dr Karl Polanyi, editor for foreign and world affairs, unloaded a large collection of newspaper clippings marked in red and blue pencil from a briefcase bulging with papers to the point of shapelessness. It appeared that this truly cosmic briefcase contained every possible available piece of information relating to economic and political events reported anywhere in the world during the past week. Or not yet reported. I well remember the many Tuesdays when Karl Polanyi, interrupted by loud derision from the rest of the editorial team, recited the complicated names of unknown Chinese revolutionary generals. Nobody was interested in these characters—until events projected them onto the front pages of the world's press.

The purpose of these weekly Tuesday morning meetings of the editors and staff was to monitor new developments, determine editorial policy, but most especially to select the themes of the economic and political Notes (*Glossen*) which were the lead items of every issue of the *Volkswirt*. The fact that this exercise was treated with such importance and seriousness gave the journal its own very special character.

In Austria, where journalism treats economic and political affairs from strictly partisan and pedestrian positions with no coverage of European or exotic contemporary world events, these well-intentioned persons of varying political party affiliation gathered weekly to exchange opinions until there was a consensus on what was to be done. This journal, limited in its readership and heavy on figures and statistics, was edited with a magnificent sense of its importance. Every word was written as if the fate of the country, indeed the fate of all humanity, depended on it.

It is a sign of a truly excellent publication that every editorial conference should begin with a devastating critique of the previous issue. At 11 o clock on Tuesday morning, every member of the editorial team is deeply disappointed and depressed. So many mistakes! So many erroneous judgements! There is criticism that a note was not correctly placed, a sentence redundant, an expression misconceived. These errors are corrected in the following issue; apologies are extended where an injustice was perceived to have been done to somebody—a practice foreign to Austrian journalism. Debates were conducted with everyone speaking at the top of his voice, not only because one of the participants was hard of hearing, but because everybody was very temperamental. But differences of opinion were resolved; there was never a real quarrel, nor was a word ever spoken in anger. It was a discussion of well-informed individuals who respected—and even liked—each other.

The composition of the editorial team has changed over the years. First and foremost was the departure from Vienna of Dr Gustav Stolper and his wife Toni. The energy which Stolper brought to the editorial team, and the priceless assistance of his capable and hardworking wife Toni, could ill be spared. Stolper's departure left Walter Federn, founder of the *Volkswirt*, alone as publisher. This represented a significant increase in workload, with longer work days and shorter holidays. His incredible capacity for work was legendary. But it was his fund of knowledge of economic affairs, his judgment in matters of policy, and his clarity of mind which contributed even more than his tireless capacity for hard work. He is and has been for 20 years the real backbone of the journal. He is as strong, straight and sensitive as a backbone.

Walter Federn leads the editorial team, not because he owns the journal—none of the team think of him as employer or entrepreneur—but because he is the best person for the job. He not only founded the journal, he built it page by page, line by line. Today it is impossible to differentiate between the person of Walter Federn and the modest, high-spirited, thorough, explosive and quarrelsome *Volkswirt*.

The regular members of the editorial team at the weekly Tuesday meetings are now Dr Karl Polanyi, Dr Franz Klein who handles domestic politics and financial affairs, Josef Jellinek who specializes in questions of social policy, and the representative of the journal in Prague, Dr Adalbert Worliczek, who is intimately familiar with the politics of his country and never shuns controversy. Hofrat Dr Adolf Drucker contributes on legal matters and participates in editorial meetings from time to time. Last but not least, we have Dr Braun and Dr Gartenberg who cover the stock exchange and fiscal affairs.

In the five years which have passed since Gustav Stolper discovered the questionable talent of the author of these lines, this inveterate world traveller has spent more time in Brazil, Fiji, the West Indies and California than in Austria. But he is immensely proud of the fact that in a small office in the Porzellangasse, grotesquely stuffed with papers, a vacant *fauteuil* awaits the return of the wanderer. That chair is his anchor in the world of Austria's public affairs, his journalistic homeland.

Pardon me for speaking so much about myself. As I travel in some far corner of the world, the little country of Austria seems very far away. The newspapers I read carry hardly a word about Austria; and when there is news, it is usually painful. Sometimes the wind seems to carry the sweet scent of decay across the oceans. But when I receive an old issue of the *Volkswirt* sent to me in Honolulu, Dominica or Hollywood, I know everything about Austria that is worth knowing. I know what is happening there and how it relates to events in the wider world. I recognize in the *Glossen* the style of one or other of my friends, and I am brought up to date by the fearless, knowledgeable and thoughtful opinions of the editorial collective. I know that conservative readers will scream that the journal is too "red" (socialist), and socialists will write obsequious rebuttals. I see Walter Federn smiling into his lovable grey beard, Polanyi riding a favourite hobby horse, Klein throwing foreign expressions around, Jellinek being factual and statistical—the dear old circus still going on. There is still an Austria and there is still somebody who takes it seriously.

Translated by Kari Polanyi Levitt, February 1998.
Published in the *Osterreichische Volkswirt*, Vol. 26, No. 4, 1928.

Chapter Thirty

VORGARTENSTRASSE 203: EXTRACTS FROM A MEMOIR
Felix Schaffer

The text which follows consists of recollections by Dr. Felix Schaffer of a "Seminar" on "Socialist Accountancy" which met at the home of Karl and Ilona Polanyi in Vienna in the 1920s. This (unpublished) German text of over 100 single-spaced typed pages was written in 1964/66 in the form of letters to Ilona and Kari Polanyi Levitt. It is an important document which records Karl Polanyi's attempts to construct an economic model of a socialist economy on two tracks: a price-forming exchange economy and an administered "purchasing power" economy. Schaffer suggests that Polanyi's intellectual struggle with this polarity gave rise to his later distinction between "formal" and "substantive" approaches to the study of economies, and to his thesis of the "double movement" of the self-protection of society from the disintegrating effects of a "self-regulating" market economy.

The passages selected from the Schaffer memoir are digressions from his account of conversations with Polanyi on economic theory, in which he recalled memories of the Polanyi apartment in the Vorgartenstrasse: the family, visitors, key events and personalities which shaped our lives in Vienna from 1924 until my father's departure for England in 1933.

In correspondence with Felix Schaffer, following the death of my mother in 1978, he repeated that it was his belief that Karl Polanyi's later work was an organic development of his earlier work in Vienna. "I am already getting old," he wrote, "you have much to do to preserve the intellectual heritage of your parents." I did not understand, at the time, how much work remained to be done. Over the years, I have re-read Schaffer's long manuscript many times, and have long waited for the opportunity to share some of its contents with friends and scholars who are interested in understanding the origins—and the unity—of my father's world of thought.

As is evident from the obituary published in *Co-Existence* in 1964, I fully share Felix Schaffer's belief that Karl Polanyi's ideas were conceived in Vienna. There he observed the world economic crisis of the inter-war years as a working journalist with the *Oesterreichische Volkswirt*, and conducted an informal "seminar" on socialist accountancy from 1923 until his departure for England in 1933.   —Kari Polanyi Levitt

You, Ilona, know that we met on the premises of a socialist student organization in the D'Orsaygasse some fifty years ago. I was then 22 and quite immature. The place was close to my parents' home. Aside from my interest in questions of socialism, I had time on my hands because I was a bank employee, on strike. The power of the state was decidedly hostile to the [Social Democratic][1] Party. The police broke up a demonstration of bank employees in the Strauchgasse with unaccustomed brutality. But, at that time, whoever was arrested was immediately released, provided a party or trade union functionary of sufficient influence was able to intervene. During the strike, I read a notice in the D'Orsaygasse advertising a seminar on Guild Socialism. The venue was on the first floor of the rather dilapidated building, in a room situated above the large meeting hall where Julius Deutsch, more that a year later—and nine years before 1934—declared: "We [the Social Democratic Party] are too weak to engage in civil war." At that time fascism was not as obviously proximate as it was to become a few years later.

Like many other socialist university students, I was stimulated by [Ludwig von] Mises into thinking about price formation in a socialist economy. Mises prophesied the demise of a socialist economy on account of the absence of market prices. As you can imagine, we did not know how to counter his arguments, because we didn't understand the issues. His case seemed convincing. Like others, I wished to learn more about socialist price formation, and attended the "Seminar" with high expectations. You were there for the first evening. You seemed incredibly young. I thought you were not yet 20. We were ten to begin with; but soon we were only four (Alsegg, Bock, Pick and myself).

With endless patience, Karl tried to explain to us that in a socialist economy there would have to be a democratic way of appraising the efforts put forth by citizens in their capacity as producers of the goods and services required by them as consumers. Not surprisingly, as time passed, attendance at the seminar diminished. That was probably the reason why, after several weeks, you moved the seminar to your apartment. It also saved you from having to go out in the evening. Thus I came to your home, and met your family. By that time you were already in the Vorgartenstrasse. Kari was just beginning to walk, when I first saw her. The district was new to me. It took me some time to get my bearings, but eventually I was standing in front of your door, on the second floor. A woman with a smiling face opened the door. It was Erzsi, the faithful domestic helper, a pillar of the household. Forty years later, having experienced the problems of learning a foreign language on arriving in New Zealand, I am still amazed at her knowledge of German. She probably had no formal education in this foreign language, but she spoke it well, if with an unmistakable [Hungarian] accent. If you are still in contact with her, please convey my greetings and very best wishes. On that first evening, she led me to the centre room with its two windows that looked onto the Reservegarten [nursery garden] of the City of Vienna. Then, it could not be seen because it was already dark. The seminar was already in session. Karl was critiquing the moneyless command economy of Neurath. In this "model" (as we would now call it) producers and consumers were not represented in two independent associations. Decisions on production and consumption were taken by a central authority. In such an economy, he argued, it is impossible to separate the "natural (economic) cost" from the "social cost" deriving from citizen rights. [There followed a long quotation from Polanyi's article on the Socialist Calculation problem.]

That was the essence of the argument put forward that evening, I don't know whether I was able to follow it. My attention wandered to the pictures on the walls of men in splendid uniforms, hardly consistent with the realm of socialist ideas under discussion. The pictures belonged to Nene, Ilona's mother. Later, when I had already known her for several years, she explained that they were of Hungarian nobles of a lineage so ancient that they had no titles, because they predated the award of titles. She herself was of noble family and was "high class" personified. Behind her initial reserve, there was deep goodness, even self-denial. Her small room was a museum, with photographs of Hungarian magnates, beautiful old samovars, and various small artefacts proclaiming that she came from a world which had disappeared, or was in the process of disappearing. Her room was a sanctuary into which she withdrew when reality became too heavy a burden to bear. (And of course, she had time.) She was accustomed to say: *"Meine Waffe ist die Hoeflichkeit"* [my defense is courtesy: *"Hoeflichkeit,"* like "courtesy," deriving from the imperial and royal court]. Nene told me many things: that Karl worshipped you Ilona, and that she greatly admired him. She knew that the old world, and with it the magnates in their splendour (the thousand-year-old upper classes, as she called them) were destined to disappear. The wife of the Hungarian Prime Minister, she related, had announced that there was no point in repairing the [leaky] windows of their official residence, because "the Bolsheviks will soon come." (That happened twenty years later.) Nene once described the glories of the family castle, with all the servants, etc. "But everything is mortgaged to the bank," she added. Her strong attachment to her family made it difficult for her to contemplate the disappearance of those times without sorrow. But her sense of justice brought her to the side of progress. After 1934 she did all she could to help. The first decree of the fascist regime after February 12, 1934, was the suspension by the [formerly socialist] municipal administration of Vienna of the right to work ...granting the city the right to dismiss its employees. Nene went to the [newly appointed] deputy mayor to intervene on my behalf [the gentleman in question was a former member of the Hungarian gentry, and one-time dancing partner of Nene]. I will never forget the efforts this good lady made in that matter. When she was unable to see him in the *Rathaus* [City Hall], she took up a position in front of his private residence until he and his family returned from their Sunday outing. He could no longer evade her. On another occasion, she went to the police on behalf of Trude Kurz [a close friend of Ilona's, imprisoned for political activities] and told the official that he must grant her an audience, because it was a Christian duty to defend the persecuted. The official was obliged to agree. Whether her efforts were effective, we do not know. [Trude Kurz, or Gertrude Kurz de Lara, was released shortly before the *Anschluss*, escaped to France, and from there in 1940 went to Mexico where she became a Professor of Physics at the National University of Mexico.] The last time I spoke with Nene was in 1938, shortly before we planned to emigrate, and I asked her to write to you. She expressed her disgust with the Nazis: "It is a disgrace how they treat the Jews." It was a courageous expression of opinion, because the walls had Gestapo ears. Shortly after the Nazis came to Vienna, I was arrested. When I was released in 1939, she was no longer in Vienna.

Regrettably, I was unable fully to comprehend Karl's *Weltanschauung* at that time—partly because I was preoccupied with technical economics, partly because I was not sufficiently mature. When he discussed metaphysical subjects with me, it was like throwing peas against the wall. But strange as it may seem, much of what he said remained with me; his words came back, years later. I remember that he told me that he had discussed questions of methodology with his brother Michael. He mentioned this several times, to emphasise that choice in economic theory had nothing to do with psychology. Psychology was just one of many ways to treat economic choice. Karl sometimes worried about the breadth of his interests. "I am too much of a polymath, that's why I can't bring anything to a conclusion," he once told me. But it was precisely the diversity of his interests together with your political engagement, Ilona, which made your home the political and scholarly "salon" where several of your friends received formative experiences which carried them through to later work. I knew only a few of your circle. Philosophy, literature and aesthetics were often discussed with *Grossvaterchen* Aurel Kolnai [who wore an elegant long beard]. Here he found a non-materialistic orientation which combined Marx with Kant. (Karl followed Max Adler, or so it seemed to me).

Another visitor to your "salon" who was indebted to Karl was Karl Popper. He was one of the few who was employed by the Educational Institute of the City of Vienna at a time when there was terrible unemployment and it was very difficult for teachers to find a job. He also gave instruction in philosophy. I think he got a prize in Vienna at the time of *Heimwehr* fascism, which enabled him to leave for New Zealand as a lecturer. There he helped us get permission to immigrate for which we are greatly indebted to him. I think he is now a professor in London. I have not read his books because they are not in my field, but I feel that the influence of the Vorgartenstrasse would be evident at least on *Historismus*. Please convey our greetings, if you are in contact with him. Another of the visitors I remember very well was Hans Zeisel. I can still recall the many occasions when Karl lectured him on issues relating to the theory of knowledge. I don't know what happened to him, and others like Paul Lazarsfeld and Ludwig Wagner. I only hope that they survived the fascists.

I did not participate in many of the discussions with these truly very gifted individuals, because my understanding of the subjects was limited, and I was still somewhat immature. I listened intermittently, or played with Kari who was then still called "Baby" or *Hasenhund*. When I first saw her she had barely started walking, and could not see over the round brown table in the living room. Her own room was on the right, and also had two windows with a view of the Vorgartenstrasse. That's where we amused ourselves when there was no space in the living room, or when she was not with her grandmother. Often we played on the floor in the living room with books and newspapers which were in plentiful supply. We made hats, boats and birds out of the papers. Used exercise books and typing paper were stronger, and they made better beaks which could open and shut by themselves. In the summer we sometimes sat in the garden. Kari and I walked up and down by the grilled fence, looking out at the street where there was much to see—people, cars, dogs, cats, pigeons and sparrows. In the beginning, Kari could not say my name too well. This is how I came to be called "Wawi," a name that has stayed with me through the years. No wonder that, growing up in this beautiful atmosphere, she has your spirit. Your conversation, the people in the street going to work in the morning, the red flag which fluttered in the wind every first of May from the window of the living room, were surely impressions which helped shape her life in the image of humanity. With her sense of justice, Grandmother Nene could no longer defend the Old

Order. For you Ilona, her daughter, revolt was a necessity. For Kari, the New was taken for granted. Shortly after Karl went to England in November 1933, Nene and Kari came to visit us. Nene brought a christening present for our son, then four months old. It was a silver spoon embossed with her family crest, the *"Nenelöffel,"* which is still in the family. We spoke about the dangers of fascism, a storm cloud on the horizon. Three months later, the last remnants of democracy disappeared. Kari went to England. That was for the best. I have only seen pictures of her. She and one of her children bear a remarkable likeness to Karl. We wish her and her family all the best. Perhaps she remembers some of what I have written about the Vorgartenstrasse.

You, Ilona, have an intimate knowledge of his (Karl's) life. So you can judge whether I am right, that there were at least two occasions on which he threw up a promising career because it was not consistent with his principles. The first was when he quit the legal profession. I think that was just before the [Great] War. About this I know only the little he told me. Of the second occasion, I can say more. It was in the autumn of 1933, when the increasingly fascist tendencies of the Austrian government resulted in a conflict between the editorial position of the *Volkswirt* and Karl's principles. He left for London. Fearlessly he assumed the risk of giving up his employment, so as not to compromise his principles. However difficult it must have been at the time, his principled action was our good fortune. Because if he had bent to the political demands of the time, he would almost certainly have fallen into the hands of the Nazis, and would not have survived. My family and I were sorry that we did not emigrate after the events of 1934. Only with your help did we escape with nothing worse than a black eye. [Several months in Buchenwald concentration camp!]

I believe that economic theory was for Karl, at least at that time, a tool which could show how a socialist economy could function within a price system. (The works of Bohm Bawerk, Menger, Schumpeter, Wicksteed and Wieser he considered inadequate.) "We must establish the minimal conditions under which an exchange economy can function," he said, pacing up and down between the door of your bedroom, past the green tiled stove and the round table and the door opposite which opened onto the bedroom with two windows. I remember the scene exactly. Kari was playing on the floor with various books. Some she used to build houses with; others served as a stool to sit on. "This is my daughter's reading matter," he said. You, Ilona, were sitting at the round table. Kari busied herself removing books from the book case [which had glass doors and large marble lions on top, one right, one left]. The bookcase was less full than usual, so the title and author of a fat book was exposed to view. I cannot remember the title, but the author's name was Pikler. I think he was Professor of Roman Law at the University of Budapest where Karl had studied. Karl once related how he had to describe some kind of institution, and that Pikler seemed to like his paper. Karl thus came to his notice: "We expect to hear from you," the professor told him. Karl also recalled the occasion when a lecture by Professor Pikler was interrupted by hecklers. "The customary fist fight followed. We accompanied Pikler home, to make sure that nothing would happen to him." This, Karl told me, was the incident which sparked the foundation of the Galilei Circle [the Hungarian student movement]. The members were of course a minority of the student body, and the situation was not easy for them. I seem to remember that Karl was the first president. Surely then he was already known for his abilities, or he would not have been chosen for such a responsible and noteworthy position. I think that, even before the foundation of the Galilei Circle, links had been established between the left-oriented students and faculty.

In the context of another discussion on economics, I noted that Karl again returned to the concept of "man as a social being" [*Vergesellschafte Mensch*] a concept which I believe was the logical foundation of all his work. In the area of economic theory, this was the key concept in terms of which he developed and clarified its assumptions. Regrettably, he never published his findings. This was characteristic. He was too modest to seek publication. His mother, Cecile Polanyi, once complained to me, as I accompanied her home late one evening: "Whenever he has the opportunity to become well-known, he will have none of it." That was in June or July 1926. The evening was warm, and she stayed until it cooled down a little. I rode with her [on the streetcar] all the way to her house, which was on the Hitzinger Hauptstrasse. It was like the first time I came to your home. I had hardly ever been in the neighbourhood before. However, four years later we lived quite close by and visited the Szecsi family several times. I fear that only one daughter, Maria Szecsi—who resembled the grandmother and also her uncle Karl—survived the Nazis. I remember your brother-in-law Egon Szecsi very clearly. But I came to know him much better in Buchenwald. Like Jellinek, he was happy that you and your family were safely in England. For himself, he was not very optimistic, and sadly he was right. But he bore his fate with heroism. In those terrible circumstances, he strove to maintain his spiritual equilibrium, and he succeeded. He used to discuss political and economic events with us, in so far as one was able to learn what was happening from the newspapers available in the camp. "These Nazis are peculiar," he once told us. "They have different orientations towards different sectors of society. The capitalists are treated wonderfully; here the Nazis are quite bourgeois. But the Jews are treated in the same way that the Bolsheviks treat the capitalists." I recalled these words when I read Karl's "Essence of Fascism." Nazism undertook to repress democracy in order to install a corporative capitalism under the guise of racial pseudomysticism. Of course, we recognised the achievement of full employment. Szecsi often spoke about the dependence of the German economy on external trade to gain access to basic raw materials, and the limitations of autarky which must, sooner or later, come into play. The evidence of this was demonstrated in our everyday existence, because many things in the camp were "*Ersatz*" [of substitute material] which could not really replace foreign products. For example, our prisoner uniforms, which weren't too bad in appearance, but provided little protection against the rain. The material was liable to disintegrate. Moreover, when wet, they gave off an odour reminiscent of lime. Szescsi repeatedly drew attention to the limitations of these *ersatz* products. For him, it was evidence of the incapacity of the Nazi regime to sustain itself in the long run. How it would meet its end, he could not predict, nor could anybody else in 1938, prior to the outbreak of war. But he was always, except regarding himself, confident and optimistic. I believe he died of pneumonia, which is hardly surprising given the sort of conditions where people were forced to work outside in almost any kind of weather. May he rest in peace! My very best wishes to the remaining members of his family. I remember all of them very well.

All of this was some twelve or thirteen years after the time when Karl was working on the conditions essential for a price-forming socialist economy. At the time, nobody could have dreamed of what was to come, certainly not I. We believed we had endless time for tranquil reflection. Price formation in a socialist economy was then considered to be the central problem of socialism. The purpose of the socialist model ("construction," as Karl called it) was to arrive at a process of price formation in which the purchasing power available to individuals was independent of their contributions to the national product. The objective was a social and economic order which could be interpreted as "the deliberate subordination of the economy to the ends of the human community." (Here again I cite Kari). Essentially, he was doing what Oscar Lange and others were doing at the same time, or later—filling the formal body of marginal utility economics with historical (institutional) content. (I think the image was Schumpeter's). But the content was to be socialist.

I believe that the young Hugh Gaitskell, whom I remember rather vaguely, presented a lecture to Mises's seminar on the subject of socialist accountancy in 1933. His presentation was certainly influenced by Karl's work. [Hugh Gaitskell, a British post-war Opposition Leader, was then a graduate student in economics at the University of Vienna, a close friend and frequent visitor to the Vorgartenstrasse]. I clearly remember when Karl cited Wieser in this connection; I think it was in 1925. Wieser's book in hand, he was sitting in the centre room on the grey covered divan between the bookcase and the window. It was the evening of April 30, and the red flag was already in place at the window. In front of the divan was a desk covered with manuscripts and newspaper cuttings for the *Volkswirt,* and sometimes also books. One of the books was a collection of essays by Wieser, one of which predicted that socialists would abandon their aversion to marginal utility theory because it is not incompatible with a socialist economy. On the contrary, Wieser predicted, socialists would lay claim to or "occupy" marginal utility theory in order to use it for their purposes. Karl was certainly one of the first who, in searching for a theory of socialist price formation, "occupied" marginal economics. Although he did not, to the best of my knowledge, publish his work, his "occupation" of economic theories which were at that time rejected by most socialists as bourgeois, must be put on record.

"With a lot more work, something may come of all this," he said one evening after recapitulating the problem of the two stocks [of goods and purchasing power]. He was in bed, recovering from influenza which almost turned into pneumonia, but fortunately passed without further complications. On the night table beside the bed were several books. Behind the bed was the door to Nene's room. On the bed was a ginger-coloured kitten, an addition to the household to keep Kari company. The kitten was so young and so small that its meanderings on the bedspread eventually caused it to fall between the bed and the wall, where its feeble high pitched meowings finally induced Karl to reach down to place it back on the bed. The kitten grew up to become a large male cat. In the following summer, the cat declared his independence in Klosterneuburg. Meantime it was still winter, and Karl was happy that the "terrible headaches" connected with the flu had eased. He was back in form. This was apparent when one of the listeners to Karl's exposition of his theory asked in a timid voice: "So what about the Marxist theory of value?" Karl replied:

> Well, what I am saying validates only the subjective school. Once we assume scarcity, the Marxist theory becomes redundant. But if we assume an absence of scarcity, then only the Marxist theory has explanatory value. In the circumstances of the capitalism of the 19th century, which Marx described, the capitalists believed in the unlimited supply of labour. This was of course a

capitalist illusion, but Marx took it *seriously* as revealing of implications for the future of capitalism. In the absence of scarcity, he required an "objective" explanation of value. Under these assumptions, but only under these assumptions, does Marxist value theory have a role to play.

Notwithstanding his critique of the "objectification" of labour, Karl's interpretation of the Marxist theory of value presaged his later work. In *The Great Transformation* he similarly took the self-regulating market economy *seriously* as a mechanism supposedly functioning without hindrance from intervention. He showed that the market economy, on account of its internal economic dynamic, would of itself become unworkable. Society would have to devise defensive interventions to moderate the functioning of capitalism, until by the end of the 19th century very little of liberal capitalism remained. "Nineteenth century civilization has collapsed" (as you know, this was the first sentence of *The Great Transformation*). I suggest that the approach of "taking capitalism seriously" led towards the great Marxist schema which shows that unregulated capitalism (and Marx always assumed an unregulated capitalism) would ultimately become unworkable and would disappear.

Karl's thesis on market economy and Marxist theories of the breakdown of capitalism seem to me to be closely related. I make this observation because I am concerned to show that Karl's later work was already taking shape decades earlier. Regrettably, as far as I know, nothing of this is published. I believed that his "reading" of Marx is not well understood, because he rejected not only the labour theory of value but all the orthodoxies of Marxism. The comments were made as we were leaving the Seminar on a warm June or July summer evening in 1924. We were walking along the Vorgartenstrasse in the direction of the Lasallestrasse. Everybody was silent. I myself, and I am sure the other comrades, savoured the wonderful fragrance of the plants in the Reservegarten bordering the Vorgartenstrasse. As we reached the corner of the Lasallestrasse, one of them (I think it was Bock) broke the silence: "What is left of Marx?" After a while, one of them (I don't know who) said: "Essentially, nothing!" If we had been a little older (all of us were under 25) and consequently more mature, at least one of us would have answered: "Essentially, everything!" The "everything" would have referred to the historical approach. Although Karl was occupied with marginal utility theory, he was conscious that he was applying these theories to specific historical conditions, because he wanted to use them to develop a way to embody price making markets in a socialist context. Years before, as you, Kari, wrote in your fine article, "he crossed the line into the disciplines of economic sociology and economic anthropology"; his approach was already "substantive" because he was interested in specific historical economic institutions. And this was Marxist; it followed him throughout his whole life. Here also, we see the connections between his earlier and later work.

From this digression, let me return to your home in the Vorgartenstrase, where you, Kari, spent such wonderful childhood years. The discussions were frequently interrupted by the ringing of the telephone, located on the wall above the desk between the two windows. Usually the call came from the *Volkswirt*, often from the publisher, Walter Federn. The *Volkswirt* was, as you know, a bourgeois publication, but one not ill-disposed towards the Left, especially social democracy. Karl could work there comfortably without compromising his principles. Federn was a Liberal, but not in the sense of economic liberalism. For him, liberalism signified above all what the French Revolution had declared to be human rights. Freedom of speech was for him a life-giving force. In some respects he reminded me of Nene. Like her, he emanated mildness, goodness and dignity. With his fine small nose and greying beard he resembled a biblical patriarch in modern dress. Always a convinced democrat, in emigration after 1938 he called himself a socialist. His position became increasingly difficult with the rising tide of Austrian reaction. Shortly before or just after February 1934, when the diminished remnants of the democratic republic in Austria came under increased pressure, he was forced to step down as publisher, although he was permitted to remain on the editorial team. In the difficult years of 1934-38, he went to the limits of what was possible. In 1938, as a "non-Aryan" he was obliged to leave the journal. Fortunately, he escaped the Nazis. I think he lived long enough to witness the collapse of fascism. In 1938-39, in Buchenwald, I came to know his nephew who miraculously survived seven years of concentration camps. He was unspeakably happy that his uncle was safe and sound.

Walter Federn introduced Karl to the *Volkswirt* in the summer of 1924. The reason seems to have been that Gustav Stolper, long time co-publisher with Federn, had moved to Germany to found a similar weekly, the *Deutsche Volkswirt*. Federn could not have found a better replacement for Stolper, and he surely knew it. "Polanyi is the most congenial person I have ever known," he told me, when I visited him briefly, shortly before I was arrested in 1938. In fact, Karl soon became Federn's alter ego. "At first it was a little difficult," he once said, "but later it became easy." Karl was senior editor responsible for international affairs. Every day, *The Times*, *Le Temps*, the *Frankfurter Allgemeiner Zeitung*, and the *Arbeiter Zeitung*, were delivered to the house. Karl marked articles or news items with coloured pencils, cut them out, and packed them into his legendary briefcase every Tuesday morning, for the weekly editorial meeting at the *Volkswirt*. There the contents of the next issue and the subject matter of the *Glossen* were decided. The *Glossen* were composed in a uniform style—"they all must look the same," Karl once told me as he was working on one of them, "nobody must be able to know who wrote what." I think Karl enjoyed his work enormously at the *Volkswirt*. He was far more than editor for international affairs. He was really Federn's right hand. At times he was formally designated as Editor-in-Chief. When Federn was ill or on vacation, Karl acted as publisher, and following the Tuesday editorial meetings he presided over informal discussions on the implementation of editorial decisions at the neighbouring Cafe Bauernfeld.

Although Karl was always available to the *Volkswirt* and had no fixed hours of work, I think these were happy times for all of you. The "Glossen" had to be written impersonally, but in his signed articles he was free to write as he pleased. Displaying profound knowledge of the material, but written in an easy style, his articles attracted attention and were read regularly by his opponents.

The impersonally written "Glossen" sometimes posed problems when they had to deal with hot political topics. I recall the occasion when in March 1927 a burglary at the Arsenal revealed a cache of *Schutzbund* arms. It was suspected that it was a set-up and the evening paper carried a headline suggesting a *putsch*. Karl had to write the "Glossen" concerning the incident. "That is difficult," he said, leaning against the green-tiled stove. But eventually he dictated it to Ilona seated at the typewriter. I think, dear Ilona, that you also worked at the *Volkswirt* for a time. In 1924, I believe, you wrote your impressions of a visit to fascist Italy, in three articles for the *Volkswirt*. This was just before, or just after, the murder of Mateotti. I remember how eagerly Karl awaited your return. "Now she has already crossed the border," he told me, one evening when I was visiting him.

It was winter. Thick snow lay on the Reservegarten facing your house. But one could not see it because the windows were covered with heavy blankets. The bitter north winds were blowing across the open space straight toward the house, frustrating the efforts of the green-tiled stove to maintain a normal room temperature. But this did not trouble Karl. "Technical difficulties cannot stand in the way of whatever is to be done," he once told me, and that applied on this occasion also. Oblivious to the raging winter storm, he paced up and down between the two doors of the centre room, frequently stopping by the green stove, and continued: "Yes, purchasing power is a means that is not related to any material commodity. It is only necessary that it consist of homogeneous units. It is required only for purposes of accounting. This is essentially what Knapp has called 'materially valueless money.'"

Over the divan on which he was sitting there was a picture. "That is my beloved father," he once told me. His had evidently been a prosperous home. Karl told me that from early childhood he and his brothers received excellent instruction in foreign languages. From everything I heard I gathered that Karl spent his youth in a well-to-do milieu, above the average level of the middle class. But this period of his life came to a sudden end. "Suddenly we were poor. And there was this uncle who declared that the young man should work and look after the family." "I gave lessons," he went on, presumably meaning in addition to his own studies, "these went on until I broke down. Of course I recovered, but I never regained my previous capacity for work." I think Karl's aversion to small mindedness, greed and poverty, which he ascribed in part to the bourgeois capitalist order, were the result of these terrible experiences.

As I remember, Karl returned to further developing his Theorem in 1926, after a brief stay in hospital. Possibly a (mistaken) diagnosis of fatal liver disease aggravated the "terrible headaches" and "congestions" which tormented him. In any event, I know that he was admitted to the Sophienspital in the 7th district in April 1926. (I don't think I am mistaken, but you, dear Ilona, will certainly know better.) I visited him and found people from the *Volkswirt* there. Although he was officially on the sick list, he maintained contact with the paper. The weeks passed, and fortunately nothing serious was found. They gave him new eye-glasses, which probably helped ease the headaches. I still remember, dear Ilona, how happy you were when he was back at home, in time for the First of May. I remember you vacationed in the Waldviertel in the summer of 1926, and Karl was feeling much better. He told me that, for the first time since the war, he rode a horse. In the autumn, back in Vienna, he resumed work on the Theorem.

While Karl continued to work on his Theorem, the contradiction of "purchasing power vs. exchange economy" as two distinct spaces, in each of which different questions could be posed and solved, was not logically sustainable. This was a disappointment for Karl, but proved to be of great significance for his future work because it led him to use both approaches in his later historical and empirical research. Over the years, the "double movement" thesis slowly evolved. He was reluctant to publish his Theorem, at least while in Vienna. "I would like to publish the Theorem," he once told me in 1929, when we were in the summer resort of Klosterneuburg, "if there were more to it, but regrettably, I don't think there is much there."

By this time he was already occupied with what Professor McIvor, in his Preface to *The Great Transformation*, called "re-writing history." He increasingly switched from the "formal" to the "substantive" approach, and became an "economic historian" as you, dear Kari, said in your article in *Co-Existence*. But the "formal" theory of the exchange economy proved fruitful in his investigation of the "substantive" economy, as he called it. Assuming an "exchange economy" without interference or intervention, he asked: what would be the result? The assumption of a self-regulating exchange economy approximated 19th century experience. Here is the link between his later work and the "Theorem" developed in Vienna. The identification of the "exchange economy" with the "self-regulating market" is evidenced in *The Great Transformation*:

> ...no market economy separated from the political sphere is possible, yet it was such a construction which underlay classical economics since David Ricardo, and apart from which the concepts and assumptions were incomprehensible. Society, according to this "lay-out," consisted of bartering individuals possessing an outfit of commodities—goods, land, labour and their composites. Money was simply one of the commodities bartered more often than another, and hence acquired for the purpose of use exchange.

These problems were treated in evening courses which he gave at the *Volkshochschule* from 1928, or possibly earlier. Perhaps through the *Volkswirt*, he came to know Professor Walter Schiff. I seem to remember that he mentioned that as early as 1925 he undertook some research together with Dr. Schiff on mixed economic enterprises, or some similar subject. He was so many-sided that no subject area could satisfy him. Dr. Schiff was at the time president of the *Volkshochschule*, an organisation for adult education which before February 1934 was closely, although not officially, associated with the Social Democratic Party. Schiff was then statistical advisor to the City of Vienna. [Dr. Schiff was an eminent social statistician who pioneered the compilation of household incomes and expenditures by categories of income and family size. Felix Schaffer worked as his assistant, and the manuscript describes his career and personality in considerable detail. Schiff was vice-president of the Federal Bureau of Statistics, when he fell victim to the mass dismissals of civil servants during the stabilisation and structural adjustment (*Sanierung*) of 1923. He was forced into premature retirement. Schaffer wrote that Schiff never forgave the capitalist establishment; a life-long liberal, he joined the Social Democratic Party in protest. As time progressed, he became increasingly radical. He told Schaffer in 1933 that the true liberals (Bohm Bawark, Menger and Wieser) would never have thought of governing without parliament by means of a wartime emergency powers: "They really believed in the civil rights of citizens."]

The connection with Schiff was of importance for Karl, because Schiff was always looking for competent instructors for his *Volkschochschule*, and was of course happy to attract a person of Karl's qualities to give a course. The preparation of lectures forced him to organise his thoughts on market economy more systematically, and commit them to paper—perhaps not unimportant for his later work on *The Great Transformation*. In the following two or three years, Karl's work expanded considerably. In addition to his duties at the *Volkswirt*, which became increasing difficult with the rise of reaction after 1927, there was now the course for the *Volkshochschule*, which I think was somewhere around the Zirkusgasse, nearer to his home. Previously, in 1925-26, we could visit Karl from Thursdays on, without disturbing him. But this became ever less possible. In increasing measure, I found the house full of people with whom I had little in common on account of my single-minded interests. The reverse was also true. That gave me many opportunities to sit with Nene in her room. If the visible signs of times gone by were evident from the pictures of the magnates in the centre room, this was even more so in Nene's room. Her room was, as I have already told you, a museum. The pictures on the wall, the finely crafted tea things, the china cups and little treasured items in the glass cupboard, the writing desk, all were redolent of a world which was vanishing, notwithstanding the efforts of the ruling classes of Hungary to stem the tide. Sometimes I sat in her room without speaking; at other times she related much about her life and the circles from which she came. Although the room reminded one intensely of times long gone, there was no sense of her rejecting her past, despite the undeniable injustices of the old order. That was the magic of Nene's presence. Her personality imposed the stamp of tranquillity, goodness, tolerance, and modest distinction. I think of her with deepest respect, thankfulness and nostalgia. As with Karl and you, Ilona, I did not appreciate the full meaning of much she told me until years later. She would surely have approved the changes in Hungary which she recognised as the unavoidable consequences of the past. May she rest in peace!

Although Karl was engaged in an increasing number of activities, he continued his investigations in the area of economic theory. The family was at the time on summer vacation in Klosterneuburg, Wienerstrasse 13. I remember one hot July day. I came early in the afternoon. Kari was sleeping. Dear Nene told me that you had company. She dressed Kari after she woke, and I helped. Then Karl came into the room: "OK, let us continue" ...[the discussion of price formation in an exchange economy]. We went into the garden behind the house. "I am returning to the horse market (the example of Bohm Bawerk, *The Positive Theory of Capital*, Vol.1, p.272) where the owners of horses are offering to sell for the maximum number of guilders they can obtain from the buyers." [There follow three pages of discussion.] It was probably not his disappointment with the "Theorem" that terminated the discussion. I think he could not concentrate any more, because all of us were preoccupied with other matters. This beautiful warm afternoon was shortly after the 15th of July [1927]. As you know, on that day there was a spontaneous demonstration of workers in Vienna [including many members of the Social Democratic Party]. It was in protest against a recent incident when members of the *Heimwehr* or a similar right-wing organisation broke up a socialist meeting in Schattendorf (Burgenland), resulting in deaths. The police fired upon the peaceful demonstration in Vienna, leaving nineteen dead. The incident was proof that the executive power of the state could be exercised against the Left, including the Social Democratic Party. For good reason, July 15 has been seen as the beginning of the counter revolution which achieved its aims seven years later with the dissolution of the Social Democratic Party; soon thereafter followed the end of the First Republic. After 1927, your home became, more than ever, a political and intellectual salon, with the political aspect obviously in the forefront. For Karl, work at the *Volkswirt* became increasingly difficult, if I am not mistaken. While the *Volkswirt* maintained its independence as far as was possible given the rising tide of reaction, I have the sense that, more and more, every word that Karl wrote had to be carefully weighed. Uninhibited writing in full security of freedom of speech was a thing of the past. By 1930, the rise of reaction was exacerbated by the onset of the world economic crisis. Karl's explanations were historical. I believe he argued that the crisis was implicit in the mechanisms of the post-war market economy, and that the re-establishment of the gold standard was a contributory cause. I think he wrote about this in the *Volkswirt*, and spoke about it in the courses he gave at the *Volkshochschule*. I remember a lecture he gave to a social democratic organisation in the spring of 1932 on the role of the gold standard. In the 1930s, the crisis was a general topic of discussion. Bourgeois optimism as to impending recovery was shattered in May 1931 with the collapse of the *Kredit Anstalt*, which precipitated international bank failures. On a sunny morning in May 1931, when this news broke, I went to see Schiff with an invitation to a Seminar requiring his signature. He greeted me with: "Capitalism is collapsing." The "collapse" proved to be a factor in its reconstitution—in a fascist form—though we were still three years away from fascism in Austria.

Few in the working-class movement could imagine that we would ever be forced into illegality. Freedom of speech was still existant, and an event like the Seminar still possible. The topic was Karl's "Theorem," and his world of thought attracted the intellectual interest of socialist students. In 1930, a Marxist student group, strongly influenced by Max Adler and with close connections to the Social Democratic Party, approached Karl [and Schaffer] to lecture on this topic. The lectures took place on two successive Fridays, and were held on the premises of the socialist student association in the Werdertorgasse. Afterwards, a comrade who lived in the area invited us to tea. Adele and I were reluctant to accept, because we had to get up early next day to go to work—at that time, two-day weekends were exceptional in Austria—but we went, and it was a very nice finish to the seminars. Some people began to sing, and Ludwig Birkenfeld who was then, I believe, the representative of the student association, sang the "Volga Boatman," the *Warschawianka*, and other movement songs in the original language. I still wonder sometimes what happened to the members of the student association.

Schiff had attended the seminars. He said that he found the topic very interesting, but too large for just two lectures. For two years or more, the Seminar met every Saturday morning at his home, where the relationship of a purchasing-power economy to price formation in a socialist economy was discussed. Soon it became evident that the way prices were set in the Soviet Union—then half way through the First Five Year Plan—was quite different from the models under discussion. The Seminar eventually petered out, as prominent members including Karl could not maintain regular attendance. It was formally terminated after February 1934. But it had the effect of renewing interest in the question of socialist accountancy. In 1932, Schiff published an important book on the subject. If I remember correctly, it was largely based on the planned economy of the Soviet Union.

The Seminar was an expression of the fact that Karl occupied himself with the "Theorem" in the 1930s, although he repeatedly stressed his limitations. In 1928 Hans Meyer published his solution to the so-called "imputation" problem. As is well known, there were two solutions to this problem in the Austrian school of economics. [There follow three densely argued pages of discussion of Boehm Bawerk's and Wieser's competing approaches.] Karl thought he saw a way to combine both of these by his "Theorem." He did actually write a paper. He gave me a copy, but said he was not yet ready to send it out. Another reason why he hesitated to submit the paper for publication may have been the hostile reception accorded his lecture to the Economic Association in December 1932.

After your return from vacation in Yugoslavia in the Spring of 1933, political developments made ever larger claims on Karl's time. The *Volkswirt* stood by its liberal convictions, and opposed the government which had dissolved parliament and declared a state of emergency in March. Earlier bourgeois demands for the dissolution of democracy and the institution of fascism (the so-called *Standestaat*) which had been foiled in 1929, were back on the agenda. The *Volkswirt* stood for democracy. The defenders of democracy warned that "war on two fronts"—against both social democracy and the Nazis—could only result in the Nazification of Austria. At the start of rule under the state of emergency, Karl could still write for the journal, although he had to weigh his words cautiously. I particularly remember an article titled "Reconstituting the State" (*Staatengruendung*) in March or April 1933, in which he called upon the bourgeois party to abandon fascist experiments which would be worthless against the Nazis, return to constitutional government, and found the Republic of Austria anew as a democratic state. This article, written with professional expertise in masterful language, must have alerted the regime to the presence of a potentially embarrassing author. It was hardly surprising that, shortly after the imposition of emergency rule, a notice proclaiming "Under Self-Censorship" appeared at the masterhead of the *Volkswirt*. (The regime was concerned to maintain the impression that the constitution, which prohibited explicit censorship, was still in force.) "This will not be without consequences," Karl said, and as so often he was right. The area where he was still free to write as he pleased was against the Nazis. The only article which I have in my possession from this period appeared in the *Volkswirt* on October 21, 1933, under the heading "The 14th October." [The date marks the withdrawal of Germany from the League of Nations.] I have often re-read it and thought how slow humanity is to learn. (I got this expression from somewhere, I don't remember from where.) Karl presents a historical interpretation of events. He starts in 1914:

> In 1914 the Austro-Hungarian monarchy used the occasion of a political assassination as an excuse to engage in a history-making show of force to prove its right to exist. Austria-Hungary and Germany trumpeted all their well-meaning efforts to preserve peace. The defeated peoples themselves punished their imperial masters, and erected new states. A metaphysical perception of the war guilt of the Central Powers hovered over the

foundation of the new successor states, a sentiment shared by virtually all the peoples of the world during the War.

In 1919, the defeated states were absolved of guilt. The victorious powers dictated peace terms which, in every line and every clause, consciously and unilaterally assumed responsibility for the outcome. History will be judge and jury. (*Die Weltgeschichte is das Weltgericht*). Versailles did not bring peace...The Victors unleashed a peace on the world whose furies proclaimed abroad their responsibility and their guilt.

In 1933, the guilt of Versailles was extinguished. Germany delivered herself up to National Socialism. The German state adopted an ideology whose highest purpose was the destruction of the very concept of humanity. In regression from the New Testament, by reversion to the darkest pages of the insanities of the chosen people, this heathen superstition of a nomadic people celebrates, between factory chimneys and chemical plants, power stations and airfields of a nation of 65 million people, its terrifying restoration. A whole people has put its science and religion, its morality and law at the service of forces the suppression of which constituted the very foundation on which science and religion, morality and the law of civilized peoples have been built. History will deliver Judgement. (*Die Weltgeschichte ist das Weltgericht*).

National Socialism has plunged Germany and Europe into great misfortune. Like a ripe fruit, Hitler thought he could pluck Germany's rise to equality of power secretly, on the basis of the progress made toward this end during the Weimar decade. But the fruit is rotten, and the axe has cut into the root of the tree. Nations who did not hate the German people when they were at war with Germany, hate them now—even without war.

Only deliberate self-deception could nurture the illusion that the hurricane, which National Socialism has unleashed on the world, will give way to a gentle breeze.

Any commentary could only diminish the power of these sentences. The article was probably the last Karl wrote for the *Volkswirt* in Vienna. He understood that neither the *Volkswirt* nor Austria (under the state of emergency) could tolerate him any longer. He could have bent. But, as you dear Kari wrote: "his life was guided by an inner necessity to exercise freedom of action and thought." So he gave up everything for the leap into the unknown. I think it was the second time in his life, the first being when he threw up a legal career for similar reasons. In any event, his decision was our good fortune. For him, who outlived the Nazi regime by twenty years, the future offered fruitful work. My family and I would not have survived had you not helped us in England.

These ideas were certainly not in my mind when I last saw Karl in Vienna, although his departure was for me a signal of the coming of fascism. Some time earlier, it was evident that something was in the air, although I did not know what. But one day, when I sat in dear Nene's room, she said: "He will have to leave. The day before yesterday they were all here (she meant the editorial team of the *Volkswirt*) and everything was decided." And that is how it was. Shortly afterwards, Karl came in and went with me, as so often before, into the centre room, and said: "Yes, I am going. I will write for the *Volkswirt* from England as a foreign correspondent." I was not surprised, but was disappointed nevertheless. We spoke for quite a while. He simply could not remain in Austria, given the restriction of freedom. Secretly, I envied him, because I also found the regime as oppressive as an impending storm. At last, I said my farewells and departed. The next time I saw Karl was five years later, in London, where you Ilona were waiting for us at the railway station. The last words I heard him say in Vienna, which summed up the whole situation were: *Hier is fuer mich kein Boden* ["this land is not for me"].

This is the beginning of the third and last part of my memories of Karl. Here I shall summarize "The Essence of Fascism" and trace its connections with Karl's ideas in the Vienna period. I have tried to situate this essay in the totality of his work. I will continue, as you dear Ilona wrote, to maintain "the immediacy of presentation" because you seem satisfied that it should continue thus. The expressions of Karl which I have recalled, are those I remember him using in Vienna in the context of similar discussions. If I am mistaken, please correct me. For lack of space, the presentation here is limited to some of Karl's most important ideas, wherever possible in the words he used in published texts. Although having but an incomplete picture of his work, I have tended to emphasize his colourful, insightful and artistic expressions.

"We have to get Wawi out" (*Den Wawi muessen wir herausbekommen*), was your reaction to the news of my arrest by the Nazi in May 1938—as you told us, one evening in March 1939, in the house of the Grants in London. Here we learned the details of your strenuous efforts to secure us permission to enter New Zealand. Your success was our rescue. To this day it seems like a miracle, which we cannot be too thankful for. In the late afternoon of that day in March, you awaited our arrival at one of the great railway stations of London (I no longer remember which). After a warm but silent greeting, you, Ilona, went to a telephone booth, presumably to alert the Grants of our arrival. We left the railway station, and soon were on a bus. When we arrived in the suburb, it was already dark. Karl carried our small son, who was tired from the long journey, in his arms. We walked through several streets of a modern development. One of the houses was the home of the Grants who accommodated us for the night in international solidarity. Our son was put to bed, and we spent the evening together. There were other visitors present who were, I believe, also refugees. They seemed to have the same difficulties we had, speaking little or no English. But in spite of my language deficiency, I managed to read the titles of leaflets and pamphlets which lay in small piles around the room. The Grants were clearly an outpost—and a probably not unimportant one—in the Left's defence line against the rise of fascism. Shortly before this time, Czechoslovakia fell into the orbit of the Third Reich. The Spanish Civil War had concluded with the victory of the fascists. That brought a growing stream of refugees to the countries where political parties of the Left were still legal. For you and for the Grants this meant a lot of hard work.

The situation favoured closer co-operation within the Left. In this intellectual atmosphere, *Christianity and the Social Revolution* was published by Gollancz in 1935. Karl was co-editor, and he contributed an article "The Essence of Fascism." I did not see the book until forty years after it appeared. Some things which I had failed to understand in Vienna only now became clear. The essay is surely a classical presentation of the philosophical foundations of Christianity and Fascism, and as such is of lasting interest. Nene had already told me in Vienna about the appearance of this book, when I visited her. By then the apartment was empty. You had left, and even Erzsi was no longer there. Nene was in the process of liquidating the apartment, to move into a *pension*. She told me: "He delivers lectures and writes articles, and now he has brought out a book." She showed me a letter which you, dear Kari, had written to her. You wrote that you were taken in bed with the 'flu, but otherwise were fine, and that you were slowly forgetting your German. I noted the English postage stamp on the envelope, and said: "from a free land." "Yes," said Nene, "there he can write."

The purpose of the book, as explained in the introduction, was to emphasize those things that Christianity and the Left had in common. Karl did this in his essay where he demonstrated that, for Christianity as for Socialism, the value of the individual is supreme. "Personality is of infinite value," he wrote in "The Essence." (p. 369) This was for him the motivation which gave rise to the essay. It resides in the ethic that individual freedom belongs among the highest values, and gives moral unity to Karl's work. Although he stood by Christianity in the matter of the value of individual freedom, he was conscious of the fact that the Churches were in general oriented against the Left and specifically that they supported fascism. But he refused to identify Christianity with the Church. He described the Catholic Church in Austria as an "organised power" which supported reaction in the 1930s. But in certain instances, as in Nazi Germany, the Church opposed fascism.

I wish to say [further to Karl's conversations in Vienna] that his interest in objectification derived from his love of freedom. He found it inhuman that social concepts like the state, or prices, etc., which derived from human relations, should assume an existence of their own, should dominate human beings. As long ago as his seminar on guild socialism, he explained this to us. Wherever possible he sought after transparent, personal and immediate relations between people. This awakened my interest in objectification, and was the reason I chose that subject for my doctoral dissertation. As I have already noted, in reality this was Karl's work, because the theme was too difficult for me.

By way of explaining the relationship of Karl's work in Vienna to his later writings, I will start with his comments upon the early stages of my dissertation. Even now, I remember the day I first told him that I wanted to do my dissertation on the concept of objectification which dominates human beings, although it is of their own creation. Karl realized that this would entail much work on his part, yet he was enthusiastic. "That is surely a good theme," he told me, "I am happy that somebody will take it on." Then he rose from the divan which was, as you'll recall, in the corner by the window in the centre room, went to the book case, and said: "The fundamental concept is Marx's fetishism of commodities. Let us have another look at the text." He took down the first volume of *Capital* from the shelf, turned the pages, and explained the concept. The key point was that Marx perceived objectification as deriving from human relations; insofar as the self-alienation of human beings was incompatible with human dignity, objectification should not only be explained by human relations, but replaced by them.

Much later, during that evening at the Grants, we naturally spoke a great deal about emigration. I discovered that Schiff was in London, and was living not far from the Grants. I immediately phoned him. It was a strange feeling to hear his familiar voice, after so many years. He was obviously pleased, and we agreed to meet on the following day. The evening at the Grants went on late, and you got up early next morning. I think you had to catch an early train. I clearly remember our goodbye. As on the previous day at the railway station, few words were spoken. You and Karl had already reached the garden gate, when you paused. I called out: "Auf Wiedersehen." Karl replied: "Who knows if we will ever see each other again?" These were the last words I ever heard him speak. It was farewell for ever.

We stayed on at the Grants for a while longer. Then we left, and they finally had some peace. They are, as you dear Ilona wrote, "the salt of the earth," a symbol of international solidarity. Donald Grant directed us to an Underground station that was not far from the house. There, Schiff was awaiting us. In spite of the cool March morning, he was as usual without coat or hat. Quite unchanged. "Welcome to the World," he said. What he meant was that we were, in England, on soil that was free still. But for how long? That was a question many were asking themselves. He was very pessimistic. He thought war inevitable, and was very conscious of the weakness of the West. He was critical of the Chamberlain government. We spent several hours together; he came with us to the railway station, and stayed till the train left for Southampton. Here, again, it was to be farewell for ever. Like many others, he had the satisfaction of living long enough to see the downfall of fascism in the Axis countries. He died not long after his return to Vienna in 1950. He was 84. Many scenes remain in my memory. At the University, his seminar became a meeting ground for the Left after 1934. Obviously, this did not please the government. When I visited him in 1936, he told me that he had been sent into retirement on the day he reached seventy. That was not normal practice; usually it happened one year later. On another occasion, he told me: "I had a short-wave receiver installed in my radio (to listen to Radio Moscow). When I switched on, it was announced that *Schutsbuendler* comrade Birkenfeld was going to speak about the economic development of a certain island (whose name I cannot remember). It was a very interesting lecture, I was very happy to hear it." He believed that Schuschnigg's fascism would be short lived, and his prognosis was, as so often, quite correct. He was, as Karl sometimes said of people he held in high esteem, "a wonderful chap." May he rest in peace!

Soon after we parted in London in March 1939, the second world war loomed on the horizon. In those times, there were few opportunities for correspondence. Later, on a beautiful October morning in 1944 (it was a warm spring day in the Southern hemisphere) we received an air mail postcard from London. A few typewritten lines announced the publication of *The Great Transformation*. The book was not immediately available. But after some weeks, the American library received a copy. For me it was a revelation. It was the fruit of years of study, or more exactly of a tree whose roots were planted in Vienna.

The principal argument of the book—what Karl called his 'thesis'—was that the idea of a self-adjusting market (the characteristic institution of capitalism in the 19th century) implies a stark utopia.

Such an institution could not exist for any length of time without annihilating the human and natural substance of society; it would have physically destroyed man and transformed his surroundings into a wilderness. Inevitably, society took measures to protect itself, but whatever measures it took impared the self-regulating of the market, disorganised industrial life, and thus endangered society in yet another way. It was this dilemma which forced the development of the market system into a definite groove and finally disrupted the social organisation based upon it. (pp. 3-4)

[We conclude with extracts from a letter written by Schaffer to Ilona in 1966.] What I have written about Karl is surely of limited value. What I am now writing (on *The Great Transformation*) is possibly of even less value because it does not deal primarily with the "Vienna times." In broad outline, I want to reiterate my impressions. I believe that Karl's work had both a *moral* and a *logical* unity. The moral unity is the highest value assigned to each individual human being (in terms of human freedom, dignity, or whatever other expression of similar meaning). This determined the selection of the problems he chose to address: the control by human beings of such objectifications as cannot be abolished, the issue of transparency (one should be able to see the results of one's actions, and thus plan them), the responsibility of every member of society for the fate of mankind, among others. The logical unity is man as a social being (*der Vergesellschaftliche Mensch*). "For Mr. Polanyi the last word is society," McIver wrote in the Foreword to *The Great Transformation*. By this, Karl meant more than Adler's "transcendental consciousness" which enables us to understand each other and build a society. Above all, for Karl, society consisted of human relations in all their complexity and variety, embracing every kind of cultural, kinship, defence, economic, and geographic relationship. In his later writings, he showed that, with the exception of 19th century capitalism, the economy has always been "embedded" in social life. "Economics," as the primary rationale of the organisation of economic life, is the exception.

This brings his "exchange economy—purchasing power theorem" into proper perspective. Ironically, he came to the discovery of the unique character of 19th century capitalism indirectly, through the subjective theories of the Austrian school of economics of the late 19th and early 20th centuries. Here he soon discovered that there was no necessary distinction between an exchange economy and one based on monetary purchasing power. This, as I remarked, disturbed him because it seemed to invalidate his model. But in his later work he returned to the distinction between commodity money and special purpose or "managed currency" money. I have started to read Firth's *Economics of the New Zealand Maori*. There I found the following sentence: "The results and the possible contributions of the anthropologists are attracting increasing attention as it is coming to be realised that intensive observation by research workers trained in a comparative discipline may throw considerable light on our economic behaviour in our society."

Selected and translated by Kari Polanyi Levitt. Square brackets are editorial insertions by her.

Chapter Thirty-One

MECHANISMS OF THE WORLD ECONOMIC CRISIS 1931–1933[1]
Karl Polanyi

From a central European perspective, the entire post-war period—including eight years of miraculous prosperity in the United States, sustained economic growth in several other countries and the multifaceted technical, economic, currency and trade policy adventures of this whole dismal historical epoch, right down to the crash of 1929 and the world depression of 1933—is in reality one single economic crisis which manifests itself in different forms as it traverses and transforms the world. The economic crisis of the first post-war years was not resolved—just postponed. Equilibrium in one location was achieved by shifting the burden of adjustment, deliberately or otherwise, to other economic regions and sectors. When the unavoidable day of reckoning arrived, it not only reignited old smoldering fires—the crisis assumed depths and dimensions which made all previous experiences pale by comparison.

To carry this argument beyond audacious generalization inferred from random connectings of events of the past 15 years, the author is obliged to explain his methodology, and to back it up with concrete evidence.

WHY WAS IT IMPOSSIBLE FOR THE CRISIS TO CORRECT ITSELF?
What is the essence of the world economic crisis? Why has there been no self-correcting solution? How could some economies repeatedly achieve apparent stability by shifting the burden of persistent and large economic deficits in space and time? Above all, how can such an interpretation shed light on the totality of the general process within which the world economic crisis is embedded?

We may set aside the complexities of economic business-cycle theory concerned with the familiar economic fluctuations which visit us from time to time, because we are convinced that the decisive characteristics of the present crisis derive from a specific historical context. In our view, the conjunctural crisis of 1929 to 1933 is only the most dramatic phase in a general crisis which had its origins in the First World War. The unique political and sociological configurations associated with the war presented insurmountable obstacles to a self-generated recovery. The economic costs of the war were enormous. The widely-held view that the economic burden of modern warfare could not be sustained for more than three months was not unreasonable. That the war could last for four years was possible only because enormous social costs were imposed on societies by the coercive pressures of overwhelming politico-sociological forces. Only disequilibria which are confined within the strictly economic sphere are amenable to self-regulating correction. The real costs of the war far exceeded the economic capacities of societies; the scale of human and societal destruction was of such magnitude that the social fabric could not withstand the forces of adjustment within a post-war equilibrium.

The conventional view, which saw the problem exclusively in terms of the threat of social revolution, was a one sided one—although this danger was real. The political-sociological factors which made it impossible to reconstruct a new and stable post-war order were almost as complex as the national, social, ideological and political forces which engaged in the war, and terminated it with a peace imposed by the victors on the vanquished.

Statistical research has only recently revealed the true costs of the war. Despite a technological revolution and the American economic miracle, industrial production at the conjectural high point of 1929 had regressed significantly in comparison with the achievements of two generations of uninterrupted economic growth prior to 1914. In the twenty years since the outbreak of the war, industrial production should approximately have doubled. Instead, it increased by only 60 per cent. In 1933 it fell to levels below 1914. According to the dynamics of economic growth of past generations, the capacity of the economy to deliver productive output in 1933 should have been twice as high as it was. Neither the feverish but unproductive economic activity of the war years, nor the steady increase in agricultural production in the face of falling prices were able to offset the economic consequences of the war in terms of ten years of lost growth in agriculture and twenty years in industry.

THE THREE CLAIMANTS: BONDHOLDERS, WORKERS AND PEASANTS

Whether the costs of the war were greater or less than was previously believed, is inconsequential. What is clear is that the political-sociological shock of the war implied that the reconstruction of a new economic equilibrium would take many years to achieve. The social framework could be sustained only if the political leaderships were to satisfy the expectations—and prevent the disappointment of—three major claimants: the bondholder (rentier) who had financed the war and without whose confidence in currencies and credit capitalist economies could not be reconstructed; the worker who had borne the moral and political burdens of the war, and was promised a reward in terms of more rights and more bread; and the peasant who appeared to be the only bulwark against social revolution.

In the defeated countries, the rentier classes were devastated by inflation; in the victorious countries, policies designed to protect their interests eventually failed. In the defeated countries the workers likewise were not protected from the fallout of the crisis. Abstracting from societal factors, less inflexible protection of the economic interests of bondholders, workers and peasants might have yielded a more favorable outcome in purely economic terms. But in the meantime the social framework would have disintegrated.

In the victorious states, bondholder interests had priority. Their financial sacrifices had won the war; their faith in the stability of currencies and credit was the basis of the post-war reconstruction of the economy. Society could continue only if the war's command economy were completely and permanently dismantled and the free market restored.

In the defeated states, the worker had priority. Installed in the seat of political power, the worker (and ex-soldier) who had borne the greatest burden of the war, demanded the promised rights and the promised bread.

In the victorious states, the democratization of public life assumed landslide proportions. In England the number of eligible voters increased from 8 million pre-war to 28 million. Here also the war machine was fired up with promises: "Homes worthy of heroes," according to Prime Minister Lloyd George. Logistical production of war materials for the military front was accompanied by the production of slogans by the Welsh master of rhetoric. When the war ended, there were no excuses for failure to deliver on promises. In reality, nobody in Britain believed in the necessity to restrict living standards after the war. When the reality of Britain's diminished economic capacity began to dawn, it was too late. The sacrifices imposed on the whole of society to defend—and increase—the value of rentier income, dictated policies which placed the entire burden of adjustment on the working classes.

The third party of this trilogy was the peasant. After the war, only the peasant—protective of his hard-earned piece of land, accustomed to an adversarial market relationship with the town—offered secure protection against bolshevism. Economic interest and his general *weltanschauung* allied him with the forces of conservatism. But when disillusioned the peasant was capable of very different behaviour—as manifested in Bulgaria and any number of other East and South East European countries where he had no problem in participating in the division of large landed estates. The fact that revolutions do not come exclusively from the political left is a lesson that Europe has learned only in hindsight. Neither the rentier nor the worker proved as socially unassailable as the peasant in pressing his demands.

Any attempt at the restoration of economic equilibrium had to take into consideration the three directions in which claims were staked. The existence of a viable social framework demanded:

Defense of rentier income by stabilization of currencies. Protection of worker income by stabilization of real wages. Protection of peasant income by stabilization of commodity prices.

In hindsight, it is incontestable that the satisfaction of all three demands was impossible, given that economic capacity had been seriously reduced by the war. The maintenance of a viable social framework required the economically impossible. But when the viability of society comes into conflict with what is economically possible, economic possibilities are stretched in one way or another. In the long run, this is of course not sustainable. Violation of the laws of economics will sooner or later incur terrible economic costs. But in the meantime, society has been saved from disaster.

Moreover, domestic pressures on the social fabric were accompanied by external pressures created by the reconstructed post-war international political order. While we place primary emphasis on policies which sought to stabilize the domestic incomes of rentiers, workers and peasants, there is no doubt that reparations, war debts and excessively autarchistic policies contributed to the incapacity of the system to regain a new equilibrium by self-correcting economic processes. The two groups of problems are inter-dependent. Reparations and war debts determined the direction of financial and economic efforts which were as unrealistic as the domestic policies which attempted to maintain living standards beyond the capacities of the war-impoverished, capital-depleted economies. Although the eventual collapse was inevitable, it could be—and was—delayed for a while, by sacrificial interventions.

THE GREAT INTERVENTION: THE WAR

It is important to recognize that virtually the whole financial and economic history of the last fifteen years consists of interventions, whose eventually adverse consequences did not fail to manifest themselves. But these interventions were not the *cause* [original emphasis] of the crisis. The effect of such interventions—sometimes misconceived, and shortsighted in implementation—was to postpone the solution of the crisis. But postponement was not without rationale: the mother of all interventions was the war itself. All the interventions of the post-war era were no more than costly attempts to protect society against the shocks of the brutal deconstruction of the economic and social equilibrium. But they created unnecessary new disequilibria which exacerbated the consequences of the original major intervention of the war. It is impossible to comprehend the function of the interventions of the post-war era, without a clear understanding of their origins in the destruction caused by the war.

It is moreover incorrect to consider as interventions only those policies which were intended to benefit the workers or the peasants. The convenient implication here is that economic measures designed to restore the pre-war order require no further justification. Protection of the currency, no matter how artificial and draconian, is not considered interventionist; the distributional effect on rentier income is not explicitly take into account. An approach to economic stabilization which depends exclusively on the formal assertion of the sanctity of contract is of little value as a practical tool of economic and financial policy. It does not speak to the decisive question: what levels of incomes are ultimately sustainable?

The return of the pound sterling to pre-war gold parity ten years ago symbolized the mindlessness of the attempt to restore the pre-war economic order without taking into account the extent to which the war years had hollowed out economic capacities. But here also it was possible to postpone the consequences of erroneous policies.

HOW WAS POSTPONEMENT OF THE CRISIS POSSIBLE?

The excess demand of the three major categories of income earners —rentiers, workers and peasants—could be met from only three sources.

Firstly, by domestic redistribution of income in favour of the privileged classes. Where workers and peasants were favoured, the distributional burden fell on the middle classes and on industrial capital by means of property taxes and the unfairest of all taxes—the liquidation of savings by inflation. Real incomes of agricultural producers were sustained by external tariffs and other protectionist measures, at the expense of urban consumers.

Secondly, by consumption of capital. Domestic capital was eaten away by inflation and by the sale of assets to foreigners.

Thirdly, deficits and debts were financed and re-financed by renewed external borrowing and increased indebtedness. This happened on a vast scale. Countries financed their deficits by perpetual external borrowing. Weaker national economies sought assistance from stronger ones. Years of apparent stability, a run of strong growth, a deceptive appearance of equilibrium were punctuated by new economic and financial difficulties, until suddenly, at the height of the American boom, the elastic band snapped. The interdependent deficit economies went into an irreversible slide, and the whole stabilization structure collapsed.

What were the mechanisms of the world economic crisis which determined this course of events, and facilitated it?

The geographical displacement and the consequent postponement of the crisis were facilitated by post-war credit mechanisms of unique capacity and flexibility.

The nature of these credit mechanisms has not been sufficiently researched. While the world economy was destroyed by the war, resurrected after the war, and slid into uninterrupted decline at the end of 1928, the system of credits has not ceased to develop following the financial innovations introduced during the war. This paradoxical phenomenon has continued throughout the entire post-war period. An amazing mobility and magnitude of international credit was accompanied by the intermittent constriction and malfunctioning of the real economy.

Wars give birth to new ways of financing them. The victorious states financed virtually all their foreign expenditures by a series of ad hoc arrangements: the sale of overseas bonds and equity in the USA, a pound sterling backed by the United States, the securitization of all obligations payable in foreign exchange between the allied powers and a moratorium on payment until the end of the war. United in a war of life and death, the major powers mobilized weapons of credit to the ultimate degree. Never in the history of modern capitalism has credit been so politicized. One consequence has been the closer relationship between the commercial banks and note-issuing authorities (central banks) in London, New York, and Paris. The source of this ultra-modern pipeline for the distribution of credit to the whole of Europe, which brought gold to irrigate the parched plains of Central Europe, was the unfathomable wealth of America. The enormous profits which America made in the war were searching for investment. The reconstruction of Europe appeared as an excellent business opportunity which would not only revive American exports to Europe, but showed a far-sighted love of humanity. Unequalled in wealth—and inexperienced—the investors who now appeared on the scene asked only that this credit mechanism should be fueled by their resources.

If we now find it incredible that the world could have been so mistaken as to the true state of the financial balance sheet of the war, the explanation lies in part with the financial claims which were considered "good." The sum total of allied war debts was estimated at 25,000 million dollars. The Genoa conference broke up in a quarrel over the distribution of quotas of Russian petroleum interests. Lloyd George would never had made his famous proposal for floating a 25 million pound sterling public company for the reconstruction of Russia, had there not been hopes that claims on Russian war and pre-war debtors were secure financial assets. At an estimated value of 35,000 million gold francs, they were not small change! The value of all these claims has now been written down. What is remarkable is that prior to the write down, owners of these bonds thought they were rich. In 1925 after Britain and Germany had returned to the gold standard, there was talk of a 16,000 million gold mark reparations issue as if it was a normal business deal! The credit mechanisms endowed by contemporaries with virtually mythical powers, were the principal actors in the ten years postponement of the crisis.[2]

THE GENERAL PROCESS

The outcome of the war determined the geographical course of the crisis —from East to West.

There were the *defeated states* like Russia, Austria, Hungary, Bulgaria, and the succession states carved from the eastern war regions like Rumania, Yugoslavia, Czechoslovakia, Poland and Greece. Last but not least, there was Germany.

There were the *victorious states*, England, France, Belgium and Italy. And in a class by itself, there was the *super victor*, America.

1918–1924: The process starts in the East with the reconstruction of the defeated states—with assistance from the victors and America. The Austrian (1923) and the Hungarian (1924) currencies were stabilized with help of the League of Nations. At the same time, Greece, Bulgaria, Finland and Estonia were structurally adjusted ("saniert"). Rumania, Poland, Czechoslovakia and Yugoslavia received French credits; even Russia was a candidate for economic assistance. The high point was the restoration of the gold standard in Germany, rooted in the Dawes Plan and finance of Dawes loans, almost half of American provenance. The reinstatement of the gold standard stripped the defeated states of the secret reserves of inflationary finance. Their structural deficits were increasingly covered by foreign loans; the burden of these debts was thus transferred to the victorious states, whose currencies were at this time far from stable or secure.

1925–1928: Apart from the deficits of the defeated states, the victorious states had their own disequilibria. From the time of the reestablishment of the gold standard in the victor states, defense of the currency assumed top priority. By so-called central bank co-operation, England shifted the economic burden of maintaining the external value of the pound sterling to the United States. The return of the pound to gold at pre-war parity in April 1925 was secured by American short-term credits. Notwithstanding ever increasing U.S. loans extended to Germany, from this time on the secret purpose of American credit policy was not so much assistance to Europe, as support for England. The high point were the negotiations between (Bank of England governor) Montague Norman and (Federal Reserve governor) Strong in New York in May 1927. In August of that year, the United States adopted a "Cheap Credit Policy" which lasted until February 1928 and prepared the way for the Wall Street crash of October 1929. The American crypto-inflation signified effective support of the European currencies which had returned to the (fixed exchange) gold standard by availability of cheap credit.

1929–1933: The deficits of the European victors and the defeated states were effectively shifted to America and covered by the steady growth of U.S. credits over the past ten years. America financed the Dawes Plan, renegotiated British and French war debts, and reparation payments by the defeated states, and the servicing of its own loans—in addition to wasted efforts to support English stabilization, bad German investments, and the accumulation of East European private sector deficits in financial institutions in Vienna. Principal Event: the crash of the Vienna Creditanstalt Bank on 12th May 1931. The Reichsmark declined; the English pound was devalued. On April 19th 1933 the dollar was floated. The constriction of the world economy and the chaotic instability of currencies resemble conditions prevailing in the immediate aftermath of the war.

THE STABILIZATION OF THE POUND AND ITS CONSEQUENCES

Seen in this light, policies which contemporary observers regarded as erroneous were the consequences of a course of events which had its own logic. Charges of mistaken policies are revealed as inconsistent, and supposedly missed opportunities were merely alternative paths to the same undesirable outcome. The return of the pound to pre-war parity now appears as a text book example of a mistaken policy. But the repeated excuse that England did not expect France and Belgium to stabilize their currencies at devalued rates and thus to put pressure on English exports, pointed to alternative policies whose non-implementation was actually fortunate. We insist that the principal issue concerning French and Belgium exchange rate policies was not their effect on relative export prices, but their relation to the previous levels of these currencies. The essence of the matter was that France was prepared to devalue the assets of their rentier class by eighty percent. In so far as English exports, after 1926, were under competitive pressure, it was because English rentier incomes were protected (by overvalued exchange rates); also for political reasons, wages were too high.

Another example. For many years, Central Europe refused to acknowledge England's economic difficulties because it was believed that the bank rate was too low to sustain the value of the pound. In reality the bank rate never fell below 4.5 per cent—far above historically prevailing rates. A legislative reduction of the rate of interest on government bonds or a tax on wealth might have offset the problems caused by the over-valuation of the pound. A substantial increase in the bank rate would not only have aggravated the acute economic crisis in England, but would have reduced the export of capital considered essential to the maintenance of the level of British exports.[3] The fact that England continued to export capital after 1925 benefited the recently adjusted economies of East Europe. Since 1924, foreign bonds floated on the London market amounted to 785 million dollars of long-term investments in continental Europe. Increasing difficulties in maintaining the flow of outward investment made it impossible to raise the bank rate. London markets were under strong but invisible pressures. As short-term loans became due, the City depended on ever-increasing levels of short-term borrowing. The dangers of this situation were clearly spelled out in the Macmillan Report shortly before the collapse of the currency in 1931.[4]

Foreign loans floated in London in 1927 amounted to 651 million dollars; in 1928 they were reduced to 525 million and in 1929 to a mere 228 million dollars—facilitated by cheap money flowing from New York. From the start, the elastic band which tied together the evermore fragile equilibria of the deficit economies were the American credits. But the transmission belt which carried the deficits of even the strongest European economies into the credit ledgers of American financial institutions was the re-established gold standard. Stripped of the secret reserves of inflation, European national economies were forced to adjust their weakened economic capacities by adherence to the rigid rules of the gold standard. Their resulting increased indebtedness to American creditors occurred silently, but no less effectively than the negotiated loans. Whereas the stabilization in Central Europe was sustained by cheap credit available on the London money markets, the restoration of the pound at pre-war parity was sustained by nothing less than the American silent inflation of 1926 to 1929—and thus brought on the eventual collapse of the whole structure of world credit.

THE UNITED STATES AND THE DOUBLE FUNCTION OF CREDIT MECHANISMS

Perhaps the most deceptive aspect of post-war economic experience was the fabulously high standard of living of the United States in this period. This was only partly due to the real wealth of the United States. It was due also to two interventions which isolated the United States from the effects of the crisis in the rest of the world: high external tariffs and the closing of the door to immigration. Without these measures, the poverty of Europe would have spread to the United States, and a resulting new equilibrium would have settled at the mid-point between the low living standards in the defeated continental states and their high level in America. The United States could free itself from European economic pressures only by shutting out cheap labour and cheap imports. This is the fundamental reason for the unilateral flow of gold into the United States. It was the only means of payments which did not reduce American living standards.

Countless charges have been made against the United States on the basis that shortsighted policies of protectionism not only aggravated, but actually caused the crisis. A creditor state should facilitate repayment of principal and interest by opening up its markets to the exports of debtor states. The exemplar here was England. But England was a special case because British external assets were built up over generations, and repayment was factored into long-term economic adjustments to new circum- stances. British imports of raw materials and semi-manufactured good for further processing are compatible with economic structures developed over decades. Britain's patterns of trade and payment are diversified, and debtors are scattered all over the world. How can the same demand be made of a state which overnight moved from being a major debtor to the world's leading creditor, and whose overseas loans are principally *political* [original emphasis] in origin? American exports from 1914 to 1919, with attendant allied war debts, implied industrial structures tailored to the requirements of the war in Europe. The acceptance of debt repayment in the form of imported goods, immediately after the war, would have brought economic crisis to the United States. Here again, we believe that the responsibility ascribed to U.S. interventionist policies in the post-war years should more properly be ascribed to the era of war itself. It is in the course of politically motivated interventions that eventual adjustments entail new and more painful interventions.

The United States would have been wiser to have written down the face value of the 11 billion dollars of war debt owed by allied states, although this would have created a fiscal burden of long duration to finance interest payments on domestically-issued liberty bonds. But American living standards would still have been higher than those prevailing before the war. All this, however, is academic, because America not only demanded repayment of the full value of war credits, but greatly increased the level of credits extended to Europe. Nevertheless, the issue gives rise to two important reflections.

First, American living standards were higher than was justified, and a write down of war debts would have reduced them. This would also have happened if America had accepted repayment of war debts in goods and cheap labour. Second, levels of consumption of its rentiers, workers and peasants in excess of Europe's productive capacity contributed to a higher standard of living in America than would have been the case in the absence of American credits. International credit thus served a double purpose: to maintain consumption levels in Europe and also in America above equilibrium levels.

For years the Federal Reserve was charged with the sterilization of the vast sum of gold flowing into the United States.[5] While Europe was unable to expand the volume of credit on account of the continuing outflow of gold, the United States, it was said, chose to sterilize gold inflows and restrict expansion of the money supply. Europe had to choke the economy by withdrawal of credits, while America refused to extend new credits to Europe. But the opposite criticism—that American policies of unrestrained inflation and mindless capital exports were responsible for the crisis—seems to me to carry more weight. Clearly, these two accusations are mutually exclusive. But we now know that the sterilization of gold reserves was based on a misunderstanding of the true facts. The increase in gold reserves from 1921 to 1929 was accompanied by an increase in the average daily excess reserves of the commercial banks of 706 million dollars (September 1921 to September 1929). The increase in the effective volume of credit available to the economy was nine or ten times this amount.

If the charges (that the United States was restricting credit) proved anything, it was that no amount of American credit appeared sufficient to satisfy European demand. The stabilization of a series of Central and East European currencies, the draconian credit restriction requiring support of the gold value of the German mark, the increasing economic pressure on England resulting from the return of sterling to parity, the need for political bridge-financing in the period between the Dawes and Young loans, in addition to the reconstruction credits for Germany and other countries, created a near insatiable demand for American financial assistance.

This invites a critical look at the phenomenon of American crypto-inflation—without question a valid observation. But the now prevalent opinion that America is therefore responsible for the collapse of world currencies is not convincing. The actual sequence of events indicates the opposite: currencies were stable only as long as they were supported by American credits, which were accompanied by inflationary finance. When it became impossible to continue these policies, the apparent stability of European currencies vanished.

Only those who have forgotten the European cry for American help in the long years of repeated financial, economic and, last but not least, political crises, can contemplate the bitter alternative of a refusal on the part of the Americans to extend credit. However, the Americans offered no serious resistance to European enthusiasm for boundless credit expansion. Accusations leveled at Wall Street regarding excessive and wasteful South American loans, also applied in part to American credits to Europe. As in South America, Europe is witnessing the dire economic consequences of the postponement of the crisis by artificially enhanced consumption, and excess dependence on credit by debtors and creditors alike.

THE COURSE OF THE CRISIS

The decisive connection in the clarification of causes and consequences was the flow of gold to the United States. The outflow of gold did not manifest itself in perceptible pressures on the supply of credit in Europe, as long as currencies were floating.[6] Currencies backed only by paper are insensitive to the loss of gold reserves. Serious complaints about the mal-distribution of gold reserves arose only after England (1925) and France (1926) returned to gold. Repeated American credit restrictions resulting in the drain of gold to America increased the burden on European debtor states.[7] Twice America experimented with policies of "cheap money." In each case in 1925 and again in 1928—the flow of gold was reserved.[8] When the stabilization of the French franc in the spring of 1927 resulted in a huge transfer of gold from the Bank of England to the Bank of France, Montague Norman and Federal Reserve governor Strong met in New York and agreed on a new policy of cheap money to save the embattled British economy from the painful consequences of a rise in the Bank rate.

From August 1927 to February 1928, the discount rate of the New York Federal Reserve Bank was a mere 3.5 percent. The result was an enhanced economic boom in the United States and Europe, as a flow of American credits supported European currencies, and foreign investments in Germany in 1927/28 topped 2 billion dollars. In July 1928, the New York bank rate was raised to 5 per cent to check a speculative bubble on the stock market. The supply of long-term capital to Europe dried up. In the first half of 1919 the value of European bonds floated in New York was a mere 101 million dollars, compared with 499 million in the first half of 1928.

Up until 1925, American protectionist and credit policies sustained living standards in the United States and in Europe by the accepting of gold for payment of imports, and by the extension of credits. After the restoration of the gold standard in Europe, essentially in England, the debtor states could withstand the pressure on their currencies only because inflationary cheap money policies in the United States were instrumental in causing an enormous increase in foreign lending to Europe. When American inflationist policies were reversed, financial pressure on debtor states triggered the world crisis. In mid-1928, the United States and France together accounted for 58 per cent of the world's monetary gold. America ceased foreign lending. Neither gold, nor credits were available to finance payment deficits. Debtor states now had no alternative but to increase the export of goods. Since 1928/9, Europe and overseas raw materials exporting countries have flooded world markets with exports at virtually any price.[9] The trend of universally falling world prices manifested in 1929 was prelude to the world economic crisis. Then came the credit crisis of 1931, the decline in world trade in 1932, and the collapse of currencies in 1933. The geographic displacement and postponement of economic deficits had run its course. If inflation succeeded in saving the social fabric, it could not save humanity from the prolonged and painful process of economic adjustment.[10]

NOTES

1. Translated and revised by Kari Polanyi Levitt, February 1998. The original title was "Der Mechanismus der Weltwirtschaftskrise," pp.3-9 in a special issue of *Der Oesterreichischen Wolkswirt* (Wien 1933), adendum to vol.25, entitled Sonderbeilage Des Oesterreichischen Volkswirt Anlasslich Der Vollendung Seines 25. Jahrganges "Wirtschafts-Und Soziale Probleme Der Donaustaaten."

2. F. Somary, "Kapitalueberschuss und Kapitalzuschussgebiete, mechanismus und wirkungen der internationalen Kapitaluebertragungen," in *Kapital und Kapitalismus*. Berlin, 1931: 483. Compare also articles written before the collapse of the Credit-Anstalt by W. Federn in nos 8, 9, 10, 16, 17, 19 and 20 of the *Oesterreichische Volkswirt*, November 22 and 29, 1930, and nos 3, 17 and 24, January 7 and February 14, 1931.

3. J.B. Condliffe explained these capital exports as "essentially normal mechanisms of the pre-war international economic order." *The World Economic Survey*, 1930/31, p. 48.

4. "Nothing is more significant for the consequences of the war than the coexistence of an unusually long economic upswing in the United States with an unusually long depression in England. The return of the pound at pre-war parity—which distinguished England from all other major European powers—together with heavy European indebtedness to the United States are the two fundamental reasons for the Depression." F. Somary, *Wandlungen der Weltwirtschaft seit dem Kriege*. Tuebingen 1928, p. 11.

5. This journal did not join the critics. See Walther Federn, "Die Sterlisierung des Goldes," nos 16 and 17; January 17 and 24.

6. J.B. Condliffe, *The World Economic Survey*, 1931/32, p. 48.

7. *Monetary Policies and the Depression*. Institute for International Affairs, Oxford 1933, p. 8.

8. Prof. Ohlin in "Le Cours et la Phase de la Depression," *Economique Mondiale*, Geneva, 1931, p. 110.

9. Condliffe in *World Economic Survey* 1931/32, p.43; and in *Situation Economique Mondiale* 1932/33, p. 171; Prof Ohlin in *op.cit.*, p. 211.

10. Professor J.B. Condliffe, editor of the last two Economic Yearbooks of the League of Nations, lent support to our view in the most recent Yearbook for 1932/33. "The real difficulties did not manifest themselves as long as the currencies of most of the debtors states were independent of each other; exchange rates were flexible, and inter-governmental debts unregulated. But as currencies returned to the gold standard, exchange rates were fixed, and debt payments were officially negotiated, tensions in the newly reconstructed international financial mechanisms increased. For a few years from 1925 to 1929 debt service was effected without radical adjustment of national economy by means of large flows of new capital to the debtor states, principally from the United States. From 1928 and continuing in 1929, capital inflows diminished. As pressures on debtors states increased, prices declined and credits dried up, the difficulties of international adjustment precipitated the collapse of the whole structure of international payments." *Situation Economique Mondiale* 1932/33, p. 277.

Chapter Thirty-Two

"OLD, BADLY PEELED, HALF-RAW POTATOES" AND PETER F. DRUCKER'S OTHER MYTHS ABOUT KARL POLANYI

Kenneth McRobbie

The growing influence of the work of Karl Polanyi is attested by the hundreds of conference papers—many of them published[1]—and the increasing number of citations in the scholarly literature around the world. His insights in social anthropology and economic history have become "embedded" in critiques of the assault by global market forces on traditional societies, political democracy, human rights, moral values, and the very sustainability of the planet's ecosphere. Surprisingly—and regrettably—there are still some who have encountered the name of Karl Polanyi only in a widely-circulated autobiographical work by the publicist and management writer Peter F. Drucker, whose *Adventures of a Bystander* contains a chapter entitled "The Polanyis" (to which page numbers in the text refer).[2] That the myths propagated there are still current I personally have been made aware of through random contacts with informants ranging from a Taiwanese graduate of Columbia's MBA programme to an Australian anthropologist (with whom I had an altercation in the "Letters" section of *The Times Literary Supplement*).[3]

Reviewers of *Bystander* seemingly had neither the inclination nor the ability to check Drucker's facts, but were impressed by his European tone of worldly-wise familiarity with those personages he claims to have met—Freud when he was eight or nine, Thomas Mann when he was sixteen, and in his early thirties such captains of industry as Henry Luce of *Time-Life-Fortune* and Alfred Sloan of General Motors. In *The Harvard Business Review* Peter Drucker was hailed as "one of the greatest thinkers of our time" (!) whose style ("both unique and engaging") was deemed to do justice to the "amazing pageant of characters" "playing to perfection their roles" in a work that "is better than a novel." (The term "novel" was particularly well chosen, as we shall see.) The reviewer also congratulated Drucker on providing an "informed glimpse" and for "shedding light" on the first half of the last century. A reviewer in *Business Week* similarly assumed that Drucker's sketches were based on "knowledge" and "an awesome power of recall." However, a close examination of his chapter "The Polanyis" shows that the opposite is the case. Why? Assuming that Drucker did possess at least *some* "knowledge" and "power of recall"—why did he choose *not* to employ them? The answer seems to be that he was bent on subordinating reality to ideology, while raking over the still glowing embers of the Cold War. This compelled him to present his subjects—the two generations of men and women whose lives spanned some 130 years—as caricatures, in order to elevate them to the status of myth, so that they might be accomodated within his over-arching ideological myth of society against the individual, and in the case of the Polanyis, the presumption and sheer pointless of their presuming that there could be an alternative to the liberal capitalist market system.

Shortly after Drucker published his *Bystander*, Karl Polanyi's nephew—Dr. George Striker of Budapest—composed a three-page letter, dated 5 September 1980, in which he expressed indignation at the author's misleading data about his ancestors, particularly his mother Laura Polanyi Striker—concerning whom Drucker's "outrageous fabrications" have recently been definitively exposed by her biographer Dr. Judit Szapor[4]—and her three brothers. A similar protest was lodged by Thomas G. Polanyi (Boston, Mass.) against Drucker's references to his father Adolph: "His statements concerning my father are all wrong. Here I am the specialist." He then made a most perceptive remark: "I am curious about how and why such stuff gets to be written."[5] Striker had gone as far as to protest to the publisher, but to no avail, as we learn from a recent letter by his wife Barbara who has contributed a vivid memoir to the present volume.[6] Nevertheless, Dr Striker did express the hope that "rectifications will at some time lead to a correction—in public—of these falsifications of my family's history." He identified some thirty errors of fact in Drucker's chapter—with comments ranging from "sheer product of phantasy" to "libelous misstatement—and sign of gross ignorance."[7] Dr. Striker concludes: "The great number and character of the erroneous data...leave me highly sceptical about the rest of the text."

We will be better able to appreciate the seriousness of these charges if we go back, almost two decades, to a very different document: the three-page letter of 21 October 1961 from Peter Drucker to Karl Polanyi on the occasion of the latter's 75th birthday.[8] Most readers will find the compliments too fulsome, the protestations of admiration too many and too sweeping concerning Polanyi's "spell," his "great scholarly work [with its] great organizing concepts of economic history," and the heavy-handed assurances that "any book today on the Economy in society" shows "how deeply, how permanently, how profoundly you have influenced all of us." All this is far removed from the "real world" of the truly modest scholar Karl Polanyi remained all his life. However, when we turn from what Drucker wrote to Polanyi in his personal letter two years *before* his death to what he says publically about him in "The Polanyis" 17 years *later*, we notice a drastic change in tone and content. To be sure, Drucker does declare that the

Polanyis were "the most gifted," even "brilliant" family he had "ever heard of"—but the hyperbole seems designed to throw into high definition the negative things he will say of them individually and collectively. For the principal purpose of the chapter is less to extol their purported brilliance than to proclaim their failure. The members of "The Polanyis" are presented as if they were actors in a Greek tragedy. The *hubris* engendered by their brilliance inevitably brought in its train the *nemesis* of downfall! "Each one found an 'answer,'" Drucker writes, "and each then realized that it was not 'the answer.'" (127)

Drucker then proceeds to impose his ideological template upon each of the *very* different members the Polanyi family—declaring, against all the evidence, that "each [was] in search of the same goal." Thereafter, virtually everything he writes is a figment of his imagination. "Beginning with the father" with his "half-political" plan to create an "unbourgeois culture through economic development"; passing then to "the mother as well" with her alleged part in a bomb plot against the Czar and her role in isolating the children to make them "different"; "Otto" who allegedly flirted with Marxism and Mussolini; Adolph who saw in Brazil "the promise of a new society, different from the 'decadent capitalism' of Europe"; Laura who "spewed out" "tracts" for communities that would be "neither 'capitalist' nor 'Communist,' but truly 'Socialist'"; Michael who at first "looked to science to find the way out between a bourgeois capitalism that denied community and a Marxist socialism that denied freedom and the person"; finally, as we shall see, he comes to Karl. Now comes their 'fall.' "I know of no family that was so successful, measured by the standards of the world," Drucker continues —another suspect statement— "and such a failure when measured by its own expectations." The father Mihály Pollacsek became "bankrupt," and his wife Cecile "a shriveled up old lady feared for her vicious tongue"; of their children: "Otto" became "a broken, bitter old man," Adoph died "a defeated man," Laura "gave up" (at the age of twenty five!), Michael "very soon gave up on society," and Karl became "a deeply disappointed man." This panorama of failure is expressly designed to lead to Drucker's final assessment: "The Polanyis...were very minor figures, entertaining rather than important."

Why then would Drucker devote a whole chapter to persons he considers to be failures? Principally, the answer seems to be, because he wishes to hold them up to his readers—whom he has good reason to know range from students of business to members of the corporate elite—as a warning. For him, the Polanyis are mid-twentieth-century examples of 'the treason of the intellectuals.' Thus he writes, in conclusion, "what made them matter was not their lives; it was their cause and its failure."(140) Here speaks a very different Peter Drucker, no longer the birthday well-wisher but the Chairman of the Graduate School of Management Studies at New York University, one who by 1993 would have to his credit no fewer than 12 books on Management, 12 more on Economics, Politics and Society, 2 works of fiction, and an Autobiography (consisting mainly of anecdotes about the famous persons he met during his career). In his other writings he is not averse to describing how he had scaled the heights—from working for *Time-Life-Fortune*, then systems analyst of General Motors Management, to becoming the preferred author of heads of government. And *what* heads! "As Mrs. Thatcher said publicly many times," Drucker assures his readers —how one would like, here and elsewhere, documentation—"she derived her policies largely from this chapter"—"The Sickness of Government"—in which, he says, "he invent[ed] and advocate[d] 'privatization,' " noting "I originally called it *re*-privatization." As if this were not enough, Drucker adds that "the chapter...also provided the basic concepts for the policy that, between 1970 and 1980, made Japan's the world's second economic world power—or so Japan's then prime minister asserted. In fact, he devoted most of his 1970 New Year's Message to the book (and especially to this chapter)."[9]

It was on the basis of his ideological opinions that, after the deaths of the members of the Polanyi family, Peter Drucker would reinterpret, indeed reinvent, their careers. The historical context may be relevant here. It is likely that, along with the establishment elites with whom his career was intertwined, Drucker deeply resented it when his (and their) world was shaken during the late 60s and early 70s—not by the external Soviet enemy, but from within by intellectuals, professors and students. This may have convinced him to portray "the Polanyis" as belonging within the category of those who had the presumption to propose that there could—indeed, ought to be—a non-communist alternative to capitalism. Not that they actively tried to implement this imputed notion: indeed, theirs was no more than a 'thought crime' Still, contrary to the evidence, Drucker can write: "All of the Polanyis searched for another alternative." Accordingly, he makes it his purpose to devise a chart on which he traces an imaginary course taken by each member of the family towards the same fatal goal. (138) "All of them," he writes, "enlisted in the same cause: to overcome the nineteenth century and to find a new society that would be free and yet not 'bourgeois' or 'liberal'; prosperous and yet not dominated by economics; communal and yet not a Marxist collectivism." Indeed, he endows them with a single-minded intensity of purpose. "They reminded me of the Knights of the Round Table, setting out in search of the same Holy Grail, each in a different direction."

Of all the Polanyis, Karl is portrayed as the most single-minded in such a search. In his *The Great Transformation*[10] and later works, Drucker says, Karl was always searching for "the viable alternative, that is, for the good society between capitalism and communism." (137) This tendentious interpretation not surprisingly comes up short on evidence concerning what the Polanyis were *for*. No matter. Drucker will portray his "knights" bearing black blazons. For to him their quest was impelled less by love of the good than by hatred of what they considered to be evil. "If there was one article of the faith to which all the Polanyis suscribed [sic]—from Karl's father on—it was that the 'laissez-faire' Liberals of the nineteenth-century Manchester School were wrong in their assertion that the market is the only alternative to serfdom. [Would any writer in the nineteenth century have said any such thing?] Indeed, the market creed of the Manchester Liberals may be called the hereditary enemy of the house of Polanyi." It is not difficult to hear in this the rustle of pages in a well-thumbed copy of Hayek's *The Road to Serfdom* (published in the same year as Polanyi's *The Great Transformation*). Drucker does not stop there..."Their failure is important, for it may signify the futility of the quest that has engaged Western man for the last 200 years...if not since Hobbes and Locke 100 years earlier: the quest for the one absolute 'civic religion'; for the perfect—or at least the good—society." He goes further—showing what Margaret ("there's no such thing as society") Thatcher had seen in him—when he declares that the failure of the Polanyis foreshadows the "end of the Age of the Infallible Society."[11]

But Karl Polanyi had not sought to "find" a new society. The emphasis in all his works was upon the need to acknowledge that the reality of human existence is within society, that man cannot abstract himself from it, that the economy must be made to serve human needs—and that human beings must consciously and constantly search for appropriate means, rather than accept the dictates of impersonal economic forces. Not only does Drucker reject what he misreads as Polanyi's central intellectual focus, he goes on to criticize his powers of analysis and interpretation. Formerly in 1961 he had nothing but praise for Karl's universally applied and "searching penetration"; by 1978, though, he decided that this was evident only in Polanyi's Vienna period, when he "analyzed [current political events] with an uncanny knack for seeing the importance of inconspicuous developments at an early stage." It would not last, though. For during what Drucker calls "the years of drift in England," Polanyi began fatally to "speculate," the problem being that he "had too much imagination to be good at it." In addition, "he had a naïve belief in the cunning, cleverness, and foresight of our rulers that made him see conspiracies and long-laid deep plots everywhere."

How different was Drucker's view in 1961, when he assures his "friend" that he *never lost* his talent for astute analysis. "And again, over the years, you have done this great job of illuminating a familiar landscape so as to bring out the new, the fundamental, the real in it again and again," "the one person who...was always ahead of the changing times, always ready in the morrow." Really? So Drucker *did* accept Polanyi's predictions —for thus he, scarcely believably, alleges them to be—that Hitler would not invade Austria in March 1938 but Switzerland instead, and that in 1940 the European powers (with Japan) would partition China, "the European war is just a feint." (133-4) Well, by 1978, he had made a 180-degree turn. "Karl was, it seemed to me, becoming the victim of his own cleverness." He was also becoming narrower: "He still divined the 'real truth' behind the news," but was "as ever, conspiratorial, labyrinthine as ever [sic]." (139)

This hardening of attitude on Drucker's part may explain while he piled on error upon error in "The Polanyis." It was not from forgetfulness or lack of knowledge—though the quality of his argument is certainly in line with the lack of historical judgment shows elsewhere[12]—but out of a need to refashion the life and work of the Polanyis to accord with his thesis. He claims to have met with members of the family—"four or five Polanyis I got to know personally" (127)—though this cannot be verified, except in the case of Karl Polanyi.[13] He met with Karl Polanyi over the course of more than two decades, beginning in 1927 and probably intermittently thereafter in Vienna; during 1935-39 in England ("these were the years when I began to see a good deal of Karl and to get close to him. In England we took long walks together on Sunday mornings"); during the 1940s in New York (as Drucker wrote to Karl, "I was privileged to see you again and again"); and at Bennington College, Vermont (where for a while they were colleagues on faculty and next-door neighbours). Indeed, "Karl became a close friend" (132), Drucker claims, though "good" would be more accurate. After his death in 1964, Drucker corresponded intermittently with his widow. Both Karl and Ilona were by no means averse to speaking of their family's history; nor were libraries lacking in appropriate works of reference.

Readers of previous Karl Polanyi Conference publications—including the present one with its several chapters of biographical data—will be able to ascertain the true facts concerning the Polanyi family. Thus, they will be able to confirm that in Drucker's chapter even some of *the names* of members of the family are wrong, while others are omitted; also, that all *the birth- and death-dates* (with one exception), where they are given at all, are wrong.[14] Building on this insecure foundation, Drucker proceeds to invent—for the family's members—lives they never lived. In all, there are no fewer than one hundred and sixty eight errors of fact, plus others of interpretation, in a chapter of no more than eighteen pages. It will be enough here to indicate the outlines of this misrepresentation with its schematic trajectory of rise and fall. Thus, Polanyi's father is credited, at some length, with having been "a tough guerilla fighter" in the 1848 War of Liberation—though that was the year of his birth! His wife Cecile is introduced as a Russian countess and bomb-maker—though really she was the daughter of a rabbinical scholar in Vilna, who became a jeweller's assistant in Vienna. Their "eldest child" is introduced as "Otto," who is described, over the best part of a page, as a machine designer in Germany, owner of a factory in Italy, ardent Marxist, then patron and friend of Benito Mussolini. So who was Drucker's source for this fascinating information? Not "Otto," for Drucker admits he never met him; nor Karl Polanyi, for Drucker reports that he found him "reluctant to talk about his brother." No wonder, for there was no such person![15] The 'real' eldest son Adolf, contrary to what Drucker alleges—as confirmed in 2004 by his son, Mr. Thomas Polanyi—

was not a qualified "engineer," did not go to Brazil in 1919 (but in 1939), and was not a leading figure in that country's industrial development, nor in its cultural renaissance. His sister Laura most certainly did not, according to her son Dr. George Striker, pursue a short-lived career as author and editor on peasant culture and communes (which, Drucker claims, influenced the future Marshall Tito and even the founders of the first Israeli kibbutz); in fact, though Drucker said she never wrote a line after the age of twenty-five, her most productive period was towards the end of her life in New York, when she undertook definitive research on the early career of a founder of the State of Virginia, Captain John Smith.[16] It is perhaps significant that Drucker has least to say on the life and work of the (at that time) best-known member of the family, the scientist and philosopher Michael Polanyi (whose son John resides in Toronto), probably because widely available reference works would have made any reshaping of his career easily detectable.

When we turn to the sections on Karl Polanyi, the page or so describing his youth in Hungary makes very disturbing reading for anyone acquainted with the truth. Errors occur in virtually every line. For Drucker's attempt to make Polanyi out to have been a politician is contradicted by the historical record, and by Karl's later deep regret that he had *not* engaged in politics—"I had no talent that way, no interest even."[17] Thus, he most certainly was *not* co-founder of the Hungarian Liberal Party together with Count Michael Károlyi (whom he had *not* met, and who, anyway, was *not* of that party); he was *not* "elected to parliament," *nor* called into the cabinet in 1918 by prime minister Count Károlyi (who had *not* recently returned from exile because he *never* was exiled, having served in the army); *nor* was Polanyi (being then in hospital) appointed Minister of Justice.

This wholly fictitious account—which is embellished with superlatives—seems to have but one purpose: to present Karl Polanyi as having had a brilliant past, in order that Drucker may contrast it with his—equally fictitious—decline (and implied imminent fall) during his life in emigration. Thus, already in Vienna, Drucker asserts, Polanyi "at first seemed to have burned himself out at an early age," "one of the casualties" of unfulfilled promise (his father allegedly confirms). Of Polanyi's time in England, Drucker says they were "not very good years." However, "a turning point" did come in 1941 in the U.S. when Polanyi received a two-year appointment as a research scholar at Bennington College, Vermont. There he finished his one and "only book"—as Drucker condescendingly puts it—which however "created enough of a stir" to earn him an appointment in 1947 at Columbia University when "already past sixty." Thereafter, in Drucker's mistaken version of Polanyi's life, it was downhill all the way.

Ignoring that this was in many ways the most fruitful and fulfilling phase of his life, Drucker insists that "Karl was a deeply disappointed man," who "retreated into footnotes...and into academic busyness." [sic] (138) To make such a statement, it was necessary for Drucker to ignore

Karl's success gained through "his greatest gift—teaching"[18] in instituting a new course on General Economic History on which he lectured to enthusiastic classes of returned veterans. Instead, Drucker portrays him as a dry-as-dust recluse. "Soon he would turn antiquarian, concerned with minutiae, with textual criticism and emendation, and with 'scholarship' for its own sake. Where earlier he had been prone to sweeping generalizations, he increasingly became a footnote hound." Even stranger —if possible—is the charge that "the only politics that now engaged his interest were increasingly the subterranean power struggles and intrigues in the Columbia faculty." (Actually, the evidence shows that it was *Drucker* who concerned himself with these.[19]) Even before retirement, Drucker says, Polanyi's career was fast declining. "He wrote less and less...and even the little he wrote was published, by and large, after his death by his friends and disciples." (139) (This "little" actually amounts, as the publications record shows, to a very great deal.) It is easy now to understand George Striker's indignation when this travesty of an intellectual portrait concludes, as it must, on a note of bathos. "By the time he died," Drucker says of Polanyi, "he himself may well have forgotten the promise he had held out in *The Great Transformation* twenty years earlier." (139) His fate was to become one of whom "not more than a handful of people ever heard." (131)

By now it will have become clear that Drucker's real concern is not with truth and objectivity, but with fabricating interpretations. When he describes himself as "the bystander [who] sees things neither actor nor audience notices" and his work as "an intensely subjective book."(p.1), he imagines that he is possessed of a higher truth than that which mere objectivity could reveal. This subjective truth is conveyed in an impressionistic 'style' which resembles that of the Viennese *feuilleton* with which he was brought up. Indeed, the entire volume is totally lacking in documentation, footnotes (except for one, to one of his own books), and anything pertaining to scholarly standards. This is no accident. In a revealing later comment, Drucker delivers himself of the following: "I consider the obscurantism of today's intellectuals equally to be betrayal and treason...In large part they bear the blame for the debasement of culture, especially in the USA...what passes for scholarship is nothing but arrogance."[20] Certainly, obscurity is not what comes to mind when reading his suppositions, privileged anecdotes and exaggerations, presented in the florid style of the practising journalist he once was in Europe and later with *Time-Life-Fortune* publications. Yet he came to regard himself, as one who "respect[s] language" in the tradition of Karl Kraus—no less! —for whom "language was morality" and "integrity," for whom to corrupt language was "to corrupt society and individual alike." (*Ibid*, pp.455-6) He likens himself to the Danish philosopher Soren Kierkegaard for whom, he says, "language is aesthetics and aesthetics is morality," and even the author of *1984*: "Long before George Orwell I...knew that the corruption of language...is both a sin and a crime." (*Ibid.*)

Stylistic excess is carried to ludicrous lengths in Drucker's portrayal of Karl Polanyi as a sort of eccentric, counter-culture character. Thus Drucker describes his first encounter in 1927 with Polanyi at an editorial board meeting of the *Oestereichische Volkswirt* [sic] (that he elsewhere also twice misspells its title is curious indeed).[21] Readers may contrast his caricature with the account of editorial board meetings provided by Richard A. Bermann—that indeed may have served as Drucker's source—elsewhere in this volume.[22] Allegedly, Karl was no less than one hour and forty minutes late, of which Drucker observed "it was clear that waiting for Karl Polanyi was nothing unusual." (124) Then, outside the closed door, Drucker says, he heard "a peculiar rhythmic chant...as if someone were shouting at the top of his lungs a lot of nonsense syllables"; thereupon Polanyi entered, "all the while continuing to chant" "the names of Chinese generals and politicians." "In the same bellowing voice he shouted at top speed" [sic] his plans for future articles, then "he chanted all these nonsense syllables again." Certain that he is entertaining his readers, Drucker repeats this nonsense —twice. Thus in 1940, he says, Polanyi "still talked at machine-gun speed and in the rhythmic chant with which...he had intoned the names of Chinese warlords," and in 1958 he had the same booming laugh, and "still had the habit of chanting strange names at the top of his voice. Only [now]... they increasingly became the strange names of...sites in Asia Minor or the titles of local officials..."

Much in the same vein, Drucker transforms the real Polanyi—who was, as contemporary photos show, a man of average build, one known to be of less than average strength[23]—into "a very large man [who] burst into the room," "carrying what looked like a small steamer trunk under each arm," with more—much, much more—in the same vein.[24] This caricature is succeeded by one of an unacknowledged Karl Polanyi in the UK where he supposedly wrote only for "obscure little magazines," who in the USA traveled "in near squalor" on lecture circuits (133); in Bennington, Vermont, he lived in a "tiny cottage," and in New York he supposedly wore "layers of frayed and threadbare sweaters" in an airless apartment "each of its grimy and ill-maintained rooms piled from floor to ceiling" with books and papers. This, then, is his portrait of the "friend" of whom Drucker wrote: "Dr.Polanyi has been my teacher more than any other man—both as a scholar and as a human being."[25]

But to return to that "Austrian Economist" editorial board meeting of December 25, 1927. At its conclusion, according to Drucker, he was invited to lunch with the Polanyi family—he seems not to be aware that the address was Vorgartenstrasse 203. Of this occasion, where he claims to have been, and what he asserts that he saw, heard, and even ate, are so totally at odds with probability, as to confirm doubts concerning the veracity of everything else he writes of "The Polanyis." First, his description of where Polanyi resided bears no resemblance, neither then nor now, to the nature of the district, the aspect of the house, or even the number of the floor on which the apartment was located. Second, no less credible is his story that Polanyi donated *all* that he earned as an editor to "Hungarian refugees" (this at a time long after the 1919-20 wave of emigration). This ignores the fact that Polanyi's editorial responsibilities, research and teaching activities would have left him little time for additional employment—which would have had to be full-time in order to provide enough money to support a household numbering *five* (plus frequent visitors). The story is alleged to have emanated from Polanyi's wife Ilona Duczynska—and thus seems designed to illustrate the political fervour for which she was renowned (and which caused her to take a firm stand against Drucker's views). However, it has certainly appealed to historians who share something of Drucker's ideological outlook.[26] Third, there is the myth of "the old, badly peeled, half-raw potatoes" which Drucker says—calling it the "worst meal of my life"—furnished forth the Polanyis' Christmas dinner table. Let us scotch this, once and for all. (1) Felix Schaffer's comprehensive 100-page memoir[27] on life and work in the household makes no mention of any such Spartan fare (or Spartan anything else), nor do reports by other visitors to the household. (2) There was a full-time live-in Hungarian cook, Erzsi, who had been with the family for 30 years, in whose national culture such a dish—whether the potatoes were completely peeled or well-cooked—would not count as food. (3) Ilona's mother Helene being of gentry background—not "a baroness" as Drucker calls her—was a fastidious lady with a firm sense of proprieties and standards, and was the fulltime housekeeper; even in the impecunious early years of her marriage, she had provided more nourishing fare for her daughter. (4) There is the testimony of Karl's daughter Kari who still clearly recollects being taken regularly as a child to the market to purchase all that was appropriate for the above-average Central European fare that was the basis of family meals. (5) In case there are still some who are inclined to regard this alleged meal as resulting from food shortages in Vienna, it should be remembered that those were for the most part immediately post-war. Moreover, Drucker's own statement that the supposed meal was "the worst" he ever had, is intended to make it clear that more normal food was available—but was not being provided for ideological reasons. Now perhaps this whole story can be struck from the Polanyi family record.

The number and seriousness of Drucker's errors of fact and interpretation make it difficult to credit that he could regard himself as Karl Polanyi's "close friend." Still, he did perform a useful service when he recommended Karl for appointment, to the President of Bennington College—or, as he self-dramatizingly puts it: "At this point Providence moved, and it moved through me!" It is less easy to accept Drucker's claim that he assisted Polanyi in the organizing and writing of *The Great Transformation*. He seems to feel confident enough to say as much, feeling that he had the edge on the older man in terms of publications. Indeed, Drucker writes at considerably greater length about his own books than he does about Karl's. Thus, he describes his first published student essay, then Polanyi's invitation to write three pages for the *OV* (overruled), and throughout the chapter devotes two-and-a-half pages to his own publications—but only one page to Polanyi's *The Great Transformation* (and nothing to his other writings). Having published his "first major book" in 1939—a work "conceived years earlier," he adds unnecessarily—in the early 1940s (" a turning point for Karl") while working on his second book, Drucker says: "I would test my ideas on Karl [who] was always interested, encouraging, and enthusiastic." From this experience, allegedly, Polanyi learned something. Their conversations, Drucker says, "forced him [Polanyi] to clarify his own thoughts": whereupon, "both of us soon realized that Karl had a major book in his head, still disorganized, disjointed, and unfocused but of real stature." By 1942, having finished *that* book, Drucker was able—"I was between books and had ample time"—to be of assistance to Karl who "was just starting to write his book and needed an audience and critic." Two or three times a week, so he says, Drucker went to Karl's "tiny cottage," and "listened" to what was to become "the only book Karl Polanyi ever finished." Polanyi's view of their association was somewhat different. In the "Author's Acknowledgements" he confirms what other sources suggest: that the book "was begun and finished in England" though "written in America."[28] He thanks several friends, including two "colleagues" from Bennington: Horst Mendershausen (whose "general sympathy added to the usefulness of his advice"), and Peter Drucker (who together with his wife was "a source of sustained encouragement, notwithstanding their wholehearted disagreement with the author's conclusions.") (A letter from Drucker, of 16 April 1944, confirms this: "I disagree as sharply as ever with the last few chapters.") In addition to these measured statements, the book's prefatory "Dedication" accords priority to Polanyi's wife—ignored by Drucker—who was then also teaching at Bennington: "To my beloved wife Ilona Duczynska I dedicate this book which owes all to her help and criticism." (*TGT*, p.v)

Omissions are another species of error. Thus Drucker finds it possible to pass over Karl's entire body of work, except for *The Great Transformation*. To this he devotes several perceptive sentences,[29] while stressing its restricted appeal: "This was—and is—a novel thesis, and one that is still highly controversial," "sociologists do, by and large, while economists do not, accept it." (136-7) This is the work which Drucker regards—terming it "both 'anti-capitalist' and 'anti-Marxist' "—as evidence for his argument that economic history was no more than a "vehicle for Karl's search for the alternative to capitalism and communism." He goes further. He claims that Karl continued to pursue "this alternative" during his last years at Columbia. "He still talked of the search for the 'alternative' and of harmony between human freedom and economic development. He still expected to find the 'alternative' every time he tackled the study of a new primitive or early culture. And then, for a few weeks, he was young again and enthusiastic." (139) It did not last, though. For, as Drucker fully expected, the only evidence to be found, he says, pointed to the contrary! Thus, "the more Karl delved into prehistory, primitive economics, and classical antiquity, the more proof did he find for the hated and despised market creed of Ricardo and Bentham, and also of Karl's bogeymen, Ludwig von Mises and Frederick Hayek of the Austrian School." (That even a professor of management studies could seriously expect that the "economy" of archaic societies would provide "proof" of the 19th century market system again calls into question the writer's motives.) As a result, Drucker goes on—in a passage which presents a Polanyi totally different from the untiring enthusiast recollected by graduate students and colleagues close to him in those years—he "came to give up on society and despair of it." (140)

From early on, significant ideological differences between the two men were apparent. To their credit, perhaps, this did not prejudice their long-standing—if not "close"—friendship, one which seems to have been more trusting and more open on Karl's side.[30] Polanyi felt free to speak with Drucker concerning his research—a little too free, it seems, there being a hint of wounded *amour propre* in Drucker's description of how, when he called at Polanyi's New York apartment, Karl immediately started talking about *his* work: "Wasting no time on preliminaries such as enquiring after my work..." The younger man was able to shrug off whatever criticisms Polanyi made, because his career—which he describes, in letters to Karl, in terms of books published and invitations extended—was highly successful. When his second book was published (1942), Drucker recalls, Polanyi was "totally out of sympathy with what I called 'a conservative approach'"—though in his 1961 letter he thanked Polanyi for pointing out "the weaknesses of a facile conservatism." More serious was their difference, in relation to the market system, on the issue of freedom. The concluding Chapter 21 of *The Great Transformation* ("Freedom in a Complex Society") deals with this issue in a fashion which Drucker rejects: "It was my willingness to settle...for an adequate, bearable, but free society that Karl...criticized and rejected as a tepid compromise." Exactly how "we would maintain freedom," along the lines Drucker says, is not clear, in view of his acceptance that it would only be "by paying a price: the disruption, the divisiveness, and alienation of the market." (140)

By 1952 it must also have been clear to both men that Drucker's whole-hearted support of America's role in the Cold War and drive for world hegemony further deepened the differences between them. This is suggested in the correspondence between Drucker and Ilona Duczynska, following the publication of his *Harper's* magazine article "Frontier for This Century."[31] There he set forth a policy for how his adopted country—"we" and "us" occur throughout—could bring industrialization to the world's underdeveloped "agrarian" societies ("bankrupt, economically as well as culturally"), where "leadership...must be the fixed star of American foreign policy." The values, beliefs and methods of the process would be American including "American business morality," the purpose of which would be to obtain "raw materials intended mainly for American use." Also, "it should be [an] extremely profitable and attractive business, especially for the larger American companies."

Ilona Duczynska took it upon herself to respond to Drucker's article, on the basis of her extensive research into peasant life and land reform. She was diametrically opposed to Drucker's giving priority to the interests of an imperial power, and to his willingness to impose urban industrial patterns on agrarian societies. In her letter of May 15, 1952, she says of his article: "It rather asks for being taken to pieces (premises included) which I will certainly try to do...from the 'underdeveloped' point of view." Drucker's reply of June 2, strongly hints—if with mock obsequiousness—at longstanding differences between them. "I do not have to tell you that to be taken that seriously by you is a very great compliment indeed. Incidentally, I believe that it is the first time in the twenty-five years we have known each other that you have taken anything I have written seriously enough to want to answer it. To feel that finally I have come up to your exacting standards—at least to the point where you want to criticize me—makes me feel very proud."[32] The episode concluded with Drucker plainly acknowledging (September 24) that "The differences, as you and I quite clearly brought out...are deeply moral."

The principal difference between them derived from Drucker's opposition to socialism—even as a challenge—to his 'end of history' view of market capitalism. This is apparent throughout his work: from his dismissal of the "upper-class proletarian chic" of Victor Gollancz's "Left Book Club"—the distinguished series in which Karl Polanyi's first book[33] (ignored by Drucker) appeared—together with the Fabians as "a bunch of power-hungry, ultra rationalists" speaking "the illiterate jargon of the Marxists"—to his portraying as failures the only socialists in his autobiography: Karl Polanyi (who ended up "deeply disappointed") and Noel Brailsford (who "ceased to matter"). (70,175)

Other differences cut just as deeply, in the areas of means—namely, the use of reason—and ends, relating to the wellbeing of society as a whole. Drucker's curious devaluing of reason occurs as early as his first book. There, seemingly taking pride in "NOT" being an economist,[34] Drucker declares that the First World War, the Great Crash, the Depression and subsequent events demonstrated that "existence in this society is governed... by blind, irrational, and demonic forces."[35] To the extent that human agency is identified at all, it is represented for Drucker by the "masses" who are responsible for the rise of totalitarianism through seeking "a real order." Out of their despair is created a new "leadership principle"—"they worship a demon when they have no God." A decade later, Drucker still claimed that "man-made demons haunt our world." This time, though, they caused "the profound spiritual crisis of Western man," and "our frightening moral numbness."[36] Professing to being influenced by Kierkegaard, he proclaimed: "The specific disease of the modern West is the falling apart of human existence—the denial of life as both spirit and flesh, and denial of the meaningfulness of each for the other."[37] He then opts for the masses' solution—the leadership principle—though at first in a spiritualized form: "Political action is no substitute for the great Prophet who shall call this generation to repentance, for the great Saint who shall turn our vision back to the source of all light, or for the great poet who shall sing again of the greatness and dignity of Man."[38] (One can hardly imagine this sort of stuff finding a publisher today.) However, the Austrian-born Drucker's sensitivity towards literature is to be doubted, in view of his ignorance of the international reputation of "Robert Musil, the Austrian writer whose book *The Man without Qualities* [is] almost forgotten today." (*Bystander*, 58)

Later, he abandoned this unconvincing vision—for, coming back down to earth, he opted for the U.S. corporate version: namely, "CEO Supermen." The only drawback is, "the supply is both unpredictable and far too limited."[39] No matter. The future will be in the hands of the few, he does not doubt. "Top management will in fact be the company," he declares, for "everything else can be outsourced." (*Ibid*, p.230) The technique of leadership to which he looks had evolved within the business corporation, which he says has "brilliantly proved itself," prophesying that it will be the model for a seemingly endless number of "totally new social institutions." These will be the key to the human condition, making possible a new type of integration of the individual, community, and society in some future "Society of Organizations."

Almost half a century after expressing concern for the "individual dimension of man" (in his Kierkegaard article), Drucker hailed "the collapse of Marxism"—"the end of the belief in salvation by society"—as vindicating his belief that 'society' was opposed to 'the individual.'[40] Indeed, this was the key to what he deemed to be the Polanyis' failure. In his concluding peroration, Drucker comes to bury the Polanyis rather than to praise them. "This might well mean that society itself—that Great Baal and Moloch of modern man—might become secondary, and society's organization no more important, in the end, and no more controversial, than infallible religion became in the Age of Society that is now fading." Thus, the Polanyis' failure to find an alternative beyond capitalism and communism "might well foreshadow the end of the Age of the Infallible Society." (140) According to his thinking, the "end" of society "makes possible renewed emphasis on the individual"—though certainly not in terms of the "inwardness" of which he wrote earlier. Rather, the "fall" of communism inspired Drucker to disinter the Manchester liberal free market economy view of human nature and motivation. Thus, what is important for him is what the individual is expected to do for himself, through "a return to individual responsibility." (*Ibid*, p.13) He still seems to be under the impression—against all the evidence—that the market can deliver material benefits to all. That its rewards, far from being the infamous "trickle down," have already swollen to Niagara proportions; insisting that "over the past 75 years the proletarian [has been converted] into a middle-class bourgeois with near-upper-class income."[41] But by no means all. For in his 2001 "The Next Society," Drucker addresses, not without relish, the coming of renewed competition in the knowledge-based society, predicting that there will be "psychological pressures and emotional traumas of the rat race. There can be winners only if there are losers." (p.212) This hard-eyed glimpse of the future is very different from the vision which graces the closing pages of *The Great Transformation*.

It may be their contrasting responses to death that reveal most clearly what separates the two writers. For Drucker, the fact of death means that "the individual basically remains in despair," "only if society makes individual life meaningless, can a person die without despair."[42] Such fearful concern for one's own life, Polanyi would dismiss as "childish, unavailing complaints," before concluding, in the final paragraph of *The Great Transformation*:

> Resignation was ever the fount of man's strength and new hope. Man accepted the reality of death and built the meaning of his bodily life upon it. He resigned himself to the truth that he had a soul to lose and that there was worse than death, and founded his freedom upon it. (p.258B)

To Polanyi, this is what will serve man in his "task" which is, we note, *directed towards others*—namely, "to remove all removable injustice and unfreedom...[thus] creating more abundant freedom for all..."

One would like to think that Drucker has by now reached that stage in his life when men naturally ponder meanings, purposes, and ends. And that he will reconsider his youthful dismissal of Polanyi's deeply pondered final chapter, and draw consolation from memories of friendship with its ever generous author.[43]

NOTES
1. Beginning with *The Life and Work of Karl Polanyi. A Celebration*, edited by Kari Polanyi Levitt. Montreal: Black Rose Books, 1990.
2. New York: Harper & Row, 1978.
3. November 22, December 20, 2002; March 21, April 11, 2003.
4. Judit Szapor of the University of Ottawa, "Laura Polanyi 1882-1959. Narratives of a Life. *Polanyiana* (Budapest) vol.6, no.2, 1997 observes that Drucker's account is "based almost entirely on his imagination"; in her Letter (*Polanyiana*, vol.8, nos.1-2, 1999) she further criticizes Drucker's "outrageous fabrications" and "nonsense."
5. Letter of March 20, 1994 to Kari Polanyi Levitt (daughter of Karl Polanyi). Kari Levitt has often pointed out the errors in Drucker's chapter.
6. Barbara Striker writes (letter to *Polanyiana*, November 18, 1998) that her husband "had written many a letter to Harper & Row, demanding correction, all of which the Publisher sent to Drucker, who did not acknowledge his errors and was naturally unwilling to make any corrections."
7. His epithets represent a crescendo of indignation: "no," "not," "never" and "untrue" followed by "complete fake," "grave mistake," "another gross mistake," "completely unknown in the family," "sheer product of phantasy," "libelous misstatement—and sign of gross igno-

rance," "ridiculous," "perfectly absurd to assume," "this is a lie and a libel," "libelous statement," "plain untruth," "apparently Drucker never bothered to check his facts," "what a superficial work!" concluding with "again a gross misstatement of well-known historical facts."

8. Peter F. Drucker, 138 North Mountain Avenue, Montclair, New Jersey.

October 21, 1961

My Dear Karl,

I am not the oldest of your friends, admirers and disciples. I have never in a formal sense, been a 'student' of your. Yet I hope that I shall be allowed to join with all your friends and students on this occasion and send you the very warmest wishes on your seventy-fifth birthday.

It is now almost thirty-four years since I first came under your spell. You probably have long forgotten the occasion—I shall never forget it, as long as I live. It was in many ways the most important encounter in my life, certainly of my life as a writer and a student. Way back in 1927 I was, myself still a boy a of eighteen, permitted to sit in at an editorial meeting of the "*Oestereichischer Volkswirt*" [sic] at which the year-end issue was being discussed. I had heard your name before. I had read you often—for the "*Oestereichischer Volkswirt*" [sic] was the economic and political journal on which I had been raised. But for the first time I then heard you talk, heard you, in pure improvisation, give an analysis of the contemporary world which, in its breadth, in its world view, and in its searching penetration to the fundamentals, was something utterly new to me, and utterly breathtaking. I am quite sure I did not understand one-tenth of what you said—I did not know enough about China then, about the gold standard, about economic history—or about any of the many other areas your talk touched upon and used [sic] to present the picture of a world on the brink of dissolution.

Yet this short morning changed my own outlook, and my own attitude. I was probably already prepared—a few months earlier I had left home and had begun to live by myself, to work as a young clerk in a foreign country, and to study law on the side. And these few months had (or so it seemed in retrospect) created considerable doubt and uncertainty in my mind—a mind brought up in the certainties of a comfortable nineteenth century Liberalism which even the catastrophic events of my childhood—World War I and the years following it—did not really disturb. Your discussion, no matter how much of it went by me, suddenly made me realize that I lived in a different world, that I had no foundation under my feet, and that I had been looking at pretty picture postcards rather than at reality.

And again, over the years, you have done this great job of illumination a familiar landscape so as to bring out the new, the fundamental, the real in it again and again.

I could—perhaps I should—talk about the many specific insights I owe to you. But there are many who have learned more from you—I am afraid I have not been a good student. But I doubt whether anyone has been more deeply formed by your influence and your friendship.

Precisely, perhaps, because my area of work as well as my temperament are so unlike yours, the influence has been all the stronger. If I were to characterize it, it has continually forced me both to face up to the reality of basic change as against a facile conservatism, and to the reality of basic continuity in needs, institutions and values of mankind, as against a facile believed [sic] in 'progress' and good intentions.

If I were to sum it up—and to sum up thereby your one great quality, the quality that peoples of such different interests, such different opinions and such different origins brought together as your admirers and disciples—it is that quality of being eternally young, eternally ready to see the new, and yet reflect it against the truly permanent, the true wisdom of history and morality.

But perhaps at this occasion I might also be allowed to reminisce a little about our personal relationship. It has been a singularly intermittent one. It began when the difference in our ages—almost twenty-five years—was so great as to rule out, on the face of it, anything that could be called 'friendship.' Yet, as you have done with everyone else, you treated the callow youth as if he were your contemporary and your friend. You have always been able to do this. My daughter, now a grown and married woman of twenty-three, will never forget how, when she was barely two years old, during a Vermont summer, you used to come into her room in the morning and talk to her of Rousseau and of Speenhamland, as if she were your contemporary and your equal in learning. (In fact 'Rousseau' and Spenhamland' [sic] are her earliest childhood memories.) Over the years we have met and parted a good many times. A few meetings in Vienna were followed by years during which we did not see each other—and we have, it seems, never corresponded. Then again a few short meetings in England around 1934 and 1935—and again years without direct contact. Then that short but intensive period, just before and during the early years of World War II, when you and Ilona were in Bennington and when you, over here for a short visit at first, joined us for one peaceful summer—the summer before the Storm—and when we then later moved up to Bennington ourselves and spent one happy, snowbound winter as next door neighbours. And then finally the years in New York during which I was privileged to see you again and again and to watch the development of your great scholarly work, the development of the great organizing concepts of economic history.

In many ways you are the only person I know who, during these long years, has not had to change his basic position, his basic principles, his basic touchstone of right and wrong. And in many ways you are the one person who during these long turbulent years was always ahead of the changing time, always already in the morrow. You were always younger than the youngest of your students; and always wiser than the most accomplished of your colleagues, whether in scholarship or in political analysis. You have not founded a 'School'—this is reserved for those who confine themselves to a narrow area rather than to those who, like you, provide seminal ideas and fundamental integrity to whatever they touch. There will not, I am afraid, be any street named after you (though I understand that the United Nations have a proposal before them to change the name of Dahomey to Polanyia—after all you invented this particular country). But in a great many houses—in a great many disciplines, a great many areas of study, a great many traditions of political thought and analysis—there will always be room—small perhaps but important—which is the room you created, the room that is furnished with ideas, principles, and above all with a moral courage, which you provided. One has only to open a book today on the role of the Economy in society, on the rhythm of economic or social development, or on the ideas that inform economic history, to see how deeply, how permanently, how profoundly you have influenced all of us. But more than this, and in its own way more lasting too, is the powerful, the lasting, the normative impact you have had on all of us who have been privileged, over these long years, to come under your influence, and to enjoy the privilege and the great and abiding pleasure of being your students—and that has always meant also your friends.

Again all my very warmest birthday wishes. Forever yours [signed] Peter.

    Dr. Karl Polanyi,

    Pickering, Ontario

9. *A Functioning Society. Selections from Sixty-Five Years of Writing on Community, Society, and Polity.* New Brunswick (USA): Transaction Publishers, 2003. Part 3 "The Sickness of Government," "Introduction," p.53.

10. Subtitled: *The Political and Economic Origins of Our Time.* New York: Rinehart & Co., 1944.

11. "But just as the failure of a whole generation of brilliant thinkers to find the new synthesis between Catholicism and Protestantism in the late sixteenth and early seventeenth centu-

ries foreshadowed the end of the Age of Infallible Religion fifty years later, so the failure of the brilliant Polanyis to find the alternative beyond capitalism and communism might well foreshadow the end of the Age of the Infallible Society." (140)

12. Historical error is not confined to "The Polanyis." Thus, Drucker alleges that Europe's 13th and 16th centuries (the High Middle Ages and the Late Renaissance) were "totalitarian periods of darkness and despair." (*The End of Economic Man. A Study of the New Totalitarianism*. With an Introduction by H.N.Brailsford. New York: The John Day Co., 1939, p.262. Two decades later, though, he had second thoughts (*Post-Capitalist Society*, New York: HarperCollins, 1993, pp.1-2). In *Bystander* Drucker declares that "sexual repression...did not exist in the Austria...in which Freud grew up." (92)

13. Drucker also observes, "I got to know all the Polanyis except Otto, but Karl alone became a close friend." (132) In the 1920s, he claims, Cecile "was the first member of the family I met" (128); "I did see quite a bit of Adolph" in the 1950s in New York (130). Thus, he appears not to have met Laura, even though she lived in New York.

14. The Parents: "Michael Polanyi" (actually Mihály Polacsek), born "between 1825 and 1830" (b.1848), died "around 1900" (d.1905); "Cecilia" (Cecil Wohl), n.d. (1862-1939). The Children: "Mousie" (actually Laura) n.d. but references suggest 1880 (b.1882), died "late 1960s" (d. 1959); "Otto" (who did not exist), naturally n.d. born in the "early 1870s," was "still alive in the mid-thirties"; Adolf, n.d. references suggest 1871 (b.1883), "died within a year" following a meeting "in the 1950s" (d.1966); Karl, n.d. references correctly suggest 1886–964; Michael, "not born until 1891" (b. 1891 correct), "ending...in the 1960s" (d.1976); no reference is made to to Sophie (b.1888), or Pál (who died aged ten). Also: Ilona Duczynska (Karl's wife), n.d. "seventeen" in 1917 (b.1897); Kari, Karl's daughter, n.d. "about eight" in 1927, (b.1923).

15. It is just possible that "Otto" was confused with a distant relative Odön Pör who, however, had no such career.

16. See Laura Polanyi Striker, "Captain John Smith's Hungary and Transylvania," in Bradford Smith, *Captain John Smith; His Life and Legend*. Philadelphia: New York, 1953, Appendix, 311-347. And see *The New York Times*, December 24, 1959, for an appreciative obituary.

17. Except, very briefly in 1914, as secretary of the National Bourgeois Radical Party (not represented in Parliament). The extract is from his letter to Oscar Jászi, October 27, 1950.

18. In the words of Ilona Duczynska, "I First met Karl Polanyi in 1920...," in *Karl Polanyi in Vienna*, edited by Kenneth McRobbie and Kari Polanyi Levitt. Montreal: Black Rose Books, 2000.

19. While there is nothing in Polanyi's correspondence to substantiate this, in Drucker's *Bystander* there is cruel vignette of Columbia's President Nicholas Murray Butler. Also in a letter to Polanyi (October 22, 1957), Drucker observes: "I always, and on principles [sic], suspect Columbia of the basest of motives and of the least decent of behaviour—it has been their consistent record in my experience."

20. *The Ecological Vision. Reflections on the American Condition*. New Brunswick (USA): Transaction Publishers, 1993. [Essays written over 40 years], p.455.

21. "The first article of mine you ever saw...was ordered and bought by *you* for the "Oesteneichische Volkswirt" [sic] and appeared around 1932." (Letter to Karl Polanyi, December 4, 1962) For another misspelling(*Oestereichischer Volkswirt*") twice within four lines, see his letter to Karl Polanyi of October 21, 1961 (fn.8).

22. Richard A.Bermann, "Editorial Board Meetings of the *Oesterreichischer Volkswirt* (1928)," in *Karl Polanyi in Vienna*.

23. A war injury led to a severe hernia which family members reported caused him trouble for the rest of his life.

24. The personage who owns this voice, Drucker says, contrary to others' recollections, was "A very large man [who] burst into the room," "carrying what looked like a small steamer trunk under each arm"; he "let himself drop into a chair that almost collapsed under the shock," a cascade of papers and books coming from one receptacle, an avalanche of same from the other.

25. To Robert D. Leigh, 1940.
26. Lee Congdon, *Exile and Social Thought: Hungarian Intellectuals in Hungary and Austria, 1919-1933*. Princeton: Princeton University Press, p.233. It is unfortunate that Congdon had not read Drucker's "The Polanyis" with a more critical eye.
27. Felix Schaffer, "Vorgartenstrasse 203: Extracts from a Memoir," in *Karl Polanyi in Vienna*.
28. *The Ecological Vision*, p.455.
29. "Polanyi's identification of the social principles of economic integration: redistribution, reciprocity, and market exchange...the most important contribution...was noticed at the time only by a few." (137)
30. In 1958, a few days before going into hospital, Karl writes a long letter to Drucker in which he describes his work-in-progress, and his reduced financial circumstances, and concludes—with a degree of embarrassment reflected in his syntax—with saying that "It would be an immense relief to know that a sum...would supplement the pension as a friendly loan...[of] doll.600...repayable in a lump sum as soon as I earn again..." To this, Drucker replies (February 17, 1958): "I frankly fail to see what the problem is"; "the only intelligent thing for you to do is to borrow the money from the bank"; "the alternative would be to borrow from a member of your known family," from "several nephews and nieces who are doing very well indeed."
31. *Harper's*. March 1952, 68-74.
32. In her response of June 7 Duczynska observes that "you make a number of rather wild statements (which also have the character of premises)." To *Harper's* (June 17) she wrote: "Incidentally, the factual part of Mr.Drucker's article where land tenure is concerned will not bear scrutiny," adding that business principles would be misapplied in "a feudal (or tribal)" agrarian society. She amassed twenty-six pages of handwritten and typed comments on Drucker's article, and detailed references to selected agrarian societies. However, the magazine decided to drop the topic.
33. *Christianity and the Social Revolution*, edited by John Lewis, Karl Polanyi, Donald K. Kitchin. London: Victor Gollancz, Ltd, 1935.
34. *The Ecological Vision*, p.75. Though Drucker seems to take satisfaction in stating that he is 'NOT' an economist—he lets drop the information that he "sat at the feet" of "the greatest": namely, J.M.Keynes and Joseph Schumpeter. All his works may be said to be economistic.
35. *The End of Economic Man*. Chapter Three "The Return of the Demons," p.59.
36. *The New Society. The Anatomy of Industrial Order*. New York: Harper & Bros., 1949, 1950, p.352.
37. *The Ecological Vision*, p.428.
38. *The New Society*, p.352.
39. "The Next Society" (originally published in *The Economist*, 2001), 197-234, Part 19 of *A Functioning Society*, p.228.
40. *Post-Capitalist Society*, p.7.
41. "From Capitalism to Knowledge Society" (from *Post-Capitalist Society*, 1993), 157-167 Part 16 in *A Functioning Society*, p.158.
42. *Ibid.*, pp. 435, 428.
43. Perhaps he will also rethink his early view of "resignation" which has the opposite meaning to that on the final page of Karl's work. Thus, in 1939 Drucker wrote "In his self-imposed resignation *from society* [emphasis added], the individual...will produce new, non-economic social substance which he will endow with freedom." (*The End of Economic Man*, p.263).

Chapter Thirty-Three

TRACING POLANYI'S INSTITUTIONAL POLITICAL ECONOMY TO ITS CENTRAL EUROPEAN SOURCE
Kari Polanyi Levitt

The year 2004 marks the 60th anniversary of the publication of *The Great Transformation*. Although the book enjoyed steady and consistent sales since its publication, and many scholars of diverse disciplines and successive generations have told me that they were deeply influenced by it, there has recently been an explosion of new interest in the work of Karl Polanyi. *The Great Transformation* (1944) is now translated into fifteen languages and a Google search for Polanyi turns up some 30,000 hits.

Many authors have provided excellent expositions of the principal thesis of *The Great Transformation* and its relevance to contemporary globalisation. But none might give him more satisfaction, given his wish to engage the intellectual adversary, than to be identified as the most effective critic of the neo-liberal project for the 21st century by a senior fellow at the Cato Institute, a leading right-wing think tank. "He has emerged in recent years as a kind of patron saint of globalisation's critics. George Soros notes his intellectual debt in his acknowledgments at the beginning of *The Crisis of Global Capitalism*. Dani Rodrik of Harvard University and author of *Has Globalization Gone Too Far?* refers to him frequently. John Gray, a professor at the London School of Economics who wrote *False Dawn: The Delusions of Global Capitalism*, titled his first chapter "From the Great Transformation to the Global Free Market." These arguments are an almost perfect inversion of the truth. The tragedies of the 19th century stemmed not from an over-reliance on markets, but from a pervasive loss of faith in them."[1]

Without doubt, Polanyi's critique of the 19th century market economy and its fateful consequences resonate most strongly with critics of globalisation. In 1947, he believed universal capitalism was discredited everywhere except in the United States. He could not have imagined that the 19th century economic order would return to be acclaimed as a golden age of globalisation to serve as a model for universal capitalism.[2] It was his hope that his warnings of the destructive effects of subordinating society to the requirements of the market economy could save humanity from disasters more profound than anything experienced to date. In a letter written to a friend of his youth in 1958, six years before his death, he wrote:

> My life was a world life—I lived the life of the world. But the world stopped living for several decades, and then in a few years it advanced a century! So I am only now coming into my own, having somewhere lost 30 years on the way—waiting for Godot—until the world caught up again, caught up to me. In retrospect, it is all quite strange, the martyrdom of isolation was only apparent—ultimately, I was only waiting for myself. Now the scales are weighed against us —against you, against me—because in ten years, I would stand vindicated in my own lifetime. My work is for Asia and Africa, for the new peoples. The West should bring them spiritual and intellectual assistance; instead the west is destroying the traditions of the 19th century and is even demolishing its Victorian ideals...My ideas at last are drawing opposition and that is a good sign, I would dearly love to live to fight for them, but man is a mortal being.[3]

Fifty years had to pass before the originality of Karl Polanyi would emerge from relative obscurity to be embraced in so many quarters as a definitive critique of the fateful effects of the subordination of society to economic market criteria.[4] Not until the Asian Crisis of 1997 and disasters of instant market capitalism in Russia would his work be cited in thousands of speeches, papers, articles and policy statements.

The lessons of *The Great Transformation* were recovered, and Polanyi now features in academic discourse and journalistic comment. Among the first to cite Polanyi was the Harvard economist Dani Rodrik. His position was that proposals to construct a new financial architecture for the global economy were doomed to frustration because global capitalism is inherently impracticable, and indeed, we have never truly had a global capitalist system. The real question, he suggested, was how to make the world safe for different brands of national capitalism to prosper side by side? Until we understand this, he wrote, we cannot formulate workable solutions.

> To understand why, it helps to go back to *The Great Transformation* by the economic anthropologist Karl Polanyi, which was first published in 1944. Polanyi took issue with the nineteenth-century liberal idea of a self-regulating market. He argued that markets could not exist outside the web of social relations for long without tragic consequences. Indeed, he interpreted the turmoil of the interwar period and its aftermath—the collapse of the gold standard, the decline into protectionism and bilateralism, the rise of fascism and national socialism, and ultimately World War II—as the result of societies rising to protect themselves from the onslaught of the unregulated market.

The basic insights of the book germinated during formative years in Hungary and journalistic experience in Vienna. Ten years of teaching and research at Columbia University from 1947-1957 provided the opportunity to extend his historical research on economic livelihood back to archaic and primitive societies.

There was a constant theme in his world of thought. It was his insistence that there are no impersonal forces which absolve us from personal responsibility for the fate of fellow human beings. Ideas matter, when people cease to believe in the legitimacy of the powerful, their power is in decline.

A WORLD LIFE

Polanyi's life was indeed a 'world life', marked by three emigrations. He was born in 1886, in Vienna, but the family moved to Budapest shortly thereafter, and his formative years were Hungarian. He grew up in a comfortable upper middle-class family. His father was a civil engineer and a successful railway contractor until a prolonged season of bad weather ruined the business and the family descended into genteel poverty. His mother, daughter of a rabbinical scholar from Vilna, then in Russia, was known for her role in hosting gatherings of Budapest's literary, artistic and intellectual elite. The Polanyi children received a superb home education, including instruction in Latin and Greek, English, French, and German. Karl graduated from the University of Budapest in 1912 with a doctorate in law, the only university qualification he ever had. He was prominent in Hungarian intellectual life as the founding president of the Galilei Circle, a student movement, which undertook educational activities on a remarkable scale of 2000 classes per year. The ideology was one of Western Enlightenment, opposed to obscurantism, clericalism and the moribund political order of the Hungarian monarchy.

He was 28 in 1914 when he enlisted in the Austro-Hungarian army as a cavalry officer and served on the Russian front.[5] He was hospitalised and in 1919 he emigrated to Vienna where he was soon followed by a large exodus of Hungarians fleeing the White Terror. Among them was Ilona Duczynska; they were married in 1923. The Russian Revolution of 1917 was fighting for its existence in a prolonged civil war. Polanyi joined the wide-ranging debate on how a socialist economy could be constructed. The model he favoured was a functional form of guild socialism associated with the English social historian G.D.H. Cole and the Austro-Marxist Otto Bauer. He engaged in a debate on the feasibility of a socialist economy with Ludwig von Mises, mentor of Friedrich von Hayek, in the pages of the premier German-language social science journal, *Archiv fur Sozialwissenchaft und Sozialpolitik*. It was in this context that he studied the works of the leading exponents of the Austrian school of economics. For many years he struggled to construct a socialist economic model, which would combine economic criteria of technical efficiency with social and cultural requirements and democratic decision- making. Eventually, he abandoned this exercise and found in history and anthropology a more effective means of developing insights regarding the place of the economy in society. He remained, to the end of his life, a socialist. In a letter written a few days before his death, he wrote: "The heart of the feudal nation was privilege; the heart of the bourgeois nation was property; the heart of the socialist nation is the people, where collective existence is the enjoyment of a community culture. I myself have never lived in such a society."[6]

From 1924 his position as a senior editor of *Der Oesterreichische Volkswirt*, the leading financial and economic weekly of Central Europe, placed him in the eye of the storm of economic and political upheavals on the continent. From this observation post he followed the unravelling of attempts by the western powers to restore the pre-1914 economic order and its eventual break down in 1931, when the collapse of a major bank in Vienna triggered a financial crisis, which spread westward to England and the United States. "Conservative Twenties, Revolutionary Thirties" summarises these experiences.[7]

In 1933, when the deteriorating political climate did not permit the journal to keep a prominent socialist on their editorial staff, Polanyi left for England, but continued to write for the journal. Kari joined him in 1934. Ilona remained to engage in the struggles of the illegal opposition to Austrian fascism until 1936 when she also came to England.[8]

In his initial years in England Polanyi was associated with a small group of intellectuals and religious leaders who called themselves the Christian Left. He contributed an essay on "The Essence of Fascism" and co-edited *Christianity and the Social Revolution* (1935). Among other contributors was Joseph P. Needham.[9] To this group he brought a continental perspective and introduced them to Karl Marx's *The Economic and Philosophic Manuscripts of 1844*.[10] In 1937, recommendations by R.H. Tawney and G.D.H. Cole assisted him in obtaining employment as a tutor with the Workers' Education Association (WEA) teaching courses on international relations and English social and economic history, a subject entirely new to him. His encounter with the conditions of working-class life on overnight stays with the families who accommodated him was a profound culture shock. He contrasted the inferior status of the English working class in the richest country of Europe with the social and cultural achievements of the workers of socialist Red Vienna in impoverished post-1918 Austria. The lecture notes for his WEA classes[11] are the skeleton upon which he later developed *The Great Transformation*. Although the book was written at Bennington College, Vermont, in 1941 to 1943, it was in England that he located the origins of the disasters that befell Europe from 1914 to 1945.

From 1947 to his retirement in 1953, Polanyi taught a course in General Economic History as a visiting professor at Columbia University, and from 1953 to 1957 he co-directed an Interdisciplinary Research Project with Conrad Arensberg on economic aspects of institutional growth. The results of this research were published as *Trade and Market in the Early Empires* (1957). Several of his graduate students contributed to the volume, among others Anne Chapman. *Dahomey and the Slave Trade* with an introduction by Paul Bohannan was published posthumously with the assistance of Abraham Rotstein in 1966. A former student, George Dalton, produced the invaluable collection of essays by Karl Polanyi, *Primitive, Archaic and Modern Economies* (1968), and Harry Pearson edited a posthumous volume of Polanyi's writings, *The Livelihood of Man* (1977).

In 1950 the Polanyis made their home in Canada in Pickering, Ontario, because Ilona was blacklisted from entering the United States on the grounds of former communist activities in Hungary (1917 to 1920) and in Austria (1934 to 1936). In 1961, Karl initiated the journal *Co-existence* as a vehicle for dialogue across the Cold War divide. The editorial board included the eminent economists Joan Robinson, Gunnar Myrdal, Oskar Lange, Jan Tinbergen, P.C. Mahalanobis, Ragnar Frisch and Shigeto Tsuru. The first issue appeared shortly after his death in 1964.[12] Both my parents died in Canada and now rest in a cemetery in Budapest.

The most frequently cited biographical source on the life of Karl Polanyi is a chapter in Peter F. Drucker's memoirs, "The Polanyis."[13] In this highly entertaining exercise in imagined recollections of his friend Karl and other members of the family, almost none of the facts are correct, indeed some are manifestly absurd.[14] However, Drucker was perceptive in noting that the Polanyis sought "a new society that would be free and yet not 'bourgeois' or 'liberal'; prosperous and yet not dominated by economics; communal and yet not a Marxist collectivism." But he could not have been more wrong in dismissing Karl Polanyi as a "minor figure" whose "failure...signifies the futility of the quest for...the perfect, or at least the good society". Or in terming his research on the economic organisation of past civilizations a retreat "into academic busyness."[15]

THE GREAT TRANSFORMATION

Polanyi's thesis was that the economic and social upheavals and political tensions resulting from the utopian attempt to restore the 19th century liberal economic order, including the gold standard, after the First World War, were the essential cause of the world economic crisis and the demise of democracy in most of the states of continental Europe. Like Keynes, he understood that the gold standard was a social mechanism designed to restructure the domestic economies of debtor countries in the interest of *rentier* financiers. My other contribution to this volume, "The Great Transformation from the 1920s to the 1990s" prepared for the Fifth Karl Polanyi Conference in Vienna in 1994, explores similarities between the inter-war years and the neo-liberal project of restructuring the world to re-create the Golden Age of the 19th century.

In the rest of this paper, we review the basic concepts which underpin the narrative of *The Great Transformation*.

FICTITIOUS COMMODITIES

While markets have existed since earliest times, it was Polanyi's contention that price-making markets including the fictitious commodities of land, labour and money were an innovation more revolutionary than the mechanical inventions of early industrial capitalism. Land, labour and money are "fictitious" commodities because unlike true commodities they are not produced for sale. Natural resources including land are God-given; people do not have children to provide workers for the labour market; money is a social convention, a book-keeping entry validated by the sanctity of contract and codified in law.

The divorce of agricultural producers from their means of subsistence by the privatization (enclosure) of communal lands created a new underclass of vagabonds and paupers. The threat to social stability was countered by measures of poor relief and wage subsidy.

The critical step in the creation of an industrial proletariat in 19th century England was the abolition of poor relief by the draconian New Poor Law of 1834, which gave legal sanction to the degradation of wage labour. It was instituted by the Reform Parliament of 1832 which subordinated the landed oligarchy to the urban and industrial bourgeoisie. The result was the unleashing of productive forces and the accumulation of capital. But wages failed to rise above subsistence until the second half of the 19th century.

The classical economists were concerned with capital accumulation, economic growth and the distribution of income from production. They largely ignored the dispossession, displacement and human degradation by the destruction of social relations in which economic livelihood, social status, pride in craft, and cultural expression had previously been embedded.

Polanyi insisted that the creation of a self-regulating market by the commodification of land, labour and money required nothing less than the subordination of society to the requirements of the market economy. His central thesis was that the 19th century liberal economic order was 'economic' in a different sense from that in which all societies have been limited by the material conditions of existence. It was 'economic' in the distinctive sense that it chose to base itself on a motive never before raised to the level of justification of action and behaviour in everyday life, namely individual gain. (GT:30) Prior to the rise of industrial capitalism markets were never more than accessories of economic life. In that regard, the generalized market economy of modern capitalism stands as an exception.

Contrary to a commonly held belief, there was nothing natural or inevitable about the 19th century market system. As Polanyi demonstrated, *laissez-faire* liberalism was designed by the early English political economists and instituted by the power of the state. In a frequently quoted passage, Polanyi concluded that "*laissez-faire* was planned"—while the protective reaction against the discipline of the market was 'spontaneous.'(GT:147)

THE DOUBLE MOVEMENT

Regarding the creation of the self-regulating market, Polanyi warned, in a frequently cited passage that: "Such an institution could not exist for any length of time without annihilating the human and natural substance of society; it would have physically destroyed man and transformed his surroundings into a wilderness. Inevitably, society took measures to protect itself, but whatever measures it took impaired the self-regulation of the market, disorganized industrial life and thus endangered society in yet another way."(GT:3)

The reference here is to the 'double movement' of the explosive spread of market economy and checks to its expansion by protective civic, social and national movements. Polanyi interpreted legislation regarding public health, factory conditions, social insurance, public utilities, municipal services, and trade union rights in Victorian England as countervailing measures to check the societal effects of the unfettered expansion of capital. He noted, that on the continent, governments of widely different political complexions enacted similar measures including protection of industries and agriculture threatened by ruinous competition. These measures were instituted by state interventions at the national level. Following the First World War, social conflicts, arising from draconian financial requirements to conform to the rules of the gold standard, could not be mediated by the democratic process and resulted in the rise of authoritarian and fascist regimes in most of continental Europe.

When the world emerged from the Second World War to construct the international institutions which framed the post-war era, it was generally accepted that the market economy would have to serve national objectives of full employment and social security. Polanyi foresaw a world of regional blocks of diverse social and economic systems. The tide, it appeared, had turned against the unrestricted domination of the economy by capital. The historical swing of the pendulum had restored social control over the economy. This was the "great transformation" which closed the book on the economic liberalism of the English classical political economists.

The Bretton Woods international financial order permitted policy space for industrial countries to pursue full employment and social security financed by re-distributive fiscal arrangements. Developing countries were able to engage in import-substituting industrialization and long-term economic planning.

As Polanyi reminded us, however, the measures taken by society to protect itself could impair the functioning of the market and set in motion a counter-attack by capital to free itself from social constraints. This indeed is what has happened since the late 1970s, when declining productivity and profits, low or negative real interest rates favouring debtors and a wave of political radicalism in the South unleashed a counter-revolution favouring capital. A macro-economic regime change precipitated the Latin American debt crisis of the 1980s and the Reagan and Thatcher administrations dismantled gains made by labour in the first three post-war decades.

The liberalization of trade and capital in the last quarter of the 20th century has once again freed capital from regulation—now on a global scale. The dictates of financial capital are again governing markets. Combined with the predominance of trans-national corporations, the democratic political process in national societies has been undermined and corrupted. The provisions of the WTO regarding investment, competition, government procurement and intellectual property are specifically designed to bind states to supra-national agreements to protect investors from legislation at the national level. The struggle to protect society from the disintegrating forces of the market economy has moved to the international arena. Inequality has escalated to unprecedented levels but there are no international institutions to moderate the polarizing effects of the liberalisation of capital. Fiscal resources that sustained the welfare state in the industrialised countries are eroding. Indebted developing countries are in the grip of conditionalities, which do not permit them to follow strategies of economic development successful in the past.

A prolonged period of relative economic stability and strong economic growth in Europe and North America encouraged a reading of Polanyi's 'double movement' as a kind of self-correcting mechanism. Such illusions were shattered in the 1990s. The surge of portfolio capital seeking high returns and capital gains in the emerging markets of Asia and Latin America precipitated a series of severe financial and economic crises, most dramatically in the high growth economies of Asia.

A longer historical perspective reveals that Polanyi's 'double movement' is not a self-correcting mechanism to moderate excesses of market fundamentalism but an existential contradiction between the requirements of a capitalist market economy for unlimited expansion and the requirements of people to live in mutually supportive relations in society.

THE DISEMBEDDED ECONOMY

The concept of the disembedded economy is central to Polanyi's contention that the 19th century liberal economic order—the template of contemporary globalisation—was economic in a different sense than that in which economic livelihood was organised in all previous societies. The ultimate economic resources of labour, land and other natural resources are subject to mechanisms of supply and demand in markets for wage labour and private property. In describing the economy as a distinct and separate sphere of human activity, Polanyi wrote: "The disembedded economy...stood apart from the rest of society...In a market economy the production and distribution of material goods in principle is carried on through a self-regulating economic system of price-making markets. It is governed by laws of its own, the so-called laws of supply and demand, and motivated by fear of hunger and hope of gain."[16] Social relations of extended family, community and all other ties of traditional society are displaced by special economic institutions such as private property and the economic motive of individual gain.

Because the disembedding of the economy was socially unsustainable, Polanyi contended that society protected itself from impersonal market forces in a variety of ways.

Instability, insecurity and serious financial crises associated with globalisation have led scholars and policy-makers, including the World Bank, to embrace institutional reform and good governance. The disastrous consequences of the attempt to introduce instant market capitalism in Russia in the absence of legal and social institutions of civil society, or even basic guarantees of personal security, have drawn attention to the importance of institutional pre-requisites for a functioning capitalist market economy. In this connection, the "embedded economy" has gained currency in policy discourse and Polanyi is frequently cited. The institutional reforms advocated by the World Bank, emphasizing transparency, accountability and security of contract are indeed essential to the creation of a favourable investment climate. Markets must be embedded in such institutions. However, while accommodating the basic institutional requirements of a market economy, neoliberal policies have sought to eliminate institutions which have protected vulnerable sectors of the economy from the play of market forces such as subsidies on basic food items or granting credit to small farmers on special terms. The assumption here is that empowerment of civil society can substitute for the traditional role of the state. In reality, the rolling back of the state has *dis*-empowered civil society. The reduction of public provisions of health and education has impoverished people, and agglomerations of private economic power, including private mercenaries, have undermined public authority and the rule of law. The result has been to diminish the capacity of societies to determine the allocation of their own resources. As never before, the economic livelihood of people is beyond national control, as instanced by collapsing commodity prices, financial crises triggered by footloose capital, the relocation of production facilities to cheaper sources of labour, and the destruction of domestic food production by liberalised imports. In this regard, globalisation has *dis*-embedded economic life on an international scale, and there are, at this time, no effective international institutions which can redress the gross imbalance of power.

The disembedded economy has been dismissed by my colleague who wrote the introduction to the new edition of *The Great Transformation*. Fred Block contends that Polanyi's real discovery was the 'always embedded economy.' He is of the view that there is a basic contradiction within the text of *The Great Transformation*. He maintains that there was a shift from Polanyi's earlier Marxist influence to a later revision of his views, and that circumstances did not permit him to revise the manuscript of *The Great Transformation* to resolve this contradiction: "Polanyi glimpsed, but was not able to name or elaborate the idea of the always embedded market economy."[17] "We can make systematic use of Polanyi's insight in the GT (*The Great Transformation)* once we have 'unpacked' the text and shown the tensions between Polanyi's original Marxist architecture for the book and the new ideas he developed as he was writing them."

By discarding the disembedded economy, Block moved Polanyi into the mainstream of socio-economic discourse. The effect is to obscure the radical implications of the existential contradiction between a market economy and a viable society. There is a suggestion here that Polanyi was influenced by Marxism in the turbulent interwar years and that there was an ideological shift during the writing of the book in the United States from 1941to1943. Such an interpretation fails to understand what Polanyi accepted and what he rejected in Marx.

Polanyi shared Marx's fundamental insight into the historically limited nature of the organisation of economic life by the universalization of the market principle, including private ownership of the means of production. His account of the societal consequences of the commodification of money, land, labour and indeed the essentials of life, recalls the Marx of *The Economic and Philosophical Manuscripts* (1932). What he rejected was the Ricardian labour theory of value and the economism of historical materialism, including the Marxian theory's stages of growth. Whereas Marx anticipated the eventual breakdown of the capitalist order on account of inherent *economic* contradictions, Polanyi emphasised the contradiction between the requirements of the capitalist market economy for limitless expansion and the human requirement to be sustained by mutually supportive social relations. In Polanyi's account of this existential contradiction the outcome is not determinate. There is no grand design of progress. There are no impersonal historical forces which inevitably move humanity forward.

There is no evidence of a "theoretical shift" (Block,2001:2) in Polanyi's thinking during the writing of *The Great Transformation*. What may appear to Fred Block as a contradiction is due to his misconceptions of the relationship of Polanyi to Marx. Fortunately, we have testimony on the writing of *The Great Transformation* by its author, in a letter written to me from Bennington College, Vermont, dated February 23rd, 1941. We note that the outline of the book, as we know it, was complete at the time this letter was written, and that there was a deliberate decision to refrain from reading new material or extending beyond the original outline. Polanyi's admiration for the New Deal, formed during several visits to the United States in the 1930s, is explicit in the final passages of the letter. There is no evidence of new influences during his stay at Bennington College from 1941 to 1943.

> So about four weeks ago I began writing, and tomorrow I intend to go to New York to hand the Introduction and the first three chapters to the publishers. Curiously enough, it is not a draft, but a finished text, ready for print. Of the many surprises the writing was connected with, this is one. When Mother arrived, I had only an outline, in 25 chapters, appr. 20,000 words. I vaguely intended to amplify it and make it three times as long, before starting out to write the book. But hardly had I started out, I changed my mind and simply wrote the first chapter, which at once settled the book. Or now I knew what I had not even suspected before, namely, the length, shape and

character of the book. So, my Darling, now I can tell you. It is going to be called *Liberal Utopia, The Origins of the Cataclysm*. It will be a very straight forward, simple story, easy to read and mainly historical in character, recounting the history of English enclosures, the Industrial Revolution, Speenhamland. But the two introductory chapters will deal with the Hundred Years Peace and the 'Conservative twenties, Revolutionary thirties'. The last chapters deal with America, Russia, the history of Economic theory and the history of the theory of the liberal state, It ends up with the formulation of new concept of freedom, the reform of human consciousness, the transcending of Christianity. The structure is extremely strict and formal. The bulk of the book is called 'Rise and Fall of Market Economy' and takes some 20 chapters of the 25. It consists of three sections: A. Satanic Mill. B. Self-Protection of Society, and C. Deadlock. There will be no footnotes, but all annexes will be added at the end with all notes under chapter headings; the notes will be full, and very much part of the book; written so as to be read—with gusto, even separately. I won't do any extensive reading any more, if I can possibly avoid it, but only the reading needed to check all my statements insofar as the writing takes one beyond the original scope. The book will have appro 500 pages.

Mother was the greatest help imaginable. She typed the fresh MS pages for me so that I could at once correct them and rewrite them myself; she listened to every two or three pages as they were written, which is a tremendous thing, for it assists one to see exactly where you are. And she was so encouraging as we know only she can be. In America the title will have to be different, here *liberal* means progressive, or more precisely what *radical* meant in England, until not long ago. (By *radical* they mean here an anarchist or a communist; while the English term *liberal* is untranslatable into American unless you say *laissez-faire*, or more often *conservative*!) Hoover, e.g. is called a conservative because he is a liberal (in the English sense), while Roosevelt is called a liberal, meaning that he is for the New Deal. Therefore Liberal Utopia would be taken to mean an attack on supporters of the New Deal—which would be almost the opposite of my purpose. I intend to call it here *The Great Transformation: Origins of the Cataclysm*.

As we enter the 21st century, we witness societal disintegration manifested in genocidal wars, displaced populations, the pandemic of HIV/AIDS, ethnic and religious conflicts and irreversible damage to the natural environment that sustains life on earth. Our world is arguably more turbulent and dangerous than Polanyi's. The impulse of social protection of societies threatened by the concentration of economic, financial and increasingly military power may be mobilized by appeals to solidarities as diverse as class, race, ethnicity, caste, religious belief or nationalism. Where the conflict between the 'economic' and the 'social,' cannot be resolved there is chaos. In the so-called failed states, social and civic relations of mutual support have disintegrated.[18] It is not by coincidence that Polanyi's warning of the fateful consequences of liberating capitalist market relations from social control has such resonance today.

RECIPROCITY, REDISTRIBUTION AND EXCHANGE

We first encounter reciprocity and redistribution in chapter 4 of *The Great Transformation*, drawn from Polanyi's early readings of anthropological writings of Malinowski and Thurnwald. To introduce a measure of order into the endless variations of the organization of economic life, Polanyi posited three forms of integration: reciprocity, redistribution and exchange. To be effective as integrative mechanisms, reciprocity requires movements between designated symmetrical groupings as in kinship relations; redistribution of goods in and out of a centre requires centricity and is generally accompanied by hierarchy; and exchange requires a system of price-making markets. These patterns of integration do not derive from the summation of individual acts but are conditional on the existence of specific institutions. They do not represent stages of development; no sequence in time is implied. However, "economic systems" may be classified according to the dominant form of integration, corresponding to the manner in which labour and land are instituted in society to produce the material requirements of life. Thus, in communal societies, kinship relations of reciprocity predominate in the allocation of land and labour; in the floodwater empires, land was largely distributed and sometimes redistributed by palace or temple, and so to some degree was labour; and the rise of the market to a ruling force in the economy can be traced by noting the extent to which land and food were mobilized through exchange, and labour was turned into a commodity free to be purchased in the market."[19] We note Polanyi's consistent reference to man and nature, labour and land, toil and soil as the ultimate economic resources of every society, and the institutional modalities regarding land are no less significant than those regarding labour.

In the history of economic thought, that man and nature are the original sources of wealth is a forgotten contribution of the Austrian school of economics. The emphasis on labour as the ultimate source of value derives from English political economy, elaborated by Ricardo and appropriated by Marx. Natural resources acquire value only when labour is applied to their extraction or use. In neo-classical economics, they have value only if they are scarce; hence, the well-known paradox, that air and water have no value because they have no exchange value, and diamonds are valuable because they are scarce. The unsustainable impact of the commodification of natural resources has attracted environmental economists to Polanyi's critique of market economy and market society.[20]

Polanyi rejected Marxist historical "stages" of slavery, feudalism and capitalism based on the predominant labour regime as historically untenable. His three patterns of integration have an interesting correspondence with Samir Amin's three modes of production: the primitive communal, tributary and capitalist. It must be noted that elements of all three patterns of integration are found in every society. Reciprocity relations of kinship persist in varying degree to modern times, redistributive institutions may be found in communal societies and play a crucial role in all variants of national capitalism, and markets, as Polanyi noted, are not a new phenomenon.

RELEVANCE OF POLANYI'S HISTORICAL AND THEORETICAL CONTRIBUTION
"The Economy as an Instituted Process" is perhaps the most comprehensive account of Polanyi's attempt to construct a general theory of the organization of economic livelihood. In this approach, based on a substantive definition of economics as " man's relation to land in providing the essentials of life," the market as the principal integrative mechanism is a special case. His un-packaging of the triad of trade, market and money from the baggage of assumptions drawn from the modern market economy and formalized in mainstream economics, opened a large and promising area of research of economic institutions in archaic and primitive societies.

Because the self-regulating market is, as Polanyi illustrated, an unattainable ideal fraught with social and ecological disaster, social institutions constrain and regulate the market, and public goods are provided by the state whose fiscal operations also finance more or less comprehensive redistributive measures. Reciprocity exists beyond relations of kinship in social obligations of all kinds. International trade is not exclusively commercial, and may be motivated by political arrangements of mutual advantage. It is generally subject to international agreement. National currencies are a form of special purpose money particularly when they are not convertible. Informal arrangements of local special purpose money may facilitate exchange within a community. Barter is a form of non-market exchange, and non-market elements are present in a variety of cooperative associational or non-profit activities. When the formal economy breaks down, or otherwise fails to clear markets, non-market exchange plays a crucial role in survival strategies of individuals, communities and enterprises.

Globalisation presents a challenge of how to reconcile participation in international trade with the requirement of societies to be anchored in social and cultural institutions. When the state is unable to mediate conflict, support individual and community creativity, provide economic and social infrastructure and ensure that the gains of economic growth are shared by all, the benefits of growth will be captured by middle- and upper-income earners. Market forces of polarization will disembed the economy from traditional social relations and people will seek solidarities of community, ethnicity, religious belief or other associations of the excluded. Polanyi's rejection of economic motives of individual gain as fundamental to human nature and his research into a diversity of patterns of economic organisation suggest that economic livelihoods can be instituted in a great variety of ways. This however, is incompatible with the universalisation of the market principle. It implies a civilisational transformation in accord with the fundamental need of people to be sustained by social relations of mutual respect.

NOTES
1. Brink Lindsey, "The Decline and Fall of the First Global Economy," *Reason*, December 2001.
2. Karl Polanyi, "Universal Capitalism or Regional Planning," *The London Quarterly of World Affairs*, January, 1945.
3. Letter written to a lifetime friend, Bé de Waard,1958, cited in Kari Levitt and Marguerite Mendell, "Karl Polanyi his Life and Times," *Studies in Political Economy*, Spring 1987, issue no.22 pp. 7-39.
4. A Google search for Polanyi turns up some 30,000 hits.
5. For a useful collection of papers on the Polanyi family and Karl's contribution to Hungarian intellectual life presented at the centenary conference in Budapest 1986, see Kari Polanyi Levitt, ed., *The Life and Work of Karl Polanyi*. Montreal: Black Rose Books, 1990.
6. From a letter written to Rudolph Schlesinger, editor of the journal *Co-existence* founded by Karl Polanyi in 1964.
7. For historical documentation including memoirs on the life of the Polanyis in Vienna in the 1920s see Kenneth McRobbie and Kari Polanyi Levitt, eds., *Karl Polanyi in Vienna, The Contemporary Significance of the Great Transformation*. Montreal: Black Rose Books, 2000; pp 255-328.
8. See her book, *Workers in Arms The Austrian Schutzbund and the Civil War of 1934*. New York and London: Monthly Review Press, 1978.
9. Joseph Needham, Christian socialist, eminent scholar best known for his *Science and Civilisation in China*. Cambridge: Cambridge University Press, 1954.
10. This was first published in Germany in 1931 and smuggled out of the country to Switzerland when the Nazis came to power.
11. Available in the archive of the Karl Polanyi Institute of Concordia University in Montreal.
12. Rudolf Schlesinger, ed.,*Co-Existence*, November 1964.
13. Peter Drucker, "The Polanyis" in *Adventures of a Bystander*. New York:Harper & Row,1978, pp.123-140. Drucker came from Vienna to the United States, where he became a leading authority on the modern corporation.
14. Kenneth McRobbie's systematic conference paper, "Re-Reading an Anti-Polanyi. Peter F. Drucker on 'The Polanyis'" reveals that of over one hundred "facts" only 13 are correct.
15. Drucker, p.138.
16. In a seminal article entitled "Aristotle Discovers the Economy," Polanyi returned to a central theme of *The Great Transformation*. See Karl Polanyi, with C.M.Arensberg and H.W.Pearson, *Trade and Market in the Early Empires*. Glencoe, Illinois: Free Press, 1957.
17. Fred Block, "Karl Polanyi and the Writing of the Great Transformation," presented at the Eighth International Karl Polanyi Conference, Mexico City 2001,on *Economy and Democracy*.
18. James Putzel, "Politics, the State, and the Impulse for Social Protection: the Implication of Karl Polanyi's Ideas for Understanding Development and Crisis," *Crisis Working Paper* no.18, Oct. 2002 http://www.crisisstates.com/Publications/wp/wp18.htm.
19. Polanyi, "The Economy as an Instituted Process," in *Trade and Markets in the Early Empires*, p.255.
20. Herman Daley and others.

LIST OF CONTRIBUTORS

Amin, Samir. The Third World Forum, Dakar.
Andor, László. Department of Political Science, Budapest University of Economic Sciences.
Bermann, Richard A. Editorial Board of the *Oesterreichische Volkswirt*, Vienna.
Block, Fred. Department of Sociology, University of California, Davis.
Bodnár, György. Institute of Literature, Budapest.
Cangiani, Michele. Faculty of Arts and Philosophy, Università di Venezia.
Chavdarova, Tanya. Department of Sociology, Sofia University.
Czjzek, Eva. Translator, Vienna.
Drainville, André. Department of Political Science, Université de Laval, Québec.
Duczynska Polanyi, Ilona. Rosebank, Pickering, Ontario.
Gábor, Eva. Department of Philosophy, Technical University of Budapest; The Michael Polanyi Liberal Philosophical Association.
Gyurgyák, János. Editor-in-Chief, Osiris Publishers, Budapest.
Hettne, Björn. Peace and Development Research. University of Goteburg.
Helleiner, Eric. Department of Political Science, York University, Toronto.
Juhász, Ferenc. Poet, Budapest.
Konrád, György. Novelist, essayist, and sociologist, Budapest.
Konstantinov, Yulian. Bulgarian Society for Regional Studies, Sofia.
Kregel, J.A. Department of Economics, Università di Bologna.
Litván, György. Institute of History, Budapest.
Lomnitz, Larissa Adler. Research Institute in Mathematical Applications, National Autonomous University of Mexico.
Matjan, Gregor. Institute for Advanced Studies, Vienna.
McRobbie, Kenneth. Department of History, University of British Columbia.
Mendell, Marguerite. Institute of Political Economy, Concordia University, Montréal.
Müller, Birgit. Centre nationale de la recherche scientifique, IRESCO, Paris.
Pfabigan, Alfred. Institute of Philosophy, University of Vienna.
Pirker, Reinhard. University of Economics and Business Administration, Vienna.
Polanyi, Karl. Rosebank, Pickering, Ontario; Department of Economics, Columbia University.
Polanyi Levitt, Kari. Department of Economics, McGill University; Department of Economics, The University of the West Indies, Jamaica.
Schaffer, Felix. Vienna; Department of Economics, University of Auckland.
Scott, Alan. Department of Sociology, University of East Anglia.
Striker, Barbara. Scientist, Budapest.
Vezér, Erzsébét. Institute of Literature, Budapest.

CRITICAL PERSPECTIVES ON HISTORIC ISSUES

Inspired by Karl Polanyi's work entitled *The Great Transformation* (1944), a whole generation of leading international scholars and critics carry on in the Polanyi tradition. This series, ISSN: 1195-1869, from the work of the Karl Polanyi Institute of Political Economy at Concordia University in Montréal, is the result.

ARTFUL PRACTICES: Political Economy of Everyday Life
Henri Lustiger-Thaler, Daniel Salée, editors

The social practices of survival are examined through case studies from Italy, the United Kingdom, Chile, Trinidad and Tobago, the United States, Canada, and Israel. Contributors include: Gavin Smith, Jane Wheelock, Enzo Mingione, Larissa Lomnitz, Ana Melnick, Menachem Rosner, Maurice Roche, S. Michael Miller, Warren Magnusson, Henri Lustiger-Thaler, Daniel Salée.

> ...enjoyable and inspiring...a colorful collection with a wide variety of well-researched case studies, fresh theoretical insights and future perspectives. —*Antipode*

HENRI LUSTIGER-THALER is Professor of Sociology at the School of Social Sciences and Human Sciences, Ramapo College of New Jersey, Mahwah, NJ. DANIEL SALEE is Professor of Political Science and Vice Principal of the School of Community and Public Affairs, Concordia University, Montreal.

    Volume 4, 1995 : 188 pages
    Paperback ISBN: 1-895431-92-1 $19.99
    Hardcover ISBN: 1-895431-93-X $48.99

CULTURE AND SOCIAL CHANGE: Social Movements in Québec and Ontario
Colin Leys, Marguerite Mendell, editors

These essays, written by activists, provide an overview of contemporary culture and politics in Canada, as well as deal with the role of social movements and the role of inter-church coalitions. Contributors include: Jean-Pierre Deslauriers, Colin Leys, Marguerite Mendell, Gregor Murray, Mona-Josee Gagnon, Laurie Adkin, Serge Quenneville, Rosemary Warskett, Micheline De Seve, Gragory Baum, Joe Mihevc, Michael McConkey, Henri Lustiger-Thaler, Louis Favreau, John Clark.

> The diversity of the topics reflects the multiplicity of political struggles. The editors correctly let the chapters speak for themselves.
> —*Canadian Book Review Annual*

COLIN LEYS is a Professor of Political Studies at Queen's University at Kingston. MARGUERITE MENDELL is Professor of Economics at the School of Community and Public Affairs, and Principal of the Karl Polanyi Institute of Political Economy, at Concordia University, Montreal.

    Volume 2, 1993 : 230 pages
    Paperback ISBN: 1-895431-28-X $19.99
    Hardcover ISBN: 1-895431-29-8 $48.99

CRITICAL PERSPECTIVES ON HISTORIC ISSUES

ECONOMY AND SOCIETY: Money, Capitalism and Transition
Fikret Adaman, Pat Devine, editors

Reinterprets the history of economic thought and re-examines monetary theory in general. Contributors include: László Andor, Ayse Buðra, Jeffrey Carpenter, Gibin Hong, Bob Jessop, Tadeusz Kowalik, Roger Krohn, Larissa Lomnitz, Yahya Madra, Sina Mandalinci, Jérôme Maucourant, Patrice Meyer-Bisch, Jean-Yves Moisseron, Surendra Patel, Hélène Pellerin, James Stodder, Ngai-Ling Sum, Behzad Yaghmaian.

FIKRET ADAMAN is Associate Professor at Bogazici University, Turkey. PAT DEVINE is Senior Lecturer in Economics, University of Manchester, UK.

    Volume 11, 2001 : 524 pages
    Paperback ISBN: 1-55164-186-0 $39.99
    Hardcover ISBN: 1-55164-187-9 $68.99

EUROPE: CENTRAL AND EAST
Marguerite Mendell, Klaus Nielsen, editors

Puts the mass of changes in the former USSR and the eastern bloc into a larger historical and sociological perspective. Contributors include: John Campbell, Mihailo Crnobrnja, Agnes Czako, Endre Sik, Jerzy Hausner, Bob Jessop, Tadeusz Kowalik, Domenico Mario Nuti, Birgit Muller, Yakov M. Rabkin, Hilary Wainwright, and Claire Wallace.

MARGUERITE MENDELL is the managing editor of this series. KLAUS NIELSEN is Associate Professor of Economics and Director of the Public Administration Program, Roskilde University, Denmark.

    Volume 5, 1995 : 298 pages
    Paperback ISBN: 1-895431-90-5 $19.99
    Hardcover ISBN: 1-895431-91-3 $48.99

FROM POLITICAL ECONOMY TO ANTHROPOLOGY: Situating Economic Life in Past Societies
Colin Duncan, David Tandy, editors

Represents a better understanding of ancient people's attempts at situating economic life within society. Contributors include: David Tandy, Colin Duncan, Walter C. Neale, Walter Donlan, Ian Morris, John Adams, Vernon L. Scarborough, Makoto Maruyama, William C. Schaniel, Rhoda Halperin.

    Demonstrate the breath of Polanyi's influence. —*From My Bookshelf*

COLIN DUNCAN is Adjunct Assistant Professor of History at Queen's University, Kingston. DAVID TANDY is Associate Professor of Classics at the University of Tennessee in Knoxville.

    Volume 6, 1995 : 186 pages
    Paperback ISBN: 1-895431-88-3 $19.99
    Hardcover ISBN: 1-895431-89-1 $48.99

CRITICAL PERSPECTIVES ON HISTORIC ISSUES

HUMANITY, SOCIETY AND COMMITMENT: On Karl Polanyi
Kenneth McRobbie, editor

Based on some of Polanyi's lesser known works: his journalism, letters, articles, conversations, books long out of print, and translations of Hungarian poetry. The contributors include: Jordan Bishop, Michele Cangiani, Marguerite Mendell, Marco Eller Vainscher, Endre Nagy, Kari Polanyi Levitt, Daniel Fusfeld, Abraham Rotstein, and Kenneth McRobbie.

KENNETH MCROBBIE is a poet and historian who teaches Cultural Studies and Intellectual History at the University of British Columbia. He collaborated with Karl and Ilona Polanyi in a volume of English translations of Hungarian poetry *The Plough and the Pen.*

Volume 3, 1994 : 178 pages
Paperback ISBN: 1-895431-84-0 $19.99
Hardcover ISBN: 1-895431-85-9 $48.99

LIFE AND WORK OF KARL POLANYI: A Celebration
Kari Polanyi Levitt, editor

Although the principle concern of this book is in developing Polanyi's thinking for its significance to the practice of economics and everyday life in democratic societies, it also treats the life of Polanyi from a perspective that conveys an impression of the man, his times, and his place in the evolution of social and economic thought. Contributors include: Jósef Bognár, Erzébét Vezér, György Litván, György Dalós, Doug Brown, Peter Rosner, Lee Congdon, Walter Goldfrank, Attila Agh, Abraham Rotstein, Kari Polanyi Levitt, Endre Nagy, Alfredo Salsano, Walter C. Neale, Margaret Somers, George Dalton, Gérald Berthoud, Mihály Sárkány, Géza Komóroczy, J. Ron Stanfield, Björne Hettne, Colin Duncan, Makoto Maruyama, Ayse Bugra, Hans Zseisel.

> Polanyi's insights into the social and political impact of the market-driven economy were both timely and prescient, and have guaranteed him a place among the great thinkers of the twentieth century...a good starting place for those wanting to know more about Polanyi. —*Canadian Book Review Annual*

> ...a unique and compelling blend of the Enlightenment tradition with the more existential thinking of the twentieth century.
> —Prof. J.R. Stanfield

KARI POLANYI LEVITT taught for many years at the University of the West Indies and in the economics department of McGill University, where she is now Emeritus Professor. She co-founded the Karl Polanyi Institute of Political Economy at Concordia University, Montreal.

Volume 1, 1990 : 264 pages, photographs
Paperback ISBN: 0-921689-80-2 $19.99
Hardcover ISBN: 0-921689-81-0 $48.99

MILANO PAPERS: Essays in Societal Alternatives
Michele Cangiani, Marguerite Mendell, editors

The writers of this collection, enriched by Polanyi's understanding of economic development, propose new concepts and goals for economic projections. Contributors include: Samir Amin, Zygmunt Bauman, Gérald Berthoud, Abraham Rotstein, Ayse Bugra, Alberto Chilosi, Alfredo L. de Romana, Pat Devine, Colin Duncan, Bjorn Hettne, Tadeusz Kowalik, Alain Lipietz, Tomory Marta, J. Martinez-Alier, Mario Nuti, Ulf Olsson, Jean-Michel Servet, Claus Thomasberger and Leo Valiani.

MARGUERITE MENDELL has written and edited many books on changing economies. MICHELE CANGIANI is Professor of History at the Universita degli Studi di Venezia, Italy.

>Volume 7, 1996 : 254 pages
>Paperback ISBN: 1-55164-022-8 $19.99
>Hardcover ISBN: 1-55164-023-6 $48.99

PREHISTORY AND HISTORY: Ethnicity, Class and Political Economy
David Tandy, editor

Stretching from the Mycenaean Greeks of the second millennium to the Athenians of the fourth century B.C.E., this volume features the work of prominent scholars in the fields of classics, history, and archaeology. Essays include the study of a Bronze Age, the economy of Iron Age Cyprus, early Greek economic development, and Athens in the fourth century. Contributors include: Thomas F. Tartaron, Ruth Palmer, Jeremy McInerney, David Rupp, Astrid Möller, David W. Tandy, Darel Tai Engen.

DAVID TANDY is Professor of Classics, University of Tennessee, Knoxville.

>Volume 10, 2001 : 204 pages
>Paperback ISBN: 1-55164-188-7 $29.99
>Hardcover ISBN: 1-55164-189-5 $58.99

SOCIAL ECONOMY: International Debates and Perspectives
Eric Shragge, Jean-Marc Fontan, editors

Coming at social economy from different vantage points and raise questions which reflect these, essays link practice and policy questions to issues. Contributors include: Enzo Mingione, Michele Cangiani, Jack Quarter, Paul Leduc Browne, Andrea Levy, Kathryn Church, Benoît Lévesque and Bill Ninacs, Jean-Luc Souchet, Louis Favreau, Michael Toye.

ERIC SHRAGGE is a Professor of Social Policy and Community Organization at the School of Social Work, McGill University. JEAN-MARC FONTAN is a Professor of Sociology at Université du Québec.

>Volume 9, 2000 : 205 pages, bibliography
>Paperback ISBN: 1-55164-162-3 $24.99
>Hardcover ISBN: 1-55164-163-1 $53.99

ESSENCE OF CAPITALISM: The Origins of Our Future
Humphrey McQueen

A timely account of globalization, the consumer culture, and the historical roots of our contemporary dilemmas. By tracking the 130-year history of Coca-Cola (and a number of other large corporations), this book details all that is best, worst and most powerful about global capitalism.

> Highly recommended. All libraries. —*CHOICE Magazine*

> McQueen's engrossing book...is a through and meticulously documented history of the fortunes of the brewers, bottlers and marketers of Coca-Cola...that casts its net wide. —*Sydney Morning Herald*

> An accessible, yet agreeably densely packed 130 year exploration of capitalism...seriously entertaining. —*The Weekend Australian*

> Takes the reader not only down the main streets of capitalism but also through less familiar back lanes. A compelling read...both fascinating and empowering. —*Australian Bookseller and Publisher*

HUMPHREY McQUEEN features regularly as a commentator on Australian radio and as a contributor to various newspapers, and magazines.

399 pages
Paperback ISBN: 1-55164-220-4 $28.99
Hardcover ISBN: 1-55164-221-2 $57.99

THORSTEIN VEBLEN AND THE AMERICAN WAY OF LIFE
Louis Patsouras

Thorstein Veblen (1857-1929) was an unrelenting critic of the American way of life. In his first and best-known work, *The Theory of the Leisure Class*, Veblen defined the social attitudes and values that condoned the misuse of wealth and the variety of ways in which the resources of modern society were wasted. Though most famous for the term "conspicuous consumption"—a pattern of consumerism that more than survives to the present day—he also attacked other American institutions and traditions, but his ideas were often dismissed because of his reputation as an eccentric.

By setting Veblen's work in its social and intellectual context, and by considering Veblen not just as an economist or a sociologist—as has been the case up to now—Patsouras also examines Veblen's politics, in particular the early manifestations of American socialism and anarchism, as well as his support of labor unions. Veblen's views are then compared and contrasted with other well-known historical and contemporary thinkers.

LOUIS PATSOURAS is Professor of History at Kent State University. He is the author of *The Anarchism of Jean Grave* (Black Rose Books).

380 pages
Paperback ISBN: 1-55164-228-X $24.99
Hardcover ISBN: 1-55164-229-8 $53.99

BOOKS of RELATED INTEREST from BLACK ROSE BOOKS

PARTICIPATORY DEMOCRACY: Prospects for Democratizing Democracy
Dimitrios Roussopoulos, C.George Benello, editors

With its emphasis on citizen participation, here, presented in one volume are the best arguments for participatory democracy written by some of the most relevant contributors to the debate, both in an historic, and in a contemporary, sense. This wide-ranging collection probes the historical roots of participatory democracy in our political culture, analyzes its application to the problems of modern society, and explores the possible forms it might take. Part II, "The Politics of Participatory Democracy," covers Porto Alegre, Montreal, the new Urban ecology, and direct democracy.

The book is, by all odds, the most encompassing one so far in revealing the practical actual subversions that the New Left wishes to visit upon us. —*Washington Post*

Contributors include: George Woodcock, Murray Bookchin, Don Calhoun, Stewart Perry, Rosabeth Moss Kanter, James Gillespie, Gerry Hunnius, John McEwan, Arthur Chickering, Christian Bay, Martin Oppenheimer, Colin Ward, Sergio Baierle, Anne Latendresse, Bartha Rodin, and C.L.R. James.

DIMITRIOS ROUSSOPOULOS, a political economist who has written widely on social and politico-economic issues, is the author *The Public Place* and *Dissidence: Essays Against the Mainstream*. C.GEORGE BENELLO (1927-1987) taught sociology at Goddard College in Vermont until his untimely death.

380 pages
Paperback ISBN: 1-55164-224-7 $24.99
Hardcover ISBN: 1-55164-225-5 $53.99

---

send for a free catalogue of all our titles

C.P. 1258, Succ. Place du Parc
Montréal, Québec
H2X 4A7 Canada

or visit our website at http://www.web.net/blackrosebooks

to order books
In Canada: (phone) 1-800-565-9523 (fax) 1-800-221-9985
email: utpbooks@utpress.utoronto.ca
In United States: (phone) 1-800-283-3572 (fax) 1-651-917-6406
In UK & Europe: (phone) London 44 (0)20 8986-4854 (fax) 44 (0)20 8533-5821
email: order@centralbooks.com

Printed by the workers of
MARC VEILLEUX IMPRIMEUR INC.
Boucherville, Québec
for Black Rose Books